University of Liverpool

Withdrawn from stock

.ie o1
veek for
ig Annual
- 2678.

An Outline of the History of Economic Thought

═

ERNESTO SCREPANTI
and
STEFANO ZAMAGNI

Translated by David Field

CLARENDON PRESS · OXFORD

Oxford University Press, Walton Street, Oxford OX2 6DP

Oxford New York

Athens Auckland Bangkok Bombay
Calcutta Cape Town Dar es Salaam Delhi
Florence Hong Kong Istanbul Karachi
Kuala Lumpur Madras Madrid Melbourne
Mexico City Nairobi Paris Singapore
Taipei Tokyo Toronto

and associated companies in
Berlin Ibadan

Oxford is a trade mark of Oxford University Press

Published in the United States
by Oxford University Press Inc., New York

British Catalogue in Publication Data
Data available

Library of Congress Cataloging in Publication Data
Screpanti, Ernesto, 1948–
[Profile di storia del pensiero economico. English]
An outline of the history of economic thought/Ernesto Screpanti
and Stefano Zamagni; translated by David Field.
Includes bibliographical references and index.
1. Economics—History. I. Zamagni, Stefano. II. Title.
HN75.S47413 1993 330'.09–dc20 92–28441
ISBN 0–19–828370–9
ISBN 0–19–877455–9 (Pbk)

Printed in Great Britain
on acid-free paper by
Bookcraft (Bath) Ltd., Midsomer Norton, Avon

PREFACE

Our experience in the teaching of economics and its history has made one thing plain to us: that keeping the two subjects separate, if it was ever justified, is certainly not today. In the face of the crisis of the theoretical orthodoxies of the 1950s and 1960s, the flowering of innovations in recent years, and the numerous rediscoveries of traditional wisdoms, it is no longer an easy task to teach economic principles. We feel it necessary, therefore, to teach economic theory by paying careful attention to its history. We have tried to satisfy this need in our book, and this already says a great deal about the way it has been conceived. We have endeavoured to present traditional theories as living matter, as well as presenting modern theories as part of a historical process and not as established truths.

On the one hand, we have tried to resist the double temptation of rereading the past only in the light of the present and explaining the present only by the past, or, to be more precise, to avoid searching in the traditional theories for the seeds of the modern theories and explaining the latter as simple accumulations of knowledge. On the other hand, we have attempted to distance ourselves from the implicit banality of the great historiographical alternatives, such as 'internal' and 'external' history or 'continuism' and 'catastrophism'. We have also tried to avoid the dichotomy which still exists today, and which seems to us to cause misleading simplifications, between the 'pure' historians of thought, who dedicate themselves exclusively to studying 'facts', and the 'pure' theorists, who are only interested in the evolution of the logical structure of theories. We believe that knowledge of the 'environment' in which a theory is formed is just as important as knowledge of its logical structure, and we do not accept the view that an analysis of the emergence of a theory must be considered as an alternative to the study of its internal structure. This historical outline is, therefore, neither a collection of discoveries nor a portrait gallery.

Our choice to give a fair amount of historical weight to modern developments has entailed the problem of where to end our narrative. This cannot but be a subjective decision. We have chosen the 1970s, but we have reserved the right to break this rule each time we felt it necessary—for example, in the case of research work and debates which produced important results in the 1980s but which began earlier. The only precaution we have taken in these cases has been to avoid citing names and titles, with a few exceptions, and limiting ourselves to outlining the essential elements of the most recent theoretical developments.

The reader accustomed to traditional history books may be surprised by the large amount of space we have reserved for the thought of the last fifty years—approximately half the extent of a book that still remains (all things considered) fairly concise. If there *is* an imbalance of this type, however, we believe it is that we have dedicated too *little* space to modern theories. Quantitative historiographical research has shown, whichever index is used, that scientific production has grown at an exponential rate in the last five centuries, with the remarkable consequence that certainly more than 70 per cent of the scientists who have ever lived are living today, and perhaps a great many more. The decision to devote less than 70 per cent of our book to modern theory was, in fact, prudent.

Finally, we have no wish to avoid certain difficulties, or, rather, responsibilities, connected with our endeavour to treat the present as history. We are well aware of the danger of the attempt to be wise in the sense advocated by William James, who believed that the art lay in knowing what to leave out. We realize that this danger becomes greater the smaller the distance from the material dealt with and the larger the quantity of material about which decisions must be made; but we believe that these responsibilities must be faced. We do not know whether we have been wise in this sense, or to what degree, but we are convinced of one thing: even if we have omitted many things from this book, the resulting selection has been justified, in fact necessitated, by the importance of the material upon which we focus.

This book is not directed to a specialist public, nor solely to a student audience. We also hope to reach the educated person, or, rather, the person who wishes to educate herself or himself. Specialist training is not, therefore, necessary to understand this book; a basic knowledge of economics, however, especially the main themes of micro- and macroeconomics, would be of help. This is true for most of the book. There are, however, sections, especially those dealing with the modern theories, in which the analytical difficulties cannot be avoided without falling into the trap of oversimplification. In these cases, which we have tried to keep to a minimum, we have chosen to avoid banality and to ask the reader for a little more effort.

This knowledge of the audience to whom the book is directed may help in understanding several things about its structure; we have chosen, for example, to avoid weighing down the narrative with footnotes, a choice that has often restricted us, but which we hope will benefit the reader. On the other hand the bibliographies presented at the end of each chapter do not pretend to be complete; they contain, apart from details of works quoted from, only a short guide to further reading.

Finally, we should like to express our gratitude to the many colleagues and friends who have kindly and generously agreed to read and comment on the first drafts of our book, or on parts of it. In particular we would like to mention Duccio Cavalieri, Marco Dardi, Franco Donzelli, Riccardo Faucci, Giorgio Gattei, Augusto Graziani, Peter Groenewegen, Vinicio Guidi, Geoff Hodgson, Alan Kirman, Jan Kregel, Marcello Messori, Pierluigi Nuti, Fabio Petri, Pier Luigi Porta, Maurizio Pugno, Piero Tani, and Warren Young. Of course any inadequacies or mistakes in this book are our own sole responsibility. Our thanks also go to Andrew Schuller and Anna Zaranko of Oxford University Press for their perceptive editorial work and advice.

E. S.
S. Z.

CONTENTS

5. THE TRIUMPH OF UTILITARIANISM AND THE MARGINALIST REVOLUTION

6. THE CONSTRUCTION OF NEOCLASSICAL ORTHODOXY

8. THE YEARS OF HIGH THEORY: II

9. CONTEMPORARY ECONOMIC THEORY: I

10. CONTEMPORARY ECONOMIC THEORY: II

11. CONTEMPORARY ECONOMIC THEORY: III

INTRODUCTION

Epochs of Economic Theory

One of the most interesting and controversial of the arguments put forward by Schumpeter in *The History of Economic Analysis* is that the evolution of economic ideas does not proceed smoothly, but in jumps, through a succession of epochs of revolution and consolidation; of language confusion and 'classical' periods. This is also a useful idea for the historian of economic thought because, if true, it would provide a clear organizational framework for the subject. In fact, this idea immediately leads to an almost natural division of the history of economic thought into epochs, a division based on a succession of 'classical situations' and revolutionary periods. Here, while agreeing with Schumpeter that any periodization, 'though certainly based upon provable facts', must not 'be taken too seriously' (p. 52), we will attempt one inspired by his idea.

Modern economic science originates from a first great theoretical revolution that occurred, roughly, in the period, 1750–80. This was an epoch of great breaks with tradition; an epoch that began with Galiani, Beccaria, and Hume, continued through Genovesi, Verri, Ortes, Steuart, Anderson, Condillac, Mirabeau, Quesnay, Turgot, and the whole physiocratic movement; and reached its climax with *The Wealth of Nations*. A chaotic flow of audacious and brilliant ideas which, even allowing for the diversity of, and conflicts among, the various approaches, was driven forward by a few fundamental themes. Common to many of these authors was the revolt against mercantilism, the perception or the foreboding that there was to be a deep revolution in the economic structure of society, the faith in natural laws and in the possibility of understanding them scientifically, and, above all, the belief in free trade, which, even if it was only professed by some of the above-mentioned economists, was soon to become the basic ideology of the new science. *The Wealth of Nations* was the supreme synthesis of all this work. For twenty years after its appearance, as Schumpeter suggests, 'there is little to report *as far as analytical work is concerned*' (p. 379).

In fact, the recovery from theoretical stagnation occurred with the 'new economics', immediately after the Napoleonic wars, and was started by Ricardo. He, far from being a servile follower of Smith, set to work on the arguments which differentiated his opinions from those of the great authorities—the greatest of which was *The Wealth of Nations*. Ricardo was the first of a long series of great innovators, among the most important of whom were Sismondi, Malthus, Torrens, Bailey, Hodgskin, Thünen, Longfield, Rae, Senior, Cournot, Dupuit, List, Rodbertus, Jones, and Roscher.

The period from 1815 to 1845 was one of the richest in the history of economic thought as well as that of socialist thought. (Owen, Saint-Simon,

Fourier, Cabet, Blanqui, Rodbertus, and Proudhon all worked in this period.) It was a period of crisis, as shown by the heterogeneous nature of the theories which fought for positions in the field: Ricardian, Ricardian socialists, Continental socialists, the old German Historical School, and the 'anti-Ricardian reaction'. The last was the most heterogeneous of all, and only later was it acknowledged as the precursor of the marginalist revolution. Despite, or perhaps because of, the diverse and contrasting flows of ideas, the doctrinal counter-positions, and the Babel's tower of terminologies and concepts, this period produced a supreme wealth of seeds, some of which were soon to bear fruit, others much later.

It was J. S. Mill who restored economics as a normal science made up of established and lasting truths, and with him the epoch closed. It was followed by a new period of stagnation, if not decadence: the age of Fawcett and Cairnes in England and Bastiat in France, while in Germany the innovative spur faded away with the affirmation of the historical school. After Bastiat, Reybaud could state that work in political economy had almost been exhausted and that there was nothing else to discover. Cairnes, too, believed that the work of political economy was 'pretty well fulfilled'. It was 1870! Yet still in 1876, as Schumpeter reminds us, there was a feeling that 'though much remained for economists to do in the way of development and application of existing doctrine, *the great work had been done*' (p. 830).

Yet it was just at that time that a new revolution was breaking through. The marginalist revolution occurred between 1870 and 1890: it was opened by Menger, Jevons, and Walras, was continued by Edgeworth, Wieser, Böhm-Bawerk, Pantaleoni, and Clark, and closed by Fisher and Marshall. Also in this period, due to its revolutionary and transitional nature, there was no predominant orthodoxy; in fact, the epoch was characterized by conflict among a remarkable number of contrasting theoretical positions. First of all, there was a revival of socialist theories in the most diverse forms, from the Marxist school to the Fabians and from Christian to agrarian socialism. Institutionalism and the Young Historical School (not only German) also began during this period and were to develop more fully later. Finally, it is important to note that there were major differences in approach, among the marginalist writers themselves, which caused bitter controversies. These were so widespread that still today it is difficult to recognize a homogeneous school of thought in the early marginalist approaches. Their way of seeing the world, in any case, seemed new and unfamiliar to many theorists, and this caused a great deal of resistance. It was only in the 1890s that a new 'classical situation' was established, and a new feeling of repose spread among the economists. In fact, it was only towards the end of the century that the fundamental homogeneity of the various versions of marginalist theory was perceived by the historians of economic thought.

The great neoclassical economists of the third generation, Cassel, Pareto, and Wicksell, were lucky enough to work within what had almost become a new tradition and orthodoxy, and had no need, therefore, to be revolutionary. The next revolutionary period occurred during the years of 'high theory', in the 1920s and 1930s. It was, as G. L. S. Shackle stated, 'an immense creative spasm . . . yielding six or seven major innovations of theory, which together have completely altered the orientation and character of economics' (*The Years of High Theory*, p. 5). But perhaps there were more than six or seven: a great many of the modern theories of growth, cycle, input–output relations, firm, general equilibrium, money, expectations, employment, distribution, demand, welfare, planning, and socialism—originate from the seeds sown in those years.

Coming to the epoch in which we live, there is no doubt that a new classical situation was created during the 1950s and 1960s. Even though dissent was not completely silenced, as shown by the post-Keynesian attacks on the neoclassical theory of distribution and growth and by the clamour of the debate on capital theory, it is evident that the 'neoclassical synthesis' constituted at that time the authentic 'single track' for economic research. Beginning with the attempt to graft the Keynesian seedling onto the old trunk of marginalist theory, the neoclassical synthesis culminated in an impressive ordering of ideas and suggestions derived from the years of the high theory. Then, strengthened by the formal elegance of the Arrow–Debreu–McKenzie general-equilibrium model, the theoretical versatility of the Hicks–Modigliani macroeconomic-equilibrium model, and the analytical simplicity of the Solow–Swan growth-and-distribution model, it was able to orient economic research and economic policy in a way that no other scientific orthodoxy had been able to do. Moreover, the fact that it even managed to transform the critical potential of many dissident theories into internal debates is a demonstration of its hegemonic strength.

In effect, it was only during the 1970s and 1980s that these potential criticisms began to produce attempts at truly alternative theoretical syntheses. In fact, the last twenty years have constituted another period of theoretical confusion. A large number of theories have emerged, all, to differing degrees, imperfect, fascinating, and revolutionary. None is completely satisfactory, none dominant. From the 'new classical macroeconomics' to the non-Walrasian equilibrium theory, from post-Keynesian theories to the various neo-institutionalist approaches, and from the neo-Austrian schools to neo-Marxism (the last being subdivided into several versions, Sraffian, anti-Sraffian, regulationist, neo-Schumpeterian, neo-Keynesian, etc.), competition in modern academic markets is again strong, incessant, and almost perfect.

Thus, in more than 200 years of the history of economic thought, from the middle of the eighteenth century to the present day, there have been four great cycles of progress followed by periods of stagnation of ideas, four long revolutionary phases followed by four equally long consolidation phases. We are now right in the middle of the fifth cycle. Each cycle begins with a period of brilliant ideas, innovations, and breaks with the tradition, controversies, bitter conflicts, and terminological confusion; in short, a stimulating process of creative destruction in the production of economic ideas. Old schools disintegrate, dwarfs give way to giants, and just when one believes that economic science has attained perfection, chaos breaks out again. Later, out of that hive of activity, the need for a new synthesis gradually emerges. This is finally reached after two or three decades, and produces a new classical situation. Then, for another twenty or thirty years political economy becomes a tranquil profession again: stable academic circles form, and members of the profession return to concerns with elegance, generality, and the solution of puzzles. Research follows well-trodden paths and produces excellent textbooks, refinements, generalizations, and varied applications.

Plurality of Interpretations

The subjective nature of the criteria we have adopted to decide what is to be considered innovative or orthodox is inevitable, as is the 'qualitative' nature of the periodization derived from it. We are also aware of the inadequacy of our appeal to the authority of Schumpeter. On the other hand, the idea that economic science progresses in jumps rather than in linear progression should not cause concern; rather, the problem is how to take account of this phenomenon.

One position is represented by the so-called 'incrementalist' approach to the history of economic thought; an approach according to which 'scientific progress' has been compared—for example, by Pantaleoni—'to the growth of a snowball which rolls down a mountain slope, gathering extra snow, with its surface representing the unknown' (*Scritti varii di economia*, p. 4). This point of view implies the possibility, according to Pantaleoni, of separating economic science from its metaphysical contour, or rather, according to Schumpeter, separating analysis from visions. By thus reducing the history of economic thought to that of analysis (or 'science'), it is conceived as the narration of the slow and continual growth in knowledge: looking backwards through time, and 'starting from what economic science is *in the present moment*', its history will be a 'history of the economic truths' (Pantaleoni, p. 484). In recent times, the most convinced supporters of this point of view have been neoclassical economists such as Knight, Stigler, Blaug, and Gordon. But it is not a point of view which originated within neoclassical theory; Say and Ferrara, for example, had held it before.

Obviously, the supporters of this position do not accept that the history of economic thought proceeds in jumps and advances by revolutions. Crises, periods of stagnation, and slow-downs are admitted, but only as perverse effects of the 'metaphysical foundations' and the psychological conditions in which the individual authors formulated their theories, all factors which do not damage the substance of the scientific element. Thus their history would be a history of mistakes.

A different point of view, which has been called 'catastrophist' or 'discontinuist', is linked to Kuhn's theory of the structure of scientific revolutions. This approach, which views the evolution of knowledge as passing through revolutions and explains the latter as caused by the accumulation of anomalies within the dominant paradigms, seems extremely useful in tackling the problem we have raised. However, the application of Kuhn's arguments to the history of economic thought has encountered serious difficulties, difficulties which can be linked both to the ambiguities of the Kuhnian definition of a 'paradigm' and to its origin in the history of the natural sciences. So much so that the characteristics of a truly Kuhnian revolution in the history of economic thought have only been identified, and then not without controversy, in the Keynesian revolution. In fact, this revolution could be interpreted, not as a theoretical response to the stimulus supplied by the occurrence, in a historically determined socio-institutional environment, of some new economic facts (crisis, depression, price rigidity, or mass unemployment), but as the realization of the importance of some anomalies which had always existed and yet had always been relegated to the footnotes by the dominant paradigm. But how does this idea fit in with the fact that the Keynesian revolution was only part of the process of deep upheaval which engulfed the years of high theory? About other revolutions, many neoclassical economists deny that it is possible to find those characteristics in the marginalist revolution, and refuse even to acknowledge its revolutionary nature, believing instead that it consisted of the purification, refinement, and generalization of the truly scientific elements which were already present in classical economics. Finally, the free-trade and Ricardian revolutions cannot be analysed according to Kuhn's schema, as they were linked to a great historical event, the birth of industrial capitalism, and not determined by a logic which was strictly internal to the evolution of a paradigm.

Recently, there have also been attempts to apply Lakatos's 'methodology of the scientific research programmes' to the history of economic thought. The best-known examples are those by Weintraub and Latsis. According to this approach, a research programme will be successful if it shows itself to be *progressive*, both theoretically (being able to predict new facts) and empirically (if such predictions are confirmed). It will be abandoned when it becomes *degenerating* (needing to be modified in order to account for known facts without being able to predict new ones), and if a 'better' programme— i.e., one that is endowed with greater empirical content—is available. The attempts to apply Lakatos's approach to economics have produced interesting results with regard to research methodology, especially in the direction of weakening faith in empiricist and positivist epistemologies, and of a greater open-mindedness towards methodological pluralism. However, as far as the history of economic thought is concerned, Lakatos's approach has not produced decisively important results and has, on the contrary, represented a step backwards relative to Kuhn, who at least admitted the importance, if not the centrality, of scientific revolutions. Lakatos's approach, instead— especially because of the emphasis it places on the 'progressiveness' of successful research programmes, and on their greater empirical content relative to those which have been surpassed—seems to be moving towards a resumption of the old 'incrementalist' arguments.

Both the incrementalist and catastrophist approaches are open to criticism at the level of their common epistemological roots. They have in common a point of view which Blaug, in *Economic Theory in Retrospect*, has defined as 'absolutist' (pp. 20–1)—in the sense that the historian is only interested in the intellectual development of the theories, without being concerned with their relationships to the socio-economic conditions in which they emerged. The absolutist point of view is clearly present in the incrementalist approach, for which the evolution of thought is nothing more than a series of marginal increments of knowledge upon a stock of aquired truth. But this is also true of the catastrophist approach, in which scientific revolutions are caused by a threshold effect generated by the accumulation of anomalies within each paradigm. In both cases there is no way of linking changes in thought to changes in social and economic life.

The approach which studies the history of economic ideas in relation to socio-economic contexts in which they have arisen has been defined by Blaug as 'relativist' (pp. 20–1). With a little more verve and still more *vis polemica*, Pantaleoni called it 'mesological' (p. 491). It is a point of view which is held by a large number of institutionalist, historicist, and Marxist scholars, and, in general, by historians with non-positivist backgrounds. Mitchell, Stark, Roll, Rogin, and Dasgupta, to name a few, are all authors who have explicitly theorized and knowingly utilized the mesological approach. The epistemological foundation of this position is based—according to Roll—'on the conviction that the economic structure of any given epoch and the changes which it undergoes are the major influences on economic thinking' (*A History of Economic Thought*, p. 14).

One of the mesological approaches aims at identifying the relationships existing between economic theory and the real socioeconomic structure. And the simplest type of relationship seems to be that between a historically determined reality and a specific thought that 'reflects' it. Working along this line, Stark has proposed an interpretation of the Schumpeterian notion of 'classical situations' which leads to a simple and apparently obvious explanation of the phenomenon in question. When comparing the classical situations represented by the theories of Smith and Walras, Stark observed that, while these are two different doctrines, they are still two theories of equilibrium. He suggests that they reflect two different economic orders which prevailed in different historical epochs.

Smith's teachings thus reflected the first real historical situation in which the capitalist order was in equilibrium conditions, an equilibrium based on the small, non-mechanized factory and on an exchange economy fully developed within a national market, in which the invisible hand was able to integrate agricultural with industrial production. On the other hand, Walras's system represented an international economic order in which competition was almost perfect, both on the commodity and labour markets, at least in the most developed economies.

Stark says nothing about the other classical situations, neither does he offer clarification about what is reflected by the theoretical formulations which occur in periods of intellectual revolution. But his arguments seem perfectly compatible with the following suggestion by Shackle concerning the state of economic theory in the 1920s: these years had marked the end of 'a belief in a self-regulating, inherently and naturally self-optimizing, stable and coherent system' (p. 5). When the economists realized that they were no longer able, with the old intellectual instruments, to restore the old order of things, they began to search for new theories; in this way, by the end of the 1930s economic science 'had come to terms with the restless anarchy and disorder of the world of fact' (p. 6). This point of view has an unpleasant premise: that social reality is only the object and thought only the subject of scientific activity, such that the latter does not obey the laws which govern the former and is able to reflect them objectively. Equally unpleasant consequences would be that the evolution of economic theory is unequivocally determined by the evolution of the objective reality; and that, once again, there is (even though through a series of oscillations) a certain type of progress through the accumulation of truth.

Another group of mesological approaches considers the political element as the most important link between theory and reality. This is the well-known argument of the 'political demand' for economic ideas, according to which the emergence of specific, real economic problems stimulates the creation of political solutions and therefore of theories which are capable of scientifically justifying those solutions. Then, the theories which supply the correct solutions are grouped together and are slowly refined until an orthodox theoretical system is formed.

Myrdal developed a similar conception, but added several interesting observations concerning the role played by the process of younger generations replacing older ones within scientific communities. The study of the new facts which emerge in the course of economic evolution, would modify political attitudes, especially among young researchers. These, rather than the older upholders of the orthodoxy, would be able to change the directions of research 'under the pressure of what is becoming politically important to the society' ('Crises and Cycles in the Development of Economics', p. 20). It is in this way that recurrent theoretical revolutions would be triggered. This position, even though it has the merit of giving the right weight to the political element, has the defect of reducing the problem to the single dimension of the adjustment of theories to problems: there is still the idea that the economist observes reality as in a laboratory and is not influenced by it.

These difficulties are not encountered by Neumark, who suggests that there is normally only one choice open to solve the fundamental economic problems: the choice between two great alternatives; and that this explains not only the perpetual oscillation of the dominant positions in economic policy between state control and *laissez-faire*, protectionism and free trade, balancing the budget and deficit spending, but also the oscillation of fundamental theoretical attitudes between preferences for the conceptions of value as 'natural' and 'just', between idealistic and materialist philosophies, and between industrialism and environmentalism.

Our Point of View

This outline of the history of economic thought is not intended to be either a history of illustrious people, their lives, their work, and their personal contributions to the discovery of the truth, or a history of the errors by which the growth of scientific knowledge has occurred. We do not share the idea that economics is a 'Darwinian' discipline, an idea which claims that the last link in the evolutionary chain contains all the preceding developments, and that these can all be dismissed as irrelevant or superseded. Certainly, we do not deny the existence of some form of evolution in the process of historical change of economic ideas. However, we deny that it is a unidirectional, homogeneous, and unique development; above all, we deny that the key to understanding this process must necessarily be provided by the theories which are in fashion today.

The approach that we follow has a great deal in common with the relativist position. We wish, however, to avoid falling into certain 'mesological' naïvities and simplifications, which often contribute to the production of histories of economic thought by portraits, or treating the evolution of ideas as an appendix to the evolution of economic facts. We realize that the reality studied by the economist is not fixed like that of the natural sciences. Economic facts change through time and space: problems which appear crucial in a certain period may be irrelevant in another, and those that are considered important in one country can be completely ignored in another. This peculiarity of the subject of investigation may help to explain part of the history of economic thought, for instance, the existence of certain national peculiarities or the emergence of specific theories at certain historical moments. But this does not explain everything, and perhaps it does not explain precisely what really deserves to be studied.

More important than the peculiarities of the object under study are those of the subject itself. There is no doubt that the cultural background and the 'visions' of the scientists have a strong effect on their research activities; and still more determinant are the common ideas and values accepted by the scientific communities, as it is precisely these which select and give direction to the individuals. But, more generally, there is no doubt that it is the particular society as a whole which determines the cultural climate in which the choices available to individual scientists and the scientific community are provided and delimited. Society as a whole decrees the importance of the problems to be studied, establishes the directions in which solutions should be sought, and, ultimately, decides which theories are correct.

None of this would merit our attention if society were a homogeneous entity. But it is not. In the field of the social sciences, a theory is a form of self-understanding and self-representation of a social subject. The subjects are heterogeneous, however: there are differences of class, culture, and nationality. Moreover, the relationships in which these subjects find themselves may be conflictual. Thus society, while being a severe judge of scientific work, is not always impartial, nor does it always have clear ideas about what it wants. And if it is true that only society decides the relevance of the problems, it is also true that its decisions are often ambiguous and contradictory. For example, some people consider an unemployment rate of 5 per cent as worrying, while others believe a 10 per cent rate is normal, even 'natural'; and it is inevitable that these two different ways of thinking are connected to two contrasting economic theories. Still more fleeting and biased are the criteria by which society decrees which theories are correct, because, in the end, as there is 'only one truth', the plurality of points of view, solutions, and directions of research which society itself generates must in some way be suppressed in favour of a single theory. Obviously, the work of the scientists has an important role in establishing which theory should prevail, as there are requirements of logical coherence, generality, and explanatory power to which it is their duty to attend. They are not the kings of the castle, however, and cannot do whatever they wish.

On some subjects and fundamental problems, *base orientations* are formed which embody diverse and often contradictory points of view. These orientations give rise to strands of research which span the history of economic thought. They are like rivers on limestone which sometimes disappear underground, giving the impression that they have dried up; but they can continue their underground life for a long time, banned from academia and deprived of scientific respectability. Then they come to light again, when nobody expects it, and become more powerful and noisy until they silence their opponents. For example, consider the orientation underlying criticism of Say's Law and its use to demonstrate the impossibility of 'general gluts'. Who would have thought, considering the defeat of Malthus by Ricardo, or the sad academic destiny of Marx or Hobson, that with Keynes justice would have been done? In regard to this problem, two base orientations have always been in conflict, one leaning towards self-regulating markets, the other toward effective demand, and neither has ever gained a complete victory. Another example comes from the theory of value, where the subjectivist and objectivist orientations have clashed continuously. It seemed that Jevons had finally defeated Ricardo, but then, a century later, Sraffa put everything back into discussion. We could go on to show the alternating destinies of the quantitative and endogenous orientations in regard to the money supply, or of the macroeconomic and microeconomic orientations concerning the distribution of income, and so on.

Matters are complicated by *traditions*, that is to say, by certain types of cultural identification which link economists of different generations. Traditions may depend on the existence of certain national cultural backgrounds, on the formation of academic schools of thought, on the strength of certain political configurations, or on yet other causes. Thus, it is possible to speak, for example, of an English tradition in the field of the construction of comprehensive grand theories, a tradition which links (despite their different theoretical positions) the magnificent syncretism of Smith with those of Stuart Mill and Marshall. Or, observing the thin but strong connecting thread linking Davanzati, Montanari, Galiani, Ferrara, and Pareto, it is possible to speak of an Italian tradition in relation to the subjective theory of value. It is also possible to speak of a socialist tradition regarding value and distribution, or of a Keynesian tradition concerning economic dynamics. Traditions have an important role in guiding the scientific activity of individuals and research groups. Developments in traditions intertwine with those of the base orientations, and contribute significantly to the evolution of economic thought.

In certain historical periods, the orientations underlying some basic theoretical principles sometimes combine with a certain specific tradition to contribute to the creation of a *theoretical system*, a general theory aspiring to give a coherent and complete answer to every problem that has arisen or can arise in a defined field of investigation. The first requirement of a theoretical system is the definition of the *scope of investigation*. Then, it is necessary to determine the *fundamental principles* around which all existing and potential knowledge can be organized, the *methodological rules* that establish the way in which the research is conducted and the results evaluated, and the *linguistic canons* which allow the classification, transmission, and communication of knowledge.

The definition of the *scope of investigation* is fundamental. It contains, in a nutshell, the whole development of the system, identifies the problems to be studied, establishes which economic factors act as parameters and which as variables, chooses the research directions to be followed and those to be ignored, and, finally, instructs the scientists as to what they are prohibited from doing. The *fundamental principles* serve to hold together the parts of the theoretical system, to create a coherent and organic core doctrine, and to make it something more than a syncretic sum of diverse theories. The *methodological rules* instruct the scientists on how to move across the unknown ground of the problems to solve and of the still unproven truths. They, perhaps more than the other dimensions of a theoretical system, and in a way that often not all the researchers are perfectly aware of, make the scientists' choices homogeneous and the research results coherent. At the same time, they allow for a division of labour which may go beyond any possible planned structures of research activities.

Finally, the recomposition of the results of such a division of labour is made possible by well-determined *linguistic canons*. Perhaps these are the least explicitily codified characteristics of a theoretical system, but they are not the least important. Not only do they allow the communication of knowledge and the education of younger generations of researchers, which means the creation and reproduction of the scientific community, but, above all, they *delimit the field of discourse*. A person who is not well versed in the linguistic terminology used by the scientific community sharing a particular theoretical system, that is, a person who is unable to follow its more or less tacit rules of communication, simply does not have the right to speak, especially when the system in question is the culturally dominant orthodoxy. The history of economic thought is full of brilliant but unheeded self-taught men, living in the 'underworlds' of heretics and precursors.

In order to clarify what we mean by a *'theoretical system'*, it may be useful to give an example. Let us consider the neoclassical system. This originated towards the middle of the nineteenth century and, through phases of crises and successes, and even enduring the pressure and the centripetal forces of three or four great national traditions, it reached its first signs of systematic organization towards the end of the century. Finally, and aided by the cosmopolitan push of the American neoclassical economists, it attained its supreme synthesis towards the middle of the twentieth century. Some base orientations typical of this system manifested themselves in a subjectivist theory of value, a microeconomic theory of distribution, and a static theory of equilibrium. These and other base orientations were organized around the principle of constrained maximization of individual objectives; while the scope of investigation was reduced to the problem of the optimal allocation of scarce resources.

The basic problem for the historian of thought is: how do such systems form? Linked to this are other, equally important questions. What determines the success of a system? What causes its break up? Why in certain periods does a 'dictatorship' of a certain system arise while in others there seems to be theoretical anarchy? In the remainder of this book we have tried, within the limits set by a simple outline of the history of economic thought, to sketch a reply to these problems. Here, we will briefly explain some of the interpretative lines on which we have based our attempt.

1. Economic problems are strictly linked, so that a new theory concentrating on only one problem, or on a limited group of problems, is in a certain sense unstable. Either it makes reference to an already existing theoretical system and tries to become integrated into it and possibly to generalize the system itself, or it proposes itself as a base for the organization of a new theoretical system. A typical example is given by the Keynesian revolution, which began by claiming to be a *general theory*, but was later generalized by the system it wished to attack. The operation was accomplished by the elimination of some

of the base orientations that were present in Keynes, orientations that turned out to be incompatible with neoclassical theory. On the other hand, and precisely on the basis of these orientations, attempts were made (which are still going on) to construct, on the basis of the *General Theory*, a post-Keynesian theoretical system conceived as an alternative to the neoclassical system.

2. The success of a theoretical system implies the realization of two conditions, one internal and one external. The former concerns logical coherence, both in terms of the analytical rigour of the specific theories of which a system is formed and in terms of the relationships that link one theory to another. The latter concerns the ability of the theoretical system to respond to a certain social need. Society in certain periods of its evolution needs a *general theory* to represent it. These are periods in which order and stability predominate. The theories which are chosen must, in some way, be theories of order, equilibrium, and harmony. Therefore, not all theoretical systems are predisposed to prevail, even if they are coherent. Some, even though they are refined, rigorous, and heuristically powerful, are in any case destined to remain at the margins of the academic world. There is another reason why the second condition is more important than the first: it is always necessary, while the first is not. When society needs an organic, orthodox, general theory, it finds one. If there are diverse theoretical systems available that satisfy the same needs, the one which best satisfies the conditions of internal coherence will presumably win. And when the market does not offer a great deal, the best that exists is taken, even if the price of syncretism and analytical weakness has to be paid. This was the case, for example, with the Bastiat-type theories of 'social harmony' that prevailed in the 1850s and 1860s.

3. When a society enters a period of crisis, the prestige of the dominant theoretical system will be shaken. In a society facing a serious crisis, the need to represent the economy as an organic and ordered body is weakened; and this occurs precisely when real problems emerge for which the general theories of order are unprepared. In these periods, the pressure of the scientific community on individual researchers weakens, while methodological and doctrinal ties on scientific research are loosened. In this way, creative energies are liberated. At the same time, the research interests of the scientists are attracted and shaped more by the problems emerging from the real world than by those springing from theory. Theoretical revolutions occur in these periods. They are characterized by confusion of language; but in such a confusion the bases are laid down for the construction of new theoretical systems. However, it could also happen that old systems are revitalised. A theoretical system which enters a period of crisis does not necessarily leave the scene. The crisis itself may even contribute to the system's regeneration, a typical example being the resurgence of the neoclassical system after the crisis of the 1920s and 1930s.

4. Although the history of economic thought cannot be interpreted simply in terms of the growth of knowledge, there are, however, certain forms of progress. One type of evolution is that which occurs within a particular base

orientation. As an orientation refers to a specific problem, evolution consists in the progressive refinement of the theory accounting for the phenomenon. In this way, the objectivist theory of value progressed as it moved from Ricardo to Marx and thence to Sraffa. On the other hand, two different orientations focusing on the same problem are not comparable, as they are derived from different pre-analytical premises. In regard to the problem of the distribution of income, for example, there is an orientation, founded on the presupposition that an economy is a set of exchange relationships among *individuals*, which tends to reduce the problem to that of the determination of the prices of the productive services. There is, however, another orientation, one based on the premise that the economy is a system of functional and/or conflictual relations among social classes, which considers the distributive problem as that of dividing the national product among the classes. Now, whether one of these two orientations is able to explain a historical reality better than the other is not a question that can be resolved on the analytical level: the acceptance of one or other of the presuppositions on which the orientations are based implies a pre-analytical choice. For this reason, the transfer of hegemony from a theory that proposes a certain orientation to one that proposes a different orientation cannot be evaluated in terms of progress.

There is a second type of evolution, one which concerns theoretical systems. Here, in addition to the progress involving each of the individual components of the system, there is also progress in the overall organization of the components. In this case, progress occurs through the substitution of a specific theory by another, if the new theory integrates better with the rest of the theories making up the system. Another type of progress of a system concerns the internal substitution of partial theories by general theories. Yet another consists of the integration, in the system, of theories relating to new problems. This can happen either because the empirical research activated by the system itself leads to the discovery of new phenomena or because the system manages to focus on, and to provide solutions to, problems that have emerged in an autonomous way. Thus the progress of a system, even if it passes through theoretical revolutions, in the end always comes down to a process of analytical refinement and/or theoretical generalization. However, we are only dealing with progress of *a* system. Also, in this case it is impossible to compare different theoretical systems in terms of progress. This is both due to the incommensurability of the base orientations from which the different systems develop and because different systems define the very scope of investigation, and the problems to which they are applied, in different terms.

From the above it will be easy to understand the methodological position we have adopted in this book. Our outline of the history of economic thought is neither a history of illustrious personalities nor one of economic themes. Rather, it takes a history-of-ideas approach, whose principal aims consist, on the one hand, of understanding the context in which the ideas are formed and, on the other, of explaining how the fundamental ideas lead to the creation of particular theoretical systems.

Bibliography

On the 'absolutist' approach: M. Blaug, *Economic Theory in Retrospect* (London 1964); 'Was There a Marginal Revolution?' in R. D. G. Black and C. D. W. Goodwin (eds.), *The Marginal Revolution in Economics* (Durham, 1973); F. Ferrara, *Esame storico-critico di economisti e dottrine economiche* (4 vols., Turin, 1889); D. F. Gordon, 'The Role of the History of Economic Thought in the Understanding of Modern Economic Theory', *American Economic Review, Papers and Proceedings* (1965); F. H. Knight, *On the History and Method of Economics* (Chicago, 1956); M. Pantaleoni, *Scritti varii di economia* (Milan, 1904); J.-B. Say, *Cours complet d' économie politique pratique* (Paris 1840); G. J. Stigler, 'The Influence of Events and Policies on Economic Theory', *American Economic Review, Papers and Proceedings* (1960).

On the applications of the theories of Popper, Kuhn, and Lakatos: R. Backhouse, *A History of Modern Economic Analysis* (Oxford, 1985); M. Blaug, 'Kuhn versus Lakatos or Paradigms versus Research Programmes in the History of Economics', in S. J. Latsis (ed.), *Method and Appraisal in Economics* (Cambridge, 1976); M. Bronfenbrenner, 'The "Structure of Revolutions" in Economic Thought', *History of Political Economy* (1971); A. W. Coats, 'Is There a Structure of Scientific Revolutions in Economics?', *Kyklos* (1969); N. de Marchi (ed.), *The Popperian Legacy in Economics* (Cambridge, 1988); R. Fisher, *The Logic of Economic Discovery* (Brighton, 1986); T. W. Hutchison, 'On the History and Philosophy of Science and Economics', in S. J. Latsis (ed.), *Method and Appraisal in Economics* (Cambridge, 1976); L. Kunin and S. F. Weaver, 'On the Structure of Scientific Revolutions', *History of Political Economy* (1971); S. J. Latsis (ed.), *Method and Appraisal in Economics* (Cambridge, 1976); E. R. Weintraub, *General Equilibrium Analysis* (Cambridge, 1985).

On the 'relativist' approaches: M. Bronfenbrenner, 'Trends, Cycles, and Fads in Economic Writings', *American Economic Review* (1966); A. K. Dasgupta, *Epochs of Economic Theory* (Oxford, 1985); J. Hicks, ' "Revolutions" in Economics', in S. J. Latsis (ed.), *Method and Appraisal in Economics* (Cambridge, 1976); S. Karsten, 'Dialectics and the Evolution of Economic Thought', *History of Political Economy* (1973); J. E. King, *Economic Exiles* (London, 1988); W. C. Mitchell, *Types of Economic Theory* (New York, 1969); G. Myrdal, 'Crises and Cycles in the Development of Economics', *Political Quarterly* (1973); L. Nabers, 'The Positive and Genetic Approaches', in S. R. Krupp (ed.), *The Structure of Economic Science* (Englewood Cliffs, NJ, 1966); F. Newmark, 'Zyken in der Geschichte ökonomischen Ideen', *Kyklos* (1975); L. Rogin, *The Meaning and Validity of Economic Theory* (New York, 1956); E. Roll, *A History of Economic Thought*, 2nd edn. (London, 1946); J. A. Schumpeter, *The History of Economic Analysis* (New York, 1954); E. Screpanti, 'Cicli rivoluzioni e situazioni classiche nello sviluppo delle idee economiche', *Economia Politica*, 5

(1988); G. L. S. Shackle, *The Years of High Theory* (Cambridge, 1967); W. Stark, *The History of Economics in its Relation to Social Development* (London, 1944); 'The "Classical Situation" in Political Economy', *Kyklos* (1959).

1

The Birth of Political Economy

1.1. THE END OF THE MIDDLE AGES AND THE BEGINNINGS OF THE MODERN WORLD

1.1.1. The end of the Middle Ages and scholasticism

The feudal economy rose from the ashes of the slave economy of the Roman Empire. The relationship between owner and slave, a relationship that is only possible if the slave can produce more than he consumes, was transformed into one between owner and serf. The serf was tied to the land he cultivated and received protection from the lord in return for certain economic and political services. The ultimate control of economic activity was in the hands of the king, who could, in most cases, transfer the feuds from one lord to another. Land and labour were transferred rather than bought and sold; and this meant that there was no need for labour and land markets. Authority, faith, and tradition were enough to guarantee that the system worked well.

The relative economic security created by the feudal institutions contributed to an improvement in the living conditions of the population, if for no other reason than that the social condition of the serf was higher than that of the slave. At the same time, the formation of cities in densely populated areas and the widespread diffusion of craft workshops laid the ground for the beginnings of intense commercial activity. The figure of the independent merchant appeared, initially, in the gaps in and at the edges of the traditional economy and, later, in a new economic sphere: the free city and its markets; the seeds of the modern European city.

The growth of the city economies and of the commercial and financial traffic of the urban bourgeoisie began in the twelfth and thirteenth centuries. It was in this period that the first serious attempts at economic theorizing started. Before this there were just a few interesting ideas: Aristotle's theories of 'natural chrematistics', that is, the art of becoming rich by producing goods and services useful to life, and of 'unnatural chrematistics', which concerns enrichment from trade and usury; his distinction between the use value and the exchange value of goods, the former consisting of the ability of a good to satisfy a specific need and the latter of the quantitative relationship in which one good is exchanged for another; and his attempt to define the 'just price' of goods on the basis of the equivalence of the values exchanged.

The scholastic philosophy of the thirteenth century, whose principal exponent was Thomas Aquinas (1221–74), was explicitly linked to Aristotelian philosophy and heavily marked by the attempt to assimilate it into Christianity. Its crucial assumption was that human intelligence is able to reach the truth by means of the speculative method. There are three orders of truth to which speculation should be turned: divine law, as manifested in the revelation; natural law (*jus naturalis*), as embodied in the 'universals' which God had given to the creatures; and positive law, produced by human choices and conventions and valid for all of mankind (*jus gentium*) or for the subjects of the single states (*jus civilis*). The majority of the economic propositions of scholasticism come under *jus gentium* and only a few under *jus naturalis*. The theory of the 'just price', reduced to the *communis aestimatio* (common evaluation) of the normal price in the absence of monopoly, was derived from Aristotle. There was also a theory of the 'just wage', which was defined, again according to the *communis aestimatio* principle, as the wage which would guarantee the worker a standard of living adequate to his social condition. In connection with this, there were also signs of a just price theory which, by virtue of the principle of 'exchange of equivalents', was connected to the cost of production and, therefore, mainly to the cost of labour. A profit is included in the cost of production, but it must be fair and moderate, just enough for the merchant to look after his family and devote a little money to charity. Thus, taking into account the fact that commerce was only considered legitimate if it was useful to the collectivity, it is difficult to see little more than the notion of a wage for direction in the scholastic concept of profit.

The just price is an intrinsic property of a good, as it expresses its intrinsic value (*bonitas intrinseca*). But how this value is determined is not clear. The prevailing opinions oscillate between the theory of the efforts sustained in production and that of the capability of the good to satisfy a human need. In both cases, however, we are dealing with an objective property of the good. And it is not clear whether the propositions concerning the value of the goods are of natural law, as suggested by the theory of the *bonitas intrinseca*, or should be reduced to the *jus gentium*, as the theory of *communis aestimatio* seems to suggest. In fact, the scholasticists were not really interested in understanding what value is or how it is determined. They believed that the just price *must* be such as to guarantee *commutative* justice, that is, equal exchange, in such a way that nobody can obtain more than he gives from the exchange of goods. If this price is 'just' because it corresponds to the natural law, it is also *true*, even though it cannot be observed—and, in a certain sense, even truer than the prices at which the goods are really exchanged on the market, which can be a little higher or lower than the 'just' price itself. This is probably the distant origin of the classical theories of natural and market prices, which will be considered in Chapter 2.

Unlike real goods, which have an intrinsic value, *money* has a conventional value (*impositus*), a value imposed by the prince, and there is no doubt that the doctrine of the value of money comes within positive rather than natural law. At any rate, a conventionalist theory of money predominates in scholastic thought, and especially in the work of Thomas Aquinas, who considered money as a *standard* invented by man to measure the value of goods and facilitate trade. Money was also considered as a replaceable good which is consumed in use. In fact, the main justification for the condemnation of usury was derived from this. Thomas Aquinas took up the Aristotelian condemnation of usury and added to it a theory according to which money, as it is not a durable good which produces services, like capital goods, cannot be rented out, so that its lending cannot give the right to the collection of interest. He was against those who maintained that interest, being proportional to the duration of the loan, is produced by time, an opinion that he attacked by arguing that time is a common good. It is God's gift to mankind, and nobody has the right to appropriate it for himself or to appropriate its fruits. Finally, Aquinas made an interesting attempt to justify private property, an attempt that seems to be the first link in the long chain which, as we will see, connects scholastic thought to the seventeenth-century natural-law philosophy, and to Locke, Quesnay, Smith, and nineteenth-century socialism. God created the earth for the whole of mankind, and nobody can claim a right which deprives other men of the goods created. Private property, however, could be justified as a stimulus to work and is not in contrast with natural law, even though it is not established by it. It can be seen as a form of concession that the community gives to individuals, provided they use it as a service to the community: it is not a right of using, enjoying, and abusing (*jus utendi, fruendi, et abutendi*), but only a power of procuring and dispensing (*potestas procurandi et dispensandi*).

It is not difficult to understand the strong moralist tone of the scholastic theories and their normative function. This was a period in which the revival of commerce threatened to break up a social order which was supposed to be based on the divine will, while bringing wealth and welfare, if not to all the community, certainly to some new classes and social groups. In this situation there was a strongly felt need to keep under the community's control, wherever possible, the economic instruments by which the new wealth was accumulated: commercial profits, prices, usury loans, and private property.

The economic ideas of Aquinas, and of scholasticism in general, have little scientific value and belong to the prehistory of economic science. But they cannot be ignored in any history of this science as, after becoming part of the social doctrine of the Catholic Church, they have continued to influence economic thought for several centuries, even in writers who did not agree with them. Economists who have elaborated opposing doctrines have had to take them into consideration. An excellent example is the abbé Galiani, who, as late as the eighteenth century, at the height of the Enlightenment, was not able to formulate his own modern theory of interest without feeling the need to show its coherence with the doctrine of 'commutative' justice and the precept that prohibits usury.

1.1.2. 'Mercantile' capitalism

A slow but inexorable process of economic, social, political, and cultural transformation began around the middle of the fifteenth century, and was to last beyond the middle of the eighteenth, when all the preconditions for the birth of modern industrial capitalism had been laid down.

One of the main factors in this transformation process was the flow of gold from the Americas. The prices in Europe tripled from 1500 to 1650. The social consequences were enormous. On the one hand, there was a gradual impoverishment of those classes, aristocratic and clerical, who lived on incomes which, being fixed by custom, adjusted extremely slowly to the fall in the value of money. On the other hand, there was an unprecedented enrichment of the mercantile class, who lived on 'profits upon alienation', namely, incomes derived from the difference between the buying and selling prices of goods, a type of profit that naturally increases with inflation. This growth of the monetary wealth of the middle classes and the corresponding gradual expropriation of the old dominant classes was one of the fundamental factors in the process of primitive accumulation.

The expansion of trade, especially long-distance commerce, led to the formation of commercial and industrial centres and, gradually, to the new figure of the merchant-manufacturer, thus inducing profound changes in productive activity. The need for an increasing quantity of manufactured products and, above all, the need for greater stability in their supply led the merchants to extend their control over the production activity. Already by the end of the sixteenth century the craft model of production, where the craftsman was the owner of his tools and workshop and worked as a small independent business-man, had begun to be replaced, in the export sector, by a system of working at home, the 'putting-out' system. At first, the merchant supplied the raw materials and commissioned the craftsman to transform them into finished products, while the work continued to be done in independent workshops. In the succeeding phase, the ownership of the tools of production, and often the workshops themselves, passed to the merchant, who was then able to employ workers himself. Workers no longer sold the finished product to the merchant but instead sold their own working capacity. The textile industry was one of the first sectors in which this new method of production took place.

Thus occurred the slow formation of a modern working class, a social class whose members are deprived of control over the production process and for whom the sale of their own working capacity represents the only way of making a living. In the countryside this process was favoured by the diffusion of the putting-out system, the enclosure movement (especially in England), and the increase in the population. Furthermore, the increase in prices in the towns drastically impoverished those categories of semi-skilled craft workers who made up the lowest strata of the old guilds, and who earned, at least in part, incomes which were fixed by tradition. Such incomes were heavily cut by inflation. This social group merged with the farmers expelled from the countryside and the poor craftsmen whose goods were no longer competitive because of lack of commercial outlets.

Another important change that occurred in these three centuries was the affirmation of the modern nation states, a process triggered by the struggles between the free cities, the papacy, and the Empire which took place in Italy in the late Middle Ages. The transformation ended in the dissolution of the Holy Roman Empire, thus giving life to various national unification processes which were completed towards the end of the fifteenth century, at least in England, France, and Spain. In the following three centuries, European wars were wars among nation states, where the reason of the state prevailed over every other, even when, as with religious wars, the ideological element was very strong.

1.1.3. The Scientific Revolution and the birth of political economy

The affirmation of the supremacy of spiritual power over temporal power was one of the main ideological weapons in the struggle of the free cities against the central power. This struggle demolished the basis of the legitimacy of the order of the Empire and led to a revolutionary process which was to change the face of Europe. It was the spirit of man which emancipated itself from tradition. The cultural revolution was slow but inexorable. With Humanism and the Renaissance, man was placed at the centre of the universe and philosophy emancipated from Aristotle and Thomism. And while politics, with Machiavelli, ceased to be a branch of moral philosophy and became a science, with the Protestant Reformation it was faith, or the spiritual base of the free act, which emancipated itself from tradition and authority. Machiavelli's *The Prince* was published in 1516; Luther began preaching against the sale of indulgences in 1517.

The Renaissance also witnessed the beginning of that great process of intellectual emancipation known as the Scientific Revolution. In the sixteenth and seventeenth centuries there was a second wave in the expansion of European universities. The first wave had taken place in the late Middle Ages under the protection of the Church. Later, in the fourteenth and fifteenth centuries, the university system collapsed, mainly because of the attempt by the freer and more creative intellectuals to escape from the spiritual control of the Church and to look for employment in the royal courts and in the lay academies. During the revival of the universities in the sixteenth and seventeenth centuries, the State tended to take the place of the Church in the control of intellectual activity. In this period, the traditionally higher-ranked faculties of theology, law, and medicine, where the spiritual control fed by the wars of religion was still important, lost prestige and importance. At the same time the faculties of philosophy, relegated to an ancillary role in the Middle Ages, acquired increasing prominence.

Modern philosophy was born in the new universities, and with it science. And it was not by chance that the greatest philosophers of the period were also great scientists, or at least showed great interest in scientific research. The Scientific Revolution began with Copernicus in the first half of the sixteenth century, continued with Keplero, Galileo, Bacon, Leibnitz, Descartes, and was completed by Newton in the eighteenth century.

It was in this climate of cultural revolution that the basis of modern economic thought was laid down. While the natural sciences were freeing themselves from belief in various forms of magic, economics wished to emancipate itself from ethics and political philosophy. The process had been under way for some time when Antoyne de Montchrétien (1575–1621) announced the programme in the title of his main work, *Traicté de l'oeconomie politique* (1615), in which he sustained that economics, the 'science of acquisition', was an important part of politics, and that it should concern itself, not only with the household, but also with the State. The birth of economic science passed through two emancipation processes. The first led to the abandonment of the Aristotelian and Thomistic idea that economics should deal exclusively with the behaviour of individual economic agents and households, while the other resulted in the abandonment of scholastic metaphysics and gnosiology. We will consider them separately.

In classical Greek thought and, owing to the influence of Aristotle, in medieval philosophy, economics was considered as the art of family management. For Thomas Aquinas, *oeconomia* was simply the 'government of the house'. It was a discipline which focused on the private sphere of human action. In this role it was subordinate to ethics and political philosophy, the philosophical disciplines which studied the public activities of man. Politics was concerned with the behaviour of collective agents such as social classes, the State, and its organs, whereas economics studied the behaviour of the individual social agents, the families. The aim of the 'science' of political philosophy was the study of the political society. In relation to this, the families represented something which was considered inessential.

On the other hand, political philosophy and ethics produced knowledge, whereas economics only had practical ends. For Aristotle, as for his followers in the late Middle Ages, especially Aquinas, 'science', that is to say, speculative knowledge, consisted of the application of a rational deductive procedure to an object of study, on the basis of which propositions could be formulated and conclusions reached that would be both universal and necessary. The universality of political propositions was derived from the fact that God's will was manifested in the popular consent given to the legislative power of the governors; while the universality of ethical propositions derived from the fact that the ends of human action coincided with the ends which God had modelled for all creatures. The economic activities of a household could not be studied in this way. All the actions of the single social cells would come under either ethics or politics, and those which could not thus be classified were not worth 'scientific' study. In other words, economics was not a 'science' because it was neither ethics nor politics. Indeed, Schumpeter is right when, in his *History*, he observes that Aquinas was not interested in economic questions in themselves, and that 'it is only where economic phenomena raise questions of moral theology that he touched upon them at all' (p. 90). He is also correct when he observes that, in scholasticism, economics as a whole was never treated as a subject in itself. Aquinas considered individual commercial action as despicable. What universal propositions could be formulated on it? How could a 'science' deal with it?

Now, pretending to be *public, national*, or *political* economy, the new discipline defined itself as a science precisely because it had located its own subject of study within the sphere of public activity. With this it affirmed, among other things, its own autonomy from the new political science, which was developing at the same time. They were two independent disciplines which studied different aspects of collective action: one was concerned with the accumulation and management of wealth, the other with the accumulation and management of power. Both studied the behaviour of collective agents: still the State and its organs, but now subordinately to another social subject, the nation. From the latter the State tended to receive legitimacy, especially as the legitimacy of the papacy or the Empire had been strongly weakened. Public welfare was becoming one of the legitimating factors by which a new sphere of State activity was to be defined. Political economy was born, together with theories of economic policy, in order to give sense and efficacy to this activity.

In order to outline the second aspect of the process of emancipation of economics from Thomism, it is important to note that the birth of political economy occurred at the same time as the concept of economic science underwent a secularization process. Only when human action is no longer motivated by spiritual ends does it make sense to study it without aspiring to reach universal propositions. And it is precisely when public choices are no longer legitimated by God, but only by the ends of men and the nation, that it is possible to study them scientifically.

This secularization process, as far as political economy is concerned, was completed in the seventeenth century, when the new science was fertilized by natural-law philosophy, English empiricism, and Cartesian rationalism. But it had begun much earlier, at the time of the philosophical debates about 'universals'. The 'universals' are the essential properties of things. According to Aquinas, before existing in the mind of man, who is able to understand them by means of abstraction, universals exist in the mind of God. They also reside in things themselves, behind and at the roots of their empirical reality. It is for this reason that speculation leads to 'science': the human mind, with its speculative ability, operates on an ontological structure of the world to which it corresponds.

A different theory of knowledge was put forward by the nominalist philosophers, who denied the real existence of the universals. These, from the nominalist point of view, were purely conventional signs: the names of things and not their real essence. The principal supporters of this conception were Roger Bacon and William Ockham, to whom we owe the distant origin of modern scientific thought. The nominalist philosophers looked for knowledge in the study of the individual and empirical aspects of the things, rather than in their universal essences.

Karl Pribram has pointed out that it was some of the nominalist thinkers, above all students and followers of Ockham, who, in the late fourteenth and early fifteenth centuries, made the first attempts at scientific reasoning in economics. Jean Buridan (?1290–?1382), who tried to explain the values of goods, not as what they should be, but as what they really are; and not as substance but as relational phenomena, expressions of human needs. Nicholas Oresme (?1320–?1382), who distanced himself from Thomism by attributing a real rather than a conventional value to money, a value linked to that of the precious metals from which money was made. Oresme was also one of the first scholars to have a clear idea of 'Gresham's Law', which we will consider in the next section. And Antonio Pierozzi (1389–1459), better known as St Antoninus of Florence, who advanced a theory according to which, the value of goods, besides being dependent on the costs sustained in production, was also dependent on scarcity (*raritas*), and on the evaluation (*complacibilitas*) of the individuals. In this way he turned the doctrine of *communis aestimatio* to serve a subjectivist notion of value.

1.2. MERCANTILISM

1.2.1. Bullionism

We should immediately point out that a school of thought that defined itself as 'mercantilist' has never existed—even as a current of opinion aware of its own theoretical homogeneity. However, there is no doubt that Adam Smith was to a degree correct in placing in the category of 'trade or mercantile system' the group of economic ideas that dominated European political and commercial circles in the sixteenth and seventeenth centuries and most of the eighteenth. A common theoretical core did exist, and this not only permitted debates and dialogues but also gave a certain homogeneity to the various national economic policies. What *is* difficult is to identify a 'system' in those ideas. It would be at least necessary to admit some important differences connected with national characteristics, and also to admit a minimum of historical evolution. We have insufficient space here to consider the national differences, except for a few points which will be mentioned when necessary; however, historical evolution cannot be ignored.

For simplicity's sake, we will follow Cannan's suggestion and distinguish bullionism from mercantilism in its strict sense, even though we are well aware that this classification is a little forced.

Bullionism had dominated the opinions circulating in the European courts up to the end of the sixteenth century. It was characterized by the conviction that money, or gold, was *the* wealth. Now, there is obviously no doubt that money *is* wealth. The mistake, according to Smith, was the belief that it was the only form of wealth. However, it is doubtful that there have ever been economists who really thought in this way. Rather, there was a widespread opinion that treasure was the only type of wealth worth accumulating—an opinion which had more than a grain of truth from the point of view of the State, in an era in which wars were won with gold. This idea also accorded well with the merchant's point of view, for whom money was capital and, actually, the only type of capital capable of increasing in value. In fact, it was clear to almost every economist of the period that money was *a means* of increasing wealth and power. What many of the bullionists did not admit was the idea that that means should be used to increase the welfare of people, the wealth of nations, as Smith claimed. But why should the State and the merchants have had to pursue such an objective? In fact, the first bullionist economists, when they were not merchants, were administrators of the sovereign's private finances rather than civil servants; in other words, they were still concerned with a household economy. This was certainly true of the German cameralists, who worked at the *Kammer*, or treasury, of the sovereign; and the same was true for many of the Spanish bullionists. They had good reasons, therefore, to work towards rulers' private goals.

The real mistake made by these economists, however, and the one which distinguishes them from the mercantilists of the following century, was in the methods they suggested for achieving these objectives. A wide circulation of money within the national borders was considered to guarantee an extensive tax base; therefore, the outflow of precious metals had to be prevented. The simplest way to do this was to prohibit the export of gold and silver, a method that was applied rigorously, sometimes even ferociously, in many countries. Another measure often adopted was that of raising the purchasing power of the foreign currencies by law within the national territory, so as to induce an inflow of money from abroad. Besides this, there were also attempts to force national companies to pay for imports with goods instead of money. Finally, a measure that was used above all in Spain was that of the 'balance of contracts': buying from each foreign country an amount of goods which did not exceed the amount exported to that country.

Another bullionist 'mistake' was the tendency to seek the causes of a systematic outflow of precious metals solely in monetary factors, namely, in the deviations of exchange rates from the parity determined by the metallic content. Such deviations were attributed to illegal behaviour, forgery, and manipulations by bankers and merchants. But the Crown also, often and willingly, resorted to illegal monetary techniques, such as 'clipping', i.e. reducing the metallic content of the currency in relation to face values, or 'raising', i.e. increasing, by means of a proclamation, the official value of the currency in relation to its metallic content. There were many learned investigations in this field, some of which led to the formulation of an important economic law, 'Gresham's Law', according to which bad money drives out good. If, in a country, two types of currency circulate which have the same nominal value but different intrinsic values (because one of the two has a lower content of precious metal, because it is a forgery or worn), the public will tend to use the bad money for internal payments. The good will be hoarded, melted down, or used for international payments, and will therefore disappear from circulation.

In regard to the naming of this law, it is worth pointing out that in 1857 its discovery was attributed to Thomas Gresham (1519–79) by Henry McLeod, who later changed his mind and called it the 'Oresme–Copernicus–Gresham Law'. Gresham provided a precise formulation of the law, first in a letter to Queen Elizabeth I and later in *Information Touching the Fall of Exchange* (1558). Today, it is known that the first formulation of the law can be found in the *Tractatus de Monetis* (1519) by Nicholas Copernicus (1473–1543), even if there were some hints of it in the *Traictie de la première invention des monnoies* (about 1360) by Nicolas Oresme.

1.2.2. Mercantilist commercial theories and policies

Bullionist doctrines were still professed in the seventeenth century. For example, Gerald de Malynes (1586–1641) (*A Treatise of the Canker of England's Common Wealth* (1603); *Consuetudo vel lex mercatoria or the Ancient Law Merchant* (1622)) sought the basic causes of a disequilibrium in the balance of trade in the alterations in the exchange rate. The most interesting part of Malynes's arguments, however, is not bullionist, and can be summarized in the following way. An exchange rate which is higher than the metal parity leads to an outflow of precious metals which diminishes the amount of money in circulation in the country under consideration. This reduces prices and worsens the *terms of trade*. Consequently, the trade deficit increases. There are two interesting aspects to this way of thinking: the use (albeit in an approximate way) of the quantity theory of money, and the implicit hypothesis of a low price elasticity of imports and/or exports. We will consider this later. Less interesting is the solution proposed: the intervention of the 'royal exchanger' against illegal practices and monetary manipulations, which had, according to Malynes, the sole responsibility for the fluctuations of the rate of exchange.

Counter-arguments were advanced by two learned merchant adventurers who disdained neither science nor politics: Edward Misselden (1608–54) (*Free Trade or the Means to make Trade Flourish* (1622); *The Circle of Commerce* (1623)) and Thomas Mun (1571–1641) (*A Discourse of Trade from England into the East Indies* (1621); *England's Treasure by Forraign Trade* (written in 1630, but published posthumously in 1664)). Misselden overturned the theories of Malynes: it is the surplus or the deficit on the balance of trade which makes the rate of exchange vary, and not the other way round. Rather than worry about the exchange rate, the State should encourage exports and discourage imports. This is the gist of the mercantilist doctrine, a doctrine which was expressed perhaps more systematically by Mun than by any other contemporary economist. While Malynes placed great emphasis on the *particular* trade balances of one country with each other country, taken singly, Mun showed that what really mattered was the overall balance of trade. The inflow and outflow of gold depends on the general balance of trade, and the State should pay direct attention to this. Thus it was permissible to maintain a commercial deficit with some countries, such as those from which raw materials were imported, if this was conducive to the increase of the national production of industrial goods. Many of these goods could be sold abroad at high prices, because of the monopolistic advantages associated with the superior technology required to produce them.

From the point of view of the birth of political economy, the identification of the interests of one particular social class, the merchant class, with those of the collectivity, was extremely important. In this way economics ceased to be 'domestic economy' and became 'political'. The profits of that class, *profits upon alienation*, were obtained from an excess of the value of sales over purchases. This gap gave rise to the accumulation of money. The entire nation was considered as a great commercial company. Its net inflow of gold corresponded to the excess of its foreign sales over and above its foreign purchases. And, as with the merchant, the nation would also have to avoid keeping its stock of money idle. It had to reinvest it in the form of *stock*, in order to buy (import) the goods necessary to produce new goods; with these it would be able to increase sales (exports) and profits (trade surplus). Although production, and therefore the transformation of the imported raw materials, played an important role in this way of thinking, it was still only the excess of sales over purchases which was seen as the source of profits, for the collectivity as well as for the individual.

The theory of economic policy that sprang from this doctrine was simple. Commercial policy had to be protectionist. Export duties had to be abolished and import duties raised. Moreover, exports should be encouraged by incentives and imports hindered as far as possible and even forbidden in certain cases. These principles were rigidly followed by the French customs tariffs instituted by Colbert in 1644. England moved in this direction especially towards the end of the seventeenth century. However, certain very important exceptions were made: the import of raw materials, which were considered useful to the national industries, was not to be obstructed, while the export of important raw materials such as wool should be forbidden.

Mercantilist commercial policy also favoured national shipping; and many measures were taken aimed at reinforcing the merchant navy. The 1651 English Navigation Act, for example, prohibited the importation of goods on non-British ships. This cultural attitude also influenced colonial expansion policy, in relation especially to the demand for the mother country's products and for the supply of low-cost raw materials that were expected to come from the colonies. Finally, it is important to mention the policy of conceding privileges and monopoly rights to the great national commercial companies. The British East India Company was founded in 1600, the Dutch in 1602.

The mercantilist industrial policy aimed at encouraging productive activity within the national territories by the concession of monopolistic privileges, State subsidies, and tax exemptions to national enterprises, as well as by the importation of advanced technology, the acquisition of manufacturing secrets, and the encouragement of the immigration of skilled workers. The industrial policy even included the creation of State factories. In this field French mercantilism again excelled: Colbert brought industrial policy to obsessive levels, to the point of administrative prescription of measures relating to production and quality control.

1.2.3. Demographic theories and policies

A mercantilist theory and policy also exists in regard to demography. The problem was how to ensure an abundant labour supply to satisfy the expansion needs of the emerging industries; the policy aimed at increasing the population (we are still a long way from the Malthusian obsessions of the nineteenth century). This policy was put into practice with particular effectiveness in Germany, with the abolition of pre-existing prohibitions on some types of marriage and the awarding of prizes for large families.

It is possible to speak of a mercantilist psychosis in regard to population scarcity. Even in countries like Italy, in which there was no real scarcity of population, the demographic mania spread—so much so that the first hints of the 'population principle', later to be called 'Malthusian', did not cause a great deal of concern. For example, Giovanni Botero (1543/4–1617) outlined, in Delle cause della grandezza e magnificenza delle città (On the Causes of the Prosperity and Magnificence of Cities) (1588), the tendency of the 'generative power' of mankind to grow more rapidly than the 'nutritive power' of the nations, but concluded that this was just one more reason to develop production; in the worst case, emigration could be used as an escape valve.

This obsession with demographic growth can be explained only partially by the continual and thirsty demand for soldiers in a period of permanent warfare. There was also an economic motivation which had a certain theoretical importance. The mercantilists had a rather peculiar wage theory, according to which maximum labour supply occurs at subsistence wage-level. If wages increase above this level, the supply will diminish rather than increase. The most ingenious justification of this theory was given in terms of 'morals': workers were considered to be depraved people, attracted by vice and excesses in eating and drinking: if they were paid more than subsistence wages, this would encourage depravity and laziness and thus reduce the labour supply.

A less ideological explanation of the phenomenon should be based on an understanding of the working conditions in the emerging industries and the difference in living conditions between the countryside and the town. The first point can be simply dealt with. Only a problem of physical survival would induce the workers to accept working 13–14 hours per day. In these conditions it was understandable that an increase in the daily wage could cause an increase in the demand for leisure, and perhaps for alcohol. What could be a worse crime against Christian morality? This is the first cause of the strange shape of the labour-supply curve which the mercantilist economists had in mind. The second cause was that the rural–urban migration was of a 'push' type (caused, for example, by the enclosures) rather than 'pull' (due to the attraction of the towns), for the living conditions in the towns were worse than in the countryside. Therefore, a slight increase in industrial wages would not encourage any significant increase in the industrial-labour supply. This second factor could account for the low elasticity in the labour supply. But the supply curve would even become negatively sloped owing to the former factor.

The theory can be illustrated by making use of a supply curve such as SS in Fig. 1. w_r is the real wage, $\overline{w}_r$ the subsistence wage, N the quantity of labour, and $\overline{N}$ the full employment level. The labour supply curve is infinitely elastic at the subsistence wage-level: at that wage, all the available labour power will offer itself in order to guarantee survival. A lower wage is not possible, simply because it would not ensure survival. Once full employment has been reached, each increase in wages would allow the workers to take some time off, and the supply curve would become negatively sloped.

Let us begin from point P, a full-employment situation at the subsistence wage-level and with a demand curve such as DD. An increase of accumulation would cause the demand curve to move to $D'D'$. The wages would increase to

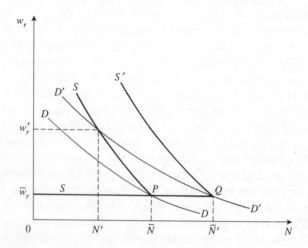

FIG. 1.

w'_r and the labour supply would be reduced to N'. In conclusion, if the enrichment of the nation is not to be slowed down by the depravity of the workers, it is necessary to ensure that the population grows at least as fast as the stock (of capital). If the supply curve shifts to SS', employment rises to $\bar{N}'$, and the wages return to $\bar{w}_r$; the new equilibrium point will be Q.

The problem of the labour market, in the period of primitive capital accumulation, was not so much that of high wages, as the manufactured products were mostly sold in imperfectly competitive markets, and therefore at remunerative prices, but rather that of a labour supply that had difficulty in keeping pace with the expansion of industry and trade. For example, Josiah Child (1630–99), who wrote *Brief Observations Concerning Trade and Interest of Money* (1668), reprinted in a modified version in 1693 as *A New Discourse of Trade*, was extremely worried about the demographical problem, as were all the mercantilists, but he was not so concerned about the problem of wages. Although he was not against a low-wage policy, Child also maintained that high wages were not generally a bad thing; or, rather, that they should be seen as a consequence of the high level of wealth of a country, while low wages would be indicative of poverty.

1.2.4. Monetary theories and policies

Let us now consider monetary theory. The mercantilists made the first formulations of the quantity theory of money. The price revolution which occurred in Europe after the discovery of America, and which caused a century-long inflationary process, could not pass unnoticed. The relationship between the increase in prices and the increase in the amount of gold in circulation had already been noticed by the early Spanish mercantilists. The first hints at this relationship were made by Martin de Azpilcueta Navarro (?–1586); a more detailed formulation was proposed by Luis de Molina (1530–1600), who touched on the problem in *De justicia et jure* (*About Justice and Law*) (1597).

One of the first formulations of the quantity theory was made by Jean Bodin (1530–96) in *Réponse aux paradoxes de Monsieur de Malestroict touchant l'enchérissement de toutes choses* (1568). Jehan Cherruyt de Malestroict had asserted, in his *Paradoxes, touchant le faict de monnaies et enchérissement de toutes choses* (1566), that the increase in prices which had occurred in France was only apparent. The prices, according to Malestroict, had increased in terms of the monetary unit, because of 'clipping'; but, as the precious-metal content of the coinage had diminished, prices had not increased at all in terms of gold. Bodin pointed out that this argument only partially explained the inflationary process: prices had increased in terms both of the monetary unit and of precious metal, and the latter factor was more important. He demonstrated, with the aid of quantitative data, that the main cause of the increase in prices was to be found in the increase in the amount of gold in circulation. After Bodin the quantity theory was adopted by many other mercantilists.

There are clear expressions of it by John Hales (b.?–1571) in *A Discourse on the Common Wealth of this Realm of England* (written 1549, published 1581), by Bernardo Davanzati (1529–1606) in *Lezione delle Monete* (*Lecture on Currencies*) (1588), and by Antonio Serra, in *Breve trattato delle cause che possono far abbondare li regni d'oro e d'argento dove non sono minere* (*A Short Treaty of the Causes which Might Make Flourish the Kingdoms where No Gold or Silver Mines Exist*) (1613).

However, from the middle of the seventeenth century there was an important theoretical change. The quantity theory was still widely accepted by the mercantilists; but it was no longer interpreted as an explanation of price levels, but rather as a theory of the level of transactions. This belief became so common that the few economists who did not accept it and remained faithful to the old quantity theory were considered almost as revolutionaries. We will consider this point in the next section, when we outline the theories of some of the forerunners of classical economics.

This change in point of view was probably connected to the end, between 1620 and 1640, of the century-long inflationary process that had begun with the discovery of America. The trend of increasing prices, which had started at the beginning of the sixteenth century, levelled out in the seventeenth and remained so until after the middle of the eighteenth. The second half of the seventeenth and the first half of the eighteenth century also represented a period of depression. The flow of gold and silver from the Americas was drastically reduced, and the struggle among the European countries to obtain precious metals almost became a 'zero sum' game.

Economists and merchants were no longer worried about inflation but about the lack of the availability of money to finance trade. A widespread idea was that 'money stimulates trade'. The increase in the inflow of precious metals caused by a surplus in the balance of trade, in a period in which it was only possible to increase internal monetary circulation by a reduction in external spending, was seen above all as the necessary condition for an increase in production and, therefore, in wealth—to the extent that protectionist policies were often linked to the advice, specifically directed to the sovereign, not to hoard money: to increase the State treasury would do nothing but take money out of circulation.

Two mechanisms were indicated by means of which the increase in the money supply would have stimulated the levels of activity. The first is a direct mechanism, consisting of the increase in incomes and consumption caused by the increase in the money supply. This argument was supported, for example, by Jacob Vanderlint (?–1740) in *Money Answers all Things* (1734) and by John Law (1671–1729) in *Money and Trade Considered* (1705). The latter clearly identified the hypothesis on which that argument was based, which was that prices do not vary in a substantial way with variations in demand (although Law limited the validity of this hypothesis to non-durable goods). In other words, the supply curve was assumed to be almost horizontal. With this, inflation, if it exists, is creeping, while its effects are in any case positive, because the increase in profits encourages further capital accumulation.

The other mechanism was indirect, and consisted of the reduction of the interest rate caused by the increase in the quantity of money. Some mercantilists had (as Keynes has pointed out) a monetary theory of interest: money is used to activate production and trade; interest is the price that is paid to obtain this use. It is also worth noting that the old term for 'interest' is 'use', a term which John Locke, at that time, still adopted as a synonym for 'interest'. This price depends on the supply and demand of money. Thus 'the abundance of money reduces usury', argued Malynes in *Consuetudo vel lex mercatoria*. Misselden, his main critic, did not disagree with him on this point when he suggested, in *Free Trade*, that 'the remedy for usury may be the abundance of money'. Cantillon observed in his *Essai* that 'it is a common idea, received of all those who have written on Trade, that the increased quantity of currency in a State brings down the price of interest, because when Money is plentiful it is more easy to find some to borrow' (p. 213).

Thus an increase in the quantity of money, *ceteris paribus*, allows for a reduction in the price of credit and therefore in the cost of financing investments, in this way encouraging economic expansion.

The level of interest was, understandably, another of the mercantilists' obsessions, due to their strong identification with the merchant's point of view. Any policy aimed at reducing the level of interest was positively evaluated, while any theory able to justify this was considered useful—so much so that many mercantilists, while adopting monetary theories of interest, did not hesitate to accept points of view from scholastic thought in order to justify measures against usury and to request state intervention aimed at lowering the rate of interest by law. Keynes found value in this mixture of theories. If value there is, it is perhaps to be found in the fact that such theories form the embryo of a monetary–institutional theory which was to be elaborated by Marx and to which the theory of Keynes himself can be traced back. If interest depends on monetary forces, its long-term trend is not an equilibrium value determined by real variables but simply an average of short-term values, an average which basically depends on institutional factors.

1.2.5. Hume's criticism

One of the principal criticisms of mercantilist thought was put forward by David Hume (1711–76) in the *Political Discourses* (1752). Hume's idea was that an increase in the circulation of money in a country with a trade surplus would increase prices (while it would reduce them in countries with a deficit). The consequent loss of competitiveness would rebalance, sooner or later, the balance of payments and halt the outflow of gold. Therefore, mercantilist commercial policies would have been, in the best of cases, short-lived. In the long run they would have been useless. From the theoretical point of view, they seemed to ignore the quantity theory of money.

The adjustment mechanism of the balance of payments theorized by Hume, and known as the price–specie-flow mechanism, was also described with a certain precision by Joseph Harris (1702–64) in *An Essay on Money and Coins* (1757–8). Later, it was accepted by the classical economists and even by Marx, not only as a criticism of mercantilism but also as a description of a general economic law. All this is rather strange, as the mercantilists were aware of the problem raised by Hume. Cantillon, for example, had clearly defined the problem thirty years before, even if, and significantly, he had limited the loss of competitiveness caused by internal inflation to the industrial sector. Moreover, he had pointed out that the increase in the imports of consumer goods directly caused by an increase in monetary incomes could also contribute to aggravating the difficulties connected with the price–specie-flow mechanism.

Mercantilist thought, however, contained all the elements necessary to rebut Hume's criticism; they had been clearly formulated even by Cantillon himself. First, the mercantilist economists were aware of the relationship that links the quantity of money to the value of transactions. As we have mentioned above, in most cases, especially in the seventeenth and eighteenth centuries, they interpreted it, not as a theory of the level of prices, but rather as a theory of the level of output. Second—and this is the argument put forward by Cantillon but already present in the work of Malynes and many other mercantilist writers—even if an increase in the quantity of money in a country with a trade surplus causes, at least partially, an increase in the level of prices (the opposite occurring in a country with a trade deficit), this could cause, owing to an improvement in the terms of trade, a further increase in the trade surplus rather than a rebalancing effect. The implicit hypothesis in this way of thinking is that of a low price elasticity of imports and exports. Under such conditions, an increase in internal prices with respect to international prices would cause an increase in the value of exports rather than causing changes in the quantities of imports and exports. Thus an improvement in the terms of trade would reflect positively on the balance of payments.

Therefore, the mercantilist theories were robust from the logical point of view, although the realism of the hypotheses on which they were based should be verified. Obviously, this is not the right place to undertake such an analysis. However, there is reason to believe that behind the theoretical jump made by Hume there was a real historical change. Probably, in the pre-industrial period the elasticity of exports was not very high, given the marked productive specialization of the various countries. In particular, the elasticity of imports of the imperialist countries must have been low, as imports mainly consisted of food supplies, raw materials, and luxury goods, which were not produced internally. However, it is probable that, as manufacturing production developed in the main capitalist countries, a certain amount of price competition gathered steam, at least for that type of production; and this could have increased the elasticity of exports and imports. It is significant that Cantillon, in 1730, limited the effects of the monetary price–specie-flow mechanism to manufacturing production. Perhaps at the time of Hume and, later, of Smith, this effect had become dominant.

1.2.6. Theories of value

The mercantilists also had, to a certain degree, a common point of view on the subject of value, at least in the sense that almost all the authors concerned with this problem in the sixteenth and the first half of the seventeenth century looked for the solution in the same direction: namely, towards utility. It was only at the end of the seventeenth century that some economists with partially mercantilist backgrounds, such as Petty and Locke, decidedly distanced themselves from the dominant view on value and looked for the solution of the problem in the costs of production. We will say more about this later.

It is not surprising that the mercantilists looked mainly to exchange as the real source of wealth and profit. In fact, the merchant earns profits, not because he controls the productive process (a control which, at least in the first phase of industrial development, was still in the hands of the craftsman), but rather because of the power he manages to exercise on the market. The merchant's profit originates from the difference between the selling and buying prices of goods. He believes, therefore, that it originates from the trading process. Thus a knowledge of the determinants of market prices is crucial in order to understand the origin and the growth of profits. Attention must be mainly focused on the forces that determine the demand for the goods, and demand is easily linked to utility.

In 1588 Bernardo Davanzati made an interesting attempt to construct a utility theory of value. In *Lezione delle monete (Lecture on Money)*, he quoted a passage from the *Natural History* by Plinius in which a story is told of a mouse sold at a very high price during the siege of a city. Davanzati explained the phenomenon by arguing that the value of goods depends on their utility and rarity. It is not absolute utility that counts, but rather utility in regard to the quantity available. The effect of greater scarcity would be to increase the use value of the goods and therefore the price at which they can be sold. This theory was taken up again in 1680 by Geminiano Montanari (1633–87), who, in the *Breve trattato del valore delle monete in tutti gli stati (A Brief Treaty on the Value of Currencies in all the States)*, asserted that 'it is the desires of men which measure the value of things', so that the prices of goods will vary, ultimately, according to changes in tastes. Desires must be related to the rarity of the objects desired. With the same amount of money, or—as we would say —given demand, the greater the scarcity of the objects the higher they will be valued. Besides this, Montanari also made an interesting attempt to establish, by making use of the principle of communicating jars, the 'law of the levelling of price' of a good in different markets, a law which was later to be called Jevons's Law.

A few years later, Nicholas Barbon (d. 1698), in *A Discourse of Trade* (1690), summarized mercantilist thought on the subject of value in the following way. First, the natural value of goods is simply represented by their market price. Second, the forces of supply and demand determine the market price. Finally, the use value is the main factor on which the market price depends. The conditions of supply play a role only in the sense that, given the demand, the price tends to rise when the supply is insufficient and vice versa.

It is understandable that, in this period, the great trading companies tried to obtain State help to ensure themselves monopoly positions. Competition among merchants reduced their market power or, in other words, their ability to control the conditions of demand (on the purchase markets) or supply (on the sales markets). Less understandable may seem the inclination of the governments to concede such privileges, or even the tendency, especially strong in France under Colbert, to bring the highest possible number of economic activities under the monopolistic control of the State. However, it is important to realize that it was precisely from the beginning of the seventeenth century that the sovereigns of the great nations began to prefer to take advice from merchants rather than from nobles. It was also the century in which the merchants began to present the principles that underpinned their own private economic activity as the principles of 'public economics'. It was in this way that economic science began.

1.3. SOME FORERUNNERS OF CLASSICAL POLITICAL ECONOMY

1.3.1. The premises of a theoretical revolution

As capitalist accumulation continued, some important changes rendered the mercantilist theoretical position increasingly inadequate in respect to the economic reality.

First, notwithstanding the efforts of the great companies to preserve their monopolistic positions, the diffusion of trade and competition tended to reduce the price differentials among regions and nations, causing a reduction in commercial profit margins. Second, the fall in profits led to an increase in capitalist control over the production process. On the other hand, in many of the old guilds the master craftsmen had already begun to transform themselves from simple workers, who operated with the help of paid apprentices, into organizers and controllers of the production process. In this way a capitalist class was born which did not originate from commerce, and whose interests were in conflict with those of the merchant manufacturers.

These changes were accompanied by a radical, even if at first gradual and confused, rethinking of the traditional way of conceiving economic facts. On the one hand, paternalistic State intervention in the economy began to be seen with suspicion. On the other, the idea made ground that prices and profits reflected the conditions of production rather than the forces of demand. In particular, the idea that the origin of profit was to be found in the production sphere began to spread. The new class of capitalist entrepreneurs needed to free itself, not only from the old economic and administrative obstacles, but also from traditional moral and ideological ties. The new philosophy of individualism, together with developments in the Protestant ethic, contributed to solving the problem by liberating egoistical and acquisitive behaviour from religious condemnation and created the premises for a new type of legitimation for economic activity. These are the bases on which the great ideological edifice of classical liberalism was to be constructed.

Towards the end of the seventeenth century and the beginning of the eighteenth, the idea that administrative restrictions on economic activity created more disadvantages than advantages for the collectivity began to spread among the economists. On the other hand, if it were true (as it was beginning to be asserted without shame), that self-interest and acquisitive behaviour produced wealth for the collectivity as well as for individuals, then the State would have to reduce its own sphere of action to the recognition and the protection of property rights, and the connected function of enforcing contractual agreements.

For the history of economic thought the dates that delimit this period could be fixed at 1662, the year in which Petty published *A Treatise of Taxes and Contributions*, and 1730–4, the years of the probable final draft of Cantillon's *Essai sur la nature du commerce en général* (posthumously published in 1755). In this period a certain number of economists, even if still under the influence of mercantilism, began to distance themselves from it in different respects and to lay the foundations for that revolution in thought from which, in the second half of the seventeenth century, was to emerge classical political economy. The most important of these forerunners were William Petty (1623–87), John Locke (1632–1704), Dudley North (1641–91), Bernard de Mandeville (1670–1733), Pierre le Pesant de Boisguillebert (1646–1714), and Richard Cantillon (d. 1734). We have not the space here to give an exhaustive account of their ideas; so we will limit ourselves to mentioning only the most innovative of their arguments, especially those which seem to anticipate future theoretical developments, while leaving out the components of their thought which were most influenced by mercantilism. We will not consider, for example, their theories on the subject of money, which, especially in Locke and Cantillon, consisted of a resumption of the traditional quantity theory, albeit with some minor developments.

1.3.2. William Petty and 'political arithmetick'

These economists were well aware of the methodological problems raised by the attempt to make economic thought a real science; and they were strongly influenced by the debate on method which had gripped seventeenth-century philosophical thought.

In particular, Petty was influenced by Bacon's thought and fascinated with experimental science. Although he realized that scientific experimentation was impossible in the social sciences, Petty aspired toward an empiricist base for economics. He believed, for example, that pure speculative reasoning must be avoided. The method suggested in *Political Arithmetick* (written between 1671 and 1676, but published in 1690) was to appeal only to empirical facts. Qualitative arguments, based on 'comparative and superlative words', must be replaced by more rigorous ones, relying on 'number, weight and measure'. This is a method based on induction from quantitative data. Here is the derivation of the name 'political arithmetik' that Petty intended to give to the new science—a science which, in the work of Petty himself and his followers, often became confused with statistics, national accounting, and demography. In economics, this methodological position has never prevailed, except perhaps in statistical economic research, which has always accompanied but never conditioned the evolution of economic thought, and, more recently, in the foundation of econometrics, or at least in a certain way of justifying it epistemologically.

The method which *did* prevail was that proposed by North in *Discourse upon Trade* (1691). A method based, with explicit reference to Cartesian philosophy, on deduction rather than induction. North believed that economics should be founded on self-evident truths. Starting from indisputable principles, it would be possible, simply by means of the rigorous use of logic, to deduce conclusions that would be as clear and evident as the premises. North's work is an early example of that habit, which has become almost a vice for a great deal of contemporary economic theory, of only analysing simple and well-defined problems so as to allow the scholar to find clear 'truths' without getting too mixed up in the facts.

Petty made an important innovation concerning the explanation of value. On the one hand, he completely abandoned the subjective theory of value; on the other, he introduced the concept of 'natural value'. The prices of commodities would tend to adjust to the natural value by means of small oscillations; yet the mechanism by which this convergence occurs was not made clear. Besides this, there was an idea of the tendency of the rates of returns to level out among the various economic activities, but this was also formulated in a rather unclear way. Petty was more lucid about the determinants of natural value, which he considered to be the costs of production. He maintained that these costs could be reduced to those of the utilization of land and labour, but later he showed a preference for a calculation of value based exclusively on embodied labour. In order to justify this, he first tried to find a unit of measure which would permit him to express the value of land in terms of labour. Later, however, he abandoned this attempt, asserting that the contribution of the land was, in any case, minimal in respect to labour, so that not a great deal would be lost by just using labour as a measure. So here we have, right from the beginning, a '93 per cent' labour theory of value, or rather 99 per cent, as

Locke suggested, even if the reasons for this were obviously different from those later to be given by Ricardo.

The search for a unit of measure to translate the value of land into labour is interesting, because in the process Petty managed to define the natural price of labour. In fact, that unit of measurement consisted of the average daily amount of food necessary to sustain a worker. The wage goods used in this calculation must be those produced in the best conditions. Here we have the embryo of the classical-Marxian theory of subsistence wages and the theory of socially necessary labour. But Petty did not explain how and why wages tended to adjust to the subsistence level. Instead, he gave only the usual mercantilist justification of why wages *must be* fixed at this level: because the labour supply would vary inversely to its price, if its price were above the subsistence level.

Petty also anticipated the classical economists on three other important questions. First, he was perceptive both in regard to the importance of the role played by the division of labour in the capital accumulation process and in regard to the relationship existing between the division of labour and market size. Second, he sketched out an idea of surplus. This was calculated by subtracting from the value of the product obtained from a given piece of land both the yield which would have been obtained from it without the application of labour and the wages paid to the employed workers. The *surplus* defined in this way was interpreted as a product of labour, as it was obtained only by the application of human energy. However, it turned out to be rent! Another anticipation of the classical theories concerned rent itself, the formation of which was explained in terms of differential returns. The origin of these, however, was to be found in the different distances of the pieces of land from the market, rather than in the various levels of fertility of the soil.

Finally, it is necessary to mention Petty's important contributions on the subject of public finance, where he anticipated several of the arguments of the later classical and free-trade theories. For example, *A Treatise of Taxes and Contributions* (1662) contains more than an embryo of the theory of some canons of taxation: clarity and certainty, economy in collection, ease in payment, and proportionality. Petty justified the last criterion by the necessity of avoiding the use of taxation to modify the distribution of income.

John Graunt (1620–74), Charles D'Avenant (1656–1714), William Fleetwood (1656–1723), and Gregory King (1648–1712) were all followers of Petty. They almost formed a school of thought and also contributed to the acceptance, at least in England, of Petty's use of quantitative methods. Their applied research was extremely interesting, and at least one important result is worth mentioning here: 'King's Law', according to which the percentage changes in the price of corn are a decreasing function of the percentage changes in the size of the harvests. This empirical law hints at the concept of price elasticity of demand.

1.3.3. Locke, North, and Mandeville

Two other scholars, John Locke and Dudley North, without being Petty's direct followers, were certainly influenced by him. One of the most important of Locke's contributions in the field of economics was his attempt to justify private property by making use of the labour theory of value. It is important because it contains, in a nutshell, all the ideological overload that the labour theory of value had to endure in its subsequent evolution. Locke's basic idea was that individual liberty implied the right to control one's own labour. This would lead to the right to own the product of *one's own* labour; moreover, as land becomes productive and acquires value only with the application of labour, the private ownership of land would also be justified. It is a justification of private property derived from natural-law philosophy. The right to control one's own labour was considered a natural right, independent of the institutional structure of the society. This was also true for the ownership of land. As, in nature, men are basically equal or, rather, their natural gifts of working ability are not fundamentally unevenly distributed, then neither the ownership of wealth, in general, nor that of land, in particular, should be unequally distributed. Locke considered this to be true in primitive societies and in general in economies in which land was not scarce, but not, however, in the England of his times.

The reason for the inequality which really existed in modern economies was to be found in the ability of money to preserve value. Money on the one hand fuels the thirst for wealth and, on the other, allows an indefinite accumulation of wealth. Therefore it would lead to an unequal distribution of land if this is scarce. But money derives its value from social conventions, and is capable of preserving value as long as people are willing to accept it as a means of payment. Thus it is the society that legitimizes an economic situation in which wealth is distributed unequally. Locke did not believe that an unequal distribution of wealth makes private property any less legitimate. It was left to the socialists of the nineteenth century, especially those of the English tradition, to bring to light all the political and social implications of this explosive mixture of value theory and natural-law philosophy. At the end of the seventeenth century it served only to give a philosophical basis to the formation of English liberalism, though not of free-trade doctrines. Locke believed that the interests of the nation were different from the sum of private interests; with all the consequences that this entailed for economic policy, especially trade policy, on which his thought did not diverge greatly from the traditional mercantilist position.

The decisive step in the direction of free trade was made by North and Mandeville. These two scholars had a disenchanted view of human nature ('the public is a beast', North stated) and refused to base politics and economics on any elevated moral philosophy. Instead, the starting-point, according to North, was the exorbitant appetites of individuals. Here is one of the first manifestations of methodological individualism in economics. The 'public' is nothing more than the sum of private citizens; and the science dealing with wealth and public welfare must begin with the appetites which individuals try to satisfy. Harmony of interests is derived solely from the fact that nobody is able to look after the interests of an individual better than the individual himself, so that if the individuals are left free, they will prosper. On the other hand, any measure that interferes with the individual's attempts to pursue private goals hinders the achievements of the public interest. This idea had drastic consequences for economic policy: if collective interest depends on private interest and the individuals are the best judges of their own interests, then the State should acknowledge this. The best policy is no policy, no laws to regulate trade, none to regulate the interest rate, nor to control the money supply.

There were also two interesting contributions to monetary theory. First, North reaffirmed the theory already proposed by Petty and Locke, according to which the 'just' level for the rate of interest is simply that to which the forces of the supply and demand for money 'naturally' lead it. In this way, all the 'usury' problems that had contaminated mercantilist theory for so long were simply swept away. In regard to the rate of interest, the monetary authorities had nothing to do but stand back and watch. Second, there is a theory of the money supply which, again, takes some of the mercantilist arguments to their extreme consequences; a theory according to which the money supply can never be inadequate for the needs of trade. The adjustment occurs through a process of hoarding (or melting down coins) when the supply exceeds the demand and dis-hoarding (or reconverting the bullion into coins) in the opposite case. North was also against sumptuary laws which, according to him, only hindered the individual in the pursuit of his own objectives and thus discouraged any private initiative.

Mandeville was of a similar opinion. In *The Fable of the Bees, or Private Vices, Public Benefits* (1714), he not only insisted that the public welfare is fostered by leaving the individual completely free to satisfy his own 'vices', for example, by giving vent to economic greed, but also considered some of the most acclaimed economic and social virtues, such as savings, as socially less useful than their opposites. Ostentatious spending, for example, created more jobs than parsimony—an argument for which Mandeville was greatly esteemed by Keynes, understandably.

1.3.4. Boisguillebert and Cantillon

On the Continent, unlike in England, the reactions against mercantilism at the end of the seventeenth and at the beginning of the eighteenth centuries assumed the form of 'agrarian protectionism'. Various scholars, such as Sébastien de Vauban (1633–1707), Pierre le Pesant de Boisguillebert and Richard Cantillon in France, Leone Pascoli and Sallustio Antonio Bandini in Italy, endeavoured to demonstrate that the State should encourage agriculture rather than protecting trade and industry. The argument they adopted was that the real wealth of a nation was made up of consumer goods, not of accumulated capital and gold, and that therefore it is the result of agricultural production and not of trade, nor of the production of 'artificial wealth'.

Boisguillebert maintained, in *Dissertation sur la nature des richesses, de l'argent, et des tributs* (1712), that, if agricultural production was to be promoted, farmers should be allowed to receive sufficient earnings, and this meant that prices should conform to the 'natural law'. So, the best way to guarantee normal prices and earnings was to *laisser faire la nature et la liberté*. These arguments led Boisguillebert to propose economic policy measures similar to those which had already been put forward by Vauban in *Projet d'une dîme royale* (1707), and which amounted to a simplification of the tax system and a liberalization at least of internal trade. In particular, in *Le Détail de la France* (1695), Boisguillebert put forward an argument that was taken up again and developed in *Le Factum de la France* (1707) and in the *Traité de la nature, culture, commerce et intérêt des graines* (1712): that consumption, especially that of landowners, was the driving force of economic growth, as it created the aggregate demand for the whole economy. Therefore it was necessary to abolish the taxes which discourage consumption, and to impose an income tax. We are already moving along the line of thought which was to lead the physiocrats to propose the *impôt unique*. It is also important to remember that Boisguillebert maintained that all incomes originated, directly or indirectly, from agricultural production.

The *laissez-faire* argument made it necessary to demonstrate the natural tendency of the economy towards equilibrium. Boisguillebert sketched out such a demonstration in various parts of his works, anticipating both the Quesnay's *tableau économique* and Say's Law; and even though it was little more than a set of intuitions, it was enough to initiate a French tradition in the theory of equilibrium.

One common characteristic of the Continental economists during this period was that, unlike most of their English colleagues, they felt no need to offer an ethical justification of private property. The ability of individuals to pursue their own interests, if they are allowed to do so, is a sufficient justification for *laissez-faire*, they maintained—to the extent that they had no hesitation in recognizing the tyrannical and violent origin of private property. This was clear in the work of Boisguillebert.

The same argument was also put forward by Cantillon in the *Essai sur la nature du commerce en général*. Of Irish origin, Cantillon worked for a long time as a banker in France and often travelled between Paris and London. This placed him in a strategic position, enabling him to absorb the best of contemporary English and French economic thought.

Cantillon took up Petty's theory of value, but reformulated it, however, by trying to base it, not exclusively on embodied labour, but on the reduction of the cost of production to the inputs of labour and land. He was clearer than

Petty in regard to the distinction between 'intrinsic value', which depends on production conditions, and 'market price', which depends on the forces of supply and demand. His explanation of the adjustment of the latter to the former was extremely clear and modern: an explanation based on the hypothesis that the market price is fixed by the seller and dynamically modified on the basis of his estimate of the demand.

Cantillon also inherited from Petty the useless search for 'parity' between land and labour, as well as the related theory of the subsistence wage as determined by the production conditions of the wage goods. Cantillon also sketched out an explanation for the convergence of real wages towards the subsistence level which could well be defined as pre-Ricardian, or, rather, pre-Malthusian: the convergence of the two types of wage would go hand in hand with the convergence of the working population towards the demand for labour. Besides this, Cantillon also offered an explanation of wage differentials which anticipated Smith's: they depend on the differences in the cost of training workers, on the differences in risk in different types of job, and on the different levels of loyalty and responsibility required by the jobs.

Cantillon also absorbed from Petty the passion for empirical research, but unfortunately we do not know the results he obtained in this field, as the statistical appendix of his work was lost. Also, his monetary theory was of English origin and clearly quantitative in nature, but moderated by an argument according to which the value of money tends to adjust itself to the production cost of gold. He described in an original way the process by which an increase in the money supply generates inflationary impulses that spread out gradually, through induced demand, in the diverse sectors and income groups. In this way, the ultimate effects of an increase in liquidity would vary according to the type of money inflow. This phenomenon has become known as the 'Cantillon effect'.

On the French side, Cantillon was strongly influenced by the agrarian protectionists and especially by Boisguillebert. The French influence was shown in his preference for land rather than labour—so much so that, where Petty had tried to reduce land to labour in order to measure value, Cantillon tended to do the opposite. He developed Boisguillebert's argument according to which rent, being an income without being a cost of production, would constitute a source of expenditure autonomous with respect to productive activity; therefore it would influence the levels of output simply as a consequence of the moods, fashions, and tastes of the aristocracy. This idea, linked to the one, derived from Petty, according to which rent is the unique component of net product, seems to justify all those who consider Cantillon a forerunner of the physiocrats.

This is not all, however. Cantillon also inherited Boisguillebert's sketch of the *tableau économique*, and integrated it into a modern theory of the three social classes (landowners, tenant-farmers, and workers) and of the *trois rentes* (rent, profit, and farmer's expenditure) which allowed him to formulate a theory of the circular flow.

Bibliography

On medieval thought: J. W. Baldwin, 'The Medieval Theories of the Just Price: Romanists, Canonists and Theologians in the Tweltfh and Thirteenth Centuries', in L. Silk (ed.), *Precapitalist Economic Thought* (New York, 1972); M. Blaug (ed.), *Saint Thomas Aquinas* (Aldershot, 1991); R. De Roover, 'The Concept of the Just Price: Theory and Economic Policy', *Journal of Economic History*, 18 (1958); R. Kaulla, *Theory of the Just Price* (London, 1940); A. E. Monroe (ed.), *Early Economic Thought* (Cambridge, Mass., 1924); J. T. Noonan, *The Scholastic Analysis of Usury* (Cambridge, Mass., 1957); G. O'Brien, *An Essay on Medieval Economic Teaching* (London, 1920); K. Pribram, *A History of Economic Reasoning* (Baltimore, 1983); J. A. Schumpeter, *The History of Economic Analysis* (Oxford, 1954).

On mercantilism: M. Blaug (ed.), *The Early Mercantilists* (Aldershot, 1991); R. C. Blitz, 'Mercantilist Policies and Patterns of World Trade, 1500–1750', *Journal of Economic History*, 27 (1967); E. Cannan, *A Review of Economic Theory* (London, 1929); H. F. Hecksher, *Mercantilism* (New York, 1955); E. A. Johnson, *Predecessors of Adam Smith* (New York, 1937); J. M. Keynes, *The General Theory of Employment, Interest and Money* (London, 1936; repr. 1973); W. E. Minchinton (ed.), *Mercantilism: System or Expediency?* (Lexington, Mass., 1969); J. Viner, *Studies in the Theory of International Trade* (New York, 1937).

On some forerunners of classical political economy: M. Blaug (ed.), *Pre-Classical Economists* (3 vols., Aldershot, 1991); R. Cantillon, *Essai sur la nature du commerce en général* (London, 1755); P. Deane, *The State and the Economic System* (Oxford, 1989); H. Higgs, 'Cantillon's Place in Economies', *Quarterly Journal of Economics*, 4 (1892); T. Hutchison, *Before Adam Smith* (Oxford, 1988); H. Landreth, 'The Economic Thought of Bernard de Mandeville', *History of Political Economy*, 5 (1975); A. H. Leigh, 'John Locke and the Quantity Theory of Money', *History of Political Economy*, 4 (1974); L. Macdonald, 'Boisguillebert, a Neglected Precursor of Aggregate Demand Theorists', *Quarterly Journal of Economics*, 68 (1954); D. North, *Discourse upon Trade*, in J. R. McCulloch (ed.), *A Select Collection of English Tracts on Commerce* (repr. London, 1954); W. Petty, *The Economic Writings*, ed. C. Hull (2 vols., Cambridge, 1899); J. J. Spengler, 'Richard Cantillon: First of the Moderns', *Journal of Political Economy* (1954); D. Vickers, *Studies in the Theory of Money, 1690–1776* (Philadelphia, 1959).

2

The *Laissez-Faire* Revolution and Smithian Economics

2.1. THE *LAISSEZ-FAIRE* REVOLUTION

2.1.1. The preconditions of the Industrial Revolution

The 35-year period from the beginning of the Austrian War of Succession in 1741 to the American Declaration of Independence in 1776 was of critical importance for the history of Europe as well as for the history of economic thought. It was a period of profound political crisis, as shown by the 25 years of war, among the most barbarous in European history, at one time or another involving each of the great powers: the Austrian War of Succession (1741–8), the colonial war between England, France, and Spain (1754–63), the Seven Years War (1756–63), and the Russian–Turkish War (1768–74). One of the main results of this political crisis was the beginning of England's military, political, and economic dominance in Europe.

An important economic transformation of this period was the spread of capitalism in the countryside, which was a fairly rapid process in France and England. In France, at least in the northern regions, Picardy, Normandy, and the province of Paris, a new social figure emerged: the *fermier*, a tenant farmer who invested his own money in the improvement of productive techniques and in the enlargement of his farm. In England, the process was facilitated by the enclosure movement which, begun more than two centuries before, experienced a real boom from 1760 onwards. Among the most important consequences were the major technical innovations in cultivation methods, the connected increase in agricultural productivity and production, and the acceleration of the expulsion of the agricultural workers from the countryside. If we add the fact that, beginning from 1740, there was an acceleration in demographic growth, it is easy to understand why the take-off of the Industrial Revolution that occurred towards the end of this period was not hindered by lack of workers (and 'means of subsistence') which had been one of the main concerns of the mercantilists. Thus industrial employment could increase rapidly from the 1770s onwards.

An important precondition for the take-off of the Industrial Revolution was the large number of technical innovations in the new industries, above all (but not only) in the textile industry: Hargreaves's spinning-jenny was invented in 1764, Watt's steam-engine in 1765, and Arkwright's water-frame in 1768.

This process was not limited to England. To give only a few more examples: in 1769 Cugnot constructed a steam-driven carriage, a prototype of the motor car, in France; while Volta in Italy invented the condensor electroscope in 1775, and constructed the electrophorus and discovered methane gas in 1776. Thus all the economic, social, and technological preconditions for industrial take-off were laid down in this period, at least in England.

Most important of all, however, were the cultural preconditions. This was the period of the eruption of that authentic cultural revolution known as the Enlightenment. The roots of this movement can be traced back to seventeenth-century England and, in particular, to the ideas of 'reason', 'experience', and 'science' with which philosophers and scientists such as Bacon, Locke, and Newton had tried to oust old idols and to sweep away traditional intellectual servitude. On the Continent, by grafting itself onto different national traditions, this movement assumed special characteristics, becoming rationalist in the homeland of Descartes and historicist in that of Vico. Its most destabilizing impact on the culture of the period occurred between 1751 and 1776, the years in which the *Encyclopédie* was published.

The Enlightenment played an important role in the history of economic thought. It supplied the philosophical bases of the attack the economists of this period were attempting against mercantilist thought. The years 1751–76 are, in fact, for economics, the years of the *laissez-faire* revolution. Mercantilism, a relatively homogeneous theoretical system that had dominated European thought for 300 years and had almost created an international scientific community, was suddenly attacked from different positions, and disappeared from the scene in a quarter of a century.

In their turn, however, the new economists did not present a homogenous theoretical approach, either within each nation or at the international level. They did begin to group themselves into authentic 'schools', or almost, such as that of the physiocrats in France and the Milan and Naples schools in Italy; but, as we will see later, there was little theoretical homogeneity among the schools and little even within them. The only argument that united them was, in fact, a negative one: their struggle against the traditional mercantilist orthodoxy and, connected to this (apart from a few exceptions), their attempt to give a scientific foundation to the *laissez-faire* doctrine. It was necessary to wait for Smith's 1776 synthesis to find the conditions that were to lead, in the following 40 years, to the formation of a new orthodoxy on a Continental scale.

2.1.2. *Quesnay and the physiocrats*

The physiocratic school that prevailed in France during this period was a true school of thought, with a doctrine to defend and propagate, a recognized master, François Quesnay (1694–1774), and a fervent group of followers.

We have insufficient space here to mention all the physiocratic economists; so we will limit ourselves to presenting the essential lines of thought of the master. His most important economic works are: the entries 'Fermiers' (1756), 'Grains' (1757), and 'Hommes' (1757), written for the *Encyclopédie*; the *Tableau économique* (1758) and the *Maximes générales du gouvernement économique d'un royaume agricole* (1758), all of which are fundamental texts of physiocratic economic thought; the article 'Droit Naturel' (1765) and the dialogue *Du commerce* (1766), in which Quesnay expressed the natural-law foundation of the *laissez-faire* and anti-mercantilist point of view of this school of thought.

The physiocratic scientific contribution was outstanding. Three points in particular are worth underlining:

(*a*) the new, revolutionary concepts of productive and unproductive labour, which were introduced in connection with a new concept of wealth; a concept by which the real source of wealth is the *net product* obtained by applying labour to land;

(*b*) the idea of interdependence among the various productive processes and the related idea of macroeconomic equilibrium;

(*c*) the representation of the economic exchanges as a circular flow of money and goods among the various economic sectors.

Quesnay assumed that the productive cycle lasted one year, and that the final product of each year was partially consumed and partially re-utilized as a necessary input for the following year. He focused on agricultural production, the only sector capable of producing a surplus over replacement costs and the only real source of wealth. The physiocrats considered the surplus as a kind of natural gift from land. The farmers, therefore, formed the 'productive class'. The people employed in manufacturing industry, on the other hand, made up the 'sterile class', not because they did not produce useful goods, but simply because the value of their output was considered to be equal to the overall value of the inputs. Finally, there was the class of landlords, or 'distributive class', whose economic role was to consume the surplus created by the productive class and to begin, by the expenditure of the rents, the circulation process of money and goods among the various economic sectors. The physiocrats called this circulation process 'distribution'. This is the derivation of the name 'distributive class': its function was to ensure an effective 'distribution' of the income and goods among the various sectors.

The *tableau économique* model is fairly simple. In one year the agricultural sector produces an output of five milliard *livres*. From this total, 1 milliard replaces the means of production consumed in the agricultural process, and 2 milliard are used to pay the wages of the farm-hands and the profits of the *fermiers* as well as to provide seeds for the following year. The other 2 milliard represent the surplus, the *produit net*. The manufacturing sector has an output and an input of 2 milliard *livres*.

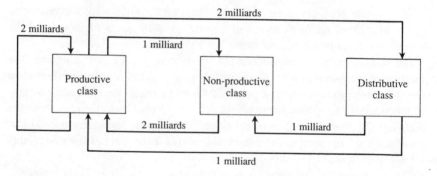

FIG. 2.

The *tableau* shows how the products of the two sectors are 'distributed' in the system and how the circulation of money ensures a continual reproduction of the system. Fig. 2 shows the three social classes and the flows of money by means of which they exchange goods. At the beginning of the year, the productive class pays 2 milliard in rent to the distributive class and 1 milliard to the sterile class to buy manufactured articles, and spends 2 milliard within the agricultural sector to buy raw materials, wage goods, and means of production. The distributive class will spend its income in the following way: 1 milliard to the sterile class and the other 1 milliard to the productive class to buy, respectively, manufactured goods and agricultural products. The sterile class, which has received 2 milliard, half from the distributive class and half from the farmers, will spend it all on the productive class to buy its inputs and necessary consumer goods. Finally, the 3 milliard that the productive class has spent outside the agricultural sector will come back to it; so that the cycle can begin again.

Quesnay derived two important political consequences from this model. The first concerns the 'natural' ability of an economic system to reproduce itself, as long as it is not obstructed by interventions of the political authorities. The reproduction equilibrium in which the system finds itself can be defined as a situation in which each sector supplies the other sectors with exactly the quantity of inputs requested, so that functional relationships are formed among the various sectors and classes which are very similar to those suggested in Menenio Agrippa's apologue. Quesnay was a medical doctor, and studied the economic system as if it were a natural organism. The equilibrium in which the economy naturally found itself was seen as a manifestation of the *natural order* of things. Here the influence of natural-law philosophy is apparent. In drawing out political implications, however, Quesnay was more coherent and extremist than Locke, who had also been strongly influenced by natural-law philosophy. With respect to the natural order, the best that could be done by the 'positive order', or the laws and institutions of organized society, was not to interfere. In this way, so it seemed, Gournay's maxim—'laissez faire, laissez passer les marchandises'—was 'scientifically proved'. In fact, the goods would go by themselves where they had to go to satisfy society's reproduction conditions, if only they were allowed to.

The second political implication of the physiocratic model concerns the doctrine of the *impôt unique*. This brought to its logical conclusions and gave a new 'scientific' basis to an argument that had already been sketched out by Vauban and Boisguillebert at the beginning of the century: that the best that could be done by the central authorities in regard to public finance was to eliminate all that complicated and inefficient fiscal apparatus, inherited from the Middle Ages, which only hindered the free circulation of goods and free private initiative, besides making tax collection expensive and difficult. The plan was to impose a single tax on the only productive factor, land, which would be paid with the net product. The other incomes would be spent on 'necessary consumption' essential to the production process, so they could not be eaten away in real terms. Taxes raised on these incomes would have been transferred and would in the end, in any case, have fallen back on rents. It would be better, therefore, to tax the latter directly.

Quesnay had numerous followers. We mention here only the most important: Nicholas Baudeau, Pierre Samuel Dupont de Nemour, Pierre Paul Mercier de la Rivière, Victor Riqueti de Mirabeau, and Guillaume François Le Trosne. But a little more has to be said about Anne Robert Jacques Turgot (1727–81) and Étienne Bonnot Condillac (1715–80), two economists who, while being influenced by physiocratic thought, distanced themselves from it in various respects. The former, in *Réflexions sur la formation et la distribution des richesses* (1766), criticized the physiocratic thesis according to which only land is able to produce a surplus. Besides this, in *Observations sur le mémoire de Saint Péravy en faveur de l'impôt indirect* (1767), he put forward some interesting ideas about the decreasing returns generated in agriculture by the intensification of investment. Finally, in *Mémoires sur la valeur et les monnaies* (1769), Turgot tried to formulate an *estimative* theory of value, based on concepts such as utility and scarcity—a theory that did not fit very well with the physiocratic conception of the *prix fondamental*, namely, the conception of cost value as determined by production conditions. It is also worth mentioning the more systematic subjective theory of value put forward by Condillac in *Le Commerce et le gouvernement considérés relativement l'un à l'autre* (1776), a theory much influenced by Galiani's work, especially in the treatment of exchange between present and future goods. Condillac differed from Galiani in that he adopted a traditional concept of utility, considering it as an intrinsic quality of goods. He also distanced himself from Turgot when he refused to accept the view that contracting parties draw the same advantage from an exchange.

Finally, it is necessary to mention some of the first important attempts to apply mathematics to economics by François Véron de Forbonnais, Pierre Dupont de Nemour, and, especially, Achylle Nicholas Isnard, in whose *Traité*

des richesses (1781) there is, perhaps, the first rudimentary, though surprisingly modern, scheme of general economic equilibrium.

2.1.3. Galiani and the Italians

The period 1750–80 has been defined by Bousquet as the *âge d'or* of Italian
economic thought. It was as if the Enlightenment in Italy had chosen economics as its favourite subject. There were numerous interesting economists
in this period, of whom we mention here only the most important. First of all,
Ferdinando Galiani (1728–87) who made, in *Della Moneta* (*On Money*) (1751),
an ambitious attempt to construct a general theory of utility value, while, in
Dialogues sur le commerce des bleds (1768), he attacked physiocratic thought
and its theories of economic policy. Next, two other Neapolitan economists:
Antonio Genovesi (1713–69), whose *Lezioni di economia civile* (*Lectures on
Civil Economy*) (1765) raised him to the position of 'head of the great family
of Italian economists'; and Gaetano Filangeri (1752–88) who, in *La scienza
della legislazione* (*The Science of Legislation*) (1780) proposed a vast illuminist project of economic and political renovation. Two economists of the
Milanese school, Cesare Beccaria (1738–94) and Pietro Verri (1728–97) should
be remembered respectively for *Elementi di economia pubblica* (*Elements of
Public Economy*) (lectures given in Milan in 1769 and 1770, but only published
in 1804) and *Meditazioni di economia politica* (*Meditations on Political
Economy*) (1771). Finally, of the work of Giammaria Ortes (1713–90), an
economist from Venice, we should at least mention *Dell' economia nazionale*
(*On National Economy*) (1774).

Galiani's most important contribution in the field of theoretical research
concerns the theory of utility value, which he took up from his Italian predecessors and developed as much as was possible in a pre-marginalist period.
He borrowed the theory, according to which value depends on the utility and
scarcity of goods, from Davanzati and Montanari, without, however, fully
acknowledging the debt. Then he made the following steps forward. First, he
argued that value is not an intrinsic quality of goods, as most of the theorists
of the cost of production tended to believe, but is a quality deriving from the
choices of economic subjects. Second, he established that it is necessary to
start from individuals in order to define these choices. Both utility and scarcity
depend on the needs of individuals. Thus, the same good has different utilities
for an individual according to the quantity of it that he has already consumed.
The more of the good consumed, the lower the utility will be, up to the point
of becoming zero. The concept was only sketched, but it was already a theory
of diminishing 'final' utility. Third—and this is perhaps the most interesting
part of his work, the part that probably led Pareto to consider him as one of
his precursors—Galiani endeavoured to study individual behaviour in terms
of choice among demanded quantities of more than one good, that is, in terms
of the composition of demand. The fundamental argument is that

value *is an idea of proportion between the possession of one thing and that of another in the mind of a man*. So, when one says that ten bushels of grain are worth one cask of wine, one expresses a proportion of equality between having one or the other; therefore men, always cautious not to be cheated out of their own pleasures, exchange one thing for another, because in the equality of exchange there is neither loss nor fraud.   (p. 39; our italics)

Except for the absence of the term 'rate of substitution', one would not be surprised to find this passage in a modern microeconomic textbook. Also note the hypothesis of individual rationality expressed in the idea of 'caution' of choices.

Not only Pareto but also other neoclassical economists could have considered Galiani an important precursor. He was well aware of the line that economic theory was taking in England in his times, and endeavoured to integrate into his work some of the arguments of the economists of that country, especially in regard to the cost of production. In doing so, however, by following a procedure of assimilation and deformation similar to that which was later to be followed by Marshall, he produced something thoroughly original. Thus he was able to state that, for the goods whose supply can be increased by the utilization of labour, value depends on the 'fatigue' (*fatica*) sustained in producing them; a view that some people have tried to interpret in terms of a labour theory of value.

To understand that it is not so, it is not even necessary to reflect on the meaning of the term *fatica*, which, in the Neapolitan dialect, while being used as a synonym for work, has a less abstract meaning with a clear implication of toil and sacrifice. It is sufficient to follow Galiani in his calculation of the contribution given by *fatica* to the value of goods. This contribution depends not only on the time and quantity of labour employed but also on its price. Already this argument is incompatitible with a pure labour theory of value. But things become even clearer when Galiani tells us that it is from the 'different values of human talents [that] the different prices for the "fatigues" originate' (p. 49). He also maintained that 'the value of talents' has to be estimated 'in the same way as for inanimate things, and that it rests on the same principles of rarity and utility taken together'. In other words, this is a theory of the 'real' cost of production measured in terms of *fatica*, or toil of labour (or, rather, labours, as talents are heterogeneous), and valued at a price that depends on the utility and scarcity of natural endowments.

Galiani also anticipated the more recent neoclassical theories of the rate of interest. He tried to explain the interest rate by linking it to the price that must be paid to equate the value of present to that of future money. The necessity of paying this price is derived from the fact that future money is valued less than present money. In fact,

among men only pleasure has a price and only comforts are bought; and, as one cannot receive pleasure without damaging and disturbing others, one pays anything else than the damage and the deprivation of the pleasure caused to others. The anxiety caused to somebody is hardship, so it is necessary to pay for this. What is called the *fruit of money*, when it is legitimate, is nothing more than the price for anxiety.   (p. 292)

Interest is the 'intrinsic price' of the 'risk' and the 'inconvenience' connected with the 'delivery of a thing with an agreement to have the equivalent back' (pp. 291–2) in such a way that there is 'equalization between present money' and future money (p. 290). Because of the risk connected with the future repayment of money (although the same point is also valid for real goods), the two sums paid at different times are evaluated as equal only if they are differentiated by the 'fruit of money'.

Finally, it is important to mention Galiani's theory of equilibrium and the political consequences he drew from it. In *Dialogues sur le commerce des bleds*, he criticized some of the physiocratic doctrines, in particular the doctrines of the net product and the single tax. He also criticized the theory of *laissez-faire*. He accepted the view that the economy tends spontaneously towards the natural order, as if it were controlled by a 'supreme hand'; but he introduced an interesting dynamic consideration, by observing that any adjustment would be achieved only in the long run. In the short run, disorders and malfunctions could well manifest themselves. But the short run could also last a long time. Therefore, there would be ample leeway and excellent reasons to try to correct those disorders and malfunctions by law. *Laissez-faire* policy would not be justified in the short run. At all events, Galiani did not admit the possibility of establishing general criteria for state intervention in the economy. The most suitable measures would depend to a large extent on the time and place in which they were taken.

This pragmatic attitude towards *laissez-faire* was also present in other Italian economists of the period. Genovesi, Beccaria, and Verri, for example, were in favour of economic freedom, which they considered from an illuminist point of view as a manifestation of the more general principle of human freedom. They justified this theoretically with the idea that nature tends to bring human things towards equilibrium if left free to do so—an idea that Genovesi supported with an argument similar to Hume's price–specie-flow mechanism. In practice, however, they limited this application of free trade to within national boundaries. In regard to foreign trade, they believed that the State had to guide and regulate the flows of imports and exports in the national interest, which might not coincide with the interests of the individual citizens. Generally speaking, it could be said that these economists had a tendency towards theoretical eclecticism and political pragmatism. For example, they took up the ideas of the French economists on the net product and, more cautiously, on the single tax, while from Galiani they adopted the theory of value. In regard to policy, especially in monetary matters, they basically remained within mercantilist thought.

Filangeri and Ortes were more extreme supporters of *laissez-faire*. The former took great steps forward in the construction of an illuminist normative system, and professed a strong faith in *laissez-faire*, justifying it with the observation that a reduction of imports would lead to reprisals by competing states and would therefore be followed by a reduction in exports. Ortes, on the other hand, justified his free-trade position with the argument that, in the absence of protectionist barriers, exports and imports of a country would tend to balance. He also constructed a vast and original theoretical system, basing it on the presupposition that national production would be limited by the size of the population, which, in turn, could not grow beyond the provisions made available by the natural endowment of the country. Ortes was also one of the many 'forerunners' of Malthus in regard to the population principle, and also anticipated the theory of decreasing returns in agriculture.

It is also worth noting some original contributions of Beccaria and Verri. Beccaria sketched out a theory of the division of labour and of increasing returns in industry, besides having an insight about the indeterminacy of prices in a duopoly. Verri developed an elementary theory of the demand curve, which he specified in the form of an equilateral hyperbola. Verri was more critical than Beccaria of the physiocrats. His criticism of the argument that the 'sterile class' did not produce a surplus was extremely interesting, and in many ways similar to the one later put forward by Smith. Verri maintained that the production of the various industries must be calculated in value, and that, in terms of value, all the activities which pay profits over and above wages and replacement costs produce a surplus.

Beccaria and Verri shared a subjectivist and hedonistic conception of economic phenomena. Starting from a sensist and materialist philosophy, they tried to explain human behaviour in utilitarian terms, by maintaining that individuals are driven, in their economic choices, exclusively by the search for pleasure and the fear of pain. It was not only in this that the two Milanese economists anticipated Bentham, but also in the proposal that the State should aim at creating—in Beccaria's words—the 'maximum happiness divided among the greatest number'. Pleasure was even thought to be measurable, and Verri considered that this could be done in monetary terms.

Some attempts to use mathematics in economic reasoning, and the ensuing methodological debates, are also interesting. Noteworthy among these initial contributions to mathematical economics was Beccaria's *Tentativo analitico sui contrabbandi* (*Analytical Essay on Smuggling*) (1764), in which there is an intelligent use of algebraic methods. Beccaria's analytical problem was taken up again and deepened by Guglielmo Silio in *Saggio sull'influenza dell'analisi nelle scienze politiche ed economiche applicata ai contrabbandi* (*Essay on the Influence of Analysis in Political and Economic Sciences as Applied to Smuggling*) (1792). Other contributions to mathematical economics in this period were made by Paolo Frisi, Luigi Valeriani Molinari, and Adeodato Ressi, besides those of Verri and Ortes, and mainly concerned the problem of the determination of price by means of the forces of supply and demand. Finally, a special mention is due to the attempt to construct a dynamic model of the adjustment process of trade in three countries, made by Giambattista Vasco in *Saggio politico della moneta* (*Political Essay on Money*) (1772).

2.1.4. Hume and Steuart.

In Great Britain, the most important contributions in this period were made by David Hume and James Denham Steuart (1712–80). The *Political Discourses* are important for the history of economic thought especially because in them, developing the ideas and methods of Petty and Locke, Hume laid the foundations for English free-trade economics. We will briefly outline the theory of the adjustment on the balance of payments based on the price–specie-flow mechanism, already mentioned in section 1.2.5. According to this theory, a surplus on the balance of trade does not produce permanent benefits, as it automatically activates a re-equilibrating process. In fact, the inflow of gold generated by the trade surplus would cause internal prices to rise, while decreasing those of the competing countries in deficit. Owing to the consequent changes in competitiveness, the trade balances would gradually adjust. The free trade implications of this theory are obvious.

In regard to money, Hume put forward a dynamic version of the quantity theory in which he recognized that an increase in the supply of money could have relevant, although temporary, real effects. He noted that the increase in prices caused by an increase in the money in circulation would be transmitted gradually from one sector to another as the initial inflow of money was spent. In this transmission process, which is extremely similar to the multiplier, the increments in expenditure can also generate, together with price increases, an expansion in production and employment. This is a remarkable acknowledgement of the validity of mercantilist theories, at least to the extent that the time-interval in which the multiplier process occurs is not well defined. It would have been sufficient to recognize, as Keynes suggested later, that life is always in transition. But nobody was able to employ this insight in defence of mercantilism.

Hume also attacked on two other fronts, and succeeded in both. First, he denied that the volume of international trade was fixed, and therefore that one country could only increase its wealth at the expense of another. Rather, he maintained that an increase in the wealth of one country—to the extent that it was an increase in real wealth, namely in the level of output—would lead, through imports, to a parallel increase in output in other countries. Second, he denied that the rate of interest would necessarily vary inversely with the money supply. Instead, he observed that it was the increase in economic activity itself that, by increasing the real capital stock of a country, would cause a decrease in the rate of profit and, as a consequence, a decrease in the rate of interest.

Hume's four fundamental arguments, the price–specie-flow mechanism, the quantity theory of money, the theory of the growth of the volume of international trade, and the explanation of the diminution of interest as a real phenomenon, were to be accepted *en bloc* by English and European thought, and were to form the pillars (even if in revised and corrected versions) of nineteenth-century free-trade theories.

If this first systematic attack on mercantilist thought was of great importance, however, its last defence, attempted fifteen years later by Steuart, was no less important. In *An Inquiry into the Principles of Political Economy* (1767), Steuart rejected the quantity theory of money along lines not dissimilar to those drawn by North. The crucial variable in the equation of exchange is the velocity of circulation, which, by means of variations of the amount of money hoarded, continually changes in such a way that the quantity of money in circulation is always adequate for the needs of trade. The volume of transactions depends on the level of output, while prices are determined by the forces of competition and the conditions of cost. Thus, the value of the transactions depends on real factors. The quantity of money exceeding the needs of trade will be hoarded. If, on the other hand, money is scarce, stocks of hoarded money will be rapidly reduced and more coins minted.

Steuart rejected the principle according to which the best way to serve the collective interest is to let private interests run free. He defined demand in terms of the need for goods accompanied by the ability to pay for them, and denied that the needs *and* the ability to pay for them are always sufficient to guarantee full employment. Furthermore, he pointed out that the introduction of machinery could create unemployment, for reasons that were not very different from those to be suggested by Ricardo half a century later: the reabsorption of the work-force into other sectors would not occur automatically. Therefore, it would be the job of the State to ensure reabsorption. In order to bring about full employment, the State would have to encourage exports by encouraging increased competitiveness of national products. Steuart suggested subsistence wages as a means to achieve this goal, but did not believe in any automatic mechanism of wage regulation, seeing this as one of the areas for government intervention.

In regard to wages, Steuart was involved in a debate that occupied English economic thought for the whole transition period from mercantilism to classical liberalism. On one side, were those who argued for the necessity to maintain wages at a low level to discourage 'vice and idleness', an old mercantilist argument which was still being put forward with force in 1757 by Malachy Postelthwayt in *Britain's Commercial Interest, Explained and Improved*. Demographic growth could help in this matter, but the State had to contribute, for example, by discouraging 'charity' towards the poor and by abolishing related laws. On the other side were those who argued that high wages could contribute to the stimulation of human effort and the improvement in working ability. Robert Wallace, Nathaniel Forster, and Thomas Mortimer were in this group; Steuart was not.

Steuart also put forward an interesting historicist theory of economic growth which has rightly been considered as the best historical justification of mercantilism. The economic growth of a nation occurs in three stages. In the first stage, the effective demand capable of driving growth is provided, above all, by the voluntary expenditure of the wealthy classes. The increase in production stimulates the introduction of machinery in industry and productive improvements in agriculture, thus prompting an increase in labour productivity. At the same time it enables the production of an agricultural surplus necessary to sustain the growth of the industrial sector. The second growth stage is reached when the country is able to produce a surplus for export. At this point luxury should give way to thrift. Growth would be sustained by the trade surplus. The third phase occurs when the country is no longer able to maintain a permanent surplus on its balance of trade. At this point, growth should return to being sustained by internal demand, and luxury could again play its role as a stimulus. In the third phase, however, there is a reduction in the rate of growth. In all three phases there is room for State intervention, both in the regulation of internal demand (for example, with sumptuary laws), and in the regulation of trade flows (with the usual mercantilist measures).

2.2. ADAM SMITH

2.2.1. The 'mechanical clock' and the 'invisible hand'

Newton's theory of universal gravitation contributed to the diffusion of the idea of an ordered and rational universe and exerted a great influence on illuminist thought. Natural phenomena, according to this idea, are reducible to the movements of atoms regulated by laws which are intrinsic to the state of nature. God created the universe together with the laws that regulate it and then he stood aside. There is no need for his continual intervention to hold the world together, as it is completely self-regulating. Furthermore, as the natural order is rational, it can be understood by human intelligence. This was the extreme outcome of a philosophical conception that had already been advanced by Descartes: rational understanding is possible, and the more abstract it is the more precise it will be. Mathematics is its most efficient and potent instrument, more powerful than observation itself. This conception, which the Scottish universities helped to spread throughout Great Britain, crossed the boundaries of the natural sciences and enjoyed enormous success even in moral philosophy, where its influence intertwined with that of natural-law philosophy. The idea of a 'natural order' played a fundamental role in the birth of classical political economy, and the conviction gained ground that human relationships were regulated by objective mechanical laws, with which positive law, which was formulated by man himself, should try its best not to interfere.

However, the influence exerted in the eighteenth century by the natural sciences over the social sciences cannot be ascribed only to the great prestige attained by the former. In fact, it can be better explained by a theoretical need which arose within the social and political thought of the period.

The central problem of European political philosophy in the period from the beginning of the Renaissance to the French Revolution was that of accounting for social life without having to resort to metaphysical presuppositions. In the Middle Ages, social consensus was maintained by two fundamental principles: authority and faith, both justified by the assumption of the existence of God. The problem of modern social thought was: how is social life possible if those two principles and their metaphysical justification are left aside?

A first answer to this question was given by Machiavelli and Hobbes: the natural egoism of man makes free social life impossible and the absolute State necessary; the principle of authority is based on the monopoly of power, and does not need to be legitimized. It is based on violence, and only obtains obedience through its strength. The citizens, mindful of a primitive 'social contract' of subjection and driven by the survival instinct and the desire for security, can do nothing else but obey. Civil society originates from repeated acts of obedience. The alternative would be social disintegration and the law of the jungle. So power gives foundation to the State, and the State makes harmonious social life possible. Now, this solution was certainly applicable to the absolutist States of the sixteenth and seventeenth centuries. It was no longer tenable after 1649, the year of the proclamation of the English Commonwealth, and, above all, after the Glorious Revolution (1688) and the Declaration of Rights (1689).

The emerging social classes created by capitalist development, and excluded from government by the absolutist States, strived to obtain what they considered to be their rights, if it is true that money is power. On the one hand, therefore, was the need for a political philosophy by which the civil society could justify itself independently of the State. On the other hand, it was necessary that such a justification take into account the real processes of wealth formation. If *Leviathan* assumed the natural egoism of individuals in order to justify the State, then it was necessary to demonstrate that a free social life is possible even in the presence of selfish individuals. Moreover, as the sphere of action of human egoism is economic activity, a change of focus from politics to economics was necessary. Finally, as a metaphysical justification had to be excluded, it was also necessary to formulate such a justification in 'scientific' rather than purely speculative terms.

Natural-law philosophy was one of the paths attempted. The followers of this view believed in a 'natural order' that presupposes the free expression of human activity. The 'positive order', based on laws and conventions, creates the State, but is only legitimate if it is not in conflict with the 'natural order'. This was a dangerous path to take, as was demonstrated by the difficulties Locke encountered in justifying the inequality in the distribution of property and wealth, and even more so by the radically egalitarian results which that philosophy was to produce in France.

A different path was attempted by the English and Scottish empiricists and 'moral-sense' philosophers. Their approach was based on the assumption of the existence of a natural 'benevolence', or 'moral sentiment', which man experiences towards his fellows. If individuals are not naturally egoistic, they tend spontaneously to associate themselves and there is no need for external intervention to give sense to social life; neither God nor the State is necessary. It is sufficient to assume a particular structure of the human psyche. Now, apart from the fact that this way of thinking succeeds in solving the problem simply by ignoring its existence, the main difficulty with it is that the assumption on which it depends, benevolence, not only runs against common sense but also is not basically different from other metaphysical assumptions; nor is it less arbitrary and easier to demonstrate.

Both Hume and Hutcheson, Smith's teacher, and Smith himself moved in this direction. Smith's main contribution, however, the one which made him the father both of economic science and of modern liberalism, came precisely at the moment when he introduced innovations within that tradition. His stroke of genius consisted, not in the rejection of the empiricist position, but in taking it to its extreme logical conclusions, by leaving out even the arbitrary hypothesis of benevolence. With the 'theorem of the invisible hand', Smith simply aimed at demonstrating that *individuals serve the collective interest precisely because they are guided by self-interest.*

A similar attempt had been made by Quesnay, a medical doctor, who, however, from the philosophical point of view, had remained tied to a natural-law position, while, in order to demonstrate the natural tendency of social agents to produce order, tried to use a biological analogy. Quesnay's natural order was very similar to Menenio Agrippa's apologue, and failed to focus on the role of individual actions in ensuring social equilibrium. The economic subjects to which Quesnay referred were collective social agents, classes of individuals, not individuals. Smith was strongly influenced by Quesnay's work, and it is possible to say that the truly 'classical' component of Smith's thought, that which was later to be developed by Ricardo and his followers, originated precisely from his attempt to assimilate some of Quesnay's fundamental ideas and to correct some of his secondary errors. However, there is a component in Smith's thought that clearly distances him from the physiocratic position, and it is that which aims at demonstrating the invisible-hand theorem. Here, collective agents disappear and the organicist analogies become meaningless. The scientific reference model is mechanics, and the objects studied are social atoms. It is not by chance that Smith is considered to be the founder of economic science not only by the classical but also by the neo-classical economists.

2.2.2. Accumulation and the distribution of income

In 1776 Smith published *An Inquiry into the Nature and Causes of the Wealth of Nations*, a milestone in modern economic thought. The work begins with an analysis 'of the causes of improvement in the productive powers of labour'—improvement immediately identified as the main condition for the growth of real wealth. The *division of labour* is a process by which a particular productive operation is subdivided into a certain number of separate operations, each of which is carried out by a different person. With the division of labour the worker's skill increases, the idle time in transferring a worker from one activity to another is reduced and, above all, technical progress is stimulated. However, the division of labour is limited by the size of the market, is only possible when the economy can produce for a sufficiently large market, and can be intensified only if the market is expanding.

In turn, the market will be larger the more the transport and communications systems are developed, the more credit and monetary instruments, are diffused, and the faster the growth in the volume of production. Smith believed there is a cumulative mechanism that operates in a capitalist system which proceeds according to the following sequence: division of labour—enlargement of the markets—increases in labour productivity, and so on; a real virtuous circle of growth.

If it is the division of labour that triggers the growth process, it is the accumulation of capital that drives it. Smith subdivided capital into *fixed capital*, consisting of machinery, plant, buildings, etc., and *circulating capital*, which is used to buy raw materials and pay for labour and energy. The *wages fund* is that part of the circulating capital which is used to pay the workers. In real terms, it is a part of the goods produced in a productive cycle which is used to pay the workers in the successive cycle. Wages are paid before the product is sold, and for the capitalist, who advances them, they are capital.

The theory of income distribution among the *social classes* plays a fundamental role in Smith's theory of growth. In fact, the three basic classes, capitalist, workers, and landlords, are distinguished both by the productive resources they hold—capital, labour, and land—and by the way in which they spend profits, wages, and rents, their respective incomes. The relationships among the types of productive resource held by the various classes, and among the ways in which their incomes are spent, constitute the essential part of Smith's theory of capital accumulation.

The landowners, who do not own productive capital, are not interested in its enlargement and have no inducement to save and accumulate capital. Their propensity to save is zero, and they make no contribution to the growth of the wealth of the nation. On the other hand, the workers only possess their labour. Both the ability of the capitalists' coalitions to influence the government and parliament and the competitive forces on the labour market push real wages down to subsistence levels. But with a subsistence wage the propensity to save must be zero. Therefore, not even the workers make a positive contribution to the growth in a nation's wealth, although they make an essential one to its production. Finally, the capitalists possess the productive capital and aim to increase it. This means they have a very high propensity to save. It follows that the higher the proportion of the national income going to profits, the higher the growth in the wealth of the nation. The general interest of the nation, therefore, coincides with that of the bourgeois class.

Smith also made an important distinction between productive and unproductive labour. The former is employed in the production of goods, the latter in the supply of personal services or in similar activities. Smith had in mind the difference existing between workers who are employed by capitalists and domestic staff who are employed by the 'leisured class'. Accumulation is the accumulation of goods. Thus productive labour is essential to sustain accumulation whereas unproductive labour is not. This means that a growing economy must reduce to a minimum the percentage of workers engaged in unproductive labour.

2.2.3. Value

Smith also made an important contribution to the explanation of the value of goods, but he did not manage to formulate a completely successful theory of value. His starting-point was to recognize that the structure of a productive process can be represented in terms of the series of quantities of labour employed to produce the goods. In fact, even the loom that is used by the worker to produce cloth has been, in its turn, produced by means of labour aided by other means of production: 'Labour, therefore, is the real measure of the exchangeable value of all commodities. The real price of everything, what everything really costs to the man who wants to acquire it, is the toil and trouble of acquiring it' (p. 133). Smith deduced from this fact that a necessary prerequisite for a good to have value is that it be produced by human labour. On the other hand, the value of a good is *measured* by the quantity of labour it is able to 'command': the value of a commodity 'to those who possess it, and who want to exchange it for some new production, is precisely equal to the quantity of labour which it can enable them to purchase or command'.

Smith clearly saw that the measure of value in labour commanded does not coincide with the amount of labour embodied in the goods. Such a coincidence could only occur

in that early and rude state of society which precedes both the accumulation of stock and the appropriation of land . . . If among a nation of hunters, for example, it usually costs twice the labour to kill a beaver which it does to kill a deer, one beaver should naturally exchange for or be worth two deer. It is natural that what is usually the produce of two days' or two hours' labour, should be worth double of what is usually the produce of one day's or one hour's labour . . . In this state of things, the whole produce of labour belongs to the labourer; and the quantity of labour commonly employed in acquiring or producing any commodity is the only circumstance which can regulate the quantity of labour which it ought commonly to purchase, command, or exchange for. (pp. 150–1)

Under these special conditions, therefore, the quantity of labour commanded coincides with the quantity of *embodied* labour.

Things change when one passes from a system in which the whole product of the labour belongs to the worker to one in which the control of the means of production, and therefore the production, is no longer in the workers' hands. When capitalists and landlords take part in the division of the product, the exchange value of a good must be such as to allow the payment of a profit and a rent besides a wage. This implies that the quantity of labour the good can pay for must be greater than that employed to produce it. In a capitalist society, therefore, embodied labour is no longer a good measure of the exchange value of goods.

Labour commanded is a relative price; it is the value of a good expressed in terms of the value of another: the labour that can be bought with it. Since Smith maintained that the price depends on the incomes paid to produce the good, he expresses it as the sum of those incomes: wages, profits, and rents. Here, for the sake of simplicity, we will ignore rent. Let us imagine an economy in which, on free land, only one good is produced, corn, for example, by means of itself and labour. The good, measured in tons, is used as a wage good as well as a capital good. Let us assume, again for simplicity, that wages are paid after the work has been done. k is the capital coefficient, namely, the quantity of seeds necessary to produce one ton of corn; l is the labour coefficient, namely, the quantity of labour-hours *directly* used to produced one ton of corn. If λ is the labour directly and indirectly embodied in a ton of corn, λk will be that embodied in k tons of grain used as seeds. Therefore:

$$\lambda = l + \lambda k = \frac{l}{1 - k}$$

Now, let r be the rate of profit, w and p the monetary wages and the monetary price of one ton of corn. p/w will be the labour commanded by it, and w/p the real wage. The price of corn will be equal to the sum of the costs sustained in producing it and the profits earned by the capitalists. The cost of labour is wl, the cost of capital pk, the profit pkr. Therefore, $p = w + pk + pkr$. Expressing the price in labour commanded:

$$\frac{p}{w} = l + \frac{p}{w} k(1 + r) = \frac{l}{1 - k(1 + r)}$$

It is easy to see that the labour commanded is greater than the embodied labour precisely because there is a profit, and that it becomes always greater as the profit rises. It is also possible to say that the price of the good is nothing more than the sum of wages and profits (and of capital) paid to produce it. It is equally clear, however, that the equation of labour commanded does not serve to determine labour commanded, which is known once the real wage is known, but only the rate of profit, which is determined *residually*. Similar results are obtained in the general case in which n goods are produced.

The theory of value based on labour commanded is correct as a price theory if it presupposes a theory of profit as a residue. On this argument, however,

Smith sometimes lets himself be led astray by misleading propositions. One of these is that an increase in wages can lead to an increase in prices, rather than to a reduction in profits; another is that profit serves as a remuneration for the risk, or even for the *disagreeableness*, faced by those who advance capital; yet another is that 'wages, profit and rent are the three original sources ... of all exchangeable value' (p. 155). Taken together, these three propositions would induce one to consider a non-residual theory of profit; which would lead to a logical error in a theory of value based on the cost of production. It is from these misleading assertions that the so-called 'additive' theory of value emerged, a theory which determines the value of a good by the sum of the incomes paid to produce it. When we speak of the mistakenness of such a theory, we are referring, not so much to the idea that the price of the good is expressed as a sum of the incomes, but to the interpretation that considers incomes as the *primary sources* of value. In such an interpretation, wages and profits would be determined by the forces of supply and demand in the 'factor' markets, so that their sum would determine the value of the good. But from the equation of labour commanded it is easy to see that, if wages and profits are predetermined, there are no more variables to determine: the equation becomes over-determined. However, Smith did not pose the problem in these terms; not only was he not completely aware of the reasons why a measure of value in labour commanded is preferable to one in embodied labour, but he did not even understand the dangers of a non-residual explanation of profit within a theory of value based on the cost of production.

2.2.4. Market and competition

The theory of labour commanded plays an important role in Smith's theory of growth. In fact, a necessary condition for the existence of a positive growth rate is that the labour commanded by the net product is higher than the quantity of labour used to produce it. In fact, only in such a case can the surplus exist which is necessary to sustain capital accumulation.

On the other hand, the additive theory of price, in that it encourages the abandonment of an explanation based on the cost of production, seems to bring back the forces of demand as fundamental determinants of the prices of goods. Coupled with a theory of profit as a normal remuneration of entrepreneurial activity, it seems to lend itself to the attempt to demonstrate the allocative efficiency (or even distributive justice) of the competitive equilibrium. Even if this line of development was followed rather more by some of Smith's followers than by Smith himself, there is no doubt that it was Smith who opened up the road. We will speak more about this in the next section.

The distinction between *market price* and *natural price* is important here. The former is the real price of a good at a given moment; the latter is that which would allow the payment of workers, capitalists, and landowners at normal rates of remuneration. The market price depends on the forces of supply and demand. In the presence of an excess of demand, the market price will rise, while it will fall if supply exceeds demand. However, 'the natural price . . . is, as it were, the central price, to which the prices of all commodities are continually gravitating' (p. 160); and this occurs precisely because competition regulates the operation of the markets.

Smith illustrated this process with an illuminating example. Let us assume that a public funeral causes an increase in the quantity demanded of black cloth. Competition among the buyers of black cloth will intensify, and this will cause an increase in the price; when the market price exceeds the natural price, the capital invested in the production of black cloth will obtain a higher return than that attainable in other industries. The capitalists who produce that good will be stimulated to expand their production, while new capital will be transferred from other uses to its production. This will cause an increase in the supply of black cloth, which at a certain moment can even exceed the demand; and this will lead to a decrease in the market price. The adjustment process will continue until the market price returns to the natural level.

The natural price is determined by the production costs, but realized on the market. The fluctuations of the market price depend on the forces of demand, but are regulated by the production conditions. The adjustment process described above is an integral part of the market mechanism by which the economy adjusts itself to its 'natural' equilibrium path. Self-interest is the driving force of the system, the force that prevents the slide into chaos. A large number of operators, a certain knowledge of the price conditions on the part of buyers and sellers, the mobility of capital, and the absence of entry barriers are all conditions that limit the ability of each single agent to influence the prices to his own advantage. Under such conditions, the market conditions ensure that exactly those goods in exactly those quantities are produced which best satisfy the final demand. In an equilibrium situation, the forces of demand provide for the distribution of capital among the various industries. While the conditions of supply determine the relative prices, the conditions of demand determine the relative quantities of goods produced.

In this view, the market is its own guardian and is capable of complete self-regulation. So that, while everybody is free to follow his personal interests, everybody is, in fact, controlled by an impersonal law. Each person is induced by an 'invisible hand' to contribute to the achievement of an economic equilibrium which was no part of his intentions: this is Smith's theorem of the invisible hand. It states that, in conditions of competitive equilibrium:

  (*a*) the productive system will produce those goods the consumers demand;
  (*b*) the chosen production methods are the most efficient;
  (*c*) the goods are sold at the lowest price possible, which is the production
     cost inclusive of a normal profit.

The main weakness of this grand construction is that it has remained unproved. In particular, Smith did not manage to demonstrate either that equilibrium exists or that it is unique and stable. In regard to these three points, however, even if they are fundamental, we should not be too hard on Smith, as even today economists are still struggling with the problems of uniqueness and stability, while those of existence have been solved only recently.

2.2.5. Smith's two souls

We conclude this brief exposition of Smith's thought by returning to an argument we mentioned at the beginning of this section. There are two different components in Smith's economic theory; let us call them *macroeconomic* and *microeconomic* components. They are tightly intertwined and it is difficult to separate them, but it is possible and useful to do so. The core of these two components consists of *the theory of surplus* and *the theory of the individualist competitive equilibrium.* The philosophical roots of the two theories are different; and it would not be difficult to trace the empiricist and moral-philosophy roots of the theory of competitive equilibrium from the influence of Hume, Hutcheson, and Shaftesbury; nor would it be difficult to trace the theory of surplus to its natural-law roots and to the influence of Locke and Quesnay. However, this is not the place to go deeper into such an argument. We will add only that, even though Smith seems perfectly aware, *at the philosophical level*, mainly of the first kind of influence, the second is no less strong, as is demonstrated by the presence in his work of the tension, typical of natural-law philosophy, between the *is* of history and institutions and the *ought to be* of the natural order. This tension was to lead Smith to foreshadow a theory of profit based on exploitation.

It is possible to link all Smith's ideas to those two theoretical components: the macroeconomic, based on the theory of the surplus, and the microeconomic, based on the theory of competitive equilibrium. The first, for example, is at the base of his theory of growth, and was in fact formulated in the attempt to adapt Quesnay's analysis to a non-stationary economy. The conceptions of the social classes, the analysis of their different types of income and expenditure behaviour, the distinction between productive and unproductive labour, the explanation of value in terms of embodied and commanded labour and, finally, the theory of profit as a residual income, are all elements of the first component. The second component, on the other hand, provides the foundation to the theorem of the invisible hand, to the idea of a competitive capitalist economy as a natural economic order, to the theory of additive prices in connection with the explanation of profit as remuneration for risk, and to the theory of wage differentials. The economic subjects which appear in this second component are no longer collective agents such as social classes, but individuals: for example, buyers and sellers of a single good who decide the quantity to demand or supply on the basis of a price they cannot modify; or single capitalists who decide to transfer investments from one sector to another in the search of a higher profit rate.

In order to understand how these two components of Smith's theory are really different, yet strictly interrelated, we will consider them at work on a specific problem: that of the explanation of the nature of labour and the level of its remuneration.

Chapter 5 of Book I of *The Wealth of Nations* begins thus:

The real price of everything, what everything really costs to the man who wants to acquire it, is the toil and trouble of acquiring it. What everything is really worth to the man who has acquired it, and who wants to dispose of it or exchange it for something else, is the toil of our own body. That money or those goods save us this toil. They contain the value of a certain quantity of labour which we exchange for what is supposed at the time to contain the value of an equal quantity. Labour was the first price, the original purchase-money that was paid for all things. It was not by gold or by silver, but by labour, that all the wealth of the world was originally purchased; and its value, to those who possess it, and who want to exchange it for some new productions, is precisely equal to the quantity of labour which it can enable them to purchase or command. (p. 133)

This famous passage has been interpreted in two completely different ways within two different streams of thought.

Ricardo and his followers, the Ricardian socialists, and Marx and the Marxists have placed the accent on the 'quantity of labour' with which the goods are produced or which is commanded by them. Here labour is intended as an investment of energy, a productive service that can be technically specified and measured in objective units, for example, working hours. This good enters into the production of others on the basis of objective technical relations, and is exchanged with others on the basis of objective exchange relations. Its productive role and its value are independent from the choices of individuals and from psychological factors. The determination of its price and its productive role can be set out in macroeconomic terms, completely ignoring single individuals. This leads to a theory of distribution that, being based on the notions of 'wage' as 'natural wage' and of 'surplus' as a 'deduction from the produce of labour', cannot but be a macroeconomic theory, and needs no microeconomic foundations. In the same way, a theory of value based on embodied or commanded labour cannot but be an objective theory of value, and needs no psychological foundations.

A completely different interpretation of the passage has been given by Jevons on the basis of theories put forward by Bentham and Gossen—an interpretation which has been accepted by all the neo-classical economists. It must be recalled, however, that Galiani had already tried to interpret the labour theory of value (of Locke and Petty) in this way. Jevons placed the accent on the 'toil and trouble' of labour. This was now defined as 'any painful exertion of mind or body undergone partly or wholly with a view to future good' (p. 189). Evidently, we are dealing with 'a case of negative utility'. Its measurement is expressed in terms of 'pain', and it is impossible to define it objectively. In fact, each individual has his own idea of how 'painful' his own work is. A theory of the price of labour based on this interpretation must have microeconomic foundations, in that it must take into consideration individual choices. Thus the theories of value and distribution that treat labour in this way cannot avoid dealing with the psychology of individuals; and they can, with good reason, be defined as subjectivist theories of value and distribution.

There is no doubt that this passage by Smith can be legitimately interpreted in both ways. But this is not all. In Chapter 10 of Book I, Smith tackles the problem of wage differentials:

The whole of the advantages and disadvantages of different employments of labour and stock must, in the same neighbourhood, be either equal or continually tending to equality. If in the same neighbourhood, there was any employment evidently either more or less advantageous than the rest, so many people would crowd into it in the one case, and so many would desert it in the other, that its advantages would soon return to the level of other employments. This at least would be the case in a society where things were left to follow their natural course, where there was perfect liberty, and where every man was perfectly free to choose what occupation he thought proper and to change it as often as he thought proper. Every man's interest would prompt him to seek the advantageous, and to shun the disadvantageous employment. (pp. 201–2)

This passage seems to prove the neoclassical interpretations correct. In fact, the reference to individual choices is clear when Smith speaks of 'every man' and of his freedom to 'choose'. The confirmation of the legitimacy of this interpretation is given by the fact that, according to Smith, the first determinant of wage differentials consists in the 'agreeableness or disagreeableness' or the 'ease or hardship' of the work. Thus, in order that 'the advantages and disadvantages of the different employments' become equal, the wage differentials must reflect the differences in hardship. This would happen under free competition, in a situation in which 'perfect liberty [existed] and where every man was perfectly free to choose'. We are referring to this point of view when we speak of the theory of *individualistic competitive equilibrium* as the *microeconomic component* of Smith's thought.

Ricardo and Marx, of course, would not agree with such an interpretation. And they would not be completely wrong. In fact, the second determinant of wage differentials consists of the high or low cost of training; and this *can* be interpreted as an objective determinant. In fact, the training costs of a labour skill, as Marx was to suggest later, are given by the quantity of labour employed to produce a certain working ability, and can be determined by referring to the 'educational technology' available in a given society in a given period, which is again an objective and macroeconomic phenomenon. We are referring to this type of interpretation when we speak of the *theory of surplus* as the *macroeconomic component* in Smith's thought.

We will see that almost all Smith's followers in the period from the publication of *The Wealth of Nations* to the end of the Napoleonic Wars developed their ideas in relation to the theory of individualistic competitive equilibrium. This fact explains why Ricardo, in order to re-establish the authority of Smith's theory of surplus, had to bring about a revolution by taking Smith himself as his favourite target. We should like to add here, for clarity, that a fundamental contribution to the theoretical development and the cultural success of the microeconomic component of Smith's thought, to the detriment of the macroeconomic side, was given by Bentham, the founder of utilitarianism. We will discuss this later.

2.3 THE SMITHIAN ORTHODOXY

2.3.1. An era of optimism

The 40 years between the publication of *The Wealth of Nations* and that of Ricardo's *Principles* was a period of enthusiasm and optimism—both for the English middle class, which was involved in the most intense phase of the Industrial Revolution, and for the Continental middle class, the French in particular, which was endeavouring to realize the Enlightenment dream. None of the intellectuals of this period, perhaps, represents this wave of enthusiasm better than William Godwin (1756–1836) and Antoine Nicholas de Condorcet (1743–94); the former with his theses about human perfectibility and his radical reform programme, which he put forward in *Enquiry Concerning Political Justice* (1793); the latter with the idea, expressed in *Esquisse d'un tableau historique des progrès de l'espirit humain* (1795), of the continual progress of scientific knowledge and the moral bases of social life.

There were also more pessimistic voices, of course. One was that of Thomas Robert Malthus (1766–1834), who, in 1798, in a polemic against Godwin's optimism, published the *Essay on the Principle of Population*. However, this was the isolated voice of a conservative pastor, a member of a class that could not be expected to be anything but pessimistic in a period in which the middle classes, its goods, its weapons, and its ideas, triumphed on every front. The 'Malthusian population principle' is a sharp and clear expression of traditional religious pessimism in the face of avaricious nature and the effects of human intemperance, which Botero, Cantillon, Ortes, and others had already expressed: the means of subsistence offered by nature grows according to an arithmetical progression, while the number of mouths to feed increases at an exponential rate. Besides this, Malthus was able to draw out the political consequences of his 'principle'. As the lower classes could not, unlike the others, use moral restraint to control the catastrophic effects of natural laws, let nature, therefore, look after itself. *Ergo*: charity and assistance to the poor must be discouraged and abolished.

From the point of view of economic theory, the population principle is important above all for the use that Ricardo and Torrens were to make of it in connection with their theories of wages. But it also had important implications for the decreasing returns in agriculture, a subject on which James Anderson (1739–1808), in *An Inquiry into the Nature of the Corn Laws* (1777), had anticipated Malthus on some important matters. We will speak more about this in the next chapter.

Malthus, at any rate, was an exception in respect to the general optimism of the post-Smithian economists. 'Post-Smithian' is perhaps the best term to define a kind of political economy that had finally found, in *The Wealth of Nations*, its *foundations*. For the first time, all over Europe, economists discovered that they were speaking the same language and had the same ideas of the aims, limits, and scope of economic science: those assigned to them by Smith.

This theoretical homogeneity, finally found after such a long search, did have its price, as is shown by the scant progress made by economic analysis in this period. But the aspect most worth highlighting in the panorama of post-Smithian economics is this: the few economists who did make some original contribution were all working within only one of the two components of Smith's thought, that of the individualistic competitive equilibrium.

2.3.2. Bentham and utilitarianism

One of these contributions was utilitarianism, the natural conclusion of a line of thought which links Bentham (1748–1832) to Shaftesbury, through Hume, Hutcheson, and Smith. We should not, however, forget the influence of Beccaria and Helvétius and the 'theologians' Priestley and Paley.

First of all, utilitarianism provided a new way of conceptualizing human motivation towards action. The increasing specialization of labour and, more generally, the nature of capitalist production had led to the consideration of individuals, not as integrated parts of an interdependent whole, but as social atoms fighting with impersonal and unchangeable market forces. As the belief spread that the economic agent is a selfish and competitive being, the idea also gained ground that all reasons for human action spring from the desire to obtain pleasure and avoid pain. This belief is the heart of *utilitarianism*, and its fundamental formulation is found in the writings of Jeremy Bentham, especially in *An Introduction to the Principles of Morals and Legislation* (1780).

The book opens with the assertion according to which every human motivation, at every place and time, can be traced back to a single principle: the desire to maximize utility—'that property of any object, whereby it tends to produce benefit, advantage, pleasure, good or happiness' or to prevent 'mischief, pain, evil, or unhappiness to the party whose interest is considered' (p. 86). By tracing all human motives back to a single principle, Bentham laid the grounds for the construction of a science of human happiness—a science endowed with mathematical precision just like physics. And he even suggested a method for the quantification of pleasures: 'The value of a pleasure or pain will be greater or less according to several circumstances: its intensity, its direction; its certainty or uncertainty; its propinquity or remoteness; its fecundity; its purity; its extent' (p. 97).

Another pillar of Bentham's theory was the idea that human beings, besides being hedonists, are also egoists: 'In the general tenor of life, in every human breast, self-regarding interest is predominant over all other interests put together... Self-preference has place everywhere' (*Economic Writings*, iii. 421).

Both ideas were to be assimilated into successive theories of utility-value. Smith had rejected the conception according to which the exchange value can be explained by the utility of goods. He used the famous example of water and diamonds (water possesses a high use value and a low exchange value, in exact opposition to diamonds) to illustrate the absence of a necessary relationship between utility and value. The neoclassical economists were to explain later that it was not the total utility of a good that determines its exchange value but the marginal utility, or rather the increase in utility which is derived from a small increment in the availability of a good. Bentham, however, had already reasoned in more or less the same way:

The terms wealth and value explain each other. An article can only enter into the composition of a mass of wealth if it possesses some value. It is by the degrees of that value that wealth is measured. All value is founded on utility ... Where there is no use, there cannot be any value. (*An Introduction* ... , p. 83)

And again:

Value in use is the basis of value in exchange ... This distinction comes from Adam Smith but he has not attached to it clear conceptions ... The reason why water is found not to have any value with a view to exchange is that it is equally devoid of a value with a view to use. If the whole quantity required is available, the surplus has no kind of value. It would be the same in the case of wine, grain, and everything else. (pp. 87–8)

The principle of marginal utility and its link with the theory of value is anticipated here, albeit in a confused way and without questioning Smith's authority to any great extent.

2.3.3. The Smithian economists and Say

Bentham was the first of the post-Smithian economists to seek the explanation of value in use value rather than in the cost of production, a tendency that may seem surprising to those who are accustomed to identifying 'classical' theory with Ricardian theory.

This tendency was extremely clear in Smith's German followers. For example, Friedrich Soden (1753–1831), in *Die Nationalökonomie* (1804), transformed Smith's distinction between use value and exchange value into that of 'positive' and 'comparative' value, maintaining that only the former is a value in the real sense; and that it depends on the utility the goods have in respect to the needs they must satisfy. Johan Freidrich Lotz (1778–1838), in *Revision der Grundbegriffe der Nationalwirtschaftlehre* (*Revision of the Fundamental Concepts of the Theory of National Economy*) (1811), pushed forward in this direction until he managed to make the comparative value, which expresses the comparison between two positive values, depend on the scarcity of goods and on the sacrifice that must be made to make them available for the satisfaction of needs.

But the person who followed this road to the point of knowingly going beyond Smith was James Maitland Lauderdale (1759–1839), who, in *Inquiry into the Nature and Origin of Public Wealth* (1804), not only rejected Smith's theory of value but also recognized the implications of such a rejection for the theory of production. With regard to value, Lauderdale concentrated his analysis on the forces of supply and demand, endeavouring to explain the latter by the subjective factors that define human needs and the former by the scarcity of the goods necessary to satisfy those needs. In regard to production, he was one of the first to put forward the argument that, to understand the role played by machinery in the productive process and in the production of wealth, it is necessary to focus not so much on its ability to co-operate with labour as on its ability to substitute for it. This view logically leads to a theory of three productive factors, labour, land, and capital and their combination in the production process.

Similar arguments were put forward in France by an economist who, unlike Lauderdale, still considered himself a follower of Smith: Jean-Baptiste Say (1767–1832), the 'optimist'. Say combined in an unusual way the two basic arguments of the Smithian theory of value, the one concerning the dependence of the variations of market prices on the forces of supply and demand and the other relating to the dependence of natural prices on the conditions of production. He thus formulated a theory which was rather more similar to that of Galiani, whose influence was still strong in France, where it had been consolidated by Condillac. The value of goods depends on the forces of demand and the costs of production. The utility of goods acts on the former, whereas the difficulties met in supplying them underlies the latter.

It is interesting to see which theories of production and distribution were linked to such a theory of value. The production of goods requires the utilization of three types of 'productive service': those of labour, capital, and land. As the value of goods depends on the demand and the efforts sustained to satisfy it, and as such efforts require the utilization of all three of the productive services, value cannot be entirely reduced to labour: all three services contribute to its formation. Furthermore, each productive service receives an income that is determined by the demand for the goods it contributes to produce. The intermediary between the product markets and the productive service markets is the entrepreneur. He compares the price that the consumers are prepared to pay for a good with the expenditure necessary to produce it, that is, with the costs of the productive services. In this way the demand for consumer goods is transformed into the demand for productive services, and the prices of the latter turn out to depend on their indirect contribution to the satisfaction of consumer needs.

The concept of the dependence of the values of goods on the prices of all the productive services, a vague rationalization of Smith's additive theory of prices, led Say almost naturally, although in a confused way, to a strange theory of distribution—strange with respect to its Smithian origin: each productive service receives a price which is equal to its productive contribution. Thus, the capitalist economy is not only efficient in the allocation of the resources with respect to demand, as stated by the theorem of the invisible hand, but also equitable in the distribution of income. There is an undoubted link between Say and Smith, but Marx was right about the nature of this link when he stated, in the *Theories on Surplus Value*, that 'Say separates the vulgar notions occurring in Adam Smith's work and puts them forward in a distinct crystallized form' (iii. 501).

Say also went beyond Smith in his attempt to justify *laissez-faire* philosophy. Although Smith restricted himself to maintaining that the greed of capitalists would lead a competitive economy to allocate the resources in such a way as to satisfy the demand for the goods on the various markets, he also pointed out that the adjustment process would have to pass through the continual appearance and disappearance of sectoral disequilibria which would never be completely eliminated. The problem remained as to whether such disequilibrium situations would compensate for each other, so as to ensure equality between aggregate supply and demand, or would generate macroeconomic malfunctioning. Smith seems to be vaguely indicating the second possibility when he theorized the tendency of the rate of profit to fall as a consequence of an excess supply of capital in all the industries.

On the contrary, Say tried to demonstrate the impossibility of a generalized excess supply. This is the famous Say's Law, also known as the '*loi des débouchés*' or 'law of markets', according to which supply always creates its own demand. Say first restricted himself to observing that the value of the aggregate production is necessarily equal to the aggregate value of the distributed incomes. This is an accountancy identity that nobody would object to. As incomes are purchasing power, it is also possible to say that the produced goods always create the purchasing power corresponding to their value. From here to say that the production always creates its own demand may seem a small step. In fact it is enormous. One must add that incomes are entirely and immediately spent—a hypothesis that Say endeavoured to justify, especially in his *Cours complet d'économie politique pratique* (1828), in an attempt to reply to the various criticisms aimed against his first formulation of the law, and taking into consideration the controversies that had developed both in England and on the Continent. However, the simplest and clearest explanation of the hypothesis on which the validity of the law depends is to be found in the *Traité d' économie politique* (1803):

It must be stressed that any commodity whatsoever, as soon as it is brought to the market, offers an outlet to other products for the whole amount of its value. In fact, when a manufacturer has produced a commodity, he has an extreme need and wish to sell it, so that its value does not dissolve in his hands. But he is no less willing to get rid of the money he obtained from the sale of the commodity, precisely in order to prevent the value of the money vanishing by remaining idle. Now, one cannot get rid of one's own money except by purchasing some product. Therefore it is clear that the very production of a commodity immediately opens an outlet to other products. (pp. 141–2)

Thus the purchasing power generated from the production process is no longer only *potential demand*; it is also, and always, *effective demand*. This leads to the conclusion that situations of *aggregate* excess supply are impossible, even when all the single markets are in disequilibrium. Say's Law excludes the possibility of crises or general gluts. At this point it still remains to be seen if it also excludes unemployment. We will return to this argument in the next chapter, when we deal with the Ricardian use of Say's Law.

Bibliography

On the French economists of the second half of the eighteenth century: M. Beer, *An Enquiry into Physiocracy* (London, 1939); M. Blaug (ed.), *François Quesnay* (Aldershot, 1991); H. Higgs, *The Physiocrats: Six Lectures on the French 'Économistes' of the 18th Century* (New York, 1952); T. Hutchinson, *Before Adam Smith* (Oxford, 1988); K. Marx, *Theories of Surplus Value* (3 vols., Moscow, 1968); R. L. Meek, *The Economics of Physiocracy* (London, 1962); J.-B. Say, *Traité d' économique politique*, 6th edn. (Paris, 1841); G. Vaggi, 'The Physiocratic Theory of Prices', *Contributions to Political Economy* (1983); *The Economics of François Quesnay* (London, 1988).

On the Italian economists of the second half of the eighteenth century; G. H. Bousquet, *Esquisse d' une histoire de la science économique en Italie: Des origines à Francesco Ferrara* (Paris, 1960); F. Cesarano, 'Monetary Theory' in F. Galiani's *Della Moneta, History of Political Economy* (1976); L. Einaudi, 'On Galiani', in Henry W. Spiegel (ed.), *The Development of Economic Thought: Great Economists in Perspective* (New York, 1952); F. Galiani, *Della Moneta* (Milan, 1963); T. Hutchison, *Before Adam Smith* (Oxford, 1988); D. Parisi Acquaviva, *Il pensiero economico classico in Italia (1750–1860)* (Milan, 1984); R. Theocharis, *Early Developments in Mathematical Economics* (London, 1961).

On the English economists of the second half of the eighteenth century: J. Bentham, *An Introduction to the Principles of Morals and Legislation*, in *A Bentham Reader*,

M. P. Mack (New York, 1969); *Economic Writings* (3 vols., London, 1952); M. Blaug (ed.), *David Hume and James Steuart* (Aldershot, 1991); T. Hutchison, *Before Adam Smith* (Oxford 1988); 'Bentham as an Economist', *Economic Journal*, 66 (1956); R. L. Meek, 'The Economics of Control Prefigured by Sir James Steuart', *Science and Society*, 22 (1958); S. R. Sen, *The Economics of Sir James Steuart* (London, 1957); W. L. Taylor, *Francis Hutcheson and David Hume as Predecessors of Adam Smith* (Durham, 1965).

On Adam Smith: R. H. Campbell and A. S. Skinner, *Adam Smith* (London, 1982); E. Cannan, 'Adam Smith as an Economist', *Economica*, 6 (1926); S. Hollander, *The Economics of Adam Smith* (Toronto, 1973); S. Jevons, *Theory of Political Economy* (Harmondsworth, 1970); A. L. Macfie, *The Individual in Society: Papers on Adam Smith* (London, 1968); C. Napoleoni, *Smith, Ricardo, Marx* (Oxford, 1975); H. M. Robertson and W. L. Taylor, 'Adam Smith's Approach to the Theory of Value', *Economic Journal*, 67 (1957); E. Rothschild, 'Adam Smith and Conservative Economics', *Economic History Review*, 45 (1992); W. R. Scott, *Adam Smith as Student and Professor* (New York, 1965); A. S. Skinner and T. Wilson (eds.), *Essays on Adam Smith* (Oxford, 1975); A. Smith, *The Wealth of Nations* (Harmondsworth, 1970); E. G. West, *Adam Smith: The Man and His Work* (New York, 1969).

3

From Ricardo to Mill

3.1. RICARDO AND MALTHUS

3.1.1. Thirty years of crisis

The 30-year period from the Congress of Vienna to the 1848 revolutions was of crucial importance for the history of Europe. It is known as the 'Age of Restoration'. In reality, it was a period of deep economic and social changes and sharp political crises; a period full of conflicts, marked as it was by the attempt of the aristocratic powers to restore the traditional absolutist order just when the Industrial Revolution was definitively undermining the economic foundations of that order. It is not surprising that, by comparison with the almost total peace in European international relations, there were almost permanent civil wars in the countries affected by most intense Conflicts of Social change.

Despite this, the Holy Alliance managed to maintain internal order in all the countries it dominated—practically all the nations of Central and Eastern Europe, including Italy and Germany. In some of these countries, political uprisings led by democratic forces occurred repeatedly and with increasing intensity during the 30-year period until the great revolutionary upheaval in 1848, but they were always defeated. The reason for this can perhaps be traced to the small mass base that the existing social structures offered the democratic movements; and underlying this situation was undoubtedly the slow process of capitalist accumulation and the relative backwardness of the economic structures of these countries.

The evolution of the political conflict assumed special characteristics in the two most advanced European countries, France and England. Their political systems were based on three great parties: reactionary, liberal, and democratic. These obviously assumed different names, programmes, and political structures in the two countries over time, but the tripartite structure remained constant throughout the period. Well-defined social forces underpinning this structure gave the parties stability and political context. These forces can be identified in Smith's three social classes: the landlords, the bourgeoisie, and the proletariat.

In the first phase, c.1815–30, which was the Age of Restoration in the strict sense, power was firmly held by the reactionary forces in the two countries. Against these, an alliance of the other two political forces formed, Whigs and Radicals in England and Orleanists and Republicans in France. This alliance provided the mass base which led, in 1830, to the July Revolution in France and the Whig election victory in England. The result of the two victories was the institution of two constitutional parliamentary regimes, albeit with very limited electoral bases. In France, the wealth requirements and the voting age were lowered so as to raise the number of electors to 240,000, just 1 per cent of the population! In England, where a parliamentary constitutional system had existed for some time, there was an electoral reform in 1832, which eradicated the system of 'rotten boroughs' (in which the sparsely populated country boroughs, controlled by the landowners, were much more highly represented in parliament than the more populous town electoral districts, where a majority of bourgeoisie and industrial proletariat lived). Furthermore, the number of electors was raised from 500,000 to 813,000.

After the reforms the 'industrialists' were satisfied, the landowners gave up their hegemony, and the proletariat had to start all over again. The democratic party became more radical in a socialist sense, and this gave the liberals one more reason to break away from the alliance. In England, some of the Radicals joined with the trade union movement to form the Chartist party, a political group that fought for the extension of political rights to the workers as a condition for the attainment of some more advanced economic and social goals. In France, a socialist movement formed that tended to differentiate itself more and more clearly from the liberal forces and, as in England, tried to unite democratic political claims with social-emancipation objectives which were incompatible with the economic structure of a capitalist system.

The class struggle, far from weakening, became more bitter after 1830. Above all, there was a qualitative change, with the conflict between the landowners and the 'industrialists' becoming less important than that between the popular masses and the privileged classes. The end result was the 1848 revolution, which in France turned into a proletarian blood-bath and the definitive attainment of the bourgeois hegemony over the whole society. In England, where the workers' movement was stronger and everybody had expected a proletarian revolution, 1848 ended in a farce, with the presentation of a Chartist petition to Parliament. In both countries, 1848 closed an era of conflict and opened one of social peace.

3.1.2. The Corn Laws

In England, the 30 years from the passing of the Corn Laws (1816) to their repeal (1846) can be defined, in terms of economic theory, as 'the Age of Ricardo'. It was at the beginning of this period that David Ricardo (1772–1823) proposed his own economic theory; and whether the economists of the period exalted, discussed, misrepresented, or criticized the Ricardian approach, it is a fact that all the English economic research of those years was involved with it. Needless to say, the controversies were bitter; in fact, they were at least as strong as the political implications of the theories in question and the violent class conflicts to which they referred.

The first fundamental class conflict involved workers and capitalists. In the next chapter we will discuss the theoretical formulations to which it gave rise. Here we will focus on another great conflict that marked English society in the period of its industrialization: that involving the landowners and the capitalists. The conflict mainly manifested itself in the battles for the control of Parliament, the real object of the fight being whether England should remain an agricultural economy or should instead accelerate the rhythm of its industrial growth. The Napoleonic wars, by drastically reducing the imports of food supplies, had provoked a substantial increase in the prices of cereals, in particular corn; the prices of manufacturing goods, on the other hand, had increased less rapidly than agricultural products and wages. In 1816, at the end of a long period of war, the landowners managed to convince Parliament to approve the famous new Corn Laws; tariffs were fixed at such a high level that corn, the foreign prices of which were much lower than the internal ones, could not enter the country at all. The economic implications of this operation are clear, and can be summarized as follows. The protectionist barriers allowed the maintenance of high land rents to the detriment of profits, given the rigidity of real wages. The opposition of the manufacturers was strong, not only because of the redistribution effects of the protectionist barriers but also because these prevented English industry from taking advantage of its higher level of productivity with respect to its European competitors.

The battle lasted for about thirty years, but in the end the persuasive force and pressure that the bourgeoisie managed to exercise at the political and cultural level led to the complete repeal of the Corn Laws. The event, which was made possible by Ricardo's decisive theoretical contribution, sanctioned the definitive hegemony of the bourgeoisie in the English society.

Ricardo's principal opponent in this battle was Thomas Robert Malthus, who supported the landowners' point of view in all the theoretical debates. The most important works of the two economists were published at about the same time: Ricardo's *On the Principles of Political Economy and Taxation* in 1817, Malthus' *Principles of Political Economy* in 1820. In reality, the economic theories of Ricardo and Malthus developed together, intertwined with each other, having in common just enough of a methodological base to allow for dialogue, while finding themselves in conflict in regard to practically every theoretical conclusion of any political importance. For this reason, the best way to understand the essentials of the two approaches is, perhaps, to study them together.

3.1.3. The theory of rent

In 1815, at the climax of the debate on the Corn Laws, five pamphlets were published: *An Inquiry into the Nature and Progress of Rent* and *The Grounds of an Opinion on the Policy of Restricting the Importation of Foreign Corn*, both by Malthus; *An Essay on the Application of Capital to Land*, by Edward West (1782–1828); *Essay on the External Corn Trade*, by Robert Torrens (1780–1864); and, finally, *An Essay on the Influence of a Low Price of Corn on the Profits of Stock*, by Ricardo. The common ground these five papers had at the analytical level, in spite of their theoretical and political differences, was the use of the theory of differential rent—a theory that seems to have been formulated independently by the first three of these economists. Ricardo himself had no hesitation in acknowledging Malthus as the founding father. However, we should not forget that the basic elements of the theory of differential rent had already been proposed by James Anderson in 1777.

In order to understand the gist of Ricardo's theoretical system, it is useful to begin with an extremely simple model of an economy in which the agricultural system only produces one good, let us say corn, by means of itself (seeds) and labour. In fact, we are not doing much injury to Ricardo by using such a simple model, as he himself implicitly used similar hypotheses in the above-mentioned pamphlet.

The levels of net corn production, G_a, G_b, G_c, G_d, G_e that can be obtained from five types of land, A, B, C, D, E, scaled in decreasing order of fertility, are shown in Fig. 3. Let us assume that a fixed quantity of seeds and a fixed quantity of labour, say, one worker, are used on each acre of land. If we begin from a situation in which only one kind of land, A, is cultivated, the production of corn net of seeds will be G_a. Let us assume that it is necessary to increase production. If the cultivation is extended to land B, the net production will

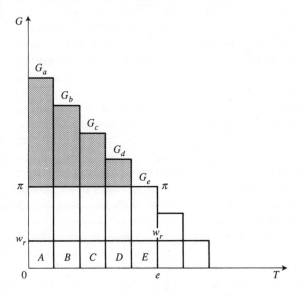

FIG. 3.

increase to $G_a + G_b$, and if land C is also cultivated the production will be $G_a + G_b + G_c$ and so forth. A movement to the right along the horizontal axis implies an increase in production and an increase in the plots of land cultivated.

Let us assume that on the least fertile of the cultivated plots there is no rent; and that the real wage w_r is fixed. If the plots of land of types A, B, C, D, and E are the only ones to be cultivated, the capitalist who works on the least fertile plot, E, will produce an amount of corn (net of seeds) equal to G_e and will make profits equal to $(G_e - w_r)$. The other capitalists, working on the more fertile land, would obtain higher profits if they didn't have to pay rent. For example, on land D the profits *would be* $(G_d - w_r) > (G_e - w_r)$. On land C they would be greater than on D, and so forth. In this case, however, competition will raise the demand for the more fertile plots; and this will allow the owners to extract higher rents; the more fertile the land, the higher the rent. In competitive equilibrium all the capitalists will earn the same profit rate since the product that can be obtained from intramarginal lands over and above that of the marginal land will be entirely swallowed up in rent. In Fig. 3 the rents are represented by the shaded area, the total wages by the area $0\,w_r w_r e$, and the profits by the area $w_r \pi \pi w_r$. This is the theory of *extensive* differential rent.

This theory was criticized by many economists, as it seemed to imply, against the evidence, that no rent is paid on marginal lands. Say criticized Ricardo in this way; Ricardo found it an easy task to defend himself, but did so only in a footnote in the second edition of the *Principles*, and in a rather too synthetic and obscure way, so that many economists continued to try to resolve the problem by using the concept of 'absolute rent'.

In order to understand why *differential* rent is also paid on the marginal pieces of land, we only have to reinterpret it as '*intensive rent*'. In this case, Fig. 3 should be read in the following way. All the land available in a country is cultivated. For simplicity, let us assume that all the plots are equally fertile. In order to obtain increases in production, there must be further investment of capital and labour on the already cultivated lands. The histogram in Fig. 3 now represents the increments in production that can be obtained as the investment of capital and labour increases. Let us assume that the capital : labour ratio is fixed. Now the horizontal axis no longer measures the area of the cultivated land (*all* the available land being cultivated), but the level of employment. A movement to the right along the horizontal axis no longer represents an extension of the cultivation given the labour : capital : land ratios, but an *intensification* of the cultivation with increases in the labour : land and capital : land ratios. It is assumed that, with the increase in production and employment, the productivity of the last employed worker will fall. G_a is the productivity of the first worker, G_b that of the second, and so forth. Therefore, the worker employed with the last investment unit, whose net productivity is G_e, will produce no rent; but a rent will be paid in any case which will be equal to the difference between the productivity of the intramarginal units and the productivity of the marginal one, as shown by the shaded area.

3.1.4. Profits and wages

Let us now consider profits. The reasoning with which Ricardo tried to demonstrate the necessity for the abolition of the Corn Laws is simple. Given the limited amount of land suitable for cultivation, if corn imports are impeded, this will force the national agriculture to increase its production by intensifying investment in agriculture, thus increasing the rent share in the national income and diminishing the profit share. This slows capital accumulation, as most of the savings necessary to finance investment come from profits. In fact, the landowners, who also earn very high incomes, do not save because the accumulation of wealth is not among their aspirations; on the other hand, the workers, who earn subsistence wages, do not save because they have nothing to save.

Ricardo did not stop here. With an excess of propagandist zeal, he even tried to extend this view to a very long-run horizon, formulating a law of the falling rate of profit. To do this, he simply assumed that technical progress would not be able, in the long run, to overcome the economic consequences of decreasing returns in agriculture. He admitted that technical innovations, by increasing the productivity of labour, could also induce increases in profits. He believed that such effects would only be temporary, however, as the increases in profits themselves would stimulate further capital accumulation, thus increasing employment, and would therefore reactivate the catastrophic effects of decreasing returns.

The distributive problem was posed by Ricardo in terms of the decreasing function linking wages to profits. Let us reconsider the equation of labour commanded which we presented on p. 59 above:

$$p/w = l + (p/w) \, k(1 + r)$$

recalling that l and k are the labour and capital coefficients, r the rate of profit, $w/p = w_r$ the real wage, and p/w the labour commanded by corn. The equation now refers to the production obtained from the marginal unit of investment. As a consequence of an intensification in cultivation, the productivity of the labour utilized at the margins will decrease and pass from $1/l$ to $1/l'$, with $l' > l$. The real wages will not change. Assume that the capital coefficient will not change either. We have:

$$p/w = l' + (p/w) \, k(1 + r')$$

It is easy to see that, given w/p and k, the rate of profit will decrease as a consequence of the decrease in labour productivity. In Ricardo's terms, it is also possible to say that the profit decreases because, as a result of the intensification of cultivation, the product share necessary to pay for the wages will increase.

In this theory, the level of real wages is taken as known. To account for this, Ricardo, following Torrens, made use of the Malthusian population principle. At each given moment, the *market wage*, which depends on the forces of supply and demand for labour, can be higher or lower than the *natural* wage. In the first case, however, the increase in the workers' welfare will stimulate the birth rate and reduce the death rate. In the second case, the opposite will occur. Thus the supply of labour tends automatically to adjust to demand. When the population and the demand for labour grow at the same rate, wages are at their natural level, i.e. the one that guarantees the workers, besides survival, the possibility of reproducing themselves at the rhythm required by the accumulation of capital. While making the necessary allowances for the possibility of secular change in the workers' 'habits and customs', Ricardo defined the natural wage as a subsistence income, and practically treated it as if it were an exogenous constant.

3.1.5. Profits and over-production

Let us return to the problem of the Corn Laws and consider Malthus' position. Ricardo had no difficulty whatsoever in acknowledging the Malthusian paternity of a great part of the theories we have discussed above, especially in regard to the determination of rent and wages. Malthus, in turn, had no difficulty in accepting Ricardo's basic conclusions. The main difference concerned the political implications of those conclusions: while Ricardo feared a fall in the rate of profit, Malthus was afraid of a rise.

Malthus' argument, cut down to the bone, runs as follows. Both workers and landowners spend almost all their incomes on buying consumer goods. Therefore, wages and rents are resolved completely into effective demand. On the other hand, profits are almost entirely saved and invested. If the profit share increases in relation to the wage share, then the labour commanded by the goods will increase with respect to that commanded by the wages fund employed to produce them. This means that the incomes paid to the workers (the wages fund) is not able to provide a level of aggregate demand sufficient to realize the value of the goods produced by them. According to Malthus, this would lead to a lack of aggregate demand, unless the rent share were sufficiently high to compensate for that lack; in such a case, the demand that does not come from the productive workers would come from the unproductive ones. The Corn Laws were welcome, therefore, if they served to redistribute incomes from profits to rents.

Ricardo had little difficulty in identifying the error in Malthus' reasoning. In *Notes on Malthus* (written in 1820, but published in 1928) he reasoned as follows: 'I may employ 20 workmen to furnish me food and necessaries for 25, and then these 25 to furnish me food and necessaries for 30—these 30 again to provide for a greater number' (ii. 429). Thus, the surplus earned by the capitalists does not reduce the aggregate demand, for the simple reason that the investments are also demand.

Malthus, to rebut this criticism, would have had to argue that the profits saved are not necessarily spent; in other words, he would have had to question the validity of Say's Law. In fact, he came close to doing this in a letter written to Ricardo himself in 1814, where he stated that he did not believe that 'the power to purchase necessarily involves a proportionate will to purchase. . . .' A nation must certainly have the power of purchasing all that it produces, but it is easy to conceive it not to have the will (in Ricardo, *Works and Correspondence*, vi. 132). Unfortunately, Malthus did not know how to make use of this insight. The only effect his letter had was to put Ricardo on guard and make him realize the key role Say's Law could play in rebutting his rival's argument. In fact, the reply he gave to Malthus' letter is extremely clear and can be summarized as follows: if there is the purchasing power, there will also be the desire to purchase; savings decisions are motivated by the desire for accumulation, so that they generate effective demand just as much as consumption decisions. In other words, savings *are* investment, the decisions to save *are* decisions to spend. Today it is clear that this is not an economic law but only an arbitrary assumption. This assumption is the foundation of Say's Law. This 'law', after it was accepted by Ricardo and advanced again in his *Principles*, became almost a dogma for classical economic theory. Even Malthus remained imprisoned by it. In fact, in his *Principles* he did not reach the point of doubting the validity of that assumption, so that his arguments on the lack of effective demand, in the end, came off worse.

In order to avoid any misunderstanding, however, it is necessary to add that Ricardo's belief in the impossibility of 'general gluts' did not imply the thesis of full employment. Say's Law, in the use made of it by the classical economists, only implied equality between aggregate supply and demand of *reproducible* goods. This equality can occur at any employment level. It states that all the produced and earned incomes are spent, but says nothing about the level of income. Ricardo, like all classical economists, was convinced that in a competitive regime, not altered by State intervention (for example, by the Poor Laws), there could be no permanent unemployment in the very long run. This was not due to Say's Law, however, but rather to the Malthusian population principle: in the long run the permanently unemployed would be unable to survive. However, in the chapter 'On Machinery' added to the third edition of the *Principles*, Ricardo admitted that technological progress could force people out of work by replacing workers by machines, without the rhythm of accumulation of fixed capital being able to reabsorb them in the short term. Note that this short term must only be considered as not longer than the period necessary for the operation of the population principle: it could well be as long as twenty years or so!

3.1.6. Discussions on value

Ricardo and Malthus found themselves in conflicting positions also in regard to value. Malthus fully accepted Smith's theory of price as a sum of incomes and, together with it, the measure of value in labour commanded. It seemed to him that the notion of labour commanded could serve excellently to demonstrate the argument about the lack of effective demand. In fact, the existence of a profit implies that the labour commanded by the goods which make up the national product is higher than the labour commanded by the wages fund utilized to produce them. This does not mean, as we have seen, that the demand is insufficient to realize production. Malthus argued just this, however, and, in doing so, slid from the concept of 'natural price' to that of 'market price'. He often used the expression 'necessary price', apparently as a synonym of 'natural price'. In reality, he was simply referring to the price necessary to stimulate a level of production equal to demand. If the demand was too low, the price of the goods would not allow for the payment of the costs of production and normal profits. In this way production would be discouraged.

If Say's Law is not assumed, this argument is applicable to all the goods produced. Thus a lack in effective demand can trigger a deflationary process that can affect both the quantities produced and the prices. In this case, however, we are dealing with market prices, not natural prices. Malthus should have limited himself to studying phenomena of disequilibrium dynamics in order to demonstrate his arguments about general gluts. In fact, his use of the concept of 'labour commanded' (which is a *natural price*) in relation to demand phenomena did nothing but increase the confusion.

Ricardo, who undertook all his own studies in terms of natural prices, found it easy to identify this confusion. Moreover, while Malthus calculated the price of the goods by adding up wages, profits, and rents, Ricardo maintained that rents do not enter into the calculation of prices, as they are determined at the margin of the cultivated land and therefore do not include the cost of the use of land.

In any case, in regard to value, Ricardo had already chosen Smith as his favourite target. Apart from the question whether rent is or is not an element in the cost of production, Ricardo rejected the additive theory of price, as it conflicted with the explanation of profits as residual income. We have already touched on this problem in the previous chapter. At this point, the theory of profit as a residue can be formulated and solved in a very simple way by the corn model. In this case, problems of valuation of the goods do not arise, and the distribution of income can be determined in physical terms. To appreciate this it is only necessary to take the equation on p. 59 and normalize it with the price of corn. With a few simple algebraic passages we obtain:

$$1 = w_r l + k(1 + r)$$

$$w_r = \frac{1}{l} - \frac{k}{l}(1 + r)$$

It can be seen that an increase in real wages, w_r, or a reduction in the productivity of labour, $1/l$, results in a reduction in profits, kr. The existence of a decreasing function linking wages to profits is a fundamental element of Ricardo's economic theory.

Problems arose when this argument had to be demonstrated in an analytical context in which wages are made up of different goods. The difficulty took various forms in Ricardo's analysis. First, when wages increase, the prices of goods must change. Smith believed that they would increase. In this case, how is it possible to argue that profits would decrease? Second, when the prices of all the goods vary, it would seem that the value of the one chosen as a measure would also vary. How is it possible to distinguish the variations of the former from those of the latter? Ricardo believed that he could overcome these difficulties by using a measure of value which is independent from the distribution of income. For this reason, he rejected the measure in labour commanded, which is *not* independent. In the first section of the first chapter of the *Principles* he adopted, as a first approximation, a measure in embodied labour, which is, in fact, independent from income distribution. Actually, the labour embodied in the net product depends solely on the techniques in use and does not change with changes in the way in which that product is distributed. Unfortunately, however, the exchange values of the goods change with the distribution of income. Therefore they do not depend only on the labour embodied in them.

Ricardo realized this problem and fought with it for all his life. He arrived at the solution when he admitted that values depend on the labour embodied in the goods *and* on the time required to bring them to the market, or, rather, on the different proportions in which the various goods are produced with labour and means of production. The solution consists in expressing that 'time' and those 'proportions' in terms of the time-structure of the labour inputs. The simplest way to understand this is to consider two goods which are produced only by labour; the techniques with which the goods are produced differ with regard to the time in which labour is kept invested in the production processes. p_1 and p_2 are the monetary prices of the two goods, l_1 and l_2 the two labour coefficients. l_1 is invested for t_1 years, l_2 for t_2. Now let us assume the monetary wage, w, is paid in advance. Then the two prices, expressed in labour commanded, are:

$$p_1/w = l_1(1+r)^{t_1}$$

$$p_2/w = l_2(1+r)^{t_2}$$

The relative value of the two goods is:

$$\frac{p_1}{p_2} = \frac{l_1}{l_2}(1+r)^{t_1-t_2}$$

It depends on the labours embodied, l_1/l_2 and the times of their investment, t_1, t_2.

Note that the relative price is a ratio between the labours commanded. This should have been the solution to Ricardo's problem. In fact, the measure in labour commanded does not conflict with the conception of profit as a residue, nor with the thesis of the existence of a decreasing function linking profits to wages.

However, Ricardo did not manage to solve this problem satisfactorily, even though he glimpsed the solution. The factor that prevented him from taking the decisive step was the notion of 'absolute value'. This notion defines a property of the goods which is intrinsic and independent of their exchange relations—a property linked to their production conditions but not to the way in which the goods themselves are distributed among the social classes. This property of goods however, if it exists, cannot have anything to do with value; yet Ricardo continued to search for the 'real' value in it. And, even though he was aware of the difficulties involved with the notion of 'absolute value' he never abandoned it. Rather, he attempted to get around the problem, as we have already mentioned, by seeking an 'invariable measure' of value: a good that, being produced in 'average' conditions with respect to the whole system, would possess the virtue, if taken as a numeraire, of making the value of the net product, and of the income shares of the various classes, coincide with the quantities of labour employed in their production. A variation in the distribution of income would cause the relative prices of the goods to vary, and would therefore change the value of the net product even without changing the quantity of labour embodied in it. According to Ricardo, however, if the prices of the goods were measured in terms of a good produced with a technique in which the ratio between 'immediate labour' and 'accumulated labour' is equal to that of the whole economic system, then the following phenomenon would occur: the increase in the prices of some goods would be compensated by the fall in prices of some others, in such a way that the value of the net product would not change. Ricardo knew that such a measure did not exist in nature, but persisted in seeking a definition that would be acceptable at least theoretically. He was fooling himself: such a measure is a chimera—in the words of Cannan—or, according to Marx, a 'squaring of the circle'.

3.2. THE DISINTEGRATION OF CLASSICAL POLITICAL ECONOMY IN THE AGE OF RICARDO

3.2.1. The Ricardians, Ricardianism, and the classical tradition

As we have already mentioned, from 1815 to 1848 Ricardo dominated English economic thought. This does not mean that a dominant Ricardian orthodoxy had formed, nor that the economists of the period were agreed about the foundations of economic science. On the contrary, it was a period of ideological turbulence, lively debates, theoretical and political oppositions, and incurable conflicts. The central position of Ricardo in this period, at least in Great Britain, was due only to the fact that no economist could ignore his thought; or rather, that nobody was able to define his own position without referring to Ricardo's, including those who accepted his authority, those who rejected and criticized it, and, finally, those who tried to use it for ends that Ricardo himself would have repudiated.

At any rate, if we are allowed to be schematic and synthetic, it is possible to group the English economists of the period into three large groups: the Ricardians, the Ricardian socialists, and the 'anti-Ricardians'. We must immediately point out, however, that we are not dealing with three schools of thought, but only with three different attitudes that unite economists of rather heterogeneous ideas. We will discuss the third group in the next section, and the second in Chapter 4.

The first group was composed of the true followers of Ricardo: economists who, although not forming a school of thought, tried, however, each in his own way, to propagate Ricardo's ideas and to build a sort of scientific orthodoxy on them. James Mill (1773–1836), a personal friend and a great supporter of Ricardo, was particularly important. In *Commerce Defended* (1808) he proposed his own version of the law of markets, while, in *Elements of Political Economy* (1821), he presented a simple and elegant synthesis of the Ricardian doctrine which contributed a great deal to its success. It is also worth mentioning the textbook by John Ramsay McCulloch (1789–1864), *The Principles of Political Economy* (1825); the methodological work of Thomas De Quincey (1785–1859), *The Logic of Political Economy* (1844); and an attempt at a mathematical formulation of Ricardian theories made by William Whewell (1794–1866) in *A Mathematical Exposition of Some Doctrines of Political Economy* (1829).

Here we must also mention Robert Torrens (1780–1864), an economist who disagreed with Ricardo on various rather important questions, but whose theoretical position was not substantially different. A major dispute concerned the theory of value. Torrens criticized the labour theory of value immediately after the publication of Ricardo's *Principles*; and his criticism played an important role in adding to Ricardo's theoretical uncertainty. Torrens put forward his own theory in the *Essay on the Production of Wealth* (1822), in which he rejected the Ricardian theory, demonstrating the uselessness of a theory of absolute value. Value, he maintained, is basically exchange value and depends on the *costs of production*; which are nothing more than the capital advanced to sustain production, including that used to pay labour. The values of the goods depend on capital, and are determined in such a way to allow the payment of a uniform rate of profit on capital.

Perhaps it is true, as some people argue, that Ricardianism only constituted an incident in the normal evolution of orthodox economic theory, an exception, a particular phenomenon, restricted historically to the first half of the nineteenth century and geographically to England. Or perhaps it is true, as others maintain, that it represented a deviation, a new budding, from the main trunk of the development of economic ideas; a trunk whose roots go back to *The Wealth of Nations* or, rather, to one of the two basic components of Smith's thought, the theory of competitive equilibrium. The branch from which Ricardianism budded was impeded in its development as an ideology of capitalist accumulation, but, instead, was later to blossom as socialist economic theory. Perhaps both points of view are right; they are not, in fact, incompatible.

There is, however, a third historical interpretation of Ricardianism that does not seem acceptable to us; an interpretation which reduces it to a normal phase in the evolution of orthodox economics. It does not seem reasonable because it tends to reduce Ricardo's theory to the theory of rent, interpreted as a first application of the principle of decreasing marginal productivity of factors. On the other hand, if this interpretation were true, why did the English forerunners of neoclassical economics, whom we shall discuss shortly, have to attack Ricardo's ideas in order to be able to assert their own?

It is easier to understand the matter if we cross the Channel to consider what was happening on the Continent. There were important forerunners of neo-classical theory also in France and Germany, but they did not need to bring about a revolution against the dominant economic thought in their respective countries to assert their own ideas. In fact, the most important of these precursors, Cournot and Dupuit in France and von Thünen and Gossen in Germany, are not considered as being opponents of classical economics. The reason is that, in England, with Ricardo, the macroeconomic component of the classical tradition prevailed, the one based on the theory of surplus, whereas in the rest of Europe, with Say, Soden, and Lotz, the microeconomic compo-nent dominated, the one based on the theory of the individualistic competitive equilibrium. Thus the Continental forerunners of neoclassical theory, in de-veloping the empiricist, mechanistic, and individualistic premises of Smithian liberalism, were able basically to remain within orthodoxy and tradition.

These four great economists, however, were almost completely ignored by their contemporaries. The main reason for this was that they took the Con-tinental classical tradition to its extreme logical conclusions and purified it from its 'classicity', and therefore were not acknowledged by those who were faithful supporters of the classical tradition. In effect, these four 'forerunners' were working in the opposite direction from that attempted by Ricardo; they tried to free the individualistic and microeconomic components of the Smith-ian approach from the theory of surplus, the equilibrium approach from the theory of conflict; but they were ahead of their times. We will discuss them in sections 3.2.3 and 3.2.4.

3.2.2. The anti-Ricardian reaction

It was probably the socialist utilization of Ricardo's theory of value and distribution that induced many economists to reject it *en bloc*. These econo-mists formed a heterogeneous group, one which it has only been possible to define in negative terms, as the 'anti-Ricardian reaction'. However, they made more original theoretical contributions than did the Ricardians—contributions that make them the precursors of the later neoclassical theoretical system.

In regard to value, the anti-Ricardian attack was initiated by Samuel Bailey (1791–1870), who, in *A Critical Dissertation on the Nature, Measure and Causes of Value* (1825), criticized the idea itself of 'absolute value'. According to Bailey, it is only possible to speak of 'relative value', a concept that does not denote anything positive or intrinsic, but just the quantitative relationship between two goods which are made objects of exchange. Now, if it only consisted of this, it would not have been a decisive criticism. In the Ricardian theoretical system absolute value, as well as the invariable measure of value, are not essential, and it is possible to dispose of them without losing any of the arguments that Ricardo considered particularly important in regard to the distribution of income. However, Bailey also hinted at another idea, one that was much more dangerous: that the value of a good is nothing more than the valuation given to it by the economic agents, and that, as a consequence, 'value' only denotes an effect produced in the mind. This meant that it was not absolute value in itself that created problems, but rather the theory that aimed at explaining value in objective terms, i.e. in terms of the production conditions of goods. This path was followed by other critics of Ricardo.

Nassau William Senior (1790–1864), for example, stated, in *An Outline of the Science of Political Economy* (1836), that value depends on the conditions both of supply and of demand. He treated the former in terms of the limitation that supply places on the satisfaction of demand, while he linked the latter to the utility of the demanded goods. Senior also came close to the idea of decreasing marginal utility when he declared: 'not only are there limits to the pleasure which commodities of any class can afford, but the pleasure diminishes in a rapidly increasing ratio long before those limits; . . . two articles of the same kind will seldom afford twice the pleasure of one' (p. 11).

The principle of decreasing marginal utility was in the air; all the anti-Ricardian economists were pondering it. Longfield, whom we will discuss later, approached it with his analysis of the influence that the 'intensity of demand' can have on prices. Richard Whately (1787–1863) and William Forster Lloyd (1794–1852), the two successors to Senior in the chair of economics at Oxford, also got very close to it. The former, in his *Introductory Lectures on Political Economy* (1831), even proposed reducing economics to 'catallactics', the science of exchange. The latter went so far along this path that he should be given credit for having invented the principle of marginal utility. In effect, the formulation of the principle Lloyd gave in *A Lecture on the Notion of Value* (1834) was fairly clear and well defined; value depends on 'a feeling of the mind, which shows itself always at the margin of separation between satisfied and unsatisfied wants' (p. 9), so that the demand for goods depends on the satisfaction they procure, and will vary in relation to the quantities the subject already holds.

All these attempts to explain value in subjective terms were motivated by the need to reject the labour theory of value. The latter, in the hands of the

Ricardian Socialists, had become a fearful political instrument, in that it seemed to imply that labour is the only source of value and therefore, since profit is a residue, it also seemed to demonstrate the exploitation of labour. Hidden behind the rejection of the objective theory of value was a rejection of the residual theory of profit. In fact, it was not that hidden. Samuel Read, in *An Inquiry into the Natural Grounds of Right to Vendible Property of Wealth* (1829), was explicit in the formulation of this anti-Ricardian research programme. Just as explicit was George Poulett Scrope (1797–1876) in his condemnation of the labour theory of value as the basis of the theory of exploitation. Profit, he maintained in his *Principles of Political Economy* (1833), must be considered as a legitimate income, in that it is necessary to remunerate the capitalist for the period of time during which capital is employed.

This was the road also taken by Senior: to try to explain profit as a premium for the sacrifice sustained in putting capital at the service of production. Here is the famous theory of 'abstinence', mother of all the neoclassical theories of capital. Senior began by postulating that labour and land are the only original productive forces. He also maintained that the utilization of capital increases the productivity of those primary factors. But a sacrifice must be made in order to supply capital, and this represents a third productive requisite: abstinence, the postponement of pleasure caused by the act of saving. Profit is its remuneration. The *rate* of profit will therefore depend on the average period of capital anticipation.

Here we have, in fact, two different explanations. One is of a psychological nature, and treats the remuneration of capital as depending on the sacrifice sustained in supplying it; the other, of a technological nature, makes the remuneration of capital depend on the contribution by investments to the increase in the productive efficiency of the other factors. Senior favoured the first explanation. The second was developed further by Samuel Mountifort Longfield (1802–84), who, in his *Lectures on Political Economy* (1834), suggested that the use of machines ease the operations of the worker; so that profit, being the sum paid for the use of the machines, should be regulated by the efficiency with which the machines ease productive activity, that is, by the efficiency of capital.

Several decades had to pass before a clear distinction could be made between the psychological and the technological theory; it was only after the marginalist revolution that it was possible to integrate them into a unitary view capable of explaining the supply of capital in psychological terms and the demand in technological terms.

3.2.3. Cournot and Dupuit

It was Say who carried the classical tradition forward in France. As we have already mentioned, he had freed himself both from the labour theory of value and from the theory of labour commanded, theories that he replaced by an explanation that relied heavily on the forces of demand and the influence of utility as the main determinants of prices.

Augustin Cournot (1801–77) followed Say in his rejection of every theory of value intended as a search for the *causes of value*. He even rejected (and this is what differentiates him from Say) a utility theory of value—a rejection motivated above all by the measurement difficulties connected with utility. However, he is linked to Say by the importance he attributed to demand in the explanation of prices. Cournot was the first scholar to be interested in the firm as such, to study its behaviour in different market situations and to pose the problem of the determination of the scale of production. It is not surprising, therefore, that his great work received no attention for several decades (which induced him to abandon economic research). In *Recherches sur les principes mathématiques de la théorie des richesses* (1838) he made the first rigorous formulation of a demand function; a function which he used to determine the price and quantity produced under monopoly.

It is the theory still found today in microeconomic textbooks. The monopolist faces a demand function of the type $D = f(p)$, where p is the price of the good. By multiplying the demand by the price, the total revenue, $R = pf(p)$ is obtained; and from this, differentiating with respect to price, the marginal revenue function, $R' = f(p) + pf'(p)$. Cournot proved that the monopolist's profit, given by the difference between revenue and costs, is at its maximum when the marginal revenue is equal to the marginal cost and the second derivative of the profit function is negative.

By introducing a second entrepreneur into the model, Cournot also laid the foundations of the theory of duopoly, even if the results he obtained in this case are less general than those obtained in his theory of monopoly. In order to explain the behaviour of the two agents, Cournot constructed two 'reaction curves'. The reaction curve of a duopolist shows the quantity he offers in relation to each level of quantity offered by the other. Assuming that the market-demand curve is *given*, that each of the two agents, at each price level, takes the level of production of the competitor as *given*, and that the costs of production are zero, Cournot proved that there is a unique equilibrium point, at which the decisions of the duopolists are compatible.

Cournot's duopoly model is illustrated in Fig. 4. The supply of duopolist A, S_a, is shown on the horizontal axis, the supply of duopolist B, S_b, on the vertical axis. $Q_a Q'_a$ is the reaction curve of the first duopolist, $Q_b Q'_b$ that of the second. If A offers the quantity H, B will offer K. But then A will modify his own decisions and offer H'. B, however, corresponding to H', will offer K'. The process will go on until it reaches point C, towards which the process will converge even if it begins from a point to its left. This is a stable equilibrium, known today as the 'Nash–Cournot equilibrium'.

Two important observations should be made. The first concerns whether such an equilibrium exists. In general, the marginal costs curves of the

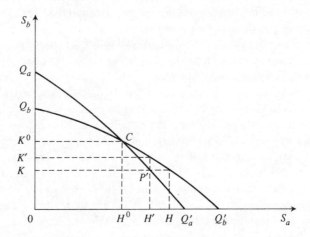

FIG. 4.

duopolists and the market-demand curve may be such that the reaction curves
do not meet in the positive quadrant or that they are parallel. By assuming zero
costs, Cournot avoided this inconvenience. Under such a hypothesis, in fact,
the equilibrium conditions depend solely on the two marginal-revenue curves;
but these are equal, since the goods supplied are homogeneous; in this case
the two reaction curves are symmetrical and intersect in the positive quadrant.
The second observation concerns the stability of equilibrium. In equilibrium,
the expectations of each duopolist about the behaviour of the other are confirmed. This is so in the sense that, if A expects B to produce exactly K^0 and
B expects A to produce exactly H^0, Cournot's equilibrium is that which emerges from such a duopoly situation. But if the firms have expectations that do
not coincide with $(H^0 K^0)$ an adjustment process needs to be considered. The
essential characteristic of the process of approaching the equilibrium point,
according to Cournot, is as follows: each firm makes a series of mistaken
assumptions about the behaviour of the other, but the size of these errors
gradually diminishes in intensity until a situation is reached in which the
expectations of reciprocal behaviour become correct. At this point the adjustment process stops. This is the sense in which the Nash–Cournot equilibrium
is stable.

Another French forerunner of neoclassical theory is Jules Dupuit (1804–66)
who, in *De l'utilité et de sa mesure* (*Of Utility and its Measurement*) (1844)
and other papers published in journals, tackled precisely the problems avoided
by Cournot. He endeavoured to study the social benefits derived from public
goods such as canals or bridges, and, above all, to evaluate the net social gains
generated by variations in tolls and rates. Dupuit was not perfectly aware of
the problems he had raised regarding the measurement of utility and the
possibility of making interpersonal comparisons of utility; but his analytical

contribution was nevertheless remarkable. He constructed a demand curve, interpreting it in terms of utility. Then he defined marginal utility and distinguished it from total utility. He assumed that the authority which supplies a good lowers the charge for it as the quantity supplied increases, so that the marginal utility of the good falls together with its price. The public benefit is measured by the sum of the intra-marginal utilities. 'Relative utility', given by the difference between total utility and marginal utility multiplied by the quantity of the good offered, will increase as the price decreases. In this way Dupuit proved that, if marginal utility is decreasing, the social benefit increases with the increase in the quantity offered. The reasoning is very similar to that which West, Malthus, and Ricardo had used to account for the increase in rent payments in relation to the increases in agricultural production. It is not by chance that, a few decades later, Marshall renamed 'relative utility' as 'consumer rent'.

Dupuit also conceptualized 'producer surplus', which, given an increasing cost curve, is the difference between the total revenue of the firm and the overall marginal costs. The total social benefit will be given by the sum of the two surpluses, that of the consumer and that of the producer.

3.2.4. Gossen and von Thünen

Also in Germany in this period, economists were working on the problems of value and utility. We have already mentioned the tendency of Smith's early German followers, such as Soden and Lotz, to distinguish between 'positive' value, which is linked to the utility of goods, and 'comparative' value, which is equivalent to Smith's 'exchange value'. There were basically two problems that two generations of German economists grappled with: how to determine exchange value on the grounds of 'positive' value, and how to explain the formation of the latter in purely subjective terms. From the point of view of the history of ideas, the solution of the problem was impeded by the Smithian origin of the notion of 'exchange value'. In fact, Smith maintained that this kind of value is a relationship between two quantities of goods, and therefore that it is an objective variable. After various attempts by Hufeland, von Hermann, and Rau, Hildebrand finally made the decisive step towards the solution by pointing out that the connection between subjective value and price presupposes that utility varies as a function of the quantity of goods.

The definitive solution was reached by Hermann Heinrich Gossen (1810–58) in 1854. In *Entwicklung der Gesetze des menschlichen Verkehrs, und der daraus fliessenden Regeln für menschliches Handeln (Development of the Laws of Human Interchange and the Resulting Rules of Human Commerce)*, Gossen argued that 'absolute value' does not exist, and that value depends on a relationship between a subject and an object. This relationship is based on utility. Gossen worked on the presupposition that the goal of an economic agent is to obtain maximum pleasure. He also formulated two laws that still today form the basis of the neoclassical theory of consumer behaviour. The *first law* establishes the principle of decreasing marginal utility: the pleasure obtained from a good decreases as the amount consumed increases until, eventually, satiety is reached. The *second law* is more important. In fact, it is a theorem derived from the assumption of maximizing behaviour and from the law of decreasing marginal utility. It states that the individual will choose to demand the various goods in such proportions that the satisfactions they give him are equal at the moment at which he stops consuming them; or, rather, that the individual will continue to exchange two goods until the values of the last units he possesses of them become equal.

Even if his explanation was a little imprecise, it remains true that Gossen had in mind what today is known as the theorem of equality of the weighted marginal utilities. Gossen also attempted to extend this theory to the labour supply by introducing the concept of 'disutility'.

Another important forerunner of neoclassical theory was Johann Heinrich von Thünen (1783–1850). In the first part of *Der Isolierte Staat* (*The Isolated State*) (1826), he put forward a theory of the location of productive activities based on the implicit use of the notion of 'opportunity cost'. Besides this he developed the theory of differential rent, proving that the level of production of a good, given demand, will be determined in such a way as to make the price equal to the production cost of the most disadvantaged firm. The surplus earned by the producers with lower costs is the rent.

In the second part of *Der Isolierte Staat* (1850), von Thünen extended this reasoning to labour and capital, formulating for the first time a complete theory of distribution based on the marginal productivity of factors. He argued that an increase in the utilization of capital and labour increases both the production and the costs, and that it will continue until the marginal productivities of factors are higher than their prices.

Von Thünen considered capital as a homogeneous factor of production, consisting of the quantity of past labour employed in the production of the means of production. He measured it in 'labour years'. He assumed that its use would raise the productivity of current labour, but at a decreasing rate. He calculated the returns of capital by differentiating a certain function at the point at which the derivative vanishes. This is the income function of the producer of capital, whose income is determined, in this way, at its maximum level. The result reached was notable at the analytical level, even though its theoretical relevance was limited by the particular hypotheses and the special form of the function with which von Thünen worked.

From those particular hypotheses, von Thünen also derived a special formula for the 'natural' wage, w^*, namely, $w^* = \sqrt{ap}$, in which a represents the subsistence level of consumption and p labour productivity. He was so strongly convinced of the importance of the formula that he wanted it inscribed on his tomb. Apart from the strangeness of the formula, von Thünen's concept of 'natural wage' deserves to be remembered above all for its originality: wages do not depend on the supply and demand of labour, nor only on the subsistence needs of the workers; they are a geometrical average of the needs and productivity of labour, and represent what must be paid to the worker in order to leave him indifferent between the choice of remaining a worker and that of becoming a capitalist-farmer (in the hypothesis that such a possibility of choice exists and land is not scarce). Von Thünen's natural wage is a *normative* concept. It is a 'just' wage in a precise sense: it is what allows the agricultural wage-earner to obtain the maximum returns from his own savings (equal to $w^* - a$) and, at the same time, what allows the independent farmer to maximize the earnings of his own investments. In other words, according to von Thünen, if the natural wage, w^*, prevailed, the worker would be a wage-earner out of free choice and not because he was forced to by need.

3.2.5. The Romantics and the German Historical School

The most ambitious attempt to criticize classical political economy did not come from any of the pre-neoclassical 'heretics' but from the Historical School, which, by putting Smith, Richardo, Say and all their followers in the same bag, criticized the idea itself that an autonomous economic science was possible.

In order to understand the sense of the historicist opposition to political economy, we must begin from its philosophical roots. While classical economics had its origins in the eighteenth-century Enlightenment, German historicism descended directly from early nineteenth-century Romanticism. It was especially in Germany that Romanticism had been accompanied by an irrationalist and organicist *Weltanschauung*. In economics it grew together with the first aristocratic and reactionary opposition to capitalist development; and with Fichte, Gentz, and Müller it opposed *laissez-faire* economics and political liberalism, both for the political consequences they implied and for the philosophical premises from which they came. The individualist and rationalist connotations of those premises were thoroughly rejected. On the contrary, the members of this school exalted the ideas of the organic unity of the nation, of the superiority of collective over individual goals, and of the historical and geographical specificity of the institutions of each country. This theoretical position has left us the bare bones of an interesting 'State' theory of money, which, if purified of the mystical elements that hampered it in those times, turns out to be in certain respects more modern than many classical theories, especially in its recognition of the conventional and institutional nature of the means of exchange.

Georg Friedrich List (1789–1846) can be associated with this stream of thought, although he did not share its reactionary political attitudes and its irrationalist philosophical premises. In *Das nationale System der politischen*

Oekonomie (*The National System of Political Economy*) (1841), List accepted a great many of the analytical premises of classical theory. However, he rejected *en bloc* its free-trade implications, for which he substituted a strongly mercantilist point of view and a theory of economic growth that gave great importance to the functional interdependence of industries and the need for uniform growth in the agricultural and industrial sectors. List not only did not reject capitalism, but tried to construct a theoretical system that, especially in its implications for trade policy, was intended to be used to foster German capitalist growth. The famous infant-industry protection strategy was brought to Europe by List who, as a political exile in the United States, had been the secretary to Henry Clay, the true inventor of that strategy. In common with the Romantics, List held the idea of the superiority of the nation's interests over those of individual citizens.

The major impact of Romantic philosophy in the field of economics occurred with the Historical School, a school that attempted to attack directly the epistemological foundations of political economy. Though there is certainly a connection between the German Historical School and Romanticism, there are many differences between them. For example, unlike the Romantic economists of the preceding generation, such as Gentz and Müller, the members of the Historical School were not all politically conservative. In fact, some criticized political economy and liberal thought from a left-wing standpoint.

The origin of the German Historical School goes back to *Grundriss zu Vorlesungen über die Staatswirtschaft nach geschichtlicher Methode* (*Compendium of Lectures on Public Economics according to the Historical Method*) (1843) by Wilhelm Roscher (1817–94). The other two founders of the school were Bruno Hildebrand (1812–78) and Karl Knies (1821–98), who, with *Die Nationalökonomie der Gegenwart and Zukunft* (*The National Economy of the Present and the Future*) (1848) and *Die politische Oekonomie vom Standpunkte der geschichtlichen Methode* (*Political Economy from the Standpoint of the Historical Method*) (1853), respectively, pushed the criticism of classical political economy much further forward than Roscher had dared to do. These three authors are the main exponents of the so-called 'Old Historical School'. This expression distinguishes them from the historicists of the following generation, who formed the 'Young Historical School'; its principal exponent was Gustav Schmoller, of whom we will speak in the next chapter. Here we present the fundamental arguments of the historical school, without dwelling on differences of opinion among individual members (which were, however, quite marked).

The basic historicist criticism of political economy touched upon its attempt to establish universal economic laws. With specific reference to the Smithian approach, the historicists denied that economic laws had the same properties as 'natural laws'. They did not deny the possibility of discovering certain economic regularities, and they also admitted that such regularities could be called 'laws'; but they did not believe that these were universally valid, nor that they were independent of the historical and geographical conditions in which they operated.

The historicists were more interested in what they called 'laws of development', that is, the regularities followed by the historical evolution of peoples and nations; here, too, they avoided constructing universal laws.

Above all, they denied the possibility of discovering economic laws by deduction. Only the inductive method was allowed: the laws of development had to be constructed by induction and analogy on the basis of the greatest possible quantity of empirical and historical data. It is clear that this type of criticism impinged not only on the theoretical tenets of Smith and Ricardo, but more generally on the simple idea that economics is a science of the same type as the natural sciences and therefore, as was to emerge later in the *Methodenstreit* at the end of the century, it refers to the neoclassical as well as to the classical approaches.

Beyond the problem of methodology there is, however, a fundamental, pre-analytical contrast between the two basic orientations. The followers of the German Historical School did not accept the idea that social behaviour depends only on the personal interests of the single individuals, or the idea that individual choices are solely based on the rational pursuit of self-interested goals. They had an organic vision of society, and upheld the presupposition that social agents are motivated by complex and multiple goals which are not all reducible to the rationality of economic calculation. Here, there is also the idea of a definite interdependence among the diverse dimensions of social action, and the conviction, therefore, that it is necessary to avoid the separation and excessive specialization of the single social sciences. From this point of view, economics was considered as only a branch of historical research.

3.3. THE THEORIES OF ECONOMIC HARMONY AND MILL'S SYNTHESIS

3.3.1. The 'Age of Capital' and the theories of economic harmony

After the defeat of the 1848 revolutions and the violent repression which ensued, the workers' movement went into hibernation and remained there for two decades. This was exactly what the industrial middle class needed. Reassured on the social front, firmly in possession of the reins of State in the principal capitalist countries, and also having laid favourable technological and cultural preconditions for economic growth, capitalism attempted its great jump forward. Hobsbawn called the 20-year period from 1850 to 1870 the 'Age of Capital'. If Great Britain had become the 'the workshop of the world', as the famous Crystal Palace exhibition in London in 1851 wished to demonstrate, there were several countries who were quite successful in their attempt to imitate the 'first industrial nation'.

Thus a certain variety in the types of industrial capitalism was created. The process of expansion involved, besides England and France, other European countries, such as Belgium, Sweden, and Germany, as well as the United States. In the latter, the necessity to supply a vast and rapidly growing market led to an early take-off of the formation of large-scale firms in the mass-production sector. Germany saw the birth of the mixed banks, financial intermediaries capable of supplying stable and consistent flows of finance to the new firms and, at the same time, of favouring the control of the market by the formation of cartels. In both countries industrial concentration increased, while limited companies began to be the preferred organizational form of large-scale firms.

Besides the 'intensification' of capitalist accumulation there was also fast geographical expansion. 'This was the period when the world became capitalist, and a significant minority of "developed" countries became industrial economies' (Hobsbawn, *The Age of Capital*, p. 29). Titanic civil-engineering projects were completed, such as the opening of the Suez Canal and the creation of national railway networks. New States and empires were founded. Finally, we should not forget that this period was dominated by a strong movement in favour of free trade, not only in Great Britain, where, after 1846, protectionism was almost completely abandoned, but also in other European countries, among which several monetary and trade agreements were created that served to encourage the growth of international trade.

Optimism spread with the growth in wealth, and the widespread social peace on which it was based allowed for important social and political reforms to be passed. The trade union movements, in return for their acquiescence or collaboration with national efforts, did achieve some conquests. For example, the ten-hour working day became law in England in 1850, whilst the recognition of the right to strike was passed in France in 1864. By and large, democratic and progressive forces were advancing all over the world. Serfdom was abolished in Russia in 1861 and slavery in the USA in 1862. Never before had capital exercised such a widespread hegemony in economic, social, political, and even cultural fields. The economists, for their part, were not to be found lacking, and did their job by producing theories of economic harmony.

We will mention here only the best-known of these economists: Frédéric Bastiat (1801–50), Henry Charles Carey (1793–1879), Francesco Ferrara (1810–1900), John Elliot Cairnes (1823–75), and Henry Fawcett (1833–1900). These economists did not make very important contributions to the evolution of economic theory, but they had great success in this period and exercised significant influence in their respective countries. It is easy to understand why. They were almost all supporters of the doctrine of the harmony of interests among the social classes; and, as that harmony was best realized, according to them, when competition was as perfect as possible, they were outspoken free-traders, arch-enemies of State intervention, and castigators of socialism. In regard to the theory of value, they tried in various ways to reconciliate the explanations based on labour and utility but did not produce significant results.

Carey, though, is a special case. He began to construct his own theoretical system in the 1830s, following a Smithian orientation and professing clear free-trade convictions. However, his influence in Europe was only felt, for example, on Bastiat, Ferrara, and Duhring, after the 1840s, and was derived from works such as *Harmony of Interests* (1851) and *Principles of Social Sciences* (1857–60). During the 1840s Carey had abandoned his earlier free-trade beliefs, replacing them by strong protectionist and nationalist propaganda. In Europe, however, only a few of his German admirers followed him along this line. Bastiat was especially influenced by his doctrine of harmony of interests, while Ferrara developed his theory of reproduction cost. The latter consisted in reducing the value of a good to the effort sustained in producing it, but the theory was not formulated in a very clear way, especially in relation to one fundamental question: if that effort should be considered in terms of subjective sacrifice or, rather, in terms of the objective cost of production.

Ferrara made interesting contributions to the economic-harmony approach, and should be remembered, if for no other reason than that he may have been the connecting link between Galiani and Pareto. Among Ferrara's important works are *Lezioni di economia politica* (*Lectures in Political Economy*) (published posthumously in 1934–5) and the prefaces to the *Biblioteca dell'economista* (1850–66), collected together and published in 1889 under the title *Esame storico-critico di economisti e dottrine economiche* (*Historical-Critical Examination of Economists and Economic Doctrines*). Ferrara developed a theory of substitutes according to which the value of a good, in relation to the value of one of its substitutes, depends on the comparison the consumer makes between the two utilities. The value emerging from such a comparison is the one at which the individual is prepared to exchange the two goods. Then, by using this theory to correct Carey's reproduction-cost doctrine, Ferrara also tried to explain, by means of the theory of exchange, the phenomena both of production and distribution. Production was considered as an exchange between the product and the productive efforts. The costs of the goods, which in competition is equal to their value, is determined by the sacrifice sustained in producing them, valued in relation to the result of the production itself: this presupposes a comparison between the disutility the individual has to bear to give up something of his own and that which he must bear if he renounces something of others'. This argument makes no use of the criterion of marginal variations, but the role of the hypothesis of substitutability, both in consumption and production, is clear. Even if the reference to classical theory in the work of Ferrara is explicit and marked, it is easy to see that here we are on the threshold of the marginalist revolution.

It is worth noting that Pareto considered Ferrara 'the best of Italian economists'. He believed that Ferrara's theory of reproduction cost had reached 'the ultimate level of perfection', only lacking in its analytical formalization. He considered it an anticipation of his own theory of optimality.

3.3.2. John Stuart Mill

The dominant economist of the 'Age of Capital' was John Stuart Mill (1806–73), philosopher, politician, social reformer, and economist. In economics Mill attempted a heroic task: a re-examination of the debates of the first half of the century with the intent of unifying its principal theoretical results. It was, above all, this effort towards theoretical 'harmonization' that determined the notable success, in the following 30 years, of his main work, *Principles of Political Economy* (1848).

But for the same reason, once the classical era had closed, his work was almost completely forgotten. Mill had tried to reconstruct the Smithian tradition by uniting two incompatible approaches: the macroeconomic theory of surplus and the theory of individualistic competitive equilibrium. All the debates that took place in the 30 years before the publication of Mill's *Principles* arose precisely from the difficulties in keeping those two approaches together. In fact, after the 1870s, they separated completely and for ever. On the one hand, the Ricardian branch developed into Marxist economics; on the other, the anti-Ricardian branch developed into neoclassical economics. Mill, who does not seem to have understood what was happening, was accused of electicism and superficiality by both parties, and was forgotten; but he does not deserve oblivion.

Mill's work is important because it is located at a central crossroads of nineteenth-century European culture. In his work several currents of thought and theoretical problems meet. This characteristic places it in the middle of the long transition process from classical to neoclassical economic thought, and gives the impression of eclecticism. But the indications of the direction (a well-defined direction) in which to seek solutions are always fairly clear, even if they are often obscured by references to authors who were moving in the opposite way. All Mill's difficulties were derived, apart from the complexity of the arguments tackled, from his fear of breaking with tradition. His theoretical difficulties arose from a combination of perceiving the new and lacking the courage to break with the old. Mill himself, in his *Autobiography* (1861), defined his own work as the constant effort to 'construct bridges and clear roads' in the theories of his predecessors.

In his youth Mill was a member of the Utilitarian Society, and collaborated in the *Westminster Review*, the Society's publication. The Society was made up of young Radicals who fought for the most extensive realization of liberal and democratic principles. The philosophical bases of this radicalism were made up by Bentham's utilitarianism, with all that it implied in terms of individualism, rationalism, the justification of *laissez-faire* in economics and of liberalism in politics. Bentham's influence on Mill, however, was tempered by the opposing influence of Romantic thought, Coleridge's in particular. Mill obviously rejected the political implications of such thought, but derived from it, on the one hand, the need to base action and political thought on a strong philosophy of history and, on the other, the refusal to reduce human choices and behaviour to the economic dimension alone.

In the essay *Utilitarianism* (1863), Mill rejected two of the fundamental assumptions of Bentham's philosophy: the one according to which the reasons for human action can all be reduced to self-interest and to the selfish search for the maximum pleasure; and the other that the single individual is the only judge of his own interest. The first argument permitted Mill to link himself with the traditional English and Scottish 'moral-sense' philosophers. Mill maintained that an increase in personal pleasure could also be derived from participation in the happiness of others. In this way he justified, from a utilitarian perspective, the rationality of behaviour motivated by feelings of humanity and solidarity. The other argument was still more important, in that it allowed relevant, if not substantial, departures from the *laissez-faire* principle. In fact, in some cases he accepted State intervention in the economy— for example, in education, in the regulation of the working day, and in assistance to the poor. In these cases, Mill maintained that the public authorities knew the interests of individuals better than they themselves, a clear anticipation of the modern 'merit goods' doctrine.

More generally, however, utilitarianism had been interpreted by placing at its base the criterion of the maximization of the welfare of the maximum number of people; and Mill's reformism pushed ahead to the point of maintaining that such an objective should be pursued even at the cost of reducing the welfare of some individuals. He derived this argument from the natural-law component of another philosophical tradition, one that linked him to Locke. In fact, he justified private property with the same argument as Locke had used, the right of individuals to possess the products of their own labour. But he criticized the abuses of this right, and especially the glaring inequality in the distribution of property, which he explained in terms of historical and institutional influences. Any interventions aimed at the correction of such defects were therefore considered legitimate. For example, he proposed progressive death duties.

Mill did not consider such conclusions to be in conflict with the laws of economics. In fact, he admitted, as had done Smith and Ricardo, the natural character of the laws of production, but denied, as did the socialists and the historicists (for example, Richard Jones, an interesting English historicist of whom we will speak in the next chapter), the natural character of the laws of distribution. Thus, while he exalted competition and the market, which would allow the natural laws of production to operate in the best possible way, he was not against the encouragement of profit-sharing schemes, and co-operative work, as well as the development of small farming communities.

Mill considered himself a friend of the working classes, as well as of other categories of outcasts and oppressed, and thought that history was working for the final realization of a society he defined as 'socialist'; but he did not consider himself a socialist. In fact he fought, in his own way, against the socialism of his times, so much so that he felt the need to demonstrate the fallacy of the socialist doctrines from the point of view of economic science. In order to understand these aspects of Mill's thought, we need to enter the heart of his political economy and, in particular, his theories of profit and wages.

3.3.3. Wages and the wages fund

There were traces of the wages-fund doctrine already in Smith's work. However, the theory was developed, above all, by Ricardo's followers, who tried to use it to overcome some difficulties of the Ricardian theory of the natural wage. The use of the population principle to account for the tendency of the market wage to adjust towards its natural level posed two crucial problems which seemed to undermine the idea itself of a natural wage as a centre of gravitation. First of all, it was necessary to define the subsistence wage in physiological terms, otherwise it would have been impossible to explain the ability of a fall in the market wage to adjust the growth of the labour supply by means of variations in the *death rates*. But all the classical economists, including Smith and Ricardo, admitted that the subsistence wage also depended on the habits and customs of the working population, that is, on social and cultural factors as well as biological ones. Second, if it is admitted (as was the normal practice), that habits and customs could also change as a result of changes in the level of income, the natural wage could vary, in the long run, as a function of the market wage. Therefore it could not be considered as a centre of gravitation for the latter.

Even if we ignore these two problems, however, the adjustment mechanism which enabled the natural wage to regulate the oscillations of the market wage would require extremely long periods, definable over several generations. In this way, the natural wage loses its relevance. What sense did the classical exercises in comparative statics have if the states that could be compared presuppposed periods of a quarter of a century or more? On the other hand, if these exercises referred to the time-span of the duration of a productive cycle, generally assumed to be a year, then the wage and its changes could not be anything but those determined by the market. We shall see in the next chapter, when we consider Marx, which was the only coherent way out of this problem—coherent, that is, with the classical approach.

The path taken by the Ricardians was that of abandoning the concept of the natural wage and relegating the subsistence wage to the simple role of a minimum limit of the market wage. The path was opened by McCulloch and followed, with variations, by Torrens, Cairnes, Mill, and others. In order to explain the theory in the simplest way, we will refer to an economy which produces one consumer good and one capital good by means of labour and capital. Let L be the labour force, L^* its full employment level, w_r the real wage, $\overline{w}_r$ its minimum subsistence level, and K capital. We will take the price of the consumer good as numeraire.

As production requires time, it is necessary, at the end of every productive cycle, to 'set aside' a part of the product to sustain the workers during the successive cycle: this is the *wages fund*. Let us define it as $W = w_r L$. Its size depends on three factors: the amount of profits, the capitalists' propensity to save, and the techniques in use. The classical economists took as given, at each moment, the last two factors. Then, if *the distribution of income is known*, it is possible to determine the wages fund, let us say, at level $\overline{W}$. It follows that wages and employment level are inversely related:

$$w_r = \frac{\overline{W}}{L}$$

This relationship is represented in Fig. 5 by curve $\overline{W}$, together with a very simple labour supply function, $\overline{L}$, corresponding to the one implicitly used by the classical economists.

As can be seen in Fig. 5, there is only one wage-level that guarantees full employment (and the full utilization of capital), and this is w_e. The Ricardian economists tended to interpret w_e as a market wage, and to consider it as determined by the forces of supply and demand. But such an explanation runs up against a series of logical difficulties. If the technique is given, the capital : labour ratio, K/L, is known. At the moment in which the productive process terminates, the structure and level of output are known. If it is decided to set aside a certain wages fund, $\overline{W}$, it is also automatically decided how to share out the investments between technical capital and wages funds. Thus $K/\overline{W}$ will also be known. Therefore the level of employment and wages are both determined, and independently of the labour supply. If the latter, by chance, were equal to the 'demand', then the wage level would be w_e, but it would not be a market wage. However, if the supply and demand of labour, let us say L^* and L_d, do not coincide, then the wage rate will be w_d; but neither is this a wage determined by the forces of supply and demand. In fact, the market would tend to bring wages towards w_e. This point cannot be reached, however, because, given $\overline{W}$ and K/W, K is also given; and given K/L at the level K/L_d, an increase in employment beyond L_d is impossible owing to a lack of capital.

The wages-fund theorists, including Mill, vaguely realized this difficulty and often tried to avoid it by letting K/L vary. This was a new path that would eventually have led to the neoclassical theory of wages. But large steps had to be taken; in particular, it was necessary to interpret $\overline{W}$ as a demand schedule for labour and make it depend on a production function in which the substitutability between labour and capital was admissible. The Ricardian economists were not equipped for such a leap.

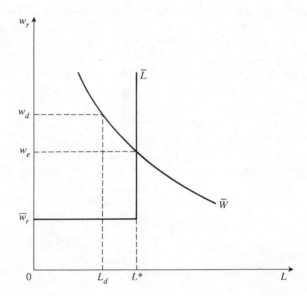

FIG. 5.

Let us return to Mill; and, in order to avoid these difficulties, let us assume that, by chance, $L^* = L_d$ and $w_e = w_d$. Now we can see how Mill used the theory in a 'labourist' way. In the 'short run' the trade unions can do nothing to modify wages, which depend solely on the techniques in use and the capitalists' investment decisions. In fact, an increase in the wages above w_e would lead to a reduction in employment (and in the utilization of capital). But then, if competition exists, the excess in labour supply will bring the wages back to their 'equilibrium' value. The workers, according to Mill, will only be able to influence wages in the 'long run'. Over time, $\overline{W}$ and $\overline{L}$ shift to the right. Wages increase if $\overline{W}$ moves more than $\overline{L}$. Therefore they would grow faster the higher the rhythm of accumulation and the lower the rate of population growth. This explains why Mill suggested that his trade union friends should preach less revolution and more contraception.

Later on, however, Mill changed his mind. The criticisms levelled against him by William T. Thornton (in *On Labour*, 1869), and by other economists, made him understand the anti-trade union use that could be made, and, in effect was being made, of his theory. But his recantation was not complete. It was presented in a review of Thornton's book published in the *Fortnightly Review* in May 1869, and it consisted of the rejection, not of the theory itself, but of two of the hypotheses that qualified it. Mill admitted that it was not necessary to take as given the distribution of income and the propensity to save of the capitalists. Thus wages could increase if the consumption of luxury goods and/or the profit share decreased. However, a real limit to the increase of the wages would still remain, a limit represented by the fact that this increase could lead entrepreneurs to bankruptcy.

3.3.4. Capital and the wages fund

More than for the explanation of wages, Mill's theory of the wages fund is important for the explanation of profit and of the role played by capital in the production process. From the point of view of the history of economic thought, this aspect of Mill's theoretical system is important for the role it played in the transition from the classical to the neoclassical approach.

In the *Essays on Some Unsettled Questions in Political Economy*, written between 1829 and 1831 (but published in 1844), Mill tackled some of the problems of the Ricardian theory of value. In this work, without dissociating himself from Ricardo, he argued that value did not only depend on labour; and that this was so because the value of the means of production and wage goods depends, in turn, not only on the wages advanced to produce them but also on the profits earned by the capitalists. From this, Mill derived a theory of value based on the cost of production which differed from Ricardo's above all in abandoning the search for an invariable measure of value. The theory was along rather similar lines to those followed by Torrens. However, it still contained the Ricardian rejection of the additive theory of prices, and this is what really counted.

The decisive turn occurred in the *Principles*, when Mill, precisely in order to oppose the socialist theories of exploitation, was forced to abandon Ricardo. In fact he maintained that the workers do not have a right to the whole product, because it is not only labour that contributes to the creation of the value of goods, but also the abstinence necessary to render capital available. Labour is only one of the requirements of production, and this cannot be undertaken without the aid of machinery and the advance of the wages fund. Capital is the other requirement of production, and it is the result of the abstinence from consumption on the part of the capitalists.

But in our analysis . . . of the requisites of production, we found that there is another necessary element in it besides labour. There is also capital; and this being the result of abstinence, the produce, or its value, must be sufficient to remunerate, not only all the labour required, but the abstinence of all the persons by whom the remuneration of the different classes of labourers was advanced. The return for abstinence is profit. (p. 280)

Mill explicitly referred to Senior:

As the wages of the labourer are the remuneration of labour, so the profits of the capitalist are properly, according to Mr. Senior's well-chosen expression, the remuneration of abstinence—they are what he gains by forbearing to consume his capital for his own uses, and allowing it to be consumed by productive labourers for their uses. For this forbearance he requires a recompense. (p. 245)

Here we have an extension of the 'wages fund' concept to include all capital. The primary requisite of the production process, according to Mill, is still labour (although sometimes land is also taken into consideration). Capital is nothing else but the wages fund set aside in preceding periods in order to sustain the workers who produce the means of production. These advances create a profit. Ricardo would not have disagreed with all this. But, according to Ricardo, capital does not contribute to the creation of *value*, and profit is not the remuneration of a productive service. Mill's theoretical jump consisted of the use of the abstinence theory to explain profit. In fact this was subdivided into various components: a management salary, a risk premium, and a re-muneration for abstinence. The last was taken to coincide with interest. Mill, in this way, was able to speak a Ricardian language and say that the *profit*, *net* of these three components, is a residue. However, he did say something that Ricardo would never have admitted when he stated that interest remun-erates a productive contribution.

This theory is similar to Senior's. Mill, however, included in abstinence not only the sacrifice connected to the renunciation of a given *flow* of income but also the sacrifice inherent in the renunciation of the consumption of capital stock already accumulated. In this way interest is explained as the remunera-tion, not of savings, but, more precisely, of capital.

Obviously, the economists of the Austrian school would have greatly ap-preciated such an interpretation of the theory of the wages fund. In effect, some of them considered the neoclassical theory of capital, at least in the version based on the notion of 'production period', precisely as an extension of the wages fund theory. What prevented Mill from taking the wages fund doctrine to its extreme logical consequences? Basically he lacked two ideas, which are, in fact, the core of the Austrian theory of capital: first the hypo-thesis that it is possible to combine labour and capital in different proportions; second, the hypothesis that the productive contribution of capital decreases with the increase in the period in which the wages fund is kept invested.

Of course, Mill can also be considered a forerunner of the English neoclas-sical school besides the Austrian one. Apart from the possibility of linking the wages fund theory to Jevons's theory of capital, another line of ancestry unites Mill to the neoclassical school, and it is that which links him to Marshall. In regard to the role played by the forces of demand and production in determining prices, Mill, as usual, started from Ricardo in distinguishing between two categories of goods: those which are absolutely limited in supply, and those for which the supply is susceptible to indefinite mutiplication without increases of costs. The value of the goods of the first type depends solely on the forces of demand, while the value of those of the second type depends solely on the cost of production. However Mill admitted that there is a third type of goods, one for which the supply is susceptible to multiplication but not without increases of costs. The value of these goods would still depend on the cost of production, but now only in the most unfavourable existing circumstances. Mill was think-ing about something similar to a 'generalization' of the role played by the decreasing returns of land, but he did not go deeper into this question. The step that still had to be made was to show that the 'most unfavourable circumstances' of the production process depend on the quantity produced. This, on the one hand, would have presupposed the hypothesis of variable returns of the productive factors and, on the other, would have implied that price depends both on forces of demand and on conditions of production.

We should like to conclude this brief exposition of Mill's thought by presenting his theory of the falling rate of profit. This will serve to give an idea of how his reformism was linked to a strong and optimistic philosophy of history, as well as to show that there was at least one thing in which Mill remained basically a classical economist: his ability to link the abstract theories to extremely important historical and political problems.

Mill believed, as did Smith, Ricardo, and Marx, that the rate of profit was governed by an inevitable tendency to fall, in the very long run. Unlike the others, however, he evaluated the 'phenomenon' optimistically. He had his own peculiar idea of the final goal of capital accumulation:

In contemplating any progressive movement . . . the mind is not satisfied with merely tracing the laws of the movement; it cannot but ask the further question, to what goal? . . . When the progress ceases, in what conditions are we to expect that it will leave mankind? (p. 452)

The answer is:

I cannot . . . regard the stationary state of capital and wealth with the unaffected aversion so generally manifested towards it by political economists of the old school. I am inclined to believe that it would be, on the whole, a very considerable improvement on our present condition. (p. 453)

The basic cause of the tendency towards the stationary state was to be found in the increase in wealth caused by capitalist accumulation. Such an increase would mean that the sacrifice of consumption connected to capital accumulation would become progressively less painful. Therefore, the remuneration for abstinence would gradually diminish. In the end, a society would be created in which there would exist so much wealth that there would no longer be any need for or stimulus towards further capital accumulation. Thus the vision of socialist society would have been realized: with zero interest, nobody would earn more than the product of their own labour. This would not lead to the abolition of private property, but only to the final realization of its 'natural' distribution. In fact, natural law would justify private property by the right of the individual to the possession of the product of his own labour. This law would only be realized when the capitalists' gains disappeared.

Mill did not criticize private property, nor the capitalist regime of the times in which he lived, but only its imperfections and abuses. He did not, however, consider these 'imperfections' unfounded: they were historically justified. Certainly, it was necessary to correct some of the excesses and injustices of the capitalist system which he observed. But, for the rest, he thought it was enough to leave history to take its course. There is certainly a good reason why Mill has been considered as one of the fathers of Fabian, or, rather, *cunctator*, socialism.

3.4. ENGLISH MONETARY THEORIES AND DEBATES IN THE AGE OF CLASSICAL ECONOMICS

3.4.1. The Restriction Act

In 1797, facing the consequences of a serious financial crisis, the British government passed a Restriction Act that suspended the convertibility of sterling and gave life to a monetary system which was in open conflict with the orthodox monetary doctrines. Immediately there was a sort of revolt on the part of the most important *laissez-faire* economists, and a theoretical controversy started which showed no signs of exhaustion until 1821, when convertibility was re-established. After this the heated discussions recommenced, but took a new direction.

The climax of the controversy occurred around 1810, the year in which the *Report of the Select Committee on the High Price of Gold Bullion* was presented to Parliament. The famous 'Bullion Committee' had been formed in February 1810 to investigate the reasons for the depreciation of sterling that had occurred in the first ten years of the century. And, both in the formulation of the problem and in the political solutions suggested, it revealed a clear stance in favour of one of the contending parties—the bullionist—which was the position assumed by most orthodox economic observers of the period. The two most important exponents of the bullionist approach were Henry Thornton (1760–1815) and David Ricardo.

The former, undoubtedly the most acute monetary theorist of the period, we will discuss in section 3.4.3. Here we will discuss Ricardo's ideas as expressed mainly in *The Price of Gold* (1809) and in *The High Price of Bullion, a Proof of the Depreciation of Bank Notes* (1810). The choice is justified by the fact that the rigour and simplicity of Ricardo's arguments were more successful than the reasonableness and realism of Thornton's, and went on to constitute the hard core of the theoretical principles of the bullionists.

The existence of a persistent gold premium, i.e. a positive difference between the market price and the mint price of gold, was the crux of the problem. Ricardo considered this to be clear evidence of currency depreciation, and the effect of excessive note issues by the Bank of England, an excess made possible by the inconvertibility regime. In order to demonstrate these arguments, he observed that the exchange rate of the pound with the most important European currencies had long remained below the parity determined by the mint price of gold. This phenomenon was also linked to the excess of issues by the Bank of England.

At the basis of these beliefs, however, there was no accurate analysis of the specific economic factors underlying the observed monetary and foreign exchange phenomena: economic growth, foreign trade trends, crises, the war, etc. Instead, there was a rigid and abstract application of the theory of the price–specie-flow mechanism formulated by Hume in the eighteenth century.

The exchange rate between two convertible currencies cannot diverge from the ratio between the gold parities except within the strict limits of the 'gold points', limits constituted by the costs for transporting and insuring the gold sent abroad. If the exchange rate of sterling with respect to the dollar fell below the lower gold point, it would be in the interest of English importers and speculators to convert sterling into gold and send the ingots to America. This would reduce, on the London market, the demand for dollar bills of exchange and the supply of sterling, and would arrest the depreciation of sterling. At the same time it would reduce the amount of sterling in circulation and decrease internal prices. If the initial depreciation of sterling was caused by an excess of issues and the consequent excess of imports, the price–specie-flow mechanism would adjust it automatically. This mechanism, however, could not work if sterling were inconvertible. In this case, a permanently undervalued exchange rate would be possible which could be below the lower gold point. And, as this phenomenon would occur together with the impossibility of reducing the amount of sterling in circulation by means of its conversion into gold, Ricardo and the bullionists took it as proof of the existence of an excess of issues.

They analysed the relationship existing between an excess of issues and a high gold price in a similar way. If the currency was convertible, a difference between the market price and the mint price of gold would not be possible because, as soon as such a divergence arose, the merchants would find it profitable to go to the mint to change sterling into ingots and sell the gold on the market. In this way the supply of gold on the market would change so as to eliminate any premium immediately. At the same time, any excess in the amount of money in circulation would be automatically eliminated owing to its conversion into gold. Therefore, argued Ricardo and the bullionists, the existence of a permanent gold premium in an unconvertibility regime is evident proof of an excess of issues.

The bullionists considered the Restriction Act as illicit government interference into the affairs of the private sector. In fact, the Bank of England was a private institution, even if it had been given some legal monopolistic privileges. It should have been managed according to the principles of sound administration of a private firm. The convertibility of the banknotes which it issued would, in any case, oblige it to behave correctly. With the Restriction Act the government had changed the rules of the game in its own favour and loosened the administrative rigour of the bank, thus causing a great deal of damage to the private citizens. In fact, inconvertibility permitted the financing of an excess of State spending and generated sharp increases in aggregate demand in monetary terms. In real terms, however, government expenditure was not an addition to private expenditure but a substitute for it. In fact, inflation would redistribute wealth from creditors to debtors and also, therefore, from the private to the State sector if its budget were in deficit. At the same time, it would create forced savings, reducing the quantity of consumer goods produced and inflating their prices.

The 'Bullion Committee', which, as already mentioned, was dominated by the bullionists, presented a report that was clearly in favour of the return to convertibility. However, ten years had to pass before the government decided to listen to its advice. The fact is that, in practice, things progressed in a rather different way from that envisaged by orthodox theory; and this is one of the most illuminating examples, in the history of economic thought, of how the political sensibility and the experience of merchants, bankers, and politicians can sometimes outweigh the doctrinal rigidity of theoretical economists.

From 1793 to 1815 England was involved in a series of wars with France which required the mobilization of all its political, military, and economic resources. Continual and heavy financing of the allies, besides maintaining the army, led to periodic draining of gold from the vaults of the Bank of England. Furthermore, the difficulties of the war and the Continental blockade made the export channels increasingly arduous and the supply of raw materials and wage goods more costly. Add to that an exceptional series of bad harvests, and it is easy to understand the real roots of the monetary problems debated by the economists.

In fact, it was the detailed attention to the real problems that characterized the theoretical approach of the anti-bullionists, from William Pitt (the younger), Chancellor of the Exchequer at the time of the Restriction Act, to Charles Bosanquet, Robert Torrens, and Robert Malthus. They maintained that the undervaluation of the exchange rate was due to exceptional exogenous factors, such as financing of the allies, overseas military expenditure, the fall in exports, the increase in the value of imported commodities, and the bad harvests. The maintenance of convertibility would probably permit the rebalancing of the balance of trade, but would produce more damaging effects than the illness it was supposed to cure; while the limit on the expansion of the money supply would force the government to limit the public debt, thus giving deflationary impulses to the economy. Moreover, further impulses of the same type would arise from difficulties with the balance of payments. In fact, the rebalancing of foreign accounts would require a reduction in the money supply and a decrease in incomes and internal prices. This would lead to drastic reductions in production and employment; phenomena which, in effect, often occurred in that period in the form of financial and productive crises. Could Great Britain, in the political conditions in which it found itself, allow itself the luxury of deflation?

In regard to the problem of inflation, the anti-bullionists adopted a clearly anti-monetarist viewpoint. The causal link in the equations of exchange, they argued, goes from prices to the money supply and not vice versa. The inflationary impulses come from the real economy, from bad harvests and imports, while the money supply adjusts passively to demand. They even maintained that it was impossible for the Bank of England, and the provincial issuing banks, to issue more bank notes than were necessary to sustain the needs of commerce, provided they were restricted to discounting only 'real bills'. This argument had already been put forward by Adam Smith. 'Real bills' are trade bills issued against transactions of real goods. When they are discounted, the banks issue money (banknotes or deposits) that has been stimulated by the flow of real transactions. This type of money creation does not permanently modify the stock of money, because, when the bill is due, the debt is paid back and the corresponding sum of money is taken out of circulation. Credit is only renewed to finance new transactions. According to this theory, the *flow* of new money is very elastic with respect to the flow of income, so that the stock of money in circulation is always adequate for the needs of transactions.

This is the substance of the famous 'real-bills doctrine'. It is not a completely wrong theory; but the anti-bullionists applied it mistakenly. They tried to use it to demonstrate the impossibility of an excess of the money supply in relation to the *real* needs of transactions, that is, the impossibility for the money supply to cause inflation. This argument was unsustainable in that period for three main reasons: first, because the English economy, with the wind of the Industrial Revolution in its sails, and right in the middle of a war, was passing through a period of almost permanent full employment; second, because speculation mainly operated on goods, so that it was difficult for the banks to distinguish 'real bills' from those generated by speculative operations; third, because the Bank of England was prohibited by the usury laws from lending at a rate above 5 per cent. In this context, it is easy to understand why the real-bills doctrines worked excellently in periods of stagnation but failed completely in periods of boom and speculation. When 'over-trading' occurred, the rate of profit, the market rate of interest, and the rate of returns on speculative operations were undoubtedly over the official 5 per cent rate, and therefore there was no efficient brake to the expansion of credit.

The anti-bullionists undervalued the effect that, with full employment, an extremely elastic credit supply could have in fuelling inflation, and this gave their critics an easy time. Interpreting the crises as forms of exaggerated reaction to the excesses of speculation, the critics pointed to the high elasticity of the money supply as the main cause of cyclical instability. As soon as the economic restrictions imposed by the war were loosened, therefore, convertibility was restored almost without opposition.

3.4.2. The Bank Charter Act

Immediately after the end of the Napoleonic era the English economy entered into a long phase of stagnation, which was characterized by a succession of brief periods of expansion, culminating in ephemeral explosions of speculative euphoria, and long periods of crisis, with sharp decreases in employment, production, and prices. The most serious crises occurred in 1816–22, 1825–31, 1836, 1839–42, and 1847–8.

There were two causes at the root of the first of these crises: the reduction of public spending connected to the end of the war and, perhaps more important, the monetary changes caused by the decision to return to convertibility. There had been a drastic cut in Bank of England issues during 1817–19, when preparations were being made for the return to gold; but the cuts were even more drastic in 1819–21, when the parliamentary decision was put into practice. Ricardo's critics immediately attributed the responsibility of the crisis to his monetary theory; and Ricardo had difficulty in defending himself. He argued that the blame should be attributed to the drastic and rapid way in which the Bank had undertaken the return to convertibility, forgetting that he himself, in the preceding years, had stated in Parliament that the restoration of the Gold Standard would have to be extremely rapid. In any case, the 1825 crisis and, with the passing of time, all the other crises that followed served to convince a growing number of economists of one fact: that the simple maintenance of convertibility was not sufficient to maintain monetary stability. The problem, therefore, was how to establish the rules of behaviour to which the Bank of England would have to conform.

The debate on this problem, which began immediately after the 1825 crisis and went on until the end of the 1840s, involved two schools of thought: the currency school, which linked itself to the bullionist tradition, and the banking school, which basically continued the anti-bullionist tradition, even though it accepted some of the arguments of the old bullionist views. The main exponents of the former were Thomas Joplin (?1790–1847), Samuel Jones Lloyd (Lord Overstone) (1796–1883), and Robert Torrens, who had passed over to the enemy after fighting in the ranks of the anti-bullionists in the second decade of the century. The main members of the banking school were Thomas Tooke (1774–1858), John Fullarton (?1780–1849) James William Gilbart (1794–1863), and, with a certain ambiguity, John Stuart Mill. Here we can mention only a few of the important works on monetary theory which came out in this period. For the currency school: *An Analysis and History of the Currency Question* (1832) by Joplin and *Tracts and Other Publications on Metallic and Paper Currency* by Overstone (collected together and edited by McCulloch in 1857). For the banking school: *An Inquiry into the Currency Principle* (1844) by Tooke and *On the Regulation of Currencies* (1844) by Fullarton.

The governors of the Bank of England, who previously had inclined towards the anti-bullionist position, from the 1820s onwards began to reorientate towards the currency school. In this way, their policy gradually conformed to the precepts of this school, culminating in the adoption of the famous Palmer's Rule (named after John Horsley Palmer, then Governor of the Bank of England). The policy of the Bank of England was to cover a third of its liabilities with the gold reserves and the rest with bills. But this was only in 'full-money' conditions, i.e. when it was believed that the quantity of money in circulation was adequate for the needs of transactions. The existence of this situation was verified by observing the exchange rate which, in presence of 'full money', should be stable. When the exchange rate began to worsen, the Bank abandoned the rule of the one-third gold reserve ratio, and let its liabilities vary with the gold reserves themselves. In this way, a drain on gold would cause, in any case, a shrinkage in the amount of money in circulation, but the deflationary impulse would be contained. Even though this kind of behaviour had been inspired by the principles of the currency school, the followers of that school were still not satisfied, and for two main reasons.

The first problem was that the Bank of England reserved to itself the right to modify the composition of its own liabilities, when it reduced their size, by letting the burden of the contraction fall more heavily on deposits than on banknotes. As the currency-school thinkers had a restricted definition of money, limiting it to currency, i.e. coinage and banknotes issued by the Bank of England and the provincial banks, they argued that Palmer's Rule did not allow perfect 'metallic fluctuation'. The principle of 'metallic fluctuation', established at that time by the currency school, claimed that the amount of money in circulation had to oscillate as if it were entirely made up of gold. Therefore, the quantity of banknotes would have to vary in the same measure as the gold reserves. Now, it was this rule that could be infringed if the Bank of England reserved the right to modify the composition of its liabilities when it reduced them, offloading part of the shrinkage on deposits.

The second problem was that Palmer's Rule itself, besides the flexibility with which it was applied, made it difficult to assign to the management of the Bank that function of automatic dampening of economic fluctuations which the currency school had recommended. Many economists of this school, headed by Overstone, had adopted a cyclic theory in which monetary permissiveness played an essential role. In expansion phases, they maintained, the Bank of England quickly adjusted the supply to the demand of money, so fuelling inflation, speculation, and euphoria. Then, when the crisis and panic arrived, the Bank, in order to protect its own reserves, was forced to take drastic measures, thus deepening the crisis.

The currency-school theorists proposed two fundamental measures to overcome these difficulties. The first, in part inspired by a proposal put forward by Ricardo in *Plan for the Establishment of a National Bank* (written in 1823 and published posthumously in 1824) consisted of the division of the Bank of England into two departments: a banking department, with the credit function, and an issue department, with the sole task of issuing banknotes. In this way, it was thought that the oscillations in gold reserves could not be offloaded on deposits, and would be completely resolved in variations in the issues of banknotes. This would have ensured perfect 'metallic fluctuation'. The second measure concerned the abolition of the fixed gold reserve ratio. The bank would have to use a cover in bills only for a fixed amount. For the rest, its issues of banknotes had to be covered by gold. In this way the reserve ratio would have changed automatically and anti-cyclically, increasing during years of prosperity, when the reserves increased, and decreasing when they decreased in the phases of crisis.

The 1844 Bank Charter Act (also known as the 'Peel Act', after the name of the Chancellor of the Exchequer who proclaimed it), fully adopting the currency-school view, divided the Bank of England into two departments, and established that the cover in bills of the liabilities of the issue department had to be £14 million.

Let us now consider the theories of the banking school. The exponents of this school accepted some of the currency school's arguments, for example, the dogma of the superiority of the Gold Standard to an inconvertible paper money regime. However, they disagreed on nearly every other question of any theoretical importance, especially in regard to the definition of money, which they formulated in much less restrictive and more modern terms than their opponents, including in the stock of money, besides currency, deposits and bills of exchange. The banking school maintained that both the amounts of deposits and bills change with transactions; that the money supply is endogenous, and that the Bank of England is incapable of controlling it efficiently. Not only this, but they argued that even the circulation of banknotes is outside the control of the Bank. They supported this view by using the old 'real-bills' doctrine, now renamed the 'doctrine of reflux'.

At this time the banking school had two new weapons with which to defend its own arguments: convertibility had been re-established and, from 1833, the 5 per cent limit for the discount rate had been abolished. Thus, at least in principle, an excess in the demand for credit for speculative purposes could be hindered by an increase in the discount rate. On the other hand, if an excess of issues had to be measured by the gold premium, as Ricardo and his followers had argued, then no excess of issues could exist in a convertibility regime. In fact, as soon as the paper money showed signs of being undervalued with respect to gold, it would have flowed back to the Bank to be converted. This would have arrested its depreciation and eliminated the excess of liquidity. The problem with this type of argument is that Ricardo's principle, that the depreciation of money is measured with precision by the gold premium, is generally not valid; and even if it is in a fiat money regime, it certainly is not in a regime of convertibility. In such a regime, money can become devalued with respect to all goods with the exception of gold, which tends to maintain its market price equal to the mint price.

But this is a secondary problem. The arguments of the banking school contained elements of truth even if the doctrine of the impossibilty of the inflationary effects of an excess money supply was not valid. In fact, with an extensive definition of money, what really matters is the supply of the total monetary mass. Now the theorists of the banking school were certainly right in maintaining that the overall money supply was very elastic and out of the control of the Bank. In fact, this was the main reason why the monetary strait-jacket constituted by the Bank Charter Act did not manage to obstruct to any significant degree the movements of the English economy. The adjustments of the money supply to the needs of capital accumulation occurred by variations in deposits and credit, despite the strictness of the rules the department of issues had to follow. Besides, there was always the possibility of suspending the Act in periods of serious crisis, as actually happened in 1847, 1857, and partially in 1866.

Finally, we should point out that, over time, the facts increasingly demonstrated the prevalently ideological nature of the Gold Standard doctrine, at least if it is understood as a theory of an *automatic* and *neutral* equilibrating mechanism of foreign trade. During the 70 years after the passing of the Bank Act, the English economy was able to expand without great problems of external equilibrium, despite a permanent trade deficit; so that there were very few difficulties in the defence of the gold reserves of the Bank of England. But the external equilibrium was maintained thanks to the adoption of a shrewd policy in regard to the discount rate, a policy that was neither automatic nor neutral, and that tended to compel the less developed countries, and especially the producers of raw materials, to pay for the adjustments when necessary.

The economists of the banking school, well aware of the industrial and financial power of the English economy, argued that the serious problems for the gold reserves originated above all from exogenous and temporary commercial difficulties. These causes of the gold drain were considered 'terminable', that is, capable of stopping by themselves. All that was asked from the Bank of England, therefore, was to maintain a large gold reserve, around £15–18 million, so as to tackle the causes of temporary drains.

Another important debate concerned the right of provincial banks to issue a paper money partially covered by the currency of the Bank of England. In the bullionist debate, the anti-bullionists had maintained that the provincial banks represented a factor in the variation of the money supply which was outside the control of the Bank of England. The bullionists, on the other hand, in their attempt to blame the governors of the Bank for all English monetary ills, had argued that the provincial banks were not autonomous factors in the variations in the money supply. In the debate about the Bank Charter Act, many members of the currency school accepted the arguments of their opponents on this point. It had become clear that the credit system based on the principle of fractional reserves generated significant multiplication effects of the central monetary impulses. Torrens, in particular, outlined the mechanism of credit multiplication quite precisely. He maintained in any case, as did a few other members of the currency school, that the mechanism only created phenomena of amplification of the monetary impulses, but did not hinder the ability of the Bank to control the overall expansion of liquidity. Most of the members of the currency school did not follow Torrens on this point; but the main reason for the inability of the Bank of England to control the overall money supply, namely, the variability of the bank reserve ratios, was not yet well understood. In any case, the prevalent opinion began to favour greater central control of the operations of the local banks and a gradual abolition of their rights of issue. This opinion was put into practice with the Bank Charter Act.

3.4.3. Henry Thornton

The economists mentioned in the preceding two sections are only a few out of the dozens and dozens who in Great Britain were concerned with monetary problems in this period. Moreover, the limitations we imposed on ourselves have prevented us from doing justice to the peculiarities of the individual contributions of the few we have mentioned. However, we must say something more precise about two economists who made the most important and original contributions: Henry Thornton and John Stuart Mill. Their monetary theories are worth discussing, if for no other reason than that they created the roots of that great English monetary-theory tradition which, passing through Marshall and his school, was to culminate in the Keynesian revolution.

Thornton was not an academic but a successful banker, who studied monetary theory for its direct implications for practical policy. He was also an influential Member of Parliament, as well as a fervent evangelist; and made an important contribution, along with Horner and Huskisson, to the drafting of the 1810 Bullion Report. Immediately after the 1797 Restriction Act he wrote a book which was full of profound insights and important theoretical innovations; a book that has been judged the greatest work on monetary theory of the nineteenth century: *An Enquiry into the Nature and Effects of the Paper Credit of Great Britain* (1802). In the debates at the beginning of the century, Thornton supported the bullionist position, rather moderately at first, but then increasingly decisively. His final points of view were expressed in a book that contains two important parliamentary speeches: *Substance of Two Speeches in the Debate in the House of Commons on the Report of the Bullion Committee* (1811).

Initially, Thornton was not against the Restriction Act, which he justified by the necessity of facing the problem of the drain of gold caused by panic and the war. He believed, however, that it should be an exceptional and temporary measure: the normal monetary system should be the Gold Standard. He was also one of the most rigorous theorists of the functioning of this system. He developed Hume's arguments on the price–specie-flow mechanism and on that basis developed the theory of the relationship existing between the depreciation of the exchange rate, the gold premium, and the excess of issues in a fiat money regime, a theory that was later to be upheld by Ricardo and his followers. We have discussed this in the previous section, and will not return to it here. We will just mention a development that Thornton brought to Hume's theory: the argument that the internal deflation capable of correcting a balance-of-payments deficit would have operated, not only on price levels, but also on the level of income and, thus, directly on the level of demand for imports of consumer goods.

Thornton was not a committed deflationist like Ricardo. He believed, with the anti-bullionists, that a depreciation of the exchange rate and the emergence of a gold premium were not always caused by an excess of issues. In special cases they could originate from exogenous and temporary factors, such as a bad harvest, an explosion of panic, or a large transfer of gold to the allies. In these cases, he argued, a contraction in the issues could aggravate the problems rather than solve them. Particularly important are his ideas on the causes of internal drain, ideas in which some elements of the liquidity preference theory are foreshadowed. Individuals hold money, not only as a means of exchange, but also as a reserve of value, so that the quantity desired depends on the state of confidence.

A high state of confidence contributes to make men provide less amply against contingencies. At such a time, they trust, that if the demand upon them for a payment, which is now doubtful and contingent, should actually be made, they shall be able to provide for it at the moment . . . When, on the contrary, a season of distrust arises prudence suggests that the loss of interest arising from a detention of notes for a few additional days should not be regarded. It is well known that guineas are hoarded in times of alarm, on this principle . . . In difficult times, however, the disposition to hoard, or rather to be largely provided with Bank of England notes, will, perhaps, prevail in no inconsiderable degree. (p. 46)

This phenomenon explains the variations in the velocity of circulation of the different monetary means. Thornton used a wide definition of money, including in it various means of exchange with different velocities of circulation, and also bills of exchange. He maintained that, in periods of crisis, not only the gold reserves of the Bank shrink but also the overall quantity of money and its velocity of circulation diminish. Therefore, the decision to reduce bank issues in order to check the drain would be a serious political error. It is important to note the remarkable implications of this argument for the theory of monetary policy. The liquidity preference theory, together with an understanding of the cyclical character of economic movements, led Thornton to attribute to the Bank of England, considered as an institution entrusted with public goals, a basic function as a lender of last resort.

Thornton was a bullionist above all in regard to the long-run effects of the movements of the monetary variables, and was inclined to believe—as we would say today—in the inefficacy of monetary policy in the long run. However, he did notice the possible *real* short-run effects of the Bank's decisions. He argued that a credit expansion, by raising prices and profits, given the stickiness of wages, could stimulate production and increase the level of employment. He also argued that the decreases in real wages caused by inflation generate forced saving ('defalcation of revenue') and induce changes in the productive structure in favour of the accumulation of stocks of goods and means of production. There is no incompatibility, in his view, between the occurrence of the real effects of the credit expansion and the phenomenon of forced saving, as the growth in demand does not act only on output or only on prices, but affects both kinds of variable. Thornton thought that the Bank of England should follow a discretionary monetary policy, with the double aim of dampening the cyclical nature of economic growth, by intervening above all in periods of crisis, and of ensuring the stability of the exchange rate. The main intervention instrument should be the interest rate.

Thornton made an important theoretical contribution in regard to the theory of interest. He observed that the usury laws forced the Bank of England to expand credit without limit when the rate of profit was above the legal 5 per cent discount rate. Anticipating Wicksell in this, he brought to light the cumulative character of the inflationary effects of this process. He also pointed out, in *Substance of Two Speeches*, the importance of the effects of inflation on the reduction of the real value of the rate of interest. For example, he argued that, with a monetary interest rate fixed at 5 per cent, a 3 per cent inflation would reduce the real interest rate to 2 per cent. In countries where there were no usury laws, however, this phenomenon would have led to an increase in the nominal rate. The political implications of this reasoning are simple: only in the absence of usury laws could the Bank of England have an effective monetary-policy instrument in the interest rate.

3.4.4. Mill on money

Mill was strongly influenced by Thornton, and explicitly recognized his authority in the theory of credit. Mill entered the field of monetary theory in 1824, supporting the bullionist positions by arguing that the price increases in the period of the French wars had been caused by the excess of issues and not by the extraordinary expenditure of the government. As early as 1826, however, in a comment on the 1825 crisis in an article published in the *Parliamentary Review*, 'Paper Currency and Commercial Distress', he distanced himself from Ricardian monetarism, advancing the argument that no excess of issues could exist in a convertibility regime. He also sketched out the idea, subsequently developed in the *Principles*, that speculation was the main cause of inflation, of credit creation, and, as a consequence, of the increase in the issue of banknotes.

Finally, in 1844, at the height of the Bank Charter debate, he intervened to support Tooke's and Fullarton's arguments with an article published in the *Westminster Review*, 'The Currency Question'. In this article he denied that the Bank Act had stabilizing effects on the real economy and on the level of prices, and presented again his 1826 arguments on the endogenous nature of the money supply and on the role played by speculation in destabilizing the system—arguments that he reinforced with the observation that only a small part of a society's 'purchasing power' was made up of currency, a larger part being represented by deposits and credit. The Bank Act would not be effective because it was unable to attack speculation, unable to avoid sharp oscillations in the rate of interest, and therefore incapable of dampening the cycles of 'excitement and depression'.

It was in the *Principles*, however, that Mill outlined his monetary theory in its most complete form, especially in the 1857 edition, in which he made significant modifications to the monetary sections. It seems that Mill accepted the quantity theory of money, which he formulated in the following way: 'the amount of goods and of transactions being the same, the value of money is inversely related to its quantity multiplied by what is called the rapidity of circulation' (p. 300). But immediately afterwards he added: 'the quantity of money in circulation is equal to the money value of all goods sold, divided by the number which expresses the rapidity of circulation'. This second formulation is remarkable precisely for its ambiguity. If interpreted as an expression of the quantity theory, it seems to prefigure the 'Cambridge equation' (see section 7.1.2), especially if importance is given to the argument (only hinted at by Mill) according to which people may decide to hold money in view of future needs. If instead, as seems reasonable, it is interpreted from the standpoint of the banking school, it alludes to the existence of a causal link between the value of transactions and the quantity of money. This is perhaps the interpretation towards which Mill himself inclined when he noted that 'many other qualifications with which the proposition must be received, that the value of the circulating medium . . . is in the inverse ratio of the quantity; qualifications which, under a complex system of credit like that existing in England, render the proposition an extremely incorrect expression of the fact' (p. 303).

Mill argued that the rate of interest depends on the supply and demand of loanable funds. The demand is made up by the expenditure for investments, plus the unproductive expenditure of landowners and government; the supply by the savings plus the bank deposits and banknotes (here Mill slightly confuses the concepts of 'stock' and 'flow'). Investment decisions are influenced by the difference between the rate of profits and the rate of interest. The latter, varying in relation to the supply and demand of loanable funds, reaches its normal equilibrium value when it becomes equal to the remuneration of the abstinence and to the expected rate of return on capital.

In *Some Unsettled Questions*, Mill had adopted the theory of forced saving. In the first edition of the *Principles* he did not mention it. In the 1865 edition, however, he admitted that inflation could encourage the creation of capital by allowing a transfer of investment from the consumer-goods sector (luxury goods) to the capital-goods sector. Besides this, and again in the *Principles*, he showed the effects of inflation on the redistribution of wealth from creditors to debtors, identifying the latter mainly in the 'productive class'.

Mill adopted from the banking school, among other things, the 'law of reflux', and tried to reinforce its usual justifications with the observation that an excess of liquidity could also be off-loaded abroad by means of a balance-of-payments deficit. He thought that such a deficit would in any case always tend to readjust automatically. In order to explain this, Mill referred to the

Humean theory of the price–specie-flow mechanism, which he enriched by developing an idea already suggested by Thornton and Overstone: that most of the adjustment of an external disequilibrium would occur by means of variations in the rate of interest. In this view, an inflow of gold caused by a trade surplus would lower the rate of interest and encourage the export of capital, and vice versa for an outflow of gold. An obvious political corollary of this theory was that the Bank of England could discretionally use interest rate manœuvres to anticipate and reinforce the automatic adjustments. This conception, which was to be later perfected, in the *Theory of Foreign Exchange* (1861), by George Joachim Goschen (1831–1907), Governor of the Bank of England in 1858, would have become one of the theoretical pillars of interest-rate policies in the Gold Standard era.

Finally, Mill had an interesting theory of the business cycle that assigned great importance to the effects of speculation and expectations. The prospects of profit generated by inflationary expectations induce an increase in the demand for credit and goods. This fuels inflation and fulfils the expectations, inducing a further speculative impulse and triggering a cumulative process of inflation and speculation. The cycle will turn down when the speculators judge that inflation has gone too far and the moment to sell has been reached. As soon as prices start to fall, panic may occur, causing the crisis to deepen. It is at this point that the central bank should intervene to slow down the contraction with an expansion of credit and a reduction in the interest rate. But the rules established by the Bank Act prevented the Bank from putting such a policy into practice, and forced it, in times of crisis, to reduce the money supply so as to defend its reserves from internal drain. Thus, that law hampered the Bank from doing what it should do in order to stabilize the economy. This gives us an idea of the reasons why Mill was against the Bank Act.

Bibliography

On the English classical economists: S. G. Checkland, 'The Propagation of Ricardian Economics in England', *Economica*, 16 (1949); A. W. Coats (ed.), *The Classical Economists and Economic Policy* (London, 1971); M. Dobb, *Theories of Value and Distribution since Adam Smith* (Cambridge, 1973); E. J. Hobsbawn, *The Age of Capital, 1848–1875* (London, 1975); D. P. O'Brien, *The Classical Economists* (Oxford, 1975); L. Robbins, *The Theory of Economic Policy in English Political Economy* (London, 1953); T. Sowell, *Classical Economics Reconsidered* (Princeton, NJ 1974); A. C. Whitaker, *History and Criticism of the Labour Theory of Value in English Political Economy* (New York, 1904).

On Ricardo: M. Blaug, *Ricardian Economics* (New Haven, Conn., 1958); C. Casarosa, 'A New Formulation of the Ricardian System', *Oxford Economic Papers*, 30

(1978); P. Garegnani, *Il capitale nelle teorie della distribuzione*, pt. i (Milan, 1960); S. Hollander, *The Economics of David Ricardo* (Toronto, 1979); C. Napoleoni, *Smith, Ricardo, Marx* (Oxford, 1975); L. L. Pasinetti, 'A Mathematical Formulation of the Ricardian System', *Review of Economic Studies*, 36 (1960); D. Ricardo, *Works and Correspondence*, ed. with introd. P. Sraffa (11 vols., Cambridge, 1951–73).

On Malthus: J. Bonar, *Malthus and His Work* (New York, 1966); R. L. Meek, 'Physiocracy and the Early Theories of Underconsumption', in *The Economics of Physiocracy* (London, 1962); M. Paglin, *Malthus and Lauderdale: The Anti-Ricardian Tradition* (New York, 1961); L. Robbins, 'Malthus as an Economist', *Canadian Journal of Economics*, 30 (1967); T. Sowell, 'Malthus and the Utilitarians', *Canadian Journal of Economics and Political Science*, 25 (1962).

On Mill: A. Bain, *J. S. Mill: A Criticism with Personal Recollections* (London, 1882); J. Hamburger, *Intellectuals in Politics: John Stuart Mill and the Philosophic Radicals* (London, 1965); A. L. Harris, 'John Stuart Mill on Monopoly and Socialism: A Note', *Journal of Political Economy*, 67 (1959); D. L. Losman, 'J. S. Mill and Alternative Economic Systems', *American Journal of Economics and Sociology*, (1971); J. S. Mill, *Principles of Political Economy* (London, 1892); M. J. Packe, *The Life of John Stuart Mill* (London, 1954); P. Schwartz, *The New Political Economy of J. S. Mill* (London, 1972); J. Viner, 'Bentham and J. S. Mill: The Utilitarian Background', *American Economic Review*, 39 (1949).

On the precursors of the marginalist revolution: R. B. Ekelund, 'Jules Dupuit and the Early Theory of Marginal Cost Pricing', *Journal of Political Economy*, 76 (1968); I. Fisher, 'Cournot and Mathematical Economics', *Quarterly Journal of Economics*, 104 (1989); B. Gordon, 'Criticisms of Ricardian Views on Value and Distribution in the British Periodicals, 1820–1850', *History of Political Economy*, 1 (1969); A. H. Leigh, 'Von Thünen's Theory of Distribution and the Advent of Marginal Analysis', *Journal of Political Economy*, 54 (1946); W. F. Lloyd, *A Lecture on the Notion of Value* (London, 1834); R. L. Meek, 'The Decline of Ricardian Economics in England', *Economica*, 17 (1950); E. Schneider, 'Johann Heinrich von Thünen', *Econometrica*, 2 (1934); P. Scrope, *Principles of Political Economy* (London, 1833); N. Senior, *An Outline of the Science of Political Economy* (London, 1836).

On Romanticism, List, and the German Historical School: F. Engel-Janosi, *The Growth of German Historicism* (Baltimore, 1944); M. E. Hirst, *Life of Friederich List and Selections from his Writings* (London, 1909); G. G. Iggers, *The German Conception of History: The National Historical Thought from Herder to the Present* (Middletown, Conn. 1968); F. K. Mann, 'The Romantic Reaction', *Zeitschrift für Nationaloekonomie*, 17 (1958); G. Vandewalle, 'Romanticism and Neoromanticism in Political Economy', *History of Political Economy*, 18 (1986); M. Weber, *Roscher und Knies und die logischen Probleme der historischen Nationaloekonomie* (Tubingen, 1922).

On the monetary debates: A. Arnon, *Thomas Tooke: Pioneer of Monetary Theory* (Aldershot, 1881); T. S. Ashton and R. S. Sayers (eds.), *Papers in English Monetary History* (Oxford, 1953); M. Caminati, 'The Theory of Interest in the Classical Economists', *Metroeconomica*, 33 (1981); B. A. Corry, *Money, Saving and Investment in British Economics 1800–1850* (London, 1962); M. R. Daugherty, 'The Currency-Banking Controversy', *Southern Economic Journal*, 33 (1942–3); F. W. Fetter, *The Development of British Monetary Orthodoxy* (Cambridge, Mass., 1965); M. C. Marcuzzo and A. Roselli, *Ricardo and the Gold Standard* (London, 1991); J. S. Mill,

Principles of Political Economy (London, 1892); L. M. Mints, *A History of Banking Theory* (Chicago, 1945); D. P. O'Brien, *The Classical Economists* (Oxford, 1975); M. Perlman, 'The Bullionist Controversy Revisited', *Journal of Political Economy*, 84 (1986); C. Rotelli, *Le origini della controversia monetaria (1797–1844)* (Bologna, 1982); W. Santiago-Valiente, 'Historical Background of the Classical Monetary Theory', *History of Political Economy*, 20 (1988); H. Thornton, *An Enquiry into the Nature and Effects of the Paper Credit of Great Britain* (London, 1802); J. Viner, 'English Currency Controversies', in *Studies in the Theory of International Trade* (New York, 1937).

4

Socialist Economic Thought and Marx

4.1. FROM UTOPIA TO SOCIALISM

4.1.1. The birth of the workers' movement

This chapter covers the same historical period as the last one and, in the same way, can be divided into two parts: the first runs from the end of the Napoleonic Wars to the 1848 revolution; the second covers the subsequent 20 years. Unlike the preceding chapter, where we dealt with capitalist growth and its economic theories, here our attention is focused on the class conflict between the workers and capitalists and the theories that emerged from this.

The modern workers' movement began with the great Luddite social uprisings of 1808–20, involving France and, especially, England, where the revolt was so strong, organized, and overpowering that the government, to put it down, had to use an army of 12,000 men.

The movement was subdued with a great deal of bloodshed in both countries, but burst out again, with a higher level of organization and political awareness in the 1820s and 1830s. In England it was organized at first by the Owenist trade unions and later by the Chartist movement, under whose banner it conducted bitter fights for objectives such as the new Poor Laws, the Reform Bill, and the reduction of the working day for women and children. In France it produced various armed insurrections at the beginning of the 1830s, some of which gave the final blow to the reign of Charles X, contributing to the ascent to the throne of Louis-Philippe, 'the bourgeois king'.

The next 10 years saw serious outbreaks of conflict in both countries. In England the climax was reached in 1842–3, while in France the struggle began again, after 10 years of respite, in 1844–6, finally exploding in the 1848 revolution. The following 20 years, initiated by the bloody defeat the workers' movement suffered in France, were, in contrast to the preceding period, years of almost complete social peace in both countries, and only in 1867–9 was there a sharp and massive resumption of the workers' struggle.

The division of this period into two sub-periods, one of acute conflict (1808–48) and the other of social peace (1848–68), corresponds more or less to that made in the previous chapter between the years of Restoration and the 'Age of Capital'. This division into two phases has been useful to frame the evolution of economic ideas. In fact, in the first phase we observed a situation of theoretical turbulence, with a succession of innovations, an overlapping of debates, and an incessant struggle among competing theories, whereas in the second period there were attempts at theoretical systemization and general-ization, and at the construction of a scientific orthodoxy. In this chapter we will outline a similar phenomenon in the evolution of socialist thought: the years of sharp conflict gave birth to a great number of new and more or less alternative socialist theories, while the period of social respite produced only the great synthesis by Marx.

4.1.2. The two faces of Utopia

The modern organized workers' movement and, with it, the basis of its view of the world were formed between 1808 and 1840. This book is not a history of political thought, and we have not the space to deal with the birth of socialist thought in general. However, some of the essential points must be dealt with in a synthetic way in a history of economic thought.

First, it is important to highlight the two extremes between which all the attempts to construct a socialist theoretical system have oscillated. As we will see in the next section, these two extremes were embodied, at the beginning of the nineteenth century, by the systems of Saint-Simon and Fourier. But it is possible to go back a few centuries, at least to the final years of the Renaissance, to trace, in humanist utopian thought, the first philosophical manifestations of that duality in social design.

On the one hand is the *Utopia-of-order* model formulated by More and other Catholic philosophers such as Campanella and Ludovico Agostini. This model inspired the first great experiment in the construction of a real 'socialist' society, the Jesuit Republic in Paraguay, with over 144,000 inhabitants at its peak, and its almost incredible duration of nearly a century, from the seven-teenth to eighteenth centuries. In this case, the Catholic view of society as a 'mystic body' prevailed. Individuals exist and also deserve to be happy, but only as parts of a metaphysical entity which, one could say, gives them life as social beings. Individual liberty is not a value in Utopia: children obey their parents, women their husbands, and everbody the patriarchs. The slaves obey the free people and the colonies the metropolis. The State dominates all. The slaves do not constitute a moral problem, as they are people who prefer slavery in Utopia to liberty outside. Neither is imperialism a problem; on the contrary, whoever is outside the ideal order deserves subjection. It is surprising that such a system could have been thought of as an ideal society; but in effect, it was just that: the ideal form of domination by society over the individual, with perfectly planned production, completely centralized decisions, and meticu-lously organized working activity, with even architecture and physical geo-graphy being forced into the strict, elegant rigour of social geometry, not to mention State intervention in the sexual sphere. The principle controlling the ownership of the means of production in the Jesuit Republic was expressed by Voltaire's lapidary sentence: people possess nothing, the Jesuits every-thing.

The rival to this design of an ideal society arose at almost the same time, around the middle of the sixteenth century, and is the *Utopia-of-freedom* model. The literary versions that exist are almost all less scholarly and refined than More's, given their folk origin, but they are all easily recognizable, in the various Lands of Cockaigne, where there is no need to work to eat; or in Doni's 'wise and mad world', where the family and money are abolished and where there is no central government or division between intellectual and manual work; or the Rabelaisian Abbey of Thélème, where there is only one rule—do what you want; and, finally, in the first attempt, which obviously collapsed immediately, by the Diggers of Everard and Winstanley to create such a Utopia during the Glorious Revolution. This is a dream of individual liberation whose philosophical basis, if it has one at all, is clearly anti-Catholic and hedonistic. Work tends to disappear, and the State with it. Its rule of political 'organization' was formulated by de Sade during the French Revolution, and is simple: 'Frenchmen, one more effort . . .!'

4.1.3. Saint-Simon and Fourier

Between one revolution and another, these two alternative models of social organization passed through European culture, without a break in continuity, from the Renaissance to the Enlightenment. In the first half of the nineteenth century they met the organized workers' movement, ceased to be dreams, and turned into projects.

Claude-Henry de Rouvroy de Saint-Simon (1760–1825) theorized better than any other socialist thinker of the period the principle of a cohesive organization of society. Overcoming 'dialectically' Enlightenment thought, and, above all, its reactionary antithesis as produced by De Maistre and De Bonald at the beginning of the century, Saint-Simon's synthesis tried to link an anti-individualistic view of society with the cult of technological and scientific progress, as if he wished to project into the future, rather than the past, the ideal of a cohesive and functional social organization. Far from wishing to realize the democratic dream of the eighteenth century and the Revolution, Saint-Simon constructed a model of a strongly hierarchical and strictly meritocratic society.

Saint-Simon despised the waste, parasitism, and anarchy of capitalism—in other words, its imperfections. His 'socialism' aspired towards a society of producers, i.e. workers, technicians, scientists, and entrepreneurs—the 'industrialists', as he called them. Saint-Simon maintained that the capitalists should be the managing élite, not because of the power derived from their wealth, but rather because of their function as innovators and organizers of the production process. The workers would obtain a gradual improvement in their living conditions, not at the expense of machines and capital, but rather by means of them.

Saint-Simon's main work, *Du système industriel*, was written in collaboration with his secretary, Auguste Comte, and was published between 1820 and 1822. In it he preached for the productive efficiency of the factory to be extended to the whole society, which would become an immense factory, with central planning of production and a distribution system based on the principle that remuneration be linked strictly to productivity.

Saint-Simon's industrial system would have finally liberated man, but from what? It is not difficult to understand that a republic such as this, in which individual liberty was so restricted in favour of the collective prerogatives, would have needed a strong religion. On the other hand, it presupposed a strong metaphysical and ethical base. It was not by chance that Saint-Simon aspired to give mankind a new catechism, the *Catéchisme des industriels*, as he entitled a book written in 1823–4, or even to found a new religion, a *Nouveau christianisme*, as he claimed in his last work in 1825. Nor was it by chance that some of his followers were reduced, in the end, to founding religious sects. Those who were more realistic dedicated themselves instead to finance or engineering, in an attempt to improve, if not mankind, at least capitalism.

At the opposite extreme to Saint-Simon is Charles Fourier (1772–1837), whose principal works are *Théorie des quatres mouvements* (1808), *Traité de l'association doméstique–agricole* (1822), *Le Nouveau monde industriel et sociétaire* (1829), and *La Fausse industrie* (1835–6). Also Fourier's thought presupposes a sort of dialectical negation of the Enlightenment, but now the connecting link is Rousseau, with his philosophy of the noble savage and his attempt to bring natural-law philosophy to its extreme logical conclusions.

It is important to point out that not only Fourier, but also the great majority of nineteenth-century socialist thinkers, accepted Rousseau's criticism of that way of reasoning typical of natural-law philosophies, aiming at establishing the right by means of the fact, a way of thinking which had enabled Locke to justify, among other things, private property and its unequal distribution.

Rousseau had turned seventeenth-century natural-law philosophy to his own philosophical ends, up to the point of denying not only the naturalness of the State and private property, but also that of the family. He believed that social inequality had been created by a drastic break from the original state of nature, a break which had created history, institutions, and civilization. Rousseau's 'state of nature' was an ideological construction aiming at showing, not the natural essence of the social being or the existing social order, but the 'should be' dimension that is inherent in it as potentiality and negation.

The theory of the noble savage in a rather naïve version, to tell the truth, is also present in Fourier's thought; in fact, it is one of his basic philosophical presuppositions. Fourier considered men to be naturally good. If they have 'perversions', it is only because society is unnatural. If individuals were allowed freely to realize their own natural wishes, they would spontaneously organize themselves in a harmonious way. *Le Nouveau monde amoureux* (written by Fourier but not published until 1967) saw the passions of individuals combine with those of others and thus ceasing to be perversions. The family, the receptacle of hypocrisy and repression, would be abolished, and with it commerce, the cancer of the economy and the cause of waste and parasitism. Consumption would be spontaneously reduced to essentials, industry reorganized, work co-ordinated in small communities and distributed according to individual abilities and wishes. Alienation would disappear, together with economic exploitation and political oppression.

It is not difficult to understand why Marx and Engels, in the *Manifesto of the Communist Party* (1848) put Fourier, as well as Saint-Simon (and this is a little more difficult to understand), in the group of utopian socialists. Marx and Engels, like almost all the other nineteenth-century socialists, avoided the two extremes, even if, like all the others, they tried to construct their own socialist system by combining Saint-Simon and Fourier.

In order to understand the sense of the doctrinal polarity embodied by Saint-Simon and Fourier and the reason for its pervasiveness within socialist thought, it is necessary to look at the real ambivalence of the problem from which socialist thought originates. The liberation of labour implies the abolition of a social relationship: that between capital and labour. Such a project of liberation has two faces. On the one hand, it can be considered as a plan for the abolition of profit and capital, on the other as a project for the abolition of wages and labour. In the first case the accent is placed on capitalist exploitation, in the second on the alienation of labour. In the first case, there is an aspiration towards an ideal society capable of ensuring distributive justice, in the second, toward a new society founded on individual liberty. In the first case, liberty is not a value; on the contrary, the principle of authority, once freed from the feudal residues that tie it arbitrarily to physical persons (the owners of capital) even in the bourgeois society, is exalted and purified when related to a technocratic organizational principle and to a meritocratic distributive criterion. In the second case it is economic equality, intended as a law of correspondence between remunerations and productive services, that becomes a disvalue, being unable to take into account the 'natural' inequality of needs and individual aspirations on which free social interaction is based.

Confused and hesitant in the face of these two opposing visions, apparently so irreconcilable and incompatible with historical possibilities, socialism in the first half of the nineteenth century seemed destined to produce only dream-worlds, vain assaults on the sky (in Europe) and vain agricultural communities (in America). It was the genius of Marx that broke the spell and founded modern socialism, in fact producing, not one, but two strokes of genius. The first consisted of interpreting the two antithetical principles of social reorganization as laws of different *historical phases*. The 'socialist' society, in which each person would be remunerated according to his or her own ability, would be only the first phase of an evolution towards a superior social organization: the 'communist' society, in which each person would only receive according to his needs. The other stroke of genius consisted of not saying a great deal more about this. Marx avoided extravagant constructions, leaving history, i.e. mankind itself, the task of realizing human ideals. It was in this way that the socialist dream, according to Engels, became 'scientific'.

4.2. SOCIALIST ECONOMIC THEORIES

4.2.1. Sismondi, Proudhon, Rodbertus

In the field of economics the socialists of the first half of the nineteenth century made important contributions, producing a series of fairly homogenous doctrines, in spite of the diversity of approaches and cultural backgrounds. The unifying element was provided by the influence of Ricardian economic theory, which, in different ways and at different levels, was felt by all the socialist economists of the period, from Sismondi to Rodbertus, from Proudhon to the Ricardian socialists.

The most important works of Jean-Charles-Léonard Simonde de Sismondi (1773–1842) are the *Nouveaux principes d'économie politique* (*New Principles of Political Economy*) (1819) and the *Études sur l'économie politique* (*Studies in Political Economy*) (1837–8). Sismondi was a theorist of the anarchy of capitalist production and a critic of Say's Law. Besides this, he considered *laissez-faire* as a capitalist weapon against the workers, who, due to competition and technical progress, were forced to accept subsistence wages and to undergo progressive impoverishment. However, the low level of workers' consumption would hamper the realization of the surplus. Thus Say's Law does not work because of the unequal distribution of income. This argument is similar to that put forward by Malthus. Sismondi, however, proposed to solve the problem by redistributing wealth, not from the capitalists to the landowners, but rather from the capitalists to the workers—an objective that could have been realized through State intervention. Without advocating violent revolutions and without demanding the abolition of private property, Sismondi's socialism aspired to construct a society dominated by small agricultural and craft producers, with an industry which distributed its profits also to the workers, land divided up into small plots, an efficient and extensive social-security system, and sharply progressive death duties.

A few years later Pierre-Joseph Proudhon (1809–65) was to follow similar lines. Of his works we should at least mention *Qu'est-ce-que la propriété?* (*What Is Property?*) (1840) and the *Système des contradictions économiques ou philosophie de la misère* (*System of Economic Contradictions, or Philosophy of Misery*) (1846). Proudhon was closer to Fourier than to Saint-Simon. He argued for the abolition, not of private property, but only of its excesses, and he exalted individual liberty against any form of State control. His socialism presupposed the ability of individuals to spontaneously organize themselves, and aimed at constructing an economy made up of artisan and industrial co-operatives. He rejected class struggle, and proposed free credit as the main instrument for the construction of socialism: by this means the workers would be able to accumulate their own capital.

A contemporary of Proudhon, but professing quite different political and economic ideas, was Johann Karl Rodbertus (1805–75). His main works are: *Zur Erkenntniss unserer staatswirtschaftlichen Zustande (On the Knowledge of Our Economic Conditions)* (1842) and *Soziale Briefe an von Kirchmann (Social Letters to von Kirchmann)* (1850–1). He was a Romantic and conservative critic of capitalism, and professed a reformist and statist socialism in which the inequality in the distribution of income could be, if not eliminated, at least reduced to decent limits. The instruments to be used to reach such a goal were, basically, taxation and the State regulation of prices. Rodbertus used the labour theory of value to demonstrate that the existence of incomes other than wages implies the exploitation of workers. Besides, he maintained that, owing to the tendency of wages to settle at subsistence level, technical progress would lead, on one side, to an increasing relative impoverishment of the workers and, on the other, towards a chronic predisposition of the capitalist system to under-consumption crises.

4.2.2. Godwin and Owen

In England the polarity between organicist and libertarian socialism was represented by the contrasting positions of Owen and Godwin.

William Godwin (1756–1836), in *Enquiry Concerning Political Justice* (1793), tried to construct his socialist theoretical system on utilitarian foundations, and arrived at a criticism of Locke's justification of private property with arguments not dissimilar to those with which Rousseau had criticized seventeenth-century natural-law philosophy. According to Godwin, each individual has only the right to possess the goods necessary to his own satisfaction; and nobody has the right to maximize his own pleasure by impairing that of others. Private property, to the degree to which it contradicts this principle of justice, is illegitimate. At its base there is only the property right and the sanction given to it by the State. Godwin maintained that individual liberty and social justice are two sides of the same coin, and that the liberation of man from oppression requires the abolition of both private property and the State. He assumed that man is rational, basically good, and in possession of the means of realizing his objectives by persuasion rather than violence.

On the contrary, the philosophy of Robert Owen (1771–1858) contained a pessimistic view of man. His most important works are *A New View of Society* (1813) and *The Book of the New Moral World* (1836). Owen did not recognize in man any natural aspiration to liberty. On the other hand, he thought that the character of man could be moulded simply by modifying his living conditions. Thus he proposed a system of social organization inspired by educational objectives, and tried to put this into practice in his own factory. He considered the factory as the nucleus around which society should be built. The factory should be co-operatively managed; production should be increased by using the most up-to-date machines; the goods should be exchanged on the basis of embodied labour; and society should provide not only for the production planning but also for the spiritual education of the producers. The ruling functions should be a prerogative of the old, and the whole hierarchy of social relations should be based on age differences. Gerontocracy is a common element of a great many of the Utopias of order; as it seemed impossible to do without a principle of authority in a society in which the people possess nothing and the Jesuits everything, a power distribution based on age seemed to be the most natural and the least unjust.

4.2.3. The Ricardian socialists and related theorists

In England, Owen's thought inspired a strong co-operative movement and, in the 1820s, a militant trade union movement which was later to converge in the Chartist party.

Three economists, followers of the Owenist movement, were known as 'Ricardian socialists': William Thompson (1783–1833), John Gray (1799–1850), and John Francis Bray (1809–95). Two more economists, Thomas Hodgskin (1787–1869) and 'Piercy Ravenston', can be loosely placed in the same group, although they differ from the preceding three above all in their political beliefs, the former being an anarchist and libertarian and the latter a conservative. We must limit ourselves here to indicating the main works of these economists: *A Few Doubts as to the Correctness of Some Opinions Generally Entertained on the Subjects of Population and Political Economy* (1812) by Ravenstone; *An Inquiry into the Principles of the Distribution of Wealth Most Conducive to Human Happiness* (1824) by Thompson; *Labour Defended Against the Claims of Capital* (1825) and *Popular Political Economy* (1827) by Hodgskin; *A Lecture on Human Happiness* (1825) by Gray; and *Labour's Wrongs and Labour's Remedy* (1839) by Bray. We will only add a few comments on some aspects of the economic doctrines they held in common; but we are well aware of the injustice we are doing them by ignoring their differences.

These economists were directly linked to the classical tradition, especially Ricardian. They accepted the labour theory of value and, combining it with a special interpretation of the natural-law doctrine of ownership, tried to use it to support a theory of labour exploitation. From Locke they took up the argument that the *source* of value is labour. They then built a model of a 'natural' society and compared it to the real society. From Locke's arguments about private property, they accepted those derived from the thesis of the natural right of each individual to possess the products of his own labour, but not those that aimed at justifying a particular historical structure of wealth distribution with the theory of social consensus and monetary convention. The Ricardian socialists did not believe that the capitalist system possesses any of those 'natural' characteristics Locke and Smith attributed to it. On the contrary, they considered it to be an artificial system, opposed to a natural-law principle of fundamental importance—that of the worker to own the product of his own labour.

The Ricardian socialists also emphasized the role played by competition in the labour market in lowering wages. Competition pushed wages towards the subsistence level and, above all, forced them to remain at a level below the 'value of labour'.

In regard to the theory of value and distribution, these economists were not so ingenuous as one might believe from Marx's criticism of them. Hodgskin in particular had a deep understanding of how the problem arose with Smith and the reasons for his analytical difficulties, and proposed a solution which could be considered as beyond criticism. He distinguished the 'natural price', defined as that prevailing in an economy regulated by natural law, and which can be expressed in terms of embodied labour, from the 'social price', defined as the one which prevails in real society, i.e. in a society in which workers do not obtain the whole produce of their labour. The 'social price' is the production price expressed in terms of labour commanded; and it is true that in a capitalist economy it is always higher than that expressed in embodied labour.

Finally, to show that the Ricardian socialists were not only concerned with 'metaphysical' problems, we should like to mention an anonymous work, published in 1821 and entitled *An Inquiry into Those Principles Respecting the Nature of Demand and the Necessity of Consumption*. The author of this paper intended to intervene in the controversy between Malthus and Ricardo about the possibility of general gluts, to demonstrate that the acceptance by Malthus of the argument that 'savings' never means 'hoarding' undermined his theory of the lack of effective demand.

He also denied, however, that Ricardo was right about the impossibility of general gluts. In fact, the author argued that the adjustment processes by which competition would have corrected the sudden changes of the channels of commerce was neither automatic nor painless in terms of profits and employment: they would require a long period of inactivity and a consequent loss of jobs at the macroeconomic level. Even worse, they would greatly reduce the scale of activity of the whole economy. The author was not very clear about the cause of the problem, but he put forward an interesting argument according to which the credit system contributes to worsen all the great fluctuations. The essay gives the impression that the author had direct knowledge, and not only theoretical, of the workings of the crisis when he argues that the reductions in bank credit cause a decrease in investment, production, and employment.

Finally, we will mention here a contemporary of the Ricardian socialists, Richard Jones (1790–1855)—although he should not really be included in this section, as he was neither a socialist nor a Ricardian. But as this section actually deals with the English forerunners of Marx, Jones does deserve to be included in it. In his two principal works, *An Essay on the Distribution of Wealth and the Sources of Taxation* (1831) and *An Introductory Lecture on Political Economy* (1833), Jones criticized Ricardo for his deductive and a priori method of reasoning, suggesting the necessity of basing theoretical generalizations, in order to make them really useful, on the observation of historical facts. He also criticized Ricardo for having constructed general laws, and presenting them as natural, when in fact they were historically limited. Jones believed that political economy should be a form of 'economic anatomy' of society, and should study the class structures and the institutional patterns that influence the production and the distribution of income in a given society in a given historical context. Therefore, the laws formulated by Ricardo were valid only in a capitalist society, especially those concerned with the formation of rent (Jones's 1831 work only dealt with rent, and was not followed up). Capitalist society represents only one phase in the historical development of humanity and is characterized by the fact that the workers are dependent on the entrepreneurial class. Jones, who was more of a conservative than a socialist, did not exclude the possibility that capitalism is a phase of an economic evolution towards a more desirable state of affairs, such as one in which workers are themselves the owners of capital. It is not surprising that Marx, in his *Theories of Surplus Value*, dedicated an entire chapter to Jones.

4.3. MARX'S ECONOMIC THEORY

4.3.1. Marx and the classical economists

Just when theories of economic harmony were spreading all over the capitalist world, Karl Marx (1818–83) was working on a 'critique of political economy'. The dates here are important. The defeat of the workers' movement in 1848 ended a cycle of struggle which had lasted for more than 30 years and opened a phase of bourgeois cultural hegemony and capitalist economic growth previously unknown in Europe. The old revolutionaries, forced into exile and political inactivity, had to find a *modus vivendi*. The road taken by Marx was to closet himself in the British Museum Library and dedicate himself to study. The revolutionary leader became an 'economist', convinced that he was still working for 'the old mole'. It was certainly a return to the 'weapon of criticism'. But the 'critique of political economy', which is the subtitle of *Capital*, must be, according to Marx, a weapon for the proletarian revolution.

The first volume of *Das Kapital* was published in 1867. The other two were published posthumously by Engels in 1883 and 1894. Marx did not have time to arrange them into a final version, and some chapters are little more than a collection of notes. Two other important works of Marx, the *Theorien über den Mehrwert* (*Theories of Surplus Value*), published in 1905, and the *Grund-*

risse, published as late as 1939–41, are also collections of more or less ordered notes.

There is a close relationship between Marx and the classical economists. In fact, he himself never had any difficulty in acknowledging the scientific merits of the great English classical economists, Ricardo in particular. The name itself, 'classical', which he attributed to them was almost a tribute from a student. By it, he intended to distinguish them from the 'vulgar' economists, the apologists of capitalism who worked to produce consensus rather than science. His definition of 'classical political economy' is simple and rigorous, and coincides with that of 'Ricardian economics': a theoretical system based on the theory of surplus, the labour theory of value, the methodology of aggregates, and the analysis of the behaviour of the social classes and their relationships. Smith's thought itself was scrutinized in the light of the Ricardian system, and did not always pass the test.

Marx considered classical political economy as a theoretical expression of the bourgeoisie in the period when the modern capitalist economy was asserting itself. The historical reference was to the English Industrial Revolution and the struggle for political hegemony that the bourgeoisie conducted in Great Britain and France between 1815 and 1848. In the struggle against the forces of aristocratic and clerical reaction, the bourgeoisie interpreted the needs of the whole society, endeavouring to present its own class interests as collective interests and the spirit of private accumulation as an instrument to increase the national wealth. The other side of the coin was that the interests of the landowners had to be shown as conflicting with those of the collectivity. This is why the classical theoretical system was based on the analysis of the social classes, the study of class conflict and the dynamics of economic aggregates resulting from the behaviour and interaction of collective agents. Marx was referring to all this when he argued that the classical economists proposed to penetrate the inner physiology of the bourgeois society. Thus, the *analytical* apparatus of classical political economy was robust, and Marx adopted it wholesale.

According to Marx, however, after 1830 came an important turning-point in the history of economic thought. The industrial bourgeoisie, as soon as it came to power with the help of the proletariat in England and France, tried to change alliance. At that moment the class conflict with the proletariat had become more important, whereas the struggle with the landowners had abated. Now the bourgeoisie needed to demonstrate that the enlightenment dream of a society of free citizens had finally been realized, that in this society there was no oppression or exploitation, that each person received what he gave, and that class conflict, or, rather the classes themselves, had no longer a reason to exist. At this point a theoretical system based on classes and class conflict no longer served; the theories of harmony of interests and of co-operating productive factors were more useful. Thus, according to Marx, as the scientific inheritance of classical political economy had been betrayed by the 'bourgeois economists', it now passed to the socialist economists. Now it was the working class which represented its interests as coinciding with those of the collectivity. This is the origin of the socialist cognitive interests in penetrating the physiology of bourgeois society. Marx believed that the proletariat had inherited science from the bourgeoisie, while waiting to inherit the world. This would explain the place of *Capital* in the history of economic thought. And this, according to Marx, accounted for his ability to recognize the limits of classical political economy; in fact, as we should not forget, Marx's theory was a 'critique of political economy'.

Marx made many specific criticisms of the classical economists, but three, in particular, are important. The first deals with their inability to explain the *nature* of profit and capital. They had posed the problem of determining the size of profits, not that of explaining its social bases, i.e. its origin in the exploitation of labour. Marx acknowledged that Smith had had an insight into the problem and that, in his distinction between embodied and commanded labour, Smith had set down the premises for the correct solution. But Marx conceded nothing more. He did not even acknowledge this in Ricardo.

The second criticism is linked to the first, and concerns the inability of the classical economists to acknowledge the historical character of capitalism. As these classical economists did not know what capital *was*, they were unable to distinguish between its technological and social dimensions. As the need to use the means of production to produce goods has always existed and always will, capital and the social order which it creates seem eternal. Marx, on the contrary, argued that capital is a social relationship: it is not simply a set of means of production, but rather, the power that their control gives to the bourgeoisie; the power to use the means of production to produce profits. Only in a particular social system, which he called 'the capitalist mode of production', do the means of production become capital. Therefore, the aim of the critique of political economy should be, on the one hand, to understand how this mode of production works and, on the other, to discover its 'laws of movement', i.e. its laws of historical evolution and transformation.

The inability of the classical, but especially the 'vulgar', economists to acknowledge the existence of exploitation at the basis of the capitalistic mode of production led them, according to Marx, to focus their attention on relationships of exchange rather than of production. This is the third important criticism. The individuals enter into an exchange relationship as autonomous subjects, for exchange is the result of their independent decisions. They also enter it as equal subjects, for exchange is always the exchange between equivalents, and the qualitative difference between the goods exchanged, for example the difference between labour and wages, is hidden by the equality of their exchange value. This is the reason why a market system seems to be a system of equality and liberty. Smith had spoken of such liberty in terms of free competition or 'perfect liberty' of the single economic agent. If individuals are equal and free, their ability to recognize and pursue their personal interests will activate the 'invisible hand', and this will reconcile the interests of all. Thus, a freely competitive exchange economy is a system of social harmony, a system in which each person has what he wants and manages to pay, i.e. what he gives. It is easy to see why Marx, who wished to explain the nature of the social relationship that ties labour to capital, focused on the sphere of production, rather than that of 'circulation' or exchange, and, in particular, the mechanisms that regulate the production of income and its distribution between wages and profits.

4.3.2. Exploitation and value

Marx's theory of exploitation aimed at bringing to light the true nature of the capital–labour relationship by unmasking the form of relationship between equivalents in which the exchange between wages and labour was presented. The worker enters the labour market as a seller of the only productive requisite he owns: his 'labour power'. As with any other good, this also has to obey the 'general law of value': in equilibrium it receives a price determined by the conditions of production. Each worker, in order to produce his working capacity, must consume a certain quantity of wage goods in the proportions determined by the consumption habits prevailing in a certain period. Thus the 'value of the labour power' is equal to the value of the means of subsistence necessary for the survival and the reproduction of the working class. The capitalist enters the labour market with the good he possesses, i.e. capital, or, rather, wages. With it he pays the 'exchange value' of the labour power and he acquires its 'use value'. After the exchange, labour becomes a means of production, and its use, given the rules established in the labour contract and the prevailing norms, is the prerogative of the capitalist. Thus the product of labour, i.e. the set of goods produced with the use of labour, belongs to the capitalist.

In the production process, labour manifests its own ability to produce goods whose value is superior to that of the labour power. The difference is the 'surplus value'. This is immediately considered as an attribute of capital, as labour has already entered the productive process as capital. Marx called 'variable' capital that part of the advances necessary to pay the 'labour power'; 'variable' because it enters into the production at a value lower than that of the goods that it produces, because it is capital which 'self-valorizes'. On the contrary, 'constant' capital is that which is advanced to buy the means of production: it transmits to the product only its own value, without adding anything.

From the surplus value the capitalist subtracts the quotas to pay for rents, interest, and other transfer payments. What remains is the profit. Here we have not the time to explain how the other payments are determined. So we will assume that they do not exist, and will consider profit as equal to the surplus value. However we will discuss interest in section 4.3.6. Thus, surplus value is the valorization of capital and belongs to the capitalist. Everything has followed market rules. The workers have received a 'just' price for the good they have sold, and the capitalists have paid for it. Yet capital has increased in value. The reason for this is that labour has the ability to produce more than is necessary for the reproduction of the 'labour power'.

This is a theory that explains *why* the production of a surplus, in a capitalist economy, takes the form of production of surplus value, i.e. of a capital attribute. This theory differs from that of the Ricardian socialists, who tended instead to *demonstrate the existence of exploitation* by arguing that, in the setting of the 'value of labour', there is a violation of the natural law according to which each good should be paid for at its own 'natural' price. Marx criticized these theories, maintaining that, in the explanation of exploitation, it is necessary to start from the idea that the 'just' or 'natural' price for labour is nothing more than that determined by the market, and not that determined by a hypothetical natural law. Thus, Marx did not even have to pose the problem of who had the 'right' to the product of labour. We will return to this matter later.

On the other hand, surplus value is produced by labour and only labour. Marx took this as obvious. He believed that the different social structures that had succeeded one another through history could change the form in which surplus value appears (e.g. profit in the capitalist economy and tithes in the feudal economy) but could not change the substance. And, in substance, *value is labour* and *surplus value is surplus labour*. These two, clearly ontological, statements were formulated by Marx, at the analytical level, by using the labour theory of value.

The value of the gross product is assumed to be equal to the labour directly and indirectly used to produce it. The value of the net product is equal to the labour directly applied, which is called 'living labour'. The value of constant capital is the same as the labour employed indirectly, and is called 'dead labour'. In a 'corn' model, λ is the labour-value of a unit of corn, l living labour, k the input of seeds, and v the value of the labour power, i.e. the labour used to produce the corn paid as a wage to one unit of labour. Thus, the values of the gross and net products are respectively equal to:

$$\lambda = l + \lambda k \quad \text{and} \quad \lambda(1 - k) = l$$

Constant capital is $C = k\lambda$; variable capital is $V = vl$; therefore surplus value is $S = l(1 - v)$. Now it is also possible to write

$$\lambda = l(1 - v) - vl + k\lambda = S + V + C$$

So, surplus value is labour. In fact, l is living labour, vl is the labour necessary to reproduce the labour power, and $l - vl$ is the labour appropriated by the capitalists. If l is a working day, vl represents the number of hours the workers work for themselves, and $l - vl$ is the number of hours they work for the capitalists. The rate of 'exploitation', or of 'surplus value', σ, is equal to:

$$\sigma = \frac{S}{V} = \frac{l - vl}{vl} = \frac{1}{v} - 1$$

and it is easy to see that it vanishes when the workers spend the whole working day working for themselves, i.e. when $v = 1$.

It may be useful, in order better to understand the Marxian theory of value and exploitation, to compare it with the theory of the Ricardian socialists and with that of Hodgskin, in particular. Furthermore, in order to frame both of these theories in a historical perspective, it is worth tracing them back to the natural-law theory of value and ownership.

The attempt to use the labour theory of value to account for the distribution of income and wealth goes back at least to seventeenth-century natural-law philosophy, if not even to scholastic thought. However, it was Locke who produced the first comprehensive formulation. Locke's theory of value and ownership can be reduced to three fundamental propositions:

(1) In the 'natural order' the value of the product is the product of labour.
(2) The relationship between value and labour is not altered by social conventions.
(3) Private property is the result of accumulation of past labour and therefore does not contradict natural law.

The first proposition is a well-known argument which is central to every ontological labour theory of value. Value is *created* by labour. Thus the value of goods coincides with embodied labour. Locke admitted the existence of a productive contribution of land, but maintained that it was insignificant and, in any case, that it could be equated to the contribution of labour by means of a few arithmetical operations. The second proposition refers to money intended as a social institution created by collective consensus. Money allows the accumulation of the products of labour beyond any immediate subsistence need and, at the same time, allows the transfer of accumulated wealth from one person to another. The third proposition is derived from the other two. As value is produced by labour, and as natural law states that each individual must possess his own labour, so private property derived from accumulated labour is legitimate. If it is distributed in an unequal way, it is only because money allows each individual to accumulate, not only the products of his own labour, but also those bought from other individuals. As the monetary convention is based on collective consensus, and as it does not alter the law of exchange based on embodied labour, private property is legitimate, even if unequally distributed.

Hodgskin converted this doctrine into a theory of exploitation by means of a simple operation: he accepted the first proposition and rejected the second. Instead of focusing his attention on the institution of money, however, he referred more specifically to the socio-institutional structure of the capitalist economy. As profits must exist in this economy, goods can no longer be exchanged at their 'natural prices', i.e. at labour values, but must be exchanged at 'social prices', which are higher than the former by the amount necessary to make profits possible. This led him to argue that the third proposition is not valid, and that private property is not just the result of the accumulation of past labour. Property is unevenly distributed because the workers are not paid on the basis of the value of their labour, and is illegitimate because goods are not exchanged at their natural prices.

Marx, for his part, accepted the first of Locke's propositions, but, given his philosophical background, rejected any reference to natural law. He substituted for the idea of natural law that of 'production in general', which, however, had the same theoretical implications as the first. 'Production in general' is a productive structure defined by abstracting from the particular institutional and social conditions in which production takes place. With 'production in general', the labour values are perfectly determined once the *productive technique* is known. They make up the 'substance of value'.

In regard to the problems connected to Locke's second thesis, Marx's position is a little more complicated. As the 'socio-economic forms' change over the course of history, so do the 'forms' of extraction of the surplus value. In the capitalist mode of production, the necessity to ensure a uniform rate of profit, required by the hypothesis of competition, implies that the goods are exchanged no longer at labour values but at 'production prices' (we will discuss this in the next section). However, changes in the form cannot alter the substance; and the substance of value remains labour. Thus, production prices redistribute value among the various productive sectors, but do not modify its amount. For this reason, and with reference to aggregate production, Marx obtained a result similar to that of Locke's second propositions. Even within a determinate socioeconomic structure, such as capitalism, the *overall* value of the product remains the product of labour, so that the *aggregate* surplus remains equal to the surplus value.

A consequence of this is that Locke's third proposition is also valid—certainly not in the sense that private property is legitimate, but undoubtedly in the sense that property is the result of an accumulation of past labour, except that it is the accumulation of other people's labour. In this way Marx managed to deal with exploitation without referring to any ethical-philosophical justification of the type put forward by the Ricardian socialists. Instead, Hodgskin formulated a theory of exploitation which implied a condemnation of profit by using natural-law arguments. However, and paradoxically, Marx distanced himself from Locke less than Hodgskin had done: in his theory, all three of Locke's propositions on value and wealth remained basically valid.

4.3.3. The transformation of values into prices

In regard to value, Marx was not a simple-minded economist. He appreciated the reasons for Smith's distinction between embodied and commanded labour, and criticized Ricardo for not having well understood the reasons why goods are not exchanged at labour values. Marx believed that goods are exchanged at 'production prices', which are prices determined in such a way as to guarantee a uniform rate of profit. In general, the ratio between the production prices of two goods does not coincide with the ratio between the quantities of labour embodied in them.

In order to understand this in the simplest possible way, let us consider an economy that produces only two goods: a capital good and a consumer good. Let k_k and k_c be the quantities of good used to produce one unit of capital good and one of consumer good respectively, l_k and l_c the inputs of living labour, λ_k and λ_c the labour values, p_k and p_c the monetary prices of production, w the money wage, and r the rate of profit. We have:

$$\lambda_k = l_k + k_k \lambda_k = \frac{l_k}{1 - k_k}$$

$$\lambda_c = l_c + k_c \lambda_k = l_c + l_k \frac{k_c}{1 - k_k}$$

$$p_k = w l_k + k_k p_k (1 + r)$$

$$p_c = w l_c + k_c p_k (1 + r)$$

The relative labour values and the relative prices are respectively:

$$\frac{\lambda_c}{\lambda_k} = \frac{l_c}{l_k} (1 - k_k) + k_c$$

$$\frac{p_c}{p_k} = \frac{l_c}{l_k} [l - k_k (1 + r)] + k_c (1 + r)$$

Only under two conditions can $\lambda_c/\lambda_k = p_c/p_k$ occur. The first is that $r = 0$; but this is irrelevant, as in a capitalist economy the profit must be positive. The second is that $k_k/l_k = k_c/l_c$, or $l_c/l_k = k_c/k_k$. In fact, by substituting k_c/k_k for l_c/l_k in the preceding two equations, $\lambda_c/\lambda_k = p_c/p_k$ is obtained.

In general, the prices diverge from the labour values because different techniques are used to produce different goods. Marx accounted for this result by saying that there are different 'organic' and 'technical' compositions of capital in the two sectors: in our example

$$k_k/l_k \neq k_c/l_c.$$

However, Marx maintained that *in the aggregate* the valuations in prices could not diverge from those in values; which means that the labour theory of value is not valid as an explanation of the exchange values of the single goods, but is still valid as an explanation of the value of the gross product and its aggregate components. This is the reason why, in the whole of the first volume of *Capital*, where Marx studied the working of a capitalist economy at the maximum level of abstraction and aggregation, he measured all the economic variables in embodied labour. His idea was that the valuation in prices would only lead to a redistribution of the overall value among the various sectors, but could not alter its aggregate size, which depends solely on the quantity of labour employed by the society to produce the gross income. A consequence of this is that the aggregate rate of exploitation could not be changed by the way in which the surplus value is shared out among the capitalists, because it is given by the ratio between the total surplus value and the total necessary labour. A final consequence is that the aggregate rate of profit could be calculated, if the technique and the real wage are known, without knowing the prices; and, as it cannot be altered by the valuations in prices, it could be applied to the costs of production of the single industries to calculate the prices themselves. In this way, the values would be 'transformed' into prices, an operation that Marx attempted in the third volume of *Capital*.

In order to understand where the difficulties of the transformation lie, we will calculate the average rate of profit in labour values and in production prices and see if the two measures coincide. The economy we are considering is stationary. Therefore, the gross product of the capital-goods sector is the same as replacements, $1 = k_k + k_c$, and the value of aggregate capital is p_k if valued in prices and λ_k if valued in labour values; furthermore, the gross production of consumer goods coincides with the aggregate net product, and its value is p_c if valued in prices and λ_c if valued in embodied labour; finally, $L = l_k + l_c$ is total employment. Then, the rate of profit calculated in prices is:

$$r = \frac{p_c - wL}{p_k}$$

and that calculated in embodied labour, ρ, is:

$$\rho = \frac{\lambda_c - vL}{\lambda_k}$$

By equating these two expressions, and keeping in mind that the real wage is $w_r = v/\lambda_c = w/p_c$, it is easy to see that the two rates of profit are equal if and only if:

$$\left(\frac{p_c}{p_k} - \frac{\lambda_c}{\lambda_k} \right)(1 - w_rL) = 0$$

and that is if $p_c/p_k = \lambda_c/\lambda_k$. The other condition, $w_r = 1/L$, means that the real wage is equal to the productivity of labour. In this case the profit is zero and $p_c/p_k = \lambda_c/\lambda_k$ holds true again. We already know that these conditions, apart from the case $r = 0$, imply equality among the organic compositions of capital. It is possible to prove that the same conclusion is reached by considering any other ratio among aggregate variables, wage share, rate of exploitation, etc.

It is possible to conclude, therefore, that in general the aggregate variables and the ratios between them are altered by the valuation in production prices. The market does not just redistribute the surplus value among the capitalists, but seems to alter its size. Thus, the actual rate of profit and the actual rate of exploitation differ from those calculated in embodied labour. The meaning of this conclusion is simple: given the wage and the technique, the rate of profit and the rate of exploitation cannot be known *before* knowing the prices of production; the determination of the latter, not being independent from the determination of the distribution of income, carries out an essential role in the determination of the former. On the other hand, the valuation in embodied labour is independent from the distribution of income, and is therefore not a correct valuation.

4.3.4. Equilibrium, Say's Law, and crises

As already mentioned, prices of production are determined in such a way as to guarantee a uniform profit rate among the various industries. They are, in a sense, equilibrium prices; in order to understand in which sense, we need to define the equilibrium conditions. Marx did this on the grounds of the analysis of Quesnay's *tableau économique*, which he studied in depth and developed into his 'reproduction schemes'. These schemes are equations defining the equilibrium conditions in terms of sectorial interdependences; and they serve to determine the flows of goods that must 'circulate' among the different productive sectors in order that each has the inputs necessary to carry out production. When the level of output in each sector guarantees a supply of goods corresponding to the demand generated by the output levels themselves, then the economy is able to reproduce itself. As Marx put it in the *Grundrisse*, an economy is able to reproduce itself when there is 'balance of demand and supply; balance of production and consumption; and what this amounts to in the last analysis, *proportionate production*' (p. 153).

With reference to our example of a two-sector economy, the reproduction conditions can be defined in the following terms. First of all, there must be equality between supply and demand for each of the two goods produced, the consumer good and the capital good. Furthermore, the exchanges of the goods must occur at prices such that the net incomes earned in each of the two sectors coincide with those spent out by the other. This means that the part of the consumer good which is not demanded by the workers and the capitalists operating in the consumer-good sector itself is equal to the demand for the consumer-good from the workers and the capitalists operating in the capital-good sector. On the other hand, the excess of output of capital goods with respect to the reinvestments in the capital-good sector must be equal to the demand for capital coming from the consumer-good sector.

These are the results reached by Marx with his '*simple* reproduction schemes'; 'simple' in that they relate to a stationary economy. For a growing economy Marx formulated some 'expanded reproduction schemes'; but we will not discuss them here.

An equilibrium such as the one just defined is a state of the economy in which supply and demand of all the goods are equal, while the goods are exchanged at the prices of production. It is a *reproduction equilibrium*, i.e. a state that guarantees the reproduction of the economy. The prices prevailing in this state depend exclusively on objective factors, such as the techniques in use and the distribution of income.

It is evident that Say's Law rules in a reproduction equilibrium. If the supply and demand are equal in each sector, they must be equal on aggregate. On the other hand, in the equations of the simple reproduction schemes the demand for consumer goods coincides with net income. This implies that income is entirely spent. In the expanded reproduction schemes, all the non-consumed profits are invested. Marx never admitted it explicitly, but in a large part of *Capital*, when he studied accumulation, 'capital in general', exploitation, the 'law of value', etc.—in other words, when he used a methodology of aggregates, valuing goods in labour value or in prices of production—he adopted Say's Law.

Yet Marx criticized this law. He formulated the reproduction schemes to demonstrate that the equilibrium defined by them could be reached only 'by chance'. The economy he studied always moves in disequilibrium. The goods are exchanged at market prices, and supply does not coincide with demand. The excess demands cause market prices to vary and the rates of profit guaranteed by the market prices differ from the 'average' rate. As aggregate demand ultimately depends on capitalists' decisions regarding production levels, it can at any time diverge from aggregate supply. The rhythm of accumulation depends, in turn, on the rates of profit. If these are low, the capitalist may decide not to reinvest all the profits earned and to 'hoard' them. In this way, part of the income produced and distributed is not spent, and this creates a situation of 'over-production', i.e. of lack of aggregate demand. This is the crisis: all goods are in excess supply, so that their value cannot be realized and the market prices and the rates of profit fall. This leads to a further disincentive to investment and a further fall in aggregate demand. In this way the crisis spreads and deepens.

All this, however, in Marx's system, does not create chaos and does not lessen the importance of the reproduction conditions as final determinants of the movement of the capitalist economy. In fact, the disequilibrium dynamic is regulated by laws that make the crises come with a certain regularity. They generate a cyclical movement which, in the long periods of accumulation, will prevent the economy from systematically diverging from the reproduction equilibrium.

4.3.5. Wages, the trade cycle, and the 'laws of movement' of the capitalist economy

The Marxian theory of cycle is based on two fundamental hypotheses:

(1) Investment is an increasing function of the rate of profit.
(2) The rate of profit is a decreasing function of wages.

If wages increase, investment will be discouraged. This will reduce the aggregate demand and trigger a crisis. The market prices will fall together with the levels of output, pushing the average rate of profit down again. Thus the crisis will deepen. However, with a reduction in investment, the demand for labour will also decrease and the 'industrial reserve army', i.e. (manifest and hidden) unemployment, will rise. As a consequence, sooner or later wages will fall. Furthermore, the crisis itself, by expelling from the market the most inefficient firms and the most obsolete machines, will contribute to raise labour productivity. Therefore, the average rate of profit will increase again, reactivating economic growth. When employment levels and wages begin to rise again, it will be the beginning of a new cycle.

The wage used in this model is the *market* wage. This is not, however, a price simply determined by the forces of supply and demand of labour. Marx explicitly admitted that 'workers' coalitions' were created precisely in order to counterbalance the effects of wage competition. Sometimes Marx reasoned in a classical manner, by treating market wages as being determined by market forces; but at other times he reasoned in his own way, by maintaining that wages were only *influenced* by market forces. His original contribution to this problem lies in his treatment of the market wage as a price fixed by collective bargaining and dependent on the power relationships among the classes. The market only acts to the degree that the variations of the 'reserve army' contribute to weaken or strengthen the trade unions. A wage determined in this way would therefore tend to oscillate.

The trend in such oscillations is represented by what Marx called the 'value of labour power', a concept corresponding to that of 'natural wage' of the classical economists. Obviously, Marx did not recognize anything 'natural' in it, even if he treated it as a subsistence wage. His wage theory differed markedly from that of the classical economists. In fact, Marx did not just admit the fundamental role played by long-term changes in workers' consumption habits, but, by recognizing the role played by trade unions in the determination of the wage *trend*, besides its oscillations, he downgraded the importance of habits and customs as *exogenous* determinants of wages.

His theory, to the degree to which it differs from the classical one, is a theory of 'normal' wages based on the power relationships among the classes. The workers enter into the conflict by trying to control the supply of labour by means of the trade unions; the capitalists enter it by trying to control the demand by means of their investment decisions. In the course of the business cycle, wages will oscillate with the levels of output. In the course of accumulation, the trend variables, including wages, will be determined by the organized strength of the workers on the one hand and technical progress on the other. In fact, in the long run the demand for labour will be strongly influenced by the ability of the capitalists to replace labour by machines—an ability which depends on the type of technical progress incorporated in the means of production.

Given that technical progress tends to substitute machines for labour, if trade unions did not exist the forces of competition would cause real wages to decrease permanently. The actions of the 'workers' coalitions' fight such a tendency. According to Marx, however, the trade unions were strong enough to contrast the effects of technical progress on wages, but not strong enough to prevent a decrease in the wage share or an increase in the rate of exploitation. This occurs because technical progress acts on the wage shares from two sides. On the one hand, given the rate of accumulation, it will depress the rate of growth of labour demand and therefore will increase the 'reserve army' (this theory, to be precise, is a development of the Ricardian theses about the occupational effects of the introduction of machines). The increase in the 'reserve army' will then slow the growth in wages. On the other hand, the use of increasingly modern machines will raise the productivity of labour. Marx believed that there is a tendency for labour productivity to increase more rapidly than real wages.

This idea is at the basis of the theory of 'increasing immiseration' of the proletariat, one of the most important 'laws of movement' of the capitalist economy. The employed workers constantly improve their own standards of living as real wages increase. However, their position with respect to the capitalist class worsens as the wage share diminishes. Furthermore, their dissatisfaction as consumers increases, as capitalist growth raises their needs more rapidly than the income necessary to satisfy them. But also their dissatisfaction at work increases as they become increasingly subordinated to mechanized work processes. At the same time, their subjection to capital rises. Finally, as the 'reserve army' increases too, the percentage of employed people in relation to the population able to work decreases. This means that the relative 'misery' of the working class as a whole increases even more than that of employed people.

The second law of movement concerns the tendency of the rate of profit to fall. The profit rate is an increasing function of the rate of exploitation and a decreasing function of the organic composition of capital. Marx believed that the processes of mechanization are undertaken to offset the negative effects of class conflict on the rate of profit. In phases of prosperity, wages increase and create the conditions for the crisis. In response, capitalists introduce machines that allow them to dismiss workers and increase productivity. Thus, the rate of profit increases again. Then, in the successive phase of prosperity the workers recover the lost ground, and so on. However, the process of mechanization, even though it raises the rate of profit following each wave of innovations, in the long run would lower it, as it would reduce the size of the cake to be shared out in relation to that of the capital invested to produce it.

In other words, behind the Marxian theory of the falling rate of profit lies the hypothesis of a fall in the output–capital ratio—a hypothesis that Marx justified, not too convincingly, with the limits that the working day would pose to the growth in the value of output, there being no limits to the growth in the value of capital.

This law can be proved quite simply in the following way. The maximum level for the rate of profit, r_{max}, is given by the aggregate output–capital ratio:

$$r = \frac{p_c - wL}{p_k} < \frac{p_c}{p_k} = r_{max}$$

Note that, when the wage rate is zero, the equality $p_c/p_k = (1 - k_k)/k_k$ holds true. The rate of profit will tend to fall if its upper limit is decreasing. Thus, the hypothesis that must be done is that technical progress always increases the quantity of means of production necessary to produce the net output.

According to Marx, another two laws can be derived from the law of the falling rate of profit. One has to do with the tendency of crises to become increasingly severe. Since, in order to overcome a crisis, capital must activate innovative processes that reduce the output–capital ratio, the ensuing crisis will always be more difficult to overcome. Given the wage increases, each crisis will bring about a greater fall in the rate of profit than the preceding crisis. This means that the combination of technological progress and class conflict will not only diminish the incentive to invest but also increase the amplitude of the oscillations around the long-run growth trend. So, sooner or later, the final crisis will arrive.

Finally, another law of movement deals with the structure of markets and the size of firms. In order to compensate for the fall in the *rate* of profit, the capitalists try to raise its *level*. This explains the push towards 'concentration' and 'centralization' of capital. On the one hand, capital accumulation and the increase in its organic composition will raise the size of firms; on the other, the *unequal* decrease in the rate of profit will allow the big fish to swallow up the little ones. According to Marx, the competitive struggle amongst capitalists is no less bitter than the class struggle between workers and capital. The final effects of competition were valued positively, however, as they would lead to the reduction in the anarchy of capitalist production and to an increase of the dimensions within which working activity is planned and organized.

The four laws of movement taken together account for the tendency of the capitalistic mode of production to create the conditions for its own overthrow. The fall in the rate of profit and the increasingly severe crises will weaken its driving force, while the growing immiseration will strengthen the will and motivation of the workers towards revolutionary change. Finally, the concentration and centralization processes will push the capitalist system towards creating the conditions of planned production. The qualitative jump will bring about an economic system in which the workers are able collectively to control productive activity. In such a new economic organization, the anarchy of capitalist production would be abolished, together with exploitation, and each person would be remunerated according to his own productive contribution, i.e. to the quantity and quality of his work. This is socialism, the first phase of communism.

4.3.6. Monetary aspects of the cycle and the crisis

Marx was very interested in the monetary aspects of economic dynamics, and studied them with a great deal of acumen, producing a particularly illuminating and modern theory of money. He believed it was important to study money in order to understand the real operation of the short-run dynamics of the capitalist economy; and thought that, even though the fundamental causes of the cycle and the crisis are real, the working of the monetary system could make its own specific contribution to the amplification of the economic fluctuations, even in the real aspects.

Marx studied in depth the English monetary debates of the first half of the nineteenth century and sided with the banking school, from whose theories he drew a great deal of inspiration. Particularly important was his acceptance of the arguments that the equation of exchanges makes the quantity of money supplied and its velocity of circulation depend on transaction needs.

The adjustment of the money supply to demand, according to Marx, occurs in part through variations in the liquid balances, i.e. in 'hoarding', which vary anti-cyclically due to the fact that money is also held for precautionary purposes. Money, he states in the *Grundrisse* is 'absolutely secure wealth' (p. 234), and serves to bring 'general wealth into safety and away from circulation'; thus 'among private individuals accumulation [of money] takes place for the purpose of bringing wealth into safety' (p. 230). Therefore, liquid balances are accumulated during the phases of contraction and decumulated during prosperity. The influence of Thornton's theory of liquidity preference is evident, and Marx explicitly recognized it when he quoted Thornton's view that 'Guineas are *hoarded* in times of distrust' (*Grundrisse*, p. 816).

But the adjustment of money to the needs of transactions does not only occur through variations in the speed of circulation; still more important is the role played by credit in the adjustment of the money supply. Marx adopted a wide definition of money, including in it, besides currency, deposits and bills of exchange. Credit plays a fundamental role in the process of capitalist accumulation. During the expansion phases there is a rapid growth, not only in production, but also in the aggregate excess demand and in market prices. In these phases the capitalists, as a whole, spend more than they earn, and a part of the purchasing power needed to finance accumulation is supplied by bank and commercial credit. The money supply is very elastic with respect to income. For this reason the rate of interest, during prosperity, rises less than the rate of profit. In this way, the monetary system fuels productive expansion in phases of rapid growth.

In these phases the capitalists' net indebtedness rises, and the risk exposure of the banking system increases with it. When the real cycle begins the downturn, owing to the increase in wages and the fall in profits, the demand for credit is kept high by speculation on goods, which is progressively fed by the increase in prices. The banks, however, at this point begin to defend their own reserves and the rate of interest climbs very fast. The turning-point of the *monetary* cycle is triggered by the change in the behaviour of the speculators. When these begin to sell, the prices and profits fall dramatically, as the demand for goods for productive purposes has already begun to weaken. Thus the *realization crisis* begins. Aggregate demand decreases, pulling down production, and the aggregate excess supply ('over-production') tends to spread. For many capitalists it becomes difficult to cover the costs of production. And for many it is difficult to collect the funds necessary to repay debts. Those who manage to find liquidity tend to accumulate it in inactive balances, 'waiting for more favourable market conditions'. The banks also behave in this way, and restrict credit advances. So the demand for money rises just when the propensity to create more of it is at a minimum. This is the liquidity crisis or the 'dearth of money'. During this crisis the intertwining of credit and debt may bring about the disastrous phenomenon of chain bankruptcies. At this stage the rate of interest reaches its maximum and the crisis touches the bottom.

When the least efficient firms have been expelled from the market and the most obsolete machines have been eliminated from the factories, when the unemployed workers have learned to moderate their grievances and the employed to accept intensified exploitation, then the conditions will have been obtained for productive recovery. At the same time, huge idle liquid balances, 'latent monetary capital', will have been accumulated. The conditions for a new credit expansion are in place. The crisis performs a fundamental function in creating both the real and the monetary conditions for recovery.

The modernity of this dynamic monetary theory is evident, as is the influence exercised on it by the English anti-bullionist and anti-currency schools. The influence, already mentioned, of Thornton's liquidity preference theory also seems notable. In the formulation of his own special version of the liquidity preference theory, however, Marx was an innovator. He established two fundamental principles which make his theory an important anticipation of Keynes's. The first of these was that it is necessary to consider the total money *stock*, rather than the *flow* of new money or credit, when studying monetary dynamics, i.e. the movements of supply and demand for finance, the changes in hoarding and in the velocity of circulation, and the oscillations in the rate of interest. From this principle comes the view that the rate of interest is the price of 'monetary capital', i.e. of the stock of money rather than the flow of credit. The second principle concerns the rate of interest. This is considered as a price, but one of a special kind, an 'irrational' form of price. This is because the market price of a real good has a dynamics regulated by the production price. The price of money, on the contrary, depends solely on the forces of supply and demand and does not possess a normal value around which to oscillate. Mill's and Ricardo's idea, that the rate of return of real capital is the equilibrium value of the rate of interest, is completely foreign to Marx's way of thinking. Marx believed that long-term movements in the rate of interest are definable only as averages of short-term movements, not as regulators of these, and that they are determined by general consensus, habits and legal traditions.

Bibliography

On Utopian thought: M. L. Berneri, *Journey through Utopia* (London, 1950); J. O. Hertzler, *The History of Utopian Thought* (New York, 1952); G. Kateb, *Utopia and its Enemies* (New York, 1963); F. E. Manuel and F. P. Manuel, *Utopian Thought in the Western World* (Oxford, 1979); L. Mumford, *The Story of Utopias* (London, 1922); G. Neagly and J. M. Patrick, *The Quest for Utopia* (New York, 1952).

On pre-Marxist socialist thought: A. Briggs, *Robert Owen in Retrospect* (Loughborough, 1959); D. W. Brogan, *Proudhon* (London, 1933); G. D. H. Cole, *Socialist Thought: the Forerunners (1789–1850)* (London, 1953); J. Kimball, *The Economic Doctrines of John Gray* (Washington, DC, 1949); C. Landauer, *European Socialism: A History of Ideas and Movements*, i (Berkeley, Calif., 1959); G. Lichtheim, *The Origins of Socialism* (New York, 1969); A. Morton, 'Un demi-siècle d'utopie: De Robert Owen et Charles Fourier à William Morris', *La Pensée*, 108 (1963); T. Sowell, 'Sismondi: A Neglected Pioneer', *History of Political Economy*, 4 (1972).

On Marx: M. Desai, *Marxian Economic Theory* (London, 1974); M. Dobb, *Political Economy and Capitalism* (London, 1940); B. Fine, *Marx's Capital* (London, 1975); P. Garegnani, *Marx e gli economisti classici* (Turin, 1981); P. Groenewegen, 'Marx's Conception of Classical Political Economy', *Political Economy*, 3 (1987); M. C. Howard and J. E. King, *The Political Economy of Marx* (Harlow, 1975); M. Lippi, *Value and Naturalism in Marx* (London, 1979); E. Mandel, *The Formation of the Economic Thought of Karl Marx*, trans. Brian Pearce (Ann Arbor, Mich., 1971); K. Marx, *Grundrisse* (Harmondsworth, 1973); W. Murray, *A Reappraisal of Marxist Economics* (New York, 1966); J. V. Robinson, *An Essay on Marxian Economics* (London, 1942); E. Screpanti, *Equilibrio e crisi nell'economia capitalistica: Un saggio sulla dinamica marxiana* (Rome, 1984); I. Steedman, *Marx after Sraffa* (London, 1977); P. M. Sweezy, *The Theory of Capitalist Development* (New York, 1956).

5

The Triumph of Utilitarianism and the Marginalist Revolution

5.1. THE MARGINALIST REVOLUTION

5.1.1. The 'climax' of the 1870s and 1880s

The quarter century from the early 1870s was a period of contradictions. On the one hand, there was a continuation or, rather, an intensification, of the process of deep structural change, which had begun during the preceding 20 years; on the other, economic difficulties of various kinds and intensity appeared that looked like the first signs of a general crisis of the capitalist system, and that made many observers speak of a 'Great Depression'.

Growth proceeded at different rates in different countries, but was everywhere accompanied by a marked increase in the concentration of capital, with a spread of collusive practices, mergers, and the formation of cartels, all factors that produced a general growth in oligopolistic power. This process was encouraged by great changes in productive techniques, which caused remarkable increases in the size of plant, especially in the mechanical, iron and steel, transport, and communications industries. Besides this, the organizational form of the limited company consolidated its position and became the privileged instrument for the mobilization and control of the huge amounts of capital needed for growth.

Social relations, in this context, began to structure themselves by taking on two different configurations in the factory and in society. Inside the firms, especially the large ones, the relations among individuals assumed a hierarchical and bureaucratized form, and this led to the first attempts at 'personnel management' and the first formulations of 'management science'. In society as a whole, on the other hand, class conflict sharpened dramatically and began to assume the form of a direct battle between powerful political and union groups capable of mobilizing vast social masses on the one side and hardened economic-interest groups on the other. In section 5.1.4 we shall say more about the widespread explosion of social conflict and the effects it produced on the moods of the dominant classes.

The unequal development of various countries also produced fiercer international competitiveness, not only in prices and technology but also in the organizational models of the firm and the national economy. This provoked both the slow decline of English industrial leadership and increased difficulties in international co-ordination, especially in capital markets. In fact, this was also a period of financial instability: serious financial crises occurred in various capitalist countries in 1873, 1882, 1890, and 1893. The English banking system, which tended to play the role of international lender of last resort, had great difficulty in keeping the situation under control, and often failed. The effects of these crises were aggravated, in many European countries, by those produced by a long agricultural depression, a depression which had been caused by the competition of American corn and which had produced a reduction in the prices of agricultural products and the incomes of the still large agricultural classes.

This was also a period of a world-wide reduction in prices and a slow-down in the growth of international trade—phenomena that should be considered in connection both with the deflationary impulses generated by the adoption of the Gold Standard by the main capitalist countries and with the increase in international competitiveness mentioned above. Nor should we forget the general movement away from the free-trade trend which had been so strong in the preceding 20 years, and the concomitant emergence of widespread attempts at protectionism. Finally, the national product grew in all countries through the storms of marked short-run business cycles. On the other hand, the long-run growth trend was weaker everywhere than in the successive 20 years (the *Belle époque*) and in most countries it was weaker even than the preceding 20 years. It is this phenomenon above all that has led some scholars to speak of a Great Depression. And if the relevance of such a point of view has been questioned by other scholars, especially by those who observed at the performances of the newly emerging powers, we should not forget that in Germany the *Grosse Depression* is usually associated with the *Bismarckzeit*, precisely the period we are studying here.

Let us return to economic thought. Three important books were published at the beginnings of the 1870s: *The Theory of Political Economy* (1871) by William Stanley Jevons (1835–82), the *Grundsätze der Volkwirtschaftslehre* (*Fundamental Principles of Political Economy*) (1871) by Carl Menger (1840–1921), and the *Éléments d'économie politique pure* (*Elements of Pure Political Economy*) (volume i in 1874 and volume ii in 1877) by Léon Walras (1834–1910): three books which marked the beginning of what was later to be called the 'marginalist revolution'. These books are so different that any attempt to group them could seem daring. In fact, they had various fundamental things in common, but time was needed to realize this. Contemporary thinkers not only did not notice it, but hardly noticed the three books at all—or, as in the case of the *Theory*, they fiercely criticized it. It seemed that these authors were to meet the same cruel fate of other great heretics and forerunners. In effect, there was an almost complete silence for a decade. The time was still not ripe for the new message to be received and appreciated. Then suddenly, in the 1880s and the first half of the 1890s, the revolution exploded. Marshall, Edgeworth, and Wicksteed in England, Wieser and Böhn-Bawerk in Austria,

Pantaleoni in Italy, and Cassel and Wicksell in Sweden all published fundamental works in the spirit of the new way of doing economic science. The revolution was completed in a decade. In the following 30 years the theories were refined and generalized. But, by this time, the old classical system was dead and buried, a new orthodoxy had asserted itself, and even if certain differences between the national schools were to last a long time, it had become clear to everybody that all over the world a single science was being studied and one language spoken; the neoclassical system had imposed itself. We will discuss this in the next chapter.

This chapter will be dedicated to the three founding fathers of marginalism, and to the meaning of the revolution begun by them. First of all, however, it is necessary to turn away from history so as to be able to give a summary of the neoclassical system and to point out some of its distinctive characteristics. Even if some elements of this picture were only to appear much later, it may be useful, in order to understand the meaning of the revolution in the 1870s and 1880s, to consider where it was all going to lead.

5.1.2. The neoclassical theoretical system

One characteristic of the new system which was apparent from the beginning was the disappearance of interest in economic growth, the great theme of the economic theories of Smith, Ricardo, Marx, and all the classical economists. Attention, instead, was focused on the problem of the allocation of *given* resources. Certainly, the basic ideas of the classical economists concerning the problem of growth continued to be influential. In lesson 36 of the *Elements*, for example, Walras put forward a theory of economic evolution that could still be considered Ricardian. The same could be said, to give another example, of the process of 'growth of wealth' described by Marshall in his *Principles*. But it is a fact that, in spite of the presence, here and there, of considerations concerning the dynamics of economic systems, the founders of the neoclassical theoretical system basically did not consider the problem of discovering the forces that determine the evolution of industrial economies. The central argument of the theoretical research in this period was the study of a static equilibrium system, that is, an economy, as J. B. Clark was to say later, 'free to find the final levels of equilibrium determined by the factors available at any given moment of time' (*The Distribution of Wealth* (1899), p. 29).

At the centre of the neoclassical system is the problem of the allocation of *given* resources among alternative uses.

In the analysis of the conditions ensuring the optimal allocation of given resources among alternative uses, the neoclassical economists identified a universally valid principle, one which was able, alone, to embrace the entire economic reality. As Robbins said: 'Scarcity of means to satisfy ends of varying importance is an almost ubiquitous condition of human behaviour. Here, then, is the unity of subject of Economic Science, the forms assumed by human behaviour in disposing of scarce means' (*An Essay on the Nature and Significance of Economic Science* (London, 1935), p. 15). The tendency to extend the basic model to every branch of economic investigation was reinforced during the course of the century until it culminated in the argument of P. A. Samuelson that there is a simple principle at the heart of all economic problems: a mathematical function to maximize under constraints.

Another characteristic that unites the three founding fathers, and one which was to remain a pillar of the neoclassical system, is their acceptance of the utilitarian approach; an approach which numbered among its forerunners Galiani, Beccaria, Bentham, Say, Senior, Bastiat, Cournot, and, above all, Gossen. In fact, the most important theoretical contribution of Jevons, Menger, and Walras lies, still more than in their complete and coherent reformulation of the utility theory of value and in the hypothesis of decreasing marginal utility, in the way they modified the utilitarian foundation of political economy. Their marginalism gave credit to a special version of utilitarian philosophy, one for which human behaviour is exclusively reducible to rational calculation aimed at the maximization of utility. They considered this principle to be universally valid: alone, it would have allowed the understanding of the entire economic reality. In this, above all, lies the revolutionary aspect of the new economic theories and not so much, as some people still maintain, in the argument that the prices of goods are determined by utility.

A third distinctive element relates to the method. The neoclassical method is based on the principle of the variation of proportions, the so-called 'substitution principle', a method which has no equivalent in classical economics. In the theory of consumption, the substitutability of one basket of goods for another is assumed; in the theory of production, the substitutability of one combination of factors for another. The analysis is carried out in terms of the alternative possibilities among which the subjects, both consumers and producers, can choose. And the objective is the same: to search for the conditions under which the optimal alternative is chosen. This method presupposes that the alternatives at stake are 'open' and that the decisions taken are *reversible*; otherwise, the substitution principle would have no rational ground.

A fourth distinctive characteristic of the neoclassical approach concerns the economic agents. If they have to be subjects able to make rational decisions with a view to maximizing an individual goal, such as utility or profit, they must be individuals, or, at the most, 'minimum' social aggregates characterized by the individuality of the decision-making unit, such as households and companies. Thus the collective agents, the social classes and 'political bodies', which the mercantilists, the classical economists, and Marx had placed at the centre of their theoretical systems, disappear from the scene.

A fifth characteristic is represented by the final attainment of an objective to which many classical economists had aspired but which nobody had ever realized completely: the historicity of economic laws. Economics was likened to the natural sciences, physics in particular, and economic laws finally assumed that absolute and objective characteristic of natural laws. The eternal nature of the problem posed by the neoclassical economists, the problem of scarcity, establishes the universal validity of the economic laws. But for this to make sense, it is necessary to remove social relations from the field of economics, exorcizing them as a superstition, a waste of time, a subject not in line with the new acquisitions of the science of the period. With the marginalist revolution also originated that reductionist project of economics which has marked all the successive neoclassical thought, a project according to which economics has no other field of research than technical relationships (the relationships between man and nature). Thus, while individualistic reductionism had led to the elimination of social classes, the anti-historicist reduction led to the elimination of social relations—which obviously meant that the study of their change also lost importance. While in the work of the classical economists and Marx the analytical apparatus was constructed with explicit reference to the capitalistic system whose laws of movement they wished to investigate, the neoclassical paradigm aimed for a complete historicity. Naturally, this was not easy to achieve. Even Walras, for example, had to use notions such as capital, interest, entrepreneur, wages—notions which make sense only in reference to the capitalist system.

Finally, a sixth important distinctive element of the neoclassical system lies in the substitution for the objective theory of value of a subjective one. At the base of the principle of subjective value is the argument that all values are individual and subjective. 'Individual' means that they are considered always as the ends of particular individuals. On the other hand, values are 'subjective' in that they arise from a process of choice: an object has value if it is desired by a subject. The principle of subjectivity implies that a value is such because somebody has chosen it as an end; whereas the principle of individuality postulates that there must be a particular individual to which that end can be attributed. In the opposite conception, that of objective value, values exist independently of individual choices. The individual can accept or reject values but he is not able to establish their cogency. An immediate and important consequence of the neoclassical approach in regard to the question of value is that the theory of the distribution of income becomes a special case of the theory of value, a problem of determining the prices of the services of the productive factors rather than of sharing out income among the social classes.

5.1.3. Was it a real revolution?

One of the most important problems posed by the marginalist revolution for the historian of ideas is whether it was a real revolution. That name, 'neoclassical system', which is now given to the theoretical system originated from the marginalist revolution, seems to prove right those who argue continuity with the preceding 'classical' theoretical system. But is the name correct? It is useful to begin precisely with this problem.

It was Marx who identified the classical theoretical system. As already mentioned, he was extremely rigorous in defining the approach and very selective in labelling the economists. The yardstick was Ricardo, but Marx went back as far as Petty and Boisguillebert to find the origins of the classical system. On the basis of his measure, the English anti-Ricardians were not considered classical, while Malthus and Say were to be taken *cum grano salis*; and even Smith was accused of a few 'vulgar notions'.

Instead, the definition of 'neoclassical system' originated with reference to the work of Marshall, from which it spread to embrace the whole of modern orthodox theory; and it is an independent definition from the Marxian one of classical economics. Marshall wished to stress the continuity of a tradition which linked him to Mill and Smith without excluding Ricardo; and he endeavoured to ignore the considerable heterogeneity of Ricardian economics with respect to that tradition.

On the other hand, the anti-Ricardian character of the marginalist revolution was extremely clear to Jevons; and there is no doubt that, if the theoretical system that originated from the revolution had been named with reference to his work, it would have been called 'anti-classical' rather than 'neoclassical'.

Now, if Marshall had been correct in rejecting any element of discontinuity between the two theoretical systems, those modern historians who deny the existence of the marginalist revolution would also be right. The idea of these historians is that, on the Continent, marginalism can be traced back, with no substantial epistemological break, to the 'classical' traditions, such as that uniting Say to Bastiat, without excluding Dupuit and Cournot, in France, or that uniting Lotz and Soden to the 'German Manchester School', without excluding von Thünen and Gossen, in Germany, or finally that uniting Galiani to Ferrara, in Italy.

England, on the other hand, would be taken as a special case. Here a particular version of the classical system developed, in the form of Ricardianism, which in a certain sense would have justified Jevons's claims of making a revolution. But then, *ex post*, Marshall turned out to be right in his rejection of the idea of a qualitative jump. Paradoxically, with this interpretation Marshall is credited with leading England out of its insularity.

But things are not exactly like this. The true precursors and founders of marginalism were not completely integrated into the classical traditions, but instead were outcasts condemned to the edges of the academic circles which cultivated orthodox theories. This is just as true for England as for the Continent (with the exception of Italy), as demonstrated by the fact not only that Jevons identified the enemy in the 'noxious influence of the authority' of Smith, Ricardo, the two Mills, Fawcett, etc., but also that Walras violently attacked Smith, Ricardo, and Mill, and when he showed a little appreciation for Say he quickly raised some qualifications (opposite to those of Marx). And both Jevons and Walras were aware that, when they paid tribute to Senior and Gossen, they were dealing with heretics.

In reality, in the orthodox pre-marginalist economic theories, from Smith and Say to Mill and to the theorists of economic harmonies, classical economic thought had evolved while preserving intact the Smithian theoretical dualism. The methodology of aggregates remained anchored to an explanation of production and distribution based on the social classes, and to a theory of value based on the costs of production; whereas microeconomic methodology remained linked to a theory of the competitive equilibrium based on the rationality, in the utilitarian sense, of individual choices. The two approaches continued to develop together for almost a century after Smith, remaining intertwined in more or less awkward ways. Ricardo had made his revolution, trying to free the former from the latter. The marginalists did the opposite. Their revolution consisted in this: they freed microeconomics, understood as a theory of rational individual choices, from classical macroeconomics. It was a revolution not only against Ricardo, but against all that was present in a confused way in the work of the other classical economists and which Ricardo had tried to bring to light. In other words, the 'classical' tradition, of which the neoclassical system proposed itself as a continuation, basically consisted in that Benthamian component which was partially already present in Smith, and later taken up again by the anti-Ricardians and by Mill; a component that Marx, instead, on the ground of the Ricardian criticisms of Smith, had defined as 'vulgar', i.e. non-classical. It was against Marx's classical economics that the marginalists made a revolution, not against that of Mill.

So different is the neoclassical theoretical system from the classical one (in the Marxian sense) that the revolution even led to a modification in the name itself of economic science, which from 1879 (at least in the Anglo-Saxon world) began to be called 'economics' rather than 'political economy'. The new term had been used sporadically in the preceding 40 years, but in 1877 and 1878 it even appeared in the titles of books by J. M. Sturtevant and by H. D. Macleod. Subsequently, Marshall and Jevons explicitly proposed it as a more serious and scientific substitute for the old term 'political economy'.

Jevons dealt with this matter in the second edition (1879) of his *Theory of Political Economy*. His proposal to substitute economics for political economy was motivated by an economic reason, one could say: one word is better than two. Later, however, phrases slipped out which reveal an inferiority complex, or spirit of emulation, in relation to mathematics. On the other hand, Jevons felt it was important to make it clear that his aspiration was to give a new name to 'a science that almost a century ago was known to French economists as *science économique*' (p. 18).

Marshall had much clearer ideas on this point. In *The Economics of Industry* (1879), written in collaboration with his wife, Mary, he explained his motivations for the change of name by putting forward the view that economics has nothing to do with political bodies and particular political interests. These are in fact two different motivations: one explicit, concerned with avoiding confusing the science with vested interests; the other implicit, but deeper, which was only later to emerge clearly, as the neoclassical system began to differentiate itself from the classical system: to avoid relating the science to 'political' or 'collective' bodies. This second reason turned into the refusal to recognize the behaviour of collective economic agents as the subject of study of economics.

As already mentioned, the study of collective agents was precisely the feature adopted by the mercantilists to found their science: no longer (domestic) economy, but *political economy*; no longer the administration of the household, but that of the State; no longer the study of the causes of the enrichment of the individuals, but that of the nation, the people, and the merchant class. It is significant that, by rejecting the 'political' nature of economics, the neoclassical economists were once more conceiving of this science as one that has to do with the *domestic* economy. In fact, it still deals with the maximization of the welfare of the household, or of the profits of the firm, which are, in fact, individual economic agents.

5.1.4. The reasons for success

Another problem the marginalist revolution poses to the historians of economic thought concerns the reasons why it occurred at that historical moment. Why not at the time of Senior, Longfield, Dupuit, Cournot, and von Thünen? And why did Jevons, Menger, and Walras not remain ingenious heretics at the edges of the academic world, as seemed to be occurring in the ten years after the publication of their works? Why was there, in the 1880s, a second generation of marginalists who gave that heresy the power of a revolutionary wave? The correct way to pose the problem of the historical sense of the marginalist revolution seems to be this: it is not the problem of finding the reasons why the fundamental works of the three great neoclassical economists were published in the early 1870s, but rather of understanding why, in a period of a few years, the message contained in those works was accepted as the 'New Testament' by the majority of the economists who counted. It is possible, with some simplification, to put forward two kinds of reason: one 'internal', the other 'external'.

The first concerns the inability of the classical orthodoxy to solve a series of theoretical problems. The labour theory of value had never been watertight, and the Ricardians' attempts to escape from the difficulties with a theory of the cost of production had only made matters worse, inducing Mill to open cracks which the marginalists had no difficulty penetrating with their corrosive criticisms. But here, generalizations were more damaging than criticisms. For example, Jevons argued that the cases of joint production, which Mill considered to be exceptions to the theory of value based on the cost of production, in fact constituted the general case. Marshall, instead, had tried to generalize the case of the goods whose production could not be increased without an increase in cost. The labour theory of value, by this time, was really only defended by Marx. Marx's version of the theory was in fact rather refined, but this did not avoid some broadsides from the neoclassical economists, as we will see later. And the weak defence set up by the Marxists (such as Hilferding) served only to discredit the theory finally, so that it lost any residue of scientific decorum.

Furthermore, the classical economists had not managed to produce a satisfactory theory of income distribution. This was a serious flaw, as the theory of distribution made up the core of the classical economic theory. The principal difficulty concerned the theory of wages, on which the whole structure was built. Once the argument is discarded that wages are forced down to the subsistence level through the operation of Malthus' population mechanism, the whole theory collapses. This was precisely one of Jevons's criticisms. On the other hand, the road taken by the Ricardians to escape from this difficulty was the theory of the wages fund, and this was even weaker and less defensible than Ricardo's own theory. It was again Jevons and Walras who put salt in the wound, by showing that the theory of the wages fund was tautological (in the best of cases) and logically inconsistent (in the worst, which were, in fact, the most widespread interpretations).

But all this is not enough to explain the success of the marginalist revolution and its rapid conquest of hegemony. The 'external' reasons are perhaps even more important than the internal ones. For some time, the Ricardian theory had been used for critical purposes by the socialist economists. In particular, the theory of surplus had been used as a foundation for a theory of capitalist exploitation. We have already mentioned that in the 1830s the 'anti-Ricardian' economists had been motivated, in their criticism of Ricardianism, by their intention to attack socialist theories. Forty years later, things were still the same. Jevons had little difficulty in linking himself to the English anti-Ricardian tradition. Walras was even more explicit when, in regard to the theory of interest, he noted: 'It has been a favourite target for socialists; and the answer which economists have given to these attacks has not, up to the present, been overwhelmingly convincing' (p. 422).

From the 1870s onwards, theoretical socialism rapidly tended to identify itself with Marxism, and unhesitatingly advanced strong claims to be a scientific theory. It was exactly against such claims that some of the second- and third-generation marginalists launched their attacks. We will limit ourselves here to mentioning the powerful 'Jevonian' attack that Wicksteed brought to bear on the Marxian theory of value in '*Das Kapital*: A Criticism' (in *To-Day*, 1884), and the even harsher one attempted by Böhn-Bawerk in *Kapital und Kapitalzins* (*Capital and Interest*) (1884–9) and in *Zum Abschluss des Marxischen Systems* (*Karl Marx and the Close of his System*) (1896). But in 1893 Pareto was already looking at the matter with more 'detachment', convinced that 'the criticism of Karl Marx no longer needed to be made', as it was by that time implicit 'in the improvements brought by political economy to the theory of value' (p. 141).

In order that the criticisms of socialism, and of Marxism in particular, should not seem too ideological, it was necessary to focus on their scientific foundations. But these were the same as those of classical economic theory. It was necessary, therefore, to 're-invent' economic science, reconstructing it on a foundation which would allow the deletion of the concepts themselves of 'social class', 'labour power', 'capitalism', 'exploitation', 'surplus', etc. from the body of the science. The theory of marginal utility provided the solution. Moreover, it seemed that it would permit the demonstration that an almost perfect kind of social organization would be realized in a competitive economy; a kind of organization in which the market rules would allow an optimum allocation to be reached and, with it, the harmony of interests and the maximization of individual objectives.

On the other hand, the resumption of a sharp and endemic social conflict made academic communities and political and cultural circles particularly receptive to the new theory. The first Workers' International was inaugurated in London in 1864, held its most important congresses in various European capitals between 1866 and 1872, and disbanded in Philadelphia in 1876. But then, in 1889 the 2nd International was founded in Paris, and this was much more fearsome and strongly influenced by Marxism. These aggregation processes of the revolutionary organizations were driven along by the powerful resumption of the workers' struggle in all the advanced capitalist countries. The period from 1868 until the mid-1870s was characterized by sharp conflict, almost as if all the repressed anger of the preceding twenty years of peace had exploded at the same time. The Paris Commune was only the tip of the iceberg of a movement which was much more widespread and longer-lasting. And the violent repressions which followed these international explosions (1872–3 in France, 1873–4 in Great Britain and Germany, 1877 in the USA and Italy) had only temporary effects. The conflict began to manifest itself again, in more or less acute forms, during the 1880s, and continued for about half the following decade.

There is thus no doubt that, when Jevons, Menger, and Walras presented a theory capable of averting attention completely from unpleasant problems, they were launching onto the market exactly the theory that was demanded. In the 1880s and 1890s, that demand was so strong that no marginalist economist had to worry about remaining on the edges of the cultural and academic worlds. A strange but eloquent fact is worth noting here. Gossen's 1854 book, which had anticipated many of the results of the marginalist revolution, had been a total publishing failure. Gossen died in 1858 with no glory. But 30 years later, a discerning Berlin publisher reprinted the book with a brief preface and a new date: 1889. It was an extraordinary success. Another curious insight, which, if nothing else, tells us a great deal about the state of mind with which the marginalists set about constructing a value-free science, was given in a letter from Auguste Walras to his son Léon on 6 February 1859:

One thing which I find most satisfying about your work plan, and with which I am in complete agreement, is your decision to keep within the most inoffensive limits with regards to proprietors. It is a wise decision and easy enough to implement. One should dedicate oneself to political economy as one would to the science of acoustics or mechanics (quoted in Leroy, *Auguste Walras*, p. 289).

Finally, it is worth observing that marginalism, while presenting itself as an alternative to the classical approach at the level of economic theory, preserved the basic philosophy of the latter on at least one essential question. Jevons, Menger, and Walras, and the vast majority of the marginalists of the following generations, were fervent supporters of *laissez-faire*. Certainly, while classical *laissez-faire* had focused on the problem of accumulation, neoclassical *laissez-faire* was orientated more towards the problem of allocative efficiency. The most advanced capitalist countries had by this time solved the problem of industrial take-off, so that the needs of accumulation were no longer felt in the terms in which they had been perceived by Smith. On the other hand, the 1870s and 1880s were marked by the 'Great Depression', the first great demonstration of the inability of capitalism to defeat the anarchy of the market. We should not be surprised, therefore, by the great success of a theory proving that the market, far from being anarchical, is the best allocator of resources, and that, if things do not work well, it is precisely because the 'workers' coalitions' hinder the functioning of the market.

5.2. WILLIAM STANLEY JEVONS

5.2.1. Logical calculus in economics

In 1874, after many years of work, Jevons published *The Principles of Science*, a powerful treatise on formal logic and scientific method destined to replace J. S. Mill's *System of Logic* (1843), a work Jevons attacked as 'an extraordinary tissue of self-contradictions'. Even though, in the *Principles*, Jevons did not intend to concern himself with the applications to the social sciences, the ideas, and above all the logical-analytical tools, that he developed there constituted the spool around which the whole of his economic works are wound. It is possible, therefore, to read in the *Theory* that economics belongs to the class of sciences which '*besides being logical, are also mathematical*' (p. 80), and that '*our science must be mathematical simply because it deals with quantities*' (p. 78).

In terms of economic theory, Jevons explicitly linked himself to Bentham. He wrote in the preface of the *Theory* that Bentham's ideas were 'the starting point of the theory given in this work' (p. 44) and later: 'In this work I have attempted to treat economy as a calculus of pleasure and pain, and I have sketched out . . . the form which the science . . . must ultimately take' (p. 44). These premises brought him to the conclusion that 'value depends entirely on utility' (p. 77), a point of view which is the opposite to that adopted by most of the classical authors. Here value stands for price. The starting-point for Jevons's analysis is the exchange process. Only two characteristics define individuals as economic agents: that subjects derive utility from the consumption of goods, and that the economic agent acts on the basis of a rational plan aiming at the maximization of utility. 'To satisfy our wants to the utmost with the least effort . . . in other words to *maximize pleasure*, is the problem of economics' (p. 101).

Jevons considered utility not as an intrinsic quality of an object but as the sum of pleasures its use allows. This meaning of 'utility' had begun to be fairly widely accepted quite a while before Jevons; it is even to be found in Bentham, who uses the term in the sense both of a physical and of a psychological attribute.

It is difficult to say whether Jevons, who had a deep knowledge of Bentham's works, was aware of this ambiguity; but it is a fact that, by giving an old term a new meaning, he contributed to the creation of a troublesome source of confusion. The confusion is particularly evident in the way in which Jevons faces the questions of the measurement and comparison of utility. On the one hand are assertions such as 'I see no means by which such comparison can be accomplished. . . . Every mind is thus inscrutable to every other mind, and no common denominator of feeling seems to be possible' (p. 85). On the other hand are several passages in which Jevons expresses the opposite view, that utility is a quantity which can be measured in a cardinal sense. We will see later which and how many problems were caused by this ambiguity.

Naturally, Jevons did not overlook production and the accumulation of capital; but when dealing with questions relating to these subjects he adopted the same conceptual apparatus and, above all, the same base orientation he had used for the theory of exchange. The essential element of his contribution to this subject is his special interpretation of the law of decreasing returns, an interpretation he put forward in his treatment of rent in Chapter 4 of the *Theory*.

In studying agricultural production, Ricardo had observed that on a given plot of land it is possible to employ alternative quantities of labour assisted by other inputs, agricultural equipment, fertilizers, and so on. Ricardo specified that it was possible to vary the proportions in which land and 'assisted labour' (i.e. labour plus capital) are employed. In this way he reached the following law (which had, however, already been formulated by Turgot): the increases in production resulting from the use of successive doses of assisted labour on the same quantity of cultivated land will first increase and then decrease.

Jevons introduced two subtle changes into the usual interpretation of the law. First, he downgraded the distinction between the extensive and the intensive case, emphasizing the latter. The classical economists, who were rather more interested in the explanation of rent than that of the prices of goods, had focused more on the *extensive* case. The *intensive* case had also been considered by them, but not without reserve—for the simple reason that, while the different productivities of plots of different quality are directly observable, the marginal productivity of a dose of input implies a change in the situation to be observed, and therefore only represents a hypothetical increase in output.

Second, the shift of interest towards the intensive case also led to an important change in the method of analysis: the reasoning had to be undertaken in terms of hypothetical rather than observable changes, and this contributed to giving credit to the thesis of symmetry between land and the other inputs. Two important consequences were derived from this thesis:

(1) The substitutability between land and assisted labour was extended from agricultural production to all types of production, even to those with no direct input of land.

(2) The substitutability was extended to all inputs, whereas for the classical economists the substitutability between land and assisted labour presupposed a strict complementarity between labour and equipment.

A final point should be mentioned. Jevons dedicated a great deal of attention to the problems of economic policy and, in particular, to the questions of social policy. In his last book, *The State in Relation to Labour* (1882), and in the collection of articles published posthumously in 1883 with the title *Methods of Social Reform*, he expressly indicated the principles that, according to him, should have guided State intervention in the economy. It is not surprising, given his starting-point, that Jevons arrived at the conclusion that the natural state of a market economy is social harmony and not class conflict. 'The supposed conflict between labour and capital is an illusion', he wrote in *The State in Relation to Labour* (p. 98); and then, appealing to a rather unclear notion of 'universal brotherhood', added: 'we ought not to look at such subjects from a class point of view, [since] in economics at any rate [we] should regard all men as brothers' (p. 104). Jevons admitted that 'workers are not the capitalists of themselves' and that this increases the complexity of the problem, since the capitalists 'come to represent a distinct interest'. However, he maintained that competition would resolve the possible conflict of interests between the two sides, as it would cause capital to be solely remunerated at the market rate of interest, while the worker would receive, in the last instance, only 'the value that he has produced'. We will see in the next chapter how this argument was taken up and developed by J. B. Clark.

Jevons's attitude towards trade unions is interesting—a severely critical attitude but not thoroughly hostile. On the one hand, he approved of the idea of trade unions acting as friendly societies in the search for better conditions for their own members; on the other, he fiercely opposed any attempt to fix wages by collective bargaining, because this would have destroyed the competitive mechanism. It was the acceptance of these two principles that led Jevons to the naïve conclusion that workers who wish to reduce their hours of work should also demand a lower wage.

Jevons obviously criticized the Ricardian theory of the inverse relationship between profits and wages as 'radically fallacious', wishing in this way to demolish the theoretical foundation of class struggle. The *Theory* is full of condemnations of Ricardo and Mill. For example: 'that able but wrong-headed man, David Ricardo, shunted the car of economic science on to a wrong line—a line, however, on which it was further urged towards confusion by his equally able and wrong-headed admirer, John Stuart Mill'. On the other hand, the book is full of praise for Malthus, Say, Senior, and Bastiat.

5.2.2. *Wages and labour, interest and capital*

Jevons's theory of the determination of the labour supply is also based on the utilititarian foundations of the theory of choice. This aspect of his analysis is one of his most notable achievements. And if it is true that it has contributed to placing Jevons in the top bracket of the 'great' figures of marginalism, it is also true that it has led to a certain undervaluation of his analyses of capital and interest, analyses which are often seen as a mere by-product of the 'grand theory' of choice. However, this opinion is, at least in part, unfounded.

The theory of the labour supply is based on the assertion that labour, both manual and intellectual, is an 'unpleasant' activity for the individual, and is undertaken only because of the greater consumption it allows. This observation may hold a grain of truth, but even today it appears, to a disenchanted eye, anything but evident outside the utilitarian framework in which it was conceived.

In Jevons's theory, the sign of the marginal utility of labour is very clear: work gives *dis*utility or negative utility, and in particular a disutility increasing with the amount of labour supplied. Jevons added to this hypothesis another, equally strong one: the worker acts autonomously, works with his own means of production, and does not depend on the employer; which implies, among other things, that the amount of labour supply is infinitely divisible and not subject to discrete changes, as is the case with dependent labour, where a contract normally fixes the hours of work. The hypothesis of infinite divisibility is essential for the application of marginal calculus, which requires infinitesimal increases of the quantities. Well aware of the 'power' and, therefore, the inevitable limits of his hypotheses, Jevons distinguished between the subjective productivity of labour, which is measured in terms of the 'psycho-physical potential' used by the worker in his activity, and the objective productivity, measured in terms of the hours worked. Obviously, the former allows for the *qualitative* differences of labour in terms of psycho-physical effort to be taken into account, but makes it impossible to measure them at an operational level; the latter, on the contrary, requires the qualitative *uniformity* of labour and has the advantage of measurability.

On the basis of these hypotheses, the application of marginal calculus produces the result that the quantity of work supplied is that for which the marginal benefit derived from the remuneration of labour equals its marginal disutility. The most interesting case is the one in which an individual is able to produce more than one good. Here it is necessary that the individual earns the same marginal benefit from each activity, and consequently that he receives the same marginal disutility from each of these. But this implies that, at least in the long run, individuals will tend to exchange goods according to a ratio equivalent to that of the marginal productivities. In the long run these should level themselves out, so that *all* the individuals who are working in a certain trade continue to do so. Such productivities must also be expressed in *subjective* terms. In this, the condition of equal marginal disutilities in the different occupations becomes an important link between the utilitarian theory of exchange and the theory of labour supply.

The mere *formal* reference to the rules of marginal calculus is not enough to make Jevons's theory a 'marginalist theory' in the deepest sense. It is known that the basic hypothesis under which marginal calculus is applicable to labour supply is that the level of utilization of all the factors of production other than labour is kept constant. Thus, it is necessary to clarify the role played by the other factors of production in Jevons's system. By doing this, one may discover that the widespread idea that Jevons's theory of capital is only a by-product of his theory of the labour supply is, in fact, unfounded.

Let us first consider the case of land, already mentioned in the previous section. Is it possible to determine rent as the remuneration of a productive activity, according to the marginalist principle, under the hypothesis of constancy of the level of utilization of the other factors? To be rigorous, the extensive case should be considered in which the amount of cultivated land is progressively increased. Jevons did deal with this case; but he focused more on the intensive case, in which the increasing amount of a given factor, labour, for example, is applied to a fixed plot of land. The intensive case represents a type of 'proof' of the theory of the labour supply, in that it constitutes an application of it.

Now, as long as land has no alternative uses, Jevons's theory works perfectly: the law of decreasing returns implies that labour will exhibit a decreasing productivity as a function of the intensity of its application. Since all labour is remunerated on the basis of the disutility of the last dose applied, a surplus will arise over the preceding doses, whose productivity is higher and disutility lower; and this surplus, to the degree to which the worker is also the landowner, is resolved in rent. In this way the theory appears to be coherent with the preceding one: intensive rent is explained in terms of the productivity of labour. But what happens when land has at least one alternative use?

In this case, the rent becomes an element of the cost of production, and this is in obvious contrast with the view of Ricardo and the other classical economists. In fact, in the preface to the *Theory* Jevons wrote: 'but when land capable of yielding rent in agriculture is applied to some other purpose, the rent which it would have yielded is an element in the cost of production of the commodity which it is employed to produce' (p. 70).

In other words, the opportunity cost of the use of land becomes an essential element in the definition of rent, and with this the theory of the labour supply is no longer sufficient to explain the level of rent. Another 'piece' of theory is necessary, one which is independent of the theory of the labour supply. And here the theory of capital appears on the scene.

Jevons considered capital, prima facie, as an aggregate of goods measured in monetary units. The role of capital in the productive process is, in the Austrian manner, that of making available an 'advance' to pay labour: the production process occurs over time and the workers are remunerated, at least in part, before the product is produced. Here Mill's influence is easy to see.

Jevons believed that an 'improvement' in the technical conditions coincides with a lengthening of the period of production—a 'proto-Austrian' view that was to become the target of many of the severest criticisms of Jevons's theory of capital. Jevons maintained that it is not the quantity of capital in itself which is remunerated, but rather the quantity of capital immobilized *for a given fraction of the period of production*; therefore a time element necessarily enters into the definition of the rate of interest. In Jevons's analysis, the cost of goods in which capital is embodied must be repaid over the period of their utilization. But how is this cost calculated? Jevons distinguishes between the amount of capital invested, (ACI) and the amount of the investment of capital (AIC). The former is the amount of 'free' capital, i.e. that which is not incorporated in goods; the latter is the product of ACI and the time for which it remains invested. If, for example, w is the total amount of wages paid for building a house and t the total investment time, then, assuming that labour is continually and uniformly distributed through time and using simple capitalization, Jevons's formula for capital is $AIC = wt/2$, and it is this magnitude that must be remunerated by interest.

Now, with simple capitalization, the average investment time, $t/2$, depends solely on the technical production conditions and is independent of the distribution of income. This means that the rate of interest, under this condition, can be expressed in terms of the average investment time. On the other hand, this is not so when compound capitalization is applied, as must be the case in a capitalist economy. It seems that Jevons was in fact aware of this problem, but he was unable to draw out the inevitable theoretical implications. The most important of these is that the marginal productivity of capital cannot be calculated as the increment of the product due to an increase in the employment of capital, when the latter is defined in the above way.

But here the problems really surface: if capital were a monetary magnitude, no difficulty would arise, since the increase in the use of capital in two different periods could be considered as a variation in a homogeneous quantity; in this case, however, it is difficult to see how a productivity could be attributed to it. On the other hand, to the extent to which capital is a monetization of an aggregate of real goods, its value depends on the price system and therefore on the level of interest that it should determine. It follows, in particular, that the value of capital depends on the distribution of income.

Thus Jevons's theoretical system, considered as a model of the operation of the whole economic system, cannot be considered acceptable. This should not be surprising, as the problems that tripped up Jevons were the same as those that have tripped up many of the better-equipped specialists of our century. The processes of logical assessment, even though difficult, are, after all, a problem of 'normal science'. It is in the 'laying of the path' that Jevons's genius emerged; and it is in these terms that his work should be evaluated.

5.2.3. English historical economics

The disintegration of classical political economy in the 1870s and 1880s is demonstrated by the fact that the marginalist criticisms of it were not isolated. In this period an increasing number of economists attacked the classical theoretical system, and this gave rise to a multiplicity of alternative theoretical directions: the socialists (of which we should remember, besides Marxism, Fabianism in England, 'agrarian socialism' in America, the 'Christian socialists' and 'chair socialists' in Germany), the institutionalists, and the historicists. Here we will focus on the last group. We will discuss Schmoller and the 'young German Historical School' later, when we will also show that the historicist polemic against Menger implied an attack on political economy *tout court*, rather than on the specific marginalist theoretical system. It was to economic science in general that the historicists attributed the vices of a historicity, deductiveness, abstraction, and one-sidedness.

It is interesting to note that in this period a similar attack was also taking place in England, the home of classical orthodoxy. The English historicists were less involved *en philosophe* than the Germans, but their criticisms were no less profound or radical. Strongly influenced by the Comtian idea of a unified social science, the English historical critics not only produced an excellent critical-methodological literature, but also opened up interesting avenues towards other fields of social research, especially sociology and economic history. We have already mentioned Richard Jones, a historicist who was a contemporary of Ricardo. Here we will consider the three most important English historicists of the following generation: Thomas Edward Cliffe Leslie (1826–88), John Kells Ingram (1823–1907), and William Cunningham (1840–1919).

Leslie greatly appreciated Smith's use of the inductive method; however, in various articles published between 1870 to 1879, and later collected together in a book, *Essays in Political and Moral Philosophy* (1879), he denied the universality of the so-called 'natural laws'. He also criticized the tendency to base economics on the simple assumption that individual behaviour is solely motivated by the thirst for wealth. Finally, he argued, acutely, that the whole of classical political economy presupposed two badly understood, yet fundamental, hypotheses: those known today as the hypotheses of complete information and perfect foresight. The validity of the classical arguments with regard to the uniformity of the rates of wages and profits, and therefore the validity of their theory of natural prices, are based on these hypotheses.

Turning to Ingram, his most important works are *The Present Position and Prospects of Political Economy*, presented to the British Association for the Advancement of Science in 1878, and *A History of Political Economy* (1893). Ingram argued that classical political economy was based on a type of abstract reasoning that completely ignores reality, as well as on an incorrect deductive method. Deduction, according to him, should be used only to check the results of induction and not to produce general theories from arbitrary assumptions. If they had used the correct method, the classical economists would have realized that their theories were valid only for a specific historical period.

Cunningham's criticisms of Marshall also took this direction. It is worth mentioning them here because they show a change of target from classical political economy to neoclassical economics. Obviously, the latter was much more deserving of historicist criticism than was the science of Smith and Mill. In one of his papers, significantly entitled *The Perversion of Economic History* (1892), Cunningham simply accused Marshall of using economic history in an incorrect way: not for acquiring knowledge by observing facts, but only for surreptitiously confirming truths obtained in a speculative way from a priori premises.

5.3. LÉON WALRAS

5.3.1. Walras's vision of the working of the economic system

The major contribution of Léon Walras (1834–1910) to economic analysis was his theory of the general economic equilibrium. Although the theme of the relationships among different markets had been studied by preceding theorists, no economist before Walras had managed to construct a general theoretical structure capable of accounting for the multiplicity of relationships linking one market to another. The actual operation of the forces of supply and demand in one market depend on the prices established in several other markets. This is why a general analysis is necessary.

The markets must be interrelated so as to make the choices of all the economic subjects compatible. A subject who is unable to achieve the goal of maximizing his satisfaction (or welfare) will have excess demands for some goods and excess supplies for others. By means of exchange, the individual will use the excess supplies to eliminate the excess demands. A state of general economic equilibrium is one in which the prices are such as to allow all individuals to maximize simultaneously their own objectives, with excess demand vanishing.

The free play of competition leads to a distribution of the factors among the productions of the various goods so as to satisfy the consumers' demands. The scarcity of productive resources in respect to the demand for goods will decisively influence relative prices. Walras rejected the classical, and especially the Ricardian, distinction between scarce and reproducible goods. He stated in the *Elements of Pure Economics*:

There are no products which can be multiplied without limit. All things which form part of social wealth . . . exist only in limited quantities . . . In the production of some things like fruit, wild animals, surface ores and mineral waters, land-services play the predominant part. In the production of other things like legal and medical services, professors' lectures, songs and dances, labour preponderates. In the production of most things, however, land-services, labour and capital services are found together. It follows, therefore, that all things constituting social wealth consist of land or personal faculties. Now Mill admits that land exists in limited quantities only. If that is also true of human faculties, how can products be multiplied without limit? (p. 399)

This passage, which is important for an understanding of the neoclassical concept of scarcity, shows a serious misunderstanding of the classical theory. In fact, Ricardo maintained that it is the single good that can be reproduced without limits, not the total of goods. The structure of the means of production, in other words, can be modified to produce any combination of products provided there is freedom of entry in all industries. Competition, intended as *a process* unfolding through time and not as a static situation in which the amount of each factor is fixed and unchangeable, will induce the capitalists to transfer their own capital from the sectors in which the rate of profit is low to those in which it is high. In this way the structure of supply will adjust to that of demand, while the quantities of capital goods will tend to settle at levels that guarantee a uniform profit rate.

In Walras's conception, the economy is made up of a plurality of agents who are present on the market either as consumers or as suppliers of productive services or as entrepreneurs. The economic process originates from the meeting, in the market, of these various agents. The productive services are transformed into goods which are bought, either by other entrepreneurs, who need them for productive uses, or by the final consumers. The latter, who have supplied the productive services to the entrepreneurs, buy produced goods from them by spending the income received in return for their productive services.

Clearly, there is no place in this model for the notion of social class. On the contrary, there are just two groups of individuals: the consumers and the entrepreneurs, distinguished solely by the different decisions they are called upon to take. The consumers decide on the composition and the level of consumption, and therefore on the level of savings; the entrepreneurs decide on the level and the composition of production and investment. The consumers' decisions do not depend on the type of income they receive, but only on the amount. The fact that an individual derives 80 per cent of his income from labour and 20 per cent from capital, or vice versa, makes no difference at all. There being no link between income categories and expenditure patterns, the links between wages and profits, on the one hand, and consumption and investment, on the other, are also cut.

At the beginning of each period, let us say one year, the economy has an initial endowment made up of a certain quantity of goods and resources, including natural resources and the goods produced in the preceding period. Each agent, at the beginning of the period, possesses a certain quantity of goods and services: as a worker he can offer a certain number of working hours, whilst as an entrepreneur he can supply services relating to the organization and control of the productive activity. Each agent tries to attain the best results from exchange. The consumer-savers try, in the first place, to determine that division of their own income between consumption and savings which will provide them with the ratio of maximum satisfaction between present and future consumption. Second, they determine the way in which their consumable income is to be shared out in the purchasing of various goods so as to obtain the maximum utility. Those who supply productive services try to obtain the best balance between the income received in payment for these services and the sacrifice involved in their supply. Finally, the entrepreneurs try to attain the maximum profit from their own activity, by endeavouring to maximize the difference between the value of the goods produced and the costs sustained in producing them.

The pursuit of their own individual objectives 'obliges' the agents to enter into exchange relationships. Let us consider first the single consumer. A part of the goods and services he consumes certainly comes from the initial endowment, but a larger part must be bought on the market. In exchange for this, he gives up money (or another means of payment) which, in turn, he gets back by selling other goods and services to other consumers and other firms. Thus, the consumer's income depends on the quantity of goods and services he sells to others and the price at which he manages to sell them. If we overlook the exchanges among consumers, we can say that they supply factors to the firms (labour, capital, and entrepreneurial ability) and receive in exchange an income which is either used to buy goods and services or stored as savings. The latter then returns to the firms through the activity of the financial intermediaries.

Let us now consider the firm. In order to fulfil its production plan, the firm uses, besides the reserves and stocks of fixed factors it already possesses at the beginning of the period, other inputs it buys from other firms and consumers. The output sold gives rise to revenues. The difference between revenues and costs represents the firm's profit, which is either distributed to the owners of the firm (i.e. to the savers-consumers) or used to buy new plant so as to increase the endowment in future periods. The total production of the system is obtained by summing the production of all the firms. Intermediate goods are clearly included in this amount. These are the goods produced by a firm and used by another (for example, the steel produced by a steel firm which is used by an engineering firm to produce a lathe). If the value of intermediate consumption is subtracted from the value of total production, the value of the final output (or the gross national product, in the terminology of national accounting) is obtained. Naturally, the value of the gross national product is equal to the value of the gross national income. In fact, if the value of the intermediate consumption is subtracted from the value of the production of the single firm, the result is the amount the firm has paid for the factors employed or, rather, the income earned from these factors. And, clearly, the sum of the incomes paid to the factors by all the firms gives us the overall income earned by all the factors.

The factors of production are the same as the stocks of goods, natural resources, and services that make up the initial endowment of the system. These are owned by the consumers or by the firms; but the firms are in turn owned by the consumers. This means that the consumers possess, directly or indirectly, all the factors, so that the final remunerations only go to them. If the profits of a firm are entirely distributed, and therefore are not stocked to provide for the needs of capital accumulation, the national income is the real purchasing power in the hands of the consumers.

5.3.2. General economic equilibrium

The central problem of Walras's theory is to show how the voluntary exchanges among individuals who are *well-informed* (each is perfectly aware of the terms of his own choices), *self-interested* (each thinks about himself), and *rational* (each tries to maximize his goals) will lead to a systematic organization of the production and the distribution of income which is *efficient and mutually beneficial*. The peculiarity of the problem is this: that the sole form of social interaction which is admitted is that realized on the market by means of voluntary exchanges. Neither trade unions nor pressure groups nor cartels nor other types of social groupings are allowed, as this would violate a fundamental requirement of the general-equilibrium model, that of perfect competition.

In order to account for the fact that the actions of the individual agents are co-ordinated on the market, it is necessary to demonstrate that prices exist that render advantageous to each individual precisely those activities and choices which satisfy his needs in an efficient way. This is why the theory of prices occupies a central position in the general-equilibrium system.

The prices are the parameters on the basis of which individual choices are made; but they are not independent of the choices themselves. On the other hand, a complex relationship is established between the prices of goods and the prices of factors. The former contributes to determining the *demand* prices of a factor used to produce goods. From the comparison between the supply price and the demand price, the market price of that factor is obtained. This, in turn, influences the supply price of the product and therefore its market price. So there is a well-articulated set of relationships between prices and quantities exchanged in regard both to inputs and to outputs. This set of relationships is in a state of general equilibrium when the prices and the quantities are such that the maximum satisfaction each agent pursues by his own choices is compatible with the maximum satisfaction pursued by all the other agents. More precisely, an economy is in a *Walrasian competitive equilibrium* when there is a set of prices such that:

(1) in each market the demand equals the supply;
(2) each agent is able to buy and sell exactly what he planned to do;
(3) all the firms and consumers are able to exchange precisely those quantities of goods which maximize, respectively, profits and utilities.

It is worth noting that, in order to obtain this result, it is only necessary to know, as initial data, the number of consumers, the number of firms, the initial endowments of resources, the consumers' preferences, and the techniques available. All the rest is left to the maximizing behaviour of the agents and to the competitive mechanism. In reality, however, two *dei ex machina* are necessary for the general equilibrium to be reached: the 'auctioneer' and the 'Sisyphus entrepreneur'. Let us see what this means.

The model of price-formation underlying Walras's theory of exchange is one of competitive bargaining. According to this model, markets are conceptualized as *auctions* (one is led to think of a French-type stock exchange), in which there are, on the one hand, stockbrokers and, on the other, the auctioneer. At the beginning of the bargaining the auctioneer 'shouts' a price vector (a price for each good) and leaves the agents to formulate their buying and selling proposals. If, in correspondence to the shouted prices, the auctioneer notices that, for each good, the supply and demand are equal, he will declare bargaining closed, and that price vector will be the equilibrium vector. If this does not happen, the auctioneer will adjust the prices according to the rule: increasing the prices of goods in excess demand and decreasing the prices of goods in excess supply. This trial and error process, which Walras called *tâtonnement*, will continue until all excesses of supply and demand have been eliminated. At this point the auction ends; the final quotations are registered as the equilibrium prices, and the supply and demand declared at such prices become binding contracts; exchanges are carried out on these terms. This is the *single-agreed-price* bargaining; the prices shouted by the auctioneer during the adjustment process are *virtual* prices; only the equilibrium ones are the prices at which exchanges actually take place. Thus, only by means of a *tâtonnement* process is it possible to reach a Walrasian general equilibrium. If, in fact, in the course of the process which leads up to the equilibrium price, the agents were allowed to exchange goods at disequilibrium prices, the individual's endowments would vary in continuation, and it would never be possible to reach a Walrasian equilibrium, which, by definition, refers to the given initial allocation of resources.

The Walrasian description of the operation of the economy uses the device of a 'ticket economy'. Walras was certainly aware of the marked institutional differences between his 'ticket economy' and a real market economy. His main objective was, however, to construct a model of an ideal economy, where social justice and the maximization of 'material welfare' were mutually compatible. He knew that this objective, while it could have been realized by his 'ticket economy', would certainly not have been possible in an authentic market economy. However, he nurtured the explicit hope that the latter could be reformed along the lines of the former.

Let us now turn to the 'Sisyphus entrepreneur'. Walras considered that a firm is in equilibrium when the profit is reduced to zero owing to the competition among entrepreneurs. In effect, in the Walrasian system there is only one category of maximizers: the consumers. The entrepreneurs, like the auctioneer, are mere co-ordinators who organize the productive activity, taking techniques and prices as given. The Walrasian entrepreneur buys the inputs at the prices fixed by the auctioneer, who looks after the adjustment process in the way described above. If the revenues are above the costs, the entrepreneur registers a profit. The existence of a profit or a loss is a sign of disequilibrium. The entrepreneur reacts to such a signal according to the rule: increase the scale of production when there is a profit and decrease it when there is a loss; 'Thus, in a state of equilibrium in production, entrepreneurs make neither profit nor loss', writes Walras (p. 225). Profit depends on exceptional circumstances; from a theoretical point of view it must simply be ignored.

Walras argued, therefore, that the choice to become an entrepreneur is purely accidental. The entrepreneur could be a capitalist who pays for the services of labour and land to the respective owners, keeping for himself a residue which is equal, in equilibrium, to the interest on the services given by his capital. Or he could be a worker who, after having paid for the services of the capital and land, obtains a residue equal, in equilibrium, to his wage. The same is true with a landowner who decides to become an entrepreneur. As profits are zero in equilibrium, the socioeconomic identity of the entrepreneur is completely irrelevant. 'They [the entrepreneurs] make their living not as entrepreneurs, but as land-owners, labourers and capitalists' (p. 225).

Walras constructed a system of simultaneous equations to describe the interaction between consumers and sellers. There are as many markets as there are goods, including the productive factors and their services. For each market, three types of equation are defined: one for demand, one for supply, and one for equilibrium. In each market of produced goods, the number of demand equations is equal to the number of consumers, while the number of supply equations is equal to the number of firms producing the good. In each factor market, the number of demand equations is equal to the number of firms multiplied by the number of goods produced by each of them, while the number of supply equations equals the number of owners of the factors. Furthermore, the 'production equations' are defined in such a way that the price of each product is equal to its cost of production, so that in equilibrium the entrepreneurs make 'neither profits nor losses'. The costs of production depend on the input prices and the technique in use. The latter is represented by some technical coefficients, assumed fixed, which express the proportion in which each input is combined with the output. Then, in the 'capitalization equations', it is assumed that the purchase price of each capital good is equal to its 'net income' discounted at the current rate of interest. And this implies an equilibrium configuration in which the rates of returns of all capital goods are uniform and equal to the rate of interest. Finally, there is an equation that determines the rate of interest with the forces of supply and demand of the *new* capital goods.

Now, a necessary but not sufficient condition for such a system of equations to have a solution is that the number of unknowns is equal to the number of equations. This raises three orders of problems of which Walras was not perfectly aware. The first originates from the capitalization equations which— to the extent that they impose a uniform rate of return on capital goods, a purchase price equal to the production price, and the equality between supply and demand of each capital good—introduce into the model an over-determination of a degree equal to the number of production equations of the new capital goods minus one. It is possible to avoid this problem by renouncing the uniformity requirement for the rate of returns and by interpreting the model in terms of temporary equilibrium. We will discuss this further below.

The second order of problems originates from the fact that one of the equations in Walras's system functionally depends on the others, so that the number of independent equations is lower than the number of unknowns. Intuitively, the matter can be explained in the following terms. If there is equilibrium in all the markets except one, this means that consumers have spent a sum of money equal to the value of the goods offered. But, given that the total value of the goods produced (the national product) equals by definition the total income earned by the consumers (the national income), there will also be equality between supply and demand in the last market. This circumstance was later to be called Walras's Law: in a general equilibrium system, if all the markets, except one, are in equilibrium and the budgets of all the agents break even, then the remaining market must also be in equilibrium. This law is the ultimate consequence of the fact that, in the Walrasian conception of the economic system, the act of demanding goods on the part of an individual presupposes that he offers goods of equal value.

Finally, we come to a third order of problems which is perhaps the most important. Walras did not take into account the fact that having 'counted' as many equations, even if independent, as there are unknowns is not enough to ensure the existence of a solution. A system of equations may have no solution at all, or may have many, even an infinity. Even in the case in which a solution exists, this may have no economic meaning, as would happen if some prices or some quantities were negative. Almost a century was to pass before the neoclassical economists managed to find the solution to this problem. We will see their results in Chapter 10.

5.3.3. Walras and pure economic science

Walras's impact on the evolution of economic theory has been enormous. No other economist before him had managed to construct a theoretical model and an analytical method which was so vast and versatile. Others, such as Quesnay and Cournot, had formulated the idea of interdependence among economic facts. But while Cournot maintained that the problem of general equilibrium was outside the scope of mathematics, Walras proved that, at least in principle, the problem could be resolved.

Notwithstanding this, his work passed almost unnoticed in France during the 25 years following its publication, and it was really only in the 1950s that the attitude of French scholars towards him began to change radically. But also outside France the reception of his work was, initially, somewhat cold, if not hostile. The relationships between Walras, on the one hand, and Jevons, Edgeworth, Wicksteed, and Menger, on the other, were certainly not the most cordial. Marshall, in his *Principles*, quoted Walras only three times and in brief passages. An exception should be made for the Italians; Pantaleoni, Barone, and especially Pareto held him in great respect, and were fervent propagandists of his work.

Walras, as Menger had done, always endeavoured to maintain a clear distinction between moral values and science. He believed that pure science had nothing to do with value judgements: 'The distinguishing characteristic of a science is the complete indifference to consequences, good or bad, with which it carries on the pursuit of pure truth' (p. 52). And Walras added, following Bentham: 'From other points of view the question of whether a drug is wanted by a doctor to cure a patient, or by a murderer to kill his family, is a very serious matter, but from our point of view, it is totally irrelevant. So far as we are concerned, the drug is useful in both cases, and may even be more so in the latter case than in the former' (p. 65). It is this radical dualism between technical and ethical judgements that was to dominate developments in economic thought.

Walras had always intended to write another two systematic treatises, one on applied and one on social economics, which would in some way have supplemented his fundamental work on pure theory. But the debilitating rhythm of work as professor in Lausanne, a position he had gained, not without difficulty, in 1870, absorbed all his energies until 1892, when he left teaching. After this he contented himself with publishing two collections of papers, entitled *Études d'économie sociale* (1896) and *Études d'économie politique appliquée* (1898).

Walras was a close observer of contemporary economic problems, favouring moderate reformism in socioeconomic matters. His political position, which he derived from his father's moral philosophy, was a mixture of traditional liberalism and the doctrine of State intervention. It is interesting that, while in regard to questions of justice he was a convinced supporter of the natural-law approach, he completely expelled the notion of natural law from economics. He never believed that, beyond observable facts, there could be a structure of economic laws capable of mirroring some natural order. As we already know, Walras was a severe critic of the classical dichotomy between natural and market prices and of everything derived from that distinction. Finally, Walras believed that economic analysis did not have, and could not have, any connection with the measures of economic policy; he always kept the normative and positive analyses clearly separated.

Walras put forward numerous articulate recommendations for economic policy. His favourite subjects were the nationalization of natural monopolies, the stabilization of prices by the monetary authorities, the capital market, whose efficiency and reliability should be ensured by the State, and the acquisition of land by the State and its concession in use to private agents in order to increase government revenues. It is worth noting the curious fact that Walras considered himself a 'scientific socialist'.

5.4 CARL MENGER

5.4.1 The birth of the Austrian School and the Methodenstreit

The label 'Austrian School' was used for the first time, with a clearly derogatory meaning, by opponents of Menger's ideas, especially the members of the German Historical School. The philosophical life of Austria in those times was still dominated by Aristotelian realism, a way of thinking which certainly must have appeared old-fashioned to people who had read Kant and Hegel. Nevertheless, it was precisely this Aristotelian background that allowed Menger to develop a theoretical perspective which the exasperated inductivism of his German contemporaries could not but reject *en bloc*. In fact, we owe to Aristotle the idea that there are qualities and facts, such as action, human nature, and other more complex phenomena, which can be understood on an a priori ground, and that it is possible to formulate 'laws' without any need to confirm them inductively. It was precisely by devoting himself to the search for the 'laws of the economy' that Menger set up, in opposition to Schmoller's German Historical School, the theoretical system of the Austrian School.

In his *Principles* (*Grundsätze des Volkswirtschaftslehre*) Menger endeavoured to reconstruct the foundations of economic science, intended as a pure theoretical discipline, so as to offer an alternative explanation of value and prices to that proposed by the classical school. If the classical economists considered value to be essentially governed by past costs, Menger considered it to be an expression of the judgement of the consumer in regard to the goods suitable to satisfy his needs. On the other hand, Menger's book and the way of doing economic science which prevailed in the German universities at that time were poles apart. Most of the German economists also criticized classical political economy, but the principal target of their criticism was method rather than content: the historical and not the theoretical approach should be followed in economics, and should be applied only to the description, classification, and collection of observed phenomena.

In the period in which Menger published the *Principles*, the 'Old' German Historical School, that of Roscher, Knies, and Hildebrand, began to give way to the 'Young' German Historical School, led by Gustav Schmoller. Menger thus had to fight on two rather different fronts: on the theoretical front, against the classical theoretical system, and on the methodological front, against the German Historical School. This is all-important in understanding Menger's complex scientific personality and, in particular, making sense of his concern for methodological matters—a concern not found either in Jevons or in Walras.

The results of Menger's battle on the second front are well known. The German economists virtually ignored the *Principles*. For about a decade after its publication, Menger remained an isolated thinker. It was not until the 1880s, with the enthusiastic work of Böhm-Bawerk and von Wieser, that a new school formed.

Gustav Schmoller (1858–1917) was the most important economist of imperial Germany and a leader of the *Kathedersozialisten*, 'chair socialists'. As the leader of the Young Historical School, Schmoller was a tenacious opponent of the axiomatic-deductive approach of the classical and neoclassical schools. His research programme, which Schumpeter has defined as the '*Schmollerprogramm*', overtly proposed to follow the line of that German tradition which, with the Cameralists and subsequently with List and the members of the Old Historical School, had already tried to create the presuppositions for an alternative theoretical approach to economics—alternative both to classical and to neoclassical economics. The principal accusation levelled against all of them was that they did not take into account, in their theoretical formulations, any knowledge of historical facts and material. Schmoller, instead, was a supporter of an interdisciplinary approach which aimed at blending the psychological, sociological, and philosophical aspects of the economic problems. By means of detailed historical research on the formation of the social classes and on the history of the Strasbourg weavers' guilds, Schmoller tried to show how political economy had to be liberated from 'false abstractions' and anchored to solid empirical foundations. In particular, he wished to focus both on the general effects produced by the process of capitalist accumulation on social classes and relationships and on the effects of *laissez-faire* principles and policies on less wealthy people.

Schmoller's main work, *Grundrisse der allgemeinen Volkswirtschaftslehre* (*Foundations of General Economic Theory*) (1900–4), however, turned out to be rather lacking on the analytical level; above all, it failed to reach its author's main objective: the formulation of a new way of doing economic theory. Schmoller's influence on the development of economic science in Germany was somewhat harmful, especially because it helped to isolate the German economists from the rest of the world for more than half a century. In fact, economists with different cultural orientations were not allowed to work in any of the German universities. This meant that the works of the new marginalist school were received by the German academic circles with almost complete silence.

This rejection of classical and marginalist theory had an immediate effect at the political level, where all approaches differing from economic historicism were silenced as '*Manchestertum*', that is to say, as orientations favourable both to the absolute liberty of economic initiative and to the progressive reduction of the role of the State.

Schmoller was a fervent supporter of enlightened and despotic sovereigns, especially the Prussian kings, whom he considered to be the only people able to defeat particularism and unify the national economy. Social reforms and distributive justice were central elements in his theoretical work. In all respects, Schmoller could be considered as a conservative in the specific Prussian sense of the term: he rejected Marxism and the liberalism of the Manchester School, but also the anti-reformist and reactionary positions, and went as far as proposing a strategic alliance between the monarchy and the working classes.

Menger's reaction to the German Historical School was harsh. The dispute between German and Austrian economists reached its climax in 1883 with the publication of Menger's *Untersuchungen-über die Methode der Sozialwissenschaften und der politischen Oekonomie insbesondere* (translated as *Problems of Economics and Sociology*, 1963), which officially opened the bitter *Methodenstreit* (struggle over method) and brought the new-born Austrian School to the attention of the international scientific community. There were two principal arguments with which the Viennese economist defended himself from Schmoller's attacks. The first was that 'pure science' is always *wertfrei*, value-free. Economics, if it wishes to be science, must keep itself free of value judgements: 'The so-called "ethical orientation" of political economy is thus a vague postulate devoid of any deeper meaning in respect both to the theoretical and to the practical problems of the latter, a confusion in thought' (p. 237). Here Menger anticipated by a few decades the famous argument of the neutrality of economic science which was later to be 'codified' in the 1932 *Essay* by Robbins.

The second argument is that economics can only scientifically deal with the behaviour of individual agents, whether they are consumers or firms. It is not possible to speak, in a scientific way, of economic aggregates. There would be no space in economic science for macroeconomics and concepts such as national interests or collective wealth. To move from the idea that individual desires are the only criteria of good and bad to the argument that social welfare is promoted and encouraged by policies aiming at maximizing the total amount of pleasure would lead to serious logical and practical difficulties. Menger, unlike Bentham, correctly perceived the technical difficulties of the reformist policies based on utilitarian principles: 'the greatest welfare for the greatest number' is not compatible with *methodological individualism*, that is, with the view that all propositions about the behaviour of the collective agents must be reducible to propositions about the behaviour of their individual components. In this sense, methodological individualism is opposed to holism or methodological organicism (at that time championed by the Historical School), according to which the collective terms of social science represent social entities which are absolutely emergent with respect to their individual constituents. Not only the members of the Historical School but also the classical economists and Marx, *according to this point of view*, were supporters of methodological holism: they believed that it is impossible to understand the operation of the economic system on the grounds of a theory of the behaviour of the single agents, and this would explain their use of the category of social class.

5.4.2 The centrality of the theory of marginal utility in Menger

In order to understand the terms of the theoretical battle fought by Menger on the other front, against classical economics, we need to reflect on the following problem: under which conditions can the principle of marginal utility be considered as the foundation of the whole of economics? The answer for Menger must be: under the condition that this principle can be extended from the limited field of exchange to the more complex problems of production and distribution. In other words, it is not enough to explain how it is possible, beginning from a *given* quantity of consumer goods, distributed among individuals in a known way, that a set of exchanges is established which, in perfect competition, maximizes the utility of the subjects and at the same time determines the equilibrium configuration of the relative prices. In order that the principle of marginal utility can form the basis of a general theory, it is necessary to extend its application to the phenomena of production and distribution. And this is where the difficulties arise.

In fact, while demand can be directly linked to its subjective determinant, which is utility, supply poses special problems. Supply is regulated by the costs that must be sustained to produce the various goods; but it seems that costs cannot be reduced to utility. The only way to preserve the *symmetry* between supply and demand would be to link costs to a certain homogeneous entity which is comparable to utility. Menger's specific contribution to economics is on this problem, and this is what distinguished him both from Jevons and from Walras.

With his theories of *imputation* and *opportunity cost*, Menger resolved costs into utility. His starting-point was a classification of goods according to their distance from final consumption: the 'higher-order goods', or the 'factors of production', derive their utility from the goods of the 'first order' (consumer goods) they contribute to produce. This indirect utility can be *imputed* to each productive factor by taking into account the marginal contribution it makes to the production process. In this way the actual cost sustained to produce a certain good becomes an *opportunity cost*, namely the cost represented by the sacrifice of utility of those other goods that could have been obtained from the resources actually used to produce the good in question. The production costs are evaluated no longer in absolute but in relative terms, i.e. in terms of sacrificed alternatives.

In conclusion, the principle of marginal utility was extended by Menger to cover the cost phenomenon and therefore the conditions of supply; so, supply and demand appear to be two aspects of the same problem and can both be explained in terms of utility. But this is not all. Since what is a cost for the firm is an income for the owners of the productive factors, the same principle is capable of explaining both the cost phenomena and the formation and distribution of income. Wages, profits, and rents depend, ultimately, on the demand and the prices of the consumer goods and are therefore determined by utility. In this way the distribution of income ceases to be a separate chapter in economic theory, as it was in the classical approach, and just becomes a section, a part devoid of autonomy, of the chapter dealing with the theory of prices.

While the other versions of marginalism needed about two decades to es-tablish that the theory of value based on marginal utility leads directly to the marginal-productivity theory of distribution, Menger reached this conclusion immediately. In particular, we owe to him the first expression of a proposition which was later to assume a central role in the debate on the neoclassical theory of distribution: if each factor receives the value of its productive contribution, the value of the total production will be perfectly 'exhausted' in the remuneration of the factors, and there will be no surplus that somebody can appropriate without having produced it. This was to be known later as the 'theorem of product exhaustion'. We will discuss it in the next chapter.

Bibliography

On the marginalist revolution: M. Blaug, 'Was There a Marginal Revolution?', *History of Political Economy*, 2 (1972); J. B. Clark, *The Distribution of Wealth: A Theory of Wages, Interest and Profits* (New York, 1899); A. W. Coats, 'The Economic and Social

Context of the Marginal Revolution of the 1870's', *History of Political Economy*, 2 (1972); M. Dobb, *Theories of Value and Distribution since Adam Smith* (Cambridge, 1973); R. S. Howey, *The Rise of the Marginal Utility School, 1870–1889* (Kansas City, 1960); E. K. Hunt, *History of Economic Thought* (Belmont, Calif., 1979); T. W. Hutchinson, 'The Marginal Revolution and the Decline and Fall of the English Classical Political Economy', *History of Political Economy*, 2 (1972); W. S. Jevons, *The Theory of Political Economy* (London, 1871; 5th edn., New York, 1969); *The State in Relation to Labour* (London, 1882); E. Kauder, *A History of Marginal Utility Theory* (Princeton, NJ, 1965); A. Marshall and M. P. Marshall, *The Economics of Industry* (London, 1879); V. Pareto, Introduction to K. Marx, *Le Capital* (Paris, 1893); G. L. S. Shackle, 'Marginalism: The Harvest', *History of Political Economy*, 2 (1972); L. Walras, *Elements of Pure Economics* (Homewood, Ill., 1954).

On Jevons: R. D. C. Black, 'W. S. Jevons, 1835–82', in D. P. O'Brien and J. R. Presley (eds.), *Pioneers of Modern Economics* (London, 1981); J. M. Keynes, *Essays in Biography* (London, 1933); D. Laidler, 'Jevons on Money', *The Manchester School*, 52 (1982); T. Peach, 'Jevons as an Economic Theorist', in *The New Palgrave: A Dictionary of Economics*, ii (London, 1987); L. C. Robbins, 'The Place of Jevons in the History of Economic Thought', in *The Manchester School*, 6 (1936); I. Steedman, 'Jevons's Theory of Capital and Interest', in *The Manchester School*, 42 (1972).

On Walras: W. Jaffé (ed.), *Correspondence of Léon Walras and Related Papers* (3 vols., Amsterdam, 1965); L. M. Leroy, *Auguste Walras*, (Paris, 1923); J. A. Schumpeter, 'Léon Walras', in *Ten Great Economists from Marx to Keynes* (London, 1966); J. Van Daal, R. E. Henderiks, and A. C. Vorst, 'On Walras' Model of General Economic Equilibrium', *Zeitschrift für Nationalökonomie* (1985); D. A. Walker, 'Walras's Theory of the Entrepreneur', *De Economist* (Holland), 8 (1986); E. Zaghini, 'Natural Prices and Market Prices: An Interpretation of the Walrasian Theory of Accumulation', *Economic Notes*, 9 (1986).

On Menger: J. R. Hicks and W. Weber (eds.), *Carl Menger and the Austrian School of Economics* (Oxford, 1973); J. J. Krabbe, A. Neutjes, and H. Visser (eds.), *Austrian Economics: Roots and Ramifications Reconsidered* (Rochester, Kent, 1988); J. A. Schumpeter, 'Carl Menger', in *Ten Great Economists from Marx to Keynes* (London, 1966); E. Streissler, 'To what Extent Was the Austrian School Marginalist?', *History of Political Economy*, 2 (1972); R. E. Wagner *et al.*, 'Carl Menger and Austrian Economics', *Atlantic Economic Journal*, special issue, (1978).

6

The Construction of Neoclassical Orthodoxy

6.1. THE *BELLE ÉPOQUE*

With the end of the immediate effects of the agrarian crisis and the 'Great Depression' which had hit Europe between the end of the 1870s and the first half of the 1890s, Europe, the United States, and Japan launched themselves into a new wave of economic growth which sustained its rhythm until the First World War, and was particularly notable for the number of technological innovations it produced. Some scholars speak of a second industrial revolution, a revolution carried over the thousands of kilometres of telephone wires and electricity poles, on the wheels of millions of bicycle, motorcycles, and cars, and on the wings of the first aeroplanes, and which produced the mysterious concoctions of synthetic chemistry from carbon derivatives. In this period the towns were bright with lights, and smooth roads were opened for the new means of transport. The mobility of the population inside and outside national borders increased enormously, almost as much as the mobility of capital, which, from the main financial centres of London, Berlin, and Paris, radiated to the most varied destinations.

New countries, which up to that time had remained at the margins of industrial growth—Sweden, Holland, Italy, Spain, Russia, Hungary, and Japan—leapt forward, while the European drive towards colonial expansion became more urgent, almost obsessive, even though it was not always economically profitable.

Although the trade union movements, by this time well-organized in many countries, were quite militant, sociopolitical institutions had become sufficiently flexible, and economic growth sufficiently self-sustaining, to allow many concessions to the workers, especially in regard to wages and working conditions, without provoking dramatic breaks in the expansive trend. This was also a period, therefore, of improvement in the standard of living of the lower classes, of urbanization, and of changes in consumption patterns.

The simultaneous industrial growth in many economic areas necessitated some form of co-ordination of international trade and finance. This requirement was met by the Gold Standard, a monetary system that had evolved over the preceding centuries and that reached its high point in this period.

With the Gold Standard, the national currencies were freely convertible into gold and the exchange rates tended to oscillate within a very thin band around the levels determined by the gold parities. This discouraged short-term capital movements, which are usually destabilizing, and encouraged, on the other hand, long-run foreign investments; at the same time it gave international trade the guarantee of safe and certain payments. It was not easy for individual countries to remain linked to the system, which required high levels of prosperity and sound monetary practices, but the periods during which this or that country left the system were brief. The Gold Standard was not such an automatic system as some literature has depicted it; but Great Britain had the financial resources and sufficient authority to put into practice the necessary adjustment mechanisms at the opportune moments.

Technological innovations, financial stability, and relative social peace produced an impressive cycle of capitalist growth that was only surpassed, in intensity, duration, and number of countries involved, by the expansion from 1950 to 1973. The large factory, the new machine age, and the aspirin won over the popular imagination. Colossal international exhibitions held in the main industrial cities of the world enjoyed enormous public success, and also influenced literature, art, architecture, and music. The *belle époque* was a period of optimism and great economic transformation, even though it was marked, on the political side, by old and renewed national antagonisms; a situation that the new, potent military weapons made available by modern industry were to fuel until it exploded in an armed conflict of unprecedented proportions. That conflict closed the *belle époque*.

The marginalist scholars working between the end of the nineteenth century and the early 1920s conquered the academic circles of almost all Western countries, and contributed to the creation of a new, dominant theoretical system. In Great Britain, Alfred Marshall (1842–1924), the most important figure of the period, established an authentic school of thought; but Francis Ysidro Edgeworth (1845–1926), Philip Henry Wicksteed (1844–1927), and Arthur Cecil Pigou (1877–1959) also made first-rate contributions. In Austria, the rapid diffusion of the 'Austrian' approach was the work of Menger's enthusiastic followers, Eugen von Böhm-Bawerk (1852–1914) and Friedrich von Wieser (1851–1926). In Italy, Maffeo Pantaleoni (1857–1924), Enrico Barone (1859–1924), and, above all, Vilfredo Pareto (1848–1923) developed and popularized Walras's teachings. In Sweden, Knut Wicksell (1851–1926) and Gustav Cassel (1866–1944) tried to blend the Austrian approach with Walrasian theory, giving rise to an original Swedish School. Finally, the two most important figures in the United States were Irving Fisher (1867–1947) and John Bates Clark (1847–1938), to whom we owe the diffusion of the neoclassical theoretical system within the American academic and cultural circles of the time.

The existence of various currents of thought and diverse national schools, often in bitter conflict among themselves, should not be undervalued. However, this should not prevent us from identifying a common denominator, a substantial unity of thought which, originating from the marginalist revolution, tended to emerge gradually and converge towards the construction of a unique theoretical system. As early as the beginning of the twentieth century, pure economic theory was able to present itself as a compact doctrinal corpus; the turning-point in the early 1870s finally produced a completely new theoretical system which still dominates the scene today.

6.2 MARSHALL AND THE ENGLISH NEOCLASSICAL ECONOMISTS

6.2.1. Alfred Marshall

By a thoroughly personal route, Marshall managed to offer the neoclassical paradigm an alternative theoretical outlet to that proposed by Jevons and, above all, a wider cultural perspective. The method of partial-equilibrium analysis was his great invention and personal contribution to economics. Unlike Walras, and the whole Continental tradition in general, Marshall tended to favour realism and the explanatory power of the theory, rather than the logical coherence and formal elegance of its results. It is for this reason that he overlooked the interrelations among markets, in order to concentrate on the equilibrium conditions of a single productive sector. His favourite analytical instruments were the concepts of 'industry' and 'representative firm'. An industry is a group of firms producing the same good; a representative firm is an 'average' firm endowed with the most important characteristics of the industry.

Of course, Marshall was aware of the numerous relationships of interdependence that link markets to each other. Walras, on the other hand, had recognized the practical usefulness of the partial-analysis method. The fact is that the two great economists were focusing on different audiences: Marshall on the intelligent common man and, especially, to the businessman (this is why the formal mathematical aspects of his work are relegated to the appendices); Walras on colleagues and scholars in general (the notable mathematical apparatus of the *Elements* is accessible only to a few). It is important to point out that Marshall applied the partial-analysis method to goods markets but not to productive-factor markets. For the latter, he too, like Walras, formulated a 'general-equilibrium' model in which the relations between the products and the factors of production play an essential role.

Marshall is the classic example of the right economist in the right place at the right time. Victorian England was sailing at full speed through the final years of the nineteenth century. And, with economic growth, a great optimism spread about the destiny of the industrial society. Real average wages increased constantly and technical progress gradually reduced the length of the working week.

A typical Cambridge intellectual, Marshall studied theology, mathematics, and physics before finally coming to economics. He arrived just about the time when English academic circles were beginning to be influenced by the theories of Darwin and Spencer. Marshall studied Darwin's theory of evolution, Christian moral philosophy, and Bentham's utilitarianism, and managed to blend these three great streams of thought into an original synthesis. The result was a philosophy of evolutionary progress which implied that the *whole* society would tend to improve in material terms, and not only the strong and courageous few, as the social Darwinists had argued. In regard to his mathematical background, Marshall certainly benefited from being taught by the great physicist Maxwell and the mathematician Clifford. It was these influences that impelled him to introduce into economics the modern diagrammatical methods of setting out theory.

Marshall's main contribution to economics is the *Principles of Economics*. The book was published in 1890, but the first draft goes back to the early 1870s, the period when the marginalist revolution was beginning. Marshall's *Principles* was an enormous success and gradually, especially in England, displaced Mill's *Principles* as the basic textbook in all the main universities; a great deal of the methodology used in that book continues to dominate microeconomics textbooks today. In particular, the famous 'Marshallian cross' has preserved its mystique. With it, the great economist tried to combine the theory of production of the classical authors with the neoclassical theory of demand which he himself had formulated.

It is important here to point out that neither Jevons nor Walras had managed directly to connect the theory of utility to the theory of demand. Instead, Marshall, with the hypothesis of a constant marginal utility of money, related the marginal-utility schedule of one good to the consumer's demand schedule, and in so doing formulated the theory of the 'consumer surplus or rent'.

The theory offered a way of measuring the return, in terms of utility, that the consumer draws from exchange activity. The idea is to compare the marginal demand price that the subject is prepared to pay for a given quantity of good with its market price. $D(q)$ is the demand curve, p is the current market price, and q the quantity demanded. At price p_0 the consumer buys q_0 by spending a sum of money equal to the area Op_0Cq_0. However, he would be prepared to pay p_2 to obtain the quantity q_2, p_1 to obtain the quantity q_1, and so on. This means that his actual outlay is lower than what he would be prepared to pay to obtain the desired quantity. Geometrically, this difference, which measures the consumer's surplus, is shown by the area of the triangle D_0p_0C in Fig. 6.

The most important scientific approach of the period in which Marshall was educated was that of Newtonian physics, an approach whose logical coherence and theoretical strength nobody doubted. The task Marshall set himself was to make economic science conform to the dominant scientific approach, highlighting the robustness of its foundations, the continuity of its growth, and the universality of its principles. This helps us to understand why he was opposed to the controversies about fundamental questions: he believed that these could weaken the scientific status of the discipline. It was for this reason that

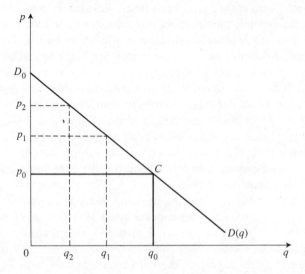

·Fig. 6

Marshall did not accept Jevons' attack on Ricardo, going so far as to argue that it was only because of an inappropriate use of language that Ricardo could have given the impression of not considering demand as a determinant of value. At the same time, Marshall maintained that the theory of supply and demand was not the scientific basis of economics. The central problem of economics, according to him, is not the allocation of *given* resources, but rather how the resources become what they are. The 'science of activities', as he called it, should have been a necessary supplement to the 'science of wants', but—as he states in the *Principles*—if one of the two 'may claim to be the interpreter of the history of man . . . it is the science of activities and not that of wants' (p. 90). Furthermore, the positive functions of competition were not defined by Marshall in terms of efficient allocation of resources, but rather in terms of the stimulus competition gives to the discovery of improved methods of production.

6.2.2. Competition and equilibrium in Marshall

The invention of the theory of perfectly competitive equilibrium has been traditionally attributed to Cournot. Cournot developed a notion of partial equilibrium by studying a market isolated from the rest of the economy. He distinguished between two kinds of equilibrium: single-producer markets and many-producer markets—in other words, a monopoly equilibrium and a competitive equilibrium. The competitive equilibrium was seen as a limiting situation, namely as the state of the market that would be realized if none of the economic agents had monopolistic power. As we saw in Chapter 5, this way of conceptualizing the competitive equilibrium was rejected by Walras. The Walrasian system assumes that the agents formulate their own plans and implement their own choices by taking prices as given. Marshall's conception of competition and equilibrium is completely different from that of Walras, and rather nearer to that of Cournot.

First of all, Marshall clearly distinguished between market behaviour and normal behaviour. The former concerns the quantity of goods actually bought and sold at a given moment and at a given price. The latter, instead, reflects what the single agent decides to buy or sell 'normally' per unit of time, over a certain time-span. The normal decisions depend on the 'normal' level of prices the agent expects to prevail during the period considered. Knowing, from experience, that the *market price* is usually different from the *normal price*, the agent will base his own daily decisions (if the day is the unit of time under consideration) on the market-price trend. However, his final aim is to realize, within the time-span considered, his own normal decisions.

The gap between market price and normal price will induce the agent to anticipate or delay the buying or selling of a certain good, but will not change his own ideas of what normal behaviour is, the latter constituting a sort of fixed reference point. Marshall considered normal prices to be subjective evaluations of the prices that are expected to prevail on the market at a particular time in the future, it is on the basis of these expected prices that the single entrepreneur decides on the size and type of plant to adopt. Marshall was very reticent about the mechanism of formation and revision of normal prices, but denied that these could be obtained in a direct way from observed market prices, as their average or by extrapolating from their past trend. If there is a causal link between market and normal prices, it seems to run from normal to market prices and not vice versa.

Second, there is a marked difference between Walras and Marshall in regard to their definitions of competition. In the Walrasian conceptualization, the agent in perfect competition is a price-taker: he considers the prices as given and not capable of being directly influenced by his own behaviour. Marshall, on the other hand, believed that a perfectly competitive market is one in which a large number of agents operate; each has objectives which conflict with those of the others, and will try to pursue them without entering into coalitions or blocs and without using special bargaining powers. Marshall's 'perfect competition' does not presuppose that each agent takes the price of goods as given, nor that the firms are identical (even though they must be 'similar'). The small differences among firms play, in Marshall's system, the same role as that of the genetic variations in Darwinian theory.

Marshall distinguished between *demand price*, p_d, i.e. the maximum price at which the demand reaches a pre-determined level, and *supply price*, p_s, i.e. the minimum price that induces the sellers to offer a quantity equal to that predetermined. Given a certain level of demand, the market is in disequilibrium if the demand price differs from the supply price. A disequilibrium situation tends to trigger the following reactions. If $p_d > p_s$, the sellers will react by increasing the volume of supply either by an increase in the production levels or by a reduction in the levels of inventories; vice versa, in the case in which $p_d < p_s$. In this way the existence of a disequilibrium produces first a variation in the quantities and only later, and as a consequence of these changes, a variation of prices. In general, Marshall's sellers prefer to increase their own profits by acting on quantities rather than on prices, for the obvious reason that price manœuvres may be difficult in situations close to perfect competition.

The method Marshall adopted led him inevitably to an analysis of the conditions of supply: in the movement towards equilibrium he admitted variations in supply, not only of the products but also of the factors, if these are reproducible. This is a point of contact with Ricardian economics, but it is only a partial contact. Marshall did not accept the producibility point of view to the point of accepting the Ricardian theory of value. He adopted a theory based on real costs, but these were restricted to labour and 'waiting', as in the work of Senior and Mill. It is not by chance that Schumpeter considered Marshall's theory of real costs as 'the olive branch presented to his classical predecessors' (*History of Economic Analysis* (London, 1954), p. 1057).

6.2.3. Marshall's social philosophy

In *The Present Position of Economics*, his inaugural lecture for the 1885–6 academic year, Marshall put forward the view that the main duty of economics is the calculation of benefits of social and industrial change, bearing in mind the fact that the same amount of money measures a greater pleasure for the poor than for the rich. This is the same as saying that overall welfare increases if the the distribution of the 'social dividend' is adjusted in favour of the poor, up to the point of levelling marginal utilities for all subjects. The defence of redistributive economic policies proceeds, according to Marshall, from the utilitarian principle that the ultimate goal of economic activity is the maximization of collective welfare.

As a good student of Mill, Marshall was the initiator, within the neoclassical stream of thought, of that tendency which tried to reconcile a moderate *laissez-faire* with a reformist programme; and, just like Mill, he rejected the argument, put forward by the most determined free-traders of the period, that the only way to improve the conditions of the poor was to stimulate the egoism of the rich. His compromise position induced him to introduce into his system of thought principles and norms which were in clear contradiction with the dominant Spencerian ideology, and which brought him more than a little criticism. In Marshall, unlike Walras, there is an inextricable interweaving among the economic, social, and ·cultural spheres of human activity, and a strong link between material and moral facts—a link that had important consequences for his way of conceiving, for example, State intervention in the economy.

Marshall was concerned to consider the main bearings in economics of the law of the struggle for existence, according to which 'those organisms tend to survive which are best fitted to utilize the environment' (p. 242). In particular, he was concerned to defeat the argument, put forward by the Social Darwinists of the period, that the State should not intervene in any way to modify the process of natural selection. From Social Darwinism however, he borrowed the evolutionist conception of history, a conception well summarized in the quotation appearing on the first page of the *Principles*: '*Natura non facit saltus.*' Human progress is slow, and moves forward in small steps. Attempts to change society quickly are doomed to failure and, if pursued, only produce misery. Marshall admitted that over the course of the slow evolution of the social institutions a particular structure could emerge which would lend itself to the exploitation of one social group by another. However, the survival of such a structure through time would prove that its merits outweighed its defects.

This argument would apply especially to modern capitalism. Notwithstanding all its social costs and injustices, capitalism ensures productive and allocative efficiency and contributes to the elevation and progress of mankind. Marshall thought that human nature, as it had developed over centuries of war and violence, and of 'sordid and gross pleasures', could not be changed in the course of a single generation. In fact, when Marshall spoke of 'sordid and gross pleasures' he had already abandoned the pure utilitarian premises. As we have seen with Mill, a social philosophy that discriminates between healthy and sordid pleasures is basically incompatible with utilitarian philosophy.

Marshall believed that the sociopolitical dimension of human action should always be taken into account by economics. The implications of this view for economic policy are notable. The State has the right and the duty to intervene in the economic sphere to regulate the market mechanism and to correct its distortions. This argument is present in all Marshall's work, but is explicitly and strongly expressed in *The Social Possibilities of Economic Chivalry* (1907). His proposals for the introduction of corrective mechanisms such as co-operative movements, profit-sharing, arbitration on wages, and similar mechanisms into the English political-economic system seemed very modern to his contemporaries.

6.2.4. Pigou and welfare economics

As Robertson has explained in *Utility and All That and Other Essays* (1952), the principal aim of economics in Marshall's Cambridge was understood in terms of welfare economics. The study of economic welfare must include, according to Marshall, the study of situations in which the market mechanism ceases to produce the beneficial effects expected from it, i.e. the study of 'market failures'. This was the main interest of Arthur Pigou, Marshall's successor as professor of economics at the University of Cambridge. In the *Economics of Welfare* (1920), Pigou stated that the object of welfare economics is represented by the circumstances most conducive to the increase of economic welfare of the world or of a specific country. The hope was to discover which type of intervention, by the government or by private bodies, would most favour such circumstances. However, Pigou made an important change in emphasis: the analysis of the operation of the competitive process and the historical perspective, which were such important elements in Marshall's system, gave way to formal analysis.

Pigou's most relevant contribution concerned his famous distinction between private and social costs. The main reason for the difference between the two categories was identified in the absence of constant returns. Pigou observed that, while industries with decreasing returns tend to become larger than is socially desirable, the industries enjoying increasing returns tend to remain too small. This led him to the conclusion that government intervention in the form of taxes and subsidies is necessary. This line of thought was first expressed in *Wealth and Welfare* (1912) and later in the more famous *The Economics of Welfare* mentioned above.

Marshall himself intervened to criticize the conclusions reached by his student in his 1912 book. He pointed out that the apparent inefficiency of industries with decreasing returns was due to the fact that Pigou was using static analysis to deal with dynamic questions. In fact, Marshall defined the law of increasing returns in terms of the improvements in the organization which usually accompany an increase in demand. And this is the meaning of the famous proposition according to which the part played by nature in production shows a tendency towards decreasing returns, whilst the part played by man shows a tendency to increasing returns; which is tantamount to saying that man continually fights to find new ways to loosen or overcome the bonds of nature. In theoretical terms, this implies a clear distinction between a static analysis, in which costs increase as a direct function of output, and a dynamic analysis, in which costs change through time owing to talent and human effort. This is exactly the road that led Marshall to admit the irreversibility of the long-run supply curve: it is not likely that economies of scale, once attained by means of general economic progress, will disappear, even if the output of the sector decreases. This implies, as Marshall had already pointed out in *The Pure Theory of Domestic Values* (1879), the impossibility of moving backwards and forwards along the same supply curve, and explains his suggestion that the curve should be redrawn each time 'great additional economies are introduced'. On the other hand, it is important to point out that with irreversible supply curves, the adjustment usually indicated in textbooks to represent the long-run equilibrium of the sector no longer makes sense. Marshall must have been aware of this, as in the fourth edition of the *Principles* he wrote: 'The Static Theory of equilibrium is only an introduction to economic studies; and it is barely even an introduction to the study of the progress and development of industries which show a tendency of increasing return' (p. 461). This insistence on growth and competition as the agents of progress is an important part of Marshall's thought—a part which was not, however, perceived by his follower, obsessed as he was with the need to confer formal rigour on his master's work.

So Pigou, in his attempt to give an authorized interpretation of Marshall, ended up by translating his long-run analysis into the language of static competition, and this was later to pass into even the most accredited micro-economic textbooks. In the course of this translation, Pigou redefined the Marshallian representative firm as one in search of an equilibrium position, and identified the Marshallian equilibrium as the perfect competitive equilibrium. Moreover, the long-run equilibrium position of the firm was made to coincide with the minimum point of the famous U-shaped long-run average-cost curve, with which the whole problem of increasing returns was reduced to a mere question of external economies. By placing the concept of the equilibrium of the firm at the centre of his analysis, Pigou was finally led to define an industry as a collection of firms in static equilibrium. It was in this way that the most interesting parts of Marshall's work, those concerned with dynamics, were left aside. All this was the work, not of an enemy, but rather of a 'loyal but faithless Marshallian', in the brilliant words of Robertson.

6.2.5. Wicksteed and 'the exhaustion of the product'

Wicksteed's name is irrevocably linked, not so much to his most ambitious work, *The Common Sense of Political Economy* (1910), but rather to *An Essay on the Co-ordination of the Laws of Distribution* (1894). This work contains the first explicit definition of the production function. There is also the first explicit formulation of the problem of the exhaustion of the product. We have already noted that we owe to Menger the idea of explaining all the distributive shares in terms of marginal productivity, but we recalled that Menger's theoretical system, at that time, fell on deaf ears in England. While it is true that there are traces of the problem in the first edition of Marshall's *Principles*, Wicksteed was the first scholar to treat the matter systematically. The same subject was tackled a few years later by Clark, Barone, and others, whom we will discuss later.

Unlike the Ricardian approach, which adopts diverse theories to explain the different distributive shares, marginalist thought uses a single law, that of marginal productivity. All the factors are considered in the same way: they all receive a share of the national income which is proportional to their respective marginal productivities. The quantity produced is determined by the sum of the resources employed, and depends on technological factors, while the re-munerations of the factors are determined by the forces of supply and demand and depend on the structure of the markets. Produced income and distributed income are therefore independent magnitudes and determined according to different rules, so that there is no reason to expect them to be always equal. On the other hand, a situation in which the sum of the distributive shares is higher or lower than unity would be unacceptable from a logical point of view. In the first case, in fact, after having paid for each resource according to its own marginal productivity, there would be a residue without an owner; in the second case, it would seem that the resources employed do not produce enough to receive a remuneration proportional to their own marginal productivity. In both cases, the logical coherence of the theory is irremediably compromised, unless one is prepared to re-introduce a non-marginalist concept to explain some type of remuneration. This is why it is necessary to prove that the product is 'exhausted' in the factor shares.

Assume for simplicity that there are only two factors of production, labour and capital. By indicating with w and r the unit prices at which their services are paid and with L and K the quantities employed, the problem is to prove that: $pY = wL + rK$, where Y denotes the volume of output and p its price. What guarantees are there that the determination of the factor prices according to the rule of marginal productivity are compatible with the equality between the value of the national product and the national income? The quantity produced, Y, is determined by the amount of the employed resources according to the production function $Y = f(K, L)$; the remunerations of the factors are determined according to the marginalist rule which states that $w = pY'_L$ and $r = pY'_K$, where pY'_L is the the value of marginal productivity of labour and pY'_K is the value of marginal productivity of capital.

The problem can be solved if it is possible to express Y in the following way: $Y = Y'_L L + Y'_K K$. In this case, in fact, multiplying both sides of the equation by p we obtain: $pY = pY'_L L + pY'_K K$. Now, a sufficient and necessary condition for $Y = Y'_L L + Y'_K K$ is that the production function is homogeneous of first degree, i.e. that it exhibits constant returns of scale. Under these conditions it is possible to apply the famous Euler theorem. But it is obvious that this solution, made to save the formal rigour of the theory, excessively restricts its field of application. However, Wicksteed did not share this point of view; on the contrary, he was so convinced of the plausibility of the hypothesis of constant returns of scale that he did not even attempt to justify it. And it was precisely against the empirical relevance of Wicksteed's conclusion that Pareto was to launch his 1897 attack: the theory is not universally valid, both because there are cases of productive processes with decreasing and increasing returns of scale and because the processes are often characterized by fixed proportions in the employment of factors, so that it is impossible to define their marginal productivities. Note that this kind of criticism does not undermine the logical structure of the theory but only its empirical relevance. In any case, apart from problems of realism, Wicksteed's solution cannot be considered adequate, as it is incomplete. It assumes a fact that is not proved: that the market laws allow for the factors to be paid according to their marginal productivities, i.e. that $w = pY'_L$ and $r = pY'_k$. What kind of market structure would guarantee this result? We had to wait first for Wicksell and then for Robinson for a decisive step forward towards a complete solution of the problem.

6.2.6. Edgeworth and bargaining negotiation

Edgeworth was a remarkable figure in the theoretical scene of those years. Thanks to his exceptional analytical ability and his mathematical background, much more solid than the standard of the period, he was undoubtedly one of the 'founding fathers' of econometrics in its original meaning of 'systematic application of mathematics to economics'. In this he played a prophetic role, anticipating what has become the undisputed research line to follow in recent years.

His main work, *Mathematical Psychics* (1881), is a short book in which in a few pages he tackles, in incredible depth, some of the burning questions in economics. To understand its meaning it is necessary to remember the great admiration, felt by Edgeworth and shared by some of his illustrious contemporaries such as Jevons and Walras, for classical mechanics, from which economics, according to this line of thought, should 'learn' the style of argument and logical reasoning so as to obtain results of the same exactness and elegance. In Edgeworth's case, such admiration was perhaps, at least in part, due to the intellectual exchanges he probably had with the great Irish physicist, William Hamilton, a family friend of Edgeworth's father. In the years in which Edgeworth was educated, Hamilton had already been working for some time on an elegant and unitary ordering of mechanics which still carries his name today. Edgeworth's arguments are difficult, as they make extensive use of techniques, such as the calculus of variations, that are still today not widely applied. Moreover, his literary style, which is rich and full of quotations but also often obscure, coupled with his natural humility and shyness, explain why, despite the consideration he enjoyed during his life, the full value of Edgeworth and his work were only understood several decades after his death. *Mathematical Psychics* should be approached in this light.

In the introduction of the book, Edgeworth made a passionate plea for mathematical economics; a plea based on the observation that economics, unlike mechanics, generally works, not with exact functional forms, but with indefinite forms of which only a few properties are specified. In other words, he considered mathematical economics as essentially a *qualitative* discipline; an idea which was to be taken up again by many different authors, among them Keynes in the *General Theory* and Samuelson in the *Foundations of Economic Analysis*.

Edgeworth is probably remembered today with more admiration for the second part of his book. In it, after having defined the economic agents as being driven only by *self-interest*, he expressed the famous theory of *bargaining negotiation*, in which the process of exchange is seen as a series of negotiations and renegotiations which only stops at the moment when the individuals are no longer motivated to revise the agreements already made. Unlike the Walrasian *tâtonnement*, in which it is the auctioneer, an almost metaphysical being, who co-ordinates the choices of the individuals, in Edge-worth's bargaining process it is the individuals themselves who, by trying very hard to reach an optimum, end by bringing the system to equilibrium. It is easy to see that this analysis is enormously more complicated than that of Walras. In particular, the problem of the *uniqueness* of the equilibrium becomes very delicate. Edgeworth realized this, and showed that in an ex-change economy with two individuals, given the initial endowments, there may be a continuum, the famous 'contract curve', of attainable Pareto-optimal points. He also noted that this curve shrinks with the increase in the number of economic agents, but that nothing definite can be concluded about its asymptotic behaviour when the number of agents changes. His contemporaries did not realize the importance of Edgeworth's bargaining theory, which was too far ahead of its times even for the subtle intelligence of Jevons and Marshall. Only in the last 30 years, with the work of Shubik, Scarf, Debreu, and Aumann, has Edgeworth's bargaining theory flourished again, giving life to 'core' theory. With this development it has been possible to determine the asymptotic structure of the set of equilibria (the multiplicity can persist asymp-totically) and to prove that bargaining can generate equilibria which cannot be obtained by means of Walras's *tâtonnement*. Besides this, the two sets of equilibria tend generally to coincide asymptotically only under certain regu-larity conditions.

Walras himself was convinced of the possibility of situations in which the competitive equilibrium is not unique; but Edgeworth's bargaining theory turned out to be more suitable for tackling the problem of the disequilibrium. As long as Walras's auctioneer is active, the system must reach equilibrium, unless some rather special conditions concerning consumer preferences and technology prevail. But in Edgeworth's world, in which single individuals make the adjustments, the system can never reach equilibrium, even in not too unusual cases, or can jump sharply from one equilibrium to another, even with small disturbances. Furthermore, the bargaining theory also shows that the adjustment mechanism can drastically modify the set of possible outcomes of the market process, an idea which only today has been fully understood, mostly thanks to the analytical apparatus of game theory.

The third and final part of Edgeworth's book deals with the classic problem of the behaviour of economic agents. Going back to Bentham, Edgeworth assumed that behaviour is aimed at the maximization of individual satisfaction and that it can be described as a procedure of constrained maximization of a utility function, for which he proposed some possible specifications. In his work, rather than referring to economics, he derived direct inspiration from the work of physio-pyschologists such as Fechner and Helmholtz. However, the problem in which he was most interested was this: how to infer the best *social* distribution of resources from the individual preferences, once these have been specified. He also assumed, not only that utility can be cardinally measured, but also that it is not necessary, in order to do this, to resort to a measurement scale with an arbitrary origin, such as the one used for temperature. He was coherent with his premises and concluded that, in order to maximize collective welfare, it was precisely those individuals who had the greatest ability to 'experience satisfaction' who should receive the greatest quantity of resources. And some limiting cases could even occur in which one individual should receive all the available resources. It is only a short step from here to the conclusion that the individuals who are at the top of the scale of evolution should be privileged, even if Edgeworth observed that, generally, the analysis of this problem cannot lead to a well-defined and fully satisfactory answer from a logical point of view.

Still today the ingenuous utilitarianism of that reasoning is not considered too implausible, and modern welfare theory is still firmly based on utilitarian foundations of this type, just a little more sophisticated. However, the shades of eugenics in Edgeworth's analysis do have a sinister sound, and certainly represent the most dated parts of his work. On the other hand, it could be said that Edgeworth, rather than wishing to prove the scientific nature of some of his ideological prejudices, wished to demonstrate that even the most complex social phenomena can be described in an 'exact' way in terms of certain pseudo-physical laws, and that the political implications of such laws had only a limited importance for him.

6.3. NEOCLASSICAL THEORY IN AMERICA

6.3.1. Clark and the marginal-productivity theory

It was Clark and Fisher who brought the new theoretical system to America, while Frank Taussig (1859–1940) was active in spreading the message. Neoclassical predominance had certainly not been attained by 1885, the year in which the American Economic Association was founded at Saratoga (NY) by a group of young economists who did not completely agree with the classical tradition. The bible of the old school was still Mill's *Principles*. In America, political economy was 'Mill' as geometry was 'Euclid'. Yet neither the Ricardian theory of rent nor Malthus' population principle seemed particularly suited to interpret the American situation, and this was another reason for the abandonment of classical economics by American economists.

Clark was undoubtedly the most influential and esteemed economist of the period. Even in his own life he was considered the principal apostle of marginalism. As a student of Knies in Heidelberg, he had been strongly influenced by the German Historical School. Both the method and spirit of that school was evident in his first work, *The Philosophy of Wealth* (1886), which included a forceful yet respectful attack on the premises of classical theory. The Ricardian system was described as 'the apotheosis of egoism'. Clark advanced the counter-proposal of State intervention to reduce the economic power of the industrialists, to enforce distributive justice, to replace competition and conflict by co-operation, and, in general, to bring the economic process under the control of moral principles.

During the next 20 years, Clark was absorbed by the intellectual challenge created by the problem of the functional distribution of income. A series of papers paved the way for his major work, *The Distribution of Wealth* (1899). In this period, Clark completely changed his orientation by embracing the neoclassical theoretical system; and the conversion was radical, as are all adult conversions. Now, the competition between egoistic individuals was seen as the vehicle of social co-operation and justice. Public interest would be served by competition, as the valuations that the market makes of goods and factors, being derived from the individual marginal utilities, would be the correct valuations for society as a whole. Finally, government intervention was invoked, not to replace competition, but to impose it with anti-trust legislation.

Underlying the marginal-productivity theory of distribution is a very simple rule: each production factor must receive a share of the national income proportional to the contribution it gives to production. Assuming that the distribution is based on the same principle for all categories of income and all individuals, it follows that all incomes can be reduced, directly or indirectly, to labour incomes. Even profit would be the compensation of a particular working ability, that of the entrepreneur, who co-ordinates production and bears the risk. Even the pure incomes from capital can be indirectly linked to labour incomes: they represent the remuneration of loaned capital, which in turn comes from accumulated savings and therefore from incomes produced, in a previous stage, by means of labour. The differences between the various forms of income, if any, are only formal; in any case, no fundamental difference depends on the fact that individuals are divided into social classes. The one exception to this rule is land rent, which is considered to be a spurious form of income, as it originates only from the scarcity of land.

After removing every sociopolitical connotation from the distributive problem, so as to be able to demonstrate that each subject receives a share of the national income proportional to his production contribution, it is necessary to postulate that the marginal productivity of a factor represents the correct measure of that contribution.

The first consequence of this theory is that the fundamental classical relationship between wages and subsistence consumption no longer applies. In fact, there is no reason to believe that, in general, the marginal productivity of labour must equal the subsistence wage.

Second, the application of a general rule such as that of marginal productivity seems to satisfy two fundamental principles: the *principle of efficiency*, since the possibility is excluded that unproductive resources can be part of the distribution of income and can continue to be produced; and the *principle of equity*, since it seems ethically legitimate that each agent receives an income in relation to what he has contributed to produce. In other words, the distribution of income is governed by a 'natural law' which attributes to every agent the amount of wealth he has contributed to produce. The notion of exploitation loses all meaning in this context.

The third important consequence is that the study of the functional distribution of income turns out to be the same as the study of the structure of factor markets, since it is in these markets that the prices of the factors and the quantities exchanged are determined. From the marginalist point of view, therefore, the problem of distribution becomes that of formulating a theory of supply and demand of factors; a theory which is *symmetrical* to that of the supply and demand of goods, and which allows the demonstration of the following proposition: the operation of the factor markets ensures that the voluntary exchanges among rational and virtually equal individuals lead to an efficient and mutually beneficial distributive setting.

The Distribution of Wealth was inspired by an ambitious project: to integrate into a single theoretical system consumption and production, capital and labour, interest, wages, and rent, marginal productivity and marginal utility. However, Clark limited his ambitions to the stationary-state case, leaving the work on dynamics to others. Clark's aggregate model was taken up again in the 1950s by Swan and Solow, in two pieces of research which marked the beginning of neoclassical growth models. These models replaced Clark's stationary state by a steady-state growth path, but their main theoretical target was no longer the distribution of income, nor the ethical justification of the marginalist principle. Yet it was reference to Clark's theory that contributed to the great controversy between the two Cambridges in the 1960s, which we will discuss in Chapter 11.

Clark's approach is not Walrasian, but it is of an aggregate type and is based on the assumption that wages and interest, i.e. the returns on capital, tend to uniformity among the various productive sectors. Competition and factor mobility should guarantee this result, but in the equilibrium described by Clark there is 'mobility without movement'. In his theory, the capital factor has to be homogeneous and malleable, so that it is possible to calculate its specific marginal productivity independently from the various technical forms assumed by the means of production in diverse allocations and over time. This 'capital' should not be confused with capital goods, which differ from industry to industry and from time to time. The latter make up, according to Clark, the specific and transient embodiment of the general and permanent factor called 'capital', i.e. the fund of savings accumulated over time. Furthermore, Clark included land in the stock of capital, a choice that aimed at eliminating *ab ovo* all the problems of Ricardo and Malthus. In a stationary state the capital stock is constant, even though the capital goods which make it up can change. From this point of view, capital is similar to labour, which remains homogeneous while different individuals enter and leave the labour force. An output is obtained from these two factors, which is also homogeneous. It is produced under conditions of constant returns to scale. In perfect competition, the marginal productivities of the factors, which depend on the respective supplies, determine wages and interest.

Clark encountered great difficulties in distinguishing between variations of labour in regard to the existing capital goods and variations of labour in regard to the 'capital' stock. He called 'rents' the returns on the existing capital goods (including land), and maintained that in equilibrium they will equal interest, i.e. the marginal productivity of 'capital'. Equilibrium here implies that the adjustment of the composition of capital goods to productive needs has been achieved. These rents are similar to Marshall's quasi-rents. Therefore they should be different from the land rent; but Clark ignored the fact that the supply of land is fixed and cannot be adjusted to demand in the way that capital goods can. Clark reserved, finally, the term 'profit' for the temporary surpluses arising from short-run dynamics.

6.3.2. Fisher: Inter-temporal choice and the quantity theory of money

Although during his life Fisher was heavily criticized, after his death his work was the object of great admiration. Time has proved Schumpeter's prediction correct: 'some future historian may well consider Fisher as the greatest of America's scientific economists up to our own day' (*History of Economic Analysis*, p. 872). Schumpeter himself gave two reasons for this evaluation. The first is that Fisher was a spokesman on several non-economic subjects: he was a follower of eugenics, a strong supporter of prohibitionism, and a versatile writer on politics. The second reason is his extraordinary knowledge of mathematics (Gibbs, the great physicist of thermodynamics, was one of his mentors); and this enabled him to make economic applications ahead of his time. Fisher was, for example, the inventor of the index numbers and a pioneer of econometrics. He was also, however, a hopeless interpreter of economic facts and a disastrous speculator on the stock exchange. In the autumn of 1929 he declared publicly that the share values had by that time reached their maximum stability, so that, operating on the basis of this presupposition, he lost not only his reputation as an economist but also almost the entire family wealth.

Over his career Fisher was interested in the same set of problems as Clark. However, his way of tackling them was different: he was less concerned about searching for an ethical basis for the market and more interested in the relevance of hypotheses and correctness of reasoning. His first theoretical contribution to economics was his 1892 doctoral dissertation, *Mathematical Investigations in the Theory of Value and Prices*, which contains a magnificent exposition of the general-equilibrium theory of Walras—an author, however, whose work he declared in the Preface that he did not know.

His main theoretical heritage is rather to be found in Jevons, Auspitz, and Lieben. The two Austrian economists had published a book, *Untersuchungen über die Theorie des Preises* (*Researches on the Theory of Prices*) (1889), which was at that time the only Austrian contribution of worth to mathematical economics. Fisher particularly admired their partial-equilibrium analysis of price under competitive conditions, an analysis which in its essence was comparable to Marshall's much more famous study. In his theory of general equilibrium, Fisher was convinced that there were deep formal analogies between thermodynamics and the economic system, and tried to apply to economics some of the innovations which Gibbs had introduced in vector calculus. Recent advances by Herbert Scarf in computational aspects of the solutions of general-equilibrium systems have in Fisher an important precursor.

Fisher's general-equilibrium model tended to overlook the problems of supply, and in particular did not take into account either capital or interest. He devoted *Appreciation and Interest* (1896) and *The Nature of Capital and Income* (1906) to the problems raised by capital. These works laid the basis for a great deal of the later work on the subject. Schumpeter believed it was 'the first economic theory of accounting, [and] the basis of modern income analysis' (p. 872). Here the notion of income as consumption was first presented; a consumption that naturally includes the consumption of the services of durable goods.

Fisher's famous theory of the determination of rates of interest is to be found in *The Rate of Interest*, published in 1907, and in the new enlarged edition of the same work, published in 1930 under the title *The Theory of Interest*. Fisher revised the original text because the critics had only focused on the role of 'impatience' as a determinant of the rate of interest, overlooking the role of 'opportunity'. In *The Theory of Interest*, he formulated what he called an 'impatience and opportunity' theory of interest, where the 'investment opportunity' was defined as 'the rate of return over cost', and where both cost and return were defined in terms of income streams. In fact, this concept was extremely similar to the Keynesian notion of 'marginal efficiency of capital', as Keynes himself was later to acknowledge. Fisher extended general-equilibrium theory to the problem of inter-temporal allocation, an extension which allowed him to anticipate some of the conclusions of the famous life-cycle model, i.e. those that explain why individuals prefer to spread their consumption over time, whatever the time-path of their expected incomes. Fisher's theory of individual savings is, basically, still accepted in the neoclassical literature today. The approach adopted by Fisher allowed him to remain above the controversies about capital and interest which were already brewing in that period. By reasoning in terms of 'investment opportunity', he had no need to assume a productive factor, 'capital', that enters as an argument into the production function. In this theory, interest is not considered as a cost of production. To understand its nature, it is necessary to assume that, starting from a situation of equality between current and planned future consumption, the individual requires a quantity of future consumption greater than that of current consumption, as a 'compensation' for an additional unit of saving. Fisher attributed this rate of compensation to 'impatience', forcefully rejecting the idea that interest represents the cost of the services of a production factor called 'abstinence' or 'waiting'. In this sense, the American economist opposed the Austrian argument, made popular by Böhm-Bawerk, that waiting contributes to increase the product. The explanation of interest is to be found in impatience; on the other hand, the brevity and uncertainty of life are the facts accounting for time preference.

In 1911 Fisher published *The Purchasing Power of Money*, which contains his contribution to monetary theory: the equation of exchanges or quantity equation, $P = (MV + M'V')/T$, where P denotes the price level, M the quantity of money in circulation, V its velocity of circulation, M' the current-account bank deposits, V' the rate of turnover of the deposits, and T the transactions. No other mathematical formula in the whole of economics, nor, perhaps, in any other discipline, with the exception of Einstein's, has ever enjoyed greater fame, a fame still intact today. It represents the traditional idea according to which variations in the money supply, if its velocity and the volume of transactions remain unchanged, will generate variations in the level of prices. This quantity equation is the origin of the theoretical apparatus of modern monetarism, a theoretical system which became popular during the 1960s, especially thanks to the work of Milton Friedman. Even if it is also true that Fisher introduced several qualifications, as we will see in Chapter 7, to take into account the adjustments of the transactions and the effects of variations in V and V', a strong and clear monetarist message still emerges from his work.

6.4. NEOCLASSICAL THEORY IN AUSTRIA AND SWEDEN

6.4.1. The Austrian School and subjectivism

Menger left the chair of economics at the University of Vienna in 1903. He was succeeded by von Wieser, 'the central figure of the Austrian School: central in time, in the ideas he professed, in his intellectual ability', as Streissler described him ('*Arma virumque cano*: Friedrich von Wieser, the Bard as Economist' (1986), p. 194). His 1914 general treatise, *Theorie der gesellschaftlichen Wirtschaft* (*Theory of Social Economy*) gave width and order to Mengerian thought. For quite some time it was used as the basic textbook of the school. Up to the beginning of the 1920s, however, Böhm-Bawerk was the most prestigious and at the same time the most controversial personality of the Austrian school. In the 10 years before the First World War it was Böhm-Bawerk's seminars, a group which included von Mises and Schumpeter, that was the main centre of theoretical formulation of the Austrian School. It is not by chance that the Marxists of the time considered Böhm-Bawerk as the intellectual enemy to defeat: it was he who represented bourgeois economics.

Böhm-Bawerk became famous not only for his theory of interest but also for his frontal attack on the Marxian labour theory of value. In 1896 (volume

III of *Capital* had been published two years before), the Viennese economist published *Zum Abschluss des Marxischen Systems* (*Karl Marx and the Close of his System*), an essay in which he aimed at stigmatizing the 'great contradiction' in Marx's work between price calculation and the labour theory of value. A talented controversialist and at the same time a man with vast practical experience (he was three times Austrian Minister of Finance), he started that tension between Marxist scholars and the neoclassical economists of the Austrian School which was to surface again, in the inter-war period, in the controversy about the possibility of economic calculation in a centrally planned economy (see section 8.5).

Böhm-Bawerk set out to extend the Mengerian theory of subjective value to the theory of capital and interest. After having published the heavy *Geschichte und Kritik der Kapitalzinstheorie* (*History and Criticism of the Theory of Interest*) in 1884, his main work, the *Positive Theorie des Kapitales*, came out in 1889. These two books make up the two parts of a treatise entitled *Kapital und Kapitalzins*. The fortunes of the Austrian School at the end of the nineteenth and the beginning of the twentieth centuries were largely due to this book. The work was to receive a mixed reception. On the one hand, the neo-Böhm-Bawerkians of the 1960s and 1970s, led by P. Bernholz and M. Faber, tried to go beyond the limits set by the analysis of their master. On the other hand, economists like L. Lachmann, on the basis of Menger's opinion (as reported by Schumpeter), judged Böhm-Bawerk's theory of capital as 'one of the biggest mistakes ever made'. Böhm-Bawerk himself, however, considered his own theory of capital and interest as a simple extension of Menger's subjective theory of value.

Böhm-Bawerk's specific contribution lies in the idea that the fundamental characteristic of every productive activity using capital, intended as a set of reproducible means of production, is that of linking the events in time-sequences. In this case, it is relations of complementarity rather than of substitutability that characterize the set of possible technological transformations. Time is considered as an irreversible succession of moments, so that the productive structure in a given instant depends not only on past investments but also on the time-sequences in which these have been made.

In other words, capital enters the production process as the *duration* of the time lapsing from the introduction, at different moments, of the original productive factors, labour and land, to the attainment of the final output. Böhm-Bawerk and all the first-generation Austrian economists, however, missed the point that there is another way in which time enters the production process: the *duration* of the interval of time in which the 'machine' surrenders its services. In fact, in the Austrian conceptualization, capital is almost always circulating capital. In it there is no place for fixed capital; this explains why their favourite examples are those of production processes such as the maturing of wine or the growing and cutting of trees. According to the celebrated terminology of R. Frisch, the time-structure of the productive process studied by Böhm-Bawerk is of the *continuous input–point output* type. We had to wait for J. Hicks's *Capital and Time* (1973) for a rigorous formulation of the fixed-capital case, i.e. of the *continuous input–continuous output* model.

Once Böhm-Bawerk had introduced the time element into the analysis of consumption and production decisions, he argued that it was possible to explain interest in these terms: as production requires time, and as individuals systematically prefer present to future goods, the production processes that use capital must generate a product which allows the payment of interest to those who, in preceding periods, have invested in the indirect productive processes. Unfortunately, the desperate attempt to bend the theory of capital to the needs of demonstrating the positivity of interest was responsible for some serious difficulties which Böhm-Bawerk never succeeded in overcoming. As von Hayek noted in *The Pure Theory of Capital* (1941), 'The treatment of the theory of capital as an adjunct to the theory of interest has had somewhat unfortunate effects on its developments, [since] the attempts to explain interest, by analogy with wages and rent, as the price of the services of some definitely given "factor" of production has nearly always led to a tendency to regard capital as a homogeneous substance the quantity of which could be regarded as a "datum" ' (p. 5). This was a notable proposition, which anticipated the essential terms of the great debate on capital theory of the 1960s.

6.4.2. The Austrian School joins the mainstream

The Austrian theoretical approach joined the mainstream of the neoclassical system in the 1920s and 1930s. In order not to break our narration, and even at the cost of being a little repetitive, we will describe in this section how this happened. However, some of the material we present here will be considered again, and in more detail, in Chapters 7 and 8, dedicated to 'The Years of High Theory'.

After the First World War, the scenario of Austrian economic theory changed dramatically and a new generation of economists came into the limelight, for example Friederich von Hayek, Gottfried Haberler, Fritz Machlup, Oskar Morgenstern, Paul Rosenstein-Rodan, and Hans Mayer. During the 1920s and 1930s, the theoretical debate was conducted between three groups of scholars which were partially overlapping. The first, led by the mathematician Karl Menger, son of the economist Carl, studied mathematical applications. In Chapter 8 we deal with the contributions by some members of this group to the problem of the existence of solutions in the general-equilibrium model. Of the other two groups, one, led by Mayer, was linked to the university. Mayer's most important contribution was his criticism of equilibrium theory, which he judged as being incapable of accounting for the sequence of actions that lead to the formation of market prices. According to him, only a 'genetic-causal' method is able to explain this sequence. This point was taken up again by the neo-Austrian research programme which we discuss in Chapter 11.

The third group was based on the famous *Privatseminar*, led by von Mises, which met at the Viennese Chamber of Commerce. This seminar group included, besides various young economists, philosophers and sociologists of the stature of Felix Kaufmann, Alfred Schutz, and Eric Voegelin. It was this group that made the first rigorous attempt to systematize the Austrian way of doing economic theory. Above all, it contributed to spreading its message outside the Viennese environment. It is important to note, however, that Menger's philosophical inspiration was not always fully accepted by the young members of the Austrian School. The replacement of the Aristotelian paradigm by a Kantian one was the major break with tradition. This was especially evident in Mises, who, while considering himself as the real heir of Menger, from the methodological and philosophical points of view had little in common with the founder of the School.

In this period Lionel Robbins, of the London School of Economics, entered into contact with the Viennese group and was much influenced by it. In 1931, Robbins invited von Hayek (1899–1992) to teach at the London School of Economics. These contacts led to the publication of *An Essay on the Nature and Significance of Economic Science* (1932), which permitted the introduction of a great many of the Austrian ideas into mainstream economics. There is no doubt that the Austrian approach dominated Robbins's *Essay*, as is shown by the fact that he only cited authors from that school. Besides this, the origin of what was to become Robbins's famous definition of economic science as 'the science which studies human behaviour as a relationship between ends and scarce means which have alternative uses' (p. 15) can be traced back to Menger's *Grundsätze*. The *Essay* was not an immediate success, as can be seen from Souter's direct attack on it in an article published in the *Quarterly Journal of Economics* the following year. The accusation was that Robbins had distanced himself from Marshall's thought: 'Professor Lionel Robbins' recent book . . . is important, not merely because it provides English and American students with an able, scholarly and succinct account of the main tenets of "the Austrian School" (it is Professor Robbins' *credo* as an adherent of that school)' (p. 377).

Hayek's arrival in London also contributed to the diffusion of the Austrian theory of the business cycle, a theory that Mises had already sketched out in 1912. The upward phase of the cycle was attributed to mistaken inter-temporal allocations caused by a 'too low' rate of interest. The mistake lies in the fact that the firms begin productive processes which imply the existence of a certain desire by consumers to postpone consumption, while in reality this is incompatible with the true pattern of their time preferences. The consequent abandonment or truncation of the processes already started then triggers the downward phase of the cycle. This model reveals, on the one hand, the typically Böhm-Bawerkian way of representing the productive process and, on the other, the Wicksellian theory of the relationship between the natural and the bank rate of interest. We will discuss this theory in the next section.

The early 1930s saw the maximum theoretical influence of the Austrian School—an influence, however, that was destined to be short-lived. Although Mayer continued to hold his chair of economics, the chair that had been held by Wieser up to the beginning of the Second World War, the group of young and brilliant economists of the circle dispersed, mainly for political reasons. Mises himself emigrated to Geneva in 1934 and then to New York. Also, many members of the group became convinced that the central ideas of their school had almost completely entered the orthodoxy at last. The eclipse of the historical approach and the decline of the anti-theoretical orientations had persuaded even the most reluctant scholars that the Austrian ideas had finally prevailed, and that there was no longer any need to fight for an 'Austrian version' of economic theory. A declaration by von Mises, in 1933, is evidence of this conviction. Subdividing economics into three schools of thought, 'the Austrian, the Anglo-American, and the Lausanne School', von Mises, referring to Morgenstern, argued that these groups of economists 'differ only in their needs of expressing the same fundamental idea and that they are divided more by their terminology and by peculiarities of presentation than by the substance of their teachings' (*Epistemological Problems of Economics*, p. 214).

Machlup held the same view. He believed that four cardinal ideas of the Austrian School had already permeated all schools of thought before the Second World War. First was *methodological individualism*, which claims that the only valid propositions of the social sciences are those that can be reduced to propositions about individual wills and actions, that all the motivations of agents and institutions are derived from individual behaviour, and, finally, that there are no immanent tendencies towards goals independent of individual desires. Second was *subjectivism*, which claims that individual actions can only be understood with reference to the knowledge, beliefs, and expectations of the individuals themselves. Third was *opportunity cost*, which suggests that the costs which influence decisions are reducible to the most important of the sacrificed alternatives when productive resources are employed for a certain aim. The last concept was that of the *time dimension* in both consumption and production activities, from which is derived the notion of 'time preference' and the hypothesis of a greater productivity of the less direct methods of production.

Successive developments, especially by Hayek, Lachmann, and Kirzner, demonstrated that this typically Austrian list of ideas was not complete. We will discuss this in Chapter 11, with reference to the contributions of the Neo-Austrian School.

6.4.3. Wicksell and the origins of the Swedish School

Wicksell in many ways is the Scandinavian Marshall. He was honest in acknowledging the contributions of others, humble in recognizing the limits of his own analysis, intelligent in avoiding illicit generalizations, and had an extraordinary ability to anticipate successive developments. Unlike Marshall, however, Wicksell did not receive great acclaim during his life, not even in his own country. It was only during the 1930s, when, on the initiative of Kahn and Keynes, *Geldzins und Gueterpreise* (*Monetary Interest and Prices of Goods*) (1898) and the two volumes of *Vorlesungen über die Nationaloekonomie* (*Lectures on National Economy*) (1901 and 1906) were translated into English, that Wicksell's name, and especially his thought, began to circulate among a wider circle of economists, so much so that in the period between Keynes's *Treatise on Money* (1930) and the *General Theory* (1936) everybody declared himself to be neo-Wicksellian.

With *Ueber Wert, Kapital und Rente* (*On Value, Capital and Rent*) (1893), the great Swedish economist produced a notable work of synthesis. Beginning from the theories of value and marginal utility of Jevons and Menger, he tried to blend Böhm-Bawerk's analysis of capital and interest with the Walrasian general-equilibrium model. He formulated a model in which the product increases with the time-interval between the introduction of inputs and the production of output. His explanation of the positivity of the rate of interest, based on the argument of the marginal productivity of waiting, is almost as important as Fisher's reformulation. He was heavily indebted, intellectually speaking, to Austrian thought and was well aware of this. In 1921 he even wrote: 'Since Ricardo's *Principles* there has been no other book—not even excepting Jevons' brilliant but somewhat aphoristic and Walras' unfortunately difficult work—which has had such a great influence on the development of economics as Menger's Grundsätze' (quoted by C. G. Uhr, 'Knut Wicksell: A Centennial Evaluation' (1951), p. 834).

In the first volume of the *Lectures*, Wicksell completed the reformulation of Böhm-Bawerk's theory of capital and interest, abandoning the measurement of capital in terms of 'average period of production' and substituting a theory in which capital is reduced to the time-structure of the inputs employed at different periods. Then he argued that this structure can undergo variations in at least two dimensions: width and height. Finally, he tried, with partial success, to develop a theory of the ways in which the time-structure of the production process changes with variations in wage-level and rate of interest. As Wicksell himself recognized with reference to the process of ageing wine, only for very special technologies is the *value* of the capital stock $V_k = \sum_{i=1}^{n} p_i K_i$ (where K_i represents the quantity of the ith capital good and p_i its price) an appropriate measure of the aggregate capital stock intended as a factor of production. That is so because V_k is a function of the rate of interest, r. The *Wicksell effect* is precisely the change in the value of the capital stock which occurs with variations in r, i.e. dV_k/dr. The expression 'Wicksell effect' was introduced by Uhr in 1951, but its importance was not appreciated until the contributions of Joan Robinson and Piero Sraffa. There is a *price Wicksell effect*—which is the revaluation of capital goods due to variations in prices—and a *real Wicksell effect*—which is the sum of the changes, expressed in value, in the physical quantities of the diverse capital goods. Their sum is:

$$\frac{dV_k}{d_r} = \sum_{i=1}^{n} \frac{dp_i}{dr} K_i + \sum_{i=1}^{n} p_i \frac{dK_i}{dr}$$

Basically, when r varies, both the prices and the physical quantities change. Now, if there were only one capital good ($n = 1$), the real Wicksell effect would always be negative, to which one could give the usual interpretation that the capital intensity of the techniques increases with a decrease in the rate of interest. But when there are diverse capital goods ($n > 1$), both Wicksell effects can be positive or negative, and so can their sum. And no commonsense interpretation can be given to this case.

Shortly before his death, Wicksell tried to introduce fixed capital in the Austrian model, which only included circulating capital—an objective that he would have been able to achieve if, rather than introducing linear depreciation, he had used the formula of exponential depreciation; but he did not have time.

Wicksell's contribution to the marginalist theory of distribution is of great importance. We have already mentioned this in the sections dedicated to Wicksteed and Clark. In his formulation Wicksell used a simple general-equilibrium model with only one good, Q, produced by the means of labour, L, and homogeneous capital, K. What was later to become famous as the Cobb–Douglas production function, $Q = L^a K^{1-a}$, was already present in the writings of the young Wicksell. Special attention should be paid to Wicksell's approach to the problem of the exhaustion of the product. Barone, in 'Studi sulla distribuzione' (*Studies on Distribution*) (published in the *Giornale degli Economisti* in 1896), had already realized that, in order to obtain the exhaustion of the product, it is sufficient for firms to activate production up to the attainment of minimum average costs. In such cases there is no need to assume first-degree homogeneity of the production function. Wicksell integrated this argument with the explicit recognition of the fact that the existence of such a minimum is the necessary condition for the existence of a long-run competitive equilibrium. In fact, only at the point of long-run minimum cost is it possible to have zero profits. Unlike Barone and Walras, who considered this solution as an alternative to that of Wicksteed, Wicksell realized that it was a generalization, since the minimum of the long-run average cost curve is characterized by 'locally' constant returns of scale. This means that competitive equilibrium implies that, at least locally, Wicksteed's technical conditions apply.

Wicksell's solution was based on the *theory of the entrepreneur*, according to which the entrepreneur contributes to the production process by means of the services of his own factors. In equilibrium these services have the same remuneration, whether they are employed by the entrepreneur in his own firm or passed on to other firms. The labour employed to organize and co-ordinate the firm will be remunerated in the same way exactly as the labour of the same quality employed in other activities and in any other firm. In fact, if the entrepreneur received a higher remuneration, everybody would wish to employ their own labour in organizational tasks and nobody would wish to be a subordinate. Obviously, in order for zero profit to be reached in this way, the number of those who possess entrepreneurial skills must be high. Even if he did not say so himself, it is plausible to think that Wicksell had in mind a stationary-state equilibrium in which the entrepreneur has no real decision-making role, and in which the organizational work is reduced to mere supervision.

Geldzins und Güterpreise and the second volume of the *Lectures* include Wicksell's most important work on monetary theory. He was one of the first to use the aggregate supply-and-demand approach to explain variations in the value of money. In most versions of the quantity theory of money the price level varies directly and in proportion to the variations in the quantity of money; but in these versions there is no relationship between the variations in the quantity of money, including bank credit, and the entrepreneurs' production decisions. Wicksell brought out this relationship and advanced the hypothesis that, in the absence of exogenous disturbances (those over which the central bank has no control, such as variations in the production of gold or the necessity to finance huge government *deficits*), the fluctuations in price level would be caused by a persistent gap between the bank (or market) rate of interest and the real (or 'natural') rate—the latter being defined as the expected rate of returns on newly produced capital goods. Wicksell came to the conclusion that, contrary to the implication of the simple quantity theory, it is the quantity of money that adjusts to the price-level movements. In his analysis, monetary equilibrium requires the satisfaction of the three following conditions:

(1) equality between the natural and the bank rate of interest; or rather, since the natural rate is not an observable variable, the prevalence of a market interest rate capable of guaranteeing;

(2) equality between the supply of savings and the demand for investment loans and 'real' cash balances;

(3) price stability.

We will consider the mechanism that ensures equality between the two rates of interest in section 7.1.3. Here we would like to point out that banks would be able to make a decisive contribution to the re-establishment and the maintenance of equilibrium by increasing the rate of interest in periods of inflation and decreasing it in periods of deflation.

The study of these three conditions of monetary equilibrium was to receive a great deal of attention in the late 1920s and throughout the 1930s, especially by Lindahl, Myrdal, and Ohlin. The work of these scholars together with that of some of their younger colleagues such as Lundberg and Svennilson, contributed to extending Wicksell's economic theory and to forming the Swedish (or Stockholm) School, which we will treat in more detail in Chapter 7.

Here it is important to emphasize a central characteristic of Wicksell's analysis: that for which the gap between the two rates of interest produces effects that will only be felt on the price *level*. This gap will not modify *relative* prices (because all prices and incomes will increase to the same degree), nor will it have any relevant effects on the accumulation of capital. Wicksell did not exclude the possibility that changes in the monetary rate of interest would induce the adoption of more or less capital-intensive techniques, but he maintained that these effects would be of secondary importance. In any case, the natural rate of interest could be considered constant during the cumulative process.

Another important aspect of Wicksell's thought concerns the theory of public finance and optimal taxation. In *Finanzteoretische Untersuchungen* (*Researches of Finance Theory*) (1896), Wicksell applied marginal-utility theory to the public sector of the economy, reaching, on the one hand, the formulation of the well-known principle of benefit and contributive ability as the fundamental criterion of taxation, and, on the other, the proposal to set the prices of the services of public firms according to the criterion of marginal cost. In fact, it was his 1896 work that initiated the Wicksell–Lindahl–Musgrave–Samuelson line of thought on the theory of public goods. According to this line of thought, the production of public goods should be pushed forward, to the point at which the marginal cost equals the sum of the marginal rates of substitution between public goods and private goods of all individuals interested in the public goods. With a little too much faith in honesty and in the principle of consensus, typical of the Scandinavian culture, Wicksell did not seem to realize what was later to become the problem of free-riders: each individual in a Lindahl-type market is motivated to declare that he does not draw any utility from the public good, with the aim of avoiding contributions to financing it.

Wicksell was decidedly reformist. He fought for programmes of redistribution of wealth from the rich to the poor, and this brought him quite a few problems in his academic career. No writer in the Edwardian period was nearer to the New Deal ideology than Wicksell. He rejected Marxism both as an instrument to understand the laws of movement of capitalism and as a guide to the action aimed at improving the conditions of the working class. In a rather more sophisticated manner than Marshall, Wicksell realized that a competitive equilibrium does not necessarily lead to a state of maximum social welfare, nor to a fair state. However, he anticipated the neoclassical argument that makes perfect competition a condition for Pareto optimality; and he understood that, by operating on the initial endowments of individuals, it is possible to lead the system towards a state which, besides being efficient, is also ethically acceptable. In any case, Wicksell forcefully emphasized the argument that the attainment of efficiency in no way constitutes a morally incontrovertible objective, so that there is no space in economic theory for a defence of the capitalist system.

Wicksell's anti-conformism helps us understand his fierce rivalry with Gustav Cassel, the King's tutor and a leading light in the Swedish intelligentsia. Before the 1930s, Cassel, the real pillar of Swedish conservative economics, was the economist most often quoted in the international press. In 1918 he published *Theoretische Sozialoekonomie (Theoretical Social Economy)*, a work that developed an interesting general-equilibrium model without making any reference to Walras. It also contained an important novelty: it did not use any utility functions. Cassel was a tenacious critic of the concept of marginal utility. By using the demand function as a primary concept and thus breaking the link between the utility functions and the demand functions, Cassel placed prices at the centre of his theory of resource allocation. This is perhaps why his work had such an enormous influence on economics literature up to the 1930s. Schumpeter, however, perhaps a little naughtily, was to define Cassel as '90 per cent Walras and 10 per cent water'.

6.5. PARETO AND THE ITALIAN NEOCLASSICAL ECONOMISTS

6.5.1. From cardinal utility to ordinalism

Vilfredo Pareto, a member of a family which included eminent politicians as well as revolutionaries, succeeded Walras into the chair of economics at the University of Lausanne, where he published his *Cours d'économie politique* in 1896–7. His important *Manuale di economica politica* was published in 1906. He had many research interests, including economics, sociology, and political science. His *Trattato di sociologia generale* (1916), better known in the Anglo-Saxon world as *The Mind and Society*, is a classic; and Pareto's Law on the distribution of income, a law according to which income is distributed among individuals in approximately the same way in all countries at all times, is still discussed and used today.

Here, for reasons of space, we will focus only on Pareto's fundamental contributions to economic theory: the foundation of the ordinalist statute and, in relation to this, the formulation of the Paretian criterion of optimality.

However, we should not overlook Pareto's contribution to general-equilibrium theory. According to J. Hicks, 'its famous theory of General Equilibrium is nothing else but a more elegant restatement of the doctrines of Walras' (*Value and Capital* (1939), p. 12)—an opinion shared by most people, but not completely true, considering that in the first volume of the *Cours*, the theory of general equilibrium is enriched by a section on monopolies (while Walras dealt with monopoly only in the 41st lesson, in his treatment of Cournot, without integrating it into the theory of general equilibrium). Not only this, but in the *Manuale*, Pareto gave numerous hints about what was later to be called monopolistic competition.

We have already mentioned that with the advent of the marginalist revolution there was a radical reformulation of the terms of economic discourse. In particular, opinion changed about the economic nature of productive activity, which was given its foundation in consumer choice: a certain productive configuration would be preferred to another if it satisfied individual needs in a better way.

The corner-stone of this construction is the theory of rational consumer behaviour, a theory that the early marginalists founded on the hypothesis that consumers are able to order their own needs. Gossen's famous First Law stated, in Georgescu-Roegen's formulation: 'If an enjoyment is experienced uninterruptedly, the corresponding intensity of pleasure decreases continuously until satiety is ultimately reached, at which point the intensity becomes nil' ('H. H. Gossen' (1983), p. lxxx). After having defined the utility of a good as its ability to satisfy needs, the early marginalists went on directly to postulate the existence of a function that associates a *measure* of total utility with the quantities of goods. Furthermore it was assumed that the increment in utility corresponding to each extra quantity consumed gradually decreases. This is the *principle of decreasing marginal utility*.

Now, the whole of this brilliant construction is based on one crucial assumption: that the utility an individual derives from the consumption of a good is a quantity that can be measured cardinally—a value which is unique in regard to linear transformation. Edgeworth, in *Mathematical Psychics*, had strenuously defended the cardinal measurement of utility. Deeply influenced by the discoveries of E. T. Fechner and E. H. Weber in experimental psychology, he even argued that satisfaction can be measured in terms of its atoms by means of a type of 'hedonimeter'.

Precisely because utility is identified in an intrinsic quality of objects (the property of generating happiness by satisfying needs), goods possess a utility as an intrinsic property. Happiness and welfare are objective, just as the health of a person is not subjective, as with the pleasure received from eating a good meal. For Bentham and the early marginalists, utility could be treated in the same way as an observable quantity, and considered measurable in the same way as weight is.

Towards the end of the nineteenth century another conception of utility gained ground, first cautiously and then with increasing authority: utility as an expression of preferences and therefore of individual choices. Pareto's contribution to this change in the notion of utility was decisive. In the *Cours*, the Italian economist coined the term 'ophelimity', from the Greek *ophelos* (beneficial), in order to denote 'the attribute of a thing capable of satisfying a need or a desire, legitimate or not' (p. 3). The main reason Pareto gave for his terminological innovation was that of distingushing the property of an object desired by an individual, its ophelimity, from the property of an object which is beneficial to society, its utility. For example, a weapon belongs to the first but not to the second category, whereas air and light, while useful to the human race, do not give ophelimity. This meaning of utility was used by Pareto in his monumental *Trattato*. The difference between utility and ophelimity is therefore the difference between 'socially useful' and 'desired'. For the individual, 'socially useful' is what leads to physical health or, more generally, material welfare, *le bien-être matériel*. Unpleasant medicine is useful for the patient, but it does not bring him ophelimity.

In the applications, Pareto considered ophelimity as a quantitative attribute; and it was precisely by using the cardinal nature of ophelimity that Pareto managed to demonstrate the famous theorem on the maximum ophelimity of the consumer. Pareto maintained the idea of ophelimity as a cardinal quantity even after becoming convinced that it was not necessary to measure it for consumer theory. In a letter to Maffeo Pantaleoni of 28 December 1899, he put forward the argument that an individual (or a group) always chooses, among the accessible alternatives, that which is preferable to all the other alternatives; the idea did not even cross his mind that the individual may not be able to choose. The time was still not ripe to doubt the postulate of the completeness of preferences. Thus, Pareto was able to state: 'Edgeworth and others start from the concept of the final degree of utility and end up by determining the indifference curves . . . I now leave completely aside the final degree of utility and *start* from the indifference curves. In this lies the whole novelty . . . One can start from the indifference curves, *which are a direct result of experience*'. (*Lettere*, ii. 288).

In this way the question whether utility or ophelimity are measurable became irrelevant. In the appendix to the *Manuale*, Pareto showed that it is possible to assign arbitrary (but increasing) *indexes* to the indifference curves; he thought, in this way, that he had succeeded in moving from utility to ophelimity, and from the latter to ordinal indexes, thus liberating economic theory from every 'metaphysical' element. However, he continued to consider ophelimity as cardinally measurable, in exactly the same way as his predecessors had considered utility.

In conclusion, already at the end of the century there were two distinct notions of utility in the literature, both known to all the pioneers of ordinalism, and especially to Pareto. And, by this time, almost everybody realized that, for the purposes of the theory of prices, there was no need whatsoever to use a cardinal measurement of utility. Fisher had already made this extremely clear in his *Mathematical Investigations*.

The implications of this new point of view were extremely important. On the one hand, utility only referred to the preference ordering of the individual; on the other, preferences were defined with respect to a situation of choice. In this way, the foundation of utility was placed in the virtual behaviour of an individual who has to choose. This behaviour is defined only in terms of certain conditions of consistency. All references to happiness and individual satisfaction of needs disappear, while the underlying motivations for the choices lose their importance. In the literature, terms such as satisfaction, tastes, needs, and desires continued to be used, but as heuristic devices for describing expected experiences rather than descriptions of real sensations. The utility orderings overlap with preference orderings, as the former are derived from the latter. Ordinalism finally came to the fore in the 1930s with the work of Robbins, Hicks, and Allen. However, the question naturally arises as to why such a radical change in the theory was so late in imposing itself, when all the necessary ingredients were already available at the beginning of the century. We will only be able to answer this question in Chapter 8.

6.5.2. Pareto's criterion and the new welfare economics

Once the notion of cardinal utility had been abandoned, it became obvious that there is no possibility of making interpersonal comparisons of utility. How is it possible to make judgements on alternative policy measures when individual utilities can be neither compared nor summed? As we have already mentioned, the criterion proposed by Bentham was the maximization of the sum of individual utilities, a criterion that found its widest application in Pigou's work. But once cardinality was abandoned it became necessary to find another rule in order to be able to advance social-welfare propositions.

The new criterion was discovered by Pareto: the efficiency of an allocation is maximum when it is impossible to increase one economic magnitude without decreasing another. In the specific case of social welfare, Pareto's criterion takes on the well-known formulation according to which a certain economic configuration is optimal when it is impossible to improve the welfare of an individual without worsening that of another. Such a criterion allows for the evaluation of alternative social states without any need whatsoever to use interpersonal comparisons of utility or welfare. All that is needed is to determine if each individual improves or worsens his own condition.

Walras was the first to put forward explicitly, even if in a rather unclear way, the idea that the best possible allocation of resources occurs when all goods are exchanged on perfectly competitive markets. This idea anticipated a crucial aspect of Pareto's criterion of social optimum: the *principle of unanimous evaluations of the allocations*. With the assertion that, in competitive equilibrium, all agents reach the maximum satisfaction, however this is defined, Walras had implicitly maintained that an evaluation of alternative allocations is only meaningful if there is complete consensus about it. Now, Pareto introduced a notion of social optimum which is compatible with the principle of unanimous evaluations—a notion that succeeded in crowning Walras's project, in that it proved the superiority of competitive markets with respect to other market structures. It was in 'Il massimo di utilità dato dalla libera concorrenza' ('The Maximum of Utility Given by Free Competition') (published in the *Giornale degli Economisti* in 1894) that Pareto put forward for the first time his notion of social optimum: this is an allocation that cannot be modified in order to increase the welfare of everybody. In other words, a social state is *Pareto-optimal* if and only if there is no other alternative state in which at least one individual is better off and nobody else worse off. On the other hand, a social state x is *Pareto-superior* to a social state y if and only if at least one individual is better off in x than in y without any other individual being worse off in x than y.

Now, provided it exists, is a Pareto optimum unique? Clearly not! An allocation to which no other is unanimously preferred is not necessarily the allocation unanimously preferred. There can be a multiplicity of Pareto optima, none of which is comparable with the others on the basis of the unanimity criterion. Pareto's fundamental result is the demonstration that each allocation associated with a competitive equilibrium is a social optimum in the above sense. If the allocation associated with a competitive equilibrium were unanimously preferred to *any* other possible allocation, then it would be possible to state that an equilibrium different from the competitive one is socially inferior to it. Yet it is not possible to assert the superiority, in general, of the competitive market structure, contrary to Walras's idea. However, Pareto demonstrated the superiority of perfect competition over monopoly. He then tried to compare it with other market structures, but did not obtain significant results.

6.5.3. Barone, Pantaleoni, and the 'Paretaio'.

The history of economic analysis is full of great economists whose ideas have been appreciated and assimilated only after many years, and who have lived, in the best of cases, surrounded by respect mixed with perplexity, without being able to form a 'school'. This is certainly not the case with Pareto. In spite of his despotic and intolerant attitude towards the ideas of others, he managed to surround himself with some of the best economic minds of his time, giving life to the famous 'Lausanne School'. In Italy, the diffusion of marginalism was the work of two illustrious members of the school, Enrico Barone (1859–1924) and Maffeo Pantaleoni (1857–1924).

Enrico Barone was a singular economist. He spent the years of his youth and early maturity in the army, and published some excellent works on military history. With the passing of time he showed a growing interest in economics, an interest that at first produced a gradual transformation of his historical methodology and then in 1906 culminated with his resignation from the army to dedicate himself full-time to economics.

As early as 1894, thanks to his friendship with Pantaleoni and Pareto, he collaborated on the prestigious *Giornale degli Economisti*, and many colleagues, including Walras, predicted a brilliant career for him. However, during the decade after his death the prevailing opinion was that he had, at least in part, betrayed these expectations, and that this was due, perhaps, to the excessive heterogeneity of his interests. This opinion is still sometimes expressed today. In any case, it is certain that his most famous work, the article 'Il ministro della produzione nello stato collettivista' ('The Minister of Production in the Collectivist State') (in *Giornale degli Economisti*, 1908) had to wait until 1935, the year of the publication of the English translation, thanks to Hayek's interest, for all its importance and originality to be recognized. In this article Barone raised the question whether a planner in a 'socialist' state, using a Walrasian general-equilibrium system, could obtain the same results as a decentralized economy based on private property. The answer was that the equations describing the two systems are formally equivalent, and that the only obstacle for the planner is one of computational complexity, a problem that in the competitive context is theoretically resolved by resorting to the auctioneer. All this is argued without any reference to the theory of utility, while the equivalence of the allocative results between the two systems is demonstrated with a pioneering use of Pareto optimality. Samuelson, in the *Foundations* (1947), recognized the importance of Barone's contribution in establishing the correct use of Pareto optimality as a criterion of economic efficiency.

Although his work played an important role in the debate between the supporters of the centrally planned economy and those of the market economy, Barone believed that the ideological element was absent from it. Above all, he was interested in the possibilities offered by mathematics in the search for a solution to many practical problems. Paradoxically, from this point of view, his most important work was a failure because he came to negative conclusions about the *practical* possibility of central planning based on the Walrasian theoretical system.

Other works of Barone also deserve attention, for example his studies on the theory of distribution and the problem of the exhaustion of the product, which we have already mentioned; but especially those in the field of public finance. Also in this field he was able to use Pareto's theories, above all his distribution law. He used this law to explain how the burden of taxation should be shared among the contributors. Once again, it was the practical problems that caught his imagination; on the basis of his methodological beliefs, and even though he was aware that the Pareto Law may not be stable, he defended it as a heuristic device to solve the thorny question of taxation. His relative lack of interest in theory itself meant that, when the first misunderstandings between Pareto and Walras arose, he stayed on the fence and tried to act as peace-maker, which only led him to be partially misunderstood by both.

Even today it is not possible to say how much Barone's ideas have contributed to the formulation and consolidation of the systems of thought of his two mentors, who were certainly not very generous in acknowledging their intellectual debts, while Barone tended to be exactly the opposite. Perhaps a major re-evaluation of his thought still has to be accomplished.

Let us now turn to Maffeo Pantaleoni, also a singular personality but for very different reasons. He had a fiery and volatile character and his furious opposition to any form of restriction on intellectual freedom brought him more than a few enemies. Nevertheless, he was a supporter of the Fascist regime, and shared a great many of Pareto's ideological prejudices. The two had an intense intellectual exchange which even spilled over into Pareto's interests in sociology, psychology, and public policy. Pantaleoni's brilliant and heterodox intelligence allowed him to make original incursions into a remarkable number of debates over the whole field of economics.

Pantaleoni's greatest merit may lie in his spreading within the Italian cultural world the 'new ideas' of Walras and Pareto and, more generally, the marginalist approach to economics. However, it is important to note that, from the methodological point of view, Pantaleoni was nearer to Marshall than Walras. More than one generation of Italian economists was educated with his extremely successful textbook: *Principii di Economia Pura* (*Principles of Pure Economics*) (1889), and when the English translation was published about a decade later, it enjoyed international success. In any case, in Italy, the 'new' economics was much more the economics of Pantaleoni than that of Pareto, also thanks to the flourishing and lasting school of thought he managed to create around himself.

Although he had a very different character to that of Barone, Pantaleoni shared with him an interest in practical problems. Particularly important were his applications of marginalist analysis to some classic problems of public finance, such as the financing of public spending and the theory of optimal taxation. Pantaleoni was never dogmatic in his use of the marginalist categories, and his refined eclecticism often led him to anticipate the arguments of many of the most widespread modern heterodox theories. The extraordinary accuracy of his applied analysis is clear, as is his sophisticated use of economic theory and his rare ability to understand the psychological and sociological aspects of economic phenomena.

Unlike Barone, the mathematical element never played a determinant role in his work. He believed economic reasoning to be endowed with an autonomous strength, which meant that any reference to 'more noble' disciplines was superfluous. The discipline that inspired Pantaleoni was not mechanics, but rather sociology, a science that studies diverse and complex causal factors and the complicated social-interaction patterns in which they are combined.

We must also mention here Ugo Mazzola (1863–99), author of *I dati scientifici della finanza pubblica* (*The Scientific Data of Public Finance*) (1890), a book judged by Pantaleoni as a 'lasting contribution' to the foundation of financial science, and one which was to exercise a strong influence on Wicksell's theoretical work. Mazzola was a student of Francesco Ferrara and a fervent admirer of the theories of Jevons and Menger. In 1896, together with other colleagues, he took control of the *Giornale degli Economisti* and, widening its cultural and scientific scope, transformed it into a forum of liberal thought.

The Italian economists in the first decade of the century were all, in one way or another, followers of Pareto and Pantaleoni. They concentrated their interest by and large, on applications of partial-equilibrium analysis, which they judged more likely to come to grips with reality and to produce results of practical value. Pasquale Jannaccone (1872–1959), a student of Pantaleoni and the author of *Il costo di produzione* (*The Production Cost*) (1902) made an important contribution to this line of thought. In 1916, he published an article, 'Il "paretaio"', stigmatizing the prevailing tendency among Italian economists to follow in an uncritical way the methodological canons of the Lausanne School. There is clear evidence of this in the works of Umberto Ricci (1879–1946) and Luigi Amoroso (1886–1965), even if the latter also made important contributions to general-equilibrium theory.

Bibliography

On Marshall and the English neoclassical economists: K. Bharadwaj, 'The Subversion of Classical Theory: Alfred Marshall's Early Writings on Value', *Cambridge Journal of Economics*, 2 (1978); A. K. Dasgupta, *Epochs in Economic Theory* (Oxford, 1985); P. Deane, *The State and the Economic System* (Oxford, 1989); J. Maloney, *Marshall, Orthodoxy and Professionalisation of Economics* (Cambridge, 1985); A. Marshall, *The Present Position of Economics* (London, 1885); *Principles of Economics* (7th edn., London, 1916); G. L. S. Shackle, *The Years of High Theory* (Cambridge, 1967); J. A. Schumpeter, *History of Economic Analysis* (London, 1955); *Early Writings of Alfred Marshall*, ed. J. K. Whitaker (London, 1975).

On neoclassical theory in America: E. R. Canterbury, *The Making of Economics* (Belmont, Calif., 1980); R. B. Ekelund and R. F. Herbert, *A History of Economic Theory and Method* (New York, 1975); G. Routh, *The Origin of Economic Ideas* (London, 1977); J. Schumpeter, 'Irving Fisher', in *Ten Great Economists from Marx to Keynes* (London, 1966); *History of Economic Analysis*, (London, 1955); J. Tobin, 'Neoclassical Theory in America: J. B. Clark and Fisher', *American Economic Review*, 75 (1985).

On neoclassical theory in Austria and Sweden: E. Böhm-Bawerk, *Kapital und Kapitalzins: Positive Theorie des Kapitales* (Innsbruck 1889); F. A. von Hayek, 'Bemerkungen zum Zurechnungsproblem', *Jahrbücher für Nationalökonomie und Statistik* (1926); I. Kirzner, 'Austrian School of Economics', in *The New Palgrave: A Dictionary of Economics*, i (London, 1987); J. Schumpeter, 'Eugen Böhm-Bawerk and Friedrich von Wieser', in *Ten Great Economists* (London, 1966); R. W. Souter, 'The Nature and Significance of Economic Science', *Quarterly Journal of Economics*, 47 (1933); E. W. Streissler, '*Arma virumque cano*: Friedrich von Wieser, the Bard as Economist', in N. Leser (ed.), *Die Wiener Schule der Nationalökonomie* (Vienna, 1986); L. von Mises, *Human Action* (London, 1949); *Epistemological Problems of Economics* (Princeton, NJ, 1960); *The Ultimate Foundation of Economic Science*

(Kansas City, 1962); C. G. Uhr, 'Knut Wicksell: A Centennial Evaluation', *American Economic Review*, 41 (1951); F. von Wieser, *Grundsätze der politischen Oekonomie* (Vienna, 1891); translated as *Fundamentals of Political Economy* (London, 1914).

On Pareto and the Italian neoclassical economists: G. Busino, 'Vilfredo Pareto', in *The New Palgrave: A Dictionary of Economics*, iii (London, 1987); J. S. Chipman, 'The Paretian Heritage', *Revue européenne des sciences sociales*, 6 (1976); N. Georgescu-Roegen, 'H. H. Gossen: His Life and Work in Historical Perspective', in H. H. Gossen, *The Laws of Human Relations* (Cambridge, Mass., 1983); G. L. S. Shackle, *The Years of High Theory*, chps. 7, 8 (Cambridge, 1967); A. P. Kirman, 'Pareto as an Economist', in *The New Palgrave: A Dictionary of Economics*, iii (London, 1987); W. Jaffe, 'Pareto Translated: A Review Article', *Journal of Economic Literature*, 10 (1972); V. Pareto, *Cours d'économie politique* (2 vols., Lausanne, 1896–7), *Lettere a M. Pantaleoni*, ed. G. De Rosa (3 vols., Rome, 1960); *Manuale di economia politica* (Milan, 1906; repr. following the 1909 French edn., Rome, 1965); *Trattato di sociologia generale* (Milan, 1964); G. Busino and P. Tommissen, 'A Bibliography of the Studies on Pareto', in *Jubilé du prof. V. P.* (Geneva, 1975).

7

The Years of High Theory: I

7.1.1. Economic hard times . . .

I went to university in the fateful 1930, and during the four-year course I watched the almost complete collapse of the American economy. I also had occasion, at that time, to hear my Professor of Banking, who was also the Vice-President of the New York Federal Reserve, admitting during a lecture that he did not know why the President had ordered the closure of all the banks the day before. My grandfather's bank did not open again and later my father also went bankrupt. I studied these events: my conversion can be seen from the fact that the subject of my thesis was Marxism. Having observed the incompetence and impotence of the Government, I decided to change to Economics, hoping to find there the key to understanding the events: even if this was rendered impossible by the useless orthodoxy of the period.

Thus R. M. Goodwin ('Economia matematica: Una visione personale' (1988), p. 157) explained his simultaneous conversion to Marxism and economics. This was not an isolated case; similar conversions flooded in during those years.

The entire period from the beginning of the First World War to the end of the Second was marked by crisis; a crisis which affected every sphere of bourgeois life, from the economic to the social and from the political to the cultural. The outbreak of the First World War had sown doubts about the rationality of the international capitalist system. But the most lucid minds had immediately understood the deep reasons for the conflict, and could not avoid acknowledging the truth in the arguments of those Marxist thinkers who had preached the dangers of imperialism and prophesized the great war. Then, as soon as the First World War had ended, the conditions were laid down for the Second, as Keynes and a few other enlightened thinkers immediately understood.

In the meantime, a nation-continent had attempted its escape from capitalism with the Bolshevik Revolution, an attempt which not even military intervention by the major capitalist powers was able to quell. At that time it was impossible to see where the revolution was finally going to lead. The only thing that everybody clearly saw was the practical demonstration that capitalism was not eternal and that the proletarian revolution was possible. Many and immediate were the attempts at imitation, driven on by the great wave of industrial conflict which had already affected all the major capitalist countries in the second decade of the century and which showed no signs of slowing down until the middle of the 1920s. The bourgeois terror was so great that in about fifteen years half of Europe was at the mercy of Fascism.

And if this were not enough to convince even the most optimistic of the depth of the crisis, they only had to look at the economy: the breakdown of the system of international payments, abandonment of the Gold Standard even by those countries which still supported it, competitive devaluations, harsh protectionism, the contraction in international trade; and then, increasing instability in growth, increasingly bitter crises, rampant unemployment, the Wall Street Crash, and the suicides of speculators. It seemed that all the Marxist predictions were turning out to be true, from the falling rate of profit to the increasing immiseration of the proletariat, from the deepening of the inter-imperialist contradictions to the reawakening, because of the crisis, of the revolutionary consciousness, and from the increase in the concentration of capital to the amplification of the periodic oscillations. Was the final collapse in sight?

Nobody was surprised at the weakening of the intellectual fascination of that economic orthodoxy which preached the allocative efficiency of competition and the rationality of economic agents. Nor was it surprising if the *laissez-faire* ideology could no longer recruit members, while the most enlightened economists began to theorize the necessity of abandoning free trade in order to rescue capitalism.

The economists of this period can be roughly divided into three groups. Some underwent a Goodwin-style conversion and, escaping from the fetters of the official science, began to look for alternative theoretical approaches, Marxist, institutional, or others, which seemed to promise sharper instruments with which to understand reality. A second group, on the contrary, gave up any pretence of using neoclassical theory to understand reality and tried to cultivate it as pure theory, satisfied with the puzzle-solving work it offered in abundance. Finally, there were those who, while continuing to show due respect for the official science in which they had been educated, tried to twist it to serve ends it was not suitable for, above all in the attempt to use it to explain the real world. The most eminent examples of the last category were Keynes and Schumpeter. But they were only the tip of the iceberg. Most of the economists of this group returned to the problems which had given birth to political economy: those of *macroeconomic dynamics*. It was not surprising that they lost more time than necessary in liberating themselves, often without success, from 'techniques of thought' which served more to hide than to reveal reality. Nor is it surprising that, in the end, they produced imperfect and incoherent theories.

In the next three sections of this chapter we will outline the three most important dynamic theories formulated in the years of high theory, those of Keynes, Kalecki, and Schumpeter. In the rest of this section we will consider various themes of economic dynamics to show the main directions of theoretical development from which originated the work of the three masters. And, in the next chapter, we will deal with developments in microeconomic and the general-equilibrium theory as well as with the contributions of various hetero-dox theories.

7.1.2. Money in disequilibrium

Up to now we have emphasized the static character of neoclassical analysis. In this chapter we must contradict ourselves. In fact, some dynamic macro-economic models had already been formulated in the 1890s by a few great neoclassical economists. It is interesting to note that the field in which such attempts were made was mainly that of monetary economics. It is not by chance that it happened in this way. In fact, unless money is considered as the same as any other good, monetary theory does not lend itself to a simple application of the method of maximization of individual goals in the presence of scarce resources: first, because money is not a good which is desired in itself and it is not clear what is meant by demand for money; second, because money is not a naturally scarce good and it is not obvious what is meant by supply of money; finally, because it is not evident which factors the supply and demand of money depend on, nor is it clear what is meant by monetary equilibrium.

The early neoclassical economists, who were all concerned with other matters, rather overlooked monetary problems and adopted the *equation of exchanges* as the last word in regard to the scientific explanation of the price level. As we have seen in the last chapter, in Fisher's (simplified) version, the identity

$$MV = PT$$

where M is the quantity of money, V is its velocity of circulation, P the level of prices, and T the level of transactions, becomes an explanation of the value of money once V, T, and M have been fixed exogenously. The difficulties and the interesting thing about this theory arise, as Cantillon and Hume had already pointed out, as soon as one wishes to study the *process* by which a monetary impulse affects the level of prices, that is, as soon as one wishes to tackle the problem of the value of money in dynamic terms. Fisher, Wicksell, and Mar-shall have made the most interesting attempts to solve this problem. Even though these theories were formulated in the 1890s, it is worth discussing them in this chapter, as they produced their best fruits precisely in the years of the 'high theory'.

In Fisher's theory, the variables appearing in the equation of exchanges are set at their normal value, so that the explanation emerging from the equation refers only to the 'final and permanent effects' of monetary changes. However, there are 'temporary effects' that are felt in the transition period. And it is with these effects that Fisher tried to explain economic fluctuations. When prices begin to rise, following an increase in M, the monetary interest rate is slow to adjust, so that the real interest rate falls. In this way economic activity and the creation of bank credit is stimulated. Production, pulled by demand, increases, and prices increase still more. However, the indebtedness of the economic agents also grows. Finally, when the monetary interest rate (and with it the real interest rate) rises to adjust to the reduced value of money, deflation begins; and this will have catastrophic effects owing to the high level of indebtedness artificially generated by the preceding boom.

Another great influence on the monetary thought of the 1930s, especially in England, was that of Marshall. The Marshallian version of quantity theory is represented by the famous 'Cambridge equation'. The first official formulation of this theory was made by Marshall in a testimony to the 'India Committee' in 1899. As early as 1871, while reformulating Mill's arguments on money, Marshall had already sketched out his own personal version of the quantity theory in an unpublished paper. For a long time, however, the Cambridge monetary theory remained basically an oral tradition. The key formulations came out rather late, and are to be found in an article by Pigou, 'The Exchange Value of Legal Tender Money', published in the *Quarterly Journal of Economics* (1917), and in Marshall's *Money, Credit and Commerce* (1923). The 'Cambridge equation' is:

$$M = hYP$$

where Y is the real income and h is the ratio in which individuals wish to keep liquid assets. Although h can be interpreted as the inverse of the income velocity of circulation, the original interpretation, which underlines its dependence on the decisions of economic agents, offers quite marked theoretical advantages. For example, it makes it possible to introduce into the demand function for money those 'psychological' factors, such as uncertainty and other motivations in regard to choices about personal wealth, which Keynes was later to develop into the liquidity preference theory.

Another important Marshallian idea in regard to monetary dynamics concerns periodical crises, which Marshall explained as caused by changes in the entrepreneurs's expectations in connection with credit fluctuations. This point of view was put forward for the first time in *Economics of Industry* (1879) and then taken up again in 'Remedies for Fluctuations of General Prices', published in *Contemporary Review* in 1887. Marshall tried to explain economic fluctuations by inflationary expectations. When credit expands excessively and prices rise, entrepreneurs and speculators expect further price rises; therefore they increase their demand for credit *and* goods. Thus the inflationary expectations are self-fulfilling. As monetary wages are inelastic in the short run, profits increase, investments are encouraged, and inflation is fuelled. In inflationary phases credit expands very fast, which puts the creditors in a risky position and reduces their willingness to offer further credit. At a certain point credit begins to contract and the interest rate rises. A lack of confidence spreads and speculators are forced to sell to repay debts. Thus, prices fall and real wages rise; panic creates panic, and spreads together with bankruptcies. In the end, production and employment contract. A precise type of monetary policy was derived from this theory, one based on the necessity to stabilize the price level, to control credit, and to establish an indexation of future payment contracts. Rather than Marshall, however, it was his students, especially Pigou and Keynes, who pursued this line of thought. This, for example, is the theory used by Keynes in *Tract on Monetary Reform* (1923).

7.1.3. The Stockholm School

An important source of dynamic analysis during the years of high theory was represented by Wicksell's work. We have already discussed this in the last chapter. Here we will recall the essential elements of Wicksell's contribution to monetary theory, just to introduce the theories of his followers. Towards the end of the last century and the beginning of ours, Wicksell undertook a detailed study of the nature and implications of the divergence between natural and bank interest rates and, more importantly, he formulated the nucleus of a theory which aimed to provide the basis for economic policy measures able to guarantee price stability.

In Wicksell's theory, the 'natural' interest rate is the equilibrium price of savings and investments, and, at the same time, the real rate of returns of investments. However, the ability of the banks to create credit is independent from savings, so that the market interest rate, i.e. the one applied to bank credit, can differ from the natural rate. If it is lower, the demand for credit will increase. The supply of credit will adjust, as it is fairly elastic (even if not completely, given the necessity of the banks to maintain reserves). The monetary expansion will fuel the demand for real goods and, with it, increase prices. This is a disequilibrium inflationary process in which Say's Law does not apply. As long as the difference between the natural and market interest rates lasts, aggregate demand will increase, partially dragging with it supply and generating a *cumulative process* of price increases.

In monetary equilibrium, savings are equal to investments, the market interest rate is equal to the natural one, profits are zero, and the level of prices is constant. Economic fluctuations are determined, according to Wicksell, by oscillations in the natural interest rate, which may be caused, for example, by technical progress (although he also mentioned changes in the state of confidence of the entrepreneurs), and by the tendency of the bank rate to lag behind the natural rate.

This model had an enormous influence on the monetary theory of the early nineteenth century, and was taken up and developed by various economists, especially Austrian, such as Mises and Hayek, but also American and English, such as Fisher and Keynes. In Sweden, Wicksell's teachings were developed by several scholars who went on to form, in the 1930s, the so-called 'Stockholm School', as it was named by Ohlin in 'Some Notes on the Stockholm

Theory of Saving and Investment' (*Economic Journal*, 1937). Its most important members were: Erik Robert Lindahl (1891–1960), Karl Gunnar Myrdal (1898–1986), Bertil Ohlin (b. 1899), and Erik Lundberg (b. 1907).

Lindahl developed the theory of the cumulative process in an article published in 1929 (reprinted in *Studies in the Theory of Money and Capital* (1939), with the title *The Interest Rate and the Price Level*) in which he anticipated some Keynesian arguments. He defined macroeconomic equilibrium in terms of the equality between the value of the production of consumer goods and the aggregate consumption expenditure. He argued that the Wicksellian cumulative process, in the presence of unemployment, would only partially have resulted in an increase in prices, while in part it would have generated increases in consumption and production in real terms, and therefore a reduction in unemployment.

Myrdal tried critically to develop the Wicksellian analysis in *Monetary Equilibrium* (published in Swedish in 1931, then translated into German in 1933 and into English in 1939). He maintained that *ex ante* investments, i.e. investment decisions, depend on the entrepreneurs's expectations in regard to the rate of return. Monetary equilibrium is only reached when *ex ante* investments coincide with *ex ante* savings, i.e. with the part of income which individuals decide not to consume. When the expectations of the entrepreneurs change, investments and the value of aggregate production also change, while savings adjust by means of variations in the incomes earned, the prices (of the consumer goods), and the saving ratio. In equilibrium, investments may be positive and aggregate demand may grow, so that monetary equilibrium is compatible with an increasing price-level. Vice versa it is possible, as a consequence of a restrictive monetary policy and owing to the inelasticity of money wages, that the process generates unemployment, so that equilibrium is reached at any level of employment.

The Stockholm School did not limit itself to developing the Wicksellian analysis of the cumulative processes in the field of monetary theory, but tried to extend its dynamic properties to other sectors of economic theory, contributing in this way to the birth of the modern methods of economic dynamics, to the point of anticipating some of the most recent developments of non-Walrasian economics. Besides this, there are, especially in the work of Lindahl, the basic theoretical elements of the modern notions of inter-temporal and temporary equilibrium. These notions were taken up, reformulated, and made known to the great academic public by Hicks in 1939. We will discuss this in more detail in the sections of the next chapter dedicated to Hicks. Here we will limit ourselves to outlining the evolution of these theories in Sweden. One of the first interesting contributions to the development of modern dynamics was made by Myrdal in his 1927 article, *Prisbildningsproblemet och föränderlighten*, in which expectations were introduced among the variables that determine prices. By means of expectations, future changes produce effects on economic activity before they actually occur. This leads to the fact that the determination of the equilibrium variables must include expectations of future movements. Subsequently, in another article of 1929, Lindahl, with the hypothesis of perfect foresight, defined an equilibrium in which, for each individual and each good, the expected price produces equality between supply and demand. All the expectations in regard to future evolution come true, so that the economy is in equilibrium 'through time': this is a type of inter-temporal equilibrium. A year before, but without Lindahl knowing it, Hayek had formulated the same concept.

The notion of inter-temporal equilibrium gives the appearance of a dynamic process. But it is not a true dynamics, as the determination of all the prices and all the quantities of all future periods takes place in the present time. In order to escape from this difficulty, Lindahl introduced a new concept, that of 'temporary equilibrium'. From this point of view the evolution of the economy through time occurs over a succession of periods. The basic hypothesis is that we are dealing with such brief periods of time that the factors which directly influence the prices can be considered as unchanged. The idea is that the economy is in equilibrium in each period, and that the data of that equilibrium, the factors influencing the prices, change from one period to another, like unpredictable disturbances. This type of analysis was criticized by Myrdal and Lundberg. The problem is that, in this model, the succession of the disturbances, and therefore of the equilibria, remains unexplained, while it is precisely the nature of the changes occurring in the movement from one period to another that must be explained. Lindahl recognized the difficulty, and admitted that he had endeavoured to introduce 'dynamic problems into a static context'.

It was in an unpublished paper written in 1934, and later in the article 'The Dynamic Approach to Economic Theory' (published in his 1939 book) that Lindahl made the decisive jump forward. Here he constructed a model of a sequential economy which moves in 'complete disequilibrium', and in which the prices of all goods are fixed each time by the single sellers. These prices are based on expectations that, *ex post*, usually turn out to be mistaken. Exchanges are undertaken at these prices, so that excess demands can occur on all markets. These excess demands are eliminated by means of unplanned variations in stocks, so that buyers always obtain what they demand, while the disequilibrium is only perceived by the producers. The producers, on the basis of the information thus obtained, modify their own expectations and, consequently, the announced prices for future exchanges. In this way the economy can move through a series of disequilibria without necessarily tending to adjust towards a Walrasian equilibrium. On the other hand, it could not be otherwise, as the 'complete disequilibrium' model does not use three of the fictional analytical devices of the Walrasian model: perfect price flexibility, the auctioneer, and *tâtonnement*. In Chapter 9 we will see that it was precisely the abandonment of one or other of these devices that gave birth to the modern non-Walrasian theories.

7.1.4. Production and expenditure

Around the beginning of the century, a group of trade cycle theories, quite different from those of the monetary type outlined above, became popular, especially among politicians and the general public, rather than academic economists. These theories focused on the real factors of crises and tended to cast doubts on some doctrinal taboos, such as Say's Law and the argument that the 'invisible hand' is able to ensure stability and full employment. Even if some of these theories were supported by a few orthodox economists, their origin is not within the neoclassical theoretical system but rather in that of 'the underworld of Karl Marx, Silvio Gesell, and Major Douglas' of which Keynes spoke in the *General Theory*, and in whom he found, if not precursors, at least economists who 'deserve recognition for trying to analyse the influence of saving and investment on the price level and on the credit cycle, at a time when orthodox economists were content to neglect almost entirely this very real problem' (*Treatise*, i. 161). It is possible to label these theories 'theories of real macroeconomic disequilibrium' and to divide them into two groups: those of 'over-savings' and those of 'over-capitalization'. In both cases their distant origin can be found in Marx's 'reproduction schemes', but the economists from whom the two approaches directly originated were John Atkinson Hobson (1858–1940) and Mikhail Ivanovic Tugan–Baranovskij (1865–1919)

Hobson tackled the problems of unemployment and crises in various works, among them *The Physiology of Industry* (written in collaboration with A. F. Mummery and published in 1889), *The Problem of Unemployment* (1896), *The Industrial System* (1909), and *The Economics of Unemployment* (1922). The basic argument was that the business cycle is caused by the effects that variations in the distribution of income have on the average propensity to save. In the expansion phases, prices increase and real wages decrease because of the delay with which money wages adjust. The increase in the profit share causes savings and investments to rise. The increase in productive capacity implies that the production of consumer goods will also rise; worse, as wages have difficulty in keeping pace, production will rise more rapidly than the demand. Therefore, unsold inventories will accumulate while the prices of consumer goods will drop. But this will cause profits to decrease, triggering the depression. Then, the depression itself, by causing production and income to decrease, will eliminate the excess of savings. Hobson pointed out the famous paradox or dilemma of thrift, according to which a high level of savings, while being useful for personal enrichment, is detrimental to the economy as a whole, as it reduces effective demand.

In the 1920s this paradox almost became a slogan among trade unionists, and in the progressive political circles; and it was taken up and publicized in two books whose success with the general public was just as great as their academic misfortune: *The New and Old Economics* by Major C. H. Douglas and *Profits* by W. T. Foster and W. Catchings. Keynes acknowledged that these two books had the merit of focusing on one of the fundamental problems of every theory of unemployment, even if they did not manage to solve it: the paradox of thrift.

Keynes criticized the theories of under-consumption in the same manner as Tugan-Baranovskij had many years before, with the argument that the lack of effective demand caused by low consumption can be compensated by high investment expenditure. Tugan had put this criticism forward in *Theoretische Grundlagen des Marxismus* (*Theoretical Foundations of Marxism*) (1905), where he attacked some Marxist theories of breakdown and under-consumption. In his major work, *The Industrial Crisis in Contemporary England* (published in Russian in 1894 and in German in 1901), Tugan advanced an original theory of economic crises in which investment decisions are the main cause of fluctuations.

The cyclical movements occur because of the absence of a balancing mechanism between savings and investments. The formation of savings is a relatively stable process, whereas investments tend to be carried out in clusters. In the phases of prosperity investments increase, generating effective demand for the whole economy by a process similar to that of the Keynesian multiplier. The financing of the investments over and above current savings is effected by an expansion of bank credit and by the availability of 'free' or 'loanable' capital, i.e. by the liquid funds accumulated in the preceding depression phase. The increase in investment raises the production and the productive capacity of the capital goods sector. However, in phases of prosperity the *proportion* between consumer-goods and capital-goods sectors changes in such a way that the productive capacity of the system tends to rise above consumer demand. This reduces the incentive for capital accumulation. Moreover, and this is the most important fact for Tugan, the accumulation of real capital leads to the exhaustion of loanable capital, and the supply of credit tends to slow down; the interest rate rises, and this discourages further capital accumulation. The consequences are an excess supply of capital goods and a reduction in their prices and production. Then, from this sector, deflation is transmitted to the whole economy. In the phases of crisis and depression, savings exceed investment, and are accumulated once again in the form of idle liquid balances.

Tugan-Baranovskij's model is the head—'the first and most original', as Keynes was to say—of a family of cycle models based on the relationships between savings and investment which have among their most important exponents Spiethoff, Bouniatian, Cassel, and the Keynes of the *Treatise*. We will discuss Keynes later. Here, for the sake of completeness, we will outline the models of Spiethoff and Cassel.

Arthur Spiethoff (1873–1957), immediately after the German translation of Tugan's book had come out, published an important essay, 'Vorbemerkungen zu einer Theorie der Überproduktion' ('Prelude to a Theory of Over-Production') in *Jahrbuch für Gesetzgebung, Verwaltung und Volkswirtschaft* (1902), in which he developed the theory of the Russian economist. According to Spiethoff, an investment boom can be triggered by technological innovations and the opening of new markets. During the expansion phase, the production of capital goods grows more rapidly than the production of consumer goods; employment and consumption also grow more rapidly, so that the composition of supply diverges from the composition of aggregate demand. The prices of consumer goods increase and, with these, profits. But accumulation of capital causes productive capacity to increase, and at a certain point production of consumer goods will exceed demand, thus causing prices and profits to fall. The rate of investment will decrease both because of diminished profitability and because plants have been renewed a short time before. In other words, the depression is caused by the over-capitalization of the preceding boom.

Karl Gustav Cassel (1866–1945) reproposed this model with some important modifications in *Theoretische Sozialoekonomie*. There were three main changes. The first concerns the role played by certain lags, such as those existing between investment decisions and the activation of plant and those between changes in the interest rate and investments. The second concerns the explanation, in terms similar to the accelerator mechanism, of the influence that variations in demand for consumer goods have on investments. The third regards the role played by the financial sector in amplifying economic fluctuations. A low interest rate during recovery, when profits are high, stimulates investments. Sooner or later, however, investment will overtake savings and the interest rate will rise, contributing to the inversion of the cycle. On the other hand, during the phases of depression the low level of investments with respect to savings causes the interest rate to decrease, thus paving the way for the next recovery. Monetary factors, however, are only reinforcing elements in the cyclical movement, whose real causes are to be found, as in the theories of Tugan and Spiethoff, in the disequilibria between the composition of demand and the structure of output.

It is this kind of disequilibrium which underlies almost all the non-monetary pre-Keynesian theories of the business cycle, and Keynes himself, in the *Treatise*, reasoned in these terms. We will see later that one of the essential aspects of the theoretical revolution to which Keynes gave his name consisted in going beyond this way of thinking.

7.1.5. The multiplier and the accelerator

The fourth great stream of thought in dynamic theory in the inter-war period was the study of the interaction between the multiplier and the accelerator. The principle of the multiplier can be presented, in its simplest way, by assuming the maximum aggregation possible. If ΔY represents the increment in the national income, ΔC the increment in consumption, and c the marginal

propensity to consume, then $\Delta C = c\Delta Y$. The sum of the increase in the autonomous expenditure, ΔA, and that of the induced expenditure, ΔC, is equal to
the variations in income:

$$\Delta A + \Delta C = \Delta Y$$

from which, by substituting in ΔC, we have

$$\Delta Y = \frac{1}{1-c} \Delta A$$

$1/(1-c)$ is the multiplier. If the propensity to consume is 0.8, an increase in
the autonomous expenditure of \$100 bn. will generate an increase in income
of \$500 bn. In fact, the initial expenditure of \$100 bn. generates incomes that
will be spent to buy consumer goods of the value of $0.8(100) = 80$; this generates incomes which will be spent to buy consumer goods of the value of
$0.8(80) = 0.64(100) = 64$; and so on. Therefore, the overall income generated
by the initial expenditure of 100 is equal to $100[1 + (0.8) + (0.8)^2 + (0.8)^3$
$+ (0.8)^4 + \ldots] = 500$. In fact, the sum of the numbers between the square
brackets tends towards $1/(1 - 0.8) = 5$.

Signs of a rudimentary but deep insight into the multiplier process can be
found in Marx. There is an interesting page in s. 12 of ch. 7 of the second
volume of the *Theories of Surplus Value*, in which Marx tries to explain
how a lack of effective demand in an industry with a high level of employment
can be transmitted to the entire economy through a reduction in the production of that industry and the consequent reduction in employment and
wages. The reduction in consumption which follows turns into a reduction
in demand for other industries, which, in turn, will be forced to reduce production and employment, generating a further reduction in effective demand.
This process is linked to another deflationary process, consisting of a reduction in the demand for intermediate goods and for the means of production
generated by the initial lack of demand and by the consequent reduction in
the levels of activity which gradually spreads through the whole economy.
The passage in which Marx explains this process is too brief and confused
for us to be able to speak of a theory of the interaction between the multiplier and the accelerator, or even just a clear theory of the multiplier; but it
is enough to show us that the problem had been posed long before it was
solved.

About 30 years after Marx, there were some more shrewd insights, if not
something more, in an unpublished work of 1896 by Julius Wulff and in one
by Nicolaus A. L. J. Johannsen (circulated as a paper in 1889 and published
in 1903 as *Der Kreislauf des Geldes und Mechanismus des Soziallebens* (*The
Monetary Circuit and the Mechanism of Social Life*)), which used the '*Multi-
plizirende Prinzip*', as Johannsen called it, to account for the effects produced
by an initial impulse of expenditure on the whole economy. Johannsen again
used the multiplier principle in his 1908 work, *A Neglected Point in Connection with Crises*.

However, the official date of birth of the multiplier is 1931. What happened was that the theory, or rather *a* theory, of economic policy had shown the necessity for the multiplier principle. Keynes, expressing opinions circulating in Cambridge at those times, had raised the problem in *Can Lloyd George Do It?* (written in collaboration with H. Henderson in 1929), where he had put forward the argument that an increase in employment generated by public works would not be limited to the employment directly created by public expenditure but would generate additional induced employment. In the *Treatise on Money* of the following year, Keynes reproposed the argument, but without managing to demonstrate it in a convincing way. However, by now the time was almost ripe. In 1930 the multiplier principle was used by L. F. Giblin in *Australia 1930*. Then in 1931 it was used by Jens Warming and by Ralph Hawtrey. Finally, the classic work of Richard Ferdinand Kahn (1905–89), 'The Relation of Home Investment to Unemployment', came out in the *Economic Journal* of 1931. Keynes understood immediately that it was an important missing piece in the puzzle he was trying to solve, and in 1936 he assigned it a central place in the *General Theory*.

In regard to the accelerator, for the first traces we have to go back to an article by T. N. Carver, 'A Suggestion for a Theory of Industrial Depressions', published in the *Quarterly Journal of Economics* in 1903. Then Albert Aftalion (1874–1956) expressed it clearly in 'La Réalité des surproductions générales', (*Revue d'économie politique*, 1908 and 1909) and in 'Les Crises périodiques de surproductions' (1913). Finally it appeared in an article by C. F. Bickerdike ('A Non-Monetary Cause of Fluctuations in Employment', in the *Economic Journal* of 1914), and in an article by John Maurice Clark ('Business Acceleration and the Law of Demand', *Journal of Political Economy*, 1917).

In its simplest form the accelerator principle can be presented in the following way. Let *a* be the marginal capital–output ratio, i.e. the increase in capital necessary to increase the production by a marginal amount. Then the *expectation* of an increase in the demand equal to ΔY^* will induce entrepreneurs to make investments, I, in other words to increase the capital stock by an amount equal to:

$$I = a\Delta Y^*$$

a is called the accelerator because, given that its value is normally greater than 1, the growth in capital is greater than the growth in the expected demand which induces it.

7.1.6. The Harrod–Domar model

Right from the very beginning the accelerator was used to account for economic fluctuations. But the crucial year for the cycle theories based on the accelerator was 1936, when Roy Forbes Harrod (1900–78) published *The*

Trade Cycle, in which he proposed an explanation of the business cycle which combined the accelerator and multiplier principles. Three years later Paul Anthony Samuelson (b. 1915) put some order in this subject. In an article published in the *Review of Economic Studies* ('Interaction between the Acceleration Principle and the Multiplier') and one in the *Journal of Political Economy* ('A Synthesis of the Principle of the Accelerator and the Multiplier'), by combining the two principles with some special hypotheses in regard to time-lags, Samuelson proved that it is possible to generate cyclical movements. But his demonstration was fatal for this line of research. In fact Samuelson proved that, generically, the cycles caused by the multiplier-accelerator principle could be either dampened or explosive. Both properties are undesirable from the point of view of cycle theory, as they imply that the oscillating movements, in a certain sense, tend to extinguish themselves.

More promising was the line of research opened up by Harrod in 'An Essay on Dynamic Theory', published in the *Economic Journal* of 1939. Here Harrod, still using the multiplier-accelerator interaction, tackled the problem of the instability of growth. A few years later a similar theory was formulated by Evsey David Domar (b. 1914) in various papers published in the 1940s and 1950s and later collected in *Essays in the Theory of Economic Growth* (1957). Thus the theory became known as the 'Harrod–Domar model'.

In the simplest version it is based on three equations:

$$S_t = sY_t$$

$$I_t = a\Delta Y_t^*$$

$$S_t = I_t$$

where $s = 1 - c$ is the propensity to save, and $\Delta Y_t^* = Y_{t+1}^* - Y_t$ is the expected change in demand. The multiplier principle is hidden in the first equation, while the second incorporates the accelerator principle and the third sets out the condition of macroeconomic equilibrium. The equilibrium solution is obtained by substituting from the first and second equations into the third and assuming that the variation in the expected demand coincides with the actual one, i.e. $\Delta Y_t^* = \Delta Y_t$. The warranted rate of growth, G, which guarantees equilibrium, is determined as:

$$G = \frac{\Delta Y_t}{Y} = \frac{s}{a}$$

The solution is unstable: each disequilibrium solution will tend to diverge from the warranted growth path, and no automatic adjustment mechanism is capable of rebalancing the economic system. For example, if the growth of expected demand is higher than warranted growth, the accelerator will increase investments more than necessary. The multiplier, in turn, will increase the demand at a rate higher not only than the warranted rate but also than the expected rate. Thus the expectations will be adjusted upwards and the disequilibrium will be aggravated.

Furthermore, given the growth rates of population and labour productivity, the model shows that warranted growth is not only unstable but also incapable of ensuring full employment and price stability. The sum of the rates of growth of population, n, and labour productivity, π, gives the natural rate of growth, G_n. This is the maximum rate at which the economy can grow. If demand grows at a rate higher than the natural one, this creates inflationary impulses, as actual production is not able to keep pace with demand. On the other hand, if demand grows at a rate lower than the natural one, unemployment is created. The economy will grow in a steady state, without generating inflationary or deflationary impulses, if and only if it grows at a rate coinciding with both the warranted and the natural rates:

$$G = \frac{s}{a} = n + \pi = G_n$$

But as s, a, n, and π are all exogenous magnitudes, it is difficult to see how this equality can hold true, if not by chance.

In this section we have only sketched out the essential lines of the Harrod–Domar model. We will return to it in Chapter 9, where we deal with the theoretical developments to which it gave rise in the 1950s and 1960s. However, it is necessary to say something else about Harrod here.

The English economist believed that his most important scientific contribution was the *Foundations of Inductive Logic* (1956), a book which did receive serious consideration by eminent philosophers. In the field of economics, he believed that he was most competent in the analysis of the operation of the international monetary system; but he also made important contributions to the theory of imperfect competition. Undoubtedly, however, his fame today is linked to the fact that he is the father of dynamic economics, with which he began to concern himself in 1939, even though his first work in this field dates back to 1934. As often happens with pioneering thinkers, Harrod was critical of the theoretical developments that others made from his original insights. This is true not only of the research linked to the neoclassical theory of economic growth but also, and more surprisingly, of the work connected to post-Keynesian theory. Both theories are, in fact, usually presented as extensions to the Harrod–Domar model. Yet Harrod has always refused to recognize his model as a realistic description of the actual dynamics of a capitalist economy, a dynamic which is considered as basically characterized by continual cyclical fluctuations. Undoubtedly, the almost uninterrupted growth of the Western economies from the end of the Second World War to the 1970s has contributed to legitimating the stable-growth models and left Harrod's original views in the shadows. However, the period of deep instability we are now passing through favours a general reappraisal of the economic-growth argument which may lead to a re-examination and a new appreciation of the Keynesian bases of post-Keynesian theory. From this perspective, Harrod's original work takes on new interest.

7.2. JOHN MAYNARD KEYNES

7.2.1. English debates on economic policy

During the inter-war period, as had already occurred about a century before at the time of Ricardo and Malthus, England became once again an experimental laboratory for economic theory. In this particular time and in this particular place, the interaction between theory and practical problems was uniquely strong. The public debate on economic policy concerned two principal issues: the return to the Gold Standard, and the problem of unemployment.

By around 1875 the Gold Standard had been pretty well accepted by all the main capitalist countries; and it continued to rule until the First World War. The war destroyed the system, but immediately afterwards there were attempts to rebuild it, especially in England, where strong efforts were made to restore sterling to its pre-war parity. From 1920 to 1925, when the English authorities were still working on preparations for the return to the Gold Standard, prices in that country fell by 40 per cent. In 1925 sterling was again linked to the pre-war gold parity, but the system only lasted six years. English prices were still too high and the export industries too weak. Meanwhile the United States and France were experiencing strong surpluses on their balance of payments. The United States masked them with a policy of long-run foreign loans, whereas France accumulated gold and sterling reserves. The final blow to the English Gold Standard came immediately after the 1929 crash. American loans dried up, while the Bank of France decided to convert its sterling reserves into gold. Then, in 1931, a wave of panic, caused by the collapse of the 'Credit Anstalt', spread throughout Europe. When several countries began to convert sterling reserves into gold, the Bank of England was unable to resist and the Gold Standard was abandoned. The 1930s were years of international monetary chaos, with competitive devaluations, protectionist trade policies, and deflationary monetary policies.

The main problem with the Gold Standard was that the 'automatic' adjustment processes it is assumed to entail require price flexibility, otherwise the price–specie-flow mechanism does not work. But by the last quarter of the nineteenth century, prices and wages had already become fairly rigid; and, in fact, the adjustments, effected by careful interest rate manœuvres, mainly acted on capital movements. They also led, however, to deflationary processes which affected production, the levels of real output, and employment. This kind of adjustment had become socially intolerable and politically dangerous, given the rates of unemployment experienced in all capitalist countries in the inter-war years. In England, for example, in the 1920s unemployment averaged 10 per cent and reached 22 per cent in 1931. In the United States it even touched 27 per cent in 1933.

What could be done? Nothing at all, maintained the British Government. The line prevailing in government circles was derived from that liberal ortho-doxy which preached the necessity of balancing State accounts by spending as little as possible and, for the rest, *laissez-faire* the private economy. Trying to alleviate unemployment by public works would only cause trouble. The main argument of the Treasury was that, as public expenditure had in any case to be financed from private sources, by taxation or debt, it subtracted capital from private enterprise and therefore reduced employment in the private sector by the same amount as it raised that provided by the State. This is the famous 'Treasury view'. It was put into practice by the Treasury in the second half of the 1920s and presented in Parliament by Churchill in 1929. But as early as 1913 it had received scientific backing from Hawtrey, who, in *Good and Bad Trade*, had put forward the argument according to which 'the government by the very fact of borrowing for [public] expenditure is withdrawing from the investment market savings which would otherwise be applied to the creation of capital' (p. 260). Most of the economists, though, were against this view. Robertson criticized Hawtrey's arguments in 1915, and Pigou had already criticized a view similar to that of the Treasury as early as 1908. The problem was: how was it possible to scientifically demonstrate that the Treasury view was mistaken? We do not believe we are exaggerating when we say that this was one of the main subjects of the economic-policy debate from which the Keynesian revolution arose.

Before considering Keynes, however, it is necessary to return to the theories of the business cycle, so as to show the climate and tenor of the scientific debate from which the *General Theory* finally emerged. Let us, for a moment, accept Hawtrey's version of the Treasury view: the government cannot in-crease the level of employment if it finances the additional expenditure by taxation and/or public debt. This, however, still leaves open the possibility of financing the deficit with a monetary expansion. Nothing more dangerous, argued Hawtrey. On the contrary, it is precisely in this way that the economic fluctuations responsible for unemployment would be amplified. A theory of the cycle capable of accounting this argument was put forward by Hawtrey in *Good and Bad Trade* and in *Currency and Credit* (1919). An expansion in bank credit increases expenditure, aggregate demand, and incomes, fuelling inflation, profit expectations, and investment activity. In this way expectations become self-fulfilling and the economic boom proceeds at a sustained pace, but the demand for credit (for money in general) increases beyond the capacity of the financial sector. When the bank reserves fall 'too' much, the banks increase the interest rate and reduce the supply of money. The ensuing contraction of expenditure is further amplified by the wholesaler's policy of reducing their inventories, as they work on a high debt/turnover ratio and are therefore severely hit by increases in the interest rate. The monetary contraction does not immedi-ately or completely lead to a reduction in prices, as these are sticky. Wages are also rigid. Therefore the deflation leads to a reduction in the level of output.

Hawtrey's is a 'purely monetary' theory of economic fluctuations; however, the hypothesis concerning price and wage rigidity plays an essential role in accounting for the process of the transmission of the monetary impulses to the real variables. Notice that it was precisely to this hypothesis that, some years later, attempts were made to reduce the Keynesian 'special case'. Keynes, however, was a critic of this theoretical approach. We will limit ourselves to noting this strange fact but will return to it in more detail later on.

In the 1920s, Hawtrey found himself somewhat isolated in English academic circles. In the 1930s, however, Robbins and Hayek arrived to give him a hand. Of particular importance were two works by Friederich August von Hayek (b. 1899): *Geldtheorie und Konjuncturtheorie* (*Theory of Money and Theory of Fluctuations*) (1929), translated into English in 1933, and *Prices and Production* (1931). Hayek's cycle theory endeavoured to blend a monetary theory of fluctuations similar to that of Hawtrey with Böhm-Bawerk's theory of capital and Wicksell's theory of the cumulative process. A credit expansion initially produces two effects: it lowers the interest rate and creates forced savings, increasing the purchasing power in the hands of the investors to the detriment of that available to consumers. With investment, the prices of capital goods increase too and, therefore, their production rises. Thus the length of the production period and the capital intensity of the system increases. In phases of monetary contraction the opposite processes occur, so that the labour force must be dislocated from one sector to the other. In fact, deflation reduces the period of production, increasing consumption and reducing investment. But this transformation process requires time, as capital goods cannot actually be transferred from one sector to another but must be substituted by new capital goods. During this technical substitution process, temporary unemployment is created.

On the opposing theoretical front to that of Hawtrey and Hayek were Robertson, Pigou, and Keynes. In *A Study of Industrial Fluctuations* (1915), Denis Holme Robertson (1890–1963) emphasized the real factors of the economic fluctuations, by combining an over-investment theory with a theory of the effects of technological innovations similar to that of Schumpeter. In *Banking Policy and the Price Level* (1926), he concentrated instead on the monetary aspects of the cycle, supporting the theory of forced savings. One important argument, which differentiates Robertson's theory from those of Hawtrey and Hayek, concerns the definition of the role of the banking system. Robertson argued that, besides its traditional objective of price stability, the financial sector, given its ability to influence the level of investments by means of forced savings, should also be governed with the aim of guaranteeing the level of desired savings.

Pigou was another fervent critic of the Treasury view. His explanation of the business cycle was presented in *Industrial Fluctuations* (1927). From Pigou's vast and complex theory it is worth underlining three elements above all. First is the argument that variations in the level of employment are generated by variations in the aggregate demand and, in particular, by variations in investment, by means of a propagation process based on the multiplier, even if the multiplier principle is not formally expressed. Second is the typically post-Marshallian, or rather pre-Keynesian, argument that fluctuations of investments basically depend on the profit expectations of the entrepreneur. Finally, it is important to recall that, according to Pigou, the possibility of increasing the level of employment depends on the occurrence of two institutional conditions: high elasticity of the credit supply and high flexibility of prices and wages.

7.2.2. How Keynes became Keynesian

In regard to the two fundamental problems of English economic policy of the 1920s and the 1930s, the Gold Standard and unemployment, Keynes took up a precise position right from the mid-1920s, and there is no doubt that, to a large degree, his theoretical work in the following years was motivated by the need to give scientific respectability to his political stances. Keynes began to oppose a return to the Gold Standard as early as 1923, when, in the *Tract on Monetary Reform*, he pointed out the deflationary danger inherent in the return to gold. Two years later, when the Gold Standard had been re-established, Keynes again raised his voice in *The Economic Consequences of Mr Churchill* (1925), where he argued that the pound was still too overvalued with respect to the dollar, and that consequently a return to the Gold Standard, *in the presence of rigid wages*, would have required adjustments in levels of production which would have been very damaging to the English export industries. In regard to the problem of unemployment, Keynes was a supporter of public investment programmes, at least from 1924 onwards, when, in the article 'Does Unemployment need a Drastic Remedy?', he backed the programme of employment put forward by Lloyd George and the Liberal Party. The philosophy underpinning his political attitude was put forward in *The End of Laissez Faire* (1926), in which Keynes argued the necessity of abandoning rigid free-trade orthodoxy, whose economic effects he feared just as much as 'State socialism'.

Keynes argued that there are spheres of activity in which private initiative carries out an essential economic role and in which the State should not interfere, while there are also spheres of activity in which the State operates in a better way than the private sector. He did not go very far forward in identifying the latter types of economic activity, which, basically he reduced to two: credit control and the regulation of the process of formation and allocation of savings. He put forward the idea that the State should take on the role of 'concerted and deliberate management' of the economy, albeit by means of a limited number of political instruments.

This emphasis on public management was also motivated by the fact that the Gold Standard, against which, realistically, he no longer fought after its re-establishment, created additional problems of stability for the national economy, problems that, he argued, could be resolved by a prudent macro-economic policy. This view might seem paradoxical, if one considers the fact that the Gold Standard was supported by liberal thinkers precisely for its supposed ability to produce automatic adjustments. However, Keynes considered the basic political and philosophical problem to be different: are these 'automatic' adjustments, given their effects on unemployment, not worse than the illness they wish to cure?

The crucial years for the maturation of Keynes's thought were those imme-diately after the publication of *A Treatise on Money* (1930). In 1931 the Macmillan Report came out, the product of a Commission on Finance and Industry of which Keynes was a member. The report supported a philosophy of economic policy similar to the one put forward by Keynes himself in *The End of Laissez Faire*. Furthermore, it proposed a reflationary monetary policy that seemed to have been inspired by the theory advanced by Keynes in the *Treatise*. The basic idea was that monetary expansion, by creating inflation, would stimulate profits and investments, thus pushing the economy out of the troughs of depression.

In the *Treatise on Money* Keynes had reached this theoretical conclusion by means of a rather complicated and extremely ambitious model with which he tried to integrate the results of two streams of research: on the one hand, the neoclassical theories of the cycle as a phenomenon of monetary disequili-brium, in particular Marshall's and, above all, Wicksell's theories; on the other, the theories of the production/expenditure disequilibrium which had been formulated in the heterodox 'underworlds' of Tugan-Baranovskij, Hob-son, etc.

From the latter type of model Keynes took the idea of disaggregation in two productive sectors, consumer goods and investment goods, and, above all, the idea of studying the dynamics of the economy as a disequilibrium phenom-enon, the disequilibrium being generated by a lack of correspondence between patterns of expenditure and of output. As investment decisions are not savings decisions, nor decisions to produce investment goods, the investment share in the aggregate expenditure may be higher than the share of investment goods in the aggregate output. In a disequilibrium situation such as this, the prices of investment goods will rise over and above the costs (inclusive of normal profits). Thus (extraordinary) profits will increase. If this rise in profits fuels the confidence of the capitalists, they will increase both their consumption and investment expenditure. Thus the inflation process is self-sustaining; on the one hand it spreads from the capital-goods sector to the whole economy, on the other it produces the strange and miraculous effect of the 'widow's cruse': as the expenditure of each agent is the profit of another, the higher the aggregate expenditure of the capitalists, the higher their earnings will be.

The Marshallian element of the model concerned the theory of the demand for money, which Keynes, by using the Cambridge equation, formulated in terms of the quantity of liquid assets the public wishes to hold. Developing an argument of Robertson, however, he took a step forward, by distinguishing between a demand for *cash deposits* motivated by the needs of transactions and a demand for *saving deposits* dependent on psychological factors such as the state of confidence and the level of *bearishness* of the public. The bank interest rate depends on the forces of supply and demand for money. At this point Wicksell's cumulative process enters the scene. The monetary authorities can lower the interest rate. In this way they will encourage investment and cause both prices and profits to rise, which, in turn, will make the entrepreneurs more confident and lead them to increase production.

Here is the gist of the monetary management policy Keynes supported in the 1920s. The authorities should not be concerned solely with price stability, but also, and above all, with the creation of savings. And if the two objectives conflict, price stability should be sacrificed. By means of inflation the monetary authorities would be able to induce private capitalists to create employment.

The treatise was heavily criticized. Here we will limit ourselves to outlining the most important criticism, the one raised both by Hawtrey and by the members of the circle of young Cambridge economists who met periodically to discuss Keynes's theories, especially Kahn. Basically this criticism refers to the fact that the 'fundamental equations' by means of which Keynes formulated his model are only valid under the hypothesis of full employment; thus the implications in regard to the ability of the cumulative process and the monetary policy to reflate the economy in *real* terms were a *non sequitur*. It was a simple and devastating criticism. Keynes felt the punch and, undoubtedly, this was the beginning of the theoretical travail which was to lead him to publish, six years later, *The General Theory*.

The rethinking process, however, had begun as early as 1931. For example, while the Macmillan Report adopted the theories Keynes had put forward in *The End of Laissez Faire* and in the *Treatise*, a minority of the commission, including Keynes himself, were sceptical about the possibility of curing unemployment with monetary policy. Furthermore, and still in 1931, Keynes gave some Harris Lectures in Chicago in which, for the first time, he tackled the problem of unemployment in terms of the equilibrium level of production determined by a given level of investment. In so doing he admitted, even if only in passing, that an unemployment situation can be an equilibrium.

7.2.3. The General Theory: *effective demand and employment*

The fundamental theoretical leap with which Keynes achieved his revolution consisted in the abandonment of the disequilibrium analysis typical of the *Treatise* and the adoption of a *macroeconomic-equilibrium* approach. In order to understand this change it is necessary to begin with Say's Law. Most pre-Keynesian critics had rejected this law because of its implications for the equilibrium between production and expenditure. A criticism of this type underlies all those savings–investment disequilibrium models which were to culminate in the 'fundamental equations' of the *Treatise*. In *The General Theory of Employment Interest and Money* (1936), Keynes criticized Say's Law for a different reason from the traditional one—for its implications in regard to the *direction of the causal link* connecting production and expenditure. Keynes argued that it is not production which generates expenditure and demand, but the expenditure decisions which generate demand; then production adjusts to demand. This argument has three important theoretical implications. The first is that there is no longer any reason to waste time analysing the dynamic processes by which production adjusts to demand; it is sufficient to assume they are rapid so as to be able to take them for granted; then the analysis becomes an equilibrium analysis. The second is that it is no longer necessary to focus on the dynamics of the inter-sectoral composition of production; as production quickly adjusts to demand, the changes in its *structure* can be ignored in the study of the factors determining its *level*, and this is the main justification of Keynesian macroeconomic analysis. The third is that, in order to identify the causes that determine the employment level, it is necessary to study the factors on which expenditure decisions depend.

To present the theory of effective demand in the simplest way we will use an expository device invented by Hansen. Aggregate demand is subdivided into an autonomous component, investment, I, and an induced component, consumption, C. Consumption varies with income according to function $C = C_0 + cY$. Therefore the aggregate expenditure is $I + C = I + C_0 + cY$. The three functions, $I, C, C + I$ are shown in Fig. 7. The horizontal axis represents produced and distributed income and the vertical axis represents expenditure. On the 45° line are all the points in which aggregate expenditure equals income. The equilibrium point therefore will be E, at which the $C + I$ line meets the 45° line. At this point, the expenditure generates exactly the amount of demand and production which will distribute the income, Y_e, necessary to finance the expenditure itself. As C depends on the level of income, while I is autonomous, the latter variable will determine the level of activity. The level of production determined in this way does not necessarily mean there will be full employment. However, it is an equilibrium point, in that it guarantees equality between aggregate supply and demand. Furthermore, at this point all earned incomes are spent and savings are equal to investments.

The problem is: in what sense is it possible to speak of investments as autonomous expenditure if they are, in any case, financed by the savings created by the equilibrium income? The answer on which the Keynesian revolution is based is this: it is investments that generate the necessary saving for financing, not vice versa. In fact, investment decisions are independent of the amount of available savings. Given the propensity to consume of the collectivity, a certain amount of investment will determine, by means of the multiplier, a certain level of income. The savings stemming from that level of income will be exactly sufficient to finance those investments. This can be seen clearly

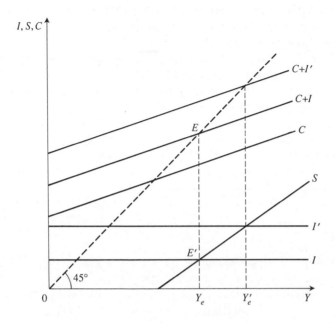

FIG. 7

from Fig. 7, where point E' represents the equality between savings and investment. The savings function is $S = Y - C_0 - cY = -C_0 + sY$. Let us assume that, starting from an equilibrium situation, investments increase by $100 bn. and that the propensity to consume is 80 per cent. The multiplier will be $1/(1 - c) = 1/0.2 = 5$. Therefore, income will increase by $500 bn. The propensity to save is 20 per cent, so that the saving created by the $500 bn. will be $100 bn., which is exactly the value of the additional investment. Fig. 7 shows that an increase in the investments from I to I' will increase the income from Y_e to Y'_e, while the savings will adjust to the new investment level.

The idea that the levels of activity and employment depend on investment decisions has two important theoretical implications. The first is that, if the level of employment depends on the *level* of investment, rather than on its *composition*, the neoclassical view that full employment is reached by means of the changes in relative factor prices, and the consequent changes in relative demand, is deprived of any theoretical relevance. We should add that Keynes did not notice this implication immediately. He outlined it in 'Relative Movements of Real Wages and Output' in *The Economic Journal* of 1939, but even then did not give it a great deal of importance. In fact, he did not fully exploit the implications of this criticism for the theory of effective demand, partly because he was more interested in constructing an alternative to orthodox theory than in criticizing it, and partly because he had not freed himself completely from the influence of that theory (for example, he continued to believe in the neoclassical postulate that links wages to the marginal productivity of labour). However, some of Keynes's students were more coherent than their master in regard to this argument—an argument which was, as we shall see later, to constitute a basic distinction, in the debates of the 1950s and 1960s, between the post-Keynesian and the neoclassical schools.

The second implication concerned the explanation of the instability of capitalism. Keynes focused on the problem of why investments did not normally settle at the level that guarantees full employment. Investments depend on the *marginal efficiency of capital*, which is a synthetic estimate of the future returns of investments, $R_t (t = 0, 1, \ldots n)$. The marginal efficiency of capital, r, is calculated as the discount rate that makes the present value of those returns equal to the cost of the capital goods:

$$K = \sum_{t=0}^{m} \frac{R_t}{(1 + r)^t}$$

The higher the expected returns from a given investment, the higher the marginal efficiency of capital. Keynes added that, *for a given state of expectations*, the marginal efficiency of capital decreases as investments increase. In order to determine the amount of investments, therefore, it is sufficient to know the interest rate, i, which is taken as an indicator of the cost of finance. The problem is that the investment returns, on the basis of which the marginal efficiency of capital is calculated, are not concrete elements, but psychological variables which depend on entrepreneurs' expectations about the future trends of the economy. However, the future is uncertain and expectations are volatile. Moods, the state of confidence, and the 'animal spirits' of the entrepreneurs play a key role in the formation of their expectations and, therefore, in investment decisions. The levels of activity and employment depend on imponderable, uncontrollable, and extremely unstable psychological factors. Fig. 8 shows various schedules of the marginal efficiency of capital, $r(F_1), r(F_2), r(F_3) \ldots$, one for each state of confidence, F_i; those which are further to the right represent the most optimistic expectations. It is easy to see that, on a given schedule, investments increase as the interest rate decreases. However, taking interest as given, investments decrease as entrepreneurs' confidence falls. This should be enough, moreover, to allow us to understand the profound difference between the notion of 'marginal efficiency of capital' and that of marginal productivity of capital, into which many neoclassical economists have tried to assimilate the former.

7.2.4 The General Theory: *liquidity preference*

The neoclassical theory considers the interest rate as a real variable that depends on technology and/or psychology, and that is determined as the price of savings. In equilibrium it equates savings and investments. We have seen

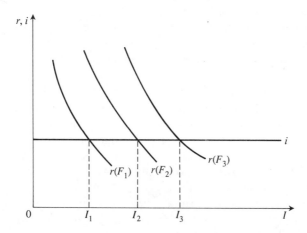

FIG. 8

that, in Keynes, savings adjust to investments through the variations in income
generated by the investments themselves. In this adjustment process the interest rate plays no role at all. Thus the double problem arises of what interest
is and how it should be determined in a theory of effective demand. Keynes's
solution was to consider the interest rate as a monetary rather than a real
variable, and to determine it by the forces of supply and demand for *money*.

In the 'Cambridge equation' the quantity theory was formulated in terms of
the quantity of liquid balances which individuals wish to keep in relation to the
real income they earn. From this point of view, money is mainly demanded for
its services in the purchasing of real goods. Purchases cannot be completely
planned, as they depend on unpredictable factors; therefore liquid reserves are
also demanded for precautionary motives. And this is the origin of the *liquidity
preference* theory. Individuals wish to hold liquid assets because the future is
uncertain. Money, the liquid asset *par excellence*, is purchasing power that
can be used at any moment to face unexpected eventualities. Therefore, individuals prefer to hold their wealth as money rather than as any other form of
asset. But money is also necessary to finance investment. The entrepreneurs
who invest more than they earn must in some way obtain the liquidity necessary to finance the investment expenditure. In order to do this they issue forms
of liabilities such as bonds, bills of exchange, and bank debts, which they try
to 'sell' in exchange for money. But why should the economic agents agree
to hold their own wealth in the form of non-liquid assets? If liquidity preference exists, the economic agents who renounce holding liquid assets must
be rewarded. Here is the *liquidity premium*: the difference between the returns
on non-liquid and liquid assets. In the simplified case which Keynes dealt
with, there is no return on money, and the liquidity premium is the same as
the interest paid on a non-liquid asset called 'security'.

In this way, the demand for money depends, not only on the level of transactions, as was suggested by the Cambridge equation with its emphasis on the precautionary and transaction motives, but also on the level of the interest rate. *Given liquidity preference*, the quantity of money that the economic agents decide to hold increases as the interest rate decreases. So, *if the monetary authorities manage to control the money supply*, they will also be able to determine the interest rate. If they have this ability they will possess an easily manageable policy instrument. We will soon see what great importance is attached to the two conditions we have emphasized above.

Monetary policy could act on the real economy by means of an 'indirect transmission mechanism' which is now called 'Keynesian' in most macroeconomic textbooks. An expansion in the money supply increases the price of 'securities' and decreases the interest rate; then, given the schedule of marginal efficiency of capital, a reduction in the cost of finance induces an increase in investments; finally, by virtue of the multiplier, incomes and employment also increase. No doubt, in Keynes there are many arguments that justify this theory of monetary policy. But it is also true that, in the 1930s, abandoning the views he had held in the previous decade, Keynes became very sceptical about the effectiveness of monetary policy. The reasons for this scepticism can be found in three factors.

First of all, it is not certain that the monetary authorities are able effectively to control the money supply. Even if in the *General Theory* Keynes assumed (although rather for explanatory convenience than for any other reason) a quantity of money fixed exogenously by the monetary authorities, on several other occasions he put forward the opinion that the money supply may adapt in a fairly elastic way to the demand and that, in fact, it is quite endogenous. Keynes was not able to exploit all the advantages that a theory of the endogenous money supply offered for his point of view. Instead, as we will see in more detail in Chapter 9, these advantages were fully exploited in more recent times by modern post-Keynesian thinkers.

A second group of doubts were derived from Keynes's consideration of the role of speculation in the determination of the interest rate. Money is demanded, not only to finance productive activity, but also to finance speculation. The liabilities issued by firms receive a price which depends solely on the forces of supply and demand. In 'normal' times, speculators behave more or less like any other economic agent, and are unable to modify the effects of the public's liquidity preference on the interest rate. When the prices of securities increase and the interest rate decreases, speculators expect that, in the future, prices and the interest rate will return to their fundamental values. Therefore they will sell securities with the intention of buying them back in the future. In this way they contribute to stabilizing the stock market. In 'abnormal' times, however—and one has the impression that Keynes believed that times are quite often abnormal on the stock market—speculators do not take into consideration the fundamental values, but try to make capital gains by speculating with a very short-run perspective. For example, they buy stocks when their prices are rising, contributing in this way to making their prices rise still more. This kind of speculation destabilizes the market and condemns to ineffectiveness the monetary policies which aim at setting the interest rate in a discretionary way. In fact, the objectives of monetary policy can be frustrated by speculators' expectations. Not only this, but the obstinacy and the strength with which a certain policy has to be put into practice to reach a certain objective could, in fact, trigger a wave of speculation and produce the opposite effects to those desired. Thus, as we have seen, the existence of a stable money demand function and the possibility of an effective monetary policy depend on two conditions: first, that the liquidity preference (of the speculators) is independent of variations in the interest rate, and second, that the monetary authorities are able to control the money supply. Keynes thought these two conditions were difficult to realize in a *laissez-faire* capitalist system, even if in the *General Theory* he did not pay any special attention to the second.

Finally, the third set of doubts concerns the possibility of influencing, to a relevant degree, investment decisions by means of monetary policy. Even if we admit that the monetary authorities are able discretionally to set the interest rate, in what degree would a variation in the latter influence the level of investment? In a minimal way, Keynes argued. It is true that investment decisions depend on the marginal efficiency of capital and on the cost of finance. But profit expectations basically depend on the moods of the entrepreneurs, and these are very unstable. When pessimism predominates, investments will be postponed until better times, and a reduction in the interest rate will not persuade entrepreneurs to change their minds. On the contrary, in phases of optimism the profit expectations are high and self-sustaining, so that it is unlikely that an increase in the interest rate will discourage investment decisions in any significant way. But things can be worse: variations in the interest rate itself may influence the formation of profit expectations. In this case it would be impossible to construct schedules of the marginal efficiency of capital curves such as those drawn in Fig. 8.

So, even if we accept that the first two sets of difficulties can be overcome and that the monetary authorities are able discretionally to modify the interest rate without destabilizing the financial markets, this does not mean that such a policy will be effective in influencing the real variables. It is easy to understand why the monetary policies upheld by Keynes's followers after the Second World War, and adopted by the main industrial nations up to the 1960s, had the simple goal of stabilizing the interest rate leaving the economic system to receive all the liquidity demanded.

Keynes's revolutionary book concludes with an important chapter on the 'social philosophy towards which the *General Theory* might lead'. In it he took up again the subjects he had dealt with ten years before in *The End of Laissez Faire*, but came to a more extreme anti-*laissez-faire* position, conceding a vast area to the exercise of State intervention in the economy. More sceptical about monetary policy than he had been ten years before, Keynes had by that time convinced himself that the right of the State to intervene in the private sector should no longer be limited to credit management and, by means of it, the savings-formation process. Instead, it should be extended to two fields in which *laissez-faire* had most clearly shown its deficiencies: the determination of the level of investments and of income distribution.

On the first subject, Keynes even reached the point of preaching some form of 'socialization of investments'. Given that the level of investments normally tend, in a *laissez-faire* regime, to lead the economy to underemployment equilibria, the State had the right, or rather the duty, to intervene in order to ensure full employment. In regard to the distribution of income, Keynes pointed out that the natural tendency of a *laissez-faire* regime is towards the determination of arbitrary and unjust distributive patterns; and he believed that the large amount of savings generated by very unequal distribution of income would only serve to keep the level of expenditure and aggregate demand at a low level, rather than supporting the capital accumulation process. The State should also intervene in this case.

It should intervene, however, without damaging the fundamental tenets on which the capitalist economy was built, as Keynes saw them: individualism and private ownership of the means of production. He had become an anti-*laissez-faire* economist but he was still a liberal. He believed that State intervention should not *abolish* the 'invisible hand' but help it to manifest itself and, in a certain sense, render it visible. This is the origin of the new philosophy of the 'administered market'.

7.3. MICHAŁ KALECKI

7.3.1. The level of income and its distribution

Michał Kalecki (1899–1970) is considered by many as a minor Keynesian and a popularizer of the Keynesian revolution. Sometimes he is recognized as being a forerunner, but not much more. On the contrary, his work is important for the history of modern economic thought, not only because he was the first to formulate the theory of effective demand, nor so much for the fact that the Kaleckian version of that theory was more realistic than the Keynesian one, but because of the centrality Kalecki assigned to the problem of the distribution of income and to the non-competitive context in which he assumed prices to be determined. His work is important, above all, because Kalecki, given his non-academic origin and his Marxist background was almost completely immune to those doctrinal restraints that on more than one occasion had confused Keynes's thought. And it has been quite rightly pointed out that, precisely for this reason, Kalecki was more Keynesian than Keynes himself.

So much so that, after the Second World War, some of Keynes's most coherent Cambridge followers, in the attempt to purify their master's work of every anti-Keynesian residue, did nothing but develop a Kaleckian version of the theory of effective demand and construct a theoretical system that could be defined as neo-Kaleckian.

We find the first formulation of the principle of effective demand in a paper published in Warsaw in 1933 entitled 'Próba teorji Konjunktury', and later published in a shorter version in *Econometrica* (1935), entitled 'A Macroeconomic Theory of Business Cycle'. Also in 1933, Kalecki published, again in Polish, a paper entitled 'On Foreign Trade and "Domestic Exports"'. In the following five years, various articles came out which were collected together in 1939 in a book entitled *Essays in the Theory of Economic Fluctuations*. Other papers and anthologies were published in the following years. Here we will limit ourselves to the *Selected Essays on the Dynamics of the Capitalist Economy 1933–1970*, published in 1971, a collection of the best of Kalecki's scientific work.

To explain Kalecki's theory of effective demand in the simplest way, we will begin with an equation which defines the national income as the sum of consumption and investment, $Y = C + I$. We will separate the workers' consumption from that of the capitalists. The former, under the assumption that the workers' propensity to consume is equal to 1, coincides with the wage-bill, W. The latter is equal to $c_p P$, where c_p is the capitalists' propensity to consume and P is the level of profits. Then:

$$I + W + c_p P = Y$$

As $W = Y - P$, it holds:

$$I + Y - P(1 - c_p) = Y$$

$$P = \frac{1}{1 - c_p} I$$

The last equation incorporates the Kaleckian version of the theorem of the 'widow's cruse': 'the capitalists may decide to consume and invest more in a given period than in the preceding one, but they cannot decide to earn more. It is, therefore, their investment and consumption decisions which determine profits, and not vice versa' (pp. 78–9). In this way profits are determined by investment decisions through a process similar to the Keynesian multiplier. In the Kaleckian version, however, the role played by the multiplier in the creation of the savings necessary to finance investments is even more clear. Since, in this model, only the capitalists save, the increase in profits generated by a given increase in investments will continue up to the point at which all the necessary funds have been created to repay the debts with which those investments were financed.

The problem now is: which level of income and employment is generated by given investment decisions? After a not very convincing first attempt, based on the hypothesis that the rate of profit, the profit margin, and the level of utilization of productive capacity vary in the same direction, Kalecki finally managed to solve the problem by making use of 'Bowley's Law'—an empirical law, discovered in 1937, according to which the wage share in the national income is constant through time. In this case also we will simplify as much as possible. If $q = P/Y$ is the profit share and this is known, then we can transform the profit equation in the following way:

$$Y = \frac{1}{1 - c_p} \frac{I}{q}$$

Given the investment level and the profit share, the lower the propensity to save of the capitalists the higher the income necessary to supply the savings required to finance investments.

One final problem remains: the determination of the profit share. Kalecki assumed three hypotheses to solve this problem:

(1) Perfect competition does not exist.
(2) Average variable costs of the firms are constant up to the point of full utilization of the plant and/or full employment.
(3) Prices are set by the firms in relation to the average variable costs and the average price prevailing in the industry in which they operate.

The basic idea is this: because of phenomena such as industrial concentration, vertical integration, productive diversification, and oligopolistic co-ordination of the markets, modern large-scale firms possess a discretionary market power; and they use this power to fix, among other things, the prices of the products. Therefore, neither variations in demand nor conditions of scarcity play an important role in explaining the movements of prices of manufactured goods. From this point of view, prices depend on variable costs, especially on the cost of labour, and on the 'degree of monopoly' existing in the various industries. The inter-sectoral diversity of the degrees of monopoly is due to the diverse degrees of industrial concentration prevailing in the various productive sectors, while the degree of monopoly in force in each sector depends on the distribution of market power among the firms of the sector.

Thus, given the degree of monopoly of the various firms, their cost curves, and their relative contributions to the output of the industry, the average profit margin of the industry depends on the average degree of monopoly and does not vary with changes in the level of output. This reasoning can be extended to the whole economy (which, for simplicity, we assume closed). Given the average profit margin of the whole economy, the profit–wage ratio is known. An increase in investment raises aggregate demand. If there is not full employment or full utilization of plant, the firms can satisfy the demand by increasing production without modifying prices. Therefore, the level of income can increase with no changes in income distribution. This depends on the structure of the markets. The lower the competition, the higher, on average, are the prices with respect to variable costs, and the higher are the profits with respect to wages. Later Kalecki reinterpreted the 'degree of monopoly' in such a way as to take into account class conflict and, in particular, the role played by wage-bargaining in the determination of the distribution of income. In this way the theory became more realistic, but its analytical structure remained basically the same.

7.3.2. The trade cycle

Unlike Keynes, Kalecki used the principle of effective demand, not within a theory of the level of *output*, but within a theory of the *business cycle*. Once he had determined the output level starting from the level of investment decisions, Keynes had accomplished his task, but Kalecki's had only just begun, as he had to solve the problem of determining the level of investments. The problem of the business cycle is that of explaining fluctuations in the level of investments.

Kalecki believed that investments depend on profit expectations and the interest rate. The latter affects investment in that it represents the cost of finance. However, in all analytical formulations of the investment function Kalecki ignored the interest rate—a simplification justified by a particular theory of the term structure of the interest rate and its changes. This theory seems to be based on a mixture of Marxian and Fisherian doctrines, even if Kalecki mentioned neither Marx nor Fisher in regard to this matter. The short-run interest rate varies pro-cyclically, as it is drawn along by real profitability. Therefore, if the profit expectations depend on the current rate of profit and the variations of the latter are stronger than the variations in the interest rate, the influence of the cost of finance on investment can be ignored, at least to the degree to which the investments are financed by short-run credit. This is Marx pure and simple. If instead investments are financed by the issue of long-run liabilities, the long-run interest rate must be taken into account. However, according to a theory already put forward by Fisher, the long-run interest rate is no more than an average of the expected short-term rates within the time of maturity of the loan. Therefore, the variations in the long-run rate are always smaller than those of the short-term rates; and, to the extent to which investments are financed with long-run debt, the influence of the variations of the cost of finance can be ignored even more legitimately.

A problem does arise here, however: if there is a permanent gap between the rate of profit and the interest rate, what prevents investments from growing indefinitely? Keynes's Solution to this problem consisted of the assumption of a decreasing marginal efficiency of capital, an assumption basically justified by the hypothesis of increasing costs in the capital-goods industry. Kalecki rejected this explanation, substituting one based on the hypothesis of 'increasing risk'—a hypothesis for which he drew inspiration from work by Marek Breit, a Polish economist with whom he had collaborated in Warsaw. This hypothesis implies that the risk of an investment increases with the ratio of investments to total wealth; in fact, it is the risk of insolvency and bankruptcy.

In one of the first versions of his model of the business cycle, Kalecki made investments depend on the national income (considered as a proxy for the amount of profits) and on the existing capital stock. The level of investments is an increasing function of national income and a decreasing function of capital stock. This is nothing more than a special version of the *principle of adjustment of the capital stock*. The cyclical movement of investments is explained by coupling this principle with some hypotheses relating to the structure of time-lags. An increase in investments raises the capital stock; this at a certain point will be judged too high to justify a further increase in investments, which then begins to decrease; when the capital stock is again considered too low, the cycle starts again. A similar model, but one applied to shipyard production, was formulated by J. Tinbergen in 'Ein Schiffbauzyklus?,' published in *Weltwirtschaftliches Archiv* in 1913. It is worth mentioning this, as Kalecki drew some inspiration from this work.

In a later version of his model Kalecki modified the investment function, making it depend not only on the level of income (by means of the savings function) but also on its *variations* and on the variations of capital stock. The new model turned out to be a generalization of the old, as well as of various other models of the multiplier-accelerator type.

It seems that, from the beginning of the 1940s, Kalecki grew increasingly dissatisfied with this kind of model, even though he continued to work on them until the 1950s. In fact, in a 1943 article on the political business cycle he took a completely different direction, opening a new research field that proved to be much more promising than that of the mechanistic models of the multiplier-accelerator type. The article in question is 'Political Aspects of Full Employment,' published in the *Political Quarterly*. In it Kalecki focused his attention on the possibility of stimulating an increase in output by means of public spending. However, he argued, such a policy would meet with opposition from 'business leaders'. This opposition could be explained both by ideological factors and by more specific political-economic factors. The point is that the maintenance of full employment would bolster workers' self assurance, re-awaken their class consciousness, weaken the disciplinary function of the fear of unemployment, stimulate strike activity, undermine the authority of the factory bosses, and, in the final analysis, could cause social and political changes judged dangerous by the dominant classes.

Class conflict encouraged by full employment would not necessarily cause a reduction in profits, given the ability of firms to immediately transfer the cost increases onto prices. 'But "discipline in the factories" and "political stability" are more appreciated by the business leaders than profits. Their class instinct tells them that lasting full employment is unsound from their point of view and that unemployment is an integral part of the normal capitalist system' (p. 141). Thus, sooner or later the government would be forced to abandon full employment policies. The consequent depression would, however, induce the resumption of expansionist policies and the cycle would begin again.

7.4. JOSEPH ALOIS SCHUMPETER

7.4.1. Equilibrium and development

Schumpeter (1883–1950) was a great admirer of Walras's work but, as Keynes with Marshall, he was hindered rather than helped by his master's work. In the end he managed to use it to serve his own ends, but not before having reinterpreted it in his own way, and he still did not succeed in drawing any great advantage from it in terms of coherence and clarity of vision. We have no room here to concern ourselves with all of Schumpeter's scientific work, or to mention his historical and sociological works. We will instead cite his three most important economic books: *Theorie der Wirtschaftlichen Entwicklung* (*Theory of Economic Development*) (1912), *Business Cycles* (1939), and *Capitalism, Socialism and Democracy* (1942).

Schumpeter considered the Walrasian model of general economic equilibrium as the greatest achievement of nineteenth-century economic science, the culminating point of a strand of research started in the eighteenth century by Quesnay. In Schumpeter's view, the general-equilibrium model aimed at studying the conditions that allow a system made up of independent economic agents to reproduce itself through time. He defined these conditions in terms of the 'circular flow' of exchanges which are established among economic agents when the choices and behaviour of each are compatible with those of all the others. The equilibrium conditions, when they are realized, allow the economic system to reproduce itself through time by maintaining its own structure unaltered. In this way, the Walrasian model of general economic equilibrium was reinterpreted as a *stationary*-equilibrium model.

According to Schumpeter, stationary equilibrium is reached by the operation of 'traditional economic agents', agents who behave in an adaptive and routine way. On the other hand, rational economic agents can follow this type of behaviour only if the economy actually moves around a stationary-equilibrium path, a situation in which there are no relevant endogenous changes. A model of this type is, according to Schumpeter, logically coherent but incapable of accounting for the really important economic phenomena such as change, growth, technical progress, or profit.

The real dynamics of the capitalist system is generated by the behaviour of a type of agent different from the traditional ones: the 'innovator entrepreneur'. He aims at making profits, and therefore cannot logically exist in a system in which 'neither profits nor losses' are admitted. The enterpreneur differs from the company manager in that he aims at introducing *new* combinations of productive factors into the productive process, while the manager simply endeavours to organize the factors efficiently on the basis of the possibilities offered by the *given* techniques. Thus the manager's income is a functional income, like the worker's, and is positive in a stationary equilibrium. The entrepreneur's income, instead, arises from a break in the stationary equilibrium. Profit is created by the difference between revenues and costs, and is a residual income activated by innovation. It originates, for example, from the possibility of introducing a new productive method which allows the production of a given good at lower cost than the competitors, or from the possibility of exploiting a new market, a new product, a new source of raw materials, or a new organizational method before the competitors. Therefore this income, which is in fact a monopoly rent, is of a *temporary* nature. Competition will induce, sooner or later, the diffusion of innovations and, with it, the gradual elimination of the entrepreneur's differential earnings. At the end of the diffusion process the economy will again approach equilibrium, the rate of growth in productivity and production will stop, and firms will again make 'neither profits nor losses'. The temporary advantages arising from the innovation have gone to the entrepreneur, but society has drawn a permanent advantage from the innovation in the form of a reduction of prices or an increase in the range of products available. The innovative process is incessant and, although no single entrepreneur can ensure himself a permanent income from a single entrepreneurial act, the class of entrepreneurs as a whole continually make profits.

A conception of the competitive process emerges from this theory which is totally different from the neoclassical one. Schumpeter found little interest in the traditional theory of atomistic and static competition. He denied the importance of the idea that there are markets characterized by a large number of competitors, and also opposed the idea that agents aim at maximizing profits in the short run by taking prices as parameters and technology as given. In the real world, Schumpeter argued, competition occurs within markets in which, usually, a few large firms operate. Each tries to make profits, not *statically*, by choosing the quantity to produce under the constraints represented by the available technology at a given moment, but dynamically, by choosing an innovative long-run strategy. It is not by accepting the technological constraints, but by breaking them, that firms compete with each other. The competitive process is one of 'creative destruction'—as Schumpeter called it—a process that triggers economic growth by continually destroying the old while creating the new.

Of course this theory does not refer to an abstract 'market economy'; rather, it takes the capitalist economic system as its own subject of study. This means that Schumpeter is closer to the classical economists and Marx than to the neoclassical economists and Walras. And, just like Marx, Schumpeter did not limit himself to defining capitalism historically, but also tried to study its structural transformations in an evolutionary way: on the one hand, the phases of its evolution and, on the other, the conditions for its transformation into something else.

He argued that the evolution of capitalism was marked by two great phases: 'competitive capitalism' and 'trustified capitalism'. The first is characterized by a large number of small firms in which the entrepreneurial function is performed by the owner of the capital, the innovative process takes place through the creation of new firms, and competition operates by means of the bankruptcies of inefficient and obsolete firms. The second, on the other hand, is characterized by the existence of large firms. Technical progress is planned by the firms themselves, and growth occurs by means of the increase in company size rather than in their number.

A problem which worried Schumpeter was this: who carries out the entrepreneurial function in trustified capitalism? To the extent to which technical progress originates in the research and development departments of large firms, the capitalist who owns the capital and the entrepreneur-innovator capitalist are no longer the same person. Innovation increasingly becomes a concern of employees and managers, if not even of research teams. In this way the bourgeois class, which had initiated the process of modern social transformation by risking its own wealth, tends to disappear, along with its ethical and political values. On the other hand, with the emergence of other social classes and values, there is the tendency to legitimize political conceptions that justify State intervention both in productive activity and in the distribution of income. In this way, while the impulse towards individualistic accumulation of capital weakens, the social drive towards the construction of an economic organization based on central planning is reinforced.

7.4.2. The trade cycle and money

Economic growth, according to Schumpeter, does not take place through time in a regular way, but through cyclical fluctuations. Or, rather, it is precisely the cyclical movement that is the regular evolutionary form of the capitalist economy. The main reason for this is that innovations tend to appear in clusters in determinate periods. These clusters of innovations, by breaking the stationary equilibrium, trigger the development process. They increase the aggregate expenditure on investment goods, and this induces increases in production levels in all industries. Prices and profits also increase, while many economic initiatives are prompted, even of a speculative nature, which would not have been judged likely to succeed in a stationary-state economy. As the diffusion process of innovations spreads, however, prices tend to adjust to costs, profits are gradually eliminated, and the economy as a whole approaches a new equilibrium. Moreover, the depression may be aggravated by deflationary impulses arising from the need of the entrepreneurs to repay the debts with which they have financed the innovations. So the economy, rather than stabilizing itself along an equilibrium path, may enter into a deep trough of depression—which serves, if for nothing else, to expel from the market all those more or less foolhardy economic initiatives made possible by the preceding period of prosperity.

The main theoretical problem of this model is this: why should innovations tend to distribute themselves unevenly over time, if inventions are distributed randomly? The solution suggested by Schumpeter is not very convincing, yet still attractive. The introduction of innovations entails breaking down strong social and psychological resistance from the traditional agents. This resistance means that the inventions are not immediately transformed into innovations, but remain, we could say, inert for a while. In this way a potential of unexploited innovations mounts up. Nevertheless, once part of the resistance has been overcome or weakened by some major innovative actions, it becomes easier for the other entrepreneurs to avoid being slowed down by the resistance. Thus many other innovations follow suit, like a swarm: one or a few make the breakthrough and all the others crowd in behind, and the innovative potential is off-loaded all at the same time.

Schumpeter believed that the duration of the cycles basically depends on the type of capital goods in which technical progress is incorporated, but it is not quite clear if the factor of periodicity is related to the duration of the capital goods or to the time necessary for the diffusion of the innovations to be completed. However, more from an empirical basis than anything else, and drawing from his deep and wide historical knowledge, he distinguished three different types of fluctuations, characterized by three different orders of periodicity: Kitchin cycles, of an average length of 40 months; Juglar cycles, which average a decade; and Kondratief cycles, lasting from 50 to 60 years.

An interesting feature of Schumpeter's theory of the business cycle concerns the monetary factors of economic dynamics. The central problem of a growing capitalist economy is that of financing innovative investments. Entrepreneurs who wish to exploit an innovation do not, generally, have the finance necessary to do so. Finance comes from profits, but innovations only produce profit after they have been activated, which is often quite a long time afterwards. Therefore, credit is necessary. The banking system does not limit itself to redistributing the savings from the savers to the users. The banks, with credit, create new money, i.e. they produce new purchasing power, liquidity added to the existing stock of money; and it is this added liquidity which allows entrepreneurs to finance innovations and society to increase the stock of real capital. In real terms, credit produces a sort of forced savings. In fact, it allows entrepreneurs to appropriate tangible resources they have not produced, and, by means of inflation, forces traditional agents to give up part of the resources they have produced. Thus, credit serves to transfer resources from consumption to investment and from less productive to more productive investments.

On the other hand, it is precisely this greater productivity of innovative investments that explains interest. For the banks, the interest rate is the selling price of credit. For the entrepreneurs it is the cost of finance. Therefore it is a monetary variable. Its existence is made possible by the existence of profits. In fact, only if there are profits are the entrepreneurs prepared to pay interest. This is why Schumpeter thought that the rate of interest had to be zero in an economy in stationary equilibrium. And this is why he was sceptical about those neoclassical theories that try to explain interest in terms of a certain *equilibrium* relationship between the (psychological) sacrifice inherent in the act of saving and the advantage derived from its productive use.

Bibliography

On the theories of the business cycle in the inter-war years: R. Backhouse, *A History of Modern Economic Analysis* (Oxford, 1985); R. M. Goodwin, 'Economia matematica: Una visione personale', in J. A. Kregel (ed.), *Il mestiere di economista* (Turin, 1988); R. A. Gordon, *Business Fluctuations* (New York, 1952); G. Haberler, *Prosperity and Depression* (Geneva, 1933); D. Hamberg, *Business Cycles* (New York, 1951); A. H. Hansen, *Business Cycles and National Income* (London, 1951); A. H. Hansen and H. Tout, 'Annual Survey of Business Cycle Theory: Investment and Saving in Business Cycle Theory', *Econometrica*, 1 (1933): R. G. Hawtrey, *Good and Bad Trade* (London, 1913); E. Lindahl, *Studies in the Theory of Money and Capital* (London, 1959; repr. New York, 1970); W. C. Mitchell, *Business Cycles: The Problem and Its Settings* (New York, 1927); W. Young, *Harrod and His Trade Cycle Group* (London, 1989).

On Keynes: E. J. Amadeo, *Keynes' Principle of Effective Demand* (Aldershot, 1989); R. Backhouse, *A History of Modern Economic Analysis* (Oxford, 1985); A. Carabelli, *On Keynes's Method* (Cambridge, 1988); A. H. Hansen, *A Guide to Keynes* (New York, 1953); S. E. Harris (ed.), *The New Economics* (New York, 1947); R. F. Harrod, *The Life of J. M. Keynes* (London, 1951); R. F. Kahn, *The Making of Keynes's General Theory* (Cambridge, 1984); J. M. Keynes, *A Treatise on Money* (2 vols., repr. London, 1971); L. R. Klein, *The Keynesian Revolution* (New York, 1961); M. P. Minsky, *John Maynard Keynes* (New York, 1975); D. E. Moggridge, *Keynes* (Glasgow, 1976); L. L. Pasinetti, 'The Economics of Effective Demand,' in *Growth and Income Distribution* (Cambridge, 1974); D. Patinkin and J. C. Leigh (eds.), *Keynes, Cambridge and the 'General Theory'* (London, 1977); J. V. Robinson, *Introduction to the Theory of Employment*, 2nd edn. (London, 1949); W. Young, *Interpreting Mr Keynes* (Cambridge, 1987).

On Kalecki: E. Eschag (ed.), 'Michał Kalecki Memorial Lectures', *Oxford Bulletin of Economics and Statistics*, 4 (1977); G. R. Feiwel, *The Intellectual Capital of M. Kalecki* (Knoxville, Tenn., 1975); M. Kalecki, *Selected Essays on the Dynamics of the Capitalist Economy, 1933–1970* (Cambridge, 1971); P. Kriesler, *Kalecki's Micro-analysis: The Development of Kalecki's Analysis of Pricing and Distribution* (Cambridge, 1987); J. Poschl and G. Locksley, 'Michał Kalecki: A Comprehensive Challenge to Orthodoxy', in J. R. Shackleton and G. Locksley (ed.), *Twelve Contemporary Economists* (London, 1985).

On Schumpeter: R. V. Clemence and F. S. Doody, *The Schumpeterian System* (Reading, Mass., 1950); H. Frisch (ed.), *Schumpeterian Economics* (New York, 1982); S. Harris (ed.), *Schumpeter, Social Scientist* (Cambridge, Mass., 1951); A. Heertje (ed.), *Schumpeter's Vision* (New York, 1981); A. Oakley, *Schumpeter's Theory of Capitalist Motion* (Aldershot, 1990); F. Perroux, *La Pensée économique de Joseph Schumpeter: Les dynamiques du capitalisme* (Geneva, 1965); C. Seidl (ed.), *Lectures on Schumpeterian Economics* (Berlin, 1984).

8

The Years of High Theory: II

8.1. THE THEORY OF MARKET FORMS

8.1.1. The first signs of dissent

Marshall's theoretical system, perhaps precisely because of his wish to understand the real world and his attempt to link social evolutionism to the utilitarian ethic, ended up by assuming an ambiguous character and provoked a critical reaction. This was due, among other things, to the vulgarized interpretations of Marshall as preached by his followers. The *Principles*, besides being a great work of economics, represents an impressive book of 'sociology' of nineteenth-century English capitalism, and is permeated by a deep sense of history. But Marshall's followers, even the most faithful, chose to develop only the analytical part of the book, ignoring its cultural and philosophical background. This unfortunate gap between Marshall's interests and those of his followers led to more than a few misunderstandings.

At Cambridge, where Marshall's influence was to last a long time, the first signs of dissent had already appeared at the beginning of the 1920s. At the centre of these criticisms was the question of the compatibility between the hypothesis of perfect competition and the partial-equilibrium method. In the *Principles*, Marshall had discussed the existence of different productive sectors characterized by decreasing, constant, and increasing costs. The long-run supply curve of the sector is not necessarily rising, but may be horizontal or falling. Now, it is impossible to establish a priori which of the three situations is most plausible or probable. It is a matter which must be ascertained case by case, with reference to the specific type of sector under consideration. However, it is possible to say, in general, that *there is no 'law' of long-run supply* establishing a direct relationship between prices and quantity, in the same way in which it is possible to speak (albeit with reserve) of a 'law' of demand establishing an inverse relationship. In the long run, and at the sector level, there is no 'law of variable proportions' which generates a rising supply curve.

The problem of the empirical identification of industries and of the various cost regimes that predominate in them was first raised by the Cambridge economic historian J. H. Clapham. In his famous article on the 'Empty Economic Boxes', published in the *Economic Journal* in 1922, Clapham pointed out the frustrations faced by applied economists in trying to utilize, in empirical research, Marshall's division of industries into the three types of increasing, constant, and decreasing costs. In the controversy that surrounded this,

Pigou, in a defence of Marshallian orthodoxy, asserted that, if empirical observation did not confirm the theory of supply based on non-proportional costs, this must be due to the backwardness of the statistical documentation.

8.1.2. Sraffa's criticism of the Marshallian theoretical system

Piero Sraffa (1890–1983) followed a substantially different line of attack in 'Sulle relazioni tra costo e quantità prodotta' ('On the Relations between Cost and Quantity Produced') (in *Giornale degli Economisti*, 1925). With the partial-equilibrium method it has to be assumed that the market investigated has to be separate from all other markets so that what happens in it does not influence the prices of the other goods in any relevant way. Now, in a sector characterized by increasing (decreasing) costs, an increase in production will cause the prices of the productive factors to increase (decrease). Therefore, if one wishes to continue to reason in terms of partial equilibrium, it is necessary to postulate that the inputs, whose prices increase (or decrease) with production, are those that are utilized *only* by the industry in question. Otherwise, the variations in their prices would modify the prices of the goods produced in other sectors. But, obviously, this is a drastic hypothesis: 'It is only possible to use the impressive construction of decreasing productivity', writes Sraffa, 'for studying a very small category of goods, those in whose production the totality of a productive factor is used up' (p. 314).

But this is not all; in order to uphold the logical coherence of the Marshallian edifice, it is also necessary to postulate that the economies (or the diseconomies) of scale are external to the firms but internal to the sector. In fact, if they were internal to the firm, the latter would be encouraged to expand (contract) its own level of activity, and would eventually become a monopolist in its industry (or pull out of the market). Both cases are incompatible with the hypothesis of competition. If, on the other hand, the economies or diseconomies were external to the sector, a partial-equilibrium analysis would no longer make sense, and it would be necessary to move to a general-equilibrium approach.

Sraffa's attack on the logical coherence of the Marshallian edifice was more devastating than criticism concerned with its scarce empirical relevance. The gist of Sraffa's criticism is that the Marshallian theory of competitive equilibrium cannot escape from the following dilemma: either it is contradictory or it is irrelevant. The only case which is logically compatible with the partial-equilibrium analysis of a perfectly competitive sector is that of constant costs. But in this case the 'classical and neoclassical synthesis' of Marshall (and of Pantaleoni, whom Sraffa also had criticized) basically led to the same results as classical economics: prices are determined exclusively by the costs of production, while the conditions of demand only contribute to determine the quantities produced. The non-substitution theorem had not yet been formulated.

Sraffa's 1925 article interested Edgeworth so much that he suggested to Keynes he should ask Sraffa to write a shorter article on the same subject for Keynes's journal. The new article appeared in 1926 in the December issue of the *Economic Journal*, with the title of 'The Laws of Returns under Competitive Conditions'. It was extremely important, both for its critical content and for the power of its positive conclusions. The article immediately provoked an appreciative reaction, especially from Keynes, and welded the friendship which brought Sraffa to Cambridge.

After a reformulation of his 1925 criticism, Sraffa noted that increasing returns are *de facto* important in industrial sectors, and consequently that the typical cost curve of these sectors is probably negatively sloped. Thus, rather than developing an analysis of competitive markets on the basis of the hypothesis of constant costs (as it would have been natural to expect) he started off along a completely different track: 'to abandon the path of free competition and turn in the opposite direction, namely, towards monopoly' (p. 542). This is the origin of the line of research known as 'the theory of market forms' which was to surface, a few years later, in the work of Robinson and Chamberlin. Sraffa pointed out the existence of market imperfections which are not simple frictions but are themselves active forces which produce permanent and even cumulative effects on prices and quantities; furthermore, he argued that these obstacles to competition are 'endowed with sufficient stability to enable them to be made the subject of analysis based on static assumptions' (p. 542). Among the obstacles to the regular operation of a perfectly competitive market, Sraffa indicated the possession of specific natural resources, legal privileges, and control of a given percentage of total production.

The criticism of the long-run partial-equilibrium analysis developed in two directions, both indicated by Sraffa himself. The dilemma created for the traditional theory of perfect competition by the assumption of decreasing costs can be solved either by introducing a demand curve for the single firm which descends from left to right, or by abandoning the partial-equilibrium approach in favour of general equilibrium, so as to be able to take into account the movements of the cost curves induced by economies external either to the firm or to the sector.

Sraffa agreed that the first of these two alternatives had a greater explanatory value. What actually prevents the unlimited growth of a firm is not, in his opinion, an increasing cost curve but a decreasing demand curve. In fact, it is true that, in the decreasing-cost sectors, the firms never become really large scale. The solution proposed by Sraffa presupposed 'the absence of indifference on the part of the buyers of goods as between the different producers'. This absence was attributed to causes such as 'long custom, personal acquaintance, confidence in the quality of the product, proximity', and implied a willingness 'on the part of the group of buyers who constitute a firm's clientele to pay, if necessary, something extra in order to obtain the goods from a particular firm rather than from any other' (p. 544). Thus, beginning with the identification of a logical difficulty within the Marshallian analysis of competition, Sraffa ended up by opening a new field of research.

8.1.3. Chamberlin's theory of monopolistic competition

In 1933 Edward Chamberlin (1899–1967) published *The Theory of Monopolistic Competition*. In this work he acknowledged that real-world markets do not operate in perfect competition, and rejected the idea of the firm as a passive price-taker. On the contrary, he maintained that the firm is able to influence the demand decisions for its own products by means of product differentiation, promotional activity, and advertising. This was the origin of a new theory, a theory of markets which are neither in perfect competition nor under monopoly (even if—as already mentioned—Pareto was the first to outline it in the *Manual*).

The theory of monopolistic competition rests on two basic assumptions:

(1) The majority of firms set their sale prices; i.e. they are price-setters: This means that single firms retain some monopoly power and, if they increase prices, they do not lose all their customers, as happens in perfect competition.

(2) There is no natural monopoly in the majority of the productive sectors; if extra profits are made in a given sector, this encourages new firms to enter; in other words, the firms operate within a context which is, to a certain degree, competitive.

There is agreement among the various authors on these points. The differences arise in regard to the conclusions that can be drawn. This is due to the fact that the entry of new firms on the market produces two contrasting effects. On the one hand, in the presence of extra profits, competition encourages the entry of new firms, which contribute to eliminate the extra profits. This process leads to the creation of 'too many' firms—too many in regard to the number of consumers. On the other hand, the entry of new firms increases the variety of products and thus raises the customers' welfare, at least to the extent to which the latter are able to choose from a wider range of products. But, since firms do not have the opportunity to appropriate the consumer surplus, as would be possible in a monopoly, they will have little incentive to differentiate the product. Which of the two effects predominates will depend on the circumstances.

Even though Chamberlin and Robinson reached the same solution in regard to the equilibrium of the single firm and the sector, there were more than a few important differences in their work, differences which Chamberlin himself underlined in Chapter 9 of the sixth edition (1950) of his book. Their theoretical roots were also different: while Robinson in the introduction of her book acknowledged Sraffa as her source of inspiration, Chamberlin took the trouble to point out that most of his conclusions had already been set out in the dissertation he had presented at Harvard in April 1927, which he had written under the supervision of Allyn Young without having first read Sraffa's article.

There are several difficulties with Chamberlin's model. First, the hypotheses of product differentiation and atomistic behaviour do not seem compatible, for the simple reason that firms are always aware of the actions and behaviour of competitors who offer close substitutes. The second difficulty is that product differentiation, in that it leads to an entry barrier, is not compatible with the assumption of free entry into the sector. Finally, product differentiation tends to make the notion of an industrial sector meaningless. More specifically, it is incompatible with the device of the 'representative firm' in the Marshallian sense, so that it becomes necessary to take into account the relationships between individual cost and demand curves, on the one hand, and market demand and supply curves, on the other.

These were the principal points raised by the critics. Stigler, in particular, argued that the definition of group of firms is ambiguous. In fact, the hypothesis that each firm neglects, or does not consider, the effects of its own decisions on the behaviour of other firms of the group, on the one hand, and the hypothesis that demand and cost curves are basically the same for every productive unit, on the other, do not justify nor even render plausible the concept of group. For the hypothesis concerning the uniformity of the demand and cost curves not to be devoid of meaning, the group must be defined in such a way as to include only firms that sell homogeneous products. But if this is the case, there is no reason to assume that the demand curves of the single firms are downward-sloping.

Other authors have focused their attention on the logical weakness of the way in which Chamberlin arrived at the determination of the long-run equilibrium position. Harrod, for example, pointed out that the Chamberlin firm, in order to determine the quantity produced and the optimum size of its plant, uses a short-run marginal-revenue curve and a long-run marginal-cost curve, and ends by setting the price at a level which encourages new firms to enter the market. In turn, this would determine a movement towards the bottom of the marginal-revenue curve. Harrod's analysis led to the conclusion that the margin of unused capacity, if it exists, is markedly less than that indicated by Chamberlin.

Of course, these sharp criticisms do not lessen the importance of Chamberlin's work, which will always remain an ingenious, if incomplete, solution to the dilemma posed by decreasing costs. Furthermore, in addition to the important notion of product differentiation which Chamberlin introduced in the theory of price, the notion of promotional sales activity is an element of undoubted realism. Not only this, but the invention of the *ex ante* and *ex post* demand curves was to give rise to a whole series of further theoretical contributions, among which it is worth recalling the L-shaped curve, widely used in the study of the structure of oligopolistic markets.

The *Theory of Monopolistic Competition* aroused considerable interest in the 1940s and 1950s. F. Machlup, R. Triffin, W. Fellner, and A. Smithies are among those who have tried to deepen and extend Chamberlin's work. It is especially worth mentioning Triffin's enthusiasm for Chamberlin's 'large-group case', intended as an analytical tool suitable for introducing imperfect competition into the general-equilibrium model, even if careful consideration shows that Triffin was rather over-enthusiastic. In fact, in *Monopolistic Competition and General Equilibrium Theory* (1949), he ran up against the problem of the determination of the number of firms operating in equilibrium.

The problem is conceptually easy to solve in conditions of perfect competition, in which the extra profits of firms operating in a given sector are a symptom that room exists for new firms. But how is it possible to establish the number of firms in conditions of monopolistic competition? It is obvious that there is no reason to postulate a tendency towards equality of costs and earnings of all firms operating under such conditions (as can be postulated, by contrast, under perfect competition). Nor are there reasons to assume that a situation can arise in which both the entry flow of firms confident of finding a favourable niche and the exit flow of firms making losses are arrested. Reading the pages Triffin dedicated to the problem of entry, it is easy to see how this fundamental problem of a general theory of market equilibria remains basically unresolved. It was T. Negishi, in 'Monopolistic Competition and General Equilibrium' (*Review of Economic Studies*, 1961), who produced the first satisfactory formulation of a model of general equilibrium in monopolistic competition. In this model, each firm sets the price of the good it produces under the hypothesis that it knows a *perceived* demand function, which may be different from the true demand function, but such that the equilibrium point belongs to both functions.

8.1.4. Joan Robinson's theory of imperfect competition

The *Economics of Imperfect Competition* by Joan Robinson (1903–83) was also published in 1933. Grand-niece of the Christian socialist F. D. Maurice and daughter of a general, Joan Robinson assimilated with ease the humanitarian and reformist spirit of Cambridge Pigouvian economics. The core of Pigou's social philosophy consisted of the idea that scientific research should aim at identifying those deficiencies of the economic system which could be remedied by government intervention. Robinson's intellectual debt to Pigou is notable, both in general (e.g. on the subject of market failures) and at more specific levels (e.g. in the explanation of the equilibrium of the industrial sector by means of specifying the equilibrium conditions for single firms). She also followed Pigou in regard to method. She herself presented her book as 'a box of tools [that] can make only an indirect contribution to our knowledge of the actual world' (p. 1). The book was directed at the analytical economist; there was nothing in it for the businessman.

Robinson's austere view of economic theory may seem strange in the light of her declaration that the principal aim of economics is to contribute to the welfare of mankind. It is certain that her book gave a powerful thrust to the development of formalism in economics, a development that Robinson was to view with dismay after her 'conversion' in the 1940s.

One achievement of Robinson was to rescue from oblivion Cournot's notion of marginal revenue. Marshall and his students, in the graphic exposition of the problem of profit maximization, had made use of the total cost and revenue curves, thus generating more than a few cases of ambiguity. The utilization of the apparatus of average and marginal curves is one of the results of Robinson's work, in which is also to be found, for the first time, the general relationship between average and marginal curves.

Robinson's specific contribution to the theory of imperfect competition concerns the celebrated tangency solution. Robinson accepted the idea of the equilibrium of the group presented in the last part of Sraffa's essay and developed it, with the help of Richard Kahn, removing the simplifying hypothesis that the number of firms, and therefore the set of products, is fixed. The resulting analysis seems more general than that of Sraffa, but also less robust. The problem lies in the demand curve. Marshall had considered a monopoly in which a single firm controls the industry; the demand curve of the industry is therefore the same as that of the monopolist. Sraffa's monopolists, by contrast, have no privileged access to the demand curve of the sector. A price increase by a firm would provoke the transfer of some of its customers towards other industries and/or towards rival producers in the same industry. Robinson realized the difficulties in Sraffa's way of treating the demand curve of the single firm, but, rather than run the risks of dealing with these, she chose to set them aside. Her stratagem was to deal with the problems posed by the interdependence among firms by postulating that these had already been resolved in a previous stage of the analysis; and this is still today a frequent practice, especially in the theory of oligopoly. Robinson was aware of the 'misdeed', but certain difficulties must be ignored if one wishes to get on with the analysis!

In the period of the publication of *The Economics of Imperfect Competition*, most economists did not perceive the deliberate sense of irony in the use of the adjective 'imperfect'. Chamberlin himself, in a 1950 article entitled 'Capitalism and Monopolistic Competition', *American Economic Review*, wrote:

Imperfect Competition followed the tradition of competitive theory, not only in identifying a 'commodity' (albeit elastically defined) with an 'industry', but in expressly assuming such a 'commodity' to be homogeneous. Such a theory involves no break whatsoever with competitive tradition. The very terminology of 'imperfect competition' is heavy with implications that the objective is to move towards perfection.   (p. 87)

The veiled accusation here is that the Cambridge economist, far from achieving a breakthrough in the theory of competitive value, gave shape to an elegant continuation of the Marshallian tradition. And yet, in the introduction to the final edition of 1969, Robinson explicitly stated that it had been her precise intention to show that, if one attempts to construct a logically coherent marginalist theory of the firm, a conclusion will be reached which is in contrast to the neoclassical view of the world: that the free operation of market forces leads to an economic structure in which unsatisfied consumers' needs and excess capacity of firms can coexist.

The argument is, in short, the following. A firm in perfect competition can sell all that it wishes without influencing the price, for the simple reason that its increasing cost curves prevent it from producing more than a small percentage of the total output. By contrast, the firm with decreasing cost curves is unable to expand its sales without lowering the price of its output. On the other hand, if the demand curve of the firm is decreasing, so will the marginal revenue curve, so that, beyond a certain point, sales will bring forth negative marginal revenues. But before this point is reached the marginal revenues will begin to be lower than the marginal costs. An attempt to expand sales reduces the profits of the firm, so that it has no interest in pushing other firms out of the market. This is the type of limited competition Robinson tried to formalize in her book.

The implications for welfare economics are worrying: the market mechanism operates in such a way that not only are the workers not paid according to the value of their marginal productivity, but even the principle of consumer sovereignty is impaired. This theory was very influential in the anti-trust policies taken up by many Western countries in the 1940s and 1950s.

Towards the end of the 1930s, Robinson changed her theoretical interests and focused on Keynesian theory, even abandoning the theoretical debate which her book had opened. In Chapter 9 we will consider the results of this shift. Here, instead, we will briefly discuss the argument put forward by Robinson in an article published in 1934 in the *Economic Journal*, 'Euler's Theorem and the Problem of Distribution'. The problem was that of the exhaustion of the product in the marginalist theory of distribution. It is an important paper, and received a great deal of attention during the 1960s. Wicksell's solution (it will be recalled) had led to the following question: what happens if the number of potential entrepreneurs is so small that, even in equilibrium, positive profits exist?

Robinson's reply was that the competitive equilibrium profit coincides with the marginal productivity of the entrepreneurial ability for the industry. Robinson began by observing that a central requirement of the theory is that the rate of remuneration of a service is proportional to its marginal productivity. This requirement cannot be satisfied by entrepreneurial ability if the marginal productivity refers to the firm. In fact, if the entrepreneurial ability is assumed to be a variable input, the problem would remain unresolved, because profit is defined as the income of the entrepreneur net of the remuneration of the variable factors, including entrepreneurial ability. Therefore, profit cannot be equal to the marginal contribution of entrepreneurial ability. Then, the latter must be considered as a *fixed* productive factor. But if this is the case, it is impossible for the profit to be proportional to the marginal productivity of the entrepreneurial ability, since a fixed factor does not have a marginal productivity. Robinson's idea was to shift attention from the firm to the industrial sector. Now, the overall output of a sector varies, in general, with variations of the number of firms. If the returns to scale of the single firms are decreasing, the overall output corresponding to the efficient allocation of a given quantity of inputs among *n* firms will be less than the output corresponding to the efficient allocation of the same quantity of inputs among $(n + 1)$ firms. The difference between these two levels of output is the physical marginal productivity for the industry of the $(n + 1)$th firm. Thus a new version of the theory of marginal productivity is derived: the rate of remuneration of the variable factors is equal to the value of the respective marginal productivities in the firms in which they are utilized, while the profit is equal to the marginal productivity of the firm for the industry to which it belongs.

Notwithstanding the ingeniousness of the construction, the basic problem, which is that of the *nature* of entrepreneurial ability, remains: what is entrepreneurial ability in a static-equilibrium context, such as the one considered in the above reasoning? The remuneration of entrepreneurial ability is positive when, as we have outlined above, entrepreneurial ability is scarce. But why, in a static world, should all the firms not have the same technological knowledge and the same organizational ability?

8.1.5. The decline of the theory of market forms

After a promising beginning, the new theory of market forms gradually fell into decline, leaving the field free for the alternative mentioned above: general-equilibrium theory. In effect, the conceptual settling of Robinson and Chamberlin, rather than opening a new phase of theoretical reflection, closed an old one. The hypothesis of perfect competition, originated within neoclassical theory to respond to the need for logical coherence, led to a restriction in the heuristic power of the theory; but the general-equilibrium theorists were well aware of this. The theory of imperfect competition aimed to overturn this scale of priorities by focusing on the realism of its hypothesis. But the theoretical apparatus used was identical to the traditional one. In particular, the traditional scheme of profit maximization was still adopted. What were the consequences?

An imperfect market is one in which the maximum sales that the firm expects is inversely related to the price of the product. The main difference between an imperfect and a perfect market is that, in the latter, a single firm can freely increase sales at the current price; and only if a large number of firms try to do the same at the same moment will the price decrease under the *impersonal* action of the market. If, on the other hand, the market is imperfect, sales can increase only if, *before and individually*, the single firms have revised their prices (here we are not considering sales expenses or product diversification). In such circumstances, the decision to decrease the price *precedes* any attempt to increase sales, and is also a *non-anonymous* decision.

Now the decision to lower the price depends both on the form of the price–quantity trade-off around the starting-point and on the cost function. In turn, the form of the trade-off depends on two conjectural elements: the characteristics of the particular market of the firm with respect to the general market in which it operates and the expected counter-moves of competitors. This means that the choice of a business strategy in imperfect market conditions includes at the same time a patrimonial and an oligopolistic aspect. The patrimonial aspect concerns the goodwill necessary for the firm to continue to exist; the oligopolistic aspect concerns the interdependence of the decisions.

It follows that, in the presence of market imperfections, the identification of the optimal position on the trade-off is separate from the decision to approach it by means of price adjustments: the decision can be blocked by the fear of sharp reactions by competitors or unforeseen responses from the particular market. The problem was brought out in an important but almost unknown article by K. Arrow, 'Toward a Theory of Price Adjustment', published in 1959 (in *The Allocation of Economic Resources*, edited by M. Abramovitz). The more uncertain the situation, the more risky the prices. This deduction has been overlooked, and continues to be so by all those, Robinson and Chamberlin included, who have dealt with the behaviour of the firm in imperfect competition with the canonical scheme of profit maximization. The basic error of this approach is to take it for granted that the *identification of the optimum coincides with the decision to realize it.* What distinguishes the actions of firms which operate in imperfect markets is, instead, the fact that they may deliberately choose not to try to reach the optimal position.

This creates tensions within the neoclassical approach, since the hypothesis ensures the existence of an equilibrium conflict with the needs of realism. The result was that the formal rigour of the Walrasian analysis of perfect competition was lost, without, however, any great gains on the interpretative level. The theory of imperfectly competitive market forms has not given the hoped-for results precisely because it was a theoretical compromise.

An attempt at rationalization had already been made by Jacob Viner in the article 'Cost Curves and Supply Curves', published in 1931 in the *American Economic Review*. Here Viner proved the envelope theorem: the long-run average-cost curve is the envelope of the short-run average-cost curves. The 'U' shape of the former was derived from the law of returns to scale, according to which unit costs decrease with the increase in plant size up to the point that the *optimum size* is reached, in which all possible economies of scale are fully exploited. Above this size, diseconomies of scale are generated and the unit cost curve begins to rise. But what causes these diseconomies of scale? It is certainly not factors of a technological nature. If it were so, in fact, they could be avoided by doubling, tripling, etc. the optimal plant size. The *deus ex machina* was found in the inefficiencies of managerial activity: the turning-point of the long-run average-cost curve was attributed to *diseconomies of scale of a managerial nature*. The large size of the firm requires management methods different from those suitable for small and average-sized firms. Therefore, if size increases with no parallel modification in management and control structures, there will sooner or later be an increase in costs because of managerial inefficiency.

It is easy to see the fragility of this line of argument. First of all, why should the management methods not also adjust to the size of the firm? After all, management ability is a resource susceptible to improvement and innovation. Indeed, in modern times, it is precisely management that has registered the greatest progress. Second, as Florence and Andrews were to point out later, the diseconomies of managerial nature, when they do appear, have little influence on the technical economies generated by the size of the plant. This means that the long-run average-cost curve would be more likely to assume an 'L' than a 'U' shape.

It was not until the 1970s, however, that these criticisms were able to develop into an alternative strand of research to the traditional neoclassical approach. This happened with the synthesis proposed by W. Novshek and H. Sonnenschein in 'Cournot and Walras Equilibrium' (*Journal of Economic Theory*, 1978), a work which can be placed between the Cournot–Marshall and the Arrow–Debreu–McKenzie lines of thought. It remains a fact, however, that the strand of research initiated by Chamberlin and Robinson has contributed to generating a special 'orthodoxy', as K. J. Arrow called it in 'The Firm in General Equilibrium Theory' (in *The Corporate Economy*, edited by R. Marris and A. Wood, 1971), that has entered and remained in the microeconomic textbooks.

8.2. THE THEORY OF GENERAL ECONOMIC EQUILIBRIUM

8.2.1. The first existence theorems and von Neumann's model

The *impasse* in which general-equilibrium theory had remained trapped in the pre-war period was due to the problem of the existence of solutions. The economists in this field had not gone much beyond counting the unknowns and the equations. In order to make further progress it was necessary for new scholars to enter the field who were 'more mathematicians than economists'.

A group with these characteristics did form, thanks to the work and support of Karl Menger (b. 1902), and became one of the most remarkable groups in the history of economic analysis. Karl Menger, son of the great Austrian economist Carl Menger, was an active member of the Vienna Circle, from which he drew the bases for an axiomatization and a definitive consolidation of the scientific work according to the *Geometry* model of the great Austrian mathematician David Hilbert (1862–1943). In the 1930s Menger established a permanent series of seminars, the *Mathematisches Kolloquium*, which were attended by many of the most important mathematicians and logicians of the period, including Gödel, Alt, von Neumann, and Tarski. At the *Kolloquium* both pure and applied mathematical works were discussed, and among the latter were some of the most important works on mathematical economics of the 1930s. In these works, it was not so much the substantial aspects of the applications of mathematics to economic problems that were discussed but rather the underlying mathematical tools, so that the great mathematicians, who were relatively inexpert in economics, were able to take part. This was the beginning of a *de facto* separation between economics and mathematical economics; the latter being considered as the application of mathematical techniques by professional mathematicians, who are mostly uninterested in economics itself. This separation is still strong today, and often has counter-productive effects on the practice of the profession.

The attitude of the participants of the *Kolloquium* towards traditional economic theory is well summed up by the contempt in which von Neumann held the works of contemporary economists, judging their mathematics 'crude and primitive', as if mathematical standards could judge the validity of economic research. Given these premises, it is easy to understand why the *Kolloquium* focused its attention on the problems of existence and, in part, of uniqueness and stability: these were the most suitable problems to be treated in purely mathematical terms.

In the beginning, however, the proof of the existence of an equilibrium for a general case was not the object of special attention; the starting-point was, instead, a case of fixed production coefficients. It was Frederik Zeuthen (1888–1959) who proposed an ingenious solution to one of the main technical difficulties of the general-equilibrium model: the constraints requiring that the quantities of utilized resources are not higher than those available take on the form of inequalities. He then introduced a 'slack' variable, measuring the value of the unused resources; in this way each constraint could be written under the form of an equality.

However, Zeuthen did not manage to demonstrate the existence of solutions, not even for the 'simplest' problem. Neither did Schlesinger (1899–1938), a successful banker fond of economics who was an active member of the *Kolloquium*. Schlesinger financed the studies of Abraham Wald (1902–50), a young mathematician of Romanian origin, who took part in the meetings from 1930 onwards. It was Schlesinger himself who assigned Wald the problem of the existence of general equilibrium. Armed with the suggestions of Zeuthen, who had also been recommended to him by Schlesinger, Wald managed to prove the existence of solutions for a stationary system of linear equations under some key hypotheses of convexity and non-saturation, hypotheses which have continued to be used in the literature. Contrary to what a great many members of the *Kolloquium* believed, the importance of Wald's result lay precisely in its having demonstrated that the existence of an equilibrium can be ensured only by imposing important restrictions on individual preferences and the technology employed, and that it is impossible to obtain it under completely 'general' mathematical hypotheses. As Debreu was later to discover, the real difficulty in the 'interesting' demonstrations of existence is exactly that of imposing restrictions on behaviour and technology that are the least arbitrary possible but are at the same time significant from the economic point of view.

With the escalation of Nazism, the *Kolloquium* disbanded. At this point, another of the 'great figures' who had attended the meetings took on a key role: Oskar Morgenstern, a fervent member of the *Kolloquium*, a great admirer of logical positivism, and a strenuous defender of the application of its precepts in the field of economic theory. Even though he also suffered the consequences of the ascent of Nazism, Morgenstern helped Wald to emigrate to the United States. When Wald arrived there he took up the study of economic statistics, partially in collaboration with Morgenstern himself, and never returned to the existence problem. Morgenstern, however, remained very active, maintaining contacts with the survivors of the *Kolloquium* and ensuring that the results of the researches of the group did not fall into oblivion. In particular, he kept strong links with John von Neumann (1903–57).

By the end of the 1920s von Neumann had already proved the existence of an equilibrium for some situations in which two individuals, who follow some 'rational' rules of behaviour, face each other. For this purpose he used a theorem which was to become extremely important, in its various versions, in many demonstrations of existence: Brouwer's fixed-point theorem. After emigrating to the United States, and working independently of Wald, von Neumann managed to extend his first results to an economy in which all variables grow at a constant rate. We will discuss this shortly. In the meantime, we must say something about his intellectual exchange with Morgenstern, which in this period reached its high point. Morgenstern was aware of the 'poverty' of economic applications of mathematical techniques and, as a good logical positivist, was considering the titanic task of creating an *ad hoc* mathematical language for economic science, a language conducive to the rigorous formulation of the economic problems, and avoiding the 'undesirable' and limiting application of differential calculus. This was the origin of game theory, whose conceptual apparatus had been developed by von Neumann in his first existence proofs. Undoubtedly, the classic book for this new language was *Theory of Games and Economic Behaviour* (1944), by von Neumann and Morgenstern. Game theory, according to Morgenstern, should be the nucleus of the new general language he hoped to give economics. Perhaps it did not achieve precisely what Morgenstern wished, but there is no doubt that it has experienced a growing success over time; and, at the moment, it is receiving a high degree of recognition in the profession, as diverse and promising uses have recently been discovered.

Now let us consider the famous 'von Neumann model', the most important, perhaps, of the results of this branch of research. It is probable that von Neumann began to think about it as early as the end of the 1920s, when he was *Privatdozent* (a university lecturer) in Berlin (see section 8.5.4). However, it was presented for the first time in 1932 in a seminar at Princeton, and it was only later that von Neumann came to hear about Wald's work. Therefore its direct link with the Viennese *Kolloquium* is not at all certain. In fact, von Neumann's article was published (in *Ergebnisse eines mathematischen Kolloquiums*) only in 1937, with the title of 'Über ein ökonomischen Gleichungssystem und eine Verallmeinerung des Brouwerschen Fixpunktsatzes'. However, it only became known to a wider academic public after it was translated into English and published, with the title of 'A Model of General Economic Equilibrium', in the *Review of Economic Studies* (1945–6). The model is based on a series of rather brave assumptions: there are diverse methods of jointly producing different commodities by means of themselves; each of these methods, called 'activities', combines the diverse commodities according to determinate coefficients of input and output; if the economy is expanding, the ratio between input and output remains constant, i.e. there are constant returns to scale; the number of activities is not lower than the number of commodities, but it is not infinite; consumption is determined by the 'necessities of life' and is included in the productive inputs without distinguishing it from other inputs; there being no unproductive consumption, all the produced surplus is reinvested; there is no other money than the numeraire; there is perfect competition, so that, in equilibrium, the non-profitable productive processes are not activated, while the commodities in excess supply have a zero price.

Von Neumann proved that, under these assumptions, there is an equilibrium which guarantees non-negative prices and activity levels. In this equilibrium the rate of interest is equal to the rate of growth, which is a consequence of the assumption that all profits are reinvested. The rate of growth is uniform in all sectors, and therefore there is 'balanced growth', which means that the composition of commodities in the gross output remains constant through time. Finally, in this equilibrium only the most efficient productive methods are activated.

The model has played an important role in several developments of economic theory. As far as the general-equilibrium theory is concerned, it was important for the application of the fixed-point theorem and for the solution it supplied to the problem of existence. In those days, von Neumann's model represented the most general of the equilibrium models for which the existence of solutions had been proved. Besides this, in the area of growth theory, von Neumann's model opened the way to the multi-sectorial and normative theories of growth of the 1950s and 1960s; for example, the famous 'turnpike theorem' is a direct application of von Neumann's model. In the theory of programming, this model has laid the foundations of the so-called 'activity analysis' and of modern methods of linear programming.

Finally, it is important to note that von Neumann's model has aroused interest even among economists who are not supporters of neoclassical theory. In fact, it has many characteristics in common with the classical and Marxian theoretical systems: for example, the treatment of workers' consumption as a technological input; the image of the 'capitalist' as a person in charge of the function of capital accumulation; a theory of value that does not make prices depend on utility or other subjective phenomena; the use of a notion of equilibrium which can be interpreted in terms of reproduction equilibrium; and, finally, the predominance of the idea of reproducibility over that of scarcity. On the other hand, various characteristics typical of the neoclassical theoretical system are absent, besides the concept of scarcity: for example, the faith in consumer sovereignty or in the predominance of the conditions of demand over those of supply in the determination of prices and quantities produced. It is also interesting to note that von Neumann's model solves one of the principal problems of Walras's schema, that of the over-determination of the system of equilibrium equations in the case in which uniformity in the rates of return of the various capital goods is required. The model solves this problem, however, by eliminating the latter's cause, which is the hypothesis of the existence of an arbitrarily given initial endowment of capital goods. This hypothesis was important in the Walrasian model, as it served to explain the remuneration of capital goods in terms of the forces of supply and demand. In von Neumann's model, the structure of the capital goods is determined endogenously and depends, as does the remuneration of capital, only on the conditions of production.

8.2.2 The English reception of the Walrasian approach

General-equilibrium theory was rather late in reaching English academic circles and initially, that is, before the advent of Hicks's work, stimulated no significant contributions.

An important event, not only for the reception of the Walrasian approach in England but, more generally, for the history of economic analysis, was the arrival of Lionel Robbins (1898–1985) at the London School of Economics in 1929, when he was offered a senior professorship at the remarkably young age of 31. In the inter-war period Robbins was, in fact, one of the most influential economists in England. This was the period in which an extraordinary generation of 'young' economists arrived on the scene—personalities of the calibre of Hicks, Kaldor, Roy Allen, and Abba Lerner. In a short time the London School of Economics became, under the driving force of Robbins, one of the most active centres for the production and discussion of economic theory on an international scale. Many of the most important economists of the time, such as Schumpeter, von Mises, Lindahl, Ohlin, and Jacob Viner, visited London in that period to discuss their research. The longest-lasting impression, however, was certainly left by Hayek, who in 1931 held a seminar course at the LSE from which he drew inspiration for his book *Prices and Production*. In the same year, he moved to London to teach at the university. All this can be at least partially explained by the atmosphere of enlightened liberalism which existed in the department under Robbins's leadership.

Thanks to the teaching of Robbins and Hayek, the LSE soon became one of the centres in which general-equilibrium theory was studied with the greatest interest. It was also Robbins who introduced Hicks to Pareto's works and offered him a course on general equilibrium. Robbins's role was basically that of patron, able as he was in looking after the interests of the 'young lions' and in ordering the results of their work within his own methodological framework. The important *Essay on the Nature and Significance of Economic Science* (1932) was one of the products of this activity. Hayek, on the other hand, was the 'prime mover' of the group's theoretical speculation.

At the centre of Hayek's thought in that period was the attempt to apply the conceptual scheme of the general-equilibrium model to the 'dynamic' analysis of cyclical fluctuations. Historical events seemed to show that the instability of the real economy depends on the instability of monetary aggregates; and yet money had difficulty in finding an active role in the Walrasian conceptual system. We discussed the truly dynamic and macroeconomic component of Hayek's theory in Chapter 7. Here we will say something about some contributions to general-equilibrium theory which he put forward, above all, in *Prices and Production*.

Despite the deficiencies of the general-equilibrium apparatus and the consequent analytical difficulties, Hayek was convinced that it was impossible to give a coherent and unitary explanation of the trade cycle without basing it on an equilibrium theory. However, the needs of dynamic analysis meant that the category itself of equilibrium, and the theoretical constructions which originated from it, had to be seriously thought out again, if not in their logical-formal dimension, at least in their *interpretative* dimension. For example, Hayek observed that in an economic context in which time does play a role, two quantities of the same good at two different moments must be considered to all intents and purposes as two different goods. On the other hand, arbitrage phenomena occur normally, not only in spatially separate markets, but also at different moments in time. It was from these suggestions that Arrow and Debreu were able to construct their famous model of *intertemporal equilibrium*, 20 years later.

Already in that period Hayek had also succeeded in causing a change of direction in economic analysis by demonstrating the crucial importance of the problem of expectations in the 'dynamic' versions of the Walrasian model: only if individuals manage to produce systematically correct predictions of the future conditions of the economic system is it possible to consider equilibrium as a 'normal' condition of the system itself. This point of view reverberated strongly in the innovative second part of Hicks's *Value and Capital* (1939). In this work Hayek's observations were translated into a new conceptual scheme which was to remain the reference point for all later theoretical elaborations of equilibrium analysis, regularly outliving each of these, as seems to have happened recently also in the case of the theory of rational expectations.

Hicks acknowledged on more than one occasion his intellectual debt to Hayek. It must be said, however, that, once the initial driving force had been exhausted, both Hicks and the majority of the 'young lions' of the LSE took up positions which were increasingly distant from that of Hayek. While Hayek was interested in the study of equilibrium processes in which, according to the Austrian tradition, the time dimension of production plays a central role, even at the cost of sacrificing the role of expectations by means of a hypothesis of perfect foresight, Hicks, and with him, albeit from quite a different position, Kaldor, Allen, and Lerner, were moving in another direction, trying to understand the way in which the process of expectation formation could influence the equilibrium characteristics of the economic system. This was a substantial opening towards the theories of disequilibrium; an opening which led Kaldor and Lerner, and later also Hicks, to abandon equilibrium methodology.

In order to understand the intellectual evolution of these economists it is necessary also to consider the influence of another 'patriarch' of the LSE, Arthur L. Bowley (1869–1957), an excellent statistician and mathematical economist, who deserves to be remembered for his *Mathematical Groundwork of Economics* (1924). His lectures helped to enrich the mathematical knowledge of the 'young lions' as well as their understanding of the work of economists such as Cournot, Edgeworth, and Pigou. In Allen's case, Bowley's teaching also ended up in a fruitful scientific collaboration which led to the production of a statistical work on the distribution of income which was for many years a standard reference point.

8.2.3. *Value and demand in Hicks*

The paper 'A Reconsideration of the Theory of Value', written with Roy Allen and published in *Economica* in 1934, the first three chapters of *Value and Capital*, and *A Revision of Demand Theory* (1956) contain the ordinalist reorganization of consumer theory. By taking note of the suggestions put forward by Pareto in the *Manuale* and in the famous 1911 article in the *Encyclopédie des sciences mathématiques pures et appliquées*, Hicks immediately realized that Edgeworth's analysis of indifference curves would allow the theory of value to discard the cumbersome concept of cardinal utility.

In order to appreciate the importance of the shift from cardinalism to ordinalism made by Hicks, it is necessary to take into account the cultural atmosphere of the period and, in particular, the new criteria which neopositivism was proposing for the foundation of scientific work—above all, the criterion that any scientific proposition must be subject to an empirical verification procedure. Now, the notion of cardinal utility was formulated for principally philosophical ends; and this was not acceptable to the new epistemological orientations. If the Benthamian philosopher found no problem whatsoever with the scientific legitimization of the categories of utilitarian theory, this was not the case for those who had been won over by the spirit of the Vienna Circle. Thus Hicks, in *Value and Capital*, was able to say: 'If one is utilitarian in philosophy, one has the perfect right to be utilitarian in one's economics. But if one is not (and few people are utilitarian nowadays), one also has the right to an economics free of utilitarian assumptions' (p. 18)

At the beginning of the 1930s, the notion of marginal utility had been definitively overtaken, at least at the LSE. In his famous 1932 'Essay', Robbins had insisted more than once on the importance of avoiding metaphysical fog. The concept of economic science as a structure of abstract relations among scarce means and ordered preferences has no need for, nor offers any space to, the remains of Benthiam utilitarianism in economics. As we have already mentioned, Pareto was one of the first to understand the epistemological anachronism of cardinalism, and it was precisely because his proposal to leave it aside was so ahead of its time that his contribution remained for a long time without any appreciable acknowledgement or follow-up. It is true that in his pioneering 'Sulla teoria del bilancio del consumatore' ('On the Theory of the Consumer Budget'), published in the *Giornale degli Economisti* in 1915, Slutsky had foreseen the use of the principle of indifference in overtaking the obsolete law of the saturation of needs, but this article did not circulate within the academic circles of the period.

In their 1934 paper, Hicks and Allen not only rediscovered Slutsky's famous result, the decomposition of the price effect into an income and a substitution effect, but, more importantly, they decreed the replacement of Gossen's first law (the law of decreasing marginal utility) by the principle of marginal substitution: as Hicks himself was to make plain later, in *Value and Capital*, all that is needed for the validity of the principle is the convexity of the indifference map. The observation that cardinal utility, far from constituting an advance on the interpretative front, actually took empirical content away from the theory, had as a consequence the abandonment, without regret, of the cardinalist approach.

8.2.4. General economic equilibrium in Hicks

The second line of research in *Value and Capital* concerns general-equilibrium theory. The influence of this line of thought on developments in economic theory was relatively modest at first, especially because the book was published in the middle of the Keynesian revolution, so that some of the most important of Hicks's arguments were discussed within a conceptual framework that was basically extraneous to, and at the same time simpler and more effective than, the method of temporary general equilibrium.

With the passing of time, however, *Value and Capital* exercised increasing influence—and not so much for its specific contributions, even though these were numerous, as for the methods adopted. The static part of the work was the first to receive attention, especially in the USA, and contributed decisively to the resumption of general-equilibrium theory. But also the dynamic part, after a long period in obscurity, was finally appreciated, so much so that the method of temporary equilibrium has become, in recent times, the main instrument of short-run neoclassical analysis.

One of the most original and important elements of *Value and Capital* is represented by the application of comparative statics to general equilibrium. Before Hicks, in fact, theorists following this approach had limited themselves to studying the existence of equilibrium solutions, without attempting to use the model to solve even the simplest problems of change, for example, the effects produced by an increase in the 'demand' or 'supply' of a determinate good or factor. This is the origin of the widespread impression of sterility of the model. The fundamental 'ingredients' that allowed Hicks to escape from the blind alley of counting the number of equations and unknowns were basically two:

(1) the principle that a group of goods can be treated as a single good if relative prices remain constant—the well-known Hicks–Leontief aggregation theorem;

(2) the idea that the qualitative results of static comparative analysis can be derived from the conditions which ensure the stability of equilibrium.

Hicks's basic objective was to construct a dynamic theory, in the sense of a theory in which 'each variable must be dated'. Static analysis was only considered as a useful, though indispensable, premise for dynamic analysis. The main difficulty in the shift from statics to dynamics comes from the fact that, while in a static context the decisions of the agents depend solely on current prices, in a dynamic context they also depend on expected prices. The instrument used by Hicks to make static analysis serve dynamic ends was Myrdal's and Lindahl's 'period' method, the effectiveness of which he had already had the opportunity of experimenting with in his 1935 paper, 'Wages and Interest: The Dynamic Problem', published in the *Economic Journal*. As we have seen in Chapter 7, in his 1927 doctoral thesis Myrdal had introduced expectations among the determinants of relative prices: future anticipated changes produce effects on the economic process before they actually take place. This leads to the fact that the determination of an equilibrium must include the consequences of future expected changes. Hicks later called Myrdal's method the 'expectations method'. On the other hand, as we also mentioned in the previous chapter, Lindahl had already opened the way for the analysis of a dynamic process in terms of a succession of temporary equilibria.

By dividing time into periods of an adequate length ('weeks') and by including among the data of a determinate period not only the traditional data of static theory (tastes, technology, and resources) but also the state of expectations, Hicks was able to use the static method to study the 'temporary equilibrium', i.e. the equilibrium reached by an economic system in one period. In particular, he tried to examine the stability and the comparative statics properties of an economy in temporary equilibrium. In this context, he treated the movement of the economic system through time as a succession of temporary equilibria, each differing both from the preceding one, owing to the accumulation of capital, technical progress, changes in consumers' tastes, etc., and from the one expected by the economic agents. And this occurs both because the agents are not able to predict the future evolution of the data and prices and because individual consumption and production plans are generally incompatible, not to mention the fact that price expectations are also in general incompatible. From this point of view, the economic system is always in temporary equilibrium, but never in equilibrium 'through time', in the sense that in each period the price vector is generally different from that predicted by the agents when they formed their production and consumption plans.

Hicks maintained that a greater inter-temporal co-ordination of decisions would have been realized with future markets, provided there were future markets for all goods. In this case, all transactions would take place at the initial moment on the basis of the current prices of all the goods (present and future), while in successive periods there would be only the practical execution of the transactions stipulated in that moment. However, the uncertainty about the temporal evolution of preferences and resources limits the potential existence of future markets for goods. Consequently, it is not possible, according to Hicks, to study the operation of a real economic system by using inter-temporal equilibrium models even if, for certain ends, it may be worth resorting to the pure model of a futures economy, where present and future markets exist for all goods.

In the second part of *Value and Capital*, therefore, Hicks not only presented an original model for studying dynamic problems, but also anticipated, with his 'futures economy', some of the most important developments of the modern versions of the theory of general equilibrium: those which try to resolve the problems of time and uncertainty, while remaining within the field of static analysis.

8.2.5. *The* IS-LM *model*

In the article 'Mr Keynes and the Classics', published in *Econometrica* in 1937 but discussed in a seminar a year before, Hicks started, immediately after the publication of the *General Theory*, that process of reabsorption of Keynes's analysis into the mainstream of orthodox theory which was to occupy the neoclassical economists for the next 30 years. Hicks apparently followed a

Marshallian approach, assuming as given the stock of capital and interpreting the principle of effective demand in terms of a model of short-run equilibrium. In reality, he presented in that article an ambitious, though simple, model of temporary general equilibrium, in which he showed how macroeconomic equilibrium can be reached simultaneously in two markets, those of money and of savings.

Hicks generalized the *General Theory* by reducing it to four equations: one for savings, $S = S(Y)$, derived from the consumption function; one for investments, $I = I(i)$, which incorporates the function of the marginal efficiency of capital; one for the demand for money, $L = L(Y, i)$, expressed in terms of the demand for transactions and speculative purposes; and one for the money supply, assumed to be given exogenously, $M = \bar{M}$. The variables Y and i represent the income and the rate of interest respectively. By equating the supply and demand for savings and the supply and demand for money, the following two equations are obtained:

$$I(i) = S(Y)$$

$$\bar{M} = L(Y, i)$$

From them the *IS* and *LM* curves, shown in Fig. 9, originate. The *IS* curve shows all the combinations of income and interest that ensure real equilibrium. For example, an increase in income will increase savings and require a reduction in the rate of interest so as to induce entrepreneurs to increase investments. In this way there is a movement towards the right along the *IS* curve. The *LM* curve shows all the combinations of income and interest at which the demand for money coincides with the supply. For example, a rise in income will increase the transaction demand for money; if the supply is given, the demand for speculative motives has to decrease; and this will occur as a consequence of an increase in the interest rate. Thus there is a movement towards the right along the *LM* curve.

At point E the two markets are in equilibrium simultaneously. Once income has been determined in this way, the employment-level may be calculated by knowing the production function. Given the monetary wage, the price-level will be determined endogenously so as to ensure equality between the marginal productivity of labour and the real wage. However, Hicks did not give a definitive solution on this aspect of the problem. As we will see in the next chapter, it was from exactly this point that Modigliani began the 'neoclassical synthesis' after the Second World War.

With this model, Hicks tried to demonstrate that the *General Theory* was not as general as Keynes believed, but only a special case of (neo)classical theory: the case of the liquidity trap. In periods of depression the interest rate would be extremely low and speculators would not be much inclined to hold non-liquid reserves; therefore, their demand for money would absorb any amount offered to them, so that any increase in the supply of money would be counterbalanced by a corresponding increase in demand, and the interest

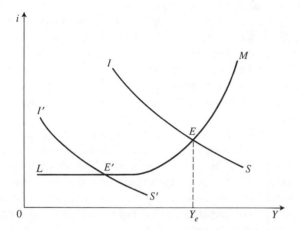

FIG. 9.

rate would not fall. In such a case, monetary policy would be totally ineffective; above all, it would be incapable of bringing the economy to full employment. It can be seen in Fig. 9 that, if $I'S'$ is valid, the equilibrium will be at point E' on the horizontal part of the LM curve; in this case an increase in the money supply will move the entire LM curve to the right, but not the equilibrium point.

In the next chapter we will see how Hicks's model was to constitute, in the 1950s and 1960s, the core of the 'neoclassical synthesis', i.e. that macroeconomic approach which, in the attempt to assimilate Keynes into orthodox theory, was to completely distort his message. It is necessary to point out, however, that Hicks during the 1960s persistently rejected this interpretation of Keynes's work.

8.3. THE NEW WELFARE ECONOMICS

8.3.1. Robbins's epistemological systematization

Welfare economics emerged, after the marginalist revolution, as a test bed for economic applications of neoclassical theory. But it dealt only with special aspects or situations of secondary importance in the economic system. Keynes tenaciously opposed welfare economics, mainly because of its inability to provide far-reaching policy suggestions for State intervention at the aggregate level; he even tried to modify its fundamental questions. Lionel Robbins was one of the first economists to perceive the importance of the Keynesian criticism of Pigou, the undisputed authority on the subject at that time, and at the beginning of the 1930s was working at the attempt to go beyond the theoretical approach which had emerged from the Cannan–Marshall–Pigou line of thought. The work of conceptual and epistemological reorganization undertaken by Robbins in this period helped the neoclassical theoretical system to resume its dominant position after the 'interlude' represented by the Keynesian revolution. The exposition of his results will allow us to answer the question we raised at the end of Chapter 6: why did the passage from cardinalism to ordinalism occur only during the 1930s if—as we have seen —all the necessary theoretical presuppositions were already available at the beginning of the century?

The point of attack of Robbins's work was his famous redefinition of the scope of economics. If, as he argued in the 'Essay on the Nature and Significance of Economic Science', 'the unity of subject of Economic Science' must be found in 'the forms assumed by human behaviour in disposing of scarce means' (p. 15), then the utility concept most suited to the study of economic welfare must be that of 'individual preferences'. Since utility, by its very nature, cannot be observed, let alone measured, Robbins argued that it deprives of scientific foundation every assertion about the effects of redistributive measures on collective welfare.

If utility is interpreted in terms of preferences, the egalitarian version of utilitarianism loses all cogency: interpersonal comparisons are arbitrary—or, rather, impossible—at the positive level, as the motivations underlying individual choices can be the most diverse and disparate. There is no way of comparing the satisfactions of different people; Robbins stated: 'of course, in daily life we do continually assume that the comparison can be made. But the very diversity of the assumptions actually made at different times and different places is evidence of their conventional nature' (p. 124). The finesse of the argument should not be missed: there is no 'fact' to which such comparisons refer; they are only expressions of more or less widely shared values in a given community, and 'can be justified on the grounds of general convenience [or] by appeal to ultimate standards of value'. In conclusion, they 'cannot be justified by appeal to any kind of positive science' (p. 125).

There was a widespread opinion, among the economists gathered together by Robbins at the LSE, that the notion of 'individual preferences' was epistemologically safer than that of 'levels of welfare'. Logical positivism had had a dramatic impact on Anglo-American social science, and the entry point in England had been the LSE. At the beginning of the century, positive epistemology had not yet begun to disturb the sleep of the economists. It was not until the philosophical settling achieved by the Vienna Circle that economists, too, began to speak of 'observability' as a demarcation criterion between science and fiction, and of neutrality with respect to value judgements as a separation criterion between science and ethics. The notion of 'individual preferences' seemed able to dispose of the concept of *inobservability* of utilities and, at the same time, to give a new foundation to the normative character of the interpersonal comparisons which motivate social policies.

Preferences can be made operational by means of a definition in terms of choice: the assertion 'the state of things x is preferred to the state of things y' is completely defined by the assertion 'the state x will be chosen by a subject if only x and y are available'. The doubt did not even cross the minds of Robbins and the other authors who followed this orientation that the *definiens*, as a conditional proposition, can perform its function only after the concept of preference has been defined. I may well prefer health to illness, but I certainly cannot choose to be well or ill. They did not notice that preferences, apart from absolute ones, have a holistic nature and therefore that the ordinalist practice of defining what is preferred in terms of what would be chosen is not immune to criticisms of an epistemological type.

It was on these presuppositions that Robbins was able to speak of a 'new' welfare economics free of any ethical assumptions. It is interesting to note, however, that, if the declared aim was that of rendering utilitarianism neutral in regard to value judgements (whatever the subjects thought had value had to be accepted), the new system produced a side-effect which is only apparently paradoxical. The preferences of a person are the product not only of biological needs but also of a socialization process. Therefore, they are determined by, and tend to reflect and reinforce, existing social relations. This means that a theory which requires the maximum satisfaction of the preferences chosen in a given social context contributes to reinforce that social context, and is therefore a theory strongly distorted in a 'conservative' sense.

8.3.2. The Pareto principle and compensation tests

There were voices of dissent but they were not many; the most insistent was that raised by L. Fraser in *Economic Thought and Language* (1937). However, the ordinalist approach of Robbins, Hicks, and Allen defeated any resistance. It is not difficult to see why. The first reason was that a central argument of the theoretical debate of the 1930s, apart from Keynesian matters, had returned to being price theory. This was a secondary consequence of Sraffa's criticism of the Marshallian system. Before that time, the problem of satisfying people's needs was seen rather as one of production and distribution. Material welfare increases if the distribution of the social dividend changes in favour of poor people, up to the point of levelling out the marginal utilities of all the people. Such a levelling process was also seen as a requirement for efficiency. Thus the defence of egalitarian economic policies was viewed as based on considerations both of efficiency and of equity, two objectives considered to be complementary and not antagonistic. It is clear that, from this approach, economists must focus on the notion of utility as 'satisfaction of needs'. If it is assumed that the needs of individuals are comparable, then utilities must also be comparable.

Thus, even though it was already known at the end of the nineteenth century that assumptions of measurement and comparison of individual utility were superfluous for a theory of prices, there was a fairly widespread opinion that they were necessary to tackle the problem of how to improve the welfare of mankind. But once the objective of economic investigation had been redefined by placing the theory of prices at its centre, the ordinalist analytical apparatus turned out to be quite sufficient. With an elegant use of Occam's razor, Hicks and Allen demonstrated, in particular, that a psychological concept such as that of marginal utility can be profitably replaced by a 'behavioural' one: that of 'marginal rate of substitution'.

The second reason for the success of the ordinalist programme was directly related to welfare economics, and was the 'discovery', in the 1930s, of the virtues of the Pareto optimality criterion, the most valuable being that there is no need for any interpersonal comparisons of utility; and this seemed to allow certain economic recommendations even when comparisons are impossible. The main recommendation was that 'the best policy is no policy'. The Pareto criterion seemed to have translated into a scientific proposition the central tenet of liberal thought. It is true, as was immediately realized, that there may be many social optima, perhaps an infinite number, and therefore that 'scientific' criteria are also needed to make a choice between them. But this did not cause much concern: the 'compensation tests' proposed by Hicks, Kaldor, Scitovsky, and Samuelson, the real theoretical novelty of the 1940s on this front, seemed to fill the gap. The works that initiated this line of research were: 'Welfare Propositions and Interpersonal Comparisons of Utility' (*Economic Journal*, 1939) by Kaldor; 'The Valuation of Social Income' (*Economica*, 1940) by Hicks; 'A Note on Welfare Propositions in Economics' (*Review of Economic Studies*, 1941–2) by Scitovsky; and, finally, chapter 8 of the *Foundations of Economic Analysis* (1947) by Samuelson.

Underlying the idea of the compensation tests is the notion of 'potential welfare', i.e. a type of welfare that takes into account all the possible redistributions which are feasible in a certain situation. Let x and y be two social alternatives—for example, to build a park (x) and not to build it (y)—and $S(x)$ and $S(y)$ indicate the set of alternatives accessible from x and y respectively. It is said that x is Hicks–Kaldor superior to y, in symbols $xHKy$, if there is an alternative $\bar{z}$ belonging to $S(x)$ such that $\bar{z}$ is Pareto superior to y, in symbols $\bar{z}Py$. The existence of such a state of affairs makes it hypothetically possible that each person is better off after alternative x has been chosen. In the example, it is possible to devise a compensation scheme based on taxes and subsidies such that those who gain from the construction of the park can compensate those who have lost out, so that, in the end, nobody is worse off and some are better off.

Unfortunately, two serious difficulties afflict the compensation tests. The first concerns their logical coherence. We will show this diagrammatically. Let $u(x)$ be the set of utility vectors generated by the set of alternatives $S(x)$. With only two individuals, A and B, $u(x)$ is represented in a diagram in which the co-ordinates represent the utility of one individual, u_A, and the utility of the other, u_B. The frontier of the shaded area in Fig. 10 is known as the utility frontier relative to x. On this frontier two points are represented: $u(x) = \{u_A(x), u_B(x)\}$ and $u(w) = \{u_A(w), u_B(w)\}$, where w denotes an alternative that belongs to $S(x)$. Clearly, B prefers w to x, so a movement from x to w implies that B must compensate A in some way. On the utility frontier relative to y are the points $u(y) = \{u_A(y), u_B(y)\}$ and $u(v) = \{u_A(v), u_B(v)\}$, where v is an alternative accessible starting from y. In terms of Fig. 10, which alternative is Hicks–Kaldor superior? Given x, it is possible to reach the alternative w, and both individuals prefer w to y. Therefore, wPy and $xHKy$. On the other hand, given y, it is possible to reach v, and both the subjects prefer the alternative v to x, so that vPx and consequently $yHKx$. The proposed criterion is logically inconsistent. Analogous problems arise from the criterion proposed by Scitovsky.

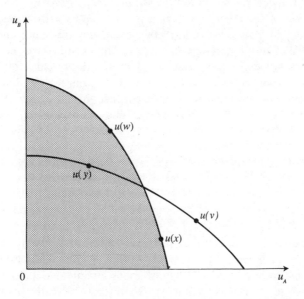

FIG. 10

The second difficulty mentioned above concerns the sense in which an increase in 'potential welfare' is important for actual welfare comparisons. Even if whoever draws advantage from a certain measure is also able to compensate whomever loses, why would this constitute an improvement? Perhaps because it is maintained that compensation must be paid? This does not really seem the right answer. In fact, if compensation is not paid, then the highest potential welfare situation can be well judged worse whenever greater consideration is attributed to the damage of those who lose rather than to the advantage of those who gain. If, instead, the compensation is paid, then, after the payment, everybody finds themselves just as well off as before and at least one is better off; a situation which clearly denotes a Pareto improvement. In this case, however, there is no need for any compensation test: the Pareto criterion is sufficient. This is the conclusion brought about by the criterion proposed by Samuelson. In other words, it is possible to conclude that the compensation tests either do not convince (when the compensation is not paid) or are redundant (when the compensation is paid). Yet it was not until the 1950s that the problem was fully realized. In this context, W. Gorman produced the key paper, 'The Intransitivity of Certain Criteria Used in Welfare Economics' (*Oxford Economic Papers*, 1955), in which he revealed the paradox of the compensation tests: they are logically coherent, and therefore acceptable, only when they are not needed.

In the meantime, within the neoclassical system, ground was gained by that vast programme of research, based on the theory of choice value, which still today provides the main frame of reference for theoretical work. The apodictic assertion advanced by Edgeworth in *Mathematical Psychics*, 'the first principle of Economics is that every agent is activated by self-interest', was still taken as true, but now it was interpreted as meaning that a person follows his own interest when it maximizes his utility. And as utility was now called on to represent choices (one alternative has more utility than another if, being able to choose between the two, the agent would opt for the first), the interpretation was advanced that what an individual chooses coincides with what is in his interest. We will see the results of this line of research in Chapter 10.

8.4. THE DEBATE ON ECONOMIC CALCULATION UNDER SOCIALISM

8.4.1. The dance begins

In most socialist interpretations of Marx's political economy, socialism is considered to be incompatible with the market. Market relationships, even in their simplest form of the exchange of goods among autonomous producers, are presented in *Capital* as the nucleus from which, logically and historically, capitalism emerged. Socialism, according to this line of thought, would not only render the market useless but would surpass it as an allocative mechanism; furthermore, it would bring to light, by means of planning, the social nature of labour. Planning would ensure the efficient allocation of resources, eliminating the absurdity of the existence of unsatisfied needs in the presence of unutilized resources.

After the October Revolution, the idea of central planning as the economic basis of socialism entered into the programmatic documents of many Communist parties. Any acceptance of the market mechanism was presented as a temporary concession, basically justified by the backwardness of the socio-economic conditions and the difficulties of the transition from capitalism to socialism. It should not be forgotten, however, that in the period of the Second

International, some of the reformist currents of Marxism, as well as some of the extreme left-wing ones, not to speak of the anarchist groups, already acknowledged the relevance of the market for the operation of a socialist economy. But with the victory of Leninism in Russia, all dissent was silenced, and socialism became identified with 'democratic centralism', 'central planning', and State ownership of the means of production.

In such a context, it is not surprising that the debates on socialism touched the theoretical front. Liberal thought entered the debate about planning and the market when von Hayek published, in an anthology entitled *Collectivist Economic Planning* (1935), an article written by von Mises in 1920, 'Die Wirtschaftsrechnung im sozialistischen Gemeinwesen' ('Economic Calculation in the Socialist Community'), in which the possibility of rational economic calculation in socialism was categorically denied: without a free market, there is no pricing mechanism; without a pricing mechanism, there is no economic calculation. The gist of von Mises' argument was that exchange relationships among produced goods, and therefore the formation of their prices, can be established only on the basis of private ownership.

Numerous attempts were made to rebut this argument in the early 1930s, by F. Taylor, H. D. Dickinson, C. Landauer, E. Heimann, and others. It is also worth recalling the challenge thrown down by Karl Polanyi against von Mises as early as 1922, during a seminar on guild socialism in Vienna held by Polanyi himself. Polanyi's attempt to construct a positive theory of the socialist economy was derived from his aversion both to the market economy and to centrally planned socialism, both of which he considered as forms of 'illiberty'. The possibility of constructing an efficient socialist economy was, in those years, the subject of the most animated discussions among economists. Von Mises, on the strength of his academic status, declared the task impossible. At any rate, all the revolutions in central Europe had been defeated, the civil war had shattered the Soviet economy, and socialism was still not on the agenda of the Soviet republics.

8.4.2. The Lange–Lerner solution

It was the Romanian economist Abba Lerner (1905–82) and, above all, the Polish economist Oskar Lange (1904–65) who gave the most vigorous reply to the arguments of von Mises and von Hayek. The 'Lange–Lerner solution' appeared in an article published by Lange in 1936–7 in the *Review of Economic Studies*, 'On the Economic Theory of Socialism', and in two articles by Lerner, 'Economic Theory and Socialist Economics' (*Review of Economic Studies*, 1934) and 'Statics and Dynamics in Socialist Economics' (*Economic Journal*, 1937). The proposed solution denied the theoretical validity of von Mises' argument by using the demonstration, elaborated by Barone in his 1908 paper, 'Il Ministro della produzione nello Stato collettivista' (*Giornale degli Economisti*, 37, translated as 'The Ministry of Production in the

Collectivist State', in *Collectivist Economic Planning*, ed. F. A. von Hayek (London, 1935)), of the virtual equivalence between central planning and the free market in the efficient allocation of resources. Lange and Lerner, on the other hand, tried to identify a 'practical' solution in the famous iterative 'trial-and-error' procedure, according to which the central planning office would undertake, practically speaking, the same function as the market. Lange formulated two alternative models. In the first, consumer goods and labour services are allocated by means of the free market on the basis of monetary prices, while in the other, inputs are assigned accounting prices. The equilibrium values of both sets of prices should be determined by means of a single iterative procedure. At each stage of the process, the planner announces a vector of non-negative prices and gives the following two orders to the managers of the State firms:

(1) Minimize the average cost of production by employing a combination of factors for which the marginal product in value of each factor equals its price.

(2) Fix the production level at the point in which the marginal cost equals the price set by the central planning office.

Similarly, by treating the announced prices as parameters, the households maximize their utility function. In this way, the functions of the demand for goods and of the labour supply are obtained. For each good and service, the planner aggregates the proposals received from the firms and households. If, for one good or service, there is positive (negative) excess demand, its price is increased (decreased). The new price vector is announced to the firms and households and the process is repeated, until all the excess demand vanishes. As Lange himself admitted, the procedure was exactly the same as Walras's *tâtonnement*.

In the second model, Lange did not assume the existence of any free market. The demand for consumer goods and the supply of labour are obtained by the planner starting from a social welfare function derived from individual preferences. The iterative process only endeavours to determine accounting prices and has a virtual nature. Once planned production has been carried out, the consumer goods can be sold on the real markets at actual prices that may not correspond to the accounting equilibrium values.

In the elaboration of the 'trial-and-error' procedure, the emphasis was placed, first of all, on the demonstration that planned socialism was able to allocate resources in the same way as a capitalist market economy. Subsequently, in the attempt to construct a normative model of *market* socialism, the project became more ambitious. However, the normative model became more vulnerable than the positive interpretation to empirical verification. In fact, while the actual behaviour of agents in capitalist markets is in no way determined by the propositions of general-equilibrium theory, the socialist managers would have to be instructed to follow the rules of the model, with all the consequences this may entail. Thus, if the equilibrium is not stable, or if the process leading to equilibrium is particularly slow, the managers would lack a reliable and effective guide; and in this case the model would lose any empirical relevance. This explains the inclusion in the market socialism model of a certain number of 'pieces' that do not exist in the capitalist market. One of the most important 'pieces' is the determination of the rate of capitalist accumulation, not by means of market processes, but directly and arbitrarily by the central office, which also fixes the rules for the distribution among the individuals of the social dividend from publicly owned land and capital. In view of these difficulties, it is not surprising that, in a further elaboration of Lange's approach, K. Arrow and L. Hurwicz, in 'Decentralization and Computation in Resource Allocation' (in R. W. Pfouts (ed.), *Essays in Economics and Econometrics* (Chapel Hill, NC, 1960)), developed the second model—a development which clearly conflicts with the recommendation made by Lange himself not to use the second model, as it was excessively 'non-democratic'.

In Lange's model, therefore, the market becomes a mere calculator to solve a system of simultaneous equations—an analogy that Lange was himself to suggest in 1965. Market socialism must be able to combine efficient allocation of productive resources (and this requires rules established by the central office to prevent mono-oligopolistic behaviour) with a distribution of income which maximizes collective welfare (and this involves the elimination of inequalities caused by private ownership of means of production). An economy that operates on the basis of these principles would be open to innovations without being liable to the disasters caused by the cyclical fluctuations. Lange certainly did not hide the difficulties connected with the realization of such a project. The most serious of these, the danger of bureaucratization of economic life and the related lack of adequate incentives for managers to follow the planner's rules, was, however, judged not to be greater than the loss in efficiency caused by mono-oligopolistic capitalism.

8.4.3. Von Hayek's criticism

This model of market socialism was violently attacked from two opposing fronts: by those opposed to the adoption of the market in the socialist system, and by those who did not accept socialism. The first type of criticism made use of the consideration that what the model of market socialism ensures is, at the most, static, certainly not dynamic, efficiency; the model had nothing to say, for example, about the problem of the full utilization of *potential* resources. Such an objective can be achieved only by central planning, which would have been necessary, in any case, to avert the strong elements of instability linked to the problems posed by economies of scale. This was the argument put forward by, among others, Maurice Dobb, in 'A Note on Savings and Investment in a Socialist Economy' (*Economic Journal*, 1939), and later by Paul Baran in 'National Economic Planning', part 3: 'Planning under Socialism' (*Survey of Contemporary Economics*, 1952); an argument which was, in the end, to force Lange himself to revise some points of his model in 'The Computer and the Market' (in *Capitalism, Socialism and Economic Growth*, C. Feinstein, 1967).

The second line of criticism, which was to have the greatest influence, was principally linked to von Hayek's arguments. His most recent essay on this subject had been 'Socialist Calculation: The Competitive Solution' (*Econometrica*, 1940). Von Mises had argued that economic calculation needed to be guided by prices. As a centrally planned economy has no productive factor markets, it is unable to provide a price guide. Lange had reacted by arguing that there was no need for the prices to be those of the market; the guide to decisions could be given by the prices announced by the central authority and taken as references by the socialist managers; these prices would be used as parameters exactly as a firm would do in perfect competitive conditions. In reply to this argument, von Hayek developed his interpretation of the operation of the market as a *discovery process*, in which information scattered among a myriad of economic agents is mobilized and used in an efficient way. This is the central message of his famous 1937 article, 'Economics and Knowledge' (*Economica*): the market is a generator of knowledge. Each individual is a unique repository, maintained Hayek, of specific elements of knowledge, and it is only through free interaction among the economic agents that this scattered knowledge is disseminated beneficially to the whole society. This basic point of opposition to socialism was justified, therefore, by the argument that such a system would attribute to an agency, endowed with incomplete information, coercive power over the sphere of individual action. Yet individuals are the only repository of the relevant information. 'How can the combination of fragments of knowledge existing in different minds bring about results which, if they were to be brought about deliberately, would require a knowledge on the part of the directing mind which no single person can possess?' (p. 53). This is tantamount to saying that the conditions (perfect information) delimiting the problem to be solved (the attainment of equilibrium) are the same as those ensuring its solution. Then the economic problem is not simply and not so much that of how to allocate *given* resources, but that of finding out 'how the spontaneous interaction of a number of people, each possessing only bits of knowledge, brings about a state of affairs in which prices correspond to costs' (p. 50). This state of affairs could be brought about by deliberate direction only by somebody endowed with the combined knowledge of all the individuals.

Recently, Hayek's 1937 contribution has been taken up again, in a completely different context, and used to criticize the theoretical relevance of the notion of perfect competition as well as to attack the centrality of the notion of equilibrium in economics. We will return to this question in Chapter 11, where we deal with the Neo-Austrian school.

8.5. ALTERNATIVE APPROACHES

8.5.1. Allyn Young and increasing returns

The problem of economic growth, which had been at the centre of the theoretical reflections of the classical economists, lost its privileged position with orthodox economists during the Victorian age. Perhaps this happened because economic growth had begun to be considered within a more general vision of human progress, so that it was no longer seen as a problem, or because it had been ousted by more pressing questions, such as those linked to the determination of prices and of remuneration of resources in situations of allocative efficiency. Finally, considerable responsibility must be attributed to the seduction exerted by the formal elegance of the neoclassical theoretical system and its ability to monopolize economists' interests; neoclassical theory deals with institutions, population, and technology, which are key elements in the growth process, only as exogenous data, the causes or factors of their change being considered outside the scope of economic science. Thus the economists wishing to study these matters have often been forced to leave the fold. This is how institutionalist economics was born.

Even the subjects of the division of labour and increasing returns, Smith's great research areas, ended up by being considered as a special and irrelevant case of equilibrium price theory. And Allyn Young, a Harvard economist, had to write, in 1928, a vehement article in the *Economic Journal* ('Increasing Returns and Economic Progress') to remind his colleagues that these were matters of fundamental theoretical importance. In the presence of increasing returns, change might be progressive and cumulative, since the forces for change are *endogenous*. Thus the actual state of the economy during any period cannot be predicted other than as a result of the sequence of events of preceding periods.

The fundamental consideration from which Young started is that any increase in the supply of goods enlarges, at least potentially, the market of other goods. Therefore, 'the extension of the market' depends on the division of labour just as much as the division of labour depends on the extension of the market.

Adam Smith's dictum amounts to the theorem that the division of labour depends in large part upon the division of labour. This is more than a mere tautology. It means [. . .] that the counter forces which are continually defeating the forces which make for economic equilibrium are more pervasive and more deeply rooted in the constitution of the modern economic system than we commonly realize. (p. 533)

The process of economic growth, according to Smith, is basically cumulative in nature. Increases in quantities produced (enlargement of the market) allow work to be divided in a better way; and to the degree to which labour is specialized, its productivity increases. Therefore, given the level of employment, further increases in production are possible which provide new growth stimuli.

What disintegrates, in the presence of increasing returns of scale, is the concept itself of long-run equilibrium. In fact, if any change in use of resources or any reorganization of productive activities creates the opportunity for a further change that would not have occurred otherwise, then the theory of the optimal allocation of resources, according to which each resource gives at the margin an equal contribution to the output whatever its use, loses any meaning. If the pattern of resource use depends on the preceding uses, the concept of economic efficiency based on the principle of the allocation of scarce means among alternative uses can no longer be maintained, except in the short run, when plants are fixed by hypothesis; Marshall seemed fully aware of the problem, to judge by his attempt to draw an 'irreversible' supply curve.

A further important consequence of the existence of increasing returns—as Kaldor observed in 'The Irrelevance of Equilibrium Economics' (*Economic Journal*, 1972)—is that, when there is an increase in the level of output, it becomes profitable to increase the capital–labour ratio: the higher the level of output, the more specialized the machinery which can be profitably used. In Young's words: 'It would be wasteful to make a hammer to drive a single nail, it would be better to use whatever awkward implement lies conveniently at hand' (p. 530). This means that the choice of the capital–labour ratio depends on extension of the market rather than on relative input prices, which is the opposite to what marginalist theory would lead us to believe.

Voices of dissent such as that of Young were heard during the inter-war period, and they were notable—it is enough to mention Schumpeter. But they were not listened to, both because neoclassical theory was evolving according to an internal logic that rendered it inaccessible to such radical and simple criticisms, and because a great many of the dissenting forces were being attracted and united by the new general short-run theories. For the same reasons, few people listened to the institutionalist economists, who began to speak up again in this period.

8.5.2. Thorstein Veblen

In the 1890s classical economics had almost completely disappeared from the scene, so that, beginning from that decade, the external attacks against political economy became criticisms of neoclassical economics. And this happened in America with the institutionalist schools. This line of thought was initiated by Veblen in the 1890s and developed by further generations of institutionalists in the following decades. In America, its development and its criticisms have always accompanied (perhaps compensating for the weaker development of Marxist criticisms) the development of neoclassical orthodoxy. It is still alive today, for example in the work of Galbraith and his followers and in some currents of the so-called 'radical political economy'. A. Gruchy has recently described the institutionalists as thinkers who 'inquired into problems such as the impact of technological change on the structure and functioning of the economic system, the power relations among economic interest groups, the logic of the process of industrialization and the determination of notional goals and priorities' ('Institutional Economics', p. 11).

In order to grasp the meaning of such a definition, we need to glance at the course of American economic history from 1880 to 1915, the most active period of the intellectual career of Thorstein Veblen (1857–1929), the 'founder' of the institutionalist approach. This period was far from being one of 'Victorian tranquillity'. Apart from the fact that the five-year period 1885–90 was like the eye of a storm between the depressions of the 1870s and 1890s, it is necessary to keep in mind that the country was involved, in that period, in adding to its already developed agricultural sector an industrial sector which was later to threaten British economic supremacy. Besides this, the 'frontier' had reached its extreme limit around 1890, and territorial expansion began to direct itself overseas (consider neocolonialism in the Caribbean, Central America, and the Pacific, and the Spanish–American War of 1898). Finally, a new wave of prosperity began around 1897, Kondratiev's 'third wave', ushering in impressive innovations in the automobile and chemical sectors. The concentration of capital, especially in the oil industry, moved ahead undisturbed, largely owing to Rockefeller, until the passing of the Sherman Act in 1890 (the first anti-trust law, although it had modest results). But the workers' movement also produced its great 'concentrations' in this period: in 1881 that great union was formed which was later to be called the American Federation of Labour, while at the end of the century a series of other trade unions, of various types and varying degrees of radicalism, arose.

At the centre of Veblen's analysis of capitalist society was the distinction between 'industry' and 'business'. The former 'produced things', the latter 'produced money'. The active agents of industry are engineers and allied professionals; the active subjects of the business world are merchants, *rentiers*, and speculators. The first group is motivated by enterprise and creative curiosity, the second by a predatory instinct towards their fellow men. The members of the second group compete with each other in terms of 'conspicuous consumption', a type of consumption that does not satisfy real needs but only feeds the desire to display one's status in the eyes of a social reference group.

It was in his famous book *The Theory of the Leisure Class* (1899) that Veblen applied his social theory to the way of life of the average American consumer. Here he showed how the instinct towards hard work could become atrophied by emulating the 'predator' (the successful businessman), and how the natural requirement of need satisfaction could be distorted by conspicuous consumption.

Veblen believed, as did Marx, that technology is the major factor in socio-economic growth, and that it is cumulative and independent of the actions and the will of the businessmen. Besides this, and again like Marx, Veblen was convinced that technical progress was accompanied by institutional changes which would lead the economy both to a state of chronic depression and to monopolistic concentration characterized by high profits and an under-utilization of resources. This state of affairs would intensify the struggle between industry and business. Veblen himself was not too clear about where such a fight would lead. However, in the final section of *The Theory of the Business Enterprise* (1904) he wrote: 'Which of the two antagonistic factors may prove the stronger in the long run is something of a blind guess ... It seems possible to say this much, that the full dominion of business enterprise is necessarily a transitory dominion' (p. 400).

This uncertainty persisted in Veblen's thought almost until he died. In *Economic Theory in the Calculable Future* (1925) he appears to suggest that the business world will prevail—from which he inferred sad omens for economic science. In the business-dominated world (he wrote in *Essays in our Changing Order* (1934)) the economic science would be 'a science of business traffic', adding that 'any technical advance can get a hearing and reach a practical outcome only if and so far as it is presented as a business proposition, that is to say, so far as it shows a convincing promise of differential gain to some business concern' (p. 13). In fact Veblen, this new Saint-Simon, considered the industrial engineer as the real progressive factor of the modern economy, and firmly believed in the existence of a fundamental conflict between engineers and capitalists. But capitalists, in Veblen's opinion, were only those who work in the financial sector.

8.5.3. Institutional thought in the inter-war years

The most important American institutionalist of the generation which followed Veblen were Wesley Clair Mitchell (1874–1948) and John Rogers Commons (1862–1944). Mitchell had been one of Veblen's students, but he was soon to distance himself from his master in his emphasis on applied research and in his caution towards theoretical generalizations. He criticized orthodox theory for the static nature of the notion of equilibrium. He also rejected the notion of perfect competition, arguing that many prices are sticky in that they are determined by institutional factors such as contracts and conventions. He focused his attention on the empirical study of business cycles, emphasizing the role played by money in their dynamics, and demonstrating the permanence of the cycle through time, a permanence that had manifested itself in the America economy despite the great changes which had affected its demographic structure, technological bases, institutional order, and financial system. Mitchell's main works are *Business Cycles and Their Causes* (1913) and *Business Cycles: The Problem and Its Settings* (1927).

Mitchell made a lasting contribution to the development of economic science, both by his work on collecting and ordering statistical data and, above all, by his refinement of the methods for their study. He carried out this activity at the National Bureau of Economic Research, an organization he founded immediately after the First World War.

Unlike Mitchell, Commons showed a greater interest in theoretical generalizations. And Commons's main works, although his research had begun before the end of the century, were published in the years of high theory: *Legal Foundations of Capitalism* came out 1924 and *Institutional Economics* in 1934. Commons's interests range from the sociology of legal institutions to the history of labour, from the theory of public economics to the theory of the conflict of interests. He believed that the study of 'collective action', i.e. of the activity (and the apparatus) of 'control of individual action', should be placed at the centre of economic theory. He argued that individuals act by maintaining strong relations of interdependence, both in conflict and in cooperation. The 'bargaining transactions' on which orthodox economics had concentrated its research were, for him, only a part (and not even the most important part) of economic transactions. More important were precisely those overlooked by orthodox theory: 'managerial transactions', i.e. those concerned with the exercise of command between superiors and inferiors, such as between employers and employees, and 'rationing transactions', i.e. those in which costs and benefits are shared out among the members of an organization, such as the collection of social contributions in a trade union, or the distribution of the tax load by the government, or the distribution of the profits of a company. All these types of transaction take place in a specific institutional and legal context which gives them sense and makes them binding. It is this context that must be studied to understand how an economy functions.

Commons had a difficult academic life, and found a stable academic position only rather late in his career, at the University of Wisconsin, where he gathered around him a group of young economists, among them A. Gruchy, S. Slichter, and J. K. Galbraith, who were to continue the institutionalist tradition.

At the beginning of the 1930s two institutional textbooks, one by W. E. Atkins and the other by Slichter, received a certain acclaim in American academic circles. There were two main reasons for this. The first was that Rexford Tugwell, editor of *The Trend of Economics* (1924), a synthesis of institutional thought, became responsible, after having taken part in Roosevelt's brains trust, for the Ministry of Agriculture of the Federal Government of Washington, a position in which he fought to defend the Welfare State. One point on which *The Trend* particularly insisted was the necessity for economic theory to examine the economic institutions (companies, the government, and interest groups) and the non-commercial as well as the pecuniary incentives for human action. All these elements, Tugwell maintained, must be considered as they were in the real world, and not as orthodox theory thought they should be. The book also recommended statistical measurement of economic phenomena, a difficult problem which the dominant theory of the period often tried to avoid. The second reason was that the University of Wisconsin became a source of ideas, as well as of practical initiatives, for American social legislation. Commons, in a certain way, was for America what Bismarck had been for Germany in the second half of the nineteenth century and Lloyd George for Britain in the early twentieth. His group of economists fought for the approval of the Social Security Act, a law which gave birth to the Welfare State in the USA, and which, as a consequence of the harsh reaction of the entrepreneurs, marked the beginning of an important change in the relationship between the profession and the entrepreneurial world. From this point on, the economists no longer accepted the simple role of rationalizing the economic situation of their times, as had happened in the past and as had been criticized by Veblen.

Veblen had been a pessimistic and critical institionalist. Commons, on the other hand, tended to emphasize the positive aspects of the American economy. He believed that the main defects of that particular capitalist system could be remedied by means of wise institutional reforms. However, beyond specific differences of opinion and research, some common characteristics unite them in the institutional approach. First is their emphasis on the 'open' nature of the economic system, which led them to adopt a broad definition of the field of investigation of economics and to reject its definition as the science of efficient allocation of resources among alternative uses. Second, in order to explain the way in which economic systems function and grow, institutional change was considered rather more important than that which Knight was to call 'the mechanics of the price system'. However, we must note that institutionalist criticism of the 'mechanics of the price system' dealt with its inadequacy and not, at that time, with its wrongness. Simply, according to the institutionalists, the market cannot be considered as the *only* institution able to lead a society towards economic growth. Third, the institutionalists maintained that it was reductive to base economics on the analysis of the behaviour of single economic agents, leaving aside social influences on the decision processes. If political economy wishes to concern itself with change and the evolutionary aspects of the economic system, it must focus on the complex interactions between individual behaviour and the institutional context.

Two important consequences at the level of economic analysis are derived from these principles: first, that individualism is inadequate as an explanatory device, and second, that equilibrium analysis is irrelevant; economic science should study social processes occurring through historical time rather than analysing the equilibrium positions of individual choices.

Here, we should like especially to mention Gunnar Myrdal (1898–1986), an unconventional economist who, as we have already seen, began his career within orthodox theory. We have already mentioned the importance of his *Monetary Equilibrium* (1931) in regard to developments in monetary theory. In 1930, Myrdal published in Swedish *The Political Element in the Formation of Pure Economic Doctrine* (the German edition was published in 1932 and the first English edition in 1953). In 1932 he experienced a radical conversion. As he himself wrote in the preface to the English edition of this book, his conversion occurred after he had realized there was a basic weakness in his preceding work:

> But throughout the book there lurks the idea that when all metaphysical elements are radically cut away, a healthy body of positive economic theory will remain, which is altogether independent of valuations. Political conclusions can then be inferred simply by adding to the objective scientific knowledge of the facts a chosen set of value premises. This implicit belief in the existence of a body of scientific knowledge independently of all valuations is, as I now see it, naïve empiricism . . . valuations are thus necessarily involved at the stage when we observe facts and carry out theoretical analysis. (p. vii)

It was from this conviction that Myrdal decided to abandon the old theoretical system to follow, in a rather personal way, an institutionalist line of research. He concerned himself with the multiple aspects of the problem of economic growth and, above all, with the relationships between countries at different levels of development. The new ideas elaborated by Myrdal after his conversion have been expressed in various papers collected in *Value in Social Theory* (1958) and in the books *Economic Theory and Underdeveloped Regions* (1957) and *Asian Drama: An Inquiry into the Poverty of Nations* (1968).

8.5.4. From Dmitriev to Leontief

Perhaps it is not possible to speak of a real Russian school of mathematical economics, but there is no doubt that the beginning of the century saw the formation of a group of Russian economists who faced certain problems of economic theory using a common methodology, mainly based on linear algebra, and following a fairly homogeneous theoretical line of thought. Their main doctrinal reference was general economic equilibrium theory; but some of the Marxist debates, especially concerning the theory of value, also provided important stimuli.

Undoubtedly, the most important exponent of this group was Vladimir Karpovich Dmitriev (1868–1913), 'the father and founder of Russian mathematical economics', who, in the *Economic Essays on Value, Competition and Utility* (published in Russian between 1898 and 1902 and collected in a single volume in 1904), proposed a reconciliation between the Ricardian theory of prices and distribution and the neoclassical theory of marginal utility. The reconciliation consisted in the demonstration that the former, even though analytically rigorous, was a special case of the latter—a special case defined by the hypotheses that production occurs in the presence of constant returns to scale, perfect competition, and the employment of only one primary input: labour. Dimitriev demonstrated that, under such hypotheses, conditions of demand only influence the composition of output while prices are determined by conditions of production. It is easy to see here the essential elements of that 'non-substitution theorem' which was later to be rediscovered in the 1950s. Dmitriev also anticipated some of the aspects of Leontief's input–output model when he tried to calculate the total labour requirements necessary for the production of the goods, those defined as 'labour values' in classical–Marxist theories. Dmitriev supplied the first general formulation of the criteria for determining such values, referring to a model of production of *n* goods, and demonstrating that, in order to calculate the labour embodied in these, it is necessary and sufficient to know the technical and direct labour coefficients. Therefore labour values, unlike exchange values, do not depend on the distribution of income, as Ricardo seems to have understood when struggling with the difficulties of the invariable measure of value. Dmitriev calculated exchange values by completely ignoring labour values, and expressed them in terms of the quantities of labour invested and capitalized in previous 'epochs' to produce the wage goods consumed by the workers. In an economy in which wage goods are produced by means of wage goods, the rate of profit is determined simultaneously with the exchange values, and depends only on the production conditions of wage goods, and not on those of luxury goods. Furthermore, the rate of profit is a decreasing function of the wages.

Dmitriev only mentioned Marx occasionally, and focused his attention on Ricardo; yet his conclusions are of great importance for the Marxist theory of value, especially in regard to the problem of the transformation of values into prices. Ladislaus von Bortkiewicz (1868–1913) immediately realized this, and wrote two important articles on the subject: 'Wertrechnung und Preisrechnung im marxschen System' ('Value Calculation and Price Calculation in Marx's System', *Archiv für Sozialwissenschaft und Sozialpolitik*, 1906 and 1907); 'Zür Berichtigung der grundlagenden theoretischen Konstruction von Marx im dritten Band des "kapital" ' ('On the Rectification of the Fundamental Theoretical Construction of Marx in the Third Volume of *Capital*', *Conrads Jahrbücher*, 1907). By formalizing a numerical solution of Tugan-Baranovskij and extending some of Dmitriev's analytical procedures, Bortkiewicz reached two important results. First, he proved that, contrary to the opinion of some of Marx's critics, the transformation is possible. The deficiencies of the procedure adopted by Marx himself were due to the inadequacy of his analytical tools and not to a defect in the theory. Second, however, he proved that precisely what made the transformation possible also made it useless; in fact, production prices can be calculated without knowing the labour embodied in the goods, so that the labour theory of value can be relegated to a purely 'auxiliary' role.

The subject was taken up again by Georg von Charasoff (1877–?) in two monographs, parts of an unfinished trilogy: *Karl Marx über die menschliche und kapitalistiche Wirtschaft (Karl Marx on Human and Capitalist Economy)* (1909), and *Das System des Marxismus (The Marxist System)* (1910). Charasoff tried to reformulate in a rigorous manner the theoretical foundations of the *Critique of Political Economy*. In regard to the transformation problem, he generalized Bortkiewicz's solution to the case of *n* goods, and proved that the transformation procedure followed by Marx was not mistaken, but only incomplete, as it could be interpreted as the first step in an iterative transformation process capable of approaching the solution of production prices. However, in this way the inessential nature of the labour theory of value emerges even more clearly. In fact, the iterative process can be initiated from any price vector, so that the vector of labour values carries out the simple role of an arbitrary vector of exchange values.

Von Charasoff discovered other interesting properties of the production-prices model. He clearly distinguished between 'basic products' and luxury products, and proved that production prices and the rate of profit only depend on the production conditions of the former. He calculated the rate of profit by means of a dual iterative process. Assuming a subsistence wage and assimilating the inputs of wage goods to those of other capital goods, von Charasoff proved that, by beginning from any vector of the quantities produced, it is possible to go back to the vectors of the quantities employed as inputs in preceding 'epochs' by means of an iterative process which converges towards a particular input vector. He called this vector *Urkapital* (primary capital). Its adoption in the productive process would generate an output vector which would differ from *Urkapital* only in regard to a scale factor. In other words, in production with *Urkapital* the goods produced are in the same proportion among themselves as the means of production, and the profit factor coincides with the scale factor that links input to output. Furthermore, if all profits are reinvested, the rate of growth of the production of *Urkapital* will coincide with the rate of profit. Another important result concerns the distribution of income, on which von Charasoff worked by assuming as given the technology and real wages, and as variable the length of the working day: he proved that, by reducing the latter, the rate of profit would fall, to reach a zero level when surplus value is nil.

Let us return to Bortkiewicz. We know that he taught in Berlin from 1901 to 1931. In 1926 he was invited by Ragnar Frisch to form a group of mathematicians and economists as the German section of what was to become the Econometric Society. We do not know a great deal about the activities of this group; but we do know that between 1926 and 1929 Bortkiewicz was in contact with Robert Remak, a German mathematician, and with Wassily Leontief, who was taking his degree in Berlin. Bortkiewicz introduced Remak to the problem of the existence of solutions for a 'circular-flow' model of *n* equations. Remak worked on this and supplied the solution in the article 'Kann die Volkswirtschaftslehre eine exacte Wissenschaft werden?' ('Can Political Economy Become an Exact Science?'), published in *Jahrbücher für Nationalökonomie und Statistik* in 1929. It was one of the first rigorous proofs of the existence of solutions for a general-equilibrium model, albeit of a very special type.

By a strange historical coincidence von Neumann was also teaching in Berlin during that period (1927–9). We have no proof of any contacts between him and Bortkiewicz's group, but we know that in that period (perhaps in 1928) von Neumann took part in one of Marschak's seminars on general equilibrium, during which he suggested the possibility of dealing with the problem of free goods by using disequations. Already at that time he had begun to think about the problems from which he was to develop the famous 'von Neumann' model.

On the other hand, we know that this model shares with those of Bortkiewicz, Leontief, and Remak that special notion of production which considers it as a 'circular process' of production of commodities by means of reproducible commodities. This idea is directly linked to the concept of 'economy as *Kreislauf*', as a circular flow. Even consumer goods, reduced to the 'necessities of life', were treated as reproducible inputs in that model. This concept was so basic and so strange for the times that von Neumann felt the need to emphasize it from the first line of his 1937 work. From this point of view, the endowments of scarce resources are simply ignored (von Neumann was explicit on this), and the problem of price determination is defined within the approach of reproducibility and not within the usual neoclassical conception of scarcity: it is the production conditions of goods that determine their prices, not their scarcity with relation to demand. This conception not only united the above-mentioned economists, but also clearly distinguished them from the mathematical economists of Menger's *Kolloquium*. Schlesinger and Wald, for example, were working within a tradition that went back to Cassel and specified the analysis of production in terms of a unidirectional process. From this point of view, production begins with the input of primary resources, non-produced goods, and ends with the production of final consumer goods, products not used as inputs.

Let us now return to Russia. There, in the 1920s, an important debate on planning was taking place from which two pioneering theoretical contributions were to emerge, one by A. V. Chayanov and the other by P. I. Popov and L. N. Litosenko. In the *Theory of the Peasant Economy* (published in Russian in 1926), Chayanov developed Dmitriev's theory, producing an input–output model for agriculture. In the same year *The Balance of the National Economy of the USSR* by Popov and Litosenko was published (edited by Popov). The aim of the research was to improve calculations for the 'material balances' on which the first attempts at planning were based. The material balances were crude accountancy instruments aimed at calculating the uses and productive requirements of various groups of goods on the basis of certain coefficients of planned inputs called 'norms'. These balances contained, in a nutshell, all the information necessary to construct input–output tables. Popov and Litosenko tried to integrate the information that could be deduced from these balances with the Marxian analysis of the reproduction schemes. In this way they managed to reformulate these schemes, dividing the two Marxian sections into twenty-two productive sectors. The results were rather primitive, but there is no doubt that the first step had been taken towards the construction of the input–output model. Leontief was well aware of the work of the two pioneers, having reviewed it in 1925, before publication. He also knew of the work of Bortkiewicz, under whom, in 1927, he had prepared his degree dissertation. In 1928 he published part of his dissertation in an article entitled 'Die Wirtschaft als Kreislauf' ('The Economy as a Circular Flow') in *Archiv für Sozialwissenschaft und Soazialpolitik*, in which he presented a small model similar to those of Bortkiewicz and Remak. In 1931, Leontief emigrated to America, where he began teaching at Harvard University. In 1931 he began the research which was to lead him to the invention of the input–output model. In 1936 he published his first important results, but it was not until 1941 that he published *The Structure of the American Economy, 1919–1929*, today considered the classic work on input–output analysis.

His work continued in the following decade, and led to the publication of *Studies in the Structure of the American Economy* (1953) and *Input–Output Economics* (1966). During the 1950s and the 1960s this new branch of economic theory caused a real research boom: a boom which gave rise to various analytical advances in regard both to empirical applications and to theoretical formulations. We will discuss these in Chapter 11.

Here we will limit ourselves to a short presentation of the most elementary and fundamental of Leontief's contributions, the static and open input–output model. The analysis assumes the knowledge, which can be deduced from empirical research and from national accountancy data, of an input–output table such as the following:

$$x = \begin{bmatrix} x_{11} & x_{12} & \dots & x_{1n} \\ x_{12} & x_{22} & \dots & x_{2n} \\ \dots & & & \\ x_{n1} & x_{n2} & \dots & x_{nn} \end{bmatrix}$$

where x_{ij} represents the amount of output of sector i used as input in sector j. Let $x = [x_1, x_2, \dots x_n]'$ be the column vector of the quantities produced in the various sectors. Then, if constant returns to scale are assumed, it is possible to divide each element of the input–output table by the corresponding element of the vector of outputs and calculate the technical coefficients. In this way, one obtains a matrix of technical coefficients, $A = (a_{ij})$, in which $a_{ij} = x_{ij}/x_j$ is the coefficient of the input of product i in sector j.

By imposing equality between supply and demand for each product, the following system of equations is obtained:

$$x = Ax + y$$

where x represents the supplies of the various products, Ax the demand for intermediate uses, $y = [y_1, y_2, \dots y_n]'$ the demand for final uses. If the economic system is 'vital', it is possible to produce a quantity of each good which is not inferior to that used as input and at least one good in a higher quantity. Then it is possible to solve the equation to determine the levels of output necessary to produce the desired final quantities:

$$x = (I - A)^{-1} y$$

where I is the identity matrix and $(I - A)^{-1}$ is 'Leontief's inverse matrix'. The ith column of such a matrix contains the output quantities of the various goods that must be activated to obtain one unit of good i in the final demand. If we multiply the preceding equation by the vector of the labour coefficients $l = (l_1, l_2, \dots l_n)$, we will find the level of aggregate employment $L = lx = l(I - A)^{-1} y$. It should be noted that the vector $l(I - A)^{-1}$ is the vector of total labour requirements necessary to produce an amount of each product which appears in the final demand; in other words, it is the vector of labour values.

We will conclude this section by mentioning Leonid Vitalevic Kantorovic (1912–86), an important Russian mathematician and economist who was a contemporary of Leontief. Among his economic works was *Mathematical Methods of the Planning and the Organization of Production* (1939), in which he traced the general and essential lines of the theory of linear programming. However, he was not able to find an efficient method for the solution of linear-programming problems, a failure which was later to be overcome by Dantzig, who thus opened the way for practical applications for this type of programming.

8.5.5. The reawakening of Marxist economic theory

The years from the publication of the first volume of *Capital* (1867) to the beginning of the new century saw the affirmation of Marxist hegemony over socialist thought. Original works produced by Marxist writers in that period were very few indeed, however, especially in the field of economics. The truth is that, as soon as Marxism became the official ideology of the German Social Democrats and, through the Second International, of the international workers' movement, it rapidly transformed itself from the critical theory it had been for Marx into a new form of orthodoxy. In this form it was only able to produce very few theoretical innovations. It was not until the 1910s that there was a reawakening of creativity among the Marxist economists. Driven on by an unrestrainable social explosion, various socialist militants tried to apply the theoretical instruments of Marxian economics to understand the nature and the evolutionary tendencies of contemporary capitalism. We have only time to mention three of the most important works of that decade: *Das Finanzkapital* (1910) by R. Hilferding, *Die Akkumulation des Kapital* (1913) by R. Luxemburg, and *Der Imperialismus* (1816) by V. I. Lenin.

Hilferding tried to account for a fundamental structural change in the capitalism of the *belle époque*: the emergence of German-type mixed banks, their intrusion into the productive sphere, and the role they played in accelerating the processes of 'concentration' and 'centralization' of capital. The other two books analysed the tendency of capital in the most developed countries to spread through international markets, generating and embittering inter-imperialist conflict, while the capitalist mode of production was extended on a world scale. Luxemburg's basic argument was that the imperialistic drive was due to the lack of effective demand generated in internal markets due to a very unequal distribution of income. Lenin's work, on the other hand, by drawing on Hobson's and Hilferding's theories, focused on the effects of monopolistic tendencies on the fall in the rate of profit, and the consequent necessity to look for the desired 'counter-tendencies' on foreign markets.

Then, in the 1920s, immediately after the Russian Revolution and before the full affirmation of Stalinism, a brief season of fervent creativity exploded in the Soviet Union. The revolution had freed intellectual energies and, at the same time, placed a series of extremely important problems on the agenda. We cannot here give the Soviet debates of the 1920s all the attention they deserve. We have already mentioned briefly the debate on planning; here we will mention two other interesting debates, on the crisis of capitalism and on the problem of socialist accumulation.

An interesting contribution by Nikolaj Dmitrievic Kondratiev (1892–1938) emerged from the debate on the crisis of capitalism. In various works published in Russian between 1925 and 1928, Kondratiev tried to give a theoretical explanation, as well as an empirical verification, of the long waves (or major cycles). Such waves had already been noted in 1901 by the Russian Marxist economist A. I. Helphand, and the study of them had already produced fruitful results, in 1913 from Pareto and from J. van Gelderen and in 1924 from S. de Wolff. It is interesting to note that three out of four of these forerunners of Kondratiev were Marxists. Kondratiev's empirical verification was not very convincing and his theoretical explanation was even less so. However, his work was noticed because it was ingenious. Based on a mixture of Tugan- Baranovskij's cycle model and Marshall's short- and long-run equilibrium theories, Kondratiev's theory endeavoured to explain different-length reinvestment cycles by means of the different lengths of periods of capital immobilization. He maintained that the major cycles, which are half a century long, are generated by capital immobilizations due to important long-run investments in infrastructure, roads, railways, etc. Kondratiev's main article on the argument was published in 1925 and translated into German in 1926. It became finally known to a wide audience when it was published in the *Review of Economics and Statistics* in 1935 with the title 'The Long Wave in Economic Life'.

Another important discussion of that period focused on the industrialization of the Soviet Union. The pearl that came out of this debate was an article by G. A. Feldman, 'Towards a Theory of the Rates of Growth of the National Income', published in 1928 in *Planovoe chozjajstvo*. Feldman began from the Marxian schemes of reproduction, which he modified by including in the two sectors producing consumer goods and fixed capital the industries producing the circulating capital used by them. He hypothesized a constant capital–output ratio in the two sectors, and posed the problem of how to share investments among them so as to obtain the maximum rate of accumulation for the economy as a whole. He concluded that the rates of capital growth in the two sectors must be equal. The principal merits of the model are not those arising from the disaggregation into two sectors, however, but rather those that refer to the aggregate relationships existing between growth in the stock of capital and growth in production. In his study of this relationship Feldman anticipated some aspects of the Harrod–Domar model of warranted growth. It is also important to note that Domar was one of the few contemporaries of Feldman who appreciated his work, from which the former was inspired to construct his own model.

Outside the Soviet Union, Marxist economic thought did not produce particularly innovative results in the inter-war years. In regard to the problem of the crisis of capitalism, old pre-war debates on the final breakdown came to light again, with interesting contributions by H. Grossmann and O. Bauer. There was also great concern with imperialism. Notable are the works of N. J. Bukharin, who reconsidered Lenin's arguments, and F. Sternberg, who developed Luxemburg's position. A particularly interesting contribution was made by M. H. Dobb, who, in *Political Economy and Capitalism* (1937), and especially in the chapter on crises, proposed a non-dogmatic version of Marxist economic theory which was full of Keynesian suggestions. Times were changing, however, and Dobb's original interpretation of Marxist theory had little success. Greater success was achieved in Marxist circles by the more orthodox and simpler synopsis of Marxist economic thought given by P. M. Sweezy in *The Theory of Capitalist Development* (1942), a book which was to become the authority on the interpretation of Marx for more then a quarter of a century.

Finally, in regard to value and profit, we should mention two important papers by K. Shibata: 'On the Law of Decline in the Rate of Profit' and 'On the General Profit Rate', published in the *Kyoto University Economic Review* in 1934 and 1939 respectively. In regard to the fall in the rate of profit, Shibata formulated a theorem according to which, if the criterion of profitability in the choice of techniques is that of cost reduction (rather than that of increasing labour productivity), then, given the wage rate, technical change will always lead to an increase in the rate of profit, whatever the nature of the innovation. A few decades later, N. Okishio, in reconsidering Shibata's theory, showed that this was not a demonstration of the fallacy of the theory of the falling rate of profit but an indication of the restrictive hypotheses on which its validity depends: wages must be increasing and the output–capital ratio decreasing. On the subject of value, Shibata took up again Bortkiewicz's solution to the problem of transformation, confirming that the calculation of labour value was not necessary to the determination of prices and the rate of profit. As had happened to Bortkiewicz in Europe 30 years before, these arguments were ignored by orthodox Marxism, not only in the West but also in Japan. In fact, they were dangerous for the labour theory of value, as they implied, if taken to their extreme logical conclusions, that the only correct solution to the problem of the transformation was its dissolution. This only became clear, however, in 1960, with the work of Sraffa.

Bibliography

On the theory of market forms: R. Backhouse, *Economists and the Economy* (Oxford, 1988); G. Bonanno, *Imperfect Competition in General Equilibrium Theory* (mimeo, Davis, Calif., 1989); E. Chamberlin, 'Public Heterogeneity and Public Policy', *American Economic Review*, 40 (1950); J. Creedy and D. P. O'Brien (eds.), *Economic Analysis in Historical Perspective* (London, 1985); P. Deane, *The Evolution of Economic Ideas* (Cambridge, 1978); R. Harrod, 'Doctrines of Imperfect Competition', *Quarterly Journal of Economics*, 48 (1934–5); J. Hicks, 'The Process of Imperfect Competition', *Oxford Economic Papers*, 6 (1954); P. J. McNulty, 'A Note on the History of Perfect Competition', *Journal of Political Economy*, 75 (1967); H. Nikaido, *Monopolistic Competition and Effective Demand* (Princeton, NJ, 1975); W. Novschek and H. Sonnenschein, 'General Equilibrium with Free Entry: A Synthetic Approach', *Journal of Economic Literature*, 25 (1987); J. Robinson, 'What Is Perfect Competition?', *Quarterly Journal of Economics*, 48 (1934–5); G. Stigler, *Monopolistic Competition in Retrospect* (London, 1949); 'Perfect Competition, Historically Contemplated', *Journal of Political Economy*, 65 (1957).

On developments in the theory of general equilibrium and welfare economics: J. Hicks, 'The Foundations of Welfare Economics' (1939), repr. in *Wealth and Welfare* (Oxford, 1981); L. Punzo, 'Von Neumann and K. Menger's Mathematical Kolloquium', in S. Chakravarty, M. Dore, and R. H. Goodwin (eds.), *John von Neumann and Modern Economics* (Oxford, 1989); J. Quirk and R. Saposnik, *Introduction to General Equilibrium Theory and Welfare Economics* (New York, 1968); V. Walsh and H. Gram, *Classical and Neoclassical Theories of General Equilibrium: Historical Origins and Mathematical Structure* (Oxford, 1980); E. R. Weintraub, 'On the Existence of a Competitive Equilibrium 1930–1954', *Journal of Economic Literature*, 21 (1983).

On the debate about economic calculation in socialism: J. Bennett, *The Economic Theory of Central Planning* (Oxford, 1989); W. Brus, *Socialist Ownership and Political Systems* (London, 1975); M. Dobb, *On Economic Theory and Socialism* (London, 1955); *An Essay on Economic Growth and Planning* (London, 1960); J. Kornai, *The Economics of Shortage* (Amsterdam, 1980); D. Lavoie, *Rivalry and Central Planning* (Cambridge, 1985); P. Murrell, 'Did the Theory of Market Socialism Answer the Challenge of Ludwig von Mises? A Reinterpretation of the Socialist Controversy', *History of Political Economy*, 15 (1983); A. Nove, *The Economics of Feasible*

Socialism (London, 1983); A. Nove and D. M. Nuti (eds.), *Socialist Economics* (Harmondsworth, 1972); J. A. Schumpeter, *Capitalism, Socialism and Democracy* (London, 1942); F. Taylor, 'The Guidance of Production in a Socialist State', in O. Lange and F. Taylor (eds.), *On the Economic Theory of Socialism* (Minneapolis, 1948).

On institutional economic thought: M. Bronfenbrenner, 'Early American Leaders: Institutional and Critical Traditions', *American Economic Review*, 75 (1985); J. Dorfman, *Thorstein Veblen and His America* (New York, 1935); J. K. Galbraith, *Economics in Perspective* (New York, 1987); A. Gruchy, 'Institutional Economics: Its Development and Prospects', in R. Steppacher *et al.* (eds.), *Economics in Institutional Perspective* (Lexington, Mass., 1977); E. K. Hunt, *A History of Economic Thought: A Critical Perspective* (Belmont, Calif., 1979); P. Mirowski, 'The Philosophical Bases of Institutionalist Economics', *Journal of Economic Issues*, 21 (1987).

On the Russian 'school' of mathematical economics: M. Egidi and G. Gilibert, 'La teoria oggettiva dei prezzi', *Economia Politica*, 1 (1984); G. Gilibert, *La trasformazione: vera storia di un falso problema* (Turin, 1982); W. Leontief, *Essays in Economics* (New York, 1966); L. Meldolesi, 'Bortkiewicz', in *The New Palgrave*, i (London, 1987); D. M. Nuti, introduction to V. A. Dmitriev, *Economic Essays on Value, Competition and Utility* (Cambridge, 1974).

On Marxist economic thought in the first half of the twentieth century: L. Colletti and C. Napoleoni (eds.), *Il futuro del capitalismo: Crollo o sviluppo?* (Bari, 1970); A. Erlich, *The Soviet Industrialization Debate, 1924–1928* (New York, 1960); N. Jasny, *Soviet Economists in the Twenties: Names to be Remembered* (Cambridge, 1972); T. Kemp, *Theories of Imperialism* (London, 1967); N. Spulber, *Soviet Strategy for Economic Growth: Selected Soviet Essays, 1924–1930* (Bloomington, Ind., 1964); P. M. Sweezy, *The Theory of Capitalist Development* (New York, 1942).

9

Contemporary Economic Theory: I

9.1. FROM THE GOLDEN AGE TO STAGFLATION

During the dark years of the Second World War people were already beginning to discuss the bases on which the world economy could be rebuilt when the war was over. Between the First and Second World Wars, not only did Great Britain lose its position of economic leadership but the backwardness of the whole of Europe became evident, while technology, capital, and organizational methods began to be massively imported from the United States. Thus the latter played a major role in determining the directions of reconstruction. There were three principal presuppositions on which the new period of prosperity was based: economic development as an instrument to solve distributive conflicts and to control Communism; European integration as an insurance against the outbreak of another world war; and international coordination as a condition for avoiding disruptive crises such as those of the interwar period.

The Marshall Plan contributed decisively to the renewed industrial development of the European countries, pushing them towards economic collaboration, supplying the means for importing indispensable raw materials, resolving the 'German question' without creating problems of reparation payments and, finally, instilling in the Europeans the wish to imitate the American way of life. Also very important were the international monetary agreements concluded at Bretton Woods in 1944, with the foundation of the International Monetary Fund and the World Bank and the signing of GATT, mechanisms designed to co-ordinate monetary and commercial measures on the world scale.

The great boom that followed was generalized, involving the old industrialized countries and some of the new, born from the process of decolonization. Naturally, the countries that had a solid industrial base were able to narrow the gap with the USA, giving rise to a real 'economic miracle'; however, most countries which were emerging at that time from their colonial past enjoyed rather limited improvement, mainly dependent on the sale of raw materials on international markets.

The push towards European integration turned out to be much more than a vague proposal: it led to the creation of the European Coal and Steel Community and later to the Common Market, and to all the other community initiatives which gave life to the new European economy. The decline of the European economies was soon arrested, with important consequences for relations not only with the USA but also with Eastern Europe, which had remained largely outside the development process.

These were the years of great exoduses of the labour force, from agriculture to industry and from the countryside to the cities. Years of great sociocultural transformations, such as the growth of urban areas, changes in consumption patterns and cultural models, increased population mobility, the large increase in the number of cars, and the achievement of a general increase in the standard of living. Trade union protests were limited, and this was partially due to the permanently high labour demand, which gave workers a strong opportunity to improve their economic position.

Such a sustained, rapid, and widespread growth had never before been experienced. The war and crises were rapidly forgotten; it seemed that there were no limits to economic and cultural expansion. When the first man landed on the moon in 1969, it seemed that any challenge could be met. Scientists and economists enjoyed enormous social prestige, and it seemed they could achieve anything that the human mind conceived.

The golden age of the 1950s and 1960s was in fact short-lived. The earthly paradise, with its abundance and harmony, was not just around the corner. It was trade union protests which first brought governments back to the harsh reality of the class struggle and made them understand that there was still a fundamental conflict, despite the rapid economic growth. Then serious disruptions in the international monetary system began to manifest themselves; and the dollar, weakened by the costs of Vietman War and by the strong growth in other industrialized countries, was no longer able to govern that system. At the beginning of the 1970s, the Gold Exchange Standard, as established at Bretton Woods, was abandoned, first by the devaluation of the dollar and then by the declaration of inconvertibility.

As far as raw materials were concerned, the situation was also reaching boiling point. Growing realization of the exhaustibility of resources and the gradual increase in the autonomy of the producing countries led to inevitable price rises which noticeably altered the terms of trade, especially in regard to oil. In this case, the existence of a small number of producer countries favoured the creation of a strong (but not omnipotent) international cartel which helped to raise the price of oil by 400 per cent in 1973, and managed to maintain it at a high and rising level in the following years.

Many countries suddenly found themselves with large balance-of-payments deficits, and had to resort to international loans and restrictive internal measures. Thus there was an increase in the foreign indebtedness of many countries and on the other hand, inflationary processes and restrictions in demand broke out. The growth rate of the world economy slowed down drastically. International co-ordination agencies showed to be incapable in dealing with the new problems.

Despite an international network of lenders of last resort at work, some dramatic bank collapses could not be avoided. There were serious stock exchange crises which, however, did not cause the avalanche effects that had been seen on previous occasions; and this was largely due to the speed and wisdom of central-bank and government interventions. There were attempts at strengthening co-ordination and monitoring of the international economy, for example by means of the creation of the European Monetary System and by the conferences of the 'Big Seven' industrialized countries. On the other hand, many countries were experimenting with new forms of industrial relations.

In general, throughout the 1970s and 1980s the international scene was characterized by strong uncertainty and instability, and this made it difficult for governments to co-ordinate and programme long-term economic policies and for large companies to formulate coherent development plans. The latter were being forced to find new organizational modules so as to make their production flows more flexible and better adapted to the consumption patterns of their customers. This process led to the construction of a network of linked companies which function in a much more complicated way than has ever been seen in the past.

Finally, growing concerns about environmental issues, especially about pollution caused by the extension of mass industrial production, have added new demands for a rethink of the development model which dominated the 1950s and 1960s.

9.2. THE NEOCLASSICAL SYNTHESIS

9.2.1. Generalizations: the IS-LM model again

In Chapter 8 we showed how attempts to normalize the Keynesian heresy began immediately after the publication of the *General Theory*. The speed of the neoclassical reply is surprising when we consider that Hicks's paper, 'Mr Keynes and the Classics', was published in 1937 and had already been presented at a meeting of the Econometric Society in 1936. Attempts at reabsorption and generalization were resumed immediately after the war, and occupied economists for another two decades. These attempts gave birth to the theoretical approach to macroeconomic problems which became known as the 'neoclassical synthesis' and which constituted the hard core of orthodox economics after the Second World War. Many scholars define this approach as 'neo-Keynesian', but this is not correct, unless the term is intended as a contraction of 'neoclassical-Keynesian'. The label used by Robinson, 'bastard Keynesian', is perhaps a little strong, but expresses the concept well. Here, however, in order to avoid misunderstandings, we will mainly use the term 'neoclassical synthesis', which seems to be the most correct. Many economists have contributed to the construction of this theoretical system, but here we will mention only the most important: William Baumol (b. 1922), James Duesenberry (b. 1918), Lawrence R. Klein (b. 1920), Franco Modigliani

(b. 1918), James Edward Meade (b. 1907), Don Patinkin (b. 1922), Paul Anthony Samuelson (b. 1915), Robert Solow (b. 1924), and James Tobin (b. 1918). We will begin by commenting on two fundamental works: Modigliani's 'Liquidity Preference and the Theory of Interest and Money' (*Econometrica*, 1944), which opened the dance, and Patinkin's *Money, Interest and Prices* (1956), especially the largely modified second edition (1965), which practically closed it.

Modigliani, in his article, developed Hicks's *IS-LM* model with the aim of formulating a more general theory than that of Keynes. He constructed a 'generalized classical' model, using Hicks's equations and limiting himself to replacing the hypothesis of fixed money wages by one of flexible wages— thereby obtaining, as special cases, the traditional (neo)classical and the Keynesian models.

The former differs from the 'generalized' model as it adopts the Cambridge quantity equation instead of the liquidity preference equation. The latter differs from it because of its hypothesis of rigid money wages. Modigliani proved that the (neo)classical model shows the usual dichotomy between the real and the monetary sectors of the economy. Flexible wages ensure that a full employment equilibrium is reached in which all the real variables depend on real factors. The neutrality of money ensures that variations in the quantity in circulation only influence the level of prices and other monetary variables. With the liquidity trap set aside as a very special case, Modigliani then showed how, given the money supply, macroeconomic equilibrium could be reached in the Keynesian model at any level of employment, so that there is no guarantee of full employment. He also showed that the hypothesis of rigid money wages caused this result. The reason is very simple: with a given money supply, the constraint on money wages becomes, in fact, a constraint on real wages. Monetary conditions determine the monetary income. Real income will vary in order to equate the marginal productivity of labour to the real wage; and there will be a different level of employment for each different wage-level.

In the years after the publication of Modigliani's article, attention was focused on the way in which wage and price flexibility manage to neutralize Keynes's theory. It had seemed to some people that there were at least two very special cases in which not even the flexibility of wages could defeat Keynes's arguments. One is the liquidity trap, already mentioned in Chapter 7. The other is that of the interest inelasticity of investments. If one hypothesizes that not only savings but also investments are independent of interest, the *IS* curve assumes a vertical position, so that no monetary policy is able to influence the level of employment. Well, it is proved that even in these cases it is necessary to assume rigidity of prices and wages in order to obtain Keynes's conclusions.

A key role in this demonstration was played by the so-called 'wealth effect', of which two types can be distinguished: the 'Pigou effect' or 'real-balance effect' and the 'Keynes effect' or 'windfall effect'. Let us assume that unemployment exists. If money wages are flexible, they will fall, and this fall will be followed by a decrease in prices. Taking the money supply as given, the liquid reserves of economic agents will increase in real terms. Then the agents will reduce their demand for money in an attempt to regain their desired liquid balances. This will cause the *LM* curve to shift to the right. A price fall corresponds to an increase in the money supply in real terms, and this occurs automatically with unemployment. Second, an increase in the real cash balances makes the economic agents feel richer and, as a consequence, induces them to increase their demand for consumer goods. This will cause the *IS* curve to move to the right, pushing the economy towards full employment. Furthermore, the increase in the money supply in real terms will cause the rate of interest to fall, and this will raise the value of financial assets. The consumers, feeling richer, are able to reduce their propensity to save and this, while pushing the *IS* curve further to the right by increasing the multiplier, will also modify the slope of the curve. Savings become sensitive to variations in the interest rate, and the *IS* curve, if it was vertical, now becomes negatively sloped.

Finally, the increase in entrepreneurs' financial wealth caused by interest rate reduction will induce them to spend more, even in investment activity. This is the Keynes effect, which implies an increase in the interest-sensitiveness of investments and therefore a further change in the slope of the *IS* curve. Moreover, if the windfall profits caused by interest rate reduction make the entrepreneurs more optimistic, then the *IS* curve will shift further to the right. In conclusion, horizontal *LM* and vertical *IS* curves cannot do any harm: if prices and wages are flexible, the economy has the strength *automatically* to bring itself towards full employment. Keynesian under-employment equilibrium is no longer admissible, not even as a special case.

It was Patinkin who settled these results within a general-equilibrium model, and who, in the above-mentioned book, managed to generalize the generalized neoclassical model of Hicks and Modigliani. The new generalization consisted, on the one hand, of the introduction of a fourth market, that of financial assets, besides those of 'national product', money, and labour, and, on the other of the introduction of a new variable in the supply and demand functions of all four goods, i.e. the price-level. This variable enters into the supply and demand functions of labour together with money wages, in such a way that only real wages count, thus eliminating any possible 'monetary illusion'. It enters the demand functions for goods, money, and bonds as well as that of the supply function of bonds, as a deflator of liquid reserves, so that only their real value counts. It is not surprising that in this model the neutrality of money and the usual neoclassical dichotomy are confirmed. The beauty of Patinkin's theory is in its clear elucidation of the hypotheses on which his conclusions depend. The two principal hypotheses concern the absence of monetary illusion and the perfect flexibility of prices on all markets. There seems to be no hope for Keynes: if interpreted within a general-equilibrium model, his general theory dissolves into nothing.

Together with this kind of generalization work, the economists of the neo-classical synthesis carried out a series of investigations on specific aspects of Keynesian theory with the aim of correcting some of its particular flaws, refining some of its peculiar theses, and adjusting the latter to the results of empirical research. From such work some debates originated which led to the discarding or amending of certain peculiarities of Keynes's theory in such a way that it finally became unrecognizable. Here we will consider four of the most important macroeconomic problems tackled in the 1950s and 1960s: those of the consumption function, the demand for money function, the theory of inflation, and the theory of growth.

9.2.2. Refinements: the consumption function

The consumption function played a fundamental role in Keynes's theory, as it allowed the identification of a simple relationship between consumption and income from which a measure of the marginal propensity to consume and the multiplier could be obtained. It is important that such a function is stable, in the sense that its parameters do not vary significantly when the magnitudes of the variables change. Only if the multiplier is stable can the Keynesian pro-cedure for explaining the variations in income and employment by autonom-ous expenditure be considered legitimate. The Keynesian consumption function in its simplest form is:

$$C = C_0 + cY$$

where C_0 is a constant, C represents consumption, and Y the disposable income (i.e. the income earned net of taxes). In this function, the average propensity to consume, C/Y, is higher than the marginal propensity, c. It is obvious that such a function cannot hold true in the long run, nor can it be applied to a long period; otherwise, it would lead to negative aggregate savings corresponding to low income-levels, such as those which occurred in nineteenth-century Europe and America.

Another function which holds true in the long run, as Simon Kuznets (1901–85) showed in *Uses of National Income in Peace and War* (1942), is a function of the following type:

$$C = bY$$

in which the marginal propensity to consume, b, coincides with the average one and is higher than that measured by c. This type of function, being well adapted to a long historical period, was soon to be known as the long-run consumption function. The other, one which is better adapted to the cross-sectional data of family budgets, became known as the short-run function.

A simple and reasonable explanation of the differences between short-run and long-run functions was offered by Duesenberry in *Income, Saving and the*

Theory of Consumption Behaviour (1949), in which he put forward the 'relative income hypothesis'. According to this hypothesis, family consumption is a function of 'relative', besides absolute, incomes. Poor families have an average propensity to consume which is higher than rich families, so that cross-section data show a decreasing average propensity to consume. When the national income increases, without any change in its distribution, the consumption of all families will increase in the same proportion, in such a way that the distribution of consumption will also remain broadly constant. In this way, the national average of the average (family) propensities to consume can remain constant through time. In other words, with a variation in the national income the short-run consumption function would shift upwards along a long-run function. This explanation, despite its reasonableness, did not have a great deal of success, perhaps because, being too faithful to the Keynesian spirit, it did not attribute great weight to the need to find a microeconomic foundation based on the assumption of maximizing behaviour of the consumers, or perhaps because neoclassical economists love sociological reductions less than psychological ones, or perhaps for both reasons.

A suggestion which achieved more success was that advanced by Tobin in 'Relative Income, Absolute Income, and Saving' (published in *Money, Trade, and Economic Growth* 1951), where he included wealth among the arguments of the short-run consumption function. His suggestion was taken up by Modigliani and Brumberg, who, in 'Utility Analysis and the Consumption Function: An Interpretation of Cross-Section Data' (published in *Post-Keynesian Economics* (1954), edited by K. K. Kurihara), put forward the so-called 'life-cycle' hypothesis. The new theory underwent various modifications and refinements in the debates that followed, but few substantial changes. It can be presented succinctly in the following way. In the presence of an additive utility function, and with decreasing marginal utility, consumers try to distribute their consumption in a uniform way over their life-span, so as not consume too much when they earn a lot and too little when they earn little. Thus, during their working years they save so as to accumulate wealth to use when they are old and when they have stopped producing income. The consumption function has two arguments: wealth, W, and 'life income', Y_v, which is what the individual expects to earn on average, annually, over his life. The function will be:

$$C = aW + cY_v$$

Kuznets's problem is easily solved if the ratio between wealth and disposable income and between life income and disposable income are assumed constant. Then the average propensity to consume, $C/Y = aW/Y + cY_v/Y$, will be constant. However, this will only happen in the long run, when it is legitimate to assume that the wealth–income ratio is constant. In the short run, on the other hand, such a relationship will oscillate considerably, and with it the average propensity to consume.

Not too dissimilar to this is Milton Friedman's (b. 1912) theory of 'permanent income', formulated in *A Theory of Consumption Function* (1957). Permanent income is defined as the present value of future wealth. As future wealth is unknown, the evaluation of permanent income depends on the expectations of the consumers. Assuming adaptive expectations, permanent income, Y_p, can be calculated as a weighted average of the incomes earned in past years—in practice, as an average of current incomes earned in the two years of the most recent past, Y and Y_{-1}:

$$Y_p = \alpha Y + (1 - \alpha)Y_{-1}$$

with $0 < \alpha < 1$. The long-run consumption function will depend on permanent income, and will be:

$$C = bY_p$$

However, in the short run the current income will differ from the permanent one because of a random transitory component. If it is lower, the short-run average propensity to consume will be greater than the long-run one, and vice versa. Thus the marginal propensity will be lower than the average propensity, and this can be explained by the fact that individuals do not know whether the variations observed in their current incomes will be maintained through time or are only transitory. Therefore, by regressing consumptions on current incomes the following function should be obtained:

$$C = C_0 + cY$$

which is the same as the simple Keynesian consumption function. But Friedman has derived it from a theory which explains it as a *highly unstable* function. The parameters of Friedman's function can vary substantially with changes in current income, as this includes a strong random and transitory component. We will see later which important role was to be assigned by Friedman, in the attack on Keynesian theory, to the instability of the consumption function.

9.2.3. Corrections: money and inflation

Another field in which the theorists of the neoclassical synthesis went beyond Keynes was that of the theory of the demand for money. In Keynes's theory, speculators carry out a key role. They speculate on the changes in the value of financial assets, forming expectations based over an extremely brief period and paying no attention to the fundamentals which should govern share prices. Such expectations assume the form of forecasts with regard to the expectations of others and, on certain occasions, when the markets are dominated by phenomena of mass psychology, they become self-fulfilling, producing instability and abrupt crashes. If the demand for money is dominated, or is influenced to a substantial degree, by speculation of this type, it will be affected by drastic changes or unexpected jumps following variations in the opinions of the speculators. As these opinions can also vary unpredictably in relation to interest rate changes, the demand function for money is extremely unstable, and is unable to provide reliable support to monetary policy. In fact, Keynes was very sceptical, not only about the efficacy, but also about the implementation of discretionary monetary policies.

The neoclassical revision of Keynes's theory of the demand for money had three main aims:

(1) to expel destabilizing speculation from the theory;
(2) to find microeconomic foundations capable of linking the aggregate demand for money to some form of individual maximization behaviour;
(3) to construct a stable function of the demand for money.

An attempt to account for the existence of a stable relationship between the transaction demand for money and the rate of interest was made by Baumol in 'The Transaction Demand for Cash: An Inventory Theoretic Approach' (*Quarterly Journal of Economics*, 1952). Baumol applied the theory of inventory decisions to the demand for money, and demonstrated that the transaction demand depends on the volume of transactions, on the costs that must be sustained to convert short-term assets into money, and, above all, on the rate of interest. This occurs because the cash balances held by firms for the normal running of business represent a cost in terms of the yields forsaken for not having invested the wealth in less liquid assets. When the rate of interest increases, this opportunity cost also increases and, all other conditions being equal, the companies are induced to reduce their cash balances. The transaction demand for money is therefore a decreasing function of the rate of interest.

More ambitious attempts to find a microeconomic foundation for monetary theory were made by Hicks and Tobin. In the 1950s a theory of portfolio selection was developed, about which we should mention at least two works by Harry Markowitz, the article 'Portfolio Selection' (*Journal of Finance*, 1952) and the book *Portfolio Selection* (1959), and one by Tobin, 'Liquidity Preference as Behaviour toward Risk' (*Review of Economic Studies*, 1958). Tobin directly tackled the problem of the speculative demand for money, and solved it by reducing it to a problem of choice in respect to risk. The holding of non-liquid assets gives a return, which is the sum of the interest and the capital gains, that cash cannot give. Economic agents formulate expectations in regard to possible capital gains, and specify these in the form of a frequency distribution. They admit the possibility that actual values might differ from expected ones, and attribute to each of these possibilities a subjective probability. Tobin assumed, for the sake of simplicity, a normal distribution, and took its mean as a measure of the expected value and its standard deviation as a measure of risk. Given the current rate of interest and the expected capital gain, the expected returns from the investment will be an increasing function of risk. As the percentage of wealth invested in non-liquid assets increases, so do the returns, but also the riskiness of the investment. The investor will have preferences concerning the way to combine returns and risk. His problem is therefore reduced to one of maximizing satisfaction, and the way in which he divides his wealth between money and non-liquid assets will depend on his risk aversion. In order to induce a typical investor, who is assumed to be averse to risk, to increase the demand for non-liquid assets and therefore to decrease the demand for money, it is necessary to increase the interest rate. Thus the speculative demand for money is a stable decreasing function of the interest rate.

After the publication of Tobin's article the research continued, especially in the direction of extending Tobin's results to portfolio choice in the presence of different kinds of asset. Important contributions were made by Hicks in various papers collected in the volume *Critical Essays in Monetary Theory* (1967). But the final word in this strand of research was again given by Tobin, who, in 'A General Equilibrium Approach to Monetary Theory' (*Journal of Money, Credit and Banking*, 1969) extended the theory of portfolio choice to the general case in which agents must choose among a vast range of financial assets. Among these Tobin included real capital stock. Furthermore he introduced a new economic variable, q, which he defined as the ratio between the market valuation of a firm and the replacement cost of its capital. This is the origin of the famous 'q-theory' of accumulation. When q increases, firms have no difficulty in finding external finance, which is abundant and cheap; therefore real investments will increase. When q decreases and the stock market valuation becomes lower than the replacement cost of capital, firms which wish to invest will find it more advantageous to buy other firms or shares in other firms on the stock exchange, rather than increase their real investments. Thus, investments are an increasing function of q. It is this q that should appear in the *IS-LM* model, rather than a generic 'rate of interest'. It remains true, however, that q depends, in any case, on the decisions of the monetary authorities about interest rate levels and structure. Therefore, the possibility that investments are insensitive to discretionary monetary policies must be excluded.

Another field of investigation in which the neoclassical synthesis tried to improve upon Keynes was the theory of inflation. On this subject Keynes had formulated a precise theory as early as the *Treatise*. And he remained basically faithful to that theory even after the publication of the *General Theory*; so much so that he reproposed it almost unchanged in *How to Pay for the War* (1940). He believed that inflation depends on the excess of aggregate expenditure over real output, and therefore that it becomes a relevant problem only in the presence of full employment. In such a situation, an excess of aggregate demand increases profits and initiates a cumulative inflationary process which, by modifying the distribution of income in favour of the capitalists, will continue until savings have increased to the level necessary to finance investments. A corollary of this theory (which, however, was developed by post-

Keynesians rather than by Keynes himself) is that, in an unemployment situation, inflation cannot be explained by the forces of demand, but only by the impulses coming from costs.

This dualistic theoretical stance, with pure demand-pull inflation in periods of full employment and pure cost-push inflation in the presence of unemployment, did not seem very elegant, and was disliked by many economists; and as soon as a pretext appeared on which to reject it, all the neoclassical Keynesian economists seized the opportunity. The pretext was offered by Alban William H. Phillips (1914–75), who, in 'The Relationship between Unemployment and the Rate of Change of Money Wage Rates in the United Kingdom, 1861–1957' (*Economica*, 1958), set out the results of an empirical investigation from which emerged the existence of a decreasing function between the growth rate of money wages and the rate of unemployment. The orthodox theoretical explanation of the 'Phillips curve' was given by Richard George Lipsey (b. 1928) in 'The Relationship between Unemployment and the Rate of Change of Money Wage Rates in the United Kingdom, 1862–1955: A Further Analysis' (*Econometrica*, 1960). The explanation was given in terms of the law of supply and demand. Wages change as an increasing function of the excess demand for labour. The rate of unemployment reflects this excess demand. In this way, the Phillips curve is reconciled with the orthodox theory of wages, except for the fact, which was later to turn out to be crucial, that it is not the variations in real wages but those in money wages that it makes depend on the excess demand.

9.2.4. Simplifications: growth and distribution

The final step that still had to be taken to complete the reabsorption of Keynes into the neoclassical theoretical system was to show that the interest rate, while being influenced by monetary forces, remained regulated by real forces; and that, in the end, it was possible to reduce it to be precisely what Keynes had denied it was, i.e. the price of the services of real capital, or the equilibrium price of savings and investments. Hicks and Modigliani, in the two above-mentioned articles on the *IS-LM* model, had already tried to reach this result. But that model, based as it was on the hypothesis of temporary equilibrium (with a given capital stock) did not lend itself to this purpose. To make interest the equilibrium price of the services of capital, it is necessary to be able to link it to the productivity of capital and make it depend on the proportions in which capital is utilized in relation to other factors. Besides this, it is essential that these proportions can be linked to the decisions of optimizing economic agents, as the equilibrium is a situation in which the individuals have maximized their own objectives. Finally, the capital stock cannot be taken as given; and it is the concept of long-run equilibrium that must be referred to. These objectives were reached (at least it seemed so at that time) by the neoclassical growth models.

We will ignore the vast amount of literature which appeared on the subject in the 1960s, and limit ourselves to mentioning the first and simplest of these models, that formulated by Solow in 'A Contribution to the Theory of Economic Growth' (*Quarterly Journal of Economics*) and by T. W. Swan in 'Economic Growth and Capital Accumulation' (*Economic Record*), both published in 1956. However, it is important to point out that, a year before, Tobin had already drawn the essential lines of this model in 'A Dynamic Aggregative Model' (*Journal of Political Economy*)

The explanation of the interest rate by the marginal productivity of capital was only one of the birds to be killed with Solow's stone. Another was the solution of a basic problem concerned with growth which had emerged from the Harrod–Domar model: that of the possibility for a capitalist economy to grow at the 'natural' rate, ensuring the maintenance of full employment. The neoclassical economists set aside the problem of stability from the very beginning by assuming that the economy always grows at the warranted rate. Then the problem of natural growth was solved by adding to the three basic equations of the Harrod–Domar model (see Section 7.1.6) an aggregate production function of the type $Y = F(K, L)$, in which Y represents the national income, K capital, and L labour. In Chapter 11, when we consider the debate on the theory of capital, we will discuss the analytical and theoretical difficulties inherent in the concepts themselves of an aggregate production function and aggregate capital. Here we will ignore them by treating capital as if it were jelly.

If constant returns of scale are assumed, the production function can be rewritten as $y = f(k)$, with $y = Y/L$ and $K = K/L$, as shown in Fig. 11. Now, it can be proved by making adequate hypotheses on the form of the production function that, given the propensity to save, there is a unique capital–output ratio which ensures equality between the warranted rate of growth and the natural rate, n. In other words, a^*, the full-employment capital–output ratio, is determined endogenously in such a way as to guarantee the equality $s/a^* = n$, or $1/a^* = n/s$.

The solution of the Harrod–Domar problem was achieved by treating the capital–output ratio as a variable, instead of as a datum. The economic meaning of this solution consists of the fact that, as the capital–output ratio is variable, entrepreneurs will choose it with the aim of maximizing their profits. The techniques will change in response to variations in factor prices. At any moment, if an unemployment situation occurs, the flexibility of real wages guarantees a reduction in the cost of labour necessary to induce the entrepreneurs to modify the techniques in such a way as to increase the demand for labour. Unemployment can only be temporary and frictional. In equilibrium, the wage rate will be equal to the marginal productivity of labour, and the economy will grow with full employment.

In the same way, any monetary disturbance which alters the rate of interest will induce entrepreneurs to modify their demand for capital in such a way as to equate its marginal productivity to the cost of finance. Thus equilibrium on

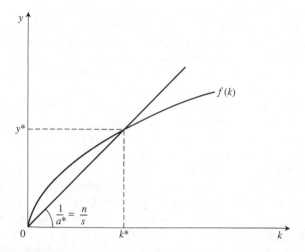

Fɪɢ. 11

the capital market will be ensured by an interest rate which rewards the productive services of capital, being equal to its marginal productivity.

The persuasiveness of this model was also linked to the fact that it also seemed to account in the simplest way for a historical phenomenon which Keynes would have had difficulty in believing in and which the Harrod–Domar model was incapable of explaining: the ability of the most advanced capitalist economies to grow by maintaining full employment, as had occurred in the 1950s and 1960s. This phenomenon did not lead the neoclassical economists explicitly to reject Keynes, but it did seem to justify their rejection of his pessimism. After all was said and done, the capitalist economy seemed able to look after itself, so that Keynesian economic policies were not needed to try to cure any incurable illness. At most they could be called up to correct some imperfections, for example when trade unions insisted in raising wages. In general, however, they were only needed to 'fine-tune' economic growth, and to minimize oscillations, so as to allow the 'invisible hand' to work with ease. On the other hand, as they were short-run policies, nothing more could be expected of them. In the same way in which Keynesian theory did not damage the neoclassical theoretical framework in any essential way, Keynesian policies would not impinge upon the operation of the market.

9.3. THE MONETARIST COUNTER-REVOLUTION

9.3.1. Act I: Money matters

While the neoclassical synthesis was being built at the Massachusetts Institute of Technology, Yale, and Harvard, Milton Friedman, at the University of

Chicago, was working on his personal reconstruction of the neoclassical system. The monetarist theory, as Friedman's reworking of the traditional quantity theory of money was to be called, progressed at the same time as the neoclassical synthesis and grew, apparently, in conflict with it, as it presented itself as a criticism of Keynes's economics, while the neoclassical economists of MIT were proclaiming themselves as 'neo-Keynesian'. The monetarist counter-revolution began in 1956, when Friedman published 'The Quantity Theory of Money: A Restatement'. This famous article was followed by other important works, later collected in *The Optimum Quantity of Money* (1969), which contains the foundations of monetarist theory.

Friedman argued that the quantity theory had to be interpreted as a theory of demand for money and not as a simple explanation of price-level. Only with the addition of specific hypotheses in regard to the supply conditions (of money and real goods) would it have been possible to use that approach to explain the price-level. He then reformulated the theory of money demand, taking into account the advances made by modern research. After various refinements, he proposed a model not dissimilar to those based on portfolio choices. He included among the arguments of the money demand function the interest rates on bonds and shares and the inflation rate (interpreted as a negative rate of returns on liquid assets), as well as wealth and other structural and institutional variables. This function contains nothing substantially new in comparison to the one used by the Keynesian neoclassical economists, and can be easily manipulated, as occurs when it is used in empirical research, in such a way as to transform it into a demand function which is only dependent on interest rate and level of income. Friedman was convinced, even more than the Keynesian neoclassical economists, that this function is extremely stable.

In a 1963 article written in collaboration with D. Meiselman, 'The Relative Stability of Monetary Velocity and the Investment Multiplier in the United States, 1897–1958' (reprinted in *Monetary Economics* (1971), edited by J. Praeger), Friedman again presented the argument of the stability of the money demand function under the form of a hypothesis on the stability (and the magnitude) of the velocity of money circulation, which he renamed the 'monetary multiplier'. He coupled this with a hypothesis on the income multiplier, which he maintained to be lower and more unstable than the monetary multiplier. He justified this hypothesis with the permanent-income theory of the consumption function. As consumption depends on permanent income, and therefore on the incomes received in past years besides that of the current year, the propensity to consume calculated on current income is lower than that calculated on permanent income. Moreover, current income always contains a transitory component which is random and extremely variable. Therefore the propensity to consume, and the Keynesian multiplier, are not only low but change markedly in response to changes in income-level. The conclusion was simple: impulses from fiscal policy, which act on the economy through the

Keynesian multiplier, are less effective than monetary stimuli, which work through the monetary multiplier.

This conclusion was reinforced by the so-called 'crowding-out thesis', a modern reformulation of the traditional 'treasury view', which Keynes had fiercely fought against. Given the money supply, an increase in public spending financed by borrowing will increase the rate of interest, and consequently 'crowd out' private investments, so that aggregate demand will not increase. On the contrary, given public spending, a rise in the money supply will increase incomes, without raising the rate of interest: *money matters*. The extreme argument about crowding-out requires a vertical *LM* curve, but, generally, an *LM* curve which is steeper than the *IS* curve is enough to be able to conclude that money is more important than real stimuli.

However, Friedman did not derive from this argument the conclusion that discretionary monetary policy is advisable. In fact, in a monumental investigation carried out in collaboration with A. J. Schwartz, *A Monetary History of the United States, 1861–1960* (1963), he believed he had demonstrated that the influence of the money supply is strong but irregular, the delay occurring between the monetary impulse and the real effects being long and variable. This means that, even though money is able to disturb the real economy, owing to the unpredictable nature of its real effects nobody would be able to use it as an instrument of discretionary policy. The best thing to do, for the monetary authorities, would therefore be to increase the money supply at the rhythm required by long-run real growth and to leave the market with the job of dealing with short-run adjustments.

9.3.2. Act II: 'You can't fool all the people all of the time'

The decisive blow against Keynesian neoclassical economics was struck, at the end of the 1960s, in two articles that attacked the theory underlying the Phillips curve: one by E. S. Phelps, 'Phillips Curve: Expectations of Inflation and Optimal Unemployment over Time' (*Econometrica*, 1967) and one by Friedman, 'The Role of Monetary Policy' (*American Economic Review*, 1968). It was pointed out that, if the Phillips curve is interpreted in terms of the laws of supply and demand, and if agents are assumed to be rational, then the rate of unemployment should not be related to the variations in *money* wage, but to the variations in real wages. The growth rate of the real wage is given by the difference between the growth rate of the money wage and the expected rate of inflation. Given certain inflationary expectations, the monetary authorities are able to reduce the level of unemployment only if they increase the money supply in such a way as to generate an inflation rate which is greater than the expected one. Thus the entrepreneurs believe in a reduction in the real wage and increase the demand for labour. The money wage will increase, and the workers, given the inflationary expectations, increase the labour supply.

A simple linear 'short-run Phillips curve' will be:

$$\dot{W} = \beta\dot{P}^e - \mu(U - U_n)$$

where $\dot{W}$ is the growth rate of money wages, $\dot{P}^e$ the expected rate of inflation, U the rate of unemployment, and U_n its 'natural' level, the latter depending on the preferences of the economic agents and on technology. In correspondence to given inflationary expectations, for example $\dot{P}^e_1$, the short-run Phillips curve will be negatively sloped, like curve I in Fig. 12. In order to obtain a level of unemployment such as $\bar{U}$ the money supply must increase in such a way that wages rise at rate $\dot{W}_1$. However, individuals are not fooled for long. When they realize that the prices have risen more than predicted, they will raise their expectations, for example to $\dot{P}^e_2 > \dot{P}^e_1$. Now, if the wages continue to increase at rate $\dot{W}_1$ the workers will reduce the supply of labour, so that, in Fig. 12, there will be a horizontal shift towards U_n. To maintain the unemployment at level $\bar{U}$, the monetary authorities must increase the monetary supply even more than before, so as to generate an inflation rate greater than $\dot{P}^e_2$.

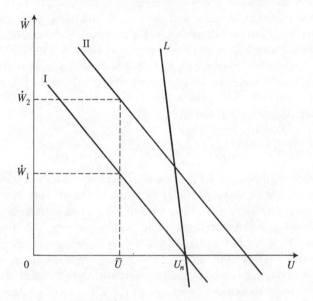

FIG. 12

This will again fool the economic agents and cause a movement towards the left along curve II (corresponding to the expectations $\dot{P}^e_2$). In conclusion, to continue to fool the economic agents the authorities must trigger and maintain an accelerated inflation process. This is the so-called 'accelerationist hypothesis'. In the presence of any rate of inflation, provided that it is constant and therefore known to the economic agents, nobody is fooled, and the economy will stabilize at the natural rate of unemployment, U_n. In the long run there is no decreasing function between unemployment and the growth rate of money wages. Or, in any case, it is an extremely weak relationship. With the 'long-run Phillips curve', the expected rate of inflation coincides with the actual one, and the curve itself will be more or less vertical, like the L curve in Fig. 12.

The long-run Phillips curve is obtained from the above formula when $\dot{W} = \dot{P} = Pe$, where $\dot{P}$ is the actual rate of inflation. Then:

$$U = U_n - (1 - \beta)\dot{P}/\mu$$

from which it can be seen that the curve is vertical, i.e. $U = U_n$, if $\beta = 1$.

In this case the monetary policy is completely ineffective as a full-employment policy and has only inflationary effects. If, however, $\beta < 1$, the long-run Phillips curve is sloped, even if less than the short-run curve. β is the 'expectation coefficient', and expresses the degree to which the actual rate of inflation depends on the expected rate. The neo-Keynesian economists argued that β depends on the size of monetary illusion: the stronger it is, the lower β will be. The difference between the Keynesian neoclassical and the monetarist neoclassical economists thus hinges on the size of β, the former wishing it to be low, the latter near to 1.

The various arguments put forward by Friedman against the Keynesian neoclassical system have always caused heated debates, as if they had been heresies. This may seem strange if one thinks that Friedman has always accepted all the theoretical foundations of the neoclassical synthesis, from the consumption function to the money demand function, from the practical importance of wealth effects to the theoretical importance of price flexibility, from acceptance of the *IS-LM* model to allegiance to general-equilibrium theory. In effect, Friedman simply limited himself to drawing out the extreme logical consequences from the premises of the neoclassical synthesis, the apparent reasons for dissent mainly concerning certain hypotheses about the size of some economic parameters, such as the propensity to consume, the money velocity of circulation, and the expectation coefficient. The real disagreement concerned, above all, the consequences of economic policy that could be drawn from the sizes of those parameters. One is almost tempted to believe Friedman when he said that all differences of opinion could be resolved by empirical research. But empirical research has never been able to resolve policy differences of this type.

How is it possible, then, to explain that towards the beginning of the 1970s monetarism finally broke through, suddenly conquering an unexpected hegemony, or almost? The reason is basically political. On the one hand, the stagflation of those years seemed to prove the monetarists right, especially in their insistence on putting the politicians on guard against the inflationary effects of Keynesian policies. Furthermore, with the accelerationist hypothesis, they called for the necessity of a long period of stagnation to reduce inflation. The monetarists, on the other hand, offered a simple remedy for all problems: block monetary expansion and deflate the economy. And this was welcomed not only by the simple-minded politicians but also by the shrewdest, such as those who, for example, while not believing the monetarist argument that the trade unions were not responsible for inflation, thought that monetarist policies could at least serve to teach them a lesson.

9.3.3. Act III: The students go beyond the master

The triumph of monetarism was short-lived: Milton Friedman had just conquered the field, after more than 15 years of struggle, when he was immediately swept away by 'neomonetarism'. 'Neomonetarism' is perhaps the most appropriate term to define that school of thought which most call, exaggerating a little, the 'new classical macroeconomics'. This school, which came to the fore towards the end of the 1970s, was explicitly and directly linked to the traditional monetarist school; but it differed from it in several respects, especially in the greater refinement of its theoretical and methodological position, but also for being more extreme, if possible, in regard to economic policy. The main exponents of this school are Robert E. Lucas Jr. (b. 1937), Thomas J. Sargent (b. 1943), and Neil Wallace (b. 1939). Lucas's most important work was published between 1972 and 1981 and later collected together in *Studies in Business Cycle Theory* (1981). Other strongholds of the 'new classical macroeconomics' are to be found in the article by Lucas and Sargent, 'After Keynesian Macroeconomics' (published in *Rational Expectations and Econometric Practice* (1981), edited by the same authors) and in the article by Sargent and Wallace, 'Rational Expectations, the Optimal Monetary Instrument, and the Optimal Money Supply Rule' (*Journal of Political Economy*, 1975).

Monetarism showed its greatest weakness precisely on those subjects with which it seemed to have routed the field. The recognition of the existence of a short-run Phillips curve had, in fact, reinforced the position of those neo-Keynesians for whom economic policy served to 'fine-tune' the economy in the short run. Moreover, the admission of the possible existence of a negatively sloped, long-run Phillips curve had demonstrated that Keynesian policies could also have lasting effects, albeit not particularly dramatic. At the political and empirical level, therefore, the differences did not seem so great. On the theoretical level, however, Friedman had made a short step forward with respect to the neoclassical synthesis when he stressed the role played by expectations in the frustration of economic policy. As already mentioned, the *IS-LM* model, interpreted as a temporary general-equilibrium model, was adopted both by the Keynesian neoclassical economists and by the monetarists. In a temporary general-equilibrium model, if futures markets are not open for all goods, the only way to account for the influence of the future on current transactions is to introduce expectations about the prices of the goods available in the future. This is what Friedman did by introducing inflationary expectations. These are expectations about the future price of those consumer goods for which there are no futures markets. Friedman, however, following Phillip

Cagan ('The Monetary Dynamics of Hyperinflation' in *Studies in the Quantity Theory of Money*, edited by M. Friedman, 1956), assumed 'adaptive expectations', a kind of expectation formed in a rather mechanical way by extrapolating from past experience. This assumption not only did not have a solid theoretical justification but was also the main reason for the expectation coefficient of the Phillips curve being different from 1; or, to put it in a different way, for the possibility that economic agents let themselves be systematically fooled. In fact, adaptive expectations can give rise to systematic prediction errors.

Lucas avoided this difficulty with one jump, by adopting the '*rational-expectations*' hypothesis—a hypothesis which had already been formulated in 1961 by John Fraser Muth (b. 1930) in a famous article published in *Econometrica* and entitled 'Rational Expectations and the Theory of Price Movements'. The main problem with adaptive expectations is that they are unable to deal with all the available information in a rational way. For example, as the formation process of adaptive expectations only takes into account past experience, the agent who follows it will ignore the announcements and the future effects of current economic-policy choices. In order to take into account these and other phenomena relevant to the decisions, the agents should reason by making use of the 'correct' economic theory. Rational expectations are formed on the basis of knowledge of all available information, and are elaborated by means of the 'correct' economic model. The 'correct' economic model is, obviously, the one accepted by Lucas. Being 'correct', it allows for the determination of the 'true' equilibrium values of the economic variables. So the hypothesis of rational expectations is *basically* the same as that of 'perfect foresight', the only difference being that it allows for stochastic disturbances—a significant difference, but not decisive from a theoretical point of view. Rational expectations do not eliminate every possible prediction error, but only admit random errors. The predictions based on rational expectations are 'true' only 'on average'.

The neomonetarists took up Friedman's hypothesis of the natural rate of unemployment and reformulated it, transforming the Phillips curve into an 'aggregate supply function'. To do this they used 'Okun's law', which postulates the existence of a decreasing function linking the unemployment rate and the difference between the growth rate of the national income and its trend. They reformulated this law in such a way as to obtain the equation $(U - U_n) = -\gamma(\dot{Y} - \dot{Y}_n)$. Here $\dot{Y}_n$ is the 'natural' growth rate of income, i.e. the one which guarantees 'natural' unemployment. By substituting this equation into that of the Phillips curve (p. 310), and assuming $\dot{P} = \dot{W}$ and $\beta = 1$, we have:

$$\dot{Y} = \dot{Y}_n + \frac{1}{\mu\gamma}(\dot{P} - \dot{P}^e)$$

from which it is easy to see that, if expectations are rational, then $\dot{P} = \dot{P}^e$ and income will grow at the natural rate. Unemployment will also stabilize at its natural rate. There will be no short-run Phillips curve, while the long-run one will be vertical. This means that any *systematic* expansive economic policy is doomed to failure. If the monetary authorities announce their decisions, or if, while not announcing them, they take them by following a model which is known to the economic agents, the latter will immediately foresee the effects of the policy and will not let themselves be fooled. In this way they will condemn it to ineffectiveness.

How is it possible, then, to explain cyclical oscillations? Not by price rigidity and market imperfections, as the Keynesian neoclassical economists maintained. The neomonetarists assumed that prices are capable of clearing the markets at any moment, i.e. that they are perfectly flexible equilibrium prices. Then there is only one possibility left. Random shocks are not predictable, nor are *non-systematic* economic policies. Therefore surprises can occur in the short run, and P may not equal P^e. But for this to occur it is necessary to assume that information is not perfect; and this is what the neomonetarists did with the so-called 'islands hypothesis', already put forward by Phelps. Economic agents work in 'local' markets that are separated from each other, as if they were islands. The first information the agents acquire concerns their specific markets. If they interpret it as being specific to these markets, when it is not, they are fooled, at least temporarily. For example, an unexpected political decision with inflationary effects will cause a general increase in prices. Each entrepreneur will observe the increase in price of his own product. If he interprets it as an increase limited to his own market, he will believe that it is a change in relative rather than absolute prices, and will be induced to increase production. Later, however, he will realize that he has been fooled and return production to its 'natural' level. Therefore economic policy can be effective in the short run, but only if it is unsystematic and unpredictable.

From this point of view, economic fluctuations are generated by unexpected exogenous shocks and are based on incomplete information. A criticism levelled against this conception is that it is only able to account for short and chaotic movements of the economic variables and not for a business cycle. In the real world the cycle is characterized by a succession of phases of various lengths in which different variables, production, employment, wages, etc. undergo fairly marked 'co-movements', i.e. they evolve through time, maintaining a strong correlation. This is the 'persistence problem'. Lucas has replied to this type of criticism in two ways. He has suggested that the 'islands' on which the economic agents operate may be so far away from each other as to require a certain time-lapse to fill the information gaps. And he has maintained that there are certain economic mechanisms, of the accelerator type for example, which tend to prolong the effects of exogenous shocks.

It was from these kinds of problem that the literature on the 'real business cycle' arose, a literature which has flourished in very recent years. Here we will limit ourselves to mentioning the two contributions which made the breakthrough and laid the ground for this line of research: 'Time to Build and

Aggregate Fluctuations' (*Econometrica*, 1982), by F. Kydland and E. C. Prescott, and 'Real Business Cycles' (*Journal of Political Economy*, 1983), by J. B. Long and C. I. Plosser. These theories preserve two fundamental hypotheses of the neomonetarist approach: economic agents with rational expectations and markets in equilibrium at each moment. However, they focus on real rather than monetary shocks as the principal factors of cyclical movements, especially on those connected with the changes in the productivity of factors and in public expenditure. An increase in productivity raises the income of the factors and, given the inputs, the level of production, whereas an increase in public expenditure raises aggregate demand and wages on the one hand and interest rate and savings on the other. In boom phases there is an increase in the labour supply, but it is not caused by an increase in wages induced by excess demand. Wages, according to this line of thought, always coincide with the marginal productivity of labour, while the supply and demand of the services of all the factors equal each other at each moment. The main reason for the 'co-movements' of wages–employment–production is the rationality of workers' behaviour. Workers plan the supply of their own factor over a fairly long period, let us say one to two years. Therefore, as they are able to predict the future evolution of incomes, they tend to work more when wages are higher and less when they are lower. And the main reason for the persistence of the effects of exogenous shocks is this phenomenon of inter-temporal substitution of leisure.

9.3.4. Was it real glory?

Right from its birth and increasingly so as it acquired an audience, the new classical macroeconomics has been inundated with criticisms. Today all its weak points are known. Here we will list those which seem to us to be the most decisive. We will just note its ability to ignore constant attacks from empirical research: not all theoretical economists take a great deal of notice of such defects, and many believe that this is not an irremediable type of defect, as empirical research is incessant and there are almost no limits to what can be asked and obtained from it. The theoretical difficulties, however, are much more serious.

There are problems above all with the notion of rationality of expectations. In neomonetarist theory this concept is basically used to reduce to a calculable risk those effects that an *unpredictable* future may cause in the present, and which Keynes defined in terms of uncertainty. The new classical economists have simply denied the existence of this problem by assuming that economic subjects are able to consider in their own calculations the whole range of possible events. In other words, they assume that no 'residual uncertainty' can exist, an assumption which is certainly difficult to swallow.

Another important problem concerns the hypothesis of stationarity of the equilibrium towards which the economy made up of national economic agents converges. The theoretical model on which rational expectations are formed must represent an economy with a fairly persistent structure. Only in this case will individuals be justified in forming expectations on the basis of an estimate of 'fundamental' variables. Furthermore, it is necessary to hypothesize that there is one and only one correct model of the economy. This is a much less obvious hypothesis than it may seem at first sight. If the type of equilibrium to which the economy should converge itself depends on expectations, there will be not one but many rational-expectation equilibria, one for every expectation which is capable of self-fulfilment. There could even be a continuum of different theories; and the economic agents could use these to formulate their own predictions without being compelled to change their minds by the events caused by their actions.

Furthermore, rational-expectation models run up against serious problems of dynamic instability. In regard to this, the neomonetarists cannot behave in the same way as Friedman, simply *assuming* that the economy is always regulated by equilibrium prices and boldly ignoring disequilibrium dynamics and the connected problems of stability. This is because, besides the usual dynamic problems posed by the traditional Walrasian equilibrium model to which they make reference, other more specific problems arise when rational expectations are introduced. For example, the solutions of many rational-expectation models are of a 'saddle-point' type: there are an infinite number of paths that tend to lead the economy away from equilibrium and only one that brings it back. The neomonetarists were not frightened by this difficulty, and simply went ahead maintaining that the economy, whatever shock it may suffer, is always and instantaneously able to bring itself back onto that single, stable path. But a convincing justification for this way of reasoning has never been given.

A further problem of stability may arise when the process of expectation formation is described in terms of learning from errors. If the equilibrium towards which the economy should move itself depends on the expectations, it is possible that the changes in expectations generated by correction of errors may cause the equilibria to change explosively. Finally, the application of the rational-expectation hypothesis to the analysis of speculative behaviour on financial markets—perhaps the only real context in which it makes sense to use this hypothesis—can cause phenomena of self-fulfilling expectations, with all that this entails in terms of speculative 'bubbles', catastrophic crashes, etc.—possibilities that Keynes had already foreseen.

With all these reasons for concern, and others we have not had room to highlight, one can ask why the new classical macroeconomics was so widely accepted in the era of Reagan and Thatcher. One answer is immediate, the simplest and perhaps the truest: it was the era of Reagan and Thatcher. The neomonetarists were able to display a large and potent artillery of rhetorical devices, among which there was even the call to logic. But the effectiveness of this artillery was brought out by the triumph of neo-conservatism in the

1970s and 1980s and, in the profession, by the groundwork undertaken by Friedman's old monetarism.

However, the main reason for the success of neomonetarism, at least within academic circles, is the role it has played in the development of an extremely prestigious tradition: the 'neoclassical synthesis'. In the evolution of that tradition, the new classical macroeconomics has represented the final point of arrival. From the neoclassical synthesis the neomonetarists accepted the fundamental theoretical reference of the Walrasian general-equilibrium model, as well as a series of other convictions of some importance, such as that for which Keynes would not have the right of citizenship in a world of flexible prices and rational individuals. Early monetarism had already knocked down a few doors, showing, on the one hand, the implications of the 'flex-price' hypothesis for the predominance of supply (as against effective demand) in determining properties of the general equilibrium, and, on the other hand, the 'natural' character of those properties. The neomonetarists have accepted both these theoretical implications of traditional monetarism. What they added, thus completing the process of disengagement from Keynes, was the rational-expectation hypothesis, the only one plausible, in fact, in a world in which subjects are perfectly rational (in the neoclassical sense) and markets perfectly competitive. Thus, beginning from the distant 'Keynesian' premises of the neoclassical synthesis, it was impossible to avoid the extreme logical conclusions of the new classical economics. And the only real difference between fathers and sons, in the end, seems to be the different degrees of naïvety with which it is possible to believe in the realism of the flex-price hypothesis.

This also leads us to note, in defence of the new classical macroeconomics (if it can be called a defence), that a great many of its weaknesses, e.g. those relating to its way of treating uncertainty, and the hypotheses dealing with stationarity of equilibrium and its dynamic properties, are also weaknesses of many other neoclassical Keynesian models. The contribution of neomonetarism in bringing these to light could be considered a merit.

Finally, there are two additions to the modern theoretical economist's equipment which are due to the neomonetarists. The first is the systematic introduction into macroeconomics of the study of the processes of endogenous formation of expectations, together with the processes of elaboration and diffusion of information, which amounts to the addition of another important theoretical instrument to the toolbox of the economist: the economics of information. The second is extremely important: it is the 'policy-evaluation proposition'. According to this proposition Keynesian economic policies are mistakenly based on econometric models whose parameters are assumed stable. The parameters of the structural forms of the models are, in fact, derived from hypotheses about the behaviour and the decision-making rules of economic agents which are far from being a justification of their stability. In particular, in defining the functions to estimate, the expectations of the decision-making agents concerning the variables of the model are usually assumed as given. But if the expectations are endogenously formed, they will change with variations in the size of the variables and, above all, with variations in economic policy decisions. This means that the structural parameters are not stable, nor independent from the policies that their stability should justify. This not only pulls the rug out from under the feet of a great many neo-Keynesian discretionary economic policies but, more generally, undermines the theoretical bases of all econometric researches that are unable to take into account the endogenous formation of expectations.

9.4. FROM DISEQUILIBRIUM TO NON-WALRASIAN EQUILIBRIUM

9.4.1. Disequilibrium and the microfoundations of macroeconomics

In the 1960s it had become almost universally clear (except to the authors of textbooks) that the Walrasian equilibrium model was not able to do justice to Keynes. Already in 1956, Patinkin, in a book which presented a theoretical *summa* of the neoclassical synthesis, *Money, Interest and Prices*, had suggested that, as there was no space for Keynes in the general-equilibrium model, it was necessary to study disequilibrium situations to account for Keynesian problems. This suggestion was taken up by two economists who, though still following the neoclassical approach, in various articles published during the 1960s launched a powerful attack against the *IS-LM* model. Their intention was to search for the microeconomic foundations of Keynesian macroeconomics in the dynamics of disequilibrium. The economists in question are Robert Wayne Clower (b. 1926) and Axel Leijonhufvud (b. 1933). Their main works are Clower's 'The Keynesian Counter-Revolution: A Theoretical Appraisal' (1965) and 'A Reconsideration of the Microfoundations of Monetary Theory' (1967), both reprinted in *Selected Readings in Monetary Theory* (1969); and Leijonhufvud's *On Keynesian Economics and the Economics of Keynes* (1968) and *Keynes and the Classics* (1969).

Clower simply proposed to remove from the Walrasian approach the idea that exchanges are made in equilibrium. In equilibrium, all decisions of individuals are realized in such a way that they are compatible with each other. For this reason, 'planned' (or 'notional' or 'potential') demand coincides with actual demand. This correspondence disappears outside equilibrium. If the prices do not clear the markets, the individuals will not be able to buy or sell their planned quantities. In this way, the actual demand will be constrained by the monetary incomes actually realized. If the latter do not allow purchase of the quantities desired, expenditure plans must be revised. Thus, a type of 'decisional dualism' occurs. On the other hand, all transactions occur with the use of money, and this allows a clear separation between the decisions concerning the goods to demand and the goods to supply. Thus, instead of the traditional budget constraint which, in equilibrium, implies that the value of the supply of services must equal that of the demand for goods, the economic agent who operates in disequilibrium must be subjected to two different constraints. The first is an expenditure constraint which requires that the purchases are sustained by (non-negative) monetary balances; the second is an income constraint, and implies that the accumulation of liquid balances is limited by the ability to generate an income by means of the sale of goods and services. Thus the workers who do not succeed in selling all the labour services they wish may also be unable to buy all the consumer goods they would like. The firms will not then be able to sell all the goods produced. In this way, the initial excess demand can be transmitted through the whole economy by means of a multiplier process similar to that conceived by Keynes.

Leijonhufvud held a similar position to that of Clower; however he insisted that the multiplier process was essentially a phenomenon of illiquidity, i.e. a process generated by the lack of liquidity (with respect to the desired balances) occurring when exchanges take place outside equilibrium. Besides this, he emphasized, rather more than Clower, the role played by informative deficiencies as generating factors of the multiplication processes. This last point is important. Clower was not clear about one crucial question: whether rejection of the Walrasian model implied the abandonment of the auctioneer or *tâtonnement* or even Walras's Law. Leijonhufvud, by focusing on the lack of information generated by prices different from those in force in the Walrasian equilibrium, identified the key element in this theoretical approach and cleared the way for the models of non-Walrasian equilibrium formulated in the 1970s. The point is that it is not *tâtonnement* that must be abandoned, but the auctioneer.

Before describing this type of model, however, we should mention another type of non-Walrasian modelling which was also developed in the 1960s: that of the 'non-*tâtonnement* processes'. We should not speak of it in this section, as it has nothing to do with any kind of Keynesian matter; but it is useful to do so, if for no other reason than to prepare the field for a comparison. In the non-*tâtonnement* processes, in fact, exactly the opposite happens to what occurs in non-Walrasian models of equilibrium, of which we will speak in the next section: *tâtonnement* disappears but the auctioneer survives. The origin of this approach goes back to two works by Frank Hahn (b. 1925) and Takashi Negishi (b. 1933). The first is 'On the Stability of Pure Exchange Equilibrium' (*International Economic Review*, 1962), by Hahn; the second, 'A Theorem on Non-*Tâtonnement* Stability' (*Econometrica*, 1962), by Hahn and Negishi. The model, originally formulated with reference to a pure exchange economy, was later extended to a production economy by F. Fisher in 'The Hahn Process with Firms but no Production' (*Econometrica*, 1974), and in 'A Non-*Tâtonnement* Model with Production and Consumption' (*Econometrica*, 1976).

In this model the economic agents are price-takers; and the prices are fixed by an auctioneer. However, exchanges can also be undertaken at prices that do not clear the markets. Therefore, some agents may be rationed. After each exchange the auctioneer will calculate new prices; and on the basis of these the agents will take further decisions and undertake further exchanges. The economy moves through a sequence of periods. The data on the basis of which decisions are taken in one period (in particular the individual endowments of goods) depend on exchanges undertaken in the preceding period. Therefore, the equilibrium to which this sequential economy leads will generally be different from the Walrasian equilibrium. In fact, the latter depends exclusively on the initial data, and is not influenced by the *process* by which equilibrium is reached.

9.4.2. The non-Walrasian equilibrium models

In the Walrasian models the economic agents are price-takers both in equilibrium and in disequilibrium. Even at disequilibrium prices they continue to ignore any possible quantitative constraint on their own decisions, as they undertake exchanges only when equilibrium prices have been reached. On the other hand, prices are perfectly flexible: they are not set by any single economic agent, but are called by the auctioneer, who decides on them by observing the excesses of demand. Thus the agents are able to use prices 'parametrically', whether they are correct or mistaken. Only they continue to revise their own decisions until they reach the correct prices, i.e. those in force in the Walrasian equilibrium. The auctioneer, for his part, continues to modify the prices until all excess demand has been eliminated. Therefore the Walrasian equilibrium is an equilibrium, both in the sense that all excess demand has vanished in correspondence to a level of output that ensures the *full utilization of resources*, and in the sense that the economic agents are not induced to change their own decisions, so that there are no forces capable of modifying the equilibrium situation.

A 'non-Walrasian equilibrium', instead, is a state in which, although part of the resources remain unutilized, there may be no stimuli to induce agents to change their decisions. It is an equilibrium only in the sense that the economy, once it has reached that state, is not pushed away from it, or, rather, in the sense that individuals have realized, in a certain sense, their own plans. An equilibrium of this type can be reached in a theoretical context in which some basic hypotheses of the Walrasian equilibrium are abandoned, especially that dealing with price flexibility. The theory which follows from this can be called the theory of 'non-Walrasian equilibrium' or 'equilibrium with rationing'; but some people continue to call it the theory of 'disequilibrium', and others the theory of the '*K*-equilibrium', as if it had something to do with Keynes.

The most interesting models of this approach were formulated in the 1970s as a development of the contributions of Patinkin, Clower, and Leijonhufvud, and are due to Robert J. Barro (b. 1944), Herschel I. Grossman (b. 1939), Jean-Pascal Benassy (b. 1948), Jean-Michel Grandmont (b. 1939), Jaques H. J. M. E. Drèze (b. 1929), and Edmond Malinvaud (b. 1923). The classic texts are: 'A General Disequilibrium Model of Income and Employment' (*American Economic Review*, 1971) and *Money, Employment and Inflation* (1976), by Barro and Grossman; 'Neo-Keynesian Disequilibrium in a Monetary Economy' (*Review of Economic Studies*, 1975) by Benassy; 'Existence of an Equilibrium under Price Rigidity and Quantity Rationing' (*International Economic Review*, 1975) by Drèze; 'The Logic of the Fix-Price Method' (*Scandinavian Journal of Economics*, 1977) by Grandmont; and *The Theory of Unemployment Reconsidered* (1977) by Malinvaud.

Here we do not have room to deal with the internal evolution of the theory, which would have been interesting as only in the most recent work has it become clear that we are actually dealing with a theory of *equilibrium*. Nor have we time to dwell upon the marked differences between the models of the various authors. We will limit ourselves to presenting the maximum common denominator. Fig. 13 shows the curves of demand, D, and supply, S, of one commodity. The Walrasian equilibrium price is p^*. At price p_0 there is an excess demand $E_0 > 0$: the scissors have a 'long side', in this case the demand, and a 'short side', the supply. The short side is that in which the sum of the desired transactions is smaller. Thus at price p_1 the excess demand is negative, $E_1 < 0$, and the short side is that of demand. q_0 and q_1 are the 'effective' supply and demand in the two cases; q^* is the 'notional' demand.

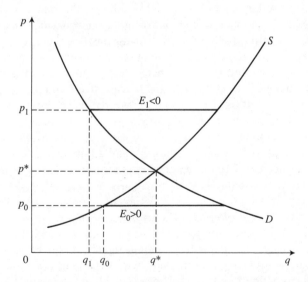

FIG. 13

Two hypotheses are made to define the method of exchange. The first is the hypothesis of *voluntary exchange*, which states that no agent is forced to exchange more than he wishes. The second is the hypothesis of *ordered markets*, or *frictionless markets*, according to which there can only be a discrepancy between desired and realized transactions for the agents who are on one of the two sides of the market. The 'short-side rule', derived from these two hypotheses, states that only the agents who are on the short side of the market succeed in realizing their plans. The agents unable to realize their own exchange plans are *rationed*. In a situation of excess supply, the sellers are rationed; in one of excess demand, the buyers are. The rationed agents are subject to quantitative constraints. Therefore, it is legitimate to assume that in the formulation of their own plans, they take into account the information concerning quantities as well as prices. A hypothesis made in Benassy-type versions is that the agents, in order to decide about the supply or the demand to present on a market, take into consideration the quantitative constraints perceived on other markets. So the worker, in deciding on the quantity of consumer goods to buy, will take into account the quantity of labour he actually sells. On the other hand, the entrepreneur will decide on the labour demand taking into consideration the quantity of goods he actually sells. In the Drèze-type versions, instead, the agents take into consideration the constraints perceived on all the markets. Now, if the prices at which the exchanges are undertaken are those determined by the Walrasian equilibrium, nobody would undergo quantitative constraints. However, if the prices are different, quantitative constraints will arise on all markets.

The key hypothesis of the non-Walrasian equilibrium models is that prices, or at least some of them, are *fixed*. It is basically for this reason that price and quantity signals enter into the functions of supply and demand. An equilibrium can be reached on the basis of such demand functions, but it is an unusual equilibrium. In it the subjects are not induced to modify their own decisions, for example by considering new or better possibilities of exchange, not because these do not exist, but because the perceived constraints induce them to believe they do not exist. Thus it is possible that unemployed workers convince themselves that there is no demand for labour, not even potentially, which is adequate to their own supply. They accept as permanent the income earned as unemployed or underemployed, and adjust their consumption demand to such incomes. The entrepreneurs, in turn, may think that the demand for goods determined in this way is normal, and therefore adjust the production and the labour demand to it. In this way the entrepreneurs justify the pessimistic evaluations of the workers, who, in turn, justify those of the entrepreneurs. A non-Walrasian equilibrium is a situation in which the 'effective' supply and demand formulated by economic agents, on the basis of price and quantity signals observed on the markets, are compatible. The demand is equal to the supply, but different from the 'notional' or 'potential' supply and demand, i.e. those that would be realized in a Walrasian equilibrium. On the other hand, the plans of the economic agents are actually fulfilled in a non-Walrasian equilibrium, and therefore there is no stimulus to modify them.

The particular kind of equilibrium which is reached will then depend on the particular hypotheses about which prices are fixed, which markets generate the quantitative constraints, and which agents are rationed. In this way, it is possible to have equilibria with 'Keynesian unemployment', in which both the prices of consumer goods and the money wages are fixed, and in which consumers are rationed on the labour market and firms on the goods markets. On the other hand, there are disequilibria with 'classical unemployment' when the *real* wages are 'too high' to guarantee full employment; in this case, while firms are rationed neither on the goods nor labour market, workers are rationed on both. There is also a particular type of equilibrium which seems able to account for the specific case considered by Keynes in the *General Theory*: that in which there are flexible prices for goods and rigid money wages. In this case, firms are not rationed on the goods markets, since prices are flexible. However, because of the unemployment generated by fixed money wages, the workers will be rationed on the labour market. And the 'Keynesian case' would be reduced to this. Is it not paradoxical that this was the fate of a line of research which originated from dissatisfaction with the neoclassical synthesis?

A strange destiny had awaited the neoclassical interpretations of Keynes. Beginning with the attempt to demonstrate that Keynes had studied a special case in which prices and/or wages are rigid, the neoclassicists created growing dissatisfaction among Keynesian economists and, through an incessant flow of polemics and counter-revolutions, they finally produced an evolution in thought which ended up by demonstrating that Keynes's case is precisely that in which prices and/or wages are rigid. The difference between the departure-point, the neoclassical synthesis, and the destination, equilibrium models with rationing, is that, in the former, Keynes was reinterpreted as a case of temporary Walrasian equilibrium, in the latter, as a case of temporary non-Walrasian equilibrium—a difference which is less remarkable than it first appears. On the other hand, in both cases, there are devastating repercussions for Keynes's *general* theory: as such, it simply does not exist.

9.5. POST-KEYNESIAN AND NEW KEYNESIAN APPROACHES

9.5.1. Anti-neoclassical reinterpretations of Keynes

It seems that there is a basic incompatibility between Keynesian and neoclassical theory. This is confirmed by the fact that all the economists who took Keynes seriously, and his conviction that he had formulated a general theory, ran up against problems with the neoclassical theoretical system.

Accepting a term which has become commonplace, even though inappropriate, we shall call the economists of this type 'post-Keynesian'. They do not make up a school of thought, nor do they share a common theoretical system. Rather, we are dealing with a group of economists with heterogeneous views, even in regard to the interpretation of Keynes. Perhaps one day a homogeneous post-Keynesian system will emerge from their work. At the moment, we must content ourselves with dividing them into two groups. The simplest classification distinguishes the European from the American post-Keynesians. The meeting point of the first group was the University of Cambridge, where a direct Keynesian tradition, formed in the early 1930s around the 'circus', has survived until very recently. The main members of this group are Richard Kahn (1905–90), Joan Robinson (1908–83), Nicholas Kaldor (1908–86), and Luigi Pasinetti (b. 1930). The second group gathered around the *Journal of Post-Keynesian Economics*. Its most important members are Paul Davidson (b. 1930), Hyman Minsky (b. 1919) and Sidney Weintraub (1919–84). A distant ancestor of all post-Keynesian economists is, however, the English economist G. L. S. Shackle (1903–1992). It is also worth mentioning another two economists who, at least partially, can be considered post-Keynesian: Lorie Tarshis (b. 1911) who, although graduating at Cambridge in Kaleckian economics, is a member of the American post-Keynesian group; and Kenneth Boulding (b. 1910), who, albeit from the other side of the Atlantic, made important contributions to the construction of the Cambridge theory of distribution. Finally we should mention Joseph Steindl (b. 1912), a 'Kaleckian' who is difficult to classify and who worked in an original way, especially on the theory of normal prices in monopoly conditions. The most recent generation of post-Keynesians, who are legion, especially in the USA, Great Britain, and Italy, are working on the difficult task of integrating the various components of post-Keynesian theories in the attempt to produce a complete and coherent theoretical system.

The most important difference between the two main groups concerns their favourite field of investigation, growth and distribution for the Europeans and monetary dynamics for the Americans. This leads to the presumption that the two groups are not basically incompatible and their theories might be complementary. Both groups, in their rejection of the neoclassical synthesis, have endeavoured to reinterpret Keynes by separating what is really Keynesian in the *General Theory* from the neoclassical and Marshallian residues. But they have taken this reinterpretation work in different directions.

The essence of Cambridge interpretation of Keynes has been well expressed in two works by Garegnani and Pasinetti. In 'Note su consumi, investimenti e domanda effettiva' (*Economia Internazionale*, 1964–5), Pierangelo Garegnani (b. 1930) put forward the idea that the principle of effective demand refers to an economy in a reproduction equilibrium. In this state, savings equal investments in such a way as to guarantee equilibrium between effective demand and the quantity supplied of *produced* goods, but not necessarily the full utilization of resources or full employment. The adjustment of savings to investments occurs through the variations in income caused by the investments themselves, and not through the determination of the interest rate. The latter is not an equilibrium value for the price of the capital services. The rejection of the neoclassical conception of interest led Garegnani to downgrade the notion of marginal efficiency of capital, and to accept the liquidity-preference theory only as an auxiliary construction, necessary to give an alternative explanation of interest. He also rejected the idea that Keynes's theory was of a short-run type, or, rather, argued that the principle of effective demand is of more value in the long run, when it makes sense to assume that the economy grows along an equilibrium path in which normal prices prevail.

Pasinetti moved along a similar interpretative line in 'The Economics of Effective Demand' (in *Growth and Income Distribution*, 1977), in which he endeavoured to reinterpret the *General Theory* from a Ricardian point of view, ending up by rediscovering in Keynes the power of the 'Ricardian vice'. By means of this, Keynes avoided being misled by the love of elegance and symmetry and aimed instead at investigating a few clear and simple causal relationships among the main economic variables. In this way he was able to identify the existence of a unidirectional causal chain which goes from money to consumption, passing through the determination of interest rate, investments, and the level of income.

Shackle's interpretation, as expressed above all in *Expectation in Economics* (1949), *Uncertainty in Economics* (1955), *Epistemics and Economics* (1972), and *The Years of High Theory* (1967), was completely different. The last book is especially important for its interpretation of Keynes. In his first works on uncertainty and 'crucial choices', Shackle rejected the probabilistic conceptions of expectations with the argument that choices, once made, destroy the possibility of repeating the experiments. The economic agents are aware of this fact, and therefore avoid formulating expectations about *all* possible events, and instead tend to focus their attention on *pairs* of objective possibilities which they judge to be particularly important. These possibilities concern events which, *ex ante* the economic agents judge potentially able (or unable) to produce surprises.

Uncertainty is also at the centre of Shackle's reinterpretation of Keynes; it is considered the principal factor of economic fluctuations and the basic cause of the intrinsically unstable nature of capitalism. The concept of marginal efficiency of capital is re-evaluated, from this point of view, but not before being reinterpreted in an anti-neoclassical sense. Shackle believes that the marginal efficiency of capital has nothing to do with the productivity of capital; instead, it is no more than a sort of 'psychic alchemy', a mental construction by means of which the entrepreneurs try to deduce from basically non-rational expectations some evaluation criteria about the convenience of investments. When facing uncertainty, intended as the awareness of the surprises that may be produced by unpredictable events, the entrepreneurs' expectations are ephemeral and volatile. This is the cause of the basic instability of capitalism. Obviously, from this point of view the liquidity-preference theory plays an important role, as, given the impossibility of reducing uncertainty to risk, money is an indispensable insurance instrument in the face of unpredictable events. As such, however, money can also contribute to economic instability, in that liquidity preference and the irrational behaviour of speculators may amplify the depressive effects of uncertainty and the lack of confidence of entrepreneurs. Therefore it is important to study the functions it accomplishes in economic activity, above all the way in which its production and control is organized.

9.5.2. Distribution and growth

A great many of the Cambridge post-Keynesian theories were developed in the 1950s and 1960s as polemics against the neoclassical growth models of the Solow–Swan type. The polemic manifested itself first of all in an attack on the neoclassical theory of capital and distribution. However, this part of the debate used as its main reference point the Sraffian theoretical approach rather than the post-Keynesian in its strict sense; and we shall therefore deal with it in Chapter 11.

The specific contribution of the post-Keynesians, instead, consisted in the formulation of an alternative theory of growth and distribution. This theory can be traced back to the 'widow's cruse' theorem, according to which the incomes earnt by capitalists ultimately depend only on their expenditure. As we saw in Chapter 7, there is a Keynesian and a Kaleckian version of this theorem. The main difference between the two concerns the level of output, which Keynes, in the *Treatise*, assumed fixed at full employment, while Kalecki maintained it to be at an underemployment level. Post-Keynesian theory was born of the attempt to extend the results of that theorem to a theoretical context in which the level of income *increases* over time.

The Kaleckian conception was developed especially in Robinson's 'open' models. The classic texts are *The Accumulation of Capital* (1956) and some articles (particularly 'Normal Prices' and 'A Model of Accumulation') collected together in *Essays in the Theory of Economic Growth* (1962). In the models of growth with unemployment and under-utilization of plant, the key hypothesis is that prices are fixed by applying the mark-up rule to direct costs, which are assumed constant. This means that, given the techniques, the distribution of income is determined by the price policies of the firms, and depends on the average degree of monopoly prevailing in the economy. In her later formulations, Robinson tried to reduce the importance attributed to the structure of markets and, by developing some of Kalecki's suggestions, focussed on the role played by trade unions. She then linked the average mark-up, and therefore the distribution of income, to the power relationships among social classes. In any case, in the presence of unemployment the distribution of income turns out to be independent of the levels of output, or its rate of growth. In the simplifying hypothesis that all wages are consumed, profits will be determined in such a way as to provide the flow of finance necessary to sustain the growth of capital. Therefore, profits depend on investments, while the rate of profit depends on the capital–output ratio and the growth rate of incomes. If neutral technical progress is assumed, in such a way as to assure a constant capital–output ratio, all that is needed to 'close' the model is knowledge of the behaviour of capitalists concerning investments. But this is exactly what the economic theory does not allow us to determine endogenously. Investment decisions depend on the 'animal spirits' of the capitalists, a social-psychological variable which has a rather more Marxian than Keynesian flavour. The economy may grow at any rate: it can be an equilibrium rate, or warranted, in the Harrod–Domar sense, but it does not necessarily ensure full employment.

Robinson considered growth with full employment as a limiting case which is difficult to obtain in a *laissez-faire* regime. This limiting case was defined, with a little irony, as the 'golden age'. A golden-age economy with neutral technical progress would grow in steady state, i.e. all the variables would grow at the same rate, including employment 'in efficiency units'. Full employment would be ensured by a growth rate of income equal to that of the stock of capital, and also equal to the sum of the growth rates of population and labour productivity. The golden-age growth model is 'closed'. In it, investment decisions are rescued from the volatile moods of the entrepreneurs and are determined endogenously in the same way as those which guarantee steady-state growth. Two hypotheses must be made to obtain this result: 'perfect foresight' and 'perfect tranquillity'. The former serves to eliminate uncertainty, the latter ensures that expectations can be formulated correctly. Both can be reduced to the *assumption* that the economy grows in a steady state. The circular nature of the argument should not be surprising. And this is one of the things that Robinson wished to show: in order to have steady-state growth, the economy must always have grown in a steady state.

Kaldor was less sceptical about the ability of the capitalist economy to grow with full employment. Thus, he made greater efforts than Robinson to account for the proper conditions of steady-state growth. His principal contributions to the construction of the post-Keynesian theory of growth and distribution are to be found in the following articles: 'Alternative Theories of Distribution' (*Review of Economic Studies*, 1956), 'A Model of Economic Growth' (*Economic Journal*, 1957), 'Capital Accumulation and Economic Growth' (in *The Theory of Capital*, edited by F. A. Lutz and D. C. Hague, 1961), and 'A New Model of Economic Growth' (written with J. A. Mirlees and published in *Review of Economic Studies*, 1962).

Kaldor preferred the Keynesian to the Kaleckian version of the widow's-cruse theorem. He believed that, in a process of growth with full employment and full utilization of capacity, it is impossible to separate the problem of income distribution from that of growth, as had occurred in Robinson's open model. The economy cannot grow, in real terms, more rapidly than the natural rate. Assume that it does not grow less rapidly. Then the growth rate of capital stock is endogenously determined. Assuming there are two classes of income-earners, the profits-earners and the wage-earners, with the former's propensity to consume lower than that of the latter, the distribution of income must be determined endogenously in such a way as to ensure flows of savings sufficient to finance investments. At any given moment, the higher the investment rate (in relation to income), the higher the profit share will be; and this is so because a higher percentage of profits are saved than of wages, and only a higher profit share is able to guarantee a higher percentage of savings on aggregate income.

This result is also valid for a growing economy. In an economy which is growing in equilibrium, the growth rate of wealth is equal to that of the capital stock.

$$\frac{S}{K} = \frac{I}{K}$$

Under the 'classical savings hypothesis', $S = s_p P$, where s_p is the propensity to save out of profits. Therefore

$$\frac{S}{K} = \frac{s_p P}{K} = \frac{I}{K}$$

from which the famous 'Cambridge distributive equation' is obtained:

$$r = \frac{g_n}{s_p}$$

The rate of profit, $r = P/K$, only depends on the expenditure decisions of the capitalists, i.e. on their propensity to save and their investment decisions, being $g_n = I/K = \Delta I/I$.

The demonstration that this result does not depend on the restrictive classical savings hypothesis was given by Pasinetti in 'Rate of Profit and Income Distribution in Relation to the Rate of Growth' (*Review of Economic Studies*, 1962). Let us consider an economy in which there are only two social classes, workers and capitalists. Their propensity to consume, s_l and s_c respectively, is such that $0 < s_l < I/Y < s_c < 1$. Then the workers will also be owners of capital, as they accumulate wealth by savings. Therefore they will earn profits (dividends and interest), besides wages. Pasinetti demonstrated that the savings made by the workers from their wages and their own profits coincide with the reduction in the capitalists' savings because the capitalists themselves do not receive all the profits. It is as if, by paying the workers part of the profits, the capitalists had partially delegated to them the function of saving. The amount the capitalists save less, the workers save more. Therefore, in regard to the financing of investments it does not matter whether the workers save or not, or whether they receive part of the profits or not. The distribution of income between wages and profits remains determined by the expenditure decisions of the capitalists, and the Cambridge equation still holds true.

A special feature of the post-Keynesian models of growth, which they share with the Harrod–Domar model, concerns the capital–output ratio which is a constant. This is not a simplifying hypothesis but, rather, an essential property of these models. In fact, by means of it, any possibility of accounting for the distribution of income on the basis of the substitution principle is radically eliminated, while a complete alternative to the Solow–Swan type of growth theory is given. Kaldor made the greatest effort to legitimate the assumption of a constant capital–output ratio, and tried to give it an empirical justification as well as a theoretical explanation. From historical observation, Kaldor came to the conclusion that in the course of its evolution capitalist accumulation had been governed by a series of empirical regularities which he defined as 'stylized facts'. Particularly important are those relating to the constancy of the wage share and the profit rate, both properties of steady-state growth models. Constancy in the capital–output ratio is also included in his list of stylized facts.

The problem is how to explain these facts. The technical-progress function was invented by Kaldor, in part, to answer this question. The function relates the growth rate of labour productivity, $\dot{y}$, with that of the capital–labour ratio, $\dot{k}$, and has the form $\dot{y} = \phi(\dot{k})$. This function is assumed to be increasing at a decreasing rate, as shown in Fig. 14. There is a point at which $\dot{y}$ and $\dot{k}$ grow at the same rate and therefore the capital–labour ratio is constant; this is point E, where the function cuts the bisector line of the quadrant. The economy tends to stabilize at this point. In fact, if it were to the left of this point, production (and aggregate demand) would grow more rapidly than the stock of capital, which would create optimistic profit expectations and would make the capitalists more dynamic. Investments, the stock of capital, and the capital–labour ratio would increase, causing a movement towards the right along the technical-progress function. If, instead, it were to the right of point E, this would mean that aggregate demand was increasing less rapidly than the stock of capital. The capitalists would expect a reduction in the rate of profit and would slow down their investment activity. The economy would again converge towards point E. At this point, not only the capital–output ratio but also the expected rate of profit must be constant (and equal to the actual one). The economy will grow in steady state, and in 'perfect tranquillity'—as Robinson would say.

We cannot close this section without mentioning a recent work by Pasinetti, *Structural Change and Economic Growth* (1981), in which, by taking up a research project already launched in 1965 in 'A New Theoretical Approach to the Problems of Economic Growth' (*Pontificia Academia Scientiarum*), he made an ambitious attempt to integrate the post-Keynesian theory of growth with some theoretical implications of the approaches of Leontief, von Neumann, and Sraffa. The post-Keynesian growth model was disaggregated in order to account for the evolution of an economy composed of various productive sectors. The population grows at a constant exogenous rate. Productivity also grows at a constant exogenous rate, but this is not uniform over the various sectors. The demand for consumer goods varies according to an Engel's Law modified to take into account new goods. The economy grows in equilibrium if it is able to ensure two conditions: first of all, productive

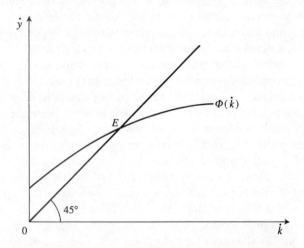

FIG. 14

capacity must grow in each sector to satisfy sectorial demand; second, aggregate demand must grow in such a way as to absorb the investment goods producible over and above the production of consumer goods.

An economy obeying these conditions will grow in 'natural' equilibrium. It will obviously be unbalanced growth. The sectorial profit rates, which are dependent on the production techniques, will not be uniform. Wages, as in other post-Keynesian models, remain determined residually.

9.5.3. Money and the instability of the capitalist economy

Even though they can be traced back to the solid tradition of the Radcliffe Report of the Committee on the Working of the Monetary System (London 1959) and, even more so, to Keynes's various ideas on the endogenous nature of the money supply, the modern post-Keynesian monetary theories were mainly formulated in the 1970s and the early 1980s. But it is worth noting that one of the first important contribution to the elaborations of these theories was given by Tobin in 1963, and it is to be found in his famous article, 'Commercial Banks as Creators of Money' (in *Banking and Monetary Studies*, edited by D. Carson), in which he sketched out some fundamental theoretical presuppositions of a theory of endogenous money supply. However, this was only an embryo of a theory, and continued for some time to live its embryonic life. Then the happy event occurred in the early 1970s, the monetarist discovery of the anticipation of money with regard to income acting as the midwife. Friedman's discovery concerned the fact that the rate of variation of the money supply occurs in cycles similar to those of income, and precede them systematically, even though at variable time-spans. The monetarist explanation was that there is a causal link from money to income—an explanation which, supported as it was by empirical evidence, went on to form one of the main points of the monetarist attack on *neo*-Keynesian theory.

The *post*-Keynesian theories, however, not only came out of this debate unscathed but were even exalted by the monetarist discovery. In fact, a theory that makes the level of income depend on the autonomous decisions of the entrepreneurs is naturally induced to assume that the money supply varies endogenously in relation to the demand for investment finance. From the post-Keynesian point of view, there is a double causal link which moves from investments to the demand for money and from investments to aggregate demand. If the money supply adjusts promptly to demand, then its variations *must* anticipate those in income. In fact, the Keynesian multiplier transmits the investment impulse to income only after a certain delay. The two most important contributions to emerge from that debate were Kaldor's 'The New Monetarism' (*Lloyds Bank Review*, 1970) and Tobin's 'Money and Income: Post Hoc ergo Propter Hoc?' (*Quarterly Journal of Economics*, 1970). The next stages in the development of post-Keynesian monetary theory were made up of several interesting contributions, for example: *Monetary Management: Principles and Practice* (1971), by A. B. Cramp; *Money and the Real World* (1972) by Davidson; various papers by Weintraub written in the 1970s and later collected in *Keynes, Keynesians and Monetarists* (1978); various papers by Minsky also written in the 1970s and collected in *Can 'It' Happen Again? Essays on Instability and Finance* (1982), as well as his *John Maynard Keynes* (1975), which is on the way to becoming a classic; and finally, *Origins of the New Monetarism* (1980) and *The Scourge of Monetarism* (1982) by Kaldor.

The endogenous nature of the money supply has ambivalent effects on the dynamics of the capitalist economy: on the one hand, it allows for growth in investment to go beyond the immediate capacity of self-financing; on the other, by doing so, it exacerbates the intrinsic instability of a *laissez-faire* regime, e.g. by creating the conditions for catastrophic financial crises and drastic interruptions in growth. Davidson pointed out that financial intermediaries and the banking system undertake an essential role in the mechanism which allows firms to mobilize resources for accumulation. The existence of a flow of savings corresponding to the desired real accumulation is neither a sufficient nor a necessary condition for that accumulation to be realized. What is necessary is that savings, or, better, finance, flows to the industrial circuit in an adequate amount, so as to prevent the liquidity preference of the public from braking the 'animal spirits' of the capitalists. The realization of this condition depends largely on the working of the banking system. So, in a period of increases in liquidity preference on the part of savers, a steady-state growth in capital stock will require an increase in the quantity of money which is higher than that needed by capital accumulation, in such a way that both the demand coming from the financial circuit and that coming from the industrial circuit is satisfied.

The destabilizing effects the structure of the financial system can have on the real economy have been studied in depth by Minsky, an economist who has recently put forward, besides an original reinterpretation of Keynes as a theorist of financial instability, an interesting theory of the crisis reminiscent of the earliest lessons of Marshall and Fisher (see section 7.1.2). At the centre of Minsky's theory is the Keynesian distinction between 'debtor risk' or the risk of the entrepreneur, which is that of not realizing his own profit expectations and, therefore, of being unable to repay his debts, and 'creditor risk', which is that of being unable to get the loans repaid. With the hypothesis of increasing risk, of Kaleckian origin, Minsky justified the existence of a decreasing curve for the marginal efficiency of capital, or the demand price of capital. Such a curve, defined over the aggregate of all the firms, and assuming the entrepreneurs' expectations given at level $\overline{E}$, is represented as $P_d(\overline{E})$ in Fig. 15. A hypothesis of increasing risk for creditors was used to justify the existence of an increasing curve of supply price of capital, such as $P_s(\overline{E})$. Curve Q is an equilateral hyperbola, and represents the expectations of self-financing at a given moment.

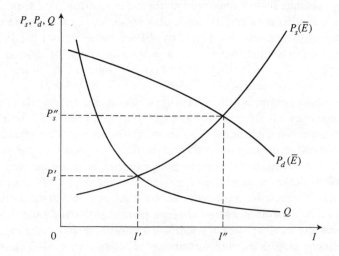

FIG. 15

If the firms limited themselves to self-financed investments, these would be fixed at level I', where the supply price, P_s', is equal to what can be paid by resorting to internal finance. But the demand price is higher; therefore, the firms are induced to expand the investments by running into debt. At the I'' level of investments the firms will run up debts to finance investments of the value of $P_s''I'' - P_s'I'$. During phases of economic expansion, the state of confidence of capitalists improves, $\overline{E}$ will increase, and the curves $P_d(\overline{E})$ and $P_s(\overline{E})$ will shift to the right. This will increase investments, but also the indebtedness and financial burdens of the firms. Thus, as the boom progresses, the *financial fragility* of the system increases. Financial fragility can be measured in terms of the ratio between indebtedness of and income produced by firms. It increases in a boom, when the risk increases of the need to refinance an increasing volume of long-term indebtedness with short-term debt. Then the expectations of a downturn in the business cycle are sufficient to cause a financial crisis. Given the high level of indebtedness and the concatenation of the debts of firms, both industrial and financial, any attempt of one of them to reinforce its own liquidity position by reducing expenditure will reflect negatively on the other firms. Besides this, any attempt to make the portfolios more liquid will increase the supply of long-run financial assets and thus lower their value. This will increase the cost of finance and give the economy further deflationary impulses. The consequences will be catastrophic: cumulative processes of reduction in investments, in income, and in the availability of internal finance, possibly accompanied by chain bankruptcies and financial crashes. So a slight downturn in the real economic cycle, even if expected, can cause a collapse. This, in Minsky's social philosophy, should justify the adoption of cautious *monetary management* policies, which is exactly the opposite to those demanded by the monetarists. And, in this view, if a crisis such as that of 1929 has never occurred since, the credit is due to the adoption of Keynesian-type monetary policies by the governments of the principal capitalist countries.

9.5.4. The new Keynesian approaches

Perhaps this is the right place to say something about the ideas developed by John Hicks after his 'conversion' around the middle of the 1960s—a conversion which requires a more extensive reinterpretation by historians than is possible in an outline such as ours. However, it is already possible to see that it must have been much more drastic than it seemed at first sight, a conversion that induced the great neoclassical economist to judge as 'a piece of rubbish' the theses on the functional distribution of income which he had himself formulated in 1932 in the *Theory of Wages* (theses which are still today taught in the orthodox economic textbooks). That same conversion led him to reconsider the general theoretical significance of methodological individualism and the hypothesis of individual maximizing behaviour, besides inducing him to reject the interpretation of Keynes based on his old *IS-LM* model. And if all this is not enough to justify the classification (albeit spurious) of the 'second Hicks' within the post-Keynesian approach, there are also some other skilful and courageous changes of attitude: his prompt acceptance of the Cambridge criticism of the neoclassical theory of capital (in *Capital and Growth*, 1965 —although it had already been anticipated in s. 24 of the mathematical appendix of *Value and Capital!*); his use of the method of vertically integrated sectors and his formulation of non-steady-state growth models (in *Capital and Time*, 1973); and, finally, his most recent reconsideration of the theory of money, in *A Market Theory of Money* (published posthumously in 1989).

But the arguments which most interest us here are those concerning Hicks's criticism of the *IS-LM* model and the elaboration of the theoretical bases of the fix-price approach. The *IS-LM* model was rejected basically for two reasons: first, because the role played by liquidity preference, as Keynes intended it, in the determination of the dynamics of employment cannot be adequately understood in a static temporary equilibrium model, such as the *IS-LM*; second, because it makes no sense to determine the macroeconomic equilibrium by means of two curves, one of which expresses a condition of flow equilibrium and the other a condition of stock equilibrium. The fix-price approach, proposed in *Capital and Growth* and taken up again in *The Crisis in Keynesian Economics* (1974), goes well beyond the traditional neoclassical argument that the results obtained by Keynes depend on the abandonment of the hypothesis of perfect competition, and also goes beyond the observation that most Keynesian macroeconomic modelling, beginning from the theory of the multiplier, presupposes an implicit hypothesis of fixed prices. Hicks's objective was much more ambitious, since he rejected *en bloc* the neoclassical theory of price formation in a competitive regime, a theory which, assuming that economic agents are all *price-takers*, needed to invent an imaginary auctioneer to account for the process of price-setting. According to the later Hicks, it is only in particular markets, speculative ones, that the traditional flex-price hypotheses make sense. In industrial goods markets, on the contrary, prices are set by the agents themselves, who modify them by responding to economic signals such as variations in wages and other prices. This does not mean that these prices are 'rigid', but only that they do not change so fast (i.e. 'instantaneously') as the neoclassical microeconomic textbooks would lead us to believe. The main consequence is that it is necessary to reject the widespread prejudice of Marshallian origin (even though Marshall was not a theorist of the auctioneer), according to which price variations predominate in short-run adjustments and quantity variations in long-run adjustments. It seems to us that this conclusion pushes the re-evaluation of Keynes thought far beyond what would have been allowed by the theoretical bases of which the Marshallian Keynes himself was aware.

The fix-price approach enjoyed wide success in the 1970s and 1980s. Apart from the non-Walrasian equilibrium models, which were, at least in part, inspired by it, or the post-Keynesian models, which adopted the fix-price hypothesis long before Hicks had reproposed it, in the last 20 years a stream of thought has developed which has placed this hypothesis at the centre of macroeconomic analysis, pushing it further along the road opened by Hicks, especially in the search for *micro*economic justifications. It is still difficult to say whether studies moving in this direction will lead to the construction of a homogeneous theoretical system. Certainly, they cannot all be assimilated into the post-Keynesian approaches, especially on account of the presence of various marginalist theoretical residues. On the other hand, all these authors have, in common with the post-Keynesians, a critical attitude towards monetarism and neomonetarism, as well as the desire to reconstruct macroeconomics on Keynesian bases. Lacking a better option, and well aware of the danger of misrepresenting particular authors by using a label, we will follow common use and group them under the term 'new Keynesian'.

The first group of these authors, which includes economists such as M. N. Baily, D. F. Gordon, C. Azariadis, and A. M. Okun, has been working on the theory of 'implicit contracts'. According to this approach, workers are more risk-averse than entrepreneurs. The latter therefore tend to take on the responsibility for that part of the risk which workers would encounter in a perfectly competitive market, where wages would change sharply. Thus they offer workers implicit contracts according to which wages are maintained stable through time. One of the main consequences of this is that, in periods of recession, the entrepreneurs, rather than reducing wage-levels, tend to dismiss some of their employees.

The most important theoretical effort in this direction has been made by Okun in 'Inflation: Its Mechanics and Welfare Costs' (*Brookings Papers on Economic Activity*, 1975) and in *Prices and Quantities* (1982), in which he tried, on the one hand, to extend the theory of implicit contracts from the labour to the product market and, on the other, to account for the formation of such contracts in terms of information cost rather than risk-aversion. It is basically because information is imperfect and expensive that agents tend to enter into long-term implicit contracts, trying in this way to save on the cost of information. Okun developed Hicks's distinction between 'flex-price' and 'fix-price', transforming it into that between 'auction' and 'customer' markets. In the former, prices are determined by supply and demand. In the latter, they are fixed by the sellers and kept stable for as long as possible, through the establishment of implicit contracts which aim at preserving a particular clientele of the firm. 'Customer' markets allow firms to economize both on the use of plant and on the cost of acquiring and supplying information about their own product markets (market research, advertising, etc.). Okun made a similar distinction to that between 'auction' and 'customer markets' with regard to the labour market, extending the theory of 'dual labour markets' already put forward by P. B. Doeringer and M. J. Piore. There exist both competitive labour markets and labour markets internal to the firm ('career markets'). In the latter, firms offer workers long-term wage contracts which are slightly higher and more stable with respect to those prevailing in the markets external to the firm. In this way the firm aims, on the one hand, to encourage the workers to be more efficient and, on the other, to keep workers' abilities within the firm. When the economy enters into a period of recession, the firms do not reduce wages, but dismiss the most inefficient and least-qualified workers.

Here we should mention three further groups of economists who have tried to attack the neomonetarists by using their own weapons and adopting the rational-expectations hypothesis. The rejection of the hypothesis of flexible prices has been their main weapon of attack.

The first of these groups is made up of economists who have investigated the theoretical implications of a fact which is obvious and yet disregarded by the neomonetarists: that labour contracts, even when indexed, are defined on a nominal basis and are, in any case, long-term contracts. Of particular importance in this line of research is the work by J. Gray ('Wage Indexation: A Macroeconomic Approach', *Journal of Monetary Economics*, 1976) and S. Fischer ('Long Term Contracts, Rational Expectations and the Optimal Money Supply Rule', *Journal of Political Economy*, 1977). The result reached by this strand of thought is that, contrary to what the neomonetarists asserted, particular monetary policy measures can be effective, even if perfectly predicted by the economic agents, simply because the duration of the labour contract and/or the level of indexation can hinder a quick and full adjustment of wages to the expected effects of the policy.

This line of thought was further developed in the theory of 'staggered' labour contracts, recently put forward by J. B. Taylor in 'Staggered Wage Setting in a Macro Model' (*American Economic Review*, 1979). In this approach all the contracts are long-term, but not all expire on the same date. Furthermore, it is assumed that the worker does not exclusively aim at maximizing his own wage, but also endeavours to maintain certain 'relativities' with other workers. Let us assume that a restrictive monetary policy leads to a reduction in the aggregate demand at time t. The workers who renew their contracts in t, having rational expectations, know that, say, at time $t + \delta$ the economic policy will become expansive again. If they accept a reduction in their nominal wage in t, this will allow for a reduction in prices. But in this way their real wages will diminish with respect to those workers who will renew their contracts in time $t + \delta$, for whom the nominal wage will not decrease between t and $t + \delta$. Therefore they will refuse a reduction in their nominal wage, so as to avoid a change in their relative position; they will prefer to accept an increase in unemployment. In this way it is possible to understand why monetary policy is able to produce real effects even in the presence of rational expectations.

Another group of theories worth mentioning here is that which has developed the analysis of costs for the adjustment of prices, or the 'small-menu costs' approach. Important contributions to this approach have been made by economists such as B. T. McCallum, N. G. Mankiw, O. J. Blanchard, N. Kiyotaki, G. Akerlof, and J. Yellen. The costs for the adjustment of prices are those a firm must sustain in order to modify the prices of its own products when conditions of demand or production vary. There are various types of cost, for example those connected with the updating of payrolls and price lists, those sustained in changing labels of products, and those caused by loss of confidence on the part of customers who face continuous price changes and over-complicated contracts. Firms try to avoid these costs, even if they are small in relation to product prices. To do so they tend to fix their prices and to hold them stable for as long as possible. So, when facing temporary changes in demand, they modify production levels, utilization of plant, and levels of inventories, rather than product prices. It is this phenomenon which gives real efficacy to short-term monetary policies.

Finally, one of the most interesting recent microeconomic approaches to the problem of unemployment is that of efficiency wages. The basic idea here is that labour productivity increases with wages. An early theory of efficiency wages in the developing countries was put forward in 1957 by J. Leibenstein in *Economic Backwardness and Economic Growth*. The argument was that, given the subsistence levels of the wages prevailing in the developing countries, an increase in them would improve the standard of living and the health of the workers and therefore would increase their work performance. In the 1970s various attempts were made to generalize this theory and extend it to industrial countries, for example by Phelps, Stiglitz, Calvo, and Solow. Finally, in the early 1980s, a comprehensive formulation was reached in works by Akerlof, Shapiro, Stiglitz, Yellen, and others.

The theory of efficiency wages is based on three principal ideas. The first is that the intensity of the work effort of each employee, and therefore the marginal productivity of labour, increases with an increase in wages. The second is that the workers' effort is also influenced by the level of unemployment, in that the fear of being dismissed for inefficiency increases with an increase in the probability of not immediately finding another job with the same pay—a probability that rises with the level of unemployment. The third hypothesis is that there is a type of asymmetric information, as firms are not able directly to ascertain the intensity of effort of each worker. In these conditions it is in the interest of firms to pay high wages to encourage workers' effort. Wages, by hypothesis, are equal to the marginal productivity of labour. However, if there is unemployment the firms are not induced to lower wages and to take on unemployed people since, if they did so, they would induce a reduction in the efficiency of the workers employed. Whereas, if aggregate demand decreases, it is not in the interest of the firms to reduce wages, since by doing so they would trigger an adverse selection process: they would lose their best workers, who would begin to look for more highly paid jobs. Thus, firms tend to leave wages unchanged and lay off the excess labour force. Furthermore, as firms are not able to ascertain individual levels of effort, they would choose to lay off workers randomly. Therefore, wages would not only be high, i.e. higher than those which would guarantee full employment, but would also be fairly rigid; and this is the simple consequence of the rational choice of the firms. On the other hand, unemployment continues to exist, as the fear of losing one's job is one of the factors that stimulates the workers' efforts. There is no Pareto efficiency in this type of equilibrium, owing to the presence of unemployment; but firms maximize profits also thanks to unemployment.

Bibliography

On the neoclassical synthesis: G. Ackley, *Macroeconomic Theory* (New York, 1961); W. Branson, *Macroeconomic Theory and Policy* (New York, 1979); F. S. Brooman, *Macroeconomics* (London, 1962); V. Chick, *Macroeconomics after Keynes* (Oxford, 1983); H. Jones, *Modern Theories of Economic Growth* (London, 1975); L. R. Klein, *The Keynesian Revolution* (New York, 1966); D. M. McDougall and T. E. Dernburg, *Macroeconomics* (New York, 1960); I. Osadchaya, *From Keynes to Neoclassical Synthesis: A Critical Analysis* (Moscow, 1974); A. Roncaglia and M. Tonveronachi, 'The Pre-Keynesian Roots of the Neoclassical Synthesis', *Cahiers d'économie politique* (1985); R. M. Solow, *Growth Theory: An Exposition* (London, 1970); H. Y. Wan, Jr., *Economic Growth* (New York, 1971); W. Young, *Interpreting Mr. Keynes: The IS-LM Enigma* (London, 1987).

On monetarism: K. Brunner, 'The "Monetarist revolution" in Monetary Theory', *Wirtschaftlisches Archiv* (1970); 'A Survey of Selected Issues in Monetary Theory,' *Schweizerische Zeitschrift für Volkswirtschaft und Statistik* (1971); F. R. Glahe, *Macroeconomics: Theory and Policy* (New York, 1973); R. J. Gordon (ed.), *Milton Friedman's Monetary Framework* (Chicago, 1970); H. G. Johnson, 'The Keynesian Revolution and the Monetarist Counter-Revolution', *American Economic Review*, 61 (1971); T. Mayer, *The Structure of Monetarism* (New York, 1978); 'Some Reflections on the Current State of the Monetarist Debate', *Zeitschrift für Nationalökonomie*, 50 (1978); A. J. Meigs, *Money Matters* (New York, 1972); M. Monti (ed.), *The New Inflation and Monetary Policy* (London, 1976); R. L. Teigen, 'Some Observations on Monetarist Analysis', *Kredit und Kapital* (1971).

On the new classical macroeconomics: D. K. Begg, *The Rational Expectations Revolution in Macroeconomics* (Oxford, 1982); K. A. Chrystal, *Controversies in Macroeconomics* (Oxford, 1979); S. Fischer, 'Recent Developments in Macroeconomics', *Economic Journal*, 98 (1988); K. Hoover, *The New Classical Macroeconomics: A Sceptical Inquiry* (London, 1988); R. Maddock and M. Carter, 'A Child's Guide to Rational Expectations', *Journal of Economic Literature*, 14 (1982); T. J. Sargent, *Macroeconomic Theory* (New York, 1979); S. M. Sheffrin, *Rational Expectations* (Cambridge, 1982); *The Making of Economic Policy: History, Theory, Politics* (Oxford, 1988); J. B. Taylor, 'Rational Expectations Models in Macroeconomics', in J. K. Arrow and S. Hankapohja (eds.), *Frontiers of Economics* (Oxford, 1985).

On disequilibrium and non-Walrasian equilibrium models: L. P. Benassy, *The Economics of Market Disequilibrium* (New York, 1982); *Macroeconomics: An Introduction to the Non-Walrasian Approach* (London, 1986); R. F. Cippà and V. Guidi, 'Temporary Equilibrium with Rationing', in M. Baranzini (ed.), *Advances in Economic Theory* (Oxford, 1982); D. Gale, *Money: In Equilibrium* (Cambridge, 1982); *Money: In Disequilibrium* (Cambridge, 1983); A. G. Hines, *On the Reappraisal of Keynesian Economics* (London, 1971); E. Malinvaud, *Théorie macroéconomique* (Paris, 1982); J. Muellbauer and R. Portes, 'Macroeconomic Models with Quantity Rationing', *Economic Journal*, 88 (1978): C. Walsh, 'New Views on Business Cycles', *Federal Reserve Bank of Philadephia* (1984).

On post-Keynesian and new Keynesian theories: P. Davidson, 'Post-Keynesian Economics', in D. Bell and I. Kristol (eds.), *The Crisis in Economic Theory* (New

York, 1981); M. Dotsey and R. G. King, 'Business Cycles', in *The New Palgrave*, i (London, 1987); A. S. Eichner, *A Guide to Post-Keynesian Economics* (Armonk, NY, 1979); A. S. Eichner and J. A. Kregel, 'An Essay on Post-Keynesian Theory: A New Paradigm in Economics', *Journal of Economic Literature*, 7 (1975); J. K. Galbraith, *Economics in Perspective* (New York, 1987); O. F. Hamouda and G. C. Harcourt, 'Post Keynesianism: From Criticism to Coherence?', *Bulletin of Economic Research*, 4 (1988); A. Klamer, 'An Accountant among Economists: Conversations with Sir John Hicks', *Journal of Economic Perspectives*, 2 (1989); J. A. Kregel, *The Reconstruction of Political Economy: An Introduction to Post-Keynesian Economics* (London, 1973); 'Post-Keynesian Theory: An Overview', *Journal of Economic Education*, 3 (1983); R. Marris, *Reconstructing Keynesian Economics with Imperfect Competition* (Aldershot, 1991); E. S. Phelps, *Seven Schools of Macroeconomic Thought* (Oxford, 1990); A. M. Okun, *Prices and Quantities: A Macroeconomic Analysis* (Oxford, 1981); J. V. Robinson and J. Eatwell, *An Introduction to Modern Economics* (New York, 1973); S. Rouseas, *Post-Keynesian Monetary Economics* (London, 1986); N. Shapiro, 'The Revolutionary Character of Post-Keynesian Economics', *Journal of Economic Issues*, 11 (1977); S. Zamagni, 'Hicks on Capital and Growth', *Review of Political Economy*, 3 (1991).

10

Contemporary Economic Theory: II

10.1 THE NEO-WALRASIAN APPROACH TO GENERAL ECONOMIC EQUILIBRIUM

10.1.1 The conquest of the existence theorem

The rise of Nazism led to a diaspora of intellectuals. All the fervour of study and debate which had enlivened Berlin and Vienna in the 1920s ended in the following decade; and the move to the West began for the most important Mittel-European economists, apart from those like Schlesinger, who committed suicide, or Remak, who died in a concentration camp. Some settled in London, but most went to the USA. At the end of the 1930s, von Neumann, Morgenstern, Wald, Leontief, Tintner, Marschak, Frisch, and many others were working in America.

The presence of these economists in the American intellectual circles of the 1940s and 1950s had many effects on the evolution of general-equilibrium theory. Even if the resumption of the American studies on this theory was stimulated, indirectly, more by Hicks's *Value and Capital* than by the contributions of the members of the Viennese *Kolloquium*, it is still true that the work of Wald, von Neumann, and Morgenstern gave a sharp impulse to that resumption. With the fixed-point theorem, Wald and von Neumann had indicated the road to be taken to solve the existence problem. Moreover, von Neumann and Morgenstern's 1944 book, the *Theory of Games and Economic Behaviour*, led (among other things) to the abandonment of traditional techniques of differential calculus and to a reorientation of mathematical economics towards the use of the techniques of convex analysis. An important contribution of that book was also the proof of the existence of solutions for a two-person zero-sum game—a demonstration later generalized to an *n*-person game by John Nash in 'Equilibrium Points in N-Person Games' (*Proceedings of the National Academy of Science*, 1950).

A decisive stimulus to the resumption of the American studies on general equilibrium was given by two works by Samuelson, one of 1941, 'The Stability of Equilibrium: Comparative Statics and Dynamics' (*Econometrica*) and one of 1947, *Foundations of Economic Analysis*. These works, by taking up Hicks's 1939 lesson, placed all the main problems of the general-equilibrium model on the agenda. Even though they did not solve any of the really important problems, neither that of existence nor that of uniqueness and even less that of stability, none the less these works indicated the road to be followed. Samuelson's argument, that all the problems faced by economics (in the neoclassical approach) can be reduced to problems of constrained maximization, was very important. Still more important was the priority he gave to the problem of dynamic stability. And perhaps only today are economists beginning to realize the importance of some of Samuelson's insights in regard to dynamics. However, two results in particular were obtained at that time: first of all, the rigorous reformulation of Walrasian *tâtonnement* in the form of a differential equation; and then the formulation of the fundamental 'correspondence principle', according to which each comparative statics exercise around an equilibrium point presupposes the dynamic stability of the equilibrium.

In the early 1950s two articles were published which demonstrated the optimality properties of a competitive equilibrium: one by K. J. Arrow (b. 1921), 'An Extension of the Basic Theorems of Classical Welfare Economics' (*Proceedings of the Second Berkeley Symposium on Mathematical Statistics and Probability*, edited by J. Neyman, 1951): and one by Gérard Debreu (b. 1921), 'The Coefficient of Resource Utilization' (*Econometrica*, 1951). In that period the two economists had begun to work together on the problem of the existence of solutions, and in 1952, at a meeting of the Econometric Society, they submitted a key paper in which the longed-for peak was finally and comprehensively conquered. The decisive instrument used in the conquest was Kakutani's fixed-point theorem. The article was then published in 1954 in *Econometrica* as 'Existence of an Equilibrium for a Competitive Economy'. We should also mention that, during that meeting of the Econometric Society, L. McKenzie (b. 1919) presented a model of competitive equilibrium of international trade in which, under less general hypotheses, he solved the existence problem by means of mathematical techniques similar to those used by Arrow and Debreu. McKenzie's paper, 'On Equilibrium in Graham's Model of World Trade and Other Competitive Systems', was also published in *Econometrica* in 1954. It is so similar to the work of Arrow and Debreu that some economists, perhaps rightly so, refer to the demonstration of the existence as the 'Arrow–Debreu–Mckenzie model'.

The Walrasian 'new testament' was written in 1959. The author was Debreu, the title, simple and lapidary, *Theory of Value*. It is useful to present a brief summary of it here, if for no other reason than to show its beauty and also, all things considered, the simplicity of the Walrasian dream come true.

The model assumes that the following data are known:

(1) the number of commodities, l;
(2) the number of producers, n;
(3) the number of consumers, m;
(4) the technology available to each producer;
(5) the physical constraints and psychological characteristics of each consumer, including tastes;

(6) the initial endowment of resources of each consumer;

(7) the share of the profits of each producer which belongs to each consumer.

The commodities are a set of goods and services specified in terms of their physical characteristics and place and time location. Thus, a good which is available today at two different locations is considered as two different commodities. The same is true for a good which is available on two different dates. Each commodity is given a price. The price vector is $p = (p_1, \ldots, p_l)$. The price is paid at the moment a deal is struck. All deals are struck at one place and at one time, even those on commodities to be delivered in the future. The prices of the latter are therefore 'futures' prices. This fact makes Debreu's model one of inter-temporal equilibrium.

It is worth pointing out here that various attempts at formalizing a general inter-temporal equilibrium model had already been made by several economists, including Frisch and Tintner. One of particular interest was made in 1943 by Debreu's teacher, Maurice Allais (b. 1911), of whom we must mention at least two important books: À la recherche d'une discipline économique: Première partie: L'Économie pure (1943) and Économie et intérêt (1947). Allais, by assuming that each economic agent is endowed with preferences with regard to both present and future consumption, also studied the optimality properties of the general inter-temporal equilibrium. In particular, in his 1943 book, Allais proved, before Arrow and Debreu, both the first and second fundamental theorems of welfare economics; while in Économie et intérêt he introduced, 11 years before Samuelson, the famous overlapping-generations model in the study of dynamic economic processes. Further developments in the inter-temporal equilibrium model are to be found in 'Capital Accumulation and Efficient Allocation of Resources' (Econometrica, 1953), an article by another famous student of Allais, Edmond Malinvaud.

Let us now return to Debreu's model. The technological constraints of producer j are represented by a production set, Y_j, which contains all the technical combinations between inputs and outputs accessible to that producer. A 'production plan' is one of these combinations, and is expressed by the vector $y_j = (y_{j1}, \ldots, y_{jl})$, in which inputs are represented by negative elements and outputs by positive ones. The producer will choose a production plan so as to maximize profit $\pi_j = p y_j$.

For each consumer, for example i, a consumption set, X_i, is defined, which contains all the combinations of commodities which the consumer can buy and sell. For some goods there are physical constraints. For example, it is impossible to sell more than a certain number of working hours per day. Furthermore, a preference ordering which expresses his tastes is defined for each consumer. Finally, given the resource endowment of consumer i, $\sigma_i = (\sigma_{i1}, \ldots, \sigma_{il})$ and his profit shares, $\theta_i = (\theta_{i1}, \ldots, \theta_{in})$, his wealth is defined, which is $w_i = p\sigma_i + \theta_i\pi$, where $\pi = (\pi_i, \ldots \pi_n)$. A 'consumption plan' for consumer i is a vector $x_i = (x_1, \ldots x_l)$ whose negative elements are the goods sold and whose positive elements are the goods bought. The consumer will choose x_i within X_i with the objective of maximizing his own satisfaction under the budget constraint $px_i < w_i$.

A state of the economy is an $(m + n)$–ple, $(x, y) = (x_1, \ldots x_m, y_1, \ldots y_n)$ which includes all the plans of action of all the consumers and producers. Each element of the $(m + n)$–ple is a vector of l elements. In such a state of the economy, the net total demand is $z = x - y - \sigma$. An equilibrium is an $(m + n + 1)$–ple, $(x^*, y^*, p^*) = (x_1^*, \ldots x_m^*, y^* \ldots y_n^*, p^*)$, such that: x^* maximizes the satisfaction of all the consumers; y^* maximizes the profits of all the producers; all and only the available resources are used, i.e. $x^* - y^* = \sigma$. The vector of equilibrium prices is p^*.

Debreu proved that this vector exists under a series of hypotheses which are no less implausible than all those adopted before him and certainly more general. Here are some of the most important. Each consumption set must be convex, so that, if two consumption plans are in one set, this will also include all their linear and convex combinations. The consumers must be insatiable, in the sense that, for every chosen consumption plan, there will always be another which is preferred. An important assumption on the production side is that the total production set, $Y = \Sigma_j Y_j$, is convex. This, together with the 'inactivity hypothesis' (i.e. $0 \in Y$), excludes the possibility of increasing returns of scale: if two production plans are in the same production set, so are all their linear combinations. Moreover, the most recent research has allowed a 'moderate' weakening of this hypothesis by admitting the possibility that single producers are able to benefit from 'moderately' increasing returns to scale. Arrow and Hahn's work in *General Competitive Analysis* (1971) has been important in this respect.

There are other particularly irksome hypotheses which concern the existence of the markets and the forecasting ability of the economic agents. As contracts are stipulated in the present, for all commodities produced and delivered not only in the present but also in the future, futures markets must exist for the commodities available in all future periods—a hypothesis of which it is not even worth raising problems of realism. In fact, Debreu did not do so. Besides this, it is necessary to assume that economic agents are endowed with perfect foresight, as they know with precision, as consumers, the future evolution of their own preferences and, as producers, the future evolution of technology.

Debreu tried to avoid this peculiarity by introducing the notion of uncertainty, but he did so in a way which was no less odd, i.e. by attributing a further specification to goods, one relating to the 'state of the world'. Thus, for example, a sack of corn available here and now would be a different commodity, not only from that available in another city now, or from that available there tomorrow, but also from that available here tomorrow in the case that there is an earthquake or any other act of God tonight. It is assumed that individuals are able to formulate plans of action with regard to all the commodities available anywhere, in all future periods, and in all possible states of the world. Besides this, it is obviously necessary to assume that there are 'contingent' markets for each possible state of the world, as all individuals must be able to make deals in them. Many believe that this is a more reasonable way to account for behaviour with regard to future events—more reasonable than perfect foresight, for example.

Finally, we mention another set of unlikely hypotheses regarding, for example, the non-existence of externalities concerning both production (external economies or diseconomies of scale) and consumption (any phenomenon of interdependence among consumers' tastes and between production and consumption, fashions, hidden persuaders, etc.).

10.1.2. Defeat on the grounds of uniqueness and stability

Even though the goal of existence had been reached, the difficulties for neoclassical economists were not over. In fact, they were only just beginning, because it was also necessary to demonstrate that the equilibrium is in some way unique and stable. There are two reasons why uniqueness and stability are *indispensable*. One is, let us say, of a philosophical nature and is fundamental. We shall discuss it in the next section. The other, of a methodological nature, will be dealt with straightaway.

The problem originates from the fact that a great deal of the reasoning with which the neoclassical economist *explains* the social meaning of the economic variables, prices, wages, etc., are the result of some comparative statics exercise. For example, in order to say that the relationship between the prices of two goods expresses their relative scarcity with respect to consumers' tastes, one simply says that it is equal to their (marginal) rates of transformation and substitution. These marginal rates are defined in terms of ratios between 'variations' of the two goods. In reality these 'variations' are defined as the differences between the values that the variables assume in two different equilibrium states, even if they are interpreted as changes around a third intermediate equilibrium. If these exercises are to be correct, as had already been pointed out by Samuelson with the correspondence principle as early as the 1940s, the equilibrium around which they are undertaken must be stable and unique. If it were not so, even a very small change around the equilibrium would lead the economy far away from it, and the various rates of substitution, transformation and the like would become meaningless. All the most important neoclassical arguments about the economic role of scarcity, the sovereignty of the consumer, the allocative efficiency of markets, etc., could no longer be sustained, for the simple reason that the concepts and the reasoning of comparative statics would no longer have any economic meaning.

Now, it is possible to obtain the desired results of stability and uniqueness, but the price in terms of the restrictiveness of the hypotheses is far too high. As early as 1936 Wald obtained results of uniqueness and stability by using some special hypotheses such as 'diagonal dominance' or 'gross substitutability'. Then in 1943 the global stability of the *tâtonnement* process under hypotheses equivalent to those of gross substitutability was proved by Allais through applying Lyapunov's second method. The gross substitutability hypothesis implies that the *aggregate* excess demand of a commodity decreases when its price increases or the price of any other commodity decreases. Diagonal dominance implies that the aggregate excess demand of a commodity is more sensitive to a change in its price than to a change in the prices of all other commodities. The results of the most recent research on this argument are not very different from those obtained by Wald and Allais. In particular, it seems that the gross substitutability hypothesis is crucial to obtain stability. In fact, it was one of the hypotheses adopted by K. J. Arrow and L. Hurwicz in their article 'On the Stability of Competitive Equilibrium I', published in *Econometrica* in 1958. In this article cases were shown of economies characterized by a stable equilibrium under various special hypotheses— but this type of reasoning was not very elegant or general. The following year, however, a general theorem of global stability was obtained which still today remains a milestone in the evolution of stability theory. It is to be found in the article 'On the Stability of Competitive Equilibrium II', published in *Econometrica* and written by K. J. Arrow, H. D. Block, and L. Hurwicz. The most important of the hypotheses on which the theorem depends concerns the continuity of the excess demand functions, and, alas, gross substitutability.

The result was received most enthusiastically and raised confidence in the possibility of generalizing it by removing some of the more restrictive hypotheses on which it depended—so much so that in the following year another four or five significant articles on this subject were published. But among these there was one by Herbert Scarf which served immediately to dishearten the optimists. It was entitled 'Some Examples of Global Instability of the Competitive Equilibrium' (*International Economic Review*, 1960), and showed cases of rather simple economies in which equilibrium existed but was unstable. One important result obtained by Scarf was the demonstration that it is possible to obtain instability simply by introducing a complementarity hypothesis, and this was considered as a confirmation of the key role of the hypothesis of gross substitutability in obtaining stability. By 1964, when M. Morishima's *Equilibrium, Stability and Growth* was published, the centrality of gross substitutability had become a more or less accepted fact.

Subsequently, there have been no great steps forward in this field of research. However, it is worth mentioning some small advances made by Arrow and Hahn in *General Competitive Analysis* (1971) and by S. Smale in 'A Convergence Process of Price Adjustment and Global Newton Methods' (*Journal of Mathematical Economics*, 1976). The attempt made in these two works consisted of the modification of Samuelson's traditional *tâtonnement* equation so as to obtain global stability without having to make very restrictive hypotheses about the excess demand functions. Unfortunately, however, it was necessary to introduce a few substitute hypotheses which were devoid of economic meaning.

The moral of the tale is now part of the official doctrine, and is that stability is not an intrinsic property of the general-equilibrium model.

Things are not very different in regard to the problem of uniqueness. Besides, the problems of stability and uniqueness are closely linked, in that, to the degree that it is possible that there are many equilibria, it is also possible that some of them are unstable. In fact, it had been clear right from the early 1950s, when Arrow and Debreu began working on the existence problem, that the general conditions used to demonstrate the existence of equilibrium were not sufficient also to guarantee uniqueness. And Debreu, more than anyone else, must have been aware of the analytical reasons for, and the theoretical implications of, this difficulty. This may explain both the rigorously axiomatic character he imposed on his research work (with the consequent refusal to listen to any criticism of irrelevance) and the almost snobbish absence from the *Theory of Value* of the usual neoclassical comparative statics exercises.

The explanation why not much faith could be placed in the possibility of solving the problem of uniqueness was provided by H. F. Sonnenschein (b. 1940) in an article published in *Econometrica* in 1972, 'Market Excess Demand Functions'. This paper was followed by others which confirmed and consolidated the results. We shall only mention three of the most important: another by Sonnenschein, 'Do Walras' Law and Continuity Characterise the Class of Community Excess Demand Functions? (*Journal of Economic Theory*, 1973); one by Debreu, 'Excess Demand Functions' (*Journal of Mathematical Economics*, 1974); and finally, the last blow, by A. P. Kirman and K. J. Koch, 'Market Excess Demand Functions in Exchange Economies with Identical Preferences and Collinear Endowments' (*Review of Economic Studies*, 1986).

In his 1972 article Sonnenschein finally demonstrated something that many people had suspected for some time: that the usual general hypotheses used to explain consumer behaviour, and from which the individual demand functions are derived, are not sufficient to place any significant restriction on the form of the aggregate demand functions. This showed that any hope of identifying general hypotheses on individual behaviour capable of generating aggregate excess-demand functions compatible with the uniqueness and stability of the equilibrium had to be given up.

To look at the problem from another angle: it is known that the results of uniqueness and stability can be obtained with some restrictive hypotheses about *aggregate* excess-demand functions; the problem is to know whether there is some set of particular assumptions about the behaviour of *individuals* which would justify such hypotheses. The answer is no. However restrictive the assumptions on individuals may be, the aggregate functions can assume practically any form. At most, it is possible to compel them to assume the properties of continuity and zero homogeneity and to obey Walras's Law.

These conditions are not sufficient to ensure the stability and the uniqueness of equilibrium. In the next section we will discuss the 'philosophical' consequences of this result.

There only remains to add something about an attempt made at that time to find, if not an escape route, at least a way to mitigate the seriousness of the problem. This attempt originated from a double hope: to be able to isolate the problem of stability from that of uniqueness, and then to be able to tame at least the latter. Such hopes were raised by the observation that, while with stability it was desirable to have global results, in the case of uniqueness a few local results might be sufficient. This was the road taken by Debreu in two important articles published in the 1970s: 'Economics with a Finite Set of Equilibria' (*Econometrica*, 1970), and 'Regular Differentiable Economies' (*American Economic Review*, 1976).

A 'regular economy' is one with a discrete set of equilibria. This means that each equilibrium has a neighbourhood in which it is unique. This excludes the most dangerous situation: that in which, near one equilibrium, there can be an infinite number of other equilibria—a situation which would make the state of equilibrium indeterminate. Moreover, the set of irregular economies that could possibly exist must be negligible. Finally, regular economies must be structurally stable, so that a small change in the parameters cannot generate a catastrophic change in the equilibria.

By making use of Sard's powerful theorem and by adopting two particularly unlikely hypotheses, Debreu succeeded in demonstrating that regular economies have a set of equilibria which are not only discrete but also *finite*; that irregular economies make up a negligible set; and, finally, that the set of equilibria depends on their parameters, not only in a continuous but also in a differentiable way. The two unlikely hypotheses on which these results depend are as follows: first, the individual demand functions must be differentiable; second, all the goods must be 'desirable', i.e. when their price approaches zero, the average excess demand for them tends to become infinite. Now the hypothesis of differentiability seems rather brave. Economists are used to treating it as if it were normal, but this does not mean it is sensible; it only means that the economist's education is generally successful in developing special gifts in the suspension of his critical faculties. First, the differentiability hypothesis presupposes that individuals are able to formulate a precise demand, for example with regard to the variation in the price of cars, not only for any number of cars but for any fraction of them; then, even worse, it implies that it is possible to determine the rate of variation of the demand for cars corresponding to every infinitesimal variation in price. And even more ridiculous, if possible, is the hypothesis of desirability; which implies that, for example, when the price of water approaches zero, individuals will tend voluntarily to drown themselves or to try to hoard the seas. But the real problem of the theory of regular economies is not so much in the unrealistic hypotheses as in the fact that it does not help to solve *the* problem. In fact, once it has been proved that equilibria are not infinite, one still has to prove that they are dynamically stable. What can we do with the equilibria, even if they are 'few' in number, if they persist in moving the economy away from themselves?

10.1.3. The end of a world?

The general-equilibrium model has been under critical fire ever since it appeared on the scene; critics have never shown any signs of tiredness, and have been just as determined as supporters have been in ignoring the criticisms. The mass of critical literature has become so great that it is impossible to deal with it in one section of a book such as this. Here we shall restrict ourselves to presenting a schematic summary of the criticisms, and of responses to them, without drawing up a list of specific contributions or of specific authors.

The most widespread criticism is obviously that which calls for the need for realism, or for explanatory or forecasting power. This has also, perhaps, been the most heeded; but it has never proved decisive. Now, the fact that the general-equilibrium model is based on extreme hypotheses cannot be disputed—with its atomistic competition, the absence of externalities, the insatiability, the desirability, the differentiability, the futures and contingent markets for all the goods, and so on and so forth. What is its explanatory and forecasting power? What does it describe? What use is it? Why is it necessary to study it?

The first group of answers to these questions came from Anglo-American economists such as Arrow, Hahn, Townsend, and Roy Weintraub, to mention only those who have made the most recent contributions. Given their positivist backgrounds, these economists have been especially sensitive to this type of criticism. The counter-arguments they advanced can be basically reduced to four types. First, even though it is true that the general-equilibrium model in itself has no explanatory power, *for the time being*, there is no reason to despair; research moves forward, loosening and generalizing hypotheses, and this process can lead to an increase in the degree of realism, so that the 'research programme', of which that theory is the 'hard core', may turn out to be *progressive* in the end. Second, the general-equilibrium model already fulfils a fundamental heuristic function, as it is able to inspire a great deal of research and applied work in specific fields of economic theory in which it is possible to reach, and, in fact, have been reached, notable results in the field of forecasting. Third, the general-equilibrium model represents, *vis-à-vis*, a great deal of research and many applications in specific fields, a general framework of theoretical reference, and acts as a deep structure capable of holding together theoretical pieces which are heterogeneous and independent of each other. Finally, the theory of general equilibrium can be used as a taxonomic instrument to classify different types of real economies, if appro-

priate restrictions are applied to them, such as the number and type of markets which are assumed to be open, the degree of competition, and the
length of the temporal horizon within which it is assumed that the decisions
are taken.

Now all these arguments are rather weak, and for the same basic reason:
that they are referring to something different from the model they wish to
justify, rather than to the properties of the model itself. The first argument is
only an appeal to the hope that the theory could, in future, become something
which it is not today. The second would be valid only if it could be demonstrated that those research projects and specific applications inspired by the
general-equilibrium model have actually been helped by it and have not
reached sound results, by chance, despite the model. The third should demonstrate that many of the results obtained in the field of specific applications
could not be accommodated within a different general theoretical system.
Finally, the weakness of the fourth lies in the fact that the special worlds that
can be obtained by rejecting some hypotheses of the general-equilibrium
model—for example, the hypothesis of flexible prices so as to obtain non-
Walrasian equilibria, or that of exchanges in equilibrium to obtain non-
tâtonnement processes—are, in fact, the result of a negation of that model, and
it is hard to see how this can be considered as one of its virtues.

But there is another way of answering the question, 'What does the general-
equilibrium model describe?'—one that resorts to a drastic answer: 'Why
should it describe anything?' It is no accident that this is the path chosen,
above all, by economists educated along the lines of the rationalist and conventionalist heritage of the homeland of Descartes and Poincaré; we can cite
the names of Debreu and Malinvaud, but not that of Allais, their master, who
has always been more sensitive to the requirements of empirical research and
practical applications. Debreu, more rigorously than the others, and by following an approach inspired by the epistemological stance of the 'Bourbaki'
group, has set out the general-equilibrium model in terms of a strictly axiomatic theory. A 'pure' economic theory such as the Walrasian one, is an
abstraction. As such, it has no need to justify its own hypotheses by induction,
nor to test them by empirical research; and it is necessarily 'irrealistic'. This
is just as true for general-equilibrium theory as for any other. Is the post-
Keynesian, steady-state growth model more realistic? Or Sraffa's standard
commodity? Or Marx's reproduction schemes, or Quesnay's *tableau économique*? A pure theory is not an imitation, reflection, or description of
reality, but a metaphor, or, in Samuelson's well-chosen term, a parable. It is
this attitude that has justified the neoclassical and all the other theoretical
economists in continuing to work on theory by ignoring the problems of the
realism of hypotheses.

From here, however, the debate moves onto new ground: that of *relevance*.
Any theory, however pure, is never neutral in the types of problem it helps
the economist to focus on or in the way in which it helps him to solve them.

The general-equilibrium model has often been criticized as completely inadequate to tackle the really important problems: growth, change, the economic role of institutions, the behaviour of collective agents, etc. Today, while every neoclassical economist is ready to accept this criticism, none will consider it as decisive. The general-equilibrium model, its supporters maintain, is not suitable to tackle these problems, which should be passed over to other sciences, such as sociology, history, and political science; but it is better suited than any other to tackle the problem of efficient allocation of scarce resources. Why should this problem be considered irrelevant? And who decides which problems are relevant? Is the fact that society has placed its best universities and richest research institutes at the neoclassical economists' disposal devoid of all meaning?

Obviously, this immediately leads us on to a third battlefield—the ideological one, in which it is mainly the Marxist critics who have distinguished themselves. It is true, they say, that the neoclassical theoretical system, of which the general-equilibrium model is the heart, reigns supreme in all the academic institutions of the capitalist world; but this demonstrates neither that it is a valid representation of that world nor that it is really useful in tackling important problems. Rather, it is only a representation in which the ruling classes recognize themselves. Is it not, perhaps, a model aiming to demonstrate the intrinsic tendency towards order and efficiency of a world made up of free, egoistic, and equal individuals? And to hide the fact that equality and liberty are only the formal attributes of the agents who meet on the market? One need only glance at the production system to realize that the individuals who are *really* free and equal are those who own the means necessary to avoid working and to exercise control over the work of others.

Inspiration for the general-equilibrium model can be traced back to Smith's theory of the individualistic competitive equilibrium; a theory that has been greatly improved over the following two centuries, while keeping its substance intact. According to this view of the world, social order is the result of the interaction of a multiplicity of autonomous, self-interested, and rational individual agents. These enter into relationships among each other, not through the operation of the institutions, social groups, or other super-individual entities but by means only of the market. The fact that we are dealing with *individual* subjects is of key importance. In the neo-Walrasian theory they are called consumers and producers. And even producers, i.e. firms, are considered as individual decision-making agents, rather than organizations, as common sense would suggest. In this theory, in fact, the individuals who participate in the activity of the firm meet and take decisions before the activity begins, and they meet on the market. The entrepreneur buys goods and services; the workers and the savers sell them. After this, production starts. The resources, the goods, and the services bought by the entrepreneur enter into the activity of the firm, but not the individuals who have sold them to the firm. The decision-making subject of the firm remains an individual. On the market, goods are exchanged at values that are not influenced by any single agent, and depend only on the scarcity of the goods themselves in relation to consumers' needs. These exchange relations, by ensuring maximum satisfaction to each agent, guarantee an efficient allocation of resources.

All things considered, it is fairly irrelevant that this impressive construction expresses a biased point of view. After all, why shouldn't one be able to choose one's point of view? In fact, ideological criticism has proved incapable of discouraging the general-equilibrium theorist from looking after his own subject in his own way. A truly effective criticism would be that of demonstrating the *inconsistency* of the construction itself, its inability to explain what it wants to explain, starting from its own premises. It seems to us, however, that this criticism has never been raised, either by Marxists or by other anti-neoclassical economists.

It is a strange quirk of history, though, that it was the neoclassical economists themselves who finally produced the decisive criticism. And this was like reaching safe harbour after a tormented voyage which had lasted two centuries.

For the grand construction of the individualistic competitive equilibrium to be valid, it is necessary to demonstrate that the market is able actually to lead the economy towards a state of equilibrium. It must be only the market, and not any social institution or collective agent; otherwise, the essential individualistic premise would be undermined. This is the fundamental problem, which Galiani and Smith thought they had 'solved' by assuming that the adjustment processes in disequilibrium are regulated by a 'supreme' or 'invisible hand'; which Walras thought he had 'solved' by assuming that the *tâtonnement* process is regulated by the ghost-like presence of an 'auctioneer', and which the modern followers of Smith and Walras have shown that it is impossible to solve.

In fact, the meaning of recent advances concerning the problem of stability and uniqueness is this: the behaviour of individuals is not sufficient to give the invisible hand the strength it needs to lead the market towards equilibrium. In order to reach a stable equilibrium, it is necessary to advance strong hypotheses on the behaviour of certain *aggregate* variables; and the knowledge of the criteria of individual behaviour alone is not enough in itself to justify any of these hypotheses. This simply means that an individualistic competitive economy *is not possible*, for it does not possess the necessary strength to reach equilibrium, not even when regulated by the auctioneer's 'supreme hand'. Thus the 'scientific' basis of the theory of *laissez-faire* and orthodox economic doctrine is simply lacking. Awareness of the seriousness of this problem is fairly widespread today, at least among economic experts. As early as 1969, for example, John Hicks warned one of the present authors, his student at Oxford, not to be too enthusiastic about the proofs of existence, as the theory would, in any case, run into the problem of stability. But it is true that many neoclassical economists tend to relegate the discussion of these problems to footnotes, to *obiter dicta*, and to verbal exchanges. Recently however, the crucial importance of this question has been brought to light by B. Ingrao and G. Israel in 'General Economic Equilibrium: A History of Ineffectual Paradigmatic Shift' (*Fundamenta Scientiae*, 1985) and in *The Invisible Hand* (1990).

The reactions of neoclassical economists to this revelation took the form of feeling that a radical change in course was needed; but it is not clear which direction should be taken.

On the one hand there has been an attempt to resort to modal logic and counter factuals. This was the road taken, for example, by Hahn in *On the Notion of Equilibrium in Economics* (1973). The general-equilibrium model does not describe actual reality, it is said, but only a *possible* ideal world. This does not make it less useful to economists: it could be used to teach them not to make hasty declarations with regard to the effectiveness of the invisible hand, and to understand the real world by observing its differences from the possible world. For example, it would be possible to understand why permanent unemployment exists in the real world simply by reflecting on the unlikely nature of the hypotheses which enable the general-equilibrium model to eliminate it.

This type of argument cannot be upheld, however, for two reasons. First, the conditions with which the existence of the general equilibrium is demonstrated are only sufficient and not necessary. This means that, if the proposition 'If *A*, then *B*' is true, the proposition 'non-*B* because non-*A*' is not necessarily true. The latter is the type of argument which should enlighten us about actual economic reality by telling us why it does not correspond to the possible ideal world of the general-equilibrium model. Well, this enlightenment is precluded. But there is an even more serious problem arising from the impossibility of demonstrating the stability of the *individualistic* equilibrium. The general-equilibrium model describes, not a possible world, albeit unreal, but, on the basis of its own hypotheses, an *improbable* world. It does not tell us that an individualistic equilibrium must be reached if the usual hypotheses on competition, convexity, and so forth are applied, but that it may not be reached, even by using these hypotheses, or, rather, precisely because of the most fundamental of them, those defining its individualistic nature. Therefore, the proposition itself, 'If *A*, then *B*', cannot be upheld; not because the world represented by *A* does not exist in reality but because its representation, *A*, is not warranted in theory.

The other position is even more pessimistic. It has been recently put forward by Alan P. Kirman in a paper whose title tells us everything: 'The Intrinsic Limits of Modern Economic Theory: The Emperor Has No Clothes,' (*Economic Journal*, 1989). Kirman believes that the only way to escape from the impasse following the collapse of the foundations of competitive-equilibrium theory is to abandon methodological individualism—which is tantamount to saying; 'Let Samson die with all the Philistines'.

Methodological individualism in its *weak versions* is an epistemological criterion that serves to identify the subject and the research method of economic science. It states that, whatever the phenomenon studied by economics, it must be possible to define it as the result of a certain set of decisions or behaviour by individual agents. This does not exclude the possibility of there being social phenomena which can be described in terms of collective behaviour, and of there being collective agents, social classes, institutions, etc. It only means that the economist who studies them must account for them in terms of the decisions of the individuals who have created them and are part of them. Thus, for instance, collective actions cannot be anything other than the results of the actions and interactions of the individuals who participate in them. This position is shared by almost all non-neoclassical economic theorists, the only exceptions, perhaps, being some members of the German Historical School and a few physiocrats.

The neo-Walrasian point of view, on the other hand, is based on a *strong version* of methodological individualism: *only individual agents exist*, and their social relationships are not mediated by any institution other than the market. This market, however, is anything but an institution, which is why it must be governed by an invisible hand or an auctioneer.

It is not the weak version, however, but rather the strong version of methodological individualism which must be abandoned. This is not a problem for the vast majority of economists, but only for the 'orphans' of Walras.

Nor is it permissible to escape from this difficulty in the simplistic way that some have suggested: by restricting oneself to adding a hypothesis of gross substitutability or diagonal dominance to the usual individualistic hypotheses. This is so basically for two reasons. First, because gross substitutability and diagonal dominance cannot be justified in economic terms, not even in terms of institutions or collective agents. The second reason is that *in general* those hypotheses are not acceptable, or, rather, it is not possible to exclude problems of complementarity, at least if one is referring to a capitalist economy, as Hicks had already understood in 1939, well before the recent debate on the reswitching of techniques.

10.1.4. Temporary equilibrium and money in general-equilibrium theory

The developments in general-equilibrium theory following the Arrow–Debreu–McKenzie model have not led to the formation of a new theoretical body of knowledge, but to the modification, and sometimes the elimination, of this and that postulate of the original model. In these developments the concept of *temporary* equilibrium has been particularly important, both from the point of view of the internal consistency of equilibrium theory and in relation to the possibility of using it to study all those phenomena that are typical of a monetary economy, especially inflation and unemployment. The modern resumption of Hicks's concept of temporary equilibrium comes from the work of K. Arrow and F. Hahn, *General Competitive Analysis* (1971) and, above all, those of J. M. Grandmont, 'Temporary General Equilibrium' (*Econometrica*, 1977) and *Money and Value* (1983).

The starting-point of the theory of temporary equilibrium has been the abandonment of the assumption that there is a complete system of markets, an assumption which is unattractive at both the empirical and the conceptual level. Roy Radner, in 'Competitive Equilibrium under Uncertainty,' (*Econometrica*, 1968), has studied sequential economies in which transactions are made on any date, and in which the incompleteness of the markets makes it impossible to reduce economic activity to a single set of initial exchanges, as happens in inter-temporal equilibrium. Thus, instead of a timeless equilibrium, there is a 'succession of temporary equilibria'. As we mentioned in section 8.2.4, at the basis of the Hicksian conception of temporary equilibrium is the device of the 'week', a period within which the economy reaches an equilibrium position. As the economic process occurs through time, and as there is only a limited number of futures markets, all the economic agents take decisions relating to a certain instant (the current 'week') subject to their plans and expectations about the future (successive 'weeks'). In particular, they decide, for example, to save, by reducing today's consumption, if they expect the prices of goods to fall in the future. Such conjectures may or may not be realized; if not, the agents will be forced to revise their plans according to the new data. In spite of this, the present decisions, already taken on the basis of incorrect expectations, once carried out, cannot be changed. In this way, future expectations, whether right or wrong, will influence the present equilibrium.

A *temporary equilibrium*, even though it is a general equilibrium at every given instant of the economic process (in each 'week'), changes through time as agents check their own expectations and revise their own plans. Grandmont used Hicks's temporary-equilibrium scheme to introduce money into the general-equilibrium model. If goods are perishable and therefore cannot be transferred from one period to another, individuals will be forced to ask for money to transfer their own savings through time. In this way, money carries out a *reserve-of-value* function: it allows individuals to transfer their own wealth from one period to another or, if necessary, from one place to another, or even from one state of nature to another. If individuals receive a certain quantity of money in each period, just like any other type of good, then money becomes, to all intents and purposes, part of the equilibrium scheme, without the possibility of separating the economy into a 'real part' and a 'monetary part', as in the case of the traditional dichotomy. Thus the amount of money present in the system will affect the determination of the prices of the various goods. In Grandmont's model, inflation is not a purely monetary phenomenon, caused by a simple excess in the money supply, but is strictly linked to real phenomena and to the expectations of the agents.

The reserve-of-value function is not, however, the only one accomplished by money. Historically, money developed as a means of exchange to facilitate the organization of the processes of decentralized exchange, processes in which there is no personification of the market such as that represented by the auctioneer.

If it makes no sense to introduce money into a model such as the Walrasian one, where, at each moment, it is certain that the exchanges will take place in equilibrium with the full satisfaction of all agents, it becomes, however, extremely important to use this instrument when it is assumed that exchanges take place in a series of physically separated 'markets' which are not in perfect communication. Thus, even considering the function of money as a *means of exchange* there are valid reasons to introduce it into the general-equilibrium model. As in the preceding case, however, it is necessary to modify the structure of the reference model, by abandoning, at least in part, the Walrasian world: for example, by admitting that exchanges among individuals can also occur outside equilibrium. This road has been followed by, among others, F. Fisher in *Disequilibrium Foundations of Equilibrium Economics* (1983).

There are many other recent examples of attempts to introduce money into more or less modified models of general equilibrium. Worth mentioning are those of F. Hahn (*Equilibrium and Macroeconomics* (1985) and *Money Growth and Stability* (1985). These attempts emphasize the function of money, either as a reserve of value or as a means of exchange (or even its role in speculative activity). In the present state of knowledge, however, this problem has still not found a definitive and fully satisfactory solution. The general-equilibrium model owes its strength and its weakness to the metaphor of the auctioneer, a *deus ex machina* who carries out the co-ordination role necessary to make the plans of the single agents mutually compatible. Money, once introduced, plays a co-ordinating role in the exchanges in which it partially replaces the role of the auctioneer and may conflict with it. The coexistence of a 'real' view, emphasizing the role of the auctioneer, and a 'monetary' view, stressing the role of money in the co-ordination of economic activities, is therefore an awkward one, if not contradictory. As long as this contradiction is not resolved in a theoretically satisfactory way, the introduction of money into the general-equilibrium model will be, to a certain degree, artificial. Considering the practical importance of issues such as inflation and unemployment, it is not surprising that the present state of the general-equilibrium model with money still gives rise to serious doubts and fiery debates.

10.2. DEVELOPMENTS IN THE NEW WELFARE ECONOMICS AND THE ECONOMIC THEORIES OF JUSTICE

10.2.1. The two fundamental theorems of welfare economics

Let us now turn to the normative component of the neoclassical theoretical system. With the full incorporation of utilitarianism into economic theory, welfare economics originated as a partially autonomous branch of research. There are three basic principles of utilitarian philosophy. The first concerns the *evaluation of alternative situations*, and states that the only correct basis for such evaluations is the welfare or the satisfaction that the economic agents derive from doing what they prefer doing. This first component is called 'welfarism'. The second principle concerns the *basis of choice of the actions*, and states that actions must only be compared or evaluated on the basis of the consequences they produce; no consideration must be reserved for the intentions of the agents, or, rather, for motivations which are different from welfare. This component of utilitarianism is known as 'consequentialism': the value of the action is entirely determined by the value of its consequences. The third principle deals with the way of organizing the welfare of single agents, and states that the aggregation criterion must be that of the sum of the individual welfares. This component is known as 'sum-ranking': the evaluation of alternative social states is made in terms of the sum of the individual utilities associated with them. Over time, these three fundamental principles of Benthamian doctrine have been reformulated and interpreted in different ways. In particular, with the emergence of ordinalism, the third principle was replaced by the Pareto criterion.

It was Roy Harrod who made the important distinction, in 'Utilitarianism Revised' (*Mind*, 1936), between act-utilitarianism and rule-utilitarianism. Later, John Harsanyi, in *Rational Behaviour and Bargaining Equilibrium* (1977), laid down the basis for neo-utilitarianism with his distinction between 'ethical preferences' and 'personal preferences'. In the following paragraphs, we shall try to explain the sense in which the new welfare economics continues to have utilitarian foundations, and discuss the problems these foundations pose. We will discover that the birth of the theory of social choices is linked to such problems. Arrow's 1951 book, *Social Choice and Individual Values*, represents a turning-point in the history of welfare economics.

The first modern formulation of the relationship between the Walrasian equilibrium and Pareto optimality is in a paper by A. Bergson, 'A Reformulation of Certain Aspects of Welfare Economics' (*Quarterly Journal of Economics*, 1937–8). During the 1930s and the 1940s, many other authors, including Hicks, Kaldor, Lerner, and Lange, developed and refined this new branch of the discipline. However, we had to wait until the beginning of the 1950s to obtain the first rigorous proofs of a *global* result (Pareto's results were, in fact, local): a competitive equilibrium is not dominated, in the Paretian sense, by *any* feasible social allocation. And this is the meaning of the *first fundamental theorem of welfare economics*, the one which Kenneth Arrow and Gerard Debreu proved in the 1951 articles, 'An Extension of the Basic Theorems on Classical Welfare Economics' and 'The Coefficient of Resource Utilization'.

The same authors also demonstrated the converse result: given any desired optimal allocation in the Paretian sense, it is always possible, under certain conditions, to find a way to distribute the initial endowments among individuals in such a manner that the Walrasian equilibrium associated with that distribution coincides with the desired allocation. And this is the content of the *second fundamental theorem of welfare economics*: its operative meaning represents a solution to the problem of the decentralization of an optimal allocation, i.e. of indicating how it is possible to obtain a certain Pareto-optimal allocation. These two theorems, taken together, sanction a type of one-to-one correspondence between Walrasian equilibrium and Pareto optimality, which is why they are of fundamental importance. Thanks to these, Smith's invisible hand would cease to be a suggestive metaphor and would seem to become a theorem full of political consequences: the justification, not only ideological but also analytical, of *laissez-faire*.

The first theorem basically asserts that the perfectly competitive equilibrium is non-wasteful, in the sense that resources are not wasted. This results from the demonstration that a general equilibrium of production and exchange has the following three properties:

(1) efficiency in the allocation of resources among firms;
(2) efficiency in the distribution of produced goods among consumers;
(3) efficiency in the composition of the final product, in the sense that the composition of output fully coincides with the preference structure of the agents.

These properties make it possible to give prices a more complete definition than that which reduces them to exchange relations between goods. In the equilibrium configuration, the price of a good in terms of another good is, at the same time, equal to the marginal rate of substitution for all consumers and equal to the marginal rate of transformation in the production system. *Price is thus defined as the common value of relationship both of psychological and of technological equivalence.*

Clearly, depending on how goods are initially distributed among agents, there will be a different combination of goods produced and, therefore, a different general-equilibrium configuration. In other words, the determination of the point on the transformation curve and the corresponding point on the contract curve depends on the initial distribution of endowments of resources among agents. This should not be surprising. In fact, we know that all the points on the transformation curve represent an optimum for the production system, just as all the points on the exchange contract curve represent an optimum of consumption. But which of these infinite number of points is selected by the market mechanism will depend on initial endowments of resources.

It is clear that the problem that now arises is no longer a problem of efficiency, but rather one of distributive justice. And this is how the second fundamental theorem should be understood. Consider Fig. 16, which depicts Edgeworth's box diagram relating to the exchange activity between two individuals *A* and *B*.

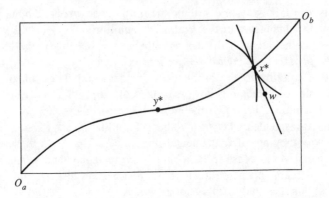

FIG. 16

If w is the initial endowment of goods, considering the co-ordinates of point w with respect to origin O_a and origin O_b, it is easy to see that A possesses much more than B. The competitive equilibrium associated with w is x^*. However, an allocation such as y^*, which also lies on the contract curve, and therefore meets the efficiency requirement, seems preferable to x^* on the basis of considerations of justice. Can the competitive mechanism, given w, lead an economy to an allocation such as y^*? The answer is provided by the second fundamental theorem of welfare economics, which ensures that a competitive market is *unbiased*, or neutral; by means of an opportune initial redistribution of resources between individuals, it is possible to reach any desired Pareto optimum as a competitive equilibrium.

Let us imagine that a central authority (a bank, for example) makes cash transfers between individuals. Each agent has an account with this bank in which all the goods he owns are listed. Let us assume that there are l goods ($j = 1, 2 \ldots l$) and m individuals ($i = 1, 2 \ldots m$). Consider an initial allocation $w = (w_1, w_2 \ldots w_m)$ and a desired allocation $y = (y_1, y_2 \ldots y_m)$, where w_i and y_i are l–ples whose elements, w_{ij} and y_{ij}, represent the endowments of goods j of individual i. The problem is as follows: is there a transfer vector $T = (T_1, T_2 \ldots T_m)$ and a price vector $p = (p_1, p_2 \ldots p_l)$ such that each individual maximizes his utility function $U_i (i = 1, 2 \ldots m)$ subject to $py_i \leqslant pw_i + T_i$? The affirmative answer is to be found in the second fundamental theorem. It is assumed that the U_i functions are individualist and monotone (increasing) and that the indifference curves are convex. y^* is any Pareto-optimal allocation for which $y_{ij}^* \geqslant 0$ for all the is and js. Then there is a transfer vector T and a price vector p, such that the pair (y^*, p) is in a competitive Walrasian equilibrium, given those transfers.

It is easy to see that the algebraic sum of the T_is must vanish. In fact, the theorem ensures that, for all the is, y^* maximizes U_i under the constraint $py_i \leqslant pw_i + T_i$. On the other hand, for the assumption of monotonicity (non-satiety) of the U_i functions, the individuals will spend all their incomes. Thus: $py_i = pw_i + T_i$. For the whole economy we will have:

$$\sum_{j=1}^{l} p_j \sum_{i=1}^{m} y_{ij} = \sum_{j=1}^{l} p_j \sum_{i=1}^{m} w_{ij} + \sum_{i=1}^{m} T_i$$

which can be rewritten:

$$\sum_{i=1}^{m} T_i = \sum_{j=1}^{l} p_j \left(\sum_{i=1}^{m} y_{ij} - \sum_{i=1}^{m} w_{ij} \right) = 0$$

Attention should be paid to what the second theorem presupposes for its validity. The central authority must know, not only the technological possibilities and the initial endowments of the single individuals, but also their utility functions. Otherwise it will not be in a position to determine the T_i transfers exactly. But if the authority knows all this, why is the market mechanism necessary? Could not the authority itself directly reach the y^* allocation without resorting to the market mechanism, for example by means of some type of planning? The answer is affirmative.

As has been forcibly shown by P. Dasgupta in 'Positive Freedom, Markets, and the Welfare State' (*Oxford Review of Economic Policy*, 1986), the following paradox seems inevitable. The second fundamental theorem of welfare economics, whilst it is called on to support the argument that the authority must avail itself of the market, is only valid in those circumstances in which there is no need to resort to the market as an allocative mechanism. This is, obviously, a fundamental paradox to which there does not seem to be a credible solution.

An important observation about the specific use of the second theorem needs to be made. The new welfare economics has used it to sanction the separation between efficiency problems and distributive-justice problems. The market is efficient as an allocative instrument. Therefore, if the distribution of welfare (or of income) following a competitive bargaining process is deemed unfair, then it is sufficient to revise the initial endowments by means of lump-sum transfers. This implies admitting the existence of a dichotomy between the moment of the production of wealth and the moment of its distribution among those who contributed to produce it. The intervention of the public authority would be justified only at the second moment and not at the first.

10.2.2. The debate about market failures and Coase's theorem

Among the many and various assumptions which must be made to demonstrate the two fundamental theorems, one (apart from the existence of complete markets) is crucial: the absence of *external effects*. Thus the following circumstances must be excluded:

(1) that the consumption choices of some agents influence the levels of utility that other agents derive from their own consumption choices;

(2) that the production functions of some firms are influenced by the production decisions of other firms.

Externalities exist when, given the existing definition of property rights, i.e.
the rights and duties of those who exercise an economic activity, the agent
who does the damage is not obliged to compensate the consumers or producers
who suffer damage as a result of his activities or, as in the case of the fields
around the beekeeper, when the owners have no right to be compensated for
the inconveniences they suffer.

The presence of externalities indicates an insufficiency in the market mechanism, in the sense that individuals' choices are made on the basis of prices and
costs that do not reflect the true value of the resources utilized. In the case of
a factory which emits smoke, the producer will act on the basis of a cost of
his activity, the *private cost*, which is lower than the *social cost*, i.e. the sum
of the private costs and the damages suffered by the others. The latter is what
he would have to sustain if he had to pay for compensation for the damage
caused to his neighbours. The result is that he will tend to increase his
production beyond the level he would have maintained if he had to pay the
social cost. This is why the market mechanism does not operate perfectly.

In short, it is possible to say that the fundamental theorems can only take
into account those categories of social interaction conveyed by the price
mechanism. The latter, in the presence of externalities, is incapable of inform-
ing the decision-makers correctly, and this deprives the competitive-equilibrium
allocations of optimality.

The cure for the inefficiencies caused by externalities lies in the introduction
of opportune corrective measures: basically, those *taxes* and *subsidies* already
mentioned by Pigou. If, in a consumption or production activity, an individual
damages others, he should have to pay a tax proportional to the damage he
has caused, while if he benefits the others he should receive a subsidy.

The solution envisaged by Pigou, and later adopted and improved by
Samuelson in the 1940s, calmed the waters troubled by those who doubted the
ability of the market to achieve an efficient allocation of resources. However,
the truce was short-lived. From the late 1950s, another line of attack against
the tenets of free-market doctrine gained ground, starting from the observation
that, for various reasons connected with the process of economic growth, the
conflict between individual action and the satisfaction of individual preferences is liable to become bitter. To get what you want and to do what you want
are incompatible whenever mass phenomena of *social interaction* are present.
Consider the case of the commons, first brought to light by G. Hardin in 'The
Tragedy of the Commons' (*Science*, 1968): individuals, each of whom is
motivated by self-interest, interfere with each other to such an extent that they
can only be better off, collectively speaking, if their behaviour is restricted;
but nobody, individually speaking, is interested in self-restriction. Also consider the case of 'positional goods' outlined by F. Hirsch in *The Social Limits
to Growth* (1977). In these situations, which become increasingly frequent as

an economy evolves, individual action is no longer a sure means of achieving individual objectives. It was, above all, Albert Hirschman and Amartya Sen who demonstrated that such objectives can best be reached either by collective action or by tying individual action to a moral code of behaviour, a 'richer' code than the mercantile moral code of which Smith and the classical economists spoke, in the sense that, besides honesty and trust, it includes benevolence.

Also consider the numerous cases described in the famous 'prisoner's dilemma'. These are cases that regularly crop up whenever 'public goods' are considered, i.e. goods characterized by the *absence of rivalry* in consumption (a number of individuals can, at the same time, benefit from a good without this reducing the utility of each individual) and by the *inexcludability* from benefits (whatever good is made available to somebody, it is not possible or worthwhile to exclude others from the benefits the good produces). The paradoxical result is that, in the case of public goods rational subjects are motivated to choose the course of action which does not maximize their welfare.

Because of the property of non-rivalry in consumption, the marginal costs of supplying the benefits of a public good are zero, so that it would seem optimal to make this available to the whole community. The community, however, has to pay for the public good. If each consumer must pay the same amount, then the consumers with the lowest marginal utility will prefer not to consume the public good, and this is sub-optimal in view of the fact that additional consumption by an individual does not increase the total cost. Thus the condition of optimality requires that each consumer pay a price equal to his marginal evaluation—a result already obtained by Wicksell and Lindahl.

What makes it impossible to reach an optimal equilibrium is the problem of the free-rider—the presence of consumers who take advantage of collective consumer goods by not participating adequately in their financing.

A further case of market failure is due to asymmetric information, and was brought to light by G. Akerlof in 'The Market for Lemons' (*Quarterly Journal of Economics*, 1970). One of the conditions for the correct functioning of markets is perfect information about the goods and services exchanged. Now, it is a fact that the buyer's knowledge is often a great deal less than the seller's. In situations of this type, the agent in possession of more information is driven by the criterion of rationality itself into a situation of moral hazard or adverse selection. The latter are those situations in which the contracting parties have different information concerning some characteristics of the contract (e.g. the quality of the product) and this is why one speaks of hidden information. Moral hazard situations, on the other hand, arise when the possible effects of a contract depend on the actions of at least one of the contracting parties, and when such actions are not perfectly observable by the other party (in this case one speaks of hidden action). In both cases the agents are motivated to give false information—to violate, in other words, the code of mercantile morality which is necessary for the correct functioning of the market. As Arrow observed, adherence to a Kantian code of professional ethics could remedy these specific forms of market insufficiency.

The fact that non-utilitarian behaviour is needed in situations in which the market and personal interest produce undesirable results has restored the notion of benevolence. The need for norms and ethical behaviour that would integrate with, and at times replace, self-interested behaviour seems one of the most interesting results of the theoretical research of the last 20 years on the foundations of free-market doctrine.

The diversity of the results derived from 'benevolent action' and the action inspired by the familiar criterion of economic rationality obliges us to reconsider the latter: what kind of rationality is one that leads to sub-optimal results? Above all, it throws serious doubts on the *logical* possibility of keeping separate the judgements of rationality, intended as judgements dealing with the relationship between choices and preferences, and moral judgements, intended as judgements about the preferences themselves. It should be noted that the impossibility of restricting the notion of rationality to judgement of the appropriateness of the means in respect to given ends is of a logical nature: it follows from the gap that social interaction produces between the intentions and the results of the action, i.e. from the gap between the expected and actual results of individual choice.

What is the moral of the story? That the principles of personal interest and mercantile morality are inadequate as instruments of social organization when phenomena of social interaction are massively present, as in the case of the highly industrialized modern economies. In these situations, the simple pursuit of self-interest no longer ensures even the attainment of economic efficiency.

A radically alternative way to tackle the problem of externalities, public goods, and informative asymmetries was suggested by Ronald H. Coase (b. 1910) in his famous article 'The Problem of Social Cost' (*Journal of Law and Economics*, 1960). In the presence of complete information on the part of the agents and in the absence of transaction costs, the consequences of externalities, asymmetries, and public goods can be corrected by means of the market itself, no recourse to other organizational principles is needed. In fact, Coase demonstrated that, if the parties involved are really able freely to negotiate about the abolition of externalities, an optimal allocation of resources can be reached independently of the initial distribution of property rights, and without any State intervention. In other words, Pigou's argument ignored (according to Coase) the possibility of agreement and therefore of a 'transaction' between the parties. If, with no costs, an act of exchange is possible between the agents whose actions generate externalities and the agents upon whom the external effects fall, then the externalities can be 'internalized', i.e. made to fall back on the party which caused them. Let us consider the case of the factory emitting polluting material and the community affected. The community, which has the right to enjoy clean air, can transfer this right by selling 'concessions' to pollute; each concession allows the factory to produce one unit more of output and the pollution associated with it. The community will continue to sell concessions as long as the marginal benefits so obtained exceed the marginal costs represented by the increase in pollution. It is clear that Coase's theorem is based on the idea that individuals can freely use their property rights as an object of negotiation, just as if they were any other good.

Coase's theorem is rather stronger than the first theorem of welfare economics. It is similar to it in that it states that, if everything, including property rights, is negotiable, then Pareto-efficient results are assured, whatever the property structure on the basis of which the subjects operate. Unlike it, however, it has no need of any hypotheses of convexity, price-taking behaviour, and complete markets. The only thing that it requires is the absence of any barrier to bargaining. Now, since Coase's theorem depends on the hypothesis that the subjects bargain in an efficient way, it is obvious that it has explanatory strength only if there is reason to believe that efficient bargaining is possible.

On this specific point, recent literature on the theory of bargaining, associated, with the names of K. Binmore, P. Dasgupta, and J. Farrell, among others, has shown that the results promised by Coase's theorem only apply in a few uninteresting cases, for instance, in the case of a modest number of agents and in the absence of transaction costs. The hopes of the scholars of the 'Chicago School' thus remain frustrated.

This does not mean that Coase has not made an important and stimulating contribution. It has contributed, to a large extent, to the rise and the diffusion of the neo-institutional approaches we consider in the next chapter.

10.2.3. The theory of social choice: Arrow's impossibility theorem

There was a double response to the 'identity crisis' faced by the new welfare economics at the beginning of the 1950s: the neo-institutional approach, and the theory of social choices. We shall concern ourselves with the latter in this section. This theory dates back to 1951, when K. Arrow published his famous *Collective Choice and Individual Values*. The book received immediate and extraordinary success, above all because of the widespread need to fill the theoretical gap opened by the success of the Keynesian theories.

It is well known that public intervention in Keynesian theory is defined, not so much by State control of economic activity, but rather by the activation on the part of the public authorities of a level of expenditure capable of stimulating the private sector to produce more. From this point of view, the problem of social choice obviously comes second. The relationship of the State with the economy is not considered in terms of the choice how to employ the resources of the society, but in terms of the satisfaction of all the interests that an increase in public spending renders compatible with each other. However, the gradual extension of the public sector after the Second World War created a new problem: the choice between different alternatives in the use of resources. In fact, beyond a certain threshold of public intervention and with structural or technological unemployment, it seems obvious that the problem of social choice can no longer be avoided. This is why Arrow's research has aroused so much interest.

The roots of the modern theory of social choices can be traced back to Illuminist thought, especially to two distinct sources: the normative study of welfare economics initiated by Bentham's works and the theory of voting and committee decisions linked to the names of Borda, Condorcet, and Rousseau. However, the influence of these two streams of thought has been different through time.

Up to the 1920s, the philosophical position of welfare economics (it was not yet called the theory of social choice) was that of classical utilitarianism. Let U_i be the utility function of person i defined over the set X of alternative social states. Then we may say that x is a least as good as state y, in symbols xRy, if and only if

$$\sum_{i=1}^{m} u_i(x) > \sum_{i=1}^{m} u_i(y)$$

Here, clearly, cardinality and interpersonal comparison of individual utilities are needed. After Robbins, the only grounds on which it was considered permissible to base judgements about social welfare was that of the $m-ple$ of individual (ordinal) utilities. These, however, could not be compared interpersonally, and thus the traditional informative apparatus of utilitarianism became untenable. In particular, since the cardinal-utility functions of the subjects had been replaced by their binary preference relations, R_i, the social-preference relation, R, could only be derived from the $m-ples$ of the individual orderings $\{R_i\}$.

It was in this context of 'information crisis' that the contribution of the other stream of thought mentioned above emerged. As it was mainly concerned with electoral methods and procedures, the theory of voting has never needed to go beyond the $m-ples$ of individual orderings. Thus the welfare economist, who, before the 1930s, had no reason to concern himself with the works of Borda, Condorcet, Lewis Carrol, and others, happened to discover, in voting theory, an instrument suitable for tackling the problem of the lack of information brought to light by the methodological changes of those years.

This convergence gave rise to the modern theory of social choice. The first steps were certainly not auspicious, to judge by Arrow's impossibility theorem. In fact, even before the failure of the approach based on the compensation tests, Harrod and Bergson, among others, had already cast doubt on the possibility of building an individualistic ordering of social states without having in some way to resort to interpersonal comparisons of welfare. Arrow's key paper in this field was the explicit and rigorous demonstration of the validity of this insight.

Here is the problem. Each individual possesses, by assumption, a well-defined ordering of preferences in regard to the set of social states. As these orderings are expressions of the systems of individual values, they do not generally coincide with each other. A 'function of social choice' is, by definition, a map from the set of all the logically possible $m-ples$ of individual orderings to the set of all possible orderings of social preferences over the various social states: $R = F(R_1, R_2 \ldots R_m)$. In deciding the ordering of social states x and y, the only admissible information is that, let us say, the ith subject prefers x to y, and the jth subject prefers y to x; but nothing allows us to suppose that someone may prefer to be in the position of i in state y rather than in the position of j in state x. Arrow demonstrated that there is no social-choice function capable of satisfying the following minimal requirements of coherence and morality:

(1) universal domain (the domain of the social-choice function must include all the profiles of *individual orderings* which are logically conceivable);

(2) independence from the irrelevant alternatives (the social choice derived from a given set of alternatives must not be influenced by the way in which individuals order the alternatives not included in that set);

(3) Pareto's condition (if all individuals prefer x to y, x must be socially preferred to y);

(4) no dictatorship (there must be no dictator who invariably succeeds in imposing his own preferences over those of the others).

The difficulty lies in this: for at least some patterns of individual orderings, the attempt to satisfy these requirements generates an ordering of social preferences which does not satisfy the property of transitivity, just as happens with the paradox of Condorcet's majority ballot. x, y, and z are three social alternatives to be chosen from on the basis of the majority criterion. It may happen that, in the comparisons between x and y, x wins; between y and z, y wins; and between x and z, z wins. Therefore there is no alternative capable of beating all the others. In fact, x loses against z which loses against y which loses against x. This means that the social choice, in so far as it cannot be rationalized by a transitive binary relation on X, does not satisfy the rationality requirement.

Thus, either one rejects at least one of the conditions imposed by Arrow on social choice (or possibly weakens it), or one changes the reference framework itself, so as to allow, for example, the utilization of an information structure which goes beyond the mere coherence of the individual preferences and their aggregation into a social-choice function dependent solely on the individual orderings. Arrow's result proved extremely important, as it demonstrates that minimal ethical-rational properties, seemingly little restrictive for assuring the democracy of the social-evaluation process, generate unbelievable results if adopted all together.

The vast literature on social-choice theory has explored both directions of research in the last twenty years. C. d'Aspremont, P. Dasgupta, P. Fishburn, C. Plott, P. Hammond, P. Pattanaik, K. May, and D. Black are some of the most representative authors of the first line of research discussed above. The major contribution to the opening of the other line of research was made by Amartya Sen (b. 1933).

10.2.4. Sen and the critique of utilitarianism

The attack of the Indian economist was directed at the 'information poverty' of Arrow's scheme. In particular, two types of information were not taken into consideration by that scheme: information about the utilities of single individuals and extra-utilitarian information. This was a consequence of Arrow's ordinalist choice—a choice implying that what matters in social decisions is solely individual preference orderings and not, for instance, the comparisons individuals themselves can make among their orderings. However, there is another constraint, implicit but no less restrictive, on the set of admissible information. In fact, Arrow's conceptualization implies that, in the definition of R, it is not possible to account for the 'objective' characteristics of the alternatives; only the way in which these are ordered by individuals must be considered. This condition, known in the literature as the 'neutrality condition', is a reflection of 'welfarism', i.e. of the view that the levels of welfare or of utility manifested by individuals are the only legitimate basis on which to achieve an aggregate evaluation of the social states. It is in conformity with the standards of welfarism that the set of relevant information contained in any social state is *reduced* to a vector of utility levels, each component of which refers to an individual.

From here, beginning from his *Collective Choice and Social Welfare* (1970), Sen developed his criticism of utilitarianism. For what reason, he asked, in deciding what is morally acceptable behaviour, or what should be the way to aggregate individuals' preferences, should the individuals' judgements be recognized as an ultimate authority? Of course, the principle of 'consumer sovereignty' is a form of respect shown towards individuals. But, apart from the fact that even utilitarians such as Harsanyi recognized the necessity of not considering certain anti-social preferences, and therefore of censuring the utility functions expressed by certain members of the collectivity, it is difficult to deny that some things have a value even if they are not desired (or preferred) by somebody. Similarly, even if there are some individuals who do not have the opportunity to manifest their preferences in regard to certain values (consider the individuals who live under an oppressive regime and do not have the courage to express their desire for freedom), nothing suspends the duty of granting them what they do not explicitly ask for. On the contrary, there are goods individuals believe they have a right to and which society cannot legitimately grant them.

In regard to rights, utilitarianism is particularly fragile, and this is for three specific reasons. First is its rather restricted view of the human personality. Second, rights cannot find a place in a theoretical structure which postulates continuity, in that they represent areas of discontinuity; areas in which an unlimited trade-off between the alternatives at stake cannot even be conceived. The third reason is concerned with sum-ranking. Clearly, in putting together the pieces of utility into a total sum, the identity and separateness of the individuals is lost, but these requirements are necessary to make possible the allocation of rights.

In conclusion, any attempt to introduce rights into the moral calculus must break with utilitarianism. The latter cannot restrict itself to the argument of ethical individualism, according to which all and only the individuals count, and all count equally. Acceptable ethical individualism implies something more than the respect of individuals; it implies respect of the individual. In exploring the territory of rights, Sen ran up against an impossibility result, formally analogous to Arrow's, but substantially more embarrassing. This is the famous argument of the 'impossibility of a Paretian liberal', put forward in 'The Impossibility of a Paretian Liberal' (*Journal of Political Economy*, 1970). The argument is that there is no social choice function (or rule) which satisfies, at the same time, the conditions of:

(1) universal domain;
(2) minimal freedom (there must be a minimal nucleus of choices belonging to the protected sphere of the individual, over which the desire or will of the individual himself must reign supreme);
(3) Pareto's condition

This is, first of all, a result which, unlike Arrow's, presupposes the specification of *only one* preference-ordering for each individual. Second, neither transitivity nor quasi-transitivity of the social preference are required here, but only its 'acyclicity', a much weaker condition which requires that, given n social alternatives $x_1, x_2 \ldots x_n$, if x_1 is preferred to x_2, x_2 is preferred to $x_3 \ldots x_{n-1}$ is preferred to x_n, then x_1 must be preferred to x_n. Third, the appeal to an increase in the utility information is not admissible in this case; and this is for the obvious reason that the libertarian conception requires that rights be taken into consideration in virtue of the *nature* of the choices at stake, i.e. of the fact that they are 'personal' questions, and not on the basis of the net utility gains connected to them. Fourth, the impossibility in question has nothing to do with the absence of extra-utilitarian information, since the minimal-freedom condition itself embodies such information. Rather, the impossibility of the Paretian liberal can be ultimately explained in terms, not of *inadequate* information, but of the *incongruent* use of the available information: the Pareto principle states that certain classes of social decisions must be exclusively based on utility information, while the liberal principle insists on conferring a primary role on extra-utilitarian information to reach some other classes of social choices. The impossibility result captures the tension between the two principles.

There have been various and numerous attempts at extending Sen's work, as well as several ingenious attempts to avoid its negative results. But it is obvious that the interest of Sen's arguments is not in their paradoxical nature but rather in their ability to show that the introduction of rights into the process of social choice poses new problems to the economist who believes that it is not necessary to gather information on the *motivations* underlying individual preferences or to take into consideration the nature of the social alternatives at stake.

10.2.5. Economic theories of justice

One of the most interesting spin-offs from research on social-choice theory has been the deep change in the way of conceiving the link between efficiency problems and distributive justice. Smith, in the *Theory of Moral Sentiments*, had maintained that justice is the main pillar of the social building.

Men are led by an invisible hand to make nearly the same distribution of the necessaries of life, which would have been made, had the earth been divided into equal portions among all its inhabitants, and thus without intending it, without knowing it, advance the interest of the society, and afford means to the multiplication of the species. (pp. 184–5)

But over the course of successive developments, the principle of self-interest ended up by attracting the attention of the economists, thus contributing to relegate the category of justice to the limbo of ethical, i.e. meta-scientific, considerations. Why was there a resurgence of interest in the subject of justice in the second half of the 1970s? Is there a connection with the great emancipation movements of those times?

We have already mentioned that utilitarianism had strong reformist political implications, at least in its early stages—consider J. S. Mill, Marshall, Wicksteed, and Pigou. It was only later, with the rise of the ordinalist statute, that it became an apology for the status quo. In particular, the belief that distributive justice and efficiency are antithetical was a consequence of the Pareto-efficiency criterion. On the other hand, if that belief is neither disturbing nor worrying, this is due to the way in which Keynesian theory laid down the terms of the relationship between efficiency and justice. In fact, in that theory, the State never enters into conflict with the market, but helps it, since public intervention simultaneously pursues objectives of equity and efficiency. An unemployment situation derived from a lack of effective demand is a clear waste of resources, and therefore both inefficient and unfair. Keynes was explicit on both points. On the other hand, the argument that there are special historical circumstances in which the State can act successfully as a neutral mediator between the classes was a really great political achievement of

Keynesianism. A higher level of public investment in a depression not only generates more jobs for the unemployed, and therefore a higher wage-bill, but it also helps the capitalists to obtain a higher level of profits.

However, this economic role of the State no longer applies when the conditions for the functioning of the model of co-operative capitalism are absent. Then Keynesian economic policy and the philosophy of the administered market enter into conflict. So it is not surprising that, starting from the 1960s, the concept of a trade-off between efficiency and justice was taken up again both by economists and by policy-makers. Arthur Okun, in *Equality and Efficiency: The Big Trade-Off* (1975), has elegantly summed up the viewpoint of the majority: 'any insistence on carving the pie into equal slices would shrink the size of the pie. That fact poses the trade-off between economic equality and economic efficiency' (p. 48). The inefficacy of the interventions in the field of distribution is depicted as a bucket with a hole: 'the money must be carried from the rich to the poor in a leaky bucket. Some of it will simply disappear in transit, so the poor will not receive all the money that is taken from the rich' (p. 91). At the root of the concept of trade-off is the idea that the market, while it is able to ensure efficiency, even though under that wide set of conditions we have mentioned, would not, however, guarantee justice.

Recently, doubts have been cast on the 'justification' approach to economic rationality, an approach that for so long has allowed the economist to work 'undisturbed' by worries concerning the fair distribution of resources and incomes. First, the various difficulties connected with the correct functioning of the market mechanism, as presented in section 10.2.2, have undermined what appeared to be the sound certainties about the ability of the market to achieve efficiency. Second, awareness spread that the societies in which we live are complex structures in which it is possible to have equal rights but unequal distribution of wealth. We are at the same time members of the 'citizenship club', in which we are recognized as equal (one head, one vote), and members of the 'market club', in which the rules provide prizes and sanctions resulting from transactions that obey no principle of social equality (one dollar, one vote). The most common tensions are those between the rights of citizenship and the rights of ownership; between rights and opportunities; between being equally free to do or to own something and having different basic abilities to do or to own something. But economic democracy and political democracy cannot diverge too much and for too long, otherwise the very foundations of the market system would be dangerously affected. This is tantamount to saying that keeping the allocative objective and the redistributive objective separate does not meet the criteria either of efficiency or of equity. This is where the growing interest in economic justice has found its justification. The project was to define an analytical framework capable of dealing at the same time with questions of efficiency and of justice, overcoming the traditional separation of the fields of research.

The various lines of attack so far put forward are mainly variants, more or less radical, of the two principal traditions of thought in the field of political philosophy, the contractualist and the utilitarian. The first, which can be traced back to the work of Hobbes, Locke, and Rousseau, conceives the State as the result of a bargaining process among self-interested agents, just as happens in a business contract between economic agents. From the utilitarian perspective, on the other hand, the State is an organization that maximizes social welfare, just as a firm maximizes its profit. Therefore the State is a sort of super-agent aiming at resolving conflicts of interest among individuals in the same way that the individual resolves his own conflicts. In the contractualist view, on the contrary, the individual can be a maximizer, but not the State, for this has the specific task of fixing the basic rules (the constitution) that legitimate individuals in pursuing their own private ends.

In his influential *A Theory of Justice* (1971), J. Rawls reawakened interest in the contractualist line of thought by putting forward an alternative procedure to the utilitarian one to express a judgement of social preferability among alternative states. A distributive pattern is 'just', according to Rawls, when it is fair, i.e. when it offers the same opportunities to all members of the collectivity, provided that, if such equality does not actually exist, the rules of the game favour the most disadvantaged groups in the assignment of resources. This is the meaning of the social-choice criterion called 'maximin': it consists of maximizing the welfare of the subjects at the lower echelons of the social scale. To reach this criterion of choice, the subjects must distance themselves—according to Rawls—from the knowledge of their own personal attributes, placing themselves behind a 'veil of ignorance'. Behind the veil, everybody finds himself in an 'original' position of total equality, in the sense that each possesses the same information about the probable effects of the different distributive rules on his own future position. Thus justice is introduced by means of the impartiality of the collective decision-making process, which operates through the information made available to the subjects in the original position. Rawls's theory is typically 'end-state-orientated', in the sense that, when evaluations must be made, it focuses on the final state.

An alternative approach, put forward by von Hayek and Nozick within the liberal tradition, developed a theory of procedural justice in which justice is defined in terms of the observance of rules and procedures by which agents may acquire resources and rights. In his illustration of the *entitlement theory*, expressed in *Anarchy, State and Utopia* (1974), R. Nozick clarified the two principles of justice in his philosophical approach: that of justice in acquisition (the initial acquisition of property must comply with the rules of the game), and that of justice in transfer (the transfer of property between different subjects must occur on the basis of a valid entitlement). Nozick's *process-orientated* approach therefore rejects consequentialism, a pillar of the utilitarian construction, according to which only the consequences of a given course of action must be taken into account.

Hayek, too, in *The Constitution of Liberty* (1960), supported the process-orientated approach: in judging the results of social institutions such as the market, attention should only be paid to the process by means of which those results are obtained; and the process is just if it respects the rules on which rational and self-interested individuals would agree. Thus, the process justifies the result; in other words, the means justify the end, and not vice versa, as in the end-state approach.

Sen tackled the problem of justice in a different way. In *On Economic Inequality* (1973) and *Commodities and Capabilities* (1985) he centred his analysis on the observation that basic values such as liberty cannot be enjoyed below certain levels of welfare. Then he suggested linking the idea of justice to the concept of 'basic capabilities', meaning the functions an individual is capable of exercising when a certain basket of goods is available to him. Thus it is not enough to consider only the amount of goods and services available to an individual; it is also necessary to ascertain whether these really enable him to satisfy his own needs. Recently Sen's approach has been widely applied in studies of poverty and, more generally, in the literature on the developing countries. A major contribution in this field has been made by Dasgupta in *An Inquiry into Wellbeing and Distribution* (1992).

The theories presented in this section offer a varied range of possible meanings of the notion of distributive justice, and therefore offer different ways of solving the trade-off problem between efficiency and justice. This plurality of positions is the result of the recognition of a simple truth: that the *political* dimension of economics sets serious problems which the economist cannot evade, whatever solution he offers. Thus the famous argument of the neutrality of economic science has been progressively abandoned. Whether this is justified from a liberal, neo-utilitarian, or neo-contractualist point of view, it remains true that the belief that economics cannot usefully exist separated from politics has been gradually spreading, and is now accepted by most scholars.

10.3. THE CONTROVERSY ON MARGINALISM IN THE THEORY OF THE FIRM AND MARKETS

10.3.1. Critiques of the neoclassical theory of the firm

The position reached by traditional neoclassical theory in regard to the nature and objectives of the capitalist firm posed several theoretical and interpretational problems. The so-called *marginalist controversy* emerged from these problems in the 1940s and lasted until the end of the 1960s. The controversy involved scholars of different theoretical orientations, who did not accept the assumption of profit maximization as a valid instrument for explaining the behaviour of the firm.

The traditional neoclassical view of the firm is based on three pillars. The first is the theory of perfect competition, a nucleus around which the analysis of other market forms has developed. The second is the argument that the long run is nothing more than the sum of many short periods, so that the firm maximizes profit in the long run if and only if it manages to maximize it period by period. The third is the conception of the firm as a 'technological black box' which produces an output by combining inputs bought on the market with the specific resources of the firm. Thus, the problem of the firm's economic performance is treated as one of an optimal combination of factors, while ignoring every organizational and institutional dimension.

With such premises, traditional theory has developed a model of perfect competition that completely excludes any serious consideration of the dynamics and life of the firm. And in fact, this model, while having a great deal to say about the price system, has little to say about the process of competition among firms and their internal organization. This model, in fact, deals not with competition but with decentralization—so much so that rather than speaking of perfect competition, we should speak of perfect decentralization. The only parameters that guide choices are exogenous tastes and technology and those determined impersonally by the market, such as prices. And as all the factors are outside the control of any single agent or institution, no central authority is able to play an allocative role in an efficient way. The 'competition' considered by the model is reduced to adjustments in quantities occurring instantaneously and without costs. Nothing evokes the notion of 'to do better than'. Besides this, decisions are taken in a context in which the knowledge of the production possibilities is perfect and free, while no attention at all is paid to the key role of management. It is obvious that in such a theoretical framework there is no place for the firm as an economic institution: the firm is nothing more than an algorithm.

As early as 1932, however, two American scholars, Adolf Berle and Gardiner Means, published *The Modern Corporation and Private Property*, a book destined to become the reference-point for all the modern theories of the firm. It was here that the concept of the separation of ownership and control was expressed and rigorously demonstrated for the first time: it is not capitalist owners but professional managers who control the large-scale firms; therefore power without ownership can exist.

In the same period, two English scholars, Robert Hall and Charles Hitch, published an essay entitled 'Price Theory and Business Behaviour' (*Oxford Economic Papers*, 1939). Their research was carried out at Oxford, and investigated the decision-making process followed by firms when faced with specific government measures. On the basis of a sample of 58 firms, the 'Oxford Economic Group' concluded that businessmen do not try to maximize profits in the way suggested by marginalist theory. Rather, they behave according to a rule, called 'full-cost rule', which in general leads to quite different results to those contemplated by traditional theory.

Although formulated from empirical research and without aiming at proposing any alternative theoretical approach, Hall and Hitch's conclusions represented a serious criticism of marginalism, the first, in fact, to come from empirical research; Sraffa's 1925 and 1926 articles contained only a theoretical attack. Then, in 1939, Paul M. Sweezy published 'Demand under Conditions of Oligopoly' (*Journal of Political Economy*), in which, by taking up the results obtained by Richard J. Kahn in 'The Problem of Duopoly' (*Economic Journal*, 1937), he formulated the famous 'kinked-demand' model in order to explain why prices in oligopolist markets tend to remain rigid and not to move in the ways predicted by traditional theory.

Various streams of research formed in the wake of this work in the 1940s and 1950s, and, although characterized by different points of view and intentions and having in common only the rejection of traditional neoclassical theory, they all aimed at giving theoretical depth to the empirical results of the Oxford Group. The most important achievements of the 'marginalist controversy' are two groups of theories: the post-Keynesian theories of the firm, linked, above all, to the names of M. Kalecki, J. Bain, P. Sylos Labini, P. W. S. Andrews, and J. Steindl, and the managerial and behavioural theories of W. Baumol, R. Marris, E. Penrose, H. Simon, and O. Williamson.

Then, from the late 1960s, the economic theory of the firm discovered problems which modified its content. Two main lines of research have emerged. The first has dealt with the nature of the firm as an organization, in particular, the question as to why the firm exists. In fact, if market transactions are the most efficient way of organizing economic activity, why do most economic activities take place within firms?—a question that Ronald H. Coase had already raised in 1937 in his pioneering article 'The Nature of the Firm' (*Economica*). The problem is to explain how an institution which is *alternative to the market* arises and, in particular, why non-atomistic firms exist. The neo-institutionalist theories which focus on these problems will be considered in the next chapter. The second line of research pursued the study of the firms' non-price policies: innovation, investment, advertising, internal employment contracts, and so on. This has led to the emergence of theories of industrial organization and evolutionary theories of the firm. It is extremely recent material, and we will simply mention it here.

10.3.2. Post-Keynesian theories of the firm

Even the scholars who accept the assumption of profit-maximization have pointed out that the objective of long-run maximization does not imply, in itself, equality between short-run marginal costs and marginal revenues. Only if the decisions taken in each period are independent of each other will short-run profit-maximization also lead to long-run maximization. The discussion on long-run profit-maximization began at Oxford. Three issues of *Oxford Economic Papers* (1954, 1955, and 1956) contained the principal works on the subject: those by J. Hicks, P. Streeten, F. H. Hahn, and H. R. S. Edwards.

The reasons for the abandonment of the marginalist principle of equality between marginal cost and marginal revenue are as follows. First, the firms do not precisely know their own demand curve; therefore, the marginalist rule cannot be applied owing to lack of information. Second, the main concern of a firm is price and not the quantity to produce; the firm sets its price on the basis of a certain criterion, and sells at that price whatever quantity the market can absorb. Finally, the application of the marginalist rule implies strong price variability, in the sense that any variation, even small, in the conditions of cost or demand causes a variation in price. But this is clearly contradicted by empirical evidence, which shows that prices of manufacturing firms tend to be rigid, despite the variations in demand and costs. As Hall and Hitch have written, 'the prices determined in this way tend to remain stable. They will change only in response to significant changes in the cost of labour or raw materials and not in response to temporary moderate variations in demand' (p. 224).

Of special importance is the case of oligopolistic markets, where the firms have both common and conflicting interests. In common they have an interest in the expansion of the sector in which they operate, since, once respective market shares have been specified, the profit of each firm grows with the health of the sector. On the other hand, it is precisely in the determination of market shares that conflict occurs. Now, among the various instruments of conflict, price competition is certainly the most dangerous. A price reduction on the part of a firm in the attempt to increase its own market share will lead to immediate retaliation, with negative effects on the level of profits of the whole sector.

The specific way in which *non-price* competition occurs depends on the characteristics and the history of the industry, the type of goods produced, the laws in force, and the general state of the economic system. In other words, the understanding of the specific forms of struggle among rival firms in oligopolistic markets cannot avoid explicit consideration of the *institutional context*. This means that it is impossible to understand the behaviour of the oligopolist firm only on the basis of the criterion of profit maximization—an argument that Nicholas Kaldor had put forward as early as 1934 in 'The Equilibrium of the Firm' (*Economic Journal*).

Large firms possess *discretional market power* because of phenomena such as vertical integration, product diversification, and oligopolistic co-ordination of the market. On the other hand, realities such as concentration, entry and exit barriers, and collusions are in contrast with the competitive mechanism conceived by neoclassical theory, as they imply that prices do not respond only to the differences in supply and demand. As there is no specific price-reaction function, there can be no convergence to an equilibrium price. From the neoclassical point of view, even in the cases of monopoly and oligopoly, prices vary as a function of the differences between supply and demand, so much so that the 'degree of monopoly' measured by Lerner's index (determined as the difference between equilibrium price and marginal cost) is defined in terms of demand elasticity. For post-Keynesians, on the contrary, prices are determined by the cost of production corresponding to a normal rate of utilization of productive capacity, and a *mark-up* added to variable costs. The problem is: what does the mark-up level depend on?

Different answers have been given by different authors. According to the exponents of the theory of entry barriers, P. Sylos-Labini, J. Bain, and F. Modigliani, who wrote, respectively, *Oligopolio e progresso technico* (1957), *Barriers to New Competition* (1956), and 'New Developments on the Oligopoly Front' (*Journal of Political Economy*, 1958), the level of mark-up is determined by the necessity of preventing the entry of potential competitors into the market. This is the limit-price theory. The level of the margin depends on factors such as degree of concentration in the industry, economies of scale, product differentiation, and cost advantage of existing firms over potential ones.

Post-Keynesian literature has stressed other factors as determinants of the mark-up. Attention, particularly during the 1970s, focused on the supply and demand for the finance necessary for investments; A. S. Eichner, the author of *The Megacorp and Oligopoly* (1976), has argued that, as it is self-finance, rather than external finance, that determines the growth of a firm in the long run, the mark-up will be calculated with the aim of expanding the firm. The idea of using investment to determine prices has enabled Eichner to lay down the bases for a new micro foundation of macroeconomic dynamics.

The post-Keynesian approach has, in recent years, found support in the work of the economic historian Alfred Chandler. In *The Visible Hand: The Managerial Revolution in the American Economy* (1977), he pointed out that the practice of *mark-up pricing* has been introduced by large firms as a technique of financial control over the huge amounts of fixed capital they have invested. By the end of the nineteenth century, large firms had already resorted to vertical integration and product diversification, above all in the areas producing primary goods. From the 1920s onwards, successive developments in this direction resulted in the diffusion of 'multi-plant' and 'multi-product' activities. In this context, mark-up pricing became the instrument with which large firms tried to decentralize their productive units into divisions or subdivisions: the price of each product must be enough to ensure a rate of return on the capital invested in the division producing that good, a rate which must be in line with the average rate of return on the total capital invested by the firm. Finally, it is worth mentioning the fact that the first historical evidence about the practices of price formation according to the full-cost rule go back to 1878, the year in which a Manchester accountant, Thomas Battersby, published a paper on the pricing procedures followed by English firms of that period. H. R. S. Edwards refers to this in 'Some Notes on the Early Literature and Development of Cost-Accounting in Great Britain' (*The Accountant*, 1937).

10.3.3. Managerial and behavioural theories

Another line of attack against traditional neoclassical theory has come from the observation of the decline of the family firm and the emergence of the limited company in modern capitalism. This has led to two important consequences. First, the control of the firm must be entrusted to professional managers. Second, since the optimal portfolio of each investor tends to be diversified among the shares of various companies, the shareholder can no longer be well informed about the events occurring in a single firm. This means that the managers of the large firms have the power to lay down company policy without any supervision by the shareholders. In an important work, *The Theory of Firm Expansion* (1959), E. Penrose pointed out that the firm, using internal and external resources, can grow up to a certain stage without any substantial barriers to expansion. In other words, it enjoys 'dynamic' economies of scale which can be realized through the acquisition of other firms or through market diversification. There is, however, a 'growth curve': beyond a certain stage, organizational costs rise and the growth rate of the firm begins to decline.

Penrose's work was an important turning-point in the theory of the firm. It replaced the traditional neoclassical viewpoint by a conception of the large firm as a *pool* of resources organized by the managers. This conception of the firm has initiated two distinct lines of research, the managerial and the behaviourial. Even though based on the same presuppositions and sharing the same ultimate goal of accounting for the 'managerial revolution', the two approaches diverge, especially in the area of methodology.

The first line of research, associated with the work of Baumol, Marris, and Williamson, maintains the principle of constrained maximization as a guarantee of the rationality of choices. The novelty, with respect to the traditional approach, is the specification of the target function. In the work of William Baumol (*Business Behaviour, Value and Growth*, 1959), for example, it is the growth rate of the firm which is maximized. But also, the influence of stock markets was explicitly taken into consideration. Robin Marris, in *The Economic Theory of Managerial Capitalism* (1964), also insisted on this point. The stock exchange is a source of finance and allows for continuous evaluation of the firm by means of the share values. On the other hand, as was pointed out by O. Williamson in *Managerial Discretion and Business Behaviour* (1964), managers do preserve a certain margin of discretion, and use it to pursue company policies which maximize their own utility. In this context, profit only acts as a constraint resulting from the need to remunerate the shareholders so as to avoid a fall in share values. The theory of takeovers developed by Marris accounts for one of the main ways in which capital markets can influence managerial behaviour: they produce a control effect. The threat of takeovers serves to discipline managers: the failure to maximize profits reduces the value of the firm on the stock market; and this may induce investors and external entrepreneurs to buy it and replace the management. The first formal study of the disciplinary role of takeovers was undertaken by S. G. Grossman and O. Hart ('Takeover Bids, the Free-Rider Problem and the Theory of the Corporation', *Bell Journal of Economics*, 1980), while C. M. Jensen and W. H. Meckling ('The Theory of the Firm: Managerial Behaviour, Agency Costs and Ownership Structure', *Journal of Financial Structure*, 1976) were the first to analyse the importance of the various ownership structures in order to determine the effectiveness of takeovers.

The second line of research, linked to the work of Herbert Simon, the pioneer of the modern theory of organizations, is characterized by the adoption of a different rationality criteria. The modern firm, Simon observed in *Administrative Behaviour* (1965), operates in a context of uncertainty and in a complex world where information and its speed of diffusion constantly increase. Its organization is the means of coping with these difficulties. More precisely, at the basis of Simon's work is the argument that the modern firm is not a well-defined 'individual entity' but rather an 'organization', a set of individuals and power centres. The decisions, in this context, result from interactions and compromises between the various centres. Therefore, only an adequate study of the interactions among the internal components of the firm would allow a definition of the firm's objectives. Such a study includes various aspects. First, the firm, as a system, is made up of individuals, but these act as 'role personifications' interacting among each other, or, rather, as elements of an information network. Second, if the firm is an 'organism' made up of various power centres, each with its own specific objective, co-ordination and control are needed to reach univocal decisions. The control theory of complex systems states that these are based on the principle of 'homeostasis', which is the ability of an organism to maintain its own structure through time, whatever the environmental variations and stimuli may be. As a 'homeostatic organism', the firm assumes forms that enable it to generate *self-regulation* processes capable of reacting to external changes so as to re-establish its internal equilibrium.

The idea is that the basic objective of a firm is 'survival'. On the other hand, the firm aims at a 'satisfactory', rather than an optimal, solution; it seeks solutions good enough for all the internal groups of the firm; and, as the firm's survival is linked to profit, it will aim at attaining a satisfactory level of profit. This is a typical example of what Simon has called *satisficing behaviour*, a concept justified by the observation that firms, in the same way as any agent, act on the basis of *bounded rationality*. Only in a stationary state will the differences in results between maximizing and *satisficing* behaviour tend to disappear, since, in such a situation, the profits which satisfy the firm will correspond, in the long run, to its opportunities to make the maximum profit. However, this is not the case in situations that change continuously, and in which knowledge is uncertain. Furthermore, the behaviour of the firm on the market is no longer guided, according to Simon, by so-called substantive rationality, but by a *procedural rationality*. This consists in attributing rationality to the procedures of behaviour as guidelines for determining economic choices. This now popular notion of procedural rationality was presented by Simon in 'From Substantive to Procedural Rationality' (in *Method and Appraisal in Economics*, edited by S. J. Latsis, 1976).

Simon's ideas gave rise to the *behaviourial approach* to the theory of the firm, of which we will mention only the book by R. Cyert and J. March: *A Behavioural Theory of the Firm* (1963). The central aim of the work of these authors was the study of the decision-making process of large firms with multiple production, operating in conditions of uncertainty and in an imperfect market. In particular, interest in organizational problems created by large-scale companies has led Cyert and March to a conception of the firm, not as a single decision-making unit with a unique objective, but as a multi-decisional organization with many objectives.

10.3.4. The neoclassical reaction and the new theories of the firm

Four lines of defence have been raised in support of marginalism during this controversy.

Milton Friedman has argued that the traditional theory of the firm has produced good and reasonable predictions, and that therefore it should be judged in a positive way. This argument derives from Friedman's methodological view that the realism of the assumptions on which a theory is based is fairly irrelevant. According to the conventional approach, the only thing that really counts is the predictions that a theory allows one to make. Basically, the entrepreneur behaves, according to Friedman, as an expert billiards player who manages to pot the ball by putting the right angle and speed on the cue ball but knows nothing of the laws of physics or the rules of geometry. Of course, this line of defence is very weak. Who guarantees that the laws the entrepreneur unconsciously follows are precisely those invented by the marginalist economists?

Marginalism's second line of defence has been to seek support in empirical research. J. Earley, for example, in 'Recent Developments in Cost Accounting and the Marginal Analysis' (*Journal of Political Economy*, 1955), has found, on the basis of a sample of 110 American companies, that modern methods of accountancy are able to supply information about marginal costs and revenues, and that this information is in fact used by the companies. This is an empirical investigation which has reached conclusions completely opposite to those reached in the studies following in the wake of Hall and Hitch.

Other authors, such as A. Alchian, who wrote 'Uncertainty, Evolution and Economic Theory' (*Journal of Political Economy*, 1950), have resorted to the Darwinian principle of survival of the fittest, to conclude that the strongest firms, those which remain on the market, are those which aim at profit maximization. The economic environment in which the firms operate selects those which aim at the maximization of profit, eliminating all the others. Thus, the economist is justified, according to Alchian, in postulating that the best hypothesis about the firm's behaviour is that of profit maximization.

Finally, a fourth line of defence claims that the hypotheses of the traditional theory of the firm are, by and large, realistic. F. Machlup is the main exponent of this view. In 'Marginal Analysis and Empirical Research' (*American Economic Review*, 1946), he pointed out that the empirical evidence against marginalism has too many shortcomings to be decisive. The declarations of businessmen that price is fixed at the level of average cost plus a mark-up does not represent any proof against the marginalist rule. This is so for the simple reason that the subjects interviewed, not knowing the language of economic theory, express themselves in an inadequate way. Besides this, there are psychological reasons why entrepreneurs should declare that the maximization of profit is not among their objectives; they wish to appear 'honest', and to show that their activities serve a social objective. The basic hypotheses of marginal theory, according to Machlup, are in the main plausible. It is true that the marginal cost and revenues are not known in an objective way by the firms; but this does not create a serious problem, given that a subjective evaluation of these curves is just as good.

In a successive work, 'Theories of the Firm: Marginalist, Behavioural, Managerial' (*American Economic Review*, 1967), Machlup made an attempt at reconciling marginalist, managerial, and behaviourial approaches. He believed that there is no radical conflict between the principle of full cost and marginalism, as that principle could be incorporated, as a special case, into marginalist theory. As long as the firm enjoys wide profit margins, there is room for the interests and wishes of the various groups which work in it, just as is theorized by the managerial and behavioural approaches. But when the wind of competition blows, and internal conflict reaches levels that erode the profit margins, to the point of threatening the survival of the firm itself, its behaviour must follow the familiar marginalist rules of maximization. The closing of the controversy in this way did not, however, prevent the vigorous resumption of interest, in the early 1970s, in the theory of full cost, nor did it prevent more recent criticisms of traditional theory from pursuing new and original paths.

One of these is the evolutionary approach to the theory of the firm initiated by the important work of R. Nelson and S. G. Winter, *An Evolutionary Theory of Economic Change* (1982). In it, the determination of the behaviour of the firm is based on the study of adaptive mechanisms. These are well known in biology, since living organisms do not follow optimal paths. An optimal result can, perhaps, be reached, under certain conditions, as an asymptotic property but not as a direct consequence of the agents' behaviour. The 'memory' of the firm is the basis of its behaviour. When the results are no longer satisfactory, the firm looks for new *routines*, either formulating them autonomously within the organization or imitating external ones. The evolutionary approach has recently become intertwined with the neo-Schumpeterian work on the firm and markets. Besides R. Nelson and S. G. Winter themselves (*Dynamic Competition and Technical Progress*, 1977), it is worth mentioning N. Rosenberg, *Inside the Black Box: Technology and Economics* (1982).

Another branch of research is the theory of industrial organization. At the basis of this is the idea that the study of the firm and markets should be carried out in terms of optimal solutions in respect, not so much to the productive constraints, but rather to the contractual constraints between the interested parties. This approach considers the firm as a nexus of contracts in which a basic role is played by the transmission of information among the members of the firm. In fact, if productive specialization ensures an increase in the productivity of the employees, it will also give rise to a problem of co-ordinating the actions of the various members of the organization, many of whom possess different information sets. Moreover, in the modern theory of the firm the interest groups are not limited to those represented by managers and the shareholders; workers, cadres, and other groups exist which have particular interests and which, because of the existence of asymmetric information, can pursue interests that are detrimental to the firm as a whole. Therefore it is necessary to investigate (as J. Tirole has pointed out in *The Theory of Industrial Organization*, 1988) how it is possible to exploit information dispersed within the firm system by finding an equilibrium among the multiple centres of interest that operate inside the firm. This shows why one of the main analytical instruments used in the varied literature on industrial organization is the principal-agent model, introduced by S. Ross ('Economic Theory of Agency: The Principal's Problem', *American Economic Review*, 1973) and by J. Mirrlees ('Notes on Welfare Economics, Information and Uncertainty', in *Contributions to Economic Analysis*, edited by M. S. Balch *et al.*, 1974; and 'Optimal Structure of Incentives and Authority within an Organization', *Bell Journal of Economics*, 1976).

Finally, another research line is that of the 'new industrial economics', whose characteristic is—as has been declared by R. Schmalensee in *The New Industrial Organization and the Economic Analysis of Modern Markets* (1982)—the abandonment of the idea that the firm is an organization which adapts, more or less passively, to given conditions. This approach aims at going beyond the famous scheme of traditional industrial economics, based on the triad structure–behaviour–performance. Productive structures, market forms, and types of company organization are not simply the result of an efficient adjustment to an external order; and this is so because the firms are able to modify the environmental conditions by their behaviour. In other words, while traditional industrial economics sees the firm as a rational adapter under the selective processes of the market, the new industrial economics sees the firm as actively seeking domination strategies (such as the strategic creation of entry and exit barriers) aimed at increasing its market power.

Bibliography

On the general equilibrium: V. Böhm, *Disequilibrium and Macroeconomics* (Oxford, 1989); G. Debreu, 'Regular Differentiable Economies', *American Economic Review*, 66, (1976); D. Gale, *Money: In Equilibrium* (Cambridge, 1983); F. H. Hahn, 'General Equilibrium Theory', in D. Bell and I. Kristol (eds.), *The Crisis in Economic Theory* (New York, 1981); 'Stability', in K. J. Arrow and M. D. Intriligator (eds.), *Handbook of Mathematical Economics*, i (Amsterdam, 1982); W. Hildebrand and A. P. Kirman, *Introduction to Equilibrium Analysis* (Amsterdam, 1976); *Equilibrium Analysis* (Amsterdam, 1988); N. Kaldor, 'The Irrelevance of Equilibrium Economics', *Economic Journal*, 82 (1972); T. J. Kehoe, 'Intertemporal General Equilibrium Models', in F. Hahn (ed.), *The Economics of Missing Markets, Information and Games* (Oxford, 1989); B. Ingrao and G. Israel, *The Invisible Hand* (Cambridge, Mass., 1990); A. Mas Colell, *The Theory of General Economic Equilibrium: A Differential Approach* (Cambridge, 1985); L. McKenzie and S. Zamagni (eds.), *Value and Capital Fifty Years Later* (London, 1991); T. Negishi, 'The Stability of a Competitive Equilibrium: A Survey Article', *Econometrica*, 30 (1962);. R. M. Starr, (ed.), *General Equilibrium Models of Monetary Economics* (New York, 1989).

On developments in new welfare economics and the theory of economic justice: F. M. Bator, 'The Anatomy of Market Failures', *Quarterly Journal of Economics*, 72 (1958); S. Bowles and H. Gintis, 'Contexted Exchange: New Microfoundations for the Political Economy of Capitalism', *Politics and Society*, 16 (1990); H. R. Cornes and T. Sandler, *The Theory of Externalities, Public Goods, and Club Goods* (Cambridge, 1986); C. D'Aspremont and L. Gevers, 'Equity and the Informational Base of Collective Choice', *Review of Economic Studies*, 44 (1977); J. de V. Graaf, *Theoretical Welfare Economics* (Cambridge, 1957); A. Feldman, *Welfare Economics and Social Choice Theory* (Boston, 1980); P. J. Hammond, 'Equity, Arrow's Conditions and Rawls' Difference Principle', *Econometrica*, 44 (1976); 'On Reconciling Arrow's Theory of Social Choice with Harsanyi's Fundamental Utilitarianism', in G. R. Feiwel (ed.), *Arrow and the Foundations of the Theory of Economic Policy* (London, 1987); J. Harsanyi, *Morality and the Theory of Rational Behaviour* (New York, 1977); I. M. D. Little, *A Critique of Welfare Economics* (Oxford, 1957); A. Okun, *Equality and Efficiency: The Big Trade-Off* (Washington, DC, 1975); A. Sen, *On Ethics and Economics* (Oxford, 1987); M. Silver, *Foundations of Economic Justice* (Oxford, 1989); A. Smith, *The Theory of Moral Sentiments*, eds. D. D. Raphael and A. L. Macfie (Oxford, 1976); J. Tinbergen, 'Welfare Economics and Income Distribution', *American Economic Review*, 47 (1957); W. S. Vickrey, 'Utility, Strategy, and Social Decision Rules', *Quarterly Journal of Economics*, 74 (1960); R. Wilson, 'Social Choice Theory without the Pareto Principle', *Journal of Economic Theory*, 24 (1972).

On the marginalist controversy and the new theories of the firm: M. Aoki, *The Co-operative Game Theory of the Firm* (Oxford, 1984); W. Baumol, J. Panzar, and R. Willig, *Contestable Markets and the Theory of Industry Structure* (New York, 1982); R. Coase, *The Firm, the Market and the Law* (Chicago, 1988); A. S. Eichner, 'P. W. S. Andrews and E. Brunner's Studies in Pricing: Review', *Journal of Economic Literature*, 10 (1978); J. Farrell, 'Information and the Coase Theorem', *Journal of*

Economic Perspectives, 1 (1987); O. Hart and B. Hölmstrom, 'The Theory of Contracts', in T. Bewley (ed.), *Advances in Economic Theory* (Cambridge, 1987); B. Hölmstrom and J. Tirole, 'The Theory of the Firm', in R. Schmalensee and P. Willig (eds.), *Handbook of Industrial Organization* (Amsterdam, 1989); M. Kamien and N. Schwartz, *Market Structure and Innovation* (Cambridge, 1982); S. Moss, *Markets and Macroeconomics* (Oxford, 1984); R. Rowthorn, 'Demand, Real Wages and Economic Growth', *Thames Papers in Political Economy*, 11 (1981); J. Stiglitz and G. Mathewson (eds.), *New Developments in the Analysis of Market Structure* (London, 1986); C. von Weizsacker, *Barriers to Entry: A Theoretical Treatment* (Berlin, 1980).

11

Contemporary Economic Theory: III

11.1. THE 'NEW POLITICAL ECONOMY' AND RELATED CONTRIBUTIONS

11.1.1. The subject of debate

Under the term 'new political economy' it is usual to include a mixed group of subdisciplines and areas of study, from public choice to new institutional economics and from behavioural economics to the economics of property rights. These are research areas that have emerged and been consolidated during the 1970s. They vary in the emphasis they place on various arguments, but they are united in an ambition to go beyond the limits placed by conventional theory on the analysis of economic effects of institutions.

Conventional theory tries to explain the choices of economic agents, their interaction, and the ensuing results at the aggregate level under a double order of assumptions. First, it is assumed that the ends and motivations of human actions are given a priori and take the form of a function to be maximized. The second order of assumptions concerns the legal-institutional structure in which individuals make their choices. The basic hypothesis here is that such a structure is a datum which conditions the choices, while it is not conditioned by them. It is true that some variants have been formulated which loosen the rigour of these hypotheses. In 'search theory', for example, the assumption that the set of alternatives is given a priori is replaced by one for which new alternatives can be generated by a search process, the cost of which is, however, known a priori. In still other variants, it is assumed that the consequences of the alternatives delimiting the range of choice of the agent are not known with certainty; however, the decision-maker possesses a joint probability distribution of the results, so that his problem becomes one of maximizing expected utilities. These, however, are, evidently, attenuations which do not modify the nature of the basic hypotheses about agents' behaviour.

The declared aim of the new political economy is to study the properties of alternative legal-institutional configurations. In this way it offers a guide to those who are interested in constitutional change. While orthodox economics examines *choice under predeterminate constraints*, and therefore aims at serving the policy-maker who operates within a given context, the new political economy examines the *choice of the constraints*, directly addressing the constituent assemblies. Monetary policy can be used as a clarifying example. The new political economy is interested not so much in establishing whether monetary expansion or restriction is required to achieve stabilization in a particular context, but rather in evaluating the properties of alternative monetary regimes (policies inspired by fixed or discretionary rules; money which derives its value from the power of the State or from a good; and so on).

The new political economy can be seen as a resumption, in modern guise, of an old Smithian project, for which the analysis of the operation of the markets was only a necessary stage towards a much more general goal: to demonstrate that, precisely because markets work well by themselves, this constitutes a normative argument in favour of a given institutional structure. According to the interpretation of James Buchanan (b. 1919), Gordon Tullock (b. 1922), and the younger von Hayek, the main exponents of this stream of thought, Adam Smith was basically concerned with comparing different institutional structures. His proposal of a 'minimal State' emerged as a solution from the comparison of the advantages and disadvantages of each alternative. In this sense, according to these scholars, the hegemony of the neoclassical paradigm is responsible for a discontinuity produced in economic science. The creation of welfare economics as a branch of study with a certain autonomy meant that economic study of the institutions was relegated to that field, in which it was undertaken, not in terms of comparative analysis, but in terms of efficiency. So, even the normative reaction against the excessive diffusion of *laissez-faire* was carried out in terms of 'market failures' rather than of comparison of different institutions.

11.1.2. Neo-institutionalism

The foundation of the *Journal of Law and Economics* in 1958 sanctioned the birth of a fruitful association between the faculty of law and the faculty of economics at the University of Chicago. It was the beginning of American neo-institutionalism. The new stream of thought was stimulated by a simple observation: that relationships among economic agents, in modern capitalist societies, are regulated by an interweaving of institutional mechanisms that are much more complex and articulated than those considered by the traditional model of perfect competition. Society is controlled by sophisticated legal systems which give rise to property rights; to criteria for the allocation of the resources of common-ownership goods or public goods; and to long-run contractual relationships capable of encouraging the maintenance through time of monopolistic or collusive structures. The aim of this branch of research was to analyse this dense intermeshing of institutional facts, to study its conditions of efficiency, and to give a microeconomic justification to it.

Beginning with these intentions, American neo-institutionalism developed into two approaches. The first, the *evolutionist* approach, found its most sophisticated expression in the system of thought formulated by von Hayek between the early 1950s and the late 1970s and, more recently, by Robert Nozick. Von Hayek made explicit reference to the eighteenth-century Scottish philosophical tradition, proposing himself as its interpreter and follower; he then arrived at the formulation of a kind of 'generalized proposition of the invisible hand'. The central argument was that, not only in the field of economic action but in the entire range of social action, free interaction among individuals develops rules of behaviour and institutional mechanisms conducive to the attainment of political order and the economic progress of society. This political and economic order was interpreted, not as the result of a conscious project finalized for collective ends, but as the spontaneous and unintentional outcome of free individual action. Von Hayek believed that institutions are the 'result of human action but not of a human plan'.

The second approach was more complex, and developed within a *contractualist* stream of thought. The various contributions to this approach made explicit reference to a theory of rational behaviour; their aim was to explain the institutional mechanisms of a society by means of a contractualist model which justifies the constitution and its operation, not only in terms of economic efficiency, but also in terms of a *consensus* based on a criterion of individual rationality. The contractualist and evolutionist approaches both deal with the interaction among economic subjects in an explicit way. Therefore, the abandonment of the neoclassical category of perfect competition, intended as competition between isolated individuals who act under parametric conditions, is deeply rooted in the neo-institutionalist approach, as is the resumption of the original classical concept of competition as rivalry between *interacting* individuals.

Another important result of neo-institutionalism was the introduction into economics of phenomena that the neoclassical economists had dismissed from their field of study. Institutions such as the moral rules of social life, long-run contracts, authority relationships, and reputation had long been confined to the research fields of other disciplines, moral philosophy, sociology, law, and political science. Neo-institutionalism helped to put these questions back on the economists' agenda.

When facing a situation of 'market failure', the contractualists attempt a solution by assuming that agents are able to organize their own social life according to a conscious plan. The 'planners' have the job of 'redesigning' the society and its institutions in such a way that all the actions are directed towards known ends. Important in this framework was L. Hurwicz's 'The Design of Mechanisms for Resource Allocation (*American Economic Review*, 1973). However, the first complete definition of this research field, which is also known as the 'Public-Choice School', is contained in *Calculus of Consent* (1962), the classic book in which James Buchanan and Gordon Tullock studied the logical foundations of constitutional democracy. The general framework is in line with the European (Continental) tradition of public finance of the last decade of the nineteenth century, a tradition which numbered among its most important members the Italian economists Pantaleoni, De Viti de Marco, Mazzola, and Montemartini and the Swedes Wicksell and Lindahl. In *Limits of Liberty: Between Anarchy and Leviathan* (1975), one of his most wide-ranging works, Buchanan studied the economic organization in a society of free individuals. His aim was to arrive at an economic constitution based on individualistic principles, where the 'constitution' is a set of rules agreed upon beforehand and according to which all the actions in the post-constitutional phase would be undertaken. Buchanan's economic constitutionalism is contractualist in the sense that the rules on which it is based presuppose consensus. It is important to note that, from the constitutionalist point of view, welfare economics should be (in the words of Schotter) 'the study of the welfare aspects of comparative social institutions' (*The Economic Theory of Social Institutions* (1981), p. 5), and not the discipline which studies the conditions for the optimal allocation of resources in a *given* institutional setting.

On the other hand, at the centre of evolutionist thought is the conviction that the success of the individual in pursuing his own aims depends on his ability to act according to rules that evolve spontaneously. The difference between the two approaches can be succinctly expressed in terms of the distinction between the 'optimal economic constitution' and the 'optimal reform path'.

A field of study where neo-institutionalism has been widely applied in the last fifteen years is that of the theory of the firm and markets. Why does the institution of the firm exist? And why is there such a great variety of types of firm, hierarchical structure, size, product diversification, and ownership structure? This is not an idle question, given that, conceptually speaking, a market economy could exist, with well-developed product specialization, even without firms. In fact, the division of labour does not necessarily imply the existence of firms. Why does the firm appear as an institution if, according to the model of perfect competition, the market is able to ensure allocative efficiency?

The problem was posed explicitly for the first time by Ronald Coase in 'The Nature of the Firm' (*Economica*, 1937), where he observed that the market has *use costs* which must be taken into consideration together with the costs of production. When the former rise above a certain level, the market enters into crisis and is replaced by the firm. In other words, the firm is an alternative to the market if information acquires value, as the market is an inefficient means of collecting and controlling information.

Coase's initial ideas have been taken up again, in recent years, by Oliver Williamson, who has used them to construct a transaction-cost approach to the theories of markets and firms. The transaction-cost approach was first laid out in *Markets and Hierarchies: A Study in the Economics of Internal Organizations* (1975) and later generalized in *The Economic Institutions of Capitalism* (1985). Williamson distinguished between *ex ante* and *ex post* transaction costs. The former are identified by the traditional category of the use costs of the market, while the latter are those arising in the phase of execution of a transaction and are due to the occurrence of circumstances which are not regulated, in advance, by the contract. The level of the costs is determined by the characteristics of the transactions, for which Williamson has identified three main dimensions. The first is *specificity*: a specific investment is required by one or both parties to the contract in order for the transaction to take place. The second dimension is *frequency*: for example, the use of a habitual supplier allows for a marked reduction in costs such as those due to quality control. The third dimension is *uncertainty*: the more uncertain the exchange, the more detailed will the contract have to be.

In conclusion, transaction costs cannot be reduced to the use costs of the market, nor exchanges to market exchanges. It is possible, for example, to speak of transaction costs in regard to the resources used to regulate the execution of employees' contracts. With this conceptual framework Williamson has been able to explain in detail the various organizational stages which the firm has passed through, from the classical Marshallian form to the large modern conglomerates.

An internal criticism of the theory of transaction costs has been recently put forward by Harold Demsetz in *Economic, Legal and Political Dimensions of Competition* (1982). Demsetz's central question was: why do firms sometimes produce their own inputs and at other times find it convenient to buy them from other firms? The question has to do not so much with the substitution between markets and firms as with the level of centralization of managerial co-ordination within and among firms. The more the firms produce internally the inputs they need, the more centralized are their managerial co-ordination systems. Demsetz observed that an increase in transaction costs does not lead to a substitution from managerial to market co-ordination, as the theory of transaction costs would imply. What happens instead is the replacement of managerial co-ordination within a few large-scale firms by managerial co-ordination in more numerous but smaller firms.

Firms buy inputs when it is more convenient than producing them themselves. Although the transaction cost is an element of the acquisition cost, it is only one element. According to Demsetz, the emphasis on transaction costs has contributed to obscure the picture by implicitly maintaining that all firms are able to produce goods and services equally well. On the contrary, it is a fact that different firms are not perfect substitutes in the production of goods; thus a firm may find it convenient to produce its own inputs even if the transaction costs are zero and the administration costs positive. Basically, the confusion derives from the fact that, while it is assumed that the information necessary for transaction purposes has a price, it becomes free when used for productive purposes.

Demsetz's approach can be considered as a natural development of the idea of the firm as a 'team production function', an idea Alchian and Demsetz had put forward in 'Production, Information Costs and Economic Organization' (*American Economic Review*, 1972). In this article Alchian and Demsetz argued that the firm originates from a particular type of 'market failure': the market is not able efficiently to organize 'team production' because it is not able to supply sufficient information to evaluate the contribution of the single factors involved in production.

Besides the transaction-cost approach, the other large research area in which the neo-institutionalist programme has developed is that of the theory of property rights. The double aim of this theory, as Alchian and Demsetz pointed out in 'The Property Rights Paradigm' (*Journal of Economic History*, 1972), is, on the one hand, to compare, in regard to efficiency, the consequences that alternative property structures can have on social allocations and, on the other, and in a rather more demanding way, to explain, on the basis of a criterion of efficiency, which structure of property rights is endogenously determined in a society beginning from a given initial situation.

The basic idea underlying this research is that, in the exchange relationships of goods and services, it is not the goods and services themselves that procure satisfaction (or utility) and that give meaning to the exchange. What really counts is what the agents have the right to do once they have entered into possession of the goods and services. This leads to a view of exchange as exchange of property rights: the value that a subject attributes to a resource depends on the property rights it enables him to command. Thus this research aims at explaining the development of the different types of property rights through time, and at answering questions such as: How does the nature of the rights an individual has at his disposal influence his behaviour? What is the explanatory value of alternative structures of property rights? Finally, and more specifically, how is it possible to explain the emergence of the firm as an alternative institution to the market by resorting to the category of property rights?

In Demsetz's original formulation, the structure of rights that exist in the capitalist firm is a reflection of the transaction costs caused by information asymmetries and the idiosyncratic nature of the actions through which individual performances materialize. The most recent theory of property rights has tackled the problem of the factors on which the optimal structure of property rights in the firm depend. For example, O. Hart and J. Moore, in 'Property Rights and the Nature of the Firm' (*STICERD Discussion Papers*, 1988), have put forward the thesis that it is the 'indispensable' agent in regard to an activity who must be the owner of that activity. This thesis is important, as it has led to the explanation of the emergence and duration of various forms of non-capitalist firms, such as co-operatives, workers' sharing companies, and non-profit organizations. In the same vein, H. Hansmann, in 'Ownership of the Firm' (*Journal of Law, Economics and Organization*, 1988), has suggested that the ownership of the firm is attributed to that agent (individual or collective) who has the lowest costs, not only transaction costs, but also the costs of running the activity. It is interesting to observe that the most recent results of this approach confirm what had been discovered in a historical perspective by

Chandler in his 1977 book and by L. Hannah in *The Rise of the Corporate Economy* (1983): that the optimal ownership structure of the firm is not unique, but that there are many of them, depending on different environmental circumstances.

11.1.3. The Neo-Austrian School and the subjectivist statute

Several meanings are attributed to the expression 'neo-Austrian economics'. For the Böhm-Bawerkian stream of thought, represented by authors such as M. Faber and P. Bernholz, the central problem is that of offering a coherent and up-to-date formulation of Böhm-Bawerk's theory of capital and interest. For other economists the expression 'neo-Austrian theory' is associated not so much with a methodology or a specific doctrine as with an ultra-liberal ideology. For these, being neo-Austrian today means basically being in favour of the free market. It is mainly to Fritz Machlup (1902–83), and to his inter-pretation of the work and thought of von Mises, as presented in *Knowledge: Its Creation, Distribution and Economic Significance* (1980–3), that we owe the diffusion of this approach—an approach which in the last few years has received a great deal of attention from von Mises' most fervent American follower, Murray Rothbard.

For yet another group of scholars, the neo-Austrian approach is charac-terized, above all, by the resumption of interest in the ideas of Menger and von Hayek in regard to the market and competition as learning and discovery processes. It is on these ideas that, over the last twenty years, a branch of study has been developed, especially in the United States, by authors such as I. Kirzner, M. Rizzo, G. O'Driscoll, and L. Lachmann. Undoubtedly, this is the most interesting stream of research of the varied neo-Austrian approach. The common and unifying element of these authors lies in the view that, owing to the subjective nature of human choice, the incessant changes in the social world, and the impossibility of acquiring and centralizing the dispersed know-ledge, an objective and predictive economic science is impossible. The aim of economic theory is, rather, that of understanding both the characteristics of human action and the interrelations among agents and institutions. More spe-cifically, the neo-Austrians aim at explaining the existence and the evolution-ary properties of the *economic order*. Therefore they refuse to reduce economics to a discipline that seeks observed regularities or mechanical laws from which quantitative predictions can be derived. Contrary to positivism, no truth obtained by direct observation is possible for the neo-Austrian school. The practical implication of this is that the theory must explain, not so much the systematic results of the market, but rather the way in which these results have been reached.

In *Competition and Entrepreneurship* (1973), Israel Kirzner developed the idea that competition is a process, not a state of things. The abandonment of the allocative scheme has generated interest in the *processes* by which individual decisions are co-ordinated on the market. The adjustment of the various individual plans, which in traditional analyses of the competitive equilibrium is simply assumed, and only studied in its equilibrium *result*, should instead be reconstructed in its dynamic process—a process that has an essentially sequential nature. Market activity appears, therefore, as a process which, given its essentially innovative and creative characteristics, is capable of generating change and producing results that cannot be known a priori. The market structure emerges from the competitive process, and its form depends on the path by which it is reached. Therefore the market is characterized by permanent disequilibrium; and it makes no sense to evaluate the advantages and disadvantages of a market economy in terms of Pareto optimality. The institutional characteristic of an economic system must be studied by examining the ways in which agents' decisions are taken and co-ordinated; clearly, this cannot be done in an equilibrium state where the decisions have already been co-ordinated by some mythical figure (the auctioneer) and the contracts are self-enforcing.

Radical views such as these presuppose radical premises. In the case in question, it is the subjectivist statute. In Chapter 5 we pointed out that subjectivism entered into economics with the marginalist revolution. Yet, while traditional neoclassical thought tended to limit its application to the study of consumer behaviour, the Neo-Austrian School tries to extend the subjectivist approach to the whole of economic research. By considering the common points of the most important works of the neo-Austrian authors, it is possible to summarize the subjectivist statute by four main points.

The first is that the economist, in trying to explain the structure and functions of the economic institutions, must be aware that he is dealing with subjects who act intentionally. This implies that the economist can conceptualize the institutions only if he recognizes himself as part of the system. Thus the social objects cannot be 'given' to observation if they are not first 'understood'. As Kirzner has emphasized in *Discovery and the Capitalist Process* (1985), the economist's pre-theoretical relationship with the institutions he studies is a necessary condition for acquiring scientific knowledge about them.

The second point is that time has a direction, so that the meaning of any evolutionary process is grasped by beginning from a certain final point. The idea itself of historical course of events originates from a model of time that assumes orientation towards an end. Thus the passage of time and the absence of change are incompatible, since the flow of time changes the expectations of the agents. Time and knowledge belong to the same category: if one accepts that time passes, one must also accept that the knowledge of economic agents changes. In traditional neoclassical theory, on the contrary, time, like space, is homogeneous in the sense that each point is equal to any other except for the position it occupies; and, just as space can be empty, time can run without the agents learning anything or modifying their expectations. G. P. Driscoll and M. Rizzo, in *The Economics of Time and Ignorance* (1985), have argued that it is precisely the spatial notion of time that has given the neoclassical economists the conceptual basis both for the notion of equilibrium and for the theory of adjustments as a succession of virtual states rather than as a historical process.

The third point is that the flow of new information is not simply added to the stock of knowledge possessed by the agents; rather, it renders obsolete at least part of the accumulated stock. This circumstance explains the impossibility, as a rule, of any asymptotic approach to an informational equilibrium— a point elucidated by L. Lachmann in *The Market as an Economic Process* (1986). Lachman has argued that action, as well as the evaluation of previous action, depends on interpretation: 'Those who speak of the "decoding of messages" lay claim to the existence of a comprehensive code book no mortal man ever possessed' (p. 46). Lachmann rejected the traditional approach to the economics of information because it limited itself to describing individual reactions to events, while the problem is to understand how information produces knowledge. This inadequacy emerges in full with the theory of rational expectations, which assumes that the agents use all the information available to them without however specifying the amount of knowledge they already possess.

Finally, the fourth point is that different individuals possess, in general, different knowledge. Just as there is a division of labour, there is also a division of knowledge. This heterogeneity of knowledge is inherent in the notion itself of decentralized economies. On the other hand, it is precisely the fact that the market process allows the transmission of knowledge from one individual to another that makes it interesting. This is the famous argument put forward by von Hayek in *Competition as a Discovery Procedure* (1968):

It is difficult to defend economists against the charge that for some 40 to 50 years they have been discussing competition on assumptions that, if they were true of the real world, would make it wholly uninteresting and useless. If anyone really knew all about what economic theory calls the *data*, competition would indeed be a very wasteful [way] of securing adjustments to these facts.   (p. 179)

As S. C. Littlechild has shown, in 'Radical Subjectivism or Radical Subversion?' (in *Time, Uncertainty and Disequilibrium*, edited by M. Rizzo, 1979), the theory of rational expectations is the most noticeable, though not the only, bad habit that leads to assuming that agents have 'convergent' expectations— convergent on an objective set of knowledge which is solely dependent on the structure of the model.

11.1.4. Game theory

Game theory was formulated as a logical instrument for investigating situations in which the results of the choices of some agents are at least partially determined by the choices of other agents with conflicting interests. This theory has been relevant, above all, in tackling the problems posed by situations of *conflict and co-operation* between *rational and intelligent* decision-makers. 'Rational' means that each agent makes his own choices with the aim of maximizing his subjective expected utility, whenever the decisions of the other agents are specified. 'Intelligent' means that each agent is in a position to know everything about the structure of the situations in which he finds himself, just like the theorist who studies them. In particular, each decision-maker knows that the other decision-makers are intelligent and rational, so that all agents perceive and respond directly to the actions of the others.

The definitive link between game theory and economic theory was only established in 1944, with the publication of *The Theory of Games and Economic Behaviour* by von Neumann and Morgenstern. We have already met these two authors in the Viennese *Kolloquium*. In their book, the tools of game theory were introduced into economic conceptualization; in this way a series of new notions and research directions originated which are still alive today: the notion of the co-operative game, in which players are able to make agreements and threats which are rationally fulfilled; the analysis of coalitions, which has resumed the pioneering studies of Edgeworth and has led to modern core analysis; the axiomatic definition of expected utility and the demonstration of its importance as a criterion of choice in uncertainty conditions; and the application of the formalism of game theory to a wide series of economic problems. Some circumstances, however, such as the novelty of the concepts and of their mathematical demonstrations, initially limited the diffusion of game theory, especially in the field of the social sciences, to which it was mainly directed. It was not until the end of the 1950s, with the publication of *Games and Decisions* (1957) by R. Luce and H. Raiffa and *The Strategy of Conflict* (1960) by T. Schelling, that game theory became widely known. It was only at that time that the first interesting economic applications appeared, especially in the United States, with the work of K. Arrow, G. Debreu, J. Harsanyi, L. Shapley, and M. Shubik.

Today the theory can deal with many categories of 'games', even if the attention of the scholars has focused on certain interesting cases. The two-person zero-sum games were among the first to receive an exhaustive general theory. Beyond their own importance, which certainly cannot be overlooked, zero-sum games have been of vital importance for game theory in that the conceptual apparatus developed to analyse them has turned out to be applicable to more general cases.

Particularly important was the notion of 'safety level', the minimum pay-off level which a player is able to guarantee himself independently of the strategies of the other. A game has *a rational outcome from the individual point of view* if the pay-off received by each player is not lower than his safety levels; if an individual is rational, he will always act in such a way as to ensure that at least that level of pay-off can be obtained with certainty. The safety level can be calculated both for the pure strategies (which are sequences of well-determined actions) and for mixed strategies (in which, in one or more stages of the game, the choice of action is made by means of a stochastic experiment, such as tossing a coin).

As early as the beginning of the century, E. Zermelo, in 'Über eine Anwendung der Mengenlehre auf die Theorie des Schachspiels' ('On an Application of Set Theory to the Theory of the Chess Game', *Proceedings of the Fifth International Congress of Mathematicians*, 1913), had already succeeded in proving that the game of chess is strictly determined. Obviously, this does not mean that the 'optimal' strategy for this game is easy to find, as every chess player knows well. In any case, Zermelo's theorem had an extraordinary importance, in that it was the prototype for the increasingly more general theorems to emerge in the following years. In practice, in order to 'export' the theorem from the field of zero-sum games, the concept of rational outcome from the individual point of view has been replaced by that of *strategic equilibrium*. A strategy brings equilibrium if it maximizes the level of pay-off obtained by a player, *given the strategies chosen by all the others*. This basic concept was introduced by John Nash in 'Non-cooperative Games' (*Annals of Mathematics*, 1951), and it is still known as the 'Nash equilibrium'. It is based on the idea that, in equilibrium, the strategies must consists of replies which are 'mutually best', in the sense that no player is able to do better than he does, *given* the actions of the other players. Nash's work permitted H. W. Kuhn to prove, in *Lectures on the Theory of Games* (1953), that every n-person perfect-information game (in which all players know the whole structure of the game, from the pay-offs to the possible moves of the others) has an equilibrium in terms of pure strategy. Despite its interest, this theorem is not particularly potent, because there is nothing to exclude the case where a game has a high number of equilibria, so that it is not clear which outcome would prevail if all the players were rational. This is what actually happens in the great majority of games. Thus a recent branch of research has tried to *refine* the set of strategic equilibria, which are generally very numerous, with the use of the most varied auxiliary criteria. The results of such research are still controversial, as there is, in fact, no 'objectively valid' criterion on which to base such a refinement process.

In a *strictly determined* game, in which there is only one rational outcome from the individual point of view in terms of pure strategy, it is certain that the outcome will prevail when all the players are rational. On the other hand, a game is *determined* if it has one rational outcome from the individual point of view in terms of *mixed* strategies. There are games which are not strictly determined but only determined; in such a case the players do not have a 'rational' choice available in terms of pure strategy, but they do have one if a wider group of mixed strategies is considered.

The most important refinements have been made by John Harsanyi in 'Games of Incomplete Information Played by Bayesian Players' (*Management Science*, 1967–8) and in 'The Tracing Procedure (*International Journal of*

Game Theory, 1975). Harsanyi introduced a more general class of games, defined as 'Bayesian games', in which the players may not know with certainty the structure of the game. R. Selten, on the other hand, introduced the notion of 'perfect equilibrium' in 'Re-examination of the Perfectness Concept for Equilibrium in Extensive Games' (*International Journal of Game Theory*, 1975). He started from the observation that quite a number of Nash equilibria are imperfect in the sense that they are based on threats of action depending on circumstances which never occur in the equilibrium situation, and which the players would never take into consideration if they could choose. The notion of 'perfect equilibrium' eliminates this kind of imperfection. An important recent synthesis of these two lines of research has been made by D. Kreps and R. Wilson with the notion of 'sequential equilibrium', in 'Sequential Equilibria' *Econometrica*, 1982.

In the case of two-person zero-sum games, things are much clearer: von Neumann's famous minimax theorem states, in fact, that, if the number of feasible pure strategies is finite, such games are determinate, or, rather, that they admit a single rational result in terms of *mixed* strategies. This theorem has had an enormous impact on the development of the subject (the demonstration itself of the existence of a competitive equilibrium has been obtained from a generalization of one of the demonstrations of the minimax theorem), and for a long period zero-sum games were considered as *the* field for the application of the theory.

The modern theory, although it has pushed the original ideas of von Neumann and Morgenstern far forward, has encountered formidable problems. For example, even in the field of co-operative games there is usually a multiplicity of possible equilibria. The number and the nature of the equilibria associated with a certain game will thus be determined by the particular interpretation of the game, the set of strategies available to the players, and the 'rationality criteria' to which they adhere. There is no universally valid criterion of choice. Each proposed criterion selects 'reasonable' equilibria for certain games; but for other games it excludes some equally 'reasonable' equilibria in order to choose some other less 'plausible' ones.

Another difficulty with the game theory of the 1950s and 1960s was that it was basically concerned with *complete* and *perfect* information games. In complete-information games, the players understand the nature of the game; in perfect-information games, on the other hand, the players know both the nature of the game and all the preceding moves of the other players. This limited the field of the phenomena which the theory was able to tackle, and therefore restricted its possible applications in economics. The theoretical developments in the 1970s and 1980s, especially the work of Harsanyi and Selten, have partially remedied this deficiency.

A recent approach has considered *repeated games*, also called *supergames*. Strategic behaviour can change if, instead of playing 'once and for all', the individuals know that the game may be repeated a certain, perhaps indefinite, number of times. A typical example is the well-known 'prisoner's dilemma', a non-zero-sum game which gives rise to a non-co-operative solution if it is played only once but which can generate co-operative behaviour if it is repeated a certain number of times. R. Luce and H. Raiffa were among the first to highlight the dilemma. This consists in the fact that an egoistic choice is rational but does not lead to the best possible solution, while the co-operative choice is irrational for the person who makes it unless the reply of the other player is also co-operative. What is best for the individual is not necessarily best for the individuals taken together. The interest in repeated games is due to a theorem, known as the 'Folk Theorem', which establishes a basic analogy between repeated games and non-repeated co-operative games by pointing out that the emergence of factors such as 'reputation' or 'credibility', which are typical of repeated games, can naturally lead the players to explore the possibilities of co-operative solutions. This is because these factors can give efficacy to the agreements and threats that make co-operation possible. An experimental verification of the theorem was given by R. Axelrod (*The Evolution of Cooperation*, 1984), who demonstrated how co-operative results tend to prevail in a game repeated an infinite number of times.

In view of the close link between 'oligopolistic indetermination' and game theory, it is not surprising that the conceptual apparatus of the latter has found a wide application in industrial economics. In his 1947 article, 'Price Theory and Oligopoly' (*Economic Journal*), K. W. Rothschild complained that, when dealing with oligopoly, economists let themselves be too influenced by analogies from mechanics and biology. Rothschild believed that in the study of oligopolist situations it is preferable to refer to those fields of research that study moves and counter-moves, the fight for power, and strategic behaviour. In fact, the use of game theory has led, in recent times, to the revaluation of concepts such as entry barriers and the relationship between the structure of the market and technical change. As M. Shubik has indicated in *Strategy and Market Structure* (1959), the most important result in this context has been the following: the causal link proceeding from the structure of the market to the behaviour and the performance has been replaced by the idea that the structure of the market, intended as the number and size of firms operating in it, is endogenously determined by the strategic interactions of the firms.

Another fruitful area of application of game theory has been that of bargaining (theories of contracts, auctions, and collective bargaining), in which two or more individuals must come to an agreement for the share of a given stake, with the constraint that, in the case of a failure to reach agreement, nobody receives anything. This problem has allowed economists to give a precise definition to a key economic notion: that of 'contractual power'. The more one party is 'anxious' to conclude an agreement, the more he will be disposed to give way. Ken Binmore's 'Modeling Rational Players' (*Economics and Philosophy*, 1987) is an important work in this context. In it, the traditional notion of 'substantive rationality' has been replaced by that of 'algorithmic rationality', which resumes and generalizes Herbert Simon's famous notion of 'procedural rationality'.

Finally, a very recent field of application of game theory is that of the theory of economic policy (monetary and fiscal policy and international economic co-operation), where Selten's 'perfection criterion' and the notion of 'sequential equilibrium' have been widely used in relation to the concepts of 'credibility' and 'reputation' of players such as governments and unions. Among the most important works on this subject are R. J. Aumann and M. Kurz, 'Power and Taxes' (*Econometrica*, 1977) and P. Dubey and M. Shubik, 'A Theory of Money and Financial Institutions' (*Journal of Economic Theory*, 1978).

The greater fertility of the economic applications of game theory by comparison with that of other mathematical instruments also depends, perhaps, on the fact that this theory was not borrowed from another discipline, but was developed within economic research, which has favoured the formulation of concepts and formal procedures well suited to the representation of social and economic interactions.

However, it is important not to forget that there are still severe limitations in the modelling within game theory. For example, the choices of the most appropriate notions of 'individual rationality' and 'game equilibrium' are multifarious and partially arbitrary. And even where a well-defined notion of equilibrium has been accepted, the problem often still remains—especially in supergames—of the multiplicity of outcomes. In any case, it remains true that game theory, because of its rigorous logical structure, enables economists to classify different types of rationality and equilibrium, and is becoming a viable alternative research approach to the neo-Walrasian one.

11.2. THE THEORY OF PRODUCTION AS A CIRCULAR PROCESS

11.2.1. Activity analysis and the non-substitution theorem

In Chapter 8 we spoke of a tradition in input–output analysis that originated at the beginning of the twentieth century in Russia with Dmitriev, and then emigrated to Germany, with von Charasoff and von Bortkiewicz. There, in the second half of the 1920s, this tradition inspired the work of Leontief and Remak. In the same chapter we also spoke of Menger's Viennese *Kolloquium*, and of the work of Schlesinger and Wald on the problem of the existence of solutions in the general-equilibrium model, and we also mentioned von Neumann's movements between Berlin and Vienna.

This line of thought was transplanted to America in the 1930s and there, after the Second World War, bore diverse and notable fruits. We have already mentioned von Neumann's contribution to the birth of game theory and of the balanced-growth models. We have also presented Leontief's research in input–output analysis. Finally, in Chapter 10 we spoke of the influence exerted by these lines of thought on the development of the neo-Walrasian approach. Now we should like to examine another two important theoretical developments which also began after the Second World War, and which can be interpreted as developments and extensions of Leontief's and von Neumann's models: activity analysis and the non-substitution theorem.

The classic work for both these theoretical developments is undoubtedly *Activity Analysis of Production and Allocation* (1951), a book edited by Tjalling Charles Koopmans (1910–84). Other works worth mentioning in this field are: *Linear Inequalities and Related Systems* (1956), edited by H. W. Kuhn and A. K. Tucker; *Linear Programming and Economic Analysis* (1959), by R. Dorfman, P. A. Samuelson, and R. M. Solow; *The Theory of Linear Economic Models* (1960), by D. Gale; and *Linear Programming and Extensions* (1963), by G. B. Dantzig. Also of importance is the first of the *Three Essays on the State of Economic Science* (1957), in which Koopmans endeavoured to link this type of analysis to the neo-Walrasian general-equilibrium theory.

Activity analysis is a generalization of von Neumann's model in terms of linear programming—a generalization consisting of the introduction of diverse scarce resources and the use of the model to solve the problem of their efficient allocation. The first ideas on linear programming, as already mentioned, go back to Kantorovic's 1939 study. But the theory only took off in 1947, after the discovery of the simplex method, an efficient way of solving a linear-programming problem. The author was George Bernard Dantzig (b. 1914), who had rediscovered linear programming independently of Kantorovic. His first important work on the argument was *Programming in a Linear Structure* (1948). A second was published in the above-mentioned 1951 book edited by Koopmans.

A linear-programming problem can be set out in the following way:

maximize $\bar{z} = px$ under the constraints $Hx \leqslant s, \quad x \geqslant 0$ (primal)

minimize $\underline{z} = ws$ under the constraints $wH \geqslant p, \quad w \geqslant 0$ (dual)

where $p = (p_1 \ldots p_m)$ and $w = (w_1 \ldots w_n)$ are of row vectors, $x = (x_1 \ldots x_m)'$, and $s = (s_1 \ldots s_n)'$ are column vectors, H is an $n \times m$ matrix. The unknowns of the problem are x and w. Depending on the meaning one wishes to attribute to the variables, diverse applications of the model can be obtained. The practical applications of linear programming have been especially important at the level of the firm. Here, however, we are interested in the theoretical applications, and the most important of these is activity analysis. In this case H is interpreted as a matrix containing a technically feasible combination of inputs in each column. Each column refers to an 'activity', each row to a resource. Generally, there are more activities than resources, $m > n$. The vector of the final goods prices is p, that of the intensities at which the activities are carried out is x. Finally, s is the quantities of available resources and w their 'shadow prices'.

Now, the primal problem consists in choosing a vector of activity levels which maximizes the level of final output, given the prices of final goods, in such a way that no more than the resources available are used. The dual problem, on the other hand, consists of the choice of shadow prices which minimize the costs of the utilized resources in such a way that the production cost of each good produced is not lower than its price. The latter condition ensures that there are no profits. The solution of the programming problem, then, will ensure that no losses are made.

The solution of the (optimal) equilibrium exists if $H \geq 0$ and if each column of H contains at least one positive element. If x^*, w^* are equilibrium values, then:

$$\max \bar{z} = px^* = w^*s = \min \underline{z}$$

which means that the net national product is equal to the value added. Furthermore, we have:

$$w^* H x^* = w^* s$$

$$w^* H x^* = px^*$$

The first of these equations implies that $w_i^* = 0$ if the demand for the resource s_i is lower than the supply; the second that $x_i^* = 0$ if the price of good i is lower than its cost. This means that the non-scarce resources are free and that the non-profitable processes are not activated. Activity analysis, therefore, serves not only to determine the intensity at which an activity is utilized but also to choose which to utilize (the most profitable) and which to leave out.

The 1951 book edited by Koopmans also included four articles on the so-called 'non-substitution theorem'. The authors were Georgescu-Roegen, Arrow, Koopmans, and Samuelson. Initially, this theorem was formulated as a theoretical application of Leontief's model. It is based on the following hypotheses: there is only one primary input, let us say labour; that input is indispensable for the production of all goods; each production process produces only one output; there are constant returns to scale and perfect competition. The problem is to choose the most profitable activity, i.e. that which minimizes costs. Now, under these hypotheses, prices and activity levels are independent, and the set of activities chosen as the most profitable to obtain a given vector of final demand remains the most profitable for the production of any other vector.

This latter result is of crucial importance. The activities are chosen by the entrepreneurs with the aim of minimizing costs; if there are no other primary inputs besides labour, there will be a unique set of activities which is the most profitable; as there are constant returns to scale, a technique which is most profitable at a certain level of activity is also so at any other level; therefore the choice of techniques does not change with variations in the composition of demand and the quantities produced, and prices depend solely on technical conditions of production.

There are two different interpretations of the relevance of this theorem. The first to be advanced interprets the term 'substitution' as a synonym for 'change of techniques'. In this case the theorem serves to demonstrate the robustness of Leontief's and similar models. The hypothesis of fixed coefficients, which appears in such models, is not restrictive, as was argued by some of Leontief's critics. In fact, the theorem demonstrates that the prevailing coefficients can be interpreted as those that have been chosen by the entrepreneurs from a vast range of technical possibilities, and that this choice is not modified by changes in final demand.

In another interpretation, the 'non-substitution theorem' aims to point out that, with variations in the composition of demand, there is no substitution among the primary factors. On the other hand, it is obvious that there cannot be substitution among primary factors when there is only one. Therefore, the relevance of the theorem would seem to lie in the fact that, when there is more than one primary factor, substitution is possible and takes place each time there is a change in consumer tastes. This seems to confirm the traditional neoclassical view that, *in general*, if the demand increases for a good with a high intensity of a certain factor, there will be an increase in the price of that good, but also in the demand and the remuneration of the factor in question, and, consequently, the prices of all the other goods will change. In general, therefore, prices depend on the demand for final goods and the scarcity of primary inputs. We will see in the next section how much caution is needed to sustain an argument of this type.

Meanwhile we should like to point out that there are cases in which the non-substitution theorem does not hold, and in which the substitution of primary factors plays no role at all. One of these is where the returns to scale are not constant. Here it is clear that variations in demand will have relevant effects on the cost of the goods and therefore also on their prices. But this has nothing to do with the substitution among primary factors. Another case is that of joint production. Here, generally, variations in demand change the convenience conditions for the activation of different processes, as a certain good can be produced jointly with some other by using different activities. Thus variations in demand can cause changes in the techniques activated and therefore in the costs and the prices of goods. But, again, this has nothing to do with substitution among primary factors.

Finally, we should like to mention three studies of the 1960s: P. A. Samuelson's 'A New Theory of Non-Substitution' (*Money, Growth and Methodology*, 1961); J. A. Mirrlees' 'The Dynamic Non-Substitution Theorem' (*Review of Economic Studies*, 1969); and J. E. Stiglitz's 'Non-Substitution Theorems with Durable Capital Goods' (*Review of Economic Studies*, 1970). In these the theory is generalized with the introduction of an interest rate, and with a special case of joint production (used machines which are not transferable from one activity to another and not employed jointly). The introduction of the interest rate modifies the results of the theorem in the sense that there is a different price system for each different value of the interest rate. The 'dynamic' character of the theorem would consist of the possibility of applying it to an economy which is growing in steady state.

11.2.2. The debate on the theory of capital

Although the possibility of substitution among primary factors is excluded under the hypotheses of the non-substitution theorem, it seems, however, possible to argue for another type of substitution: that between capital and labour. Even excluding the effects of final demand on prices, is it not possible that a significant relationship exists between demand for the 'productive factors', labour and capital, and their remunerations? If the prices of the factor services are indexes of scarcity, then the following should occur: with an increase in the wage–interest ratio, there should be an increase in the demand for the services of capital in relation to that of the services of labour. Under perfect competition the real remunerations of the factors should equal their marginal productivity; therefore, a decreasing function should link the capital intensity of the techniques to the relative cost of capital; a decrease in the marginal productivity of capital in relation to that of labour should be caused by the substitution of labour by capital.

This, apart from the concept of marginal productivity, is a very old theory. It was adopted, after the marginalist revolution, by all the important economists of the time, Jevons, Wicksteed, Clark, Böhm-Bawerk, and Wicksell. Wicksell, however (as we mentioned in Chapter 6), noticed the strangeness of certain phenomena (later called 'Wicksell effects'), and pointed out the possibility of some 'paradoxes' in the relationship between the capital intensity of the techniques and the remuneration of capital.

However, it was only in the debate of the 1950s and 1960s that this problem was solved. The debate was opened by J. V. Robinson with the article 'The Production Function and the Theory of Capital' (*Review of Economic Studies*, 1953–4), in which she put forward an argument inspired by Sraffa's introduction (1951) to Ricardo's *Principles*: that the 'degree of mechanization' of a productive technique can increase, rather than decrease, following an increase in the interest–wage ratio. Robinson also noted that the origin of this strange effect is to be found in the impossibility of measuring capital in physical terms, given its heterogeneous composition, and the consequent necessity to measure it in value. Then D. Champernowne, in a comment on Robinson's article, while acknowledging the importance of the problem, suggested that it could be solved by measuring capital by means of a 'chain index' of his own construction, although he admitted that his index might not work in some 'strange' cases. Robinson counter-attacked, especially in a section of *The Accumulation of Capital* (1956), where she pointed out that the strange relationship existing between the prices of factor services and the capital intensity of techniques is not due to purely 'financial' phenomena, as

Champernowne seemed to suggest, but can be generated by real technical change.

In that year, by a strange historical quirk, the first neo-classical aggregate growth models came to light: those of Solow and Swan, already discussed in Chapter 9. These models used exactly the same aggregate production function and the same theory of capital which had been criticized by Robinson. This certainly helped to liven up the party. In 1960 Sraffa's *Production of Commodities by Means of Commodities* was published, a book which contained, albeit in very concise form, all the elements needed to clarify the question. At the same time, Garegnani's *Il capitale nelle teorie della distribuzione* (*Capital in the Theories of Distribution*) was published, a book in which criticism of the neo-classical theory of capital was explicitly formulated.

Robinson's criticism was accepted without resistance by many neoclassical economists—for example by Morishima and Hicks, who dealt with it in *Equilibrium, Stability and Growth* (1964) and in *Capital and Growth* (1965) respectively. As late as 1962 and 1965, however, Samuelson and Levhari made attempts to resolve the problem in a different way from that suggested by Robinson. They were, for this reason, criticized by various followers of Sraffa, particularly Pasinetti and Garegnani, of whom we will mention only two of their most important articles: respectively, 'Changes in the Rate of Profit and Switches of Techniques' and 'Switches of Techniques', both published in the *Quarterly Journal of Economics* in November 1966. This issue of the journal contained various other articles on the same argument, by Levhari, Morishima, Robinson and Naqvi, Bruno, Burmeister, and Sheshinski. The most important, however, was Samuelson's 'Summing Up', in which he acknowledged the validity of the criticisms and, while trying to minimize their importance, he admitted the error inherent in the neoclassical theory of aggregate capital. This closed the debate, even if the aftermath continued until the early 1970s. The final word on this problem was given by Garegnani in 'Heterogeneous Capital, the Production Function and the Theory of Distribution' (*Review of Economic Studies*, 1970).

In order to explain this subject in the simplest way, we will use a model of an economy in which only two goods are produced, a consumer and a capital good, by means of capital and labour; it is the same model we used in Chapter 4 to clarify the Marxian problem of the transformation of values into prices:

$$p = wl_k + k_k p(1 + r)$$
$$1 = wl_c + k_c p(1 + r)$$

The price of the consumer good is taken as numeraire, w is the real wage, p the relative price of the capital good, r the rate of profit, which is equal to the rate of interest, l_k and l_c the labour coefficient in the two industries, and k_c and k_k the capital coefficients. Here, for simplicity, we will assume that all the symbols denote scalars; but in a more general interpretation, k_k can be interpreted as a matrix and p and l_k as two vectors. We will discuss this in the next section. With a few simple algebraic passages it is possible to obtain, from the two equations, a decreasing function linking wages and profit:

$$w = \frac{1 - k_k(1 + r)}{l_c - l_c\, l_k\left(\dfrac{k_k}{l_k} - \dfrac{k_c}{l_c}\right)(1 + r)}$$

Two different wage–profit curves have been drawn in Fig. 17. They represent two different productive techniques (two different systems of equations); let us call them α and β. The techniques differ in the ways in which capital and labour are combined, but it is also possible that one (or some) capital good(s) is (are) physically different in the two cases.

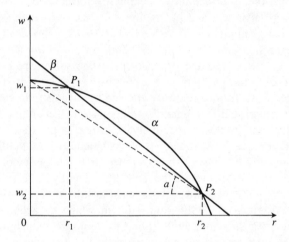

FIG. 17

The concavity of curve α implies that in the technique α it holds $k_k/l_k > k_c/l_c$, whereas curve β is linear because $k_k/l_k = k_c/l_c$. In technique α the capital–labour ratio varies with variations in the price of capital and, therefore, with variations in the distribution of income, even without a change in the productive technique. In technique β, on the other hand, the aggregate capital–labour ratio does not vary with variations in the distribution of income, as prices do not change. Graphically, the capital–labour ratio is measured, for technique β, by the slope of line β. In fact, in the case in which $k_k/l_k = k_c/l_c$ the preceding formula can be reduced to:

$$w = \frac{1 - k_k}{l_c} - \frac{k_k}{l_c}r$$

in which k_k/l_c measures the slope of line β. For technique α, instead, the capital–labour ratio is measured, for example at point p_2, by the width of angle a, and is different for every different point on curve α.

Let us now compare the two techniques in correspondence to different distributive patterns. At the points to the left of r_1, the capitalists will choose technique β as, with respect to α, it gives higher profits in relation to each wage. Technique α will be preferred at the points between r_1 and r_2, while at those to the right of r_2 technique β will be preferred again. This is the phenomenon of the 'reswitching of techniques': technique β, which had been abandoned following an increase in the rate of profit around r_1, is preferred again when the rate of profit becomes still higher, i.e. higher than r_2. At each of points P_1 and P_2 the two techniques are equally profitable and have the same price systems. Passing from technique β to α around point P_1 there is a decrease in the capital–labour ratio. This change in the capital intensity of the techniques has purely real causes, as at point P_1 the two techniques have the same price system. This phenomenon is known as the positive 'real Wicksell effect'. In the movement from technique α to β around point P_2, there is, therefore, a negative real Wicksell effect. In this case, with an increase in the rate of profit, the capital–labour ratio increases rather than decreases; and this occurs because of a real technical change. Also at the points between P_1 and P_2, the capital–labour ratio increases when the interest rate increases, but this occurs, in this case, only because the price of capital changes. This is the 'price Wicksell effect'. The phenomenon of the increase in the capital–labour ratio following an increase in the interest rate is called 'capital reversal'. It is a phenomenon that contradicts the neoclassical parable according to which the capital intensity of the techniques is a decreasing function of the ratio between the prices of the capital and labour 'factors'.

Let us now go beyond the limits set by the non-substitution theorem and admit that there are other primary inputs, e.g. land, and that each sector can produce more than one good at the same time. In this case, a variation in the composition of final demand causes the intensity of use of the primary factors to vary, as different goods use the factors in different proportions. Another neoclassical parable tells us that the intensity of use of each primary input is a decreasing function of its remuneration. This parable is derived from a 'generalization' of the classical theory of *intensive* differential rent, a generalization made by economists such as Thünen, Jevons, Wicksteed, and Clark. In the same way as land rent increases (suggests the parable) with the intensification of the use of labour per unit of land, remuneration of labour would tend to increase with the increase in use of land per labour unit.

This way of thinking can be turned upside down. If the wage–rent ratio changes in a certain direction, then the relationship between the marginal productivities of labour and land must change in the same direction. This result is ensured, not only by the hypotheses of competition and decreasing marginal productivity, but also by the assumption of maximizing behaviour by the entrepreneurs. The latter, following an increase in the ratio between the remuneration of the two factors, would tend to substitute the least expensive for the most expensive, thus changing the marginal productivities in the same direction as the remunerations and the intensities of use in the opposite direction. Unfortunately, things are not like this. If, as is obviously possible, a variation in prices and remunerations causes a technical change and therefore alters the proportions of the primary inputs, it is also true that in a capitalist economy there is not necessarily a decreasing function linking these proportions and the ratio between the factor remunerations. This is also a result which came out of Sraffa's work. However, it was explicitly brought to light by his followers, and most clearly in the essay by J. S. Metcalfe and I. Steedman, 'Reswitching and Primary Input Use' (*Economic Journal*, 1972).

11.2.3. Production of commodities by means of commodities

All the above is in Sraffa's book, but only sketched out in its essentials; it is not surprising that orthodox theory needed several years of debate in order to bring out its theoretical implications. All the same, there is more in *Production of Commodities*, and it should not be assumed that its most important theoretical implications are those dealing with orthodox theory. The fact is that this late product of the years of high theory is a concise, compact, and pared-down book which is not at all easy to understand. Nor is it easy to find the correct place for it, a place which it undisputedly occupies in the history of economic thought, given the scarcity of references supplied by Sraffa in regard to his sources. This is the problem that most concerns us here: to find the correct place for Sraffa in the history of economic thought.

The core of the model presented in the first part of *Production of Commodities* has already been presented in the two equations of the preceding section. All we have to do now is to reinterpret k_k as a matrix of technical coefficients of dimension $n \times n$, l_k as a vector of positive labour coefficients and p as a vector of relative prices. If w is known, the system of n equations simultaneously determines the rate of profit and the relative prices of $n-1$ goods.

With changes in w, the conditions of relative cost of the different commodities change, as the proportions of the utilization of labour and means of production in the diverse industries are different. Therefore, all the relative prices change. There is a decreasing function linking profit and wages similar to those drawn in Fig. 17. In general it is not a linear function, and the curve which represents it may have as many humps as the number of goods produced less one. Therefore, if there are different techniques there may be many cases of reswitching of techniques and capital reversals. Profit is not related to a productive contribution of capital; in fact, the latter cannot even be defined in Sraffa's model. In regard to distribution, the model simply states that, if one of the distributive variables is known, the other is determined residually.

In the second part of *Production of Commodities*, Sraffa introduces joint production. This makes it possible to consider fixed capital. Machines of different ages are treated as joint products of the industries which use them when they are one year younger (one year is the length of a productive cycle). It is also possible to take into consideration the use of many types of natural resource. So the model becomes more complex, and loses several of the properties it had under the hypothesis of single production with only circulating capital and labour. However, it does not lose its essentials: profit cannot be explained by the productive contribution of the capital 'factor' and its scarcity, but remains a *surplus*, the size of which depends solely on the social and technical relationships with which a given final output is produced capitalistically. This seems to us to be Sraffa's basic message.

It is necessary to begin with this result to evaluate his work in a historical perspective. In this way it is possible immediately to reject the interpretations of Sraffa's model which consider it as a special case of the neo-Walrasian general-equilibrium model. These interpretations, such as that put forward by Hahn in 'The Neo-Ricardians' (*Cambridge Journal of Economics*, 1982), have little meaning, not because they lack an analytical basis, but because, by concentrating on the formal aspects of the model, they overlook its theoretical content. According to this point of view, Sraffa's model corresponds to that special case of the inter-temporal-equilibrium model in which a uniform rate of profit is obtained. Furthermore, according to another criticism, it is a model of 'production' prices only in that it assumes constant returns to scale, and only to the degree to which it makes use of the non-substitution theorem. But Sraffa did not have to assume anything in regard to the returns to scale, because he was studying an economy in which the scale of production was assumed as given. It is true, however, that it would be necessary to say something about the returns to scale if one wished to give up that assumption, for example, when one wishes to study the adjustments of market prices to production prices, or the growth process, or to introduce some hypotheses about consumption, even if only a simple classical or Keynesian consumption function. It is also doubtful that a hypothesis different from that of constant returns could preserve the most important properties of Sraffa's theory. But these are problems that Sraffa did not pose, and it is difficult to see why a theory should be evaluated on the grounds of the things it does not state.

In reality, what makes Sraffa's model substantially different from the inter-temporal-equilibrium model are a series of important theoretical characteristics: the absence of the full-employment hypothesis, the refusal to consider prices as determined by supply and demand, and the absence of a hypothesis of an initial endowment of arbitrarily given capital goods. What distances it from the non-substitution theorem is, instead, simply its assumption of *given* quantities.

This leads us immediately into the world of the classical economists and Marx, as also suggested by the theory of profit as a surplus. The classical economists and Marx made use of a dynamic which evolves through *historical* time. They assumed as given, at a certain moment, or over a very brief period of time (e.g. a productive cycle), the technique in use and the composition of the final demand. They did not study change by assuming that *at every moment* there is the possibility of choosing between the techniques and the final consumptions prevailing in different stationary-state economies. They believed that techniques and demand change through time and differ from one period to another; but also that, in each period, in each productive cycle, there is only one technique and only one final demand. So prices can change through time; and this can also be caused by changes in the final demand, as changes in the latter induce changes in techniques. Now, almost all of Sraffa's book can be read from this point of view. The only important exception appears in the last six pages of the final chapter, where Sraffa tackles the problem of technical change by adopting the method of comparative statics. This anomaly can be interpreted as a concession, for the sake of argument, to the neoclassical economists, a concession made to demonstrate the paradoxes connected with the reswitching of techniques; and it does not seem to us to cause any problem in regard to linking Sraffa to the approach of the classical economists and Marx.

The problems lie elsewhere; and two of them deserve special attention. The first concerns the necessity of defining more clearly Sraffa's position in regard to the classical and Marxian approach. After all, there is no 'classical Marxian approach', if it is true that Marx considered himself to be a critic, albeit 'dialectical', of Ricardo and Smith. In other words, was Sraffa a 'neo-Ricardian', as some orthodox Marxists and some orthodox neoclassical economists have argued? Or was he a Marxist, as he himself and many of his followers have maintained? The second problem is this: what is the use of Sraffa's model? Some aspects of his way of thinking leave us, at first, rather perplexed. To give one example: the absence of a hypotheses in regard to constant returns scale means that analysis of the changes in the distribution of income must be undertaken by reasoning as if they could not cause changes in the composition of demand. What type of real economy can be described with such a hypothesis?

In order to clarify both these problems it is necessary to identify the level of abstraction of Sraffa's model. This level is defined, albeit with the usual cryptic conciseness, by Sraffa himself. It is defined in the subtitle of his book: *Prelude to a Critique of Economic Theory*. It is the same as the first chapter of *Capital*, 'Commodities', the real prelude to the *Critique of Political Economy*. In that chapter Marx tackled the analysis of the commodity and its value, and laid down the theoretical bases of all his successive work; he attacked the 'vulgar economists', whom he accused of looking for the explanation of the value of goods in exchange relations; and he linked himself explicitly to Ricardo in looking for it, instead, in the production sphere.

However, even though Marx had clearly pointed out that value is a *social phenomenon*, his link with Ricardo induced him to determine the value of goods by ignoring the capitalist form in which they are produced. Value, according to the theory set out in the chapter on *Commodities*, depends solely on the quantity of labour employed in its production, its social determination being reduced to the way in which society allocates working activity among the various industries. In other words, value is not influenced by the way in which production is socially structured, nor by the way in which the social classes face each other in the production sphere. Thus, for example, the value of the social product (and this is so not only in the first chapter of *Capital* but, as a consequence of the analysis undertaken in that chapter, in the whole book) does not depend on the way in which the product is distributed—a clear reminder of the Ricardian claim to measure value by making it independent from the variations in distribution. It is obvious that, in order to reach such a result, Marx had to rely on a high level of abstraction, and it is almost paradoxical that a book on 'capital' opens with a chapter in which capital is ignored. It is almost as if Sraffa had rewritten that chapter, trying to reach the maximum level of abstraction, from returns to scale, growth, disequilibrium adjustments, even from the specific institutional structure to which the type of capitalist set-up may conform historically—exactly as in the chapter on 'Commodities'. However, he made it clear once and for all that the only thing which it is impossible to ignore in determining the value of the commodities produced in a capitalist economy, is the fact that they are produced in capitalist conditions: that it is meaningless to assume, as Marx did in that chapter, that 'wages is a category that, as yet, has no existence at the present stage of our investigation' (*Capital*, i. 51); that there is no invariable measure of value in Ricardo's sense; and that the only invariable measure of value which exists, embodied labour, is not a correct measure, precisely because it is not able to take into account the capitalist nature of the production of commodities.

In other words, Sraffa took Marx seriously in his treatment of value as a *social phenomenon*—so seriously that he distanced himself from Ricardo, for this reason, more than Marx did himself. In fact, all that subtle exegetic work which he undertook in the introduction to Ricardo's *Principles* aimed at showing, among other things, the uselessness of the notion of 'absolute value' and of the 'invariable measure of value'—useless with respect to Ricardo's main theoretical aim, the theory of surplus. In *Production of Commodities* he then also demonstrated its *mistakenness*. We are sure that those last six pages of the final chapter of *Production of Commodities* which we mentioned above are, after all, only a by-product of a deeper and more profitable analysis of Marx and Ricardo. It is interesting to note that the by-product in question turned into a criticism of those neoclassical theories of capital which are linked back, through Jevons and Böhm-Bawerk, precisely to the Ricardian labour theory of value. On the other hand, the criticism of the *analytical* vices of the labour theory of value, both Marxian and Ricardian, was nothing more, in itself, than a by-product: Sraffa simply noted this in *Production of Commodities*, without giving it a great deal of importance.

It seems possible to conclude, while on the subject of the determination of profit, that Sraffa's theory does not bring to light any basic analytical differences between Ricardo and Marx, on the subject of value his work can be read in only one way: the *Prelude to a Critique of Economic Theory* seems to us just like a first chapter of *Capital* which Marx would have written if he had been a little less Ricardian and a little more Marxist.

11.3 RADICAL POLITICAL ECONOMY AND SIMILAR APPROACHES

11.3.1 Marxist economic thought before 1968

In this section we will present a group of economists who made some interesting contributions to the development of Marxist theory in the second postwar period.

The first of these is Paul Alexander Baran (1910–64). He was a Russian, son of a Menshevik militant. At a young age he absorbed the atmosphere of the fervent Soviet debates of the 1920s. He emigrated in 1928 and, after various academic misadventures in Germany and England, ended up in the United States in 1939. There he managed to obtain a safe academic position only in 1951, at Stanford University. His main work is *The Political Economy of Growth* (1957), in which he put forward the famous theory of the 'potential surplus'. While the 'effective surplus' produced in an economy is measured by the difference between current production and current consumption, the *potential* surplus is defined as the difference between the production made possible by the existing technology and the productive consumption necessary to obtain that level of production. Obviously, it is a notional quantity; it serves, however, to show the actual distortions of capitalist economies. In fact, in this type of economy the potential surplus is always greater then the actual surplus because of the importance of luxury waste consumption, unproductive labour, war damage, or the allocative inefficiencies generated by the market and the profit system.

We shall return to the concept of surplus when we consider the book written by Baran in collaboration with Sweezy. Here we shall comment on Baran's analysis of imperialism—an analysis which, distancing itself from the unrefined Marxist–Leninist work of those times, moved Marxist thought in the direction of the theory of unequal exchange as a basic mechanism in the production and reproduction of imperialism and underdevelopment. This theory inspired many further works, of which one of the most interesting is André Gunder Frank's *Capitalism and Underdevelopment in Latin America* (1967). Baran's book was also politically important: his argument that national liberation movements would contribute to liberating, not only underdeveloped countries from imperialism, but also the imperialist countries from capitalism, gave a theoretical foundation to a great many of the anti-imperialist movements of the 1960s.

Baran's arguments were developed in the book *Monopoly Capital* (1966), written in collaboration with Sweezy. We have already spoken about Paul Malor Sweezy (b. 1910) in Chapter 8, where we mentioned his summary of Marxist economic theory, *The Theory of Capitalist Development*, a book on which generations of Marxist intellectuals have been educated. Two of Sweezy's original lines of thought had already been sketched out in that book, and deal with his personal interpretation of two Marxian laws of movement: on the one hand the theory of the 'realization crises', which he reformulated by drawing on stagnationist theories of Keynesian origin and reworking them into an original under-consumption theory of depression; on the other, the law stating the tendency towards increasing 'concentration' and 'centralization' of capital, which was enriched by the experience he gained by participating in 1930s debates on the forms of non-competitive markets. Sweezy, let us recall, made an original contribution to these debates, 'Demand under Conditions of Oligopoly' (*Journal of Political Economy*, 1939), where he presented the theory of the kinked demand curve.

In *Monopoly Capital* these diverse research interests were integrated with Baran's theory of economic surplus, and produced the thesis of the *tendency of the potential surplus to grow*—a thesis which was to replace, according to the authors, the Marxian law of the falling profit rate as a fundamental explanation of the march of capitalism towards self-destruction. Capitalist accumulation causes, besides an increasing concentration of capital, a constant increase in production and productivity. Given the unequal distribution of income, a permanent feature of capitalist economies, accumulation also creates the fundamental problem of the 'absorption of the surplus' and a permanent lack of investment opportunities. The ensuing tendency towards stagnation could be counterbalanced by certain 'countervailing influences', sales expenditure, public spending, military expenditure, etc. But these, on the one hand, would contribute to various social and political problems, such as waste, inefficiency, and imperialistic wars, and, on the other, would serve to only hinder *temporarily* the intrinsic tendency towards stagnation.

Another major Marxist economist of this period was Maurice Herbert Dobb (1900–76), whose important *Political Economy of Capitalism* (1937) we have already mentioned. In 1946 he published *Studies in the Development of Capitalism*, a book which nourished the minds of entire generations of economic historians, particularly English, and gave birth to intense debates among historians and Marxist economists. One of the main arguments of the debates concerned the problem of whether the decline of feudalism had been caused by internal contradictions, as Dobb had argued, or had been caused by 'external' factors, such as the development of commerce and the relationships between town and the countryside, as was argued by Sweezy and others. The importance of this debate was not limited to the field of economic history, but also touched upon a central problem of Marxist economic theory, that of 'primitive accumulation'.

One of the main interests of Dobb, after the Second World War, was the economic theory of socialism, to which he contributed with various works, both theoretical and applied. The most important are: *Soviet Economic*

Development since 1917 (1948); *On Economic Theory and Socialism* (1955), a collection of papers which go back to the 1930s; and *Welfare Economics and the Economics of Socialism* (1969). Dobb was a critic of the theory of 'market socialism' of the Lange–Lerner type, and pointed out its essentially static and therefore unrealistic nature. Against it, he argued that, given the burdensome inheritance of productive backwardness and of inequality in the distribution of income and resources, an economy in the phase of transition to socialism must put the problems of equity and growth before that of the efficient allocation of resources.

These three heretical academics, Baran, Sweezy, and Dobb, were in fact fairly orthodox if their work is considered from the point of view of the Marxist doctrine of the period. Their orthodoxy is demonstrated mainly in their choice of the 'level of analysis' on which to focus their theoretical efforts, which was the 'intermediate' level of the analysis of economic evolution; the higher level of the 'fundamental principles' of Marxism was not even touched. In order to understand this, it may be useful to consider the 'three-level' theory put forward in the 1950s by Kozo Uno (1897–1977) to rationalize that methodological stance. Uno, an important Japanese economist of the period, or, rather, a leader of the Japanese Marxist school, put forward this theory in a book of *Principles of Political Economy*, published (in Japanese) in 1950–2 and later reprinted in an abridged form in 1964 (an English translation was published in 1980). The argument is that Marxist theory articulates itself on three levels of analysis: the first, and most abstract, faces the problems pertaining to the fundamental principles, of value, crises, laws of movement etc.; the second level delimits the field of study in regard to the evolution of the capitalist economic form, and gives rise to the so-called theory of the 'three stages' of capitalist development (mercantilism, liberalism, imperialism); the third, finally, is that of the 'concrete analysis of concrete situations'. The orthodoxy of the great Marxist economists of that period showed itself in the fact that, despite the originality with which they had tackled problems of the 'second' and 'third' levels, none of them had ever dared to move up to the highest level of wisdom, dealing with the great fundamental principles. Another symptom of their orthodoxy was the belief, which only Uno had the courage to make explicit, that the history of capitalism had ended in 1917; then began the history of the transition to socialism. But the risk of anathema was strong in those times.

It is worth pausing for a moment to consider this problem, because it constituted one of the main watersheds between traditional and modern Marxism. As early as the immediate aftermath of the Second World War, some heterodox Marxists, such as Amadeo Bordiga and Tony Cliff, had cast doubt on the socialist nature of the Soviet Union. Bordiga formulated an original theory of the Stalinist Soviet system which cut through all the contorted arguments about 'difficult transition', 'degenerated workers' State', and 'bureaucratic collectivism': the system established in the Soviet Union was simply a new form of capitalism. This argument was put forward in various papers beginning at least as early as 1946, and, in complete form, in the book *Struttura economica e sociale della Russia d'oggi* (*The Social and Economic Structure of Contemporary Russia*, 1957). Independently, Tony Cliff moved along a similar line of thought in a book which was published for the first time in 1948, and again, after various reworkings, in 1955 (*Stalinist Russia: A Marxist Analysis*). The most recent edition, entitled *State Capitalism in Russia*, came out in 1974.

This was a minority view, to say the least, in the Marxism of the 1950s and the 1960s: but time has done it justice. Charles Bettelheim (b. 1913), a scholar of Maoist orientation, (among his most important works are *Planification et croissance accélérée* (*Planning and Accelerated Growth*) (1964), and *Calcul économique et formes de propriété* (*Economic Calculation and Property Forms*) (1970), tackled the problems of the 'transition' by interpreting the economic and social transformations generated by the Soviet economic development as typical of a capitalist process. During the 1980s this point of view has become dominant in western Marxist circles, so much so that even Sweezy has moved over to this position in one of his most recent works, *Post-Revolutionary Society* (1981).

Another contemporary Marxist heretic merits mention: Ernest Mandel (b. 1923), of Trotskyist orientation, who, after a systematic but rather traditional *Traité d'économie marxiste* (1962), produced two quite original books: *Late Capitalism* (1975) and *Long Waves of Capitalist Development* (1980). Even though dealing with the 'intermediate' level of analysis, and not touching on 'fundamental' principles such as the falling profit rate, these books have helped to lead debates on the future of capitalism away from the simplifications of the theories of collapse and stagnation; besides this, they have brought the attention of the economists back to the problem of long waves.

Finally, we must mention one of the few Marxist economists of the period who has had the courage to enter the citadel of fundamental principles and clear out some commonplaces of Marxist orthodoxy. Nobuo Okishio (b. 1927), by developing some arguments already put forward by Shibata in the 1930s, has proved, among other things, that the law of the falling rate of profit is not a law at all, but only a particular theory depending on certain restrictive and unrealistic hypotheses about the nature of technical progress. At least three of his articles are important in this regard: 'Technical Change and the Rate of Profit' (*Kobe University Economic Review*, 1961), 'A Formal Proof of Marx's Two Theorems' (*Kobe University Economic Review*, 1972), and 'Notes on Technical Progress and Capitalist Society' (*Cambridge Journal of Economics*, 1977).

11.3.2. Neo-Marxist and post-Marxist approaches

1968 was a crucial year for the evolution of Marxist thought. A populous generation of young people, unscathed by ideologies and parties, suddenly approached politics. All over the world they revolted against authoritarianism, oppression, and exploitation; and, even though they sought their principal cultural references in the traditional and modern classics of Marxist thought, they did not hesitate to bring their iconoclastic fervour to bear on the 'establishment' of official socialist doctrine. Creative energies were liberated and bitter theoretical debates flared up again in the years which followed; and none of the sacred truths was spared. A new socialist economic theory, or 'radical political economy', or neo-Marxist or post-Marxist economics emerged, whatever one wishes to call it, which, at least at present, does not seem much more than an archipelago of critical theories.

Here we have no room to deal with all that is original in this theoretical magma. Therefore, to say at least something about the lines of research which seem to be the most important and promising, we have been forced to make extensive use of our scissors. So we will ignore, with very few exceptions, the work which Uno would have classified at the 'second level', even though there are interesting and original lines of research here.

The few exceptions consist of some important works which introduced innovations to traditional Marxist analysis on certain relevant theoretical questions. *The Fiscal Crisis of the State* (1973), by James O'Connor, broke away from the Marxist–Leninist simplifications about the State as a 'business committee of the bourgeoisie', and studied the role played by the modern capitalist state in the process of capital accumulation and, at the same time, the effects of class conflict on the transformations of the State itself. Harry Braverman in *Labour and Monopoly Capital* (1974), dealt with the problem of the effects of mechanization and managerial control of companies over the transformation of the labour process and class composition in modern capitalism. In *The Modern World System* (1974–80), Immanuel Wallerstein developed the Marxian analysis of 'primitive accumulation', putting forward the idea of a capitalism which can live—and, right from the outset, *did* live—only as a 'world economy', i.e. as an integrated system of international division of labour. Finally, in *Geometria dell'imperialismo* (*Geometry of Imperialism*, 1978) Giovanni Arrighi reformulated the Marxist theory of imperialism in an original general scheme capable of accounting (as special cases) for the imperialism of Hobson, Lenin, and Rosa Luxemburg, as well as those of the Vietnam War and the 'people's democracies'.

Returning to the 'first level' of analysis, we will now present in a little more detail some of the debates and theoretical developments relating to three important subjects of contemporary Marxist thought: the theory of value, the monetary circuit, and the structural change of the capitalist economy. Finally, we will mention the 'new European institutionalism', an approach which, while not being completely assimilated into the neo-Marxist approaches, does seem to maintain a certain relationship with them.

On the subject of value, the debate was reopened in 1960 by Sraffa's book, which smouldered under the ashes for a decade, burst noisily into flames in the 1970s, and was almost completely extinguished in the 1980s. Today, it seems generally accepted that the dialectic splendour of the labour theory of value must be renounced. Basically, three reasons are given for this. The first, and most important, is that this theory, the last residue of 'Ricardian naturalism' in Marx, conflicts with the truly Marxian theory, which considers value to be a 'social phenomenon'. We have already mentioned this in the section dedicated to Sraffa, and will not return to it here. We will limit ourselves to pointing out that *Value and Naturalism in Marx* (1979) by M. Lippi is the work which has most clearly tackled this aspect of the problem.

The second reason concerns the transformation problem. We have already spoken about this in the chapter devoted to Marx. Here we will restrict ourselves to reaffirming the main points. However modest the analytical claims which can be advanced in regard to the transformation procedures, it is impossible to avoid admitting that the following propositions are *in general* not valid:

(1) It is necessary to know the labour values in order to determine the production prices:
(2) Given the wage, it is possible to determine the profit rate before knowing the prices:
(3) In the transformation from values into prices, all the aggregate variables remain unchanged:
(4) In particular, the rate of profit and the rate of exploitation remain unchanged.

Marx was unaware of these difficulties. But today they are known to all, and it is almost universally accepted that, faced with these difficulties, it is impossible to remain faithful to the labour theory of value, even if there are still some people content to keep it as an 'auxiliary' theory, and others still searching for the right solution to the transformation problem.

Unfortunately, however, it is not possible to be satisfied with an auxiliary theory. In fact, there is a third reason which impels us towards the abandonment of that theory. In general, when one does not wish to be limited to the cases of single production with only circulating capital, the variables expressed in terms of embodied labour are not necessarily economically meaningful. This is the well-known phenomenon, also brought to light by Sraffa, that, in the presence of joint production and economically significant price systems, there can be negative labour values—even negative rates of exploitation in the presence of a positive profit rate. This is not a *curiosum* or a limiting case, but a possibility which may occur normally in the most general case.

Heroic attempts have been made to get around these problems, but without great success. For example, A. Medio, in 'Profits and Surplus-Value: Appearance and Reality in Capitalist Production' (in *A Critique of Economic Theory*, 1972, edited by E. K. Hunt and J. G. Schwartz), has worked out a case in which it is possible to transform values into prices respecting all, or almost all, the Marxian claims: the case of an economy without non-basic commodities, without joint production, without fixed capital; and structured in such a way as to maintain a uniform proportion between the input and output of each good. Instead, M. Morishima, in 'Marx in the Light of Modern Economic Theory' (*Econometrica*, 1974), has proved a 'fundamental Marxian theorem' for which the profit rate is positive if and only if the rate of exploitation is also positive, the labour values being positive if the prices are too. However, the definition of 'labour-value' adopted by Morishima has nothing to do with the definition of 'embodied labour' used by Marx. Furthermore (and this is more suspect), Morishima's 'fundamental Marxian theorem' is not incompatible with a marginalist theory of distribution, in which it makes no sense to speak of exploitation.

The neo-Marxists have made no song and dance about the loss of labour value. The widespread opinion today is that the theory of exploitation is independent of the labour theory of value. Thus efforts have been made to show how it is possible to account for exploitation without using the notion of 'embodied labour'. Here we will mention four of the most interesting attempts, although research is still continuing: J. Eatwell's 'Mr Sraffa's Standard Commodity and the Rate of Exploitation' (*Quarterly Journal of Economics*, 1975), I. Steedman's *Marx after Sraffa* (1975), J. E. Roemer's *A General Theory of Exploitation and Class* (1982), and S. Bowles and H. Gintis, *Democracy and Capitalism: Property, Community and the Contradictions of Modern Social Thought* (1986).

Let us turn to the other two groups of theories in which we are interested: those on the monetary circuit and structural change. Here, hoping to be justified by the fact that we are dealing with work still in progress, we will make even more drastic use of the scissors, and will avoid mentioning authors and texts (although our Bibliography will indicate a few surveys and collections).

The theories of the monetary circuit begin from the special Marxian view of the circular flow, intended as a 'circuit of commodity capital' and a 'circuit of productive capital', which make up a subset of a wider 'circuit of monetary capital'. The latter begins with the creation of purchasing power, by means of credit, and ends with its destruction, by means of payment of the debt. Money plays an essential role in the process of capitalist *production*: as it is non-produced purchasing power (unlike real goods), it allows the production process to be begun 'from nothing'. Credit is not accessible to all the economic agents, but basically only to the capitalists, who, therefore, are enabled to acquire labour and means of production without first having produced an equivalent amount in real terms. The workers, who, in practice, have no access to credit—or, at any rate, not in the way and to the extent available to the capitalists—can buy goods only after having produced them. This social asymmetry is considered by some to be an essential characteristic of the capitalist production system, and even more important than the institutional structure itself which regulates the ownership of the means of production. In fact, what really counts in the class relationship established in the productive process is not so much who owns the means of production, but rather who controls them. And they are controlled by the agents who take the investment decisions and, therefore, who have access to finance.

On the other hand, the money supply is considered endogenous, and the sector which 'deals' with it is considered an authentic productive sector: its output is liquidity, and expands and contracts in synchrony with the demand, i.e. with the overall level of economic activity. It does not, however, move in *perfect* synchrony. This may lead to realization crises and, more generally, to a strong cyclicity in the accumulation process. Here the crisis is explained, not only by the reserve function of money and the consequent possibility of excessive accumulation of liquid balances, but also, and above all, by the double asset–liability nature of money and the consequent necessity for debtors to repay, sooner or later, their debts. Due to the concatenations of the debt–credit relationships, in fact, financial crises often assume the characteristics of chain bankruptcies. Here there is a strict relationship with some post-Keynesian theories. More generally, it is possible to say that the neo-Marxian theories of the monetary circuit are derived from the attempt to assimilate into Marxist theory the theories formulated by some of the anti-neoclassical followers of Keynes; but there has also been constant reference to other, older, heretical theorists of money, such as Tooke, Wicksell, and Schumpeter. At any rate, we must point out that, even if the predominant doctrinal reference, among theorists of the monetary circuit, is Marx, not all the economists who follow this line of research, especially in France, consider themselves Marxist.

Now let us turn to the last group of theoretical problems which interest us here: those which have arisen from recent debates on long cycles. Here, perhaps, we are considering the most important theoretical innovation of the neo-Marxist political economy. What is hidden behind the debates on long cycles and is just trying to break through is the refusal to accept the legitimacy of the concept itself of the 'laws of tendential movement'. Observing the recurrent ability of history to disprove theories of history, and distrusting not only the implicit historical optimism of the neoclassical and post-Keynesian steady-state growth models but also the explicit 'optimism' of the traditional Marxist models of stagnation and collapse, the young generations of Marxists have learned to treat history and its 'laws of movement' cautiously. But they have not given up the idea that political economy, intended as the science of the capitalist mode of production, deals with long-run structural changes. However, once the illusion has been abandoned that history can be explained with some strong hypotheses on the secular trend of the rates of profit or accumulation, only two roads are left open: either renounce the analysis of long-run phenomena or tackle it in terms of recurrent structural change—or, which amounts to the same thing, of the *long cycle*.

In fact, the theory of structural change aims at endogenizing a series of economic phenomena that orthodox theory has tended to treat as parameters and exogenous data: technology, institutions, class relationships, etc. To the degree to which the ability of the capitalist system to maintain a certain accumulation 'regime' in a stable and permanent manner is denied, the necessity of drastic structural changes is acknowledged. But to the degree to which one denies any intrinsic tendency towards a final collapse, one also acknowledges the possibility of using structural change to re-establish the conditions of accumulation. This leads directly to some sort of *cyclical* theory of structural change; and, as we are concerned with the fundamental forces of change, we must be dealing with *long* cycles. At this level of analysis, moreover, the particular length of the period attributed to the cycles, 30 years, half-century, or whatever, is irrelevant, as is the idea of a regular periodicity. What really counts is this: whatever properties of the structural set-up are judged necessary to sustain accumulation, an indefinite capacity for the system to reproduce itself is denied. This implies that growth itself is able to create the necessary conditions to modify its own bases, whether social, institutional, or technological.

This methodological approach is present, in differing degrees of consciousness, in all the contemporary theories of the long cycle. The differences among them concern only the type of structural change on which attention is focused and the type of parameters which are endogenized. In this way it is possible to distinguish (just to give an idea) two large groups of theories. On the one hand are the neo-Schumpeterian theories (accepted, in recent times, also by many neo-Marxist economists), in which the emphasis is placed on technological change, on the waves of 'fundamental innovations', on the changes in 'technological paradigms', etc. On the other hand are the neo-Marxist theories in the strict sense, in which it is the changes of the institutional structures, class conflict, etc., that are endogenized. We will include in this group some versions of the 'regulation' theory, which, for the emphasis they place on the tendency of 'regulation regimes' to create the conditions for their own change of form in the long run, seem to us to belong more to the theories of the long cycle than to that of growth stages. However, recent neo-Marxist studies on the recurrent nature of structural change seem to have reabsorbed not only the traditional interest in the 'laws of movement' but also that relating to 'growth phases'.

Finally, it is worth mentioning a theoretical approach which has surfaced fairly recently, the 'new European institutionalism'. It should not be confused with American neo-institutionalism, as it did not arise as a side-shoot of neoclassical economics. On the contrary, it links itself back to the critical tradition of Veblen, at the same time paying much attention to various subjects which are dear to Marxist economics. There is also a marked interest in Schumpeter and (among the more recent economists) in authors such as Michel Aglietta, Kurt Rothschild, Janos Kornai, J. K. Galbraith, Nicholas Georgescu-Roegen, and the European post-Keynesians.

This stream of thought is like a river that numbers among its main tributaries the French 'regulation' school, various Schumpeterian approaches to economic change, including some recent 'evolutionary' lines of research on technical progress, and, finally, some of the attempts to analyse structural change which we mentioned above. The polemic against the neoclassical tradition is strong, and the rejection of methodological individualism explicit—sometimes to the point of considering conditioned and unconscious action at least as important as rational choice. The approach stresses the role played by institutions, intended as social devices created to deal with uncertainty, as mechanisms of acquisition and elaboration of information, and also as frameworks capable of moulding individual actions and producing collective behaviour. There is a certain emphasis on the indeterminism of human choices and, in relation to this, a tendency to study economic change in terms of 'evolutionary' processes of the cumulative type, in a view reminiscent of the growth theories of both Schumpeter and Kaldor. Some scholars speak, with reference to this, of 'evolutionary political economy'. The basic lines of research of this stream of thought have been laid down by G. M. Hodgson in *Economics and Institutions: A Manifesto for Modern Institutional Economics* (1988).

Predominant in the French version of this approach is the notion of the capitalist mode of production that attributes much importance to the functional nature of the set of norms and institutions which serve to 'regulate' certain regimes of wage determination and surplus extraction. There is also a marked emphasis on the historical and transitory nature of such regulation systems. It is not clear, however, if the process of their change is governed by well-defined laws of movement, and by which ones.

By and large it seems to us that these approaches to the analysis of capitalism still find some difficulty in escaping from the mist of creative inspiration, probably because of their refusal to stick to a well-defined traditional theoretical system. However, they seem to be promising perhaps because, more than other neo- or post-Marxist approaches, they are rich in important theoretical innovations.

11.3.3. Four unconventional economists

There are four economists for whom we have not found the right place in the panorama of contemporary economic schools: N. Georgescu-Roegen (b. 1906), J. K. Galbraith (b. 1908), A. O. Hirschman (b. 1915), and Richard M. Goodwin (b. 1913). We have put them together because we are convinced that their resistance to classification is a characteristic that unites and defines them more clearly than might at first appear. And we have put them with the heretics as we believe that, among the qualities that unite them, the taste for heresy is not the least important.

Georgescu-Roegen, after beginning his career in Romania as a mathematical statistician, changed to economic studies in 1934–6 at Harvard, where he was a student of Schumpeter. The first phase of his economic work focused on consumer theory, input–output analysis, and the theory of production. In this phase he published the fundamental articles 'The Pure Theory of Consumer Behaviour' (*Quarterly Journal of Economics*, 1936) and 'Choice, Expectations and Measurability' (*Quarterly Journal of Economics*, 1954). The first article, which dealt with the problems of integrability in the theory of demand, presented two important results: the demonstration that integral manifolds do not necessarily coincide with indifference manifolds (from this is derived the distinction between integrability in its mathematical and economic sense) and the demonstration that the two types of manifold can be reduced to the same thing under the postulate of transitivity of preferences. In this way Georgescu ended the discussion initiated by Pareto and Volterra about the possibility of going back to the (ordinal) utility function by beginning from the observation of market choices. The second article tackled the problem of the inexistence of the indifference map of the consumer in the presence of a lexicographic preference structure. Georgescu focused his criticism on what he called 'the ordinalist fallacy': despite appearances, the ordinalist approach is not substantially different from the cardinalist, and therefore the movement from the latter to the former would not constitute a real theoretical advance, as Robbins and others had believed.

On another research front, three contributions deserve a mention. One concerns the non-substitution theorem, which Georgescu was the first to discover. The other two concern two of the most intractable problems of macroeconomic dynamics, those of non-linearity and discontinuity, problems which he dealt with in 'Relaxation Phenomena in Linear Dynamic Models' (in Koopmans' *Activity Analysis of Production and Allocation*, 1951). In this article, on the basis of an innovative application of the theory of oscillations, Georgescu produced a fundamental result for the study of regime changes.

The second phase of Georgescu's scientific work began with the famous 1966 methodological essay, *Analytical Economics: Issues and Problems*, a book that contains a pitiless criticism of 'standard economics'. The main accusation was of having reduced the economic process to a 'mechanical analogy' and of having confined economic theory to the sphere of applicability of rational mechanics. The proposal advanced was that of a new alliance between economic activity and the natural world, a proposal which in the following years was to become his 'bioeconomic programme'. The keystone of this ambitious programme was to be found in the entropy law, 'the most economic of the physical laws', consideration of which induced Georgescu to study the survival conditions of mankind. Moving along the borders between economic and thermodynamics, in the book *The Entropy Law and the Economic Process* (1917) Georgescu formulated a new law, the 'fourth law of thermodynamics', concerning the impossibility of perpetual motion of the third type, defined as a closed system capable of carrying out work indefinitely at a constant rate. The economic implication of this law consisted of the rejection of the 'energetic dogma', a dogma according to which 'only energy counts', with no consideration for the 'material'. This line of thought later ended up in the 'funds and flows' model presented in *Energy and Economic Myths* (1976). This model was a radical alternative both to the model of the production function and to the model of activity analysis, both judged as incapable of accounting for the role played by the time element in productive activity. Recently, the funds and flows model has been receiving increased attention from both theoretical economists and analysts of productive organization. Finally, we will mention the long introductory article Georgescu wrote in 1983 to the English edition of Gossen's famous book, *The Laws of Human Relations and The Rules of Human Action Derived Therefrom*, an essay which is much more than a splendid intellectual biography, and which demonstrates not only the depth and breadth of Georgescu's knowledge of economics but also his extraordinary ability to go beyond the narrow limits within which economic discourse is often confined by official science. This may help us understand the generalized *fin de non-recevoir* of the profession in regard to Georgescu's critical message, the message of an author who was not easily confined within a rigid school of thought.

J. K. Galbraith was undoubtedly the most important exponent of contemporary institutionalist thought (not to be confused with the 'new' and neo-institutional approaches), a stream of thought which numbers among its main exponents John Adams, Kenneth Boulding, Allan Gruchy, Warren Samuels, Daniel Fusfeld, and Paul Strassman, and which has in the *Journal of Economic Issues* its most prestigious critical platform. In the groove cut by Veblen and on the basis of a very particular reading of Keynesian thought, Galbraith has explored the organizational nature and the planning methods of the company system as well as the influence of what he considers 'the technological imperatives'; but he has also concerned himself with the social formation of individual preferences, interaction between private and public spheres, and the forces that influence the formation of opinion in the public sector.

In *American Capitalism* (1961) Galbraith put forward the theory of countervailing power. According to this theory, one way to keep a social system in equilibrium, whilst reducing inequalities, injustices, and exploitation, is that of balancing the excess power held by certain socio-economic groups (large-scale companies, cartels, ownership associations, etc.) by allowing the constitution of other power-groups with opposing interests. This is a theory full of realism and wisdom, but one which could find no place within the neo-classical theoretical system. In the trilogy made up by *The Affluent Society* (1958), *The New Industrial State* (1967), and *Economic and Public Purpose* (1973), Galbraith raised the argument that the 'invisible hand' is a long way from having the beneficial effects the *laissez-faire* theorists had attributed to it. On the contrary, it leads to a sharpening of inequality in the distribution of income, to the predominance of private over public interests, to the 'squalor' of the public economy, and, finally, to a low level of research and development activities. This last point plays a fundamental role in the process of economic growth; and it is a fact, according to Galbraith, that a large part of research and development is undertaken by the large-scale companies. It is also for this reason that Galbraith has been rather sceptical about the effectiveness and utility of anti-trust policies. He believes that strategic planning is a more useful kind of public intervention in the economic sphere, and that it should not aim at coercing private activity, but at co-ordinating it and turning it to the service of the public interest. In his most recent essays, *The Nature of Mass Poverty* (1979) and *The Anatomy of Poverty* (1983), Galbraith has moved so far along this road as to reach the point of calling for State intervention systematically directed to redistributing income in favour of the poorest strata of society.

The other great master of the contemporary American *liberal* left is Albert Hirschman. He received his degree in 1937 at Trieste, where he began working on statistical demography and the Italian economy. In his first book, *National Power and the Structure of Foreign Trade* (1945), he dealt with historical and theoretical aspects of the relationship between national power and the structure of foreign trade, with explicit reference to the policies of Nazi Germany. Already in these works Hirschman had taken up a critical position in regard to several of the theoretical foundations of the dominant economic doctrine; he continued to develop his own arguments by making use of the analytical instruments of orthodox theory, but almost as if he wished to demonstrate their potential for alternative cognitive objectives. In *The Strategy of Economic Development* (1958), one of his most important books, and in *Journey toward Progress* (1963), Hirschman proposed a really heterodox analysis to tackle the problems of developing countries. *The Strategy* focused on the 'search for the *primum movens*', or the historical, psychological, and anthropological conditions for economic development. The conclusion was that development is possible even with scarce natural resources; that, in appropriate conditions, productive abilities can be learned by the whole population; and that it is not true that savings can be *chronically* insufficient, nor entrepreneurial abilities. More important is the fact that development depends on the ability to mobilize hidden, dispersed, and badly utilized resources and capabilities. Hirschman's development analysis is centred on observation of social and political aspects of growth, a line of research that found its full expression in the remarkable collection of articles *A Bias for Hope: Essays in Development and Latin America* (1971).

In 1977 Hirschman published *The Passions and the Interests*, an important book on the history of ideas which reconstructed the long sequence of thought which, initiated by Machiavelli, led to the seventeenth-century doctrine of the predominance of interests over passions. In the *Theory of Moral Sentiments*, Smith had placed the non-economic impulses at the service of economic ones, making them lose the specific autonomy they had previously enjoyed. Then, in the *Wealth of Nations*, his analysis was founded on the idea that men are mainly motivated by the desire to improve their economic conditions, and that 'sympathy' and other moral sentiments are themselves definable in relation to self-interest. This was the beginning of modern political economy: a great intellectual conquest which was, however, to bring with it a significant restriction of the field of investigation as well as an impoverishment in the conception of human nature.

Here is the first strong thesis of Hirschman's thought: it is necessary gradually to complicate the economic discipline, which, so far, has been based on over-simplified assumptions. This criticism is mainly directed towards neoclassical theory, but does not spare many alternative approaches, from Keynesian to institutionalist, from Marxist to neo-institutionalist. A constant characteristic of Hirschman's work is his refusal to respect the traditional limits of the discipline—a characteristic that has been transformed, over time, into the art of violating frontiers. This is the central message of *Essays in Trespassing: Economics to Politics and Beyond* (1981), a book which contains a strong invitation, specifically addressed to economists, to take into consideration those human actions and behaviour which cannot be reduced to the traditional notion of 'interests'.

In *Shifting Involvements* (1982), Hirschman focused on the problem of the oscillations of human involvement between the private and the public sphere. Finally, in 'Against Parsimony: Three Easy Ways of Complicating Some Categories of Economic Discourse' (*American Economic Review*, 1984) he again took up the subject of the complication of the economic discourse. This complicating process should occur by means of the introduction, into the scope of this discipline, of two fundamental modalities and two inherent tensions of the human condition. The former were 'self-reflection' and the 'voice', the protest, with which Hirschman had also concerned himself in *Exit, Voice and Loyalty: Responses to Decline in Firms, Organizations, and States* (1970). The latter concern the distinction between 'instrumental' and 'non-instrumental' modes of behaviour and that between personal interest and public morality. In this way, the economic problem would be removed from simplistic orthodox reduction to the principle of constrained maximization.

The other great heretic of this generation of economists is Richard M. Goodwin, the 'deviant Marxist', as he defined himself. He received his degree at Harvard in 1934, and was converted to Marxism under the pressure of the economic events of the great crisis; then he studied with Harrod at Oxford, where he read the proofs of the *General Theory*, which fascinated him. He returned to Harvard in 1938, and followed the lectures of Schumpeter and Leontief. There he took a Ph.D. in 1941, and taught physics and applied mathematics until 1945 and economics until 1950. Later he emigrated to Europe, where he taught in England and Italy. Marx and Schumpeter were his great spiritual fathers, as he himself acknowledged: 'only Marx had understood the truth . . . only Schumpeter had taken Marx seriously', he wrote in the preface to the Italian edition of *Essays in Economic Dynamics* (1982, pp. 12–13). This book contains the best of Goodwin's contributions to the theory of economic dynamics. Another book, *Essays in Linear Economics* (1983), contains the best of his work in the field of multi-sectorial linear modelling. Here we shall mention the most important of these articles.

In the field of the business cycle, it is worth mentioning 'The Non Linear Accelerator and the Persistence of the Business Cycle' (*Econometrica*, 1951), in which he tried to solve a fundamental problem of the cycle theory based on the interaction between the multiplier and the accelerator: that of their 'non-persistence'. Goodwin understood that this problem was essentially connected to the linearity of the models, and solved it by introducing non-linearity, obtaining the relaxation oscillations: the economy expands until it reaches full employment or full utilization of capacity; then it relaxes and enters into a depressive phase, in which it will remain until a zero level of gross invest-ments is reached.

Even more important, perhaps, was the model formulated in 'A Growth Cycle' (in *Socialism, Capitalism and Economic Growth*, 1967, edited by C. H. Feinstein), in which Goodwin used Volterra's equations to formalize the Marxian cycle theory. The philosophy of the model is that the main cause of the cycle lies in the relationship of conflict and dependence which ties together the two fundamental social classes of the capitalist economy. Each of these wishes to increase the size of its own slice of the cake. But the rules of the game prescribe that neither can take the whole cake. Neither of the two slices can increase indefinitely at the expense of the other. In the long run they will be constant; in the short run they oscillate. The mechanism ensuring the oscillation is made up by the negative effects that an increase in the wage share has on investments and the negative effects that a reduction in invest-ments has on employment.

These two articles, respectively, reveal the Harrod–Keynesian and Marxian components in Goodwin's intellectual background. The Schumpeterian com-ponent is present in another article, 'Innovation and Irregularity of Economic Cycles' (*Review of Economics and Statistics*, 1946), in which the theoretical message, according to a recent reinterpretation, lies in the demonstration of the 'resonance' effect that the irregularity of innovative investments would give to the cyclical movement. In 'Dynamical Coupling with Special Refer-ence to Markets Having Production Lags' (*Econometrica*, 1947), Goodwin attempted to account for the coexistence of cycles of different length, by coupling equations of the business cycle with equations of the building cycle. More recently, he has used the dynamic coupling to graft a Marxian short-run cycle onto a long-wave movement, explaining the latter, in a Schumpeterian manner, in terms of basic innovations and their tendency to appear in bunches.

In regard to Goodwin's other major research area, that inspired by Leon-tief's influence, the two works which seem to us the most important are 'The Multiplier as a Matrix' (*Economic Journal*, 1949), an article followed by another two on the same subject, and which gave rise to an interesting debate in the early 1950s; and 'Static and Dynamic General Equilibrium Models' (in

Input–Output Relations, 1953), where, among other things, Goodwin tried to introduce into Leontief's model an original *tâtonnement* process capable of generating small oscillations.

Goodwin has sometimes been criticized for being eclectic, a criticism which seems to us to be unjustified. It is true that he has been influenced by authors of the most diverse theoretical schools. But it is also true that he has endeavoured to bring to light some important characteristics these authors have in common: the view of capitalism as an intrinsically unstable dynamic system, awareness of the insufficiency of traditional static and equilibrium analysis as instruments to understand the laws of movement of that system, the acknowledged centrality of the behaviour of collective economic agents, and the associated judgement of irrelevance in regard to microeconomic analysis. It is also true that his research has been constantly dominated by the need to integrate ideas from those authors into an organic view. The real problem is that this research has not reached the form of a complete theoretical system. But this is a problem of all contemporary post-Keynesian and post-Marxist theoretical approaches. Goodwin's work is still in progress, however, and it is making a fundamental contribution to this approach.

Bibliography

On the new political economy and similar approaches: M. Albert and R. Halmel, *Quiet Revolution in Welfare Economics* (Princeton, NJ, 1990); S. Bowles and H. Gintis, 'The Revenge of Homo Economicus: Post-Walrasian Economics and the Revival of Political Economy', *Journal of Economic Perspectives*, (1990); G. Brennan and J. Buchanan, *The Reasons of Rules: Constitutional Political Economy* (Cambridge, 1985); J. Buchanan and G. Tullock, *The Calculus of Consent: Logical Foundations of Constitutional Democracy* (Ann Arbor, Mich., 1962); P. Dasgupta, P. Hammond, and E. Maskin, 'The Implementation of Social Choice: Some General Results on Incentive Compatibility', *Review of Economic Studies*, 46 (1979); F. Von Hayek, 'Competition as a Discovery Procedure', in *New Studies in Philosophy, Politics, Economics and the History of Ideas* (London, 1978); I. Kirzner, 'Austrian School of Economics', in *The New Palgrave: A Dictionary of Political Economy*, i (London, 1987); T. W. Hutchinson, *The Politics and Philosophy of Economics* (Oxford, 1981); R. N. Langlois, *Economics as a Process: Essays in the New Institutional Economics* (Cambridge, 1986); H. Moulin, *The Strategy of Social Choice* (Amsterdam, 1983); D. C. Mueller, *Public Choice* (Cambridge, 1989); E. S. Phelps, *Political Economy* (New York, 1985); A. H. Shand, *The Capitalist Alternative: An Introduction to Neo-Austrian Economics* (London, 1984); A. Schotter, *The Economic Theory of Social Institutions* (Cambridge, 1981).

On game theory: R. Aumann, 'Survey of Repeated Games', in R. Aumann *et al.*, *Essays in Game Theory and Mathematical Economics in Honor of Oscar Morgenstern*

(Mannheim, 1981); D. Fudenberg and E. Maskin, 'The Folk Theorem in Repeated Games with Discounting or with Incomplete Information', *Econometrica*, 54 (1986); J. Harsanyi and R. Selten, *A General Theory of Equilibrium Selection in Games* (Cambridge, Mass., 1988); E. Rasmussen, *Games and Information* (Oxford, 1989); R. Selten, 'The Chain-Store Paradox', *Theory and Decision*, 8 (1978); H. Moulin, *Game Theory for the Social Sciences* (New York, 1986).

On the models of production as a circular process, the theory of capital, and Sraffa: H. B. Chenery and P. G. Clark, *Interindustry Economics* (New York, 1959); G. C. Harcourt, *Some Cambridge Controversies in the Theory of Capital* (Cambridge, 1972); K. Marx, *Capital* (London, 1954); L. L. Pasinetti, *Lectures in Production Theory* (Cambridge, 1975); F. Petri, 'The Difference between Long Period and Short Period General Equilibrium and the Capital Theory Controversy', *Australian Economic Papers*, 17 (1978); N. Salvadori, 'Existence of Cost-Minimizing Systems within the Sraffa Framework', *Zeitschrift für Nationalökonomie*, 54 (1982); B. Schefold, *Mr Sraffa on Joint Production and Other Essays* (London, 1989); E. Screpanti, 'Sraffa after Marx: A New Interpretation', *Review of Political Economy*, 5 (1993).

On the Marxist and post-Marxist approaches: R. Arena, A. Graziani (ed.), *Production, circulation et monnaie* (Paris, 1985); M. Bronfenbrenner, 'Radical Political Economics in America', *Journal of Economic Literature*, 2 (1970); B. Chavance (ed.), *Régulation, cycles et crises dans les économies socialistes* (Paris, 1987); M. De Vroey, 'A Regulation Approach Interpretation of Contemporary Crisis', *Capital and Class*, 13 (1984); M. Di Matteo, R. M. Goodwin, and A. Vercelli (eds.), *Technological and Social Factors in Long Term Fluctuations* (Berlin, 1989); J. Foster, *Evolutionary Macroeconomics* (London, 1987); G. M. Hodgson, *Economics and Institutions: A Manifesto for Modern Institutional Economics* (Cambridge, 1988); E. K. Hunt and J. G. Schwartz (eds.), *A Critique of Economic Theory* (Harmondsworth, 1972); M. Itoh, *Value and Crisis: Essays on Marxian Economics in Japan* (London, 1980); S. Marglin (ed.), *The Rise and Fall of the Golden Age: Lessons for the 1990s* (Oxford, 1990); J. O'Connor, *Accumulation Crisis* (New York, 1984); A. Reati, *Taux de profit et accumulation du capital dans l'onde longue de l'après-guerre* (Brussels, 1990); J. Roemer, *Free to Lose* (Cambridge, Mass., 1988).

On the four 'unconventional economists': P. F. Asso and M. DeCecco, Introduction to A. O. Hirschman, *National Power and the Structure of Foreign Trade* (Berkeley, Calif., 1980); S. Bowles, R. Edwards, and W. Shepherd (eds.), *Unconventional Wisdom: Essays in Honor of John Kenneth Galbraith* (Boston, Mass., 1989); M. Di Matteo (ed.), *Celebrating R. M. Goodwin's 75th Birthday* (Siena, 1992); R. L. Heilbroner, *Behind the Veil of Economics* (New York, 1988); B. J. Loasby, *The Mind and Method of the Economist: A Critical Appraisal of Major Economists in the 20th Century* (Aldershot, 1989): L. J. Okroi, *Galbraith, Harrington, Heilbroner: Economics and Dissent in an Age of Optimism* (Princeton, NJ, 1988); S. Zamagni, *Georgescu-Roegen* (Milan, 1979).

INDEX OF SUBJECTS

INDEX OF NAMES